Communications in Computer and Information Science

501

More information about this series at http://www.springer.com/series/7899

Limin Sun · Huadong Ma
Dingyi Fang · Jinping Niu
Wei Wang (Eds.)

Advances in Wireless Sensor Networks

The 8th China Conference, CWSN 2014
Xi'an, China, October 31 – November 2, 2014
Revised Selected Papers

 Springer

Editors
Limin Sun
Chinese Academy of Sciences
Beijing
China

Huadong Ma
Beijing
China

Dingyi Fang
Northwest University
Xi'an
China

Jinping Niu
Northwest University
Xi'an
China

Wei Wang
Northwest University
Xi'an
China

ISSN 1865-0929   ISSN 1865-0937   (electronic)
Communications in Computer and Information Science
ISBN 978-3-662-46980-4   ISBN 978-3-662-46981-1   (eBook)
DOI 10.1007/978-3-662-46981-1

Library of Congress Control Number: 2015939211

Springer Heidelberg New York Dordrecht London

Printed on acid-free paper

Springer-Verlag GmbH Berlin Heidelberg is part of Springer Science+Business Media
(www.springer.com)

Preface

China Wireless Sensor Network Conference (CWSN) is the annual conference sponsored by China Computer Federation (CCF). The Eighth China Wireless Sensor Network Conference (CWSN2014) was sponsored by CCF, cosponsored by China Computer Federation Technical Committee on Sensor Network, and undertook by Northwest University of China. CWSN is the premier forum which aims to provide a high-level forum to bring together academic researchers, engineering professionals, and industry experts to exchange information, share achievements, and discuss future developments on various topics related to wireless sensor networks, which will highly promote the research and technical innovation in these fields. The papers contained in these proceedings address challenging issues in energy-efficient network infrastructure, network architecture, wireless communication systems and protocols, power control and management, resource management, positioning and location-based services, new models of sensor usage, sensor data storage, retrieval, processing and management, quality of service, fault tolerance and reliability, experience with real-world applications, security and privacy, software development, testing and debugging tools as well as simulation environments, sensor data quality, integrity and trustworthiness, performance modeling and analysis, cyber-physical systems (CPS), as well as Internet of things.

This year, CWSN received 365 submissions. After a thorough reviewing process, 64 English papers were selected for presentation as full papers, with an acceptance rate of 17.07 %. This volume contains 64 English full papers presented at CWSN 2014.

The high-quality program would not have been possible without the authors who chose CWSN 2014 as a venue for their publications. We are also very grateful to the Program Committee members and Organizing Committee members, who put a tremendous amount of effort into soliciting and selecting research papers with a balance of high quality and new ideas and new applications.

We hope that you enjoy reading and benefit from the proceedings of CWSN 2014.

January 2015

Dingyi Fang
Xiaojiang Chen

Organization

CWSN 2014 (the Eighth China Wireless Sensor Network Conference) was sponsored by CCF, cosponsored by China Computer Federation Technical Committee on Sensor Network, and undertaken by Northwest University of China.

Organizing Committees

General Chairs

Ling Gao   Vice-Chancellor of Northwest University, China
Jianzhong Li   Harbin Institute of Technology, China

Honorary Chair

Hao Dai   Chinese Academy of Engineering, China

PC Co-chairs

Dingyi Fang   Northwest University, China
Xue Wang   Tsinghua University, China
Guihai Chen   Nanjing University, China

Local Chair

Xiaojiang Chen   Northwest University, China

Program Committee

Hao Dai	Academician of Chinese Academy of Engineering, China
Mingxuan Ming	The Hong Kong University of Science and Technology, Hong Kong
Guangwei Bai	Nanjing University of Technology, China
Ming Bao	Institute of Acoustics, Chinese Academy of Sciences, China
Shaobin Cai	Harbin Engineering University, China
Fanzi Zeng	Hunan University, China
Yong Zeng	Xidian University, China
Yu Zeng	Beijing Computing Center, China
Shanfeng Chen	Nokia (China) Research Center, China
Guihai Chen	Nanjing University, China
Haiming Chen	Institute of Computing Technology, Chinese Academy of Sciences, China
Hong Chen	Renmin University of China, China

Jiaxing Chen	Hebei Normal University, China
Xi Chen	State Grid Information and Telecommunication Co., Ltd., China
Xiaojiang Chen	Northwest University, China
Zhikui Chen	Dalian University of Technology, China
Li Cui	Institute of Computing Technology, Chinese Academy of Sciences, China
Xunxue Cui	Tsinghua University, China
Xunxue Cui	Army Officer Academy of PLA, China
Zhidong Deng	Tsinghua University, China
Rong Ding	Beijing University of Aeronautics and Astronautics, China
Hongwei Du	Harbin Institute of Technology, China
Yong Fan	Beijing LOIT Technology Co., Ltd., China
Xiaoliang Fan	Lanzhou University, China
Xunli Fan	Northwest University, China
Dingyi Fang	Northwest University, China
Jian Feng	Xi'an University of Science and Technology, China
Deyun Gao	Beijing Jiaotong University, China
Hong Gao	Harbin Institute of Technology, China
Jibing Gong	Yanshan University, China
Zhongwen Guo	Ocean University of China, China
Guangjie Han	Hohai University, China
Jinsong Han	Xi'an Jiaotong University, China
He Lu	Northwest University, China
Li Hong	China University of Petroleum, China
Chengchen Hu	Xi'an Jiaotong University, China
Chengquan Hu	Jilin University, China
Yanjun Hu	Anhui University, China
Qiangsheng Hua	Tsinghua University, China
He Huang	Suzhou University, China
Liusheng Huang	University of Science and Technology of China, China
Hongbo Jiang	Huazhong University of Science and Technology, China
Ningchuan Jiang	Southeast University, China
Bo Jing	Air Force Engineering University, China
Deying Li	Renmin University of China, China
Fangmin Li	Wuhan University of Technology, China
Guanghui Li	Zhejiang A & F University, China
Guorui Li	Northeastern University, China
Jianbo Li	Qingdao University, China
Jianzhong Li	Harbin Institute of Technology, China
Jinbao Li	Heilongjiang University, China
Minglu Li	Shanghai Jiao Tong University, China
Ping Li	Changsha University of Science and Technology, China
Renfa Li	Hunan University, China
Shining Li	Northwestern Polytechnical University, China
Wei Li	Southeast University, China

Xinghua Li	Xidian University, China
Zhetao Li	Xiangtan University, China
Hui Li	Siemens China Research Institute, China
Yongzhen Liang	Southern Yangtze University, China
Wei Liang	Shenyang Institute of Automation, Chinese Academy of Sciences, China
Yaping Lin	Hunan University, China
Ming Liu	University of Electronic Science and Technology of China, China
Xingcheng Liu	Zhongshan University, China
Yunhao Liu	Tsinghua University, China
Xiang Liu	Beijing University, China
Shaohua Long	Chongqing University of Posts and Telecommunications, China
Juan Luo	Hunan University, China
Huadong Ma	Beijing University of Posts and Telecommunications, China
Jian Ma	Nanjing Research Institute of Beijing University of Technology, China
Li Ma	North China University of Technology, China
Weike Nie	Northwest University, China
Jianwei Niu	Beijing University of Aeronautics and Astronautics, China
Xiaoguang Niu	Wuhan University, China
Jian Peng	Sichuan University, China
Li Peng	Jiangnan University, China
Shaoliang Peng	National University of Defense Technology, China
Wangdong Qi	PLA University of Science and Technology, China
Depei Qian	Beijing University of Aeronautics and Astronautics, China
Fengyuan Ren	Tsinghua University, China
Xuejun Ren	Engineering College of Armed Police Force, China
Yuhui Ren	Northwest University, China
Shikai Shen	Kunming University, China
Jie Shen	Wuxi Internet of things Industry Research Institute, China
Yulong Shen	Xidian University, China
Jian Shu	Nanchang Aviation University, China
Lei Shu	Guangdong University of Petrochemical Technology, China
Guangming Song	Southeast University, China
Jinshu Su	National University of Defense Technology, China
Lijuan Sun	Nanjing University of Posts and Telecommunications, China
Limin Sun	Institute of Information Engineering, Chinese Academy of Sciences, China
Liqin Tian	North China Institute of Science and Technology, China
Shang Wang	University of Science and Technology of China, China
Jie Wang	Dalian University of Technology, China
Lei Wang	Dalian University of Technology, China
Liangmin Wang	Jiangsu University, China

Organizers

Organized by

China Computer Federation, China

Hosted by

Northwest University

China Computer Federation Technical Committee on Sensor Network

Sponsoring Institutions

Springer

Contents

Positioning and Location-Based Services in Wireless Sensor Networks

Security and Privacy

Wireless Communication Systems and Protocols

Routing Algorithm and Transport Protocols in Wireless Sensor Networks

Wireless Communication Protocols and Sensor Data Quality, Integrity and Trustworthiness

Internet of Things

Wireless Mobile Network Architecture, In-Vehicle Network

Indoor Positioning and Location-Based Services

Applications of Wireless Sensor Networks

Power Control and Management

Lifetime Optimization Algorithm with Multiple Mobile Sink Nodes for Wireless Sensor Networks

Yourong Chen[✉], Di Chen, Yaolin Liu, Zhangquan Wang,
and Tiaojuan Ren

College of Information Science and Technology, Zhejiang Shuren University,
Hangzhou, Zhejiang, China
Jack_Chenyr@163.com

Abstract. In order to overcome the energy hole problem and long data gathering latency problem in some wireless sensor networks (WSNs), lifetime optimization algorithm with multiple mobile sink nodes for wireless sensor networks (LOA_MMSN) is proposed. LOA_MMSN analyzes the constraints, establishes network optimization model, and decomposes the model into movement path selection model and lifetime optimization model with known movement paths. Finally, the two models are solved. Simulation results show that LOA_MMSN can extend the network lifetime, balance node energy consumption and reduce data gathering latency. Under certain conditions, it outperforms Ratio_w, TPGF and lifetime optimization algorithm with single mobile sink node for WSNs.

Keywords: Network lifetime · Mobile sink nodes · Optimization algorithm · Sub-gradient method

1 Introduction

In most cases all sensor nodes of WSNs are battery-powered and located in unattended or harsh environment. It is difficult or even impossible for battery replacement. Once node's energy exhausts, the node is disabled. It will affect the network operation and split the network to shorten network lifetime [1, 2]. Therefore, in WSNs, network lifetime is the important indicator of network performance. The algorithms of WSNs should save energy and maximize the network lifetime.

Some scholars research on lifetime optimization algorithm with fixed nodes for WSNs and have got some accomplishments [3–5]. In those algorithms, it is inevitably to cause unbalanced distribution of node energy consumption and energy hole problem. The problem can be overcome by sink nodes' movement. When sink node stays at some locations around which nodes distribute intensively or other key locations to gather data, all nodes have the opportunity to transmit data in the vicinity of sink node and have the same lifetime.

References [6–10] research on the network lifetime maximization problem, establish network lifetime optimization models with mobile sink node, use optimization methods to solve the models and obtain optimal scheme. Reference [11] theoretically discusses the relationship between network lifetime and maximum throughout in large scale

© Springer-Verlag Berlin Heidelberg 2015
L. Sun et al. (Eds.): CWSN 2014, CCIS 501, pp. 3–13, 2015.
DOI: 10.1007/978-3-662-46981-1_1

WSNs. However, all references [6–11] assume that the movement path of sink node is already known, and don't consider how to determine the anchors or movement path of sink node. Reference [12] searches guide agent nodes and intermediate guide nodes, analyzes TSP (traveling salesman problem), determines movement path with node cooperation, and proposes data gathering method which optimizing data transmission latency and energy. However, the algorithm doesn't consider network lifetime. Reference [13] proposes range constrained clustering (RCC). RCC divides nodes into several clusters. Sink node stays at the cluster centers to gather data. The Concorde TSP solver is used to calculate the shortest movement path of sink node through some cluster centers. Reference [14] divides network into several grids, and proposes a grid-based clustering method. References [12–14] determine the locations of mobile sink node. However, they don't consider the data gathering when sink node is moving. Whether the algorithms can obtain optimal solution still needs theoretical analysis. Reference [15] assumes that sink node stays at each grid vertex, researches on the movement path and sojourn time of sink node with known initial location, proposes a mixed integer linear programming model. But the model doesn't consider data forwarding hop limitation of sensor nodes. It can't ensure that the data gathering of sink nodes can cover all sensor nodes. Therefore, lifetime optimization algorithm with multiple mobile sink nodes for wireless sensor networks (LOA_MMSN) is proposed. It can balance the node energy consumption, reduce data transmission latency and extend the network lifetime.

The remaining parts of paper are organized as follow. In Sect. 2, we propose the system assumption and lifetime optimization model with multiple mobile sink nodes. Section 3 describes the solution of model. The simulation results are presented in Sect. 4. Section 5 provides the conclusion of the paper.

2 Establishment of Optimization Model

2.1 Assumptions

- Only 2D (two-dimension) WSNs are considered. The locations of sensor nodes are fixed. Sink nodes can move to any grid center.
- When sensor nodes are not in the data gathering range of sink nodes, they store all sensing data in cache and basically are in sleep state. When sensor nodes are in the data gathering range of sink nodes, they are in work state and transmit data to only one sink node.
- All sensor nodes can obtain their own location coordinates by installing GPS module or using other location methods.
- All sensor nodes have the same performance (sensing rate, maximum communication radius, initial energy, energy consumption parameter, etc.).
- Energy of all nodes is limited. But energy of sink nodes can be renewable.
- Each sink node gathers sensor nodes' data in multi-hop range. But the maximum hop is a fixed number and not infinitely large.

2.2 Constraints

Movement Path Constraints. Many references consider that sink node stays at one node location, gathers data and takes its responsibilities to sense. It basically limits the mobile location selection of sink node, and don't consider other locations where sensor nodes never distribute. Therefore, their algorithms obtain local optimal solutions. As is shown in Fig. 1, monitoring area is divided into several grids of the same size and each grid is numbered. The sink node can stay at each grid center to gather data. The method enlarges the selection range of sojourn locations for sink nodes.

1	2	......	n-1	n
n+1	n+2	......	2n-1	2n
⋮	⋮	⋮	⋮	⋮
(n-2)n+1	(n-2)n+2	......	n^2-n-1	n^2-n
(n-1)n+1	(n-1)n+2	......	n^2-1	n^2

Fig. 1. Grids in the monitoring area

The m-th sink node starts at initial location and finally moves back to the initial location. The initial location constraints of m-th sink node are as follow.

$$\sum_{w \in Gd} p_{s,w}^m = 1, \forall m \tag{1}$$

$$\sum_{w \in Gd} p_{w,s}^m = 1, \forall m \tag{2}$$

where, s represents $grid_s$ and initial location of m-th sink node, $grid_v$ represents the center of grid v, Gd represents the set of all grid centers. $p_{v,w}^m$ is the state indicator, which represents whether $L(grid_v, grid_w)$ appears on the movement path of m-th sink node. $L(grid_v, grid_w)$ represents the directed line segment from $grid_v$ to $grid_w$. $p_{v,w}^m = 1$ represents $L(grid_v, grid_w)$ is on the movement path of m-th sink node.

Because each sink node cyclically moves along the path, the sum of state indicators which represent from $grid_v$ to all neighbor grid centers is equal to the sum of state indicators which represent from all neighbor grid centers to $grid_v$. The state indicator balance constraint is

$$\sum_{w \in Gd \text{ and } L(grid_v, grid_w) \in Ld} p_{v,w}^m = \sum_{w \in Gd \text{ and } L(grid_v, grid_w) \in Ld} p_{w,v}^m , \forall v \in Gd, \forall m \tag{3}$$

To avoid two mutually movable grids and eliminate the subtours, the state indicator limitation constraint is

$$p_{v,w}^m + p_{w,v}^m \leq 1, \forall w, v \in Gd, \forall m \tag{4}$$

Number Constraint of Anchors. According to the state values $p_{v,w}^m$ of all grids, the state indicator ϕ_v^m of m-th sink node's sojourn location is obtained.

$$\sum_{w \in Gd} p_{v,w}^m = \phi_v^m, \forall v \in Gd, \forall m \tag{5}$$

The grid centers sink node stays are defined as anchors. Because the number of anchors in the network is fixed, the number constraint of anchors is

$$\sum_m \sum_{v \in Gd} \phi_v^m = N_a \tag{6}$$

where, N_a represents the number of anchors.

K-hop Coverage Constraint. Wireless communication environment is relative complexity. The data of sensor nodes can't reach the sink node by unlimited hop. Therefore, before planning the movement path of sink node, it is necessary to consider data gathering range of sink node and set up k-hop coverage constraint.

The distances from sensor node i to sink node and to neighbor node respectively are

$$ds_i = \min_{v \in Gd \ and \ \phi_v^m = 1} \sqrt[2]{(Px_i - gx_v)^2 + (Py_i - gy_v)^2} \tag{7}$$

$$d_{ij} = \sqrt[2]{(Px_i - Px_j)^2 + (Py_i - Py_j)^2}, j \in N(i) \tag{8}$$

where, $N(i)$ is the neighbor node set of node i, (Px_i, Py_i) represents the location coordinates of sensor node i, (gx_v, gy_v) represents the location coordinates of vth grid center.

The minimum data transmission hop h_i of each sensor node is

$$h_i = \begin{cases} 1, & ds_i < d_{\max} \\ \min_{j \in N(i)} (h_{ij}), & ds_i \geq d_{\max} \end{cases} \tag{9}$$

where, $h_{ij} = \begin{cases} 1 + h_j, d_{ij} < d_{\max} \\ \infty, \ d_{ij} \geq d_{\max} \end{cases}$. According to the definition of minimum hop, the movement path of sink node guarantees that its data gathering can cover all sensor nodes without isolated nodes. The k-hop coverage constraint is

$$h_i \leq k, \forall i \in V \tag{10}$$

Flow Constraint. The transmission data are composed of the sensing data and received data from neighbor nodes. The flow constraint is

$$\sum_{j \in N(i)} f_{ij}^m = S_i + \sum_{j \in N(i)} f_{ji}^m, \forall i \in V, \forall m \tag{11}$$

where, f_{ij}^m represents the data transmission rate between node i and node j when the data of node i aggregate to m-th sink node, S_i represents the data perceived rate of node i.

Energy Consumption Constraint. The total energy consumption of node is not larger than its initial energy in the network lifetime T_{net}. The energy consumption constraint is

$$T_{net} \sum_m \left(\sum_{j \in N(i)} f_{ji}^m E_{\text{elec}} + \sum_{j \in N(i)} f_{ij}^m (E_{\text{elec}} + \varepsilon_{\text{fs}} d_{ij}^2) \right) \leq E_{\text{initial}}, \forall i \in V, \forall m \tag{12}$$

where, E_{initial} represents the initial energy of sensor nodes, ε_{fs} represents the electronic energy consumption of amplifying unit data, E_{elec} represents the electric energy consumption of receiving or transmitting unit data.

Link Transmission Constraint. Because link bandwidth resource is limited, the total amount of link transmission data is limited. Then the link transmission constraint is

$$f_{ij}^m + f_{ji}^m \leq R_{\max}, L(i,j) \in L, j > i, \forall m \tag{13}$$

where, $R_{\max}$ represents the maximum transmission rates of nodes, $L(i,j) \in L$ represents the link between node i and node j, L represents the set of all wireless links.

2.3 Network Optimization Model

When network starts, sink node leaves from initial location to next grid center and finally moves back to initial location. The data gathering methods of sink node are mobile gathering and static gathering. The mobile gathering of sink node is that during its movement, sink node dynamically gathers data in the k-hop range. The static gathering of sink node is that it stays at some grid centers for some time. During the sojourn time, sink node statically gathers data in the k-hop range. Therefore, the network lifetime optimization model is

$$\max \quad T_{net} = \sum_c \sum_p t_p^{c,m} + \sum_c \sum_{v \in Gd} \sum_{w \in Gd} d_{vw} p_{v,w}^m / u_{v,w}^m \tag{14a}$$

$$\text{s.t.:} t^a = t^b, \forall a, b \tag{14b}$$

$$\text{Constraints (1)--(6), (10)--(13)}$$

$$t_p^{c,m} \geq 0, \forall v, c, m \tag{14c}$$

$$f_{ij}^m \geq 0, \forall i, j \in V, \forall m \tag{14d}$$

$$\phi_v^m \in \{0, 1\}, p_{v,w}^m \in \{0, 1\}, \forall v, w \in Gd, \forall m \tag{14e}$$

where, $t_p^{n,m}$ represents the sojourn time which m-th sink node stays at $grid_p$ in its c-th movement. $u_{v,w}^m$ represents the movement rate of m-th sink node along the line $L(grid_v, grid_w)$, t^a represents the work time of sink node a.

3   Model Solution

3.1   Model Decomposition

Network optimization model (14a) considers movement path selection and data routing of several sink nodes. The model has too many parameters and its solution is complicate. In the model, movement path constraints mainly limit $\sum_c \sum_{v \in Gd} \sum_{w \in Gd} (d_{vw} p_{v,w}^m)/u_{v,w}^m$ in target function. It means finding a relatively optimal path. The flow constraint, energy consumption constraint and link transmission constraint mainly limit $\sum_c \sum_p t_p^{c,m}$ in target function.

It means searching optimal network lifetime and routing solution. In order to reduce solving complication, the network optimization model (14a) is divided into movement path selection model and lifetime optimization model with known movement paths.

3.2   Movement Path Selection Model

Because of the mobile gathering efficiency of sink node is far lower than static gathering efficiency, the target of movement path selection is to minimize $\sum_c \sum_{v \in Gd} \sum_{w \in Gd} (d_{vw} p_{v,w}^m)/u_{v,w}^m$ value. But movement path constraints are too loose for path selection. It doesn't consider the node density. Therefore, the path selection of sink node also needs to consider the node residual energy and determine some anchors for sink node. The anchors are some locations around where node density is high and residual energy is large. The subtractive clustering method [16] and other methods can be used to determine anchors at which sink nodes stay to cover all sensor nodes. We use the k-means algorithm [17] to get the M numbers of clusters whose members are anchors. M represents the number of sink nodes. Each sink node needs to traverse all anchors in one cluster. The movement path selection of sink node is essentially TSP problem. It can be solved by graph theory, and other methods.

3.3   Lifetime Optimization Model

According to definition of network lifetime, when the movement paths of sink nodes are determined, the network lifetime optimization model is transformed to the model (15). Its target is to obtain the network lifetime T_{net} and node transmission rates f_{ij}^m.

$$\max \quad T_{net} = \sum_c \sum_p t_p^{c,m} + \sum_c \sum_{v \in Gd} \sum_{w \in Gd} p_{v,w}^m \tag{15}$$

s.t.: Constraints (6), (10)–(13), (14b)–(14e)

There are static gathering and mobile gathering of sink nodes. In the static gathering, the above optimization model (15) has too many parameters so that direct solution is overwhelmingly complicate. Therefore, the model is simplified. Network lifetime optimization problem is transformed to several network lifetime optimization models in which the sink node stays at different anchor. Sub-gradient method is used to solve the lifetime optimization model and the optimal scheme is obtained [18]. In the mobile gathering, neighbor nodes of sink node during its movement are defined designated gateways (DGs). The movement rate of sink node is fast and the time of mobile gathering is relatively short. In order to evaluate the data amount of mobile gathering, assume that once DGs are in the communication area of sink node, they begin to gather data in the k-1 hop range and transmit data directly to sink node. To facilitate the evaluation of gathering data amount, according to the topology of static gathering and communication time of sensor nodes which are in the 1-hop range of sink node, each link communication time is evaluated, and then the amount of node data transmission when sink node is moving is obtained.

4   Simulation Realization and Analysis

4.1   Simulation Parameters

In the simulation, network data latency of m-th sink node is the half of the data gathering period [12]. DGC is the working time (doesn't include the sleep time) that sink node successfully gathers 1Mbit data of each sensor node. The network lifetime is the number of data gathering cycle (DGC) sink nodes complete in the time when network starts to run until one node runs out of energy. Residual energy variance is the residual energy variance of all sensor nodes when one node runs out of energy.

Only the energy consumption of data wireless communication is considered. E_{elec} is 50 nJ/bit. ε_{fs} is 100 pJ/bit/m^2. d_{max} is 200 m. Edge length of simulation area is 1000 m. $E_{initial}$ is 1000 J. Sensing rate of sensor node Si is 1 Mbit/h. Link maximum transmission rate R_{max} is 5 Mbit/h. Number of grids is 30*30. Gathering hop is 2. Number of sink nodes is 2. Simulation and comparison of Ratio_w, TPGF and LOA_MMSN algorithms are realized.

4.2   Simulation Result Analysis

Firstly, node distribution, anchor distribution, and movement paths of sink nodes are analyzed. As is shown in Fig. 2, the locations of 100 sensor nodes (open circles) are generated randomly and uniformly. The 1000 m*1000 m monitoring area is divided into 30*30 number of grids. The subtractive clustering method is used and six anchors (five-pointed stars) are obtained. The anchors are divided into two clusters. Each sink node selects cluster anchors respectively and gathers the data along the shortest path.

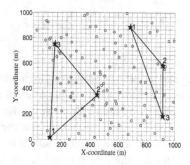

Fig. 2. Movement paths of sink nodes

Because the side lengths of grids are the same, the grid centers between two anchors are selected along the vertical direction. When their ordinates are the same, the grid centers are selected along the horizontal direction. After the process, grid movement paths of sink nodes are converted. As is shown in Fig. 3, two grid movement paths are obtained. It is the approximate solution of movement path.

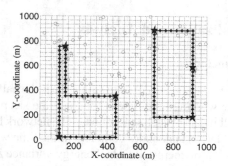

Fig. 3. Grid movement paths of sink nodes

Secondly, in order to verify the effectiveness of LOA_MMSN, Ratio_w, TPGF, LOA_SMSN and LOA_MMSN are compared. The location coordinates of 100, 120, 140, 160, 180, 200 sensor nodes are uniformly generated in the area. For each fixed number of sensor nodes, 10 different kinds of network topology are generated. The mean values of network lifetime, residual energy variance and data gathering latency are calculated to be the simulation result.

Figure 4 compares the network lifetime. LOA_MMSN comprehensively uses subtractive clustering method to obtain the anchors, uses sub-gradient method to calculate the optimal data transmission scheme and maximize network lifetime. As is shown in Fig. 4, the network lifetime of LOA_MMSN is longest. The network lifetime of TPGF is shortest.

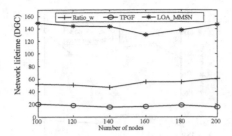

Fig. 4. Network lifetime

Figure 5 compares residual energy variance when one sensor node exhausts the energy. In LOA_MMSN, all sensor nodes have the opportunity to transmit data in the vicinity of sink node. It balances node energy consumption. All residual energy of nodes tends to 0. But in TPGF and Ratio_w, only hub nodes consume a lot of energy. Other nodes have much residual energy. Therefore, as shown in Fig. 5, the residual energy variance of LOA_MMSN is lowest. The residual energy variance of Ratio_w is largest.

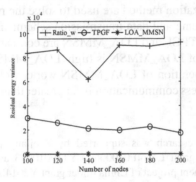

Fig. 5. Residual energy variance

Ratio_w and TPGF gather data in real time. But in LOA_MMSN, when sensor nodes are not in the data gathering range of sink nodes, they are basically in sleep state. The two types of data gathering latency can not be compared. When more sink nodes involve in data gathering, each sink node only needs to move through less number of anchors. It greatly reduces the data gathering latency. Therefore, Fig. 6 compares the data gathering latency of LOA_MMSN and LOA_SMSN (lifetime optimization algorithm with single mobile sink node). In LOA_SMSN, the number of sink node is 1, and other methods are the same as LOA_MMSN. As is shown in Fig. 6, data gathering latency of LOA_SMSN is highest. The data gathering latency of LOA_MMSN with two sink nodes is almost one half. The data gathering latency of LOA_MMSN with three sink nodes is almost one third.

In summary, LOA_MMSN can make full use of node energy to extend network lifetime, balance node energy consumption, and reduce data gathering latency.

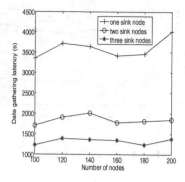

Fig. 6. Data gathering latency

5 Conclusion

In this paper, the algorithm assumptions are introduced. Then, the constraints are analyzed and network optimization model is established. Decomposition method, clustering method and optimization method are used to solve the model. The network lifetime, movement path scheme and data transmission scheme are obtained. Finally, the performance of Ratio_w, TPGF and LOA_MMSN are compared.

The time complexity of LOA_MMSN is high. LOA_MMSN needs some iteration time to converge. The operation of LOA_MMSN works well only when the energy consumption of data wireless communication is far greater than the energy consumption of solution calculation.

Acknowledgments. This research was supported by Zhejiang provincial natural science foundation of China under grant LY14F030006, LY13F010013 and Y15F030007, Zhejiang provincial education department project of China under grant Y201432498, and Zhejiang shuren university foundation of China under grant 2014R002 and 2013A31002.

References

1. Yick, J., Mukherjee, B., Ghosal, D.: Wireless sensor network survey. Comput. Netw. **52**, 2292–2330 (2008)
2. Zhang, P., Xiao, G., Tan, H.: Clustering algorithms for maximizing the lifetime of wireless sensor networks with energy-harvesting sensors. Comput. Netw. **57**, 2689–2704 (2013)
3. Hu, X.M., Zhang, J., Yu, Y., et al.: Hybrid genetic algorithm using a forward encoding scheme for lifetime maximization of wireless sensor networks. IEEE Trans. Evol. Comput. **14**, 766–781 (2010)
4. Zhu, Y.H., Shen, D.D., Wu, W.D., et al.: Dynamic routing algorithms optimizing lifetime of wireless sensor networks. ACTA Electronica Sinica. **37**, 1041–1045 (2009)
5. Shu, L., Zhang, Y., Zhou, Z., et al.: Transmitting and gathering streaming data in wireless multimedia sensor networks within expected network lifetime. Mob. Netw. Appl. **13**, 306–322 (2008)
6. Gatzianas, M., Georgiadis, L.: A distributed algorithm for maximum lifetime routing in sensor networks with mobile sink. IEEE Trans. Wireless Commun. **7**, 984–994 (2008)

7. Luo, J., Hubaux, J.P.: Joint sink mobility and routing to maximize the lifetime of wireless sensor networks: the case of constrained mobility. IEEE/ACM Trans. Netw. **18**, 871–884 (2010)
8. Zhao, M., Yang, Y.Y.: Optimization-based distributed algorithms for mobile data gathering in wireless sensor networks. IEEE Trans. Mob. Comput. **11**, 1464–1477 (2012)
9. Behdani, B., Yun, Y.S., Smith, J.C., et al.: Decomposition algorithms for maximizing the lifetime of wireless sensor networks with mobile sinks. Comput. Oper. Res. **39**, 1054–1061 (2012)
10. Emre, M.K., Kuban, A.I., Necat, A., et al.: Lifetime maximization in wireless sensor networks using a mobile sink with nonzero traveling time. Comput. J. **54**, 1987–1999 (2011)
11. Liu, W., Lu, K., Wang, J.P., et al.: Huang performance analysis of wireless sensor networks with mobile sinks. IEEE Trans. Veh. Technol. **61**, 2777–2789 (2012)
12. Rao, J., Biswas, S.: Data harvesting in sensor networks using mobile sinks. IEEE Wirel. Commun. **15**, 63–70 (2008)
13. Kumar, A.K., Sivalingam, K.M., Kumar, A.: On reducing delay in mobile data collection based wireless sensor networks. Wirel. Netw. **19**, 285–299 (2013)
14. Thanigaivelu, K., Murugan, K.: Grid-based clustering with predefined path mobility for mobile sink data collection to extend network lifetime in wireless sensor networks. IEEE Tech. Rev. **29**, 133–147 (2012)
15. Basagni, S., Carosi, A., Melachrinoudis, E., et al.: Controlled sink mobility for prolonging wireless sensor networks lifetime. Wirel. Netw. **14**, 831–858 (2008)
16. Sarimveis, H., Alexandridis, A., Bafas, G.: A fast training algorithm for RBF networks based on subtractive clustering. Neurocomputing. **51**, 501–505 (2003)
17. Wikipedia, k-means clustering, http://en.wikipedia.org/wiki/K-means_clustering
18. Madan, R., Lall, S.: Distributed algorithms for maximum lifetime routing in wireless sensor network. IEEE Trans. Wirel. Commun. **5**, 2185–2193 (2006)

Barrier Coverage with Discrete Levels of Sensing and Transmission Power in Wireless Sensor Networks

Haiming Luo[1], Hongwei Du[1]([✉]), Hejiao Huang[1], Qiang Ye[2], and Jing Zhang[1]

[1] Department of Computer Science and Technology,
Harbin Institute of Technology Shenzhen Graduate School,
Shenzhen, China
{cshmluo,cshitzhj}@gmail.com,
{hwdu,hjhuang}@hitsz.edu.cn
[2] Department of Computer Science and Information Technology,
University of Prince Edward Island, Charlottetown, Canada
qye@upei.ca

Abstract. Barrier coverage is widely used in border surveillance. Most literatures only consider sensing in barrier coverage. In this paper, we consider not only sensing but also communication in barrier coverage under a more practical environment: multi-hop wireless sensor networks. We assume that each sensor has $k+1$ adjustable sensing power levels and $k+1$ adjustable transmission power levels. Sensing data should be aggregated and transmitted to the sink node within a latency constraint. We call minimizing the individual node's maximum energy cost for barrier coverage subject to the latency constraint as the MIME problem. We propose several algorithms to solve the MIME problem. Firstly, we devise a distributed algorithm to minimize the sensing energy cost 1-local barrier coverage, then we use Divide and Conquer method to construct none-crossing k-barrier coverage. Finally we devise a heuristic algorithm to construct a data aggregation tree that satisfies nodes in barriers transmitting data to the sink node within the latency constraint. Simulations show that the proposed algorithms are efficient and outperform other existing algorithms.

Keywords: Barrier coverage · Energy efficiency · Data aggregation · Sensor networks

1 Introduction

Wireless sensor networks(WSNs) are multi-hop and self-organized networks which consist of one or multiple sink nodes and many sensor nodes. A sensor node can collect sensing data, process and transmit the data to its neighbors. The sink node is responsible to receive data from sensor nodes and inform users the environment of networks. Barrier coverage in wireless sensor networks is widely used in border surveillance. It is inspired by the moats which are used to detect and prevent

© Springer-Verlag Berlin Heidelberg 2015
L. Sun et al. (Eds.): CWSN 2014, CCIS 501, pp. 14–23, 2015.
DOI: 10.1007/978-3-662-46981-1_2

intruders trespassing [4]. Compared with area coverage or target coverage, barrier coverage has the advantage of requiring fewer sensor nodes. Sensor nodes whose sensing ranges overlap and cover the length of monitoring region form a 1-barrier coverage as shown in Fig. 1.

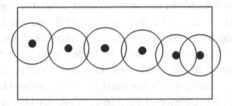

Fig. 1. An example of 1-barrier coverage.

Many literatures have studied the network lifetime and energy efficiency for area coverage and target coverage such as [6,12–15]. Like area coverage and target coverage, the network lifetime and energy efficiency are also important issues for barrier coverage. Gage et al. [1] firstly propose the concept of barrier coverage. The are two kinds of barrier coverage which are strong barrier coverage and weak barrier coverage. Kumar et al. [4] define the notion of k-barrier coverage using wireless sensor nodes and propose efficient algorithms to determine whether a region is barrier covered. They also prove the critical condition of weak barrier coverage. Liu et al. [7] prove the critical condition of strong barrier coverage. They devise an efficient distributed algorithm to construct strong barrier coverage with low communication overhead and low computation cost. Kumar et al. [8] propose optimal network lifetime strong barrier coverage algorithms. They prove an important theorem which is the optimal network lifetime of k-barrier coverage is m/k where m is the maximum number of node-disjoint paths. Ban et al. [11] define weak barrier coverage and propose a distributed algorithm for constructing weak barrier coverage. Chen et al. [9] introduce the concept of local barrier coverage and devise an efficient algorithm to construct local barrier coverage with a limitation that the crossing path of an intruder is bounded in a small rectangle box. Yang and Li [10] study the minimum energy cost k-barrier coverage problem by assuming each sensor has $l+1$ sensing power levels and propose two heuristic algorithms. The above works only consider sensing in barrier coverage. They simply treat that each sensor node can communicate with the sink node directly. However, the communication range is not large enough if a sensor node is far from the sink node. Thus we consider not only sensing but also communication in barrier coverage under multi-hop wireless sensor networks. According to [3], the communication consumes about 75 % energy of a sensor node. The communication energy efficiency is also an important factor for minimum energy cost barrier coverage problem. Du [5] states that data aggregation can reduce overall traffic given the limited bandwidth of a sensor node which saves energy. In this paper, we adopt data aggregation instead of data gathering in transmitting data to the sink node. As communication consumption is much higher than the computation cost [2], the energy cost of communication is mainly concerned with the number of hops from a sensor node to the sink node. The bigger the number of hops, the larger transmission latency. In the intruder detection, the sink node need to collect the data from sensor nodes periodically such that a transmission latency constraint is required.

Yang and Li [10] solve minimum energy cost k-barrier coverage problem by minimizing total sensing energy of sensor nodes. Based on the results of them, we extend this problem by considering another important factor communication energy cost and solve the problem in a different aspect: given the location of the sink node and sensor nodes with discrete levels of transmission power and a transmission latency constraint. Our goal is to minimize the individual node's maximum energy cost for barrier coverage subject to the transmission latency constraint by adjusting the power levels. Minimizing the individual node's maximum energy cost is significant because minimizing total energy cost does not guarantee minimizing the individual node's energy cost. If the individual node's sensing range is large, it is soon exhausted. Otherwise the individual node can last for longer time if its sensing range is small which means that there are more sensor nodes to be substituted. The contributions of our research are summarized as follows:

1. We propose an efficient distributed algorithm to minimize the sensing energy cost 1-local barrier coverage. Then based on Divide and Conquer method, we construct none-crossing k-barrier coverage.
2. Given k-barrier coverage and a transmission latency bound t_b, we construct a data aggregation tree T that satisfies nodes in barriers transmitting data to the sink node within latency t_b.

Above all we minimize the individual node's maximum energy cost for barrier coverage subject to the latency constraint. We call it the MIME problem. The rest of the paper is organized as follows: Sect. 2 presents the network model, Sect. 3 proposes algorithms for minimum sensing energy cost 1-local barrier coverage and none crossing k-barrier coverage, Sect. 4 solves the problem of minimum communication energy cost for barrier coverage. Section 5 presents our simulation results, Sect. 6 concludes this paper.

2   Network Model

We assume there are n sensor nodes randomly deployed in a monitoring region B. Each sensor node's sensing model and communication model are disk models. The radius of the sensing is denoted as R_s and the radius of the communication is denoted as R_c. Both of them have discrete power levels. The power levels vary from 0 to k where k is the maximum power level. R_c is assumed to be larger than R_s at the beginning. When the sensing power level increases, the communication power level increases correspondingly which means we always maintain $R_c > R_s$. Some definitions are shown as below:

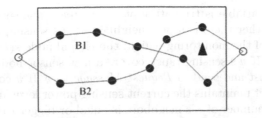

Fig. 2. An example of crossing barriers.

Definition 1. (Coverage Graph $G(V,E)$ [8]): The coverage graph is generated by the sensor network. V contains all sensor nodes and two virtual nodes while E contains all edges. There exists an edge between two sensor nodes in V whose sensing range overlaps. Two virtual nodes s and t are placed to the left of the monitoring region and to the right of the monitoring region respectively. There exists an edge between $s(t)$ and a sensor node u if u's sensing range covers the left(right) border of the monitoring region.

Definition 2. (Crossing Barriers): Two barriers B_1 and B_2 are said to be crossing barriers if and only if there is at least a pair of edges crossing in their coverage graph. Figure 2 is an example of crossing barriers.

Definition 3. (MIME Problem): The MIME problem is minimizing the individual node's maximum energy cost problem. Given a wireless sensor network N over a monitoring region B, each sensor node u has $k+1$ adjustable sensing power levels and $k+1$ adjustable transmission power levels. With a certain latency constraint t_b, our goal is to minimize the individual node's maximum energy cost for barrier coverage subject to t_b. The individual node's maximum energy cost contains the sensing energy cost and the transmission energy cost.

3   Minimum Sensing Energy Cost

In this section, we focus on minimizing individual node's maximum sensing energy cost for barrier coverage. Firstly, we propose an efficient distributed algorithm to construct 1-local barrier coverage which guarantees sensor nodes in the barriers maintain the minimum sensing power levels. Then we construct nonecrossing k-barrier coverage by the method of Divide and Conquer. Finally, we analyze the performance of our algorithms.

A. Minimum sensing energy cost 1-local barrier coverage
Minimum sensing energy cost 1-local barrier coverage is an efficient distributed algorithm. Each sensor node is assigned with the minimum sensing power level at the beginning. They increase their sensing power level progressively and maintain a boolean variable *Flag* which is used to direct themselves to adjust the sensing power level. *Flag* is set to be true initially. In Step 1, a sensor node

u whose boolean variable is true attempts to increase one sensing power level and examines whether there is a new neighbor. If u's sensing range covers the left(right) border of the monitoring region, the virtual node $s(t)$ is considered as u's new neighbor. If u's sensing range covers a new sensor node v, then it adds v to its neighbor list and sends a *Request Message* to v. If u covers none of the new sensor nodes, it maintains the current sensing power level and waits for next round. When the number of u's neighbors is equal or bigger than 2, its boolean variable is set to be false which means in the next round, it does not change its sensing power level. Because sensor node u and its current neighbors have formed local strong barrier coverage. There is no need to increase its sensing power level to find more neighbors.

In Step 2, each sensor node u handles its received messages. There are three kinds of messages which are *Request Message*, *Positive Message* and *Negative Message*. The *Request Message* is used to inquiry a sensor node's neighbor list. The *Positive Message* and the *Negative Message* are the response of *Request Message*. After receiving a *Request Message*, if the number of u's neighbors is smaller than 2, u begins to adjust its communication power lever to communicate with the sender, then it adds the sender as its new neighbor and returns a *Positive Message*, otherwise it return a *Negative Message* to the sender. When u receives a *Positive Message*, it adds the sender to its neighbor list while when u receives a *Negative Message*, it keeps its neighbor list the same. After Step 2, each sensor node goes back to the Step 1 and continues the next round.

Algorithm 1. Minimum sensing energy cost 1-local barrier coverage

---

1: **Initially** Assign the minimum power level to each sensor node. Each sensor node maintains a Boolean variable *Flag* which is set to be true.

2: **Step 1** Each sensor node u whose *Flag* is true increases its sensing power level and examines its neighbors.
    1) If u covers the border of monitoring region, u's neighbors plus one.
    2) If u covers a new sensor node v, then sends a *Request Message* to v.
    3) If u covers no new sensor nodes, do nothing and wait for next round.
    4) If the number of u's neighbors is equal or bigger than 2, set *Flag* to false.

3: **Step 2** Each sensor u receive a Message, adjust its communication power
    1) *Request Message*: If the number of u's neighbors is smaller than 2, then u's neighbors plus 1 and return a *Positive Message* to the sender. Otherwise, only return a *Negative Message* to the sender.
    2) *Positive Message*: Add the sender as a new neighbor
    3) *Negative Message*: u's neighbor list keep the same.

4: **Step 3** Go back to step 1.

5: **Output** Minimum energy cost 1-local barrier coverage.

B. None-crossing k-barrier coverage

In Kumar [8]'s study, he adopts the standard max-flow algorithm to compute the maximum number of node-disjoint paths and schedule these node-disjoint paths to construct k-barrier coverage. One node-disjoint path forms 1-barrier coverage. However, the max-flow algorithm does not guarantee none-crossing k-barrier coverage. In the coverage graph as Fig. 2, B_1 and B_2 represent two barriers. According to Kumar [8]'s optimal scheduling algorithm, B_1 works until it is exhausted, then B_2 takes the place of B_1. However, B_1 and B_2 are crossing barriers, if an intruder I is at the location as the Fig. 2 shown, then B_2 can't prevent I trespassing. Because after B_1 is exhausted, I is under B_2 which means sensor nodes in B_2 can't detect I any more. With this disadvantage, the network lifetime of barrier coverage decreases. Our goal is to construct none-crossing k-barrier coverage with the minimum energy cost.

In *Algorithm 2* we adopt Divide and Conquer method to construct none-crossing k-barrier coverage. Initially, we call *Algorithm 1* to compute a barrier B whose sensor nodes maintain the minimum sensing power level. When the density of node deployment is large enough, local barrier coverage can guarantee the global barrier coverage. Then we divide the redundant sensor nodes into two groups based on the constructed barrier B. For each group, we recursively call *Algorithm 1* to compute the next barrier until the sensor nodes of current group can not form a barrier.

Algorithm 2. Construct none crossing k-barrier coverage

1: Call *Algorithm 1* to compute a barrier B.
2: **if** B exists **then**
3:    Divide redundant sensor nodes as two groups G_1 and G_2 based on B.
4:    Continue to call *Algorithm 2* for each group.
5: **end if**
6: **Return** None crossing k-barrier coverage.

C. Performance evaluation

In each round of *Algorithm 1*, each sensor attempts to increase a sensing power level. When the number of a sensor node's neighbors is bigger or equal to 2, it does not increase its sensing power level. Such that *Algorithm 1* can converge very soon because as a sensor node's sensing range increase, it can easily find two neighbors. The biggest communication overhead of the network happens when *Algorithm 1* runs not long. At that time, the average number of neighbors of each sensor node is one. After that, the communication overhead becomes smaller and smaller. If the number of sensor nodes in the network is n, then the biggest communication overhead is $O(n)$. But most of time the communication overhead is smaller than $O(n)$.

In *Algorithm 2*, we adopt Divide and Conquer method to avoid constructing crossing barriers. In each branch, we call *Algorithm 1* to compute whether there exists a barrier. With the depth of the branch tree growing, the number of sensor nodes in each subgroup decreases. The largest communication overhead of constructing none-crossing k-barrier coverage is $O(nlogn)$. Such that our proposed algorithms for minimizing sensing energy cost barrier coverage have low communication overhead and they are efficient.

4   Minimum Communication Energy Cost

In this section, we aim to minimize the communication energy cost of the individual sensor node. In Sect. 2 we assume that the transmission power level increases corresponding with the sensing power level. After minimizing the sensing energy cost of the individual in Sect. 3, the individual sensor node maintains a low transmission power level. However, it can't guarantee that the data can be transmitted to the sink node under the latency constraint t_b. Because it needs more redundant sensor nodes as relay nodes to transmit data such that the transmission latency becomes larger. In the following study, we propose an algorithm to construct a data aggregation tree T subject to the latency constraint t_b by adjusting the individual sensor node's transmission power level.

In *Algorithm 3*, we construct a complete graph CG from G firstly. The length of each edge $e(u,v)$ is represented by the number of hops between u and v. Then we call *Kruskal* algorithm to produce an MST from CG. We can generate an aggregation tree T by substituting each edge in MST with the corresponding path in G. From Step 5 to Step 13, we modify T to satisfy the latency constraint t_b. We traverse the sensor nodes of barriers which are the source nodes one by one. We use $P_u c$ to denote a sensor node u's transmission power level and P_k to denote the maximum transmission power level. If the latency t_u from a sensor node u to the sink node s beyond t_b, then the shortest path from u to s in G is added to T. After that, if t_u still beyond t_b, then u increases its transmission power level gradually to find a shorter path to s.

Algorithm 3. Construct data aggregation tree subject to the latency constraint

1: **Input:** Coverage Graph G and the sink node s.
2: Construct a complete graph CG from G.
3: Produce an MST from CG.
4: Generate an aggregation tree T by MST.
5: **for** each node u in barriers **do**
6:   **if** $t_u > t_b$ **then**
7:     Add the shortest path from u to s to T.
8:     **while** $t_u > t_b$ and $P_u c \leqslant P_k$ **do**
9:       u increases a communication power level
10:      Find a shorter path to s.
11:    **end while**
12:   **end if**
13: **end for**
14: **Output:** The aggregation tree T with latency constraint t_b.

---

5   Simulations

In this section, we do extensive simulations by Java and Matlab to evaluate the performance of our algorithms. We present the average results from 100 separate runs of algorithms in the figures. Our simulations contains two parts:

In the first part, we compare the algorithms for the minimum sensing energy cost k-barrier coverage with two heuristic algorithms of Yang and Li [10]. The network parameters are set to the same as they do. Sensor nodes are randomly deployed in a 100×5 m rectangular monitoring region. Each sensor node has four different sensing ranges which are 0,4,6,8 and four sensing power levels which are 0,16,36,64. Yang and Li [10] study the effect of number of sensor nodes on the total sensing energy cost. Our algorithms aim to minimize the individual node's maximum sensing energy cost which is a different aspect. We add up each sensor node's sensing energy and do the comparing. In Figs. 3 and 4, "Heuristic-1" and "Heuristic-2" are two heuristic algorithms of Yang and Li [10]. "Distributed" is our proposed algorithm. We can see that "Distributed" has better performance than "Heuristic-1" and approaches to "Heuristic-2". Our distributed algorithm not only maintains minimum individual node's maximum sensing cost but also obtains low total energy cost.

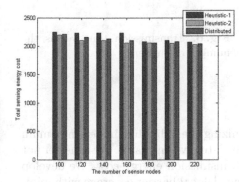 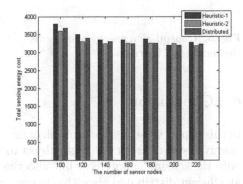

Fig. 3. Total sensing energy cost versus the number of sensor nodes with $k = 5$

Fig. 4. Total sensing energy cost versus the number of sensor nodes with $k = 8$

In the second part, we evaluate our algorithm through transmission energy cost and transmission time. We set the transmission power model: $P_c(u, v) = d^2(u,v)$. $d^2(u,v)$ is the distance in terms of number of hops between two sensor nodes u and v. We use $\max\{d(u,s) | u \in barriers\}$ to denote the longest shortest path from senor nodes in barriers to the sink node s. The latency bound ratio B_r is equal to $\alpha \Delta \max\{d(u,s) | u \in barriers\}$ where α is latency bound which varies from 1.5 to 2.5 and Δ is the maximal degree of T. Figure 5 shows the transmission energy cost versus the number of barriers, we can see that when α is strict latency bound or loose latency bound, the transmission energy costs are similar. When α is equal to 2.2 which is not strict and loose, the transmission energy cost is lower in general. Figure 6 shows the transmission time versus the number of barriers, we can see that after the number of barriers reaches to 6, the transmission time converges slowly because the transmission time is concerned with the depth of data aggregation tree T. When the number of source nodes reaches to a threshold that

T sustain, more source nodes does not increase the transmission time. When the latency bound is strict, the transmission time is smaller. This is actually expected as strict latency bound makes the depth of the aggregation tree T smaller.

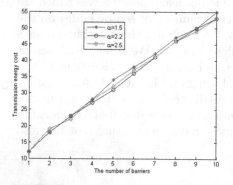

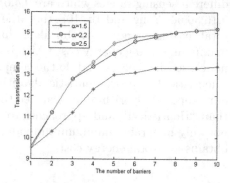

Fig. 5. Transmission energy cost versus the number of barriers

Fig. 6. Transmission time versus the number of barriers

6   Conclusion

In this paper, we study the problem of minimizing the individual node's maximum energy cost for barrier coverage subject to the latency constraint. We consider not only the sensing energy cost but also the transmission energy cost. We develop an efficient distributed algorithm to construct 1-local barrier coverage with minimum sensing energy cost. We also propose an algorithm to construct none-crossing k-barrier coverage. Then based on the methods of minimum spanning tree and shortest path tree, we construct a data aggregation tree under latency constraint by adjusting transmission power levels. For the future work, we will study the interference between neighbor barriers and construct interference-free k barrier coverage.

Acknowledgment. This work was financially supported by National Natural Science Foundation of China with Grants No.61370216, No.11371004 and No.61100191, and Shenzhen Strategic Emerging Industries Program with Grants No.ZDSY2012061312501 6389, No.JCYJ20120613151201451 and No.JCYJ20130329153215152.

References

1. Gage, D.W.: Command control for many-robot systems. In: Proceedings of the Nineteenth Annual AUVS Technology Symposium (AUVS 1992) (1992)
2. Pottie, G., Kaiser, W.: Wireless sensor networks. Commun. ACM 43(5), 51–58 (2000)

3. Mainwaring, A., Polastre, J., Szewczyk, R., Culler, D., Anderson, J.: Wireless sensor networks for habitat monitoring. In: Proceedings of the 1st ACM International Workshop on Wireless Sensor Networks and Applications, Atlanta, USA (2002)
4. Kumar, S., Lai, T.H., Arora, A.: Barrier coverage with wireless sensors. In: Proceedings of the 11th Annual International Conference on Mobile Computing and Networking (MobiCom), August 2005
5. Du, H., Hu, X., Jia, X.: Energy efficient routing and scheduling for real-time data aggregation in WSNs. J. Comput. Commun. 29(17), 3527–3535 (2006)
6. Thai, M.T., Wang, F., Du Hongwei, D., Jia, X.: Coverage problems in wireless sensornetworks: designs and analysis. Int. J. Sens. Netw. (IJSNET) 3, 191–200 (2008)
7. Liu, B., Dousse, O., Wang, J., Saipulla, A.: Strong barrier coverage of wireless sensor networks. In: Proceedings of the 9th ACM International Symposium on Mobile Ad Hoc Networking and Computing (MobiHoc) (2008)
8. Kumar, S., Lai, T.H., Posner, M.E., Sinha, P.: Maximizing the lifetime of a barrier of wireless sensors. IEEE Trans. Mob. Comput. (TMC) 9(8), 1161–1172 (2010)
9. Chen, A., Kumar, S., Lai, T.H.: Local barrier coverage in wireless sensor networks. IEEE Trans. Mob. Comput. (TMC) 9(4), 491–504 (2010)
10. Yang, H., Li, D., Zhu, Q., Chen, W., Hong, Y.: Minimum energy cost k-barrier coverage in wireless sensor networks. In: Proceeding of the 5th International Conference on Wireless Algorithms, Systems, and Applications (WASA) (2010)
11. Ban, D., Feng, Q., Han, G., Yang, W., Jiang, J., Dou, W.: Distributed scheduling algorithm for barrier coverage in wireless sensor networks. In: Proceedings of the 2011 Third International Conference on Communications and Mobile Computing (CMC), April 2011
12. Li, D., Liu, H., Lu, X., Chen, W., Du, H.: Target Q-Coverage problem with bounded service delay in directional sensor networks. Int. J. Distrib. Sens. Netw. (IJDSN) (2012)
13. Hongwei, D., Pardalos, P.M., Weili, W., Lidong, W.: Maximum lifetime connected coverage with two active-phase sensors. J. Global Optim. 56(2), 559–568 (2013)
14. Wu, L., Du, H., Wu, W., Li, D., Lv, J., Lee, W.: Approximations for minimum connected sensor cover. In: The 32nd IEEE International Conference on Computer Communications (INFOCOM) (2013)
15. Yang, M., Kim, D., Li, D., Chen, W., Du, H., Tokuta, A.O.: Sweep-coverage with energy-restricted mobile wireless sensor nodes. In: Ren, K., Liu, X., Liang, W., Xu, M., Jia, X., Xing, K. (eds.) WASA 2013. LNCS, vol. 7992, pp. 486–497. Springer, Heidelberg (2013)

Network Architecture and Deployment

3D Self-Deployment Algorithm in Mobile Wireless Sensor Networks

Chunyu Miao, Guoyong Dai, Xiao-min Zhao, Zhongze Tang,
and Qingzhang Chen[(✉)]

College of Computer Science and Technology,
Zhejiang University of Technology, Hangzhou, China
netmcy@zjnu.cn, daiguoyong@gmail.com,
{4007695, 8387667}@qq.com, qzchen@zjut.edu.cn

Abstract. The sensor deployment problem of wireless sensor networks (WSNs) is a key issue in the researches and the applications of WSNs. Fewer works focus on the 3D autonomous deployment. Aimed at the problem of sensor deployment in three dimensional spaces, the 3D Self-Deployment Algorithm (3DSD) in mobile sensor networks is proposed. A 3D virtual force model is utilized in the 3DSD method. A negotiation tactic is introduced to ensure network connectivity, and a density control strategy is used to balance the node distribution. The proposed algorithm can fulfill the nodes autonomous deployment in 3D space with obstacles. Simulation results indicate that the deployment process of 3DSD is relatively rapid, and the nodes are well distributed. Furthermore, the coverage ratio of 3DSD approximates the theoretical maximum value.

Keywords: Mobile sensor networks · Autonomous deployment · Virtual force algorithm · Nodes clustered · Density control

1 Introduction

The proliferation of wireless and mobile devices has fostered the applications of Wireless Sensor Networks (WSNs) pervaded from military to industry, agriculture and other scenarios [1]. The node deployment is a key issue in WSNs, since it seriously influences the feasibility and Quality of Service (QoS) for WSNs. Generally, the node deployment methods can be classified into static deployment scheme and dynamic deployment scheme [2]. The static deployment schemes are mainly applied in WSNs with non-mobility nodes; and it concludes determinate deployment methods and random deployment methods. In the random deployment scenario, sensor nodes are scattered via airplane or other aided measures into the Area of Interest (AOI) at which human being can't get conveniently. Random static deployment methods ensure the supervise performance via sensor node redundancy. While, the dynamic deployment methods are mainly used in a mobile WSNs (i.e. the sensor node has mobility) [3], after being scattered in AOI, the sensor nodes accomplish deployment autonomously. The autonomous deployment of mobile WSNs is a process in which the mobile sensor nodes adjust their positions dynamically according to a certain algorithm. By adopted

© Springer-Verlag Berlin Heidelberg 2015
L. Sun et al. (Eds.): CWSN 2014, CCIS 501, pp. 27–41, 2015.
DOI: 10.1007/978-3-662-46981-1_3

dynamic deployment method, the coverage performance is improved, while the overhead of hardware is decreased. However, the self-deployment scheme designing in three-dimension scenario is difficult, aside from this, the obstacle and area boundary may disturb the deployment process. Aimed at solving these problems aforementioned, we proposed a 3D self-deployment (3DSD) algorithm to fulfill the nodes autonomous deployment in 3D area with obstacles. Virtual force model is introduced in 3DSD method. The network connectivity and nodes distribution density are also concerned to provide the feasibility of 3DSD. Extensive simulations are conducted, experiment results indicate that the deployment duration of 3DSD is short comparatively, and the coverage ratio of 3DSD approximates the theoretical maximum value. The main contributions of our work can be summarized as follows: (1) The virtual force model is extended to three-dimensional space, and the optimal coverage ratio of 3D deployment is defined and calculated, (2) a density control tactic is explored, node density of each cluster is under control to ensure the node distribution of clusters is balance, (3) the network connectivity is concerned a negotiation protocol is designed to provide the practicability of 3DSD.

The rest of this paper is organized as follows. A brief introduction to the state of art of the sensor node deployment methods is presented in Sect. 2. The three-dimensional sensing model and the virtual force model are defined in Sect. 3. In Sect. 4, the 3DSD method is described in detail. Performance analysis of the proposed algorithm is provided in Sect. 5, and conclusions are drawn in Sect. 6.

2 The State of the Art

For the nodes deployment of WSN, there is a certain coverage performance criteria required to be satisfied. According to the application scenario of WSN, deployment coverage category can be classified into blanket coverage, barrier coverage and scan coverage [4]. Our work belongs to the blanket coverage. The node deployment is an enabling issue for WSN, so a large number of deployment methods are presented by scholars [5]. There mainly are three categories research methods in node deployment: incremental deployment method [6], geometric analysis method [7], and virtue force based method [7]. The incremental deployment method is appropriate for the scenario that the supervise area is unknown, but the deployment cycle is too long. Geometric analysis method can't guarantee network connectivity, and it is hard to be applied into some scenario with obstacles. Zou et al. [8] first proposed deployment method using virtual force model (VFM) in WSN. In VFM, sensor nodes are supposed subjecting to some kinds of forces come from area border, other nodes and so forth. The force balance is regarded as the final state of network. Due to the intuition and the descriptive ability of VFM, it is widely used in deployment issue of WSN [9].

The node deployment issue also can be classified into static deployment and dynamic deployment according to whether nodes have moving ability. In dynamic blanket deployment, one sub-issue is how to mend deployment holes formed in static deployment process using mobile nodes [10]. Another sub-issue is self-deployment of some mobile enabling nodes after they are launched in AOI [11]. Our work focuses on the latter. A geometric analysis method is proposed in [12], however, there still has the problem that it is hard to be employed in scenarios with obstacles. In [13], an autonomous deployment algorithm based on VFM is adopted in 2D scenario. But, for the VFM model with obstacle forces, some certain strategies should be adopted to avoid algorithm trapping into local optimum.

According to the dimensionality of AOI, the node deployment method yet can be divided into two classes: deployment in 2D space and deployment in 3D space. In 3D space deployment, there have two sub-issues, one is 3D area coverage [14] (e.g. underwater sensor deployment), and another is 3D surface deployment [15] (e.g. mountain surface deployment). Our work is about the former. A lot of applications of WSN are 3D scenario, so the autonomous deployment of mobile WSN in 3D space is of great significance [16]. It is hard to directly utilize 2D deployment method in 3D space [17], furthermore, there are fewer works focus on the 3D sensor autonomous deployment [18]. One kind of solution for 3D deployment is dimensionality reducing, but it is not suitable to autonomous algorithm. Another solution is to construct the 3D deployment model directly as [19]. However, this centralized method is lack of pervasiveness, because it only can be used in static deployment. Liu et al. [20] proposed a combined virtual force algorithm (CVF) for 3D autonomous deployment, and the performance of this algorithm is good, but the deployment cycle is comparatively long. For the autonomous deployment in 3D space, the real situation (e.g. obstacles, area boundary etc.) which can influence the deployment should be fully considered. Aside from this, both of the network connectivity and the deployment cycle should be considered. Moreover, the local optimum problem needs to be avoided [21].

3 Preliminaries

3.1 Three-Dimensional Sensing Model

We adopted a sphere perception model that node s is the center, and, R_t is the radius of the sphere. As shown in Fig. 1, within the sensing spherical region, the probability to be perceived is 1, while outside the sphere the probability to be perceived is 0. The perception function is expressed by the formula (1).

$$C(s,p) = \begin{cases} 1, & if \ d(s,p) < \, = R_t \\ 0, & otherwise \end{cases} \tag{1}$$

In Fig. 1, node P is an arbitrary point in sphere, C(s, p) represents the probability that P can be perceived by sensor node s, and d(s, p) denotes the Euclidean distance between s and point P. Every sensor nodes has the same transmission power, i.e. the same sensing radius. In fact, the 3D deployment problem, that is, how to use balls with certain radius to cover a three-dimensional space completely. We need to use fewer nodes to cover as much as possible spaces when taking the viewpoint of economic saving into consideration. Figure 2 is a schematic diagram of the ideal three-dimensional perception model in a three-dimensional perception space.

In a two-dimensional plane, seamless maximum effective coverage area of three circles is acquired when the three circles intersect at one point and their centers

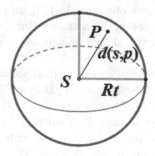

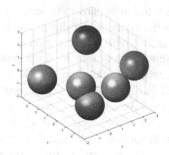

Fig. 1. Ideal 3D perception model   **Fig. 2.** Sensor nodes in 3D space

constitute a regular triangle. Compare to the two-dimensional plane, the coverage problem in three-dimensional space is more complex, and the best coverage problem in three-dimensional space is proved to be an NP-hard problem [22], but the foundational idea of the best coverage in the three-dimensional space is same as in two-dimensional. First, two definitions are proposed as following.

Definition 1 (VECA): For an arbitrary node S1, its effective coverage area VECA is the coverage space of node S1 minus the volume of the overlapping area VZ:

$$V_{ECA} = V - V_Z = \frac{4}{3}\pi r^3 - V_Z \tag{2}$$

Definition 2 (CECA): For an arbitrary node S1, its effective coverage efficiency CECA is the ratio of the VECA and the volume of node coverage area V:

$$C_{ECA} = \frac{V_{ECA}}{V} = \frac{V - V_Z}{V} = 1 - \frac{3V_Z}{4\pi r^3} \tag{3}$$

Next, let's discuss the intersection of four 1 nodes.

Theorem 1: There are four seamless topological spheres S1, S2, S3 and S4. When the four balls intersect at a point O, and the centers of the sphere constitute a tetrahedral $\Box$ S1S2S3S4 which is regular tetrahedron, the seamless maximum effective coverage space can be obtained. Its volume is $(28\sqrt{6} - 24)\pi r^3/9$.

Proof: Here we divided the positional relationship of the four sphere centers into two cases. The first one is shown in Fig. 3(a), add a ball S4 to the situation in which maximum effective coverage has been achieved by three balls. We have $S4S1 = S4S2 = S4S3 = \sqrt{2}r$, and the distances between $S1$, $S2$ and $S3$ are $\sqrt{3}r$, after calculations, the volume of the coverage space can be obtained:

$$V_4' = \frac{30\sqrt{2} + 27\sqrt{3} - 32}{12}\pi r^3 \tag{4}$$

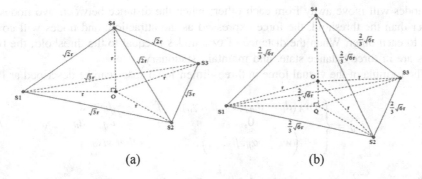

(a)   (b)

Fig. 3. The center of the sphere location map

The second case is shown in Fig. 3(b), the tetrahedral □ S1S2S3S4 is regular tetra-
hedron, and the four spheres intersect at the center of tetrahedral. $OS1 = OS2 = OS3 = OS4 = r$, $OQ = r/3$, we get $d = S1S2 = S2S3 = S3S4 = S4S1 = 2\sqrt{6}r/3$, after calculations, the volume of the coverage space under this positional relationship can be
obtained:

$$V_4'' = \frac{28\sqrt{6} - 24}{9}\pi r^3 \tag{5}$$

Obviously, it can be seen that the maximum effective coverage space with four balls
is obtained when the four sphere centers constitute a regular tetrahedron. According to
formula (2) and (3), the increment of VECA and CECA (named as VECAI and CECAI)
that a new ball is added into space can be calculated as formula (6).

$$V_{ECAI} = V_{ball} - 6 \times V_{crown} = \frac{4}{3}\pi r^3 - 2\pi h^2(3r - h) \tag{6}$$

where $h = (3 - \sqrt{6})r/3$, when h is substituted into formula (6), we get:

$$V_{ECAI} = \frac{14\sqrt{6} - 24}{9}\pi r^3 \tag{7}$$

And, the corresponding CECAI is:

$$C_{ECAI} = \frac{V_{ECA}}{V_{ball}} = \frac{7\sqrt{6} - 12}{6} = 85.774\% \tag{8}$$

3.2   Three-Dimensional Virtual Force Model

The idea of virtual force in three-dimensional is: there exit interactive forces between
every node in 3D space. According to the threshold d_{th} set in advance, when the
distance of two nodes is less than the threshold d_{th}, the force expressed as repulsion,

and nodes will move away from each other; when the distance between two nodes is greater than the threshold, the force expressed as the attraction, and nodes will come close to each other. When the distance of two nodes is equal to the threshold, the two nodes are in force balance state, and maintain stationary.

The formula of the virtual force in three-dimensional space can be described as (9):

$$\overrightarrow{F}_{ij} = \begin{cases} \left(w_A \left(d_{ij} - d_{th} \right), \alpha_{ij}, \beta_{ij}, \gamma_{ij} \right), & if & d_{ij} > d_{th} \\ 0, & if & d_{ij} = d_{th} \\ \left(w_R \frac{1}{d_{ij}}, \alpha_{ji}, \beta_{ji}, \gamma_{ji} \right), & otherwise \end{cases} \quad (9)$$

The vector $\overrightarrow{F}_{ij}$ represents virtual force of Si subjects to Sj in three-dimensional space, dij is the Euclidean distance between Si and Sj in three-dimensional space, d_{th} is the threshold value α_{ij}, β_{ij}, γ_{ij} is the direction angle of the space vector $\overrightarrow{S_i S_j}$. WA and WR are the virtual attraction coefficient and the virtual repulsion coefficient.

The forces come from not only between sensor nodes, but also between node and obstacles, this kind of force is treated as repulsion. Due to the repulsion force between node and obstacle, the node is able to be deployed around the obstacle to the open area. $\overrightarrow{F}_{iR}$ represents repulsion force that obstacles exert on Si. Furthermore, in order to take some areas needing to be covered priori into account, attractions come from these regions are introduced, the jointed force of these regions is represented as $\overrightarrow{F}_{iA}$. Then, the resultant force subjected by an arbitrary node Si is

$$\overrightarrow{F}_i = \sum_{j=1, j \neq i}^{k} \overrightarrow{F}_{ij} + \overrightarrow{F}_{iR} + \overrightarrow{F}_{iA} \quad (10)$$

where, $\overrightarrow{F}_i$ stands for the resultant force exerted on Si, and k denotes the number of sensor nodes in a specific three-dimensional space.

4   Description to 3DSD Algorithm

In this section, the explanation and analysis of some design details are illustrated, such as node density calculating, clustering strategy and movement location calculation. Finally, we explain the concrete execution steps of 3DSD.

4.1   Density Calculation

The magnitude of virtual force is determined by density of nodes and obstacles. The spherical communication area of the sensor node is divided into k sub-areas evenly, the value of k is larger, and the expression of density is more accurate. A partition of certain sensor communication area ($k = 8$) is illustrated in Fig. 4. Wherein, the red irregular object represents obstacle. The sensing radius of node S1 is r, and the communication radius is R, its communication area is evenly divided into 8 regions. Region 1 to region 4 are arranged from front to rear and from right to left in upper hemisphere, so do in lower hemisphere. Node $S2$ is in the region 2, and node $S3$ is in the region 8, the obstacle is sensed in region 5 which is shown as the blue shaded area in the figure. The node density and obstacle density are presented as following.

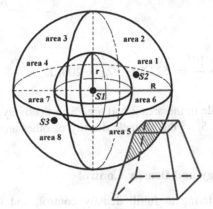

Fig. 4. Node's communication area partition (k = 8)

The node density of $S1$ can be calculated as formula (11):

$$D = \frac{N_A}{N_t} \tag{11}$$

where D denotes the node density, N_A is the number of nodes in a sub-area of $S1$, and N_t is the theoretical minimal number of nodes which locates in the sensing area and its sense range can cover the whole sub-are. N_t is a parameter that is related to the sensor node's sensing radius and communication radius. In the three-dimensional perception model, N_t can be approximately calculated based on $CECA$:

$$N_t = C_{ECA} \frac{K_m}{V_{ball}} = \frac{3C_{ECA}K_m}{4\pi r^3} \tag{12}$$

where K_m is the volume of a node's single sub-area, and r is the sensing range of a sensor node.

The density of an obstacle is defined as

$$D_o = \frac{O_m}{K_m} \tag{13}$$

where O_m is the volume of obstacles that a sensor node can detect in single sub-area, and K_m is the whole volume of one sub-area. Take Fig. 4 for instance, assuming that the communication range of $S1$ is 10 m and the sensing range is 5 m. Here, suppose that $O_m = 200$, and from formula (8), we get the CECA is 85.774 %. The node density and obstacle density can be calculated as follows.

The node density of area 2 (or area 8):

$$K_m = \frac{\frac{4}{3}\pi R^3}{k} = \frac{\frac{4}{3} \times \pi \times 10^3}{8} = 523.599, N_a = 1$$

$$N_t = \frac{3C_{ECA}K_m}{4\pi r^3} = \frac{3 \times 85.774\% \times 523.599}{4 \times \pi \times 5^3} = 0.858, D = \frac{N_a}{N_t} = \frac{1}{0.858} = 1.166$$

In area 5:

$$K_m = \frac{\frac{4}{3}\pi R^3}{k} = \frac{\frac{4}{3} \times \pi \times 10^3}{8} = 523.599, O_m = 200, D_o = \frac{O_m}{K_m} = \frac{200}{523.599} = 0.382$$

Note there is one node in the area 2 and area 8 respectively, and the obstacle only can be perceived in area 5, so the obstacle density of other area is 0.

4.2   Clustering Strategy and Density Control

Sensor nodes need clustering to fulfill density control, and the clustering strategy should be simple and efficient to decrease the deployment duration. So, the minimum ID clustering algorithm is adopted here [23].

With nodes movement, there may be appear a situation in which the member nodes and head node needing re-select. As depicted in Fig. 5, nodes form two cluster in a certain moment, i.e. S1, S2, S6, S7 and S3, S4, S5 is clustering into two groups respectively as Fig. 5(a). S1 and S3 are head node, and others are member node. In next moment (i.e. Fig. 5(b)), S3 moves to the new location, the two clusters must be re-clustered. To avoid the re-clustering process exerts too frequent, we define that cluster operation executes one time per deployment round.

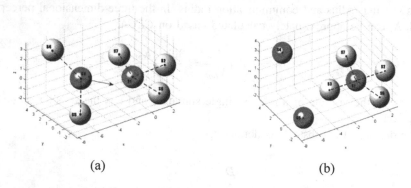

(a)   (b)

Fig. 5. Clustering after node moving

Due to the presence of obstacles, the phenomenon "regional segmentation" may be emerge, namely force that nodes subject to is balanced in local area. To solve this problem, cluster density control is adopted. After clustering is finished, the neighboring head nodes exchange the in-cluster node density. The cluster with higher density schedules some nodes to move in the cluster with lower density in case of the density difference is greater than a certain threshold. To do so, the local force balance is broke, and also, the node distribution is more even.

4.3   Decision of Target Location

There is a key issue, that is, how to calculate the target location that node needs move to. The distance and direction information can be calculated according to the received signal strength and received signal direction, based on the virtual force model proposed in Sect. 3.2, we define a virtual force vector $\vec{F}$:

$$\vec{F} = \begin{cases} (D(G - d_{th}), \alpha, \beta, \gamma), & if \quad G > d_{th} \\ 0, & if \quad G = d_{th} \\ \left(\dfrac{D}{G}, \pi - \alpha, \pi - \beta, \pi - \gamma\right), & otherwise \end{cases} \tag{14}$$

where D stands for the node density of a certain sub-area of a sensor node ($1/k$ communication area), and G denotes the Euclidean distance between source node and its neighbor in the sub-area. (α, β, γ) represent the bearings on the direction which source node points to its neighbor in case virtual force is expressed as attraction, to repulsion case, the direction angle should be $(\pi - \alpha, \pi - \beta, \pi - \gamma)$. Here, $d_{th} = 2\sqrt{6}r/3$, r is the sensing radius of nodes. The force introduced by an obstacle is calculated by another vector $\vec{F}_o$:

$$\vec{F}_o = \left(\frac{D_o}{G_o}, \pi - \alpha, \pi - \beta, \pi - \gamma\right) \tag{15}$$

where Do is the density of an obstacle in a certain sub-area, and Go denotes the Euclidean distance between the sensor node and the centroid of obstacle. After calculating the values of $\vec{F}$ and $\vec{F}_O$, we can get the value of the resultant force $\vec{F}_k$ in each sub-area: $\vec{F}_k = \vec{F} + \vec{F}_O$. Let $\vec{F}_{xk}$ represents the component of $\vec{F}_k$ on the x-axis, $\vec{F}_{yk}$ denotes the component of $\vec{F}_k$ on the y-axis, and $\vec{F}_{zk}$ is the force component of $\vec{F}_k$ on the z-axis. Then, the resultant force comes from all partitions of a certain node is

$$\left|\vec{F}_{con}\right| = \sqrt{\left(\left|\sum_{m=1}^{k} \vec{F}_{xk}\right|\right)^2 + \left(\left|\sum_{m=1}^{k} \vec{F}_{yk}\right|\right)^2 + \left(\left|\sum_{m=1}^{k} \vec{F}_{zk}\right|\right)^2} \tag{16}$$

where $\vec{F}_{con}$ is the resultant force that a node subject to. The norm of $\vec{F}_{con}$ denotes magnitude of force. Let (α, β, γ) denote the direction of virtual force, these three parameters present the included angle formed by $\vec{F}_{con}$ and the positive direction of x-axis, y-axis, and z-axis respectively. In order to facilitate the calculation, three unit vectors are introduced here, they are $\vec{e}_x = (1, 0, 0)$, $\vec{e}_y = (0, 1, 0)$ and $\vec{e}_z = (0, 0, 1)$, stands for unit vector on x-axis, y-axis and z-axis, respectively. Here, θ_x is the angle between $\vec{e}_x$ and

$\sum_{m=1}^{k} \vec{F}_{xk}$, θ_y is the angle between $\vec{e}_y$ and $\sum_{m=1}^{k} \vec{F}_{yk}$, and θ_z is the angle between $\vec{e}_z$ and $\sum_{m=1}^{k} \vec{F}_{zk}$. Then, the direction angle between the old position and the new one is

$$\alpha = \cos^{-1} \frac{\left| \sum_{m=1}^{k} \vec{F}_{xk} \right| \cdot \cos \theta_x}{\sqrt{\left(\left| \sum_{m=1}^{k} \vec{F}_{xk} \right| \right)^2 + \left(\left| \sum_{m=1}^{k} \vec{F}_{yk} \right| \right)^2 + \left(\left| \sum_{m=1}^{k} \vec{F}_{zk} \right| \right)^2}} \tag{17}$$

where k is the number of sub-areas. β and γ also can be calculated using formula (17). The distance between the new position and the old position is $d = D_{con} / \left| \vec{F}_{con} \right|$, where $D_{con} = D + DO$, it denotes the sum of node density and obstacle density in the node's communication range.

The movement range of a node calculated from resultant force may be very large, and the direction of each node is different. So, after moving, some nodes maybe isolated. Here, a negotiation strategy is adopted to ensure network connectivity.

(1) Node n_i (who has decided to move a certain distance) sent a '*ask*' message to its neighbors, the movement range and direction are included in the '*ask*' message.
(2) Neighbor node n_j (j = 1,2,...,n&&j! = i) estimates the network connectivity after n_i moving, there three cases:
  a. If there has no effect on network connectivity after movement of n_i, then, n_j sends back '*ok*' message.
  b. if the new position of n_i is out of their communication range, and neighbors $(n_j) > 2$, n_j sends back a '*suggest*' message which including a suggested moving distance d'.
  c. if the new position of n_i is out of their communication range, and neighbors $(n_j) <= 2$, n_j sends back an '*alert*' message which including a suggested moving distance d' as well.
(3) Node n_i determines the moving distance according the acknowledge message:
  a. If there is no '*alert*' message sent back. And Number(*ok*) $>= 2$ the origin distance is maintained, in case of Number(*ok*) = 1, the maximum suggested distance d' is adopted, otherwise, the secondary maximum d' is accepted.
  b. In case of there has some '*alert*' message sent back, the minimum suggested distance d' within these '*alert*' messages is accepted.

To do so, there at least have two one-hop neighbors of n_i. The negotiation introduces some communication overhead, but the 2-connected property is provided.

4.4 Steps of 3DSD

There are four stages in 3DSD algorithm, including initiation stage (step 1), selection stage (step 2, step 3), decision stage (step 4–6) and balancing stage (step 7, step 8). Each round of 3DSD deployment comprises of all these four stages. The iteration terminal condition of 3DSD is none of nodes has moved in present round. The node state has two sub-states: '*un-deployed*' and '*deployed*'. The node state is used to distinguish whether the nodes has been deployed in present round. Arguments of 3DSD are listed in Table 1.

Table 1. Input arguments of 3DSD

Arguments	Meaning
k	The number of partitions
λ	Duration of waiting for acknowledgement
τ	Upper limit of waiting for resent 'ok' message
ω	The minimum distance threshold of node movement
ε	The gap threshold of average density
r	Sensing radius of sensor node
R	Communication radius of sensor node

Each round of 3DSD can be described as follows:

Step 1   cluster state and node state are initiated.

Step 2   Each node sent its location to one-hope neighbors to update adjacency list.

Step 3   Each node calculates the node density according to adjacency list of itself, and calculates obstacle density. Then the movement target location is acquired.

Step 4   Each node broadcasts '*ask*' message to its neighbor, and determines the final movement target location according to the received acknowledgement message.

Step 5   After movement, repeat clustering process for all nodes, and member nodes report whether they have moved or not to the head node.

Step 6   The in-cluster node density is calculated by head node, and is sent to all two-hope neighbored head nodes.

Step 7   A certain nodes are scheduled from the cluster with higher density to the cluster with lower density in case of the density difference reaches the threshold.

Step 8   The algorithm is terminated if none of nodes moved and no density adjustment occurrence, otherwise go to step 1.

The node state is kept as '*deployed*' during deployment in following cases.

(a) There are obstacles in the route of node moving on, such that the movement can't accomplish.
In this case, the node that cannot accomplish its movement alters its destination in origin orientation. The distance between the destination and the obstacle surface is ω.

(b) The distance between destination and present location is smaller than the threshold ω.

Here, ω is an input argument, it used as a threshold, and it plays a critical role for the terminating of deployment. Its value is set as the *0.1* times communication radius of sensor node, such that the deployment duration and the coverage ratio are balanced, according to simulation experiment.

5 Simulation and Analysis

5.1 Simulation Environments

The size of the AOI is set as 80 m × 80 m × 80 m. In order to calculate the volume of the obstacles and the coverage ratio, the AOI is divided into grids, and the grid area is 1 m × 1 m × 1 m. We assume that the sensing range is 10 m, and the communication range is 20 m. In the simulation, the success rate of sending and receiving messages is 100 %. There are several obstacles in this three-dimensional space, and they are randomly placed. In order to facilitate the calculation of obstacle density, the shapes of the obstacles are set as rectangular in simulation. The boundaries of the three dimensional space are also treated as an obstacle.

5.2 Effect and Evaluation

In the three dimensional space with obstacles, 120 nodes are sown randomly in the center of the area. Then, the deployment commence. These 120 nodes finally are deployed evenly to the whole space with the attraction and repulsion, the effect of the algorithm implementation is shown in Fig. 6.

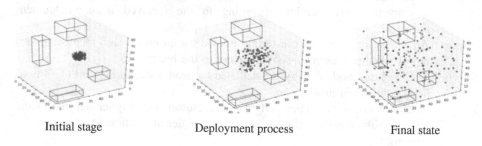

| Initial stage | Deployment process | Final state |

Fig. 6. Execution Effect of 3DSD

Two most important indicators to assess deployment algorithm are coverage ratio and deployment rounds. Figures 7 and 8 are the results of the execution of 3DSD.

Still in the previous environment of 3D space, the number of nodes increased from 5 to 120, the abscissa is number of nodes, the ordinate are the coverage ratio and deployment rounds respectively. We can see that with the gradual increase of the number of nodes, both coverage and deployment rounds show ascendant trend. The number of nodes in a linear relationship with the coverage, and the number of nodes is proportion to the deployment rounds. When there are 120 nodes in the AOI, the highest coverage rate can reach 82 %. But the theoretical calculated value of the highest

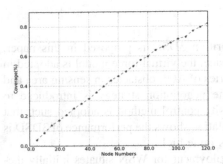

Fig. 7. Coverage ratio variation

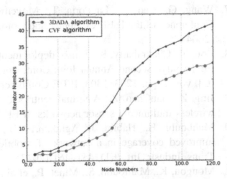

Fig. 8. Deployment round variation

coverage rate is 88 %, the nearly 6 % of the error is caused by the system parameter setting and the too big grid.

5.3   Comparison with CVF

The CVF algorithm [20] also focuses on how to maximize the coverage ratio in 3D space by autonomous tactic. Comparisons are conducted between the CVF and our 3DSD algorithm. The two comparison indicators are coverage ratio and deployment time (i.e. deployment round), as shown in Figs. 9 and 10 respectively. The network coverage performances of these two methods are similar. The deployment rounds of these two methods are both increased when sensor nodes increased. But, the deployment time of 3DSD is less than the CVF. The reasons are clustering and density control tactics introduced in 3DSD, and the terminal criteria of 3DSD is threshold judgment, while the terminal criteria of CVF is round-movement judgment. The time of deployment becomes important when the coverage ratio of deployment algorithm is close to the theoretical maximum.

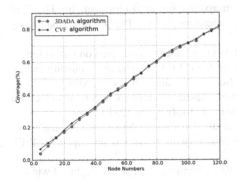

Fig. 9. Comparison of coverage ratio

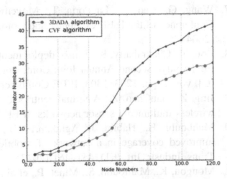

Fig. 10. Comparison of iteration variation

6 Conclusion

A distribution autonomous deployment algorithm 3DSD is proposed in this paper. Aimed at the node deployment issue in 3D space, the virtual force model is adopted in 3DSD method. The forces come from boundaries of AOI, obstacles in sensing area and the sensitive area are totally considered. The negotiation strategy is introduced to provide network connectivity. The node density control method is adopted such that the density between clusters is balanced. Simulation shows the performance of 3DSD is preferable, and the coverage ratio of 3DSD is quite high.

The work focuses on 3D autonomous deployment for WSN situates initially theoretical stage yet. In the future, a 3D irregular sensing model will be considered.

Acknowledgements. This research was supported by The National Natural Science Foundation of China (61379023).

References

1. Akyildiz, F., Su, W., Sankarasubramaniam, Y., Cayirci, E.: Wireless sensor networks: a survey. Comput. Netw. **38**(4), 393–422 (2002)
2. Ko, R.S.: Analyzing the redeployment problem of mobile wireless sensor networks via geographic models. Wirel. Commun. Mob. Comput. **13**(2), 111–129 (2013)
3. Chang, Y., Zhang, S., Zhang, Y.: Uncertainty-aware sensor deployment strategy in mixed wireless sensor networks. Int. J. Distrib. Sens. Netw. **2013**, 1–9 (2013). Article ID:834704
4. Gage, D.W.: Command control for many-robot systems. In: Proceedings of the 19th Annual AUVS Technical Symposium (1992)
5. Kulkarni, R.V., Venayagamoorthy, G.K.: Bio-inspired algorithms for autonomous deployment and localization of sensor nodes. IEEE Trans. Syst. Man Cybern. Part C Appl. Rev. **40**(6), 663–675 (2010)
6. Lin, Z., Zhang, S., Yan, G.: An incremental deployment algorithm for wireless sensor networks using one or multiple autonomous agents. Ad Hoc Netw. **11**(1), 355–367 (2013)
7. Wang, G., Cao, G., La Porta, T.: Movement-assisted sensor deployment. In: The 23rd Conference of the IEEE Computer and Communications Society (INFOCOM), Hong Kong (2004)
8. Zou, Y., Chakrabarty, K.: Sensor deployment and target localization based on virtual forces. In: Twenty- Second Annual Joint Conference of the IEEE Computer and Communications [C], vol. **2**, pp. 1293–1303. IEEE Computer Society, Washington D.C. (2003)
9. Jing, Z., JianChao, Z.: A virtual centripetal force-based coverage-enhancing algorithm for wireless multimedia sensor networks. IEEE Sens. J. **10**(8), 1328–1334 (2010)
10. Mahboubi, H., Habibi, J., Aghdam, A.G., et al.: Distributed deployment strategies for improved coverage in a network of mobile sensors with prioritized sensing field. IEEE Trans. Industr. Inf. **9**(1), 451–461 (2013)
11. Mougou, K., Mahfoudh, S., Minet, P., et al.: Redeployment of randomly deployed wireless mobile sensor nodes. In: Vehicular Technology Conference (VTC Fall) 2012, pp. 1–5. IEEE, Quebec City (2012)
12. Bartolini, N., Calamoneri, T., La Porta, T.F., Silvestri, S.: Autonomous deployment of heterogeneous mobile sensors. IEEE Trans. Mob. Comput. **10**(6), 753–766 (2011)

13. Li, J., Zhang, B., Cui, L., et al.: An extended virtual force-based approach to distributed self-deployment in mobile sensor networks.Int. J. Distrib. Sens. Netw. **2012**, Article ID:417307 (2012)
14. Yu, X., Liu, N., Huang, W., et al.: A node deployment algorithm based on van der waals force in wireless sensor networks. Int. J. Distrib. Sens. Netw. **2013**, Article ID:505710 (2013)
15. Jin, M., Rong, G., Wu, H.: Optimal surface deployment problem in wireless sensor networks. In: Proceedings of INFOCOM 2012, pp. 2345–2353 (2012)
16. Zhang, C., Bai, X., Teng, J., et al.: Constructing low-connectivity and full-coverage three dimensional sensor networks. IEEE J. Sel. Areas Commun. **28**(7), 984–993 (2010)
17. Al-Turjman, F.M., Hassanein, H.S., Ibnkahla, M.A.: Comput. Commun. **36**(2), 135–148 (2013)
18. Huang, C.F., Tseng, Y.C., Lo, L.C.: The coverage problem in three-dimensional wireless sensor networks. In: Proceedings of GLOBECOM 2004, pp. 3182–3186 (2004)
19. Huadong, M., Xi, Z., Anlong, M.: A coverage enhancing method for 3D directional sensor networks. In: Proceedings of INFOCOM 2009, pp. 2791–2795 (2009)
20. Liu, H., Chai, Z.J., Du, J.Z., et al.: Sensor redeployment algorithm based on combined virtual forces in three dimensional space. ACTA Automatica Sinica **37**(6), 713–723 (2011). (in Chinese with English abstract)
21. Chang, R.S., Wang, S.H.: Self-deployment by density control in sensor networks. IEEE Trans. Veh. Technol. **57**(3), 1745–1754 (2008)
22. Williams, R.: The Geometrical Foundation of Natural Structure: A Source Book of Design. Dover, New York (1979)
23. Gerla, M., Tsai, J.T.-C.: Multicluster, mobile, multimedia radio network. ACM Baltzer J. Wireless Netw. **1**(3), 255–265 (1995)

A Low Redundancy and High Coverage Node Scheduling Algorithm for Wireless Sensor Networks

Ying Xu[✉] and ZengRi Zeng[✉]

College of Computer Science and Electronic Engineering, Hunan University,
Changsha 410082, Hunan, People's Republic of China
hnxy@hnu.edu.cn, 363148834@qq.com

Abstract. In order to efficiently use node's energy and prolong node's life time in wireless sensor networks (WSN), this paper presents a low redundancy and high coverage (LRHC) node scheduling algorithm. In LRHC, based on the characteristics of the cellular, the WSN network is divided into a number of cellular to help the selection of active nodes. A new triangle cover method has been theoretically analyzed and proposed to solve the coverage holes problem for the first time. In addition, during the scheduling, a new active node will be the substitute for the active node near to death, which guarantees the stability of network coverage quality. The experimental results demonstrate that the proposed LRHC algorithm reduces the required nodes to satisfy a certain coverage quality, and improves the life time and ensures the high coverage quality of the network compared with some existing algorithms.

Keywords: WSN · Node scheduling · The coverage hole

1 Introduction

With the rapid development of wireless communications and sensor technology, Wireless Sensor Network (WSN), the core technology of the internet of things, has become a hot research topic [1–5]. A typical WSN which consists of a large number of sensor nodes is able to collect and send information within a monitoring area [6]. Over the last decade, WSN has been widely studied and applied in many fields, such as the environmental monitoring [7], the battlefield, the medical diagnosis, the habitat monitoring of animals [8–11], etc. A large-scale WSN is normally deployed by a group of high-density sensor nodes. A sensor node's energy is limited due to the usage of battery and the replacement of battery for distributed sensor nodes is impractical. A key to the success of a WSN application is for the purpose of minimizing energy consumption of the nodes energy consumption and prolong the life time of the network [12] as long as possible, which has attracted much research attention.

In the literature, the researchers have proposed a lot of solutions and algorithms for the sensor nodes scheduling problem in WSN. By using accurate location information of nodes to judge whether a node covers other redundant nodes, we can select some redundant nodes to be dormant, so as to prolong the network's life time. In [13], the dismissal unqualified rules (i.e. off-duty eligibility ride) are proposed to compute the

© Springer-Verlag Berlin Heidelberg 2015
L. Sun et al. (Eds.): CWSN 2014, CCIS 501, pp. 42–51, 2015.
DOI: 10.1007/978-3-662-46981-1_4

angle and the coverage redundancies of nodes according to the location and communication information of nodes. Zhang [14] discussed the network coverage and the topology structure, and proposed an Optimal Geographical Density Control (OGDC) algorithm. OGDC calculates the redundancies of coverage according to nodes' position information. However, through the GPS [15–18] or a compass to get the location information consumes a majority of node energy and also makes the network system become more complex. At present, the triangular lattice node sequence which optimizes the coverage performance and deployment of nodes has been proposed in the literature [16]. However, the demand of the precise location of the node consumes a lot of power which reduces the lifetime of a WSN [14–18]. Therefore, aiming to extend the life cycle of a WSN, the node scheduling algorithms without requiring the geographic information become the research focus. In [19], a light weight deployment-aware scheduling (LDAS) method was proposed, which achieves the probability of coverage by acquiring the number of neighbor nodes within two-hops (i.e. twice the sensing range of a node). LDAS algorithm ignores the disturbance among nodes due to the high node density, which leads to the appearance of a lot of redundant nodes. Based on the high probability to active status of boundary nodes, the relationship between the coverage area and the tolerance coverage area has been analyzed in [20], and a Tolerable Coverage Area based Node Scheduling (TCA) algorithm is then proposed. Although TCA solves the fast dying speed of boundary nodes, however, it does not consider the interference among a large number of nodes within the monitoring area, thus the coverage redundant problem still exists.

Based on [19, 20], there are two improvements in [21]: (1) introducing the parameter of relative residual energy E_{remain} to optimize the cover tolerable decision strategy; (2) improving the distribution of nodes' status by using the "pre-active" and "rollback" status, and then an ECONS is proposed. Due to the randomly selection of candidate nodes, it could not guarantee to obtain a satisfied quality of coverage each time.

For these problems in the literature, a new low redundancy and high cover (LRHC) node scheduling algorithm has been designed based on the cellular network model in this paper. The LRHC algorithm searches suitable active nodes according to characteristics of the cellular network. After the node scheduling, when the node dead occurs, a sleeping node compensation will immediately start. This compensation solves both the uneven selection of nodes and the unstable threshold settings, which provides continuous coverage and ensures the coverage quality.

The rest paper is organized as follows. In Sect. 2, we describe the relate work. Section 3 presents the proposed LRHC node scheduling algorithm. We evaluate our algorithm by experiments and summarize the obtained results in Sect. 4. Finally Sect. 5 concludes our work in this paper.

2 The Related Work

In [19–21], the node is scheduled after the end of the previous round of scheduling, which may make the energy of active nodes in this round is insufficient to support till the end of this round, the coverage holes thus occur.

In [19, 21], the relative residual energy value is to decline constantly with the consuming of nodes energy, then the probability of node entering the active state becomes smaller. Since E_{remain} is the ratio of the residual energy, those nodes may never enter the active state when some residual energy becomes very small and little change in the threshold value. So when $E_{remain} \times B_i/E_r$ within a region is less than a given threshold, the region will cause a coverage hole.

In [19–21], because of a large number of nodes deployed within the monitoring area, the judge interference among these nodes may result in some nodes to sleep at the same time, which reduces the coverage quality of the network.

In [19–21], the probability P of node i to sleep, is calculated as $p_i = 1-n0.609^{n-1}-(n/6-0.109)^{n-1}$ [19], in which n represents the quantity of neighboring nodes in the active status. For instance, if n is 9, $p_i = 0.8297$, it means that if node i wants to sleep, more neighboring nodes are needed to be active. And when many these active nodes focus on one place, it causes not only the coverage hole, but also the redundancy. Based on the above observations, we propose a low redundancy and high coverage node scheduling algorithm by using idea of the cellular network. Since we can theoretically prove that the cellular network model can provide a complete coverage of the target area with minimized number of active sensor nodes in a WSN network.

3 The Low Redundancy and High Coverage Node Scheduling Algorithm

As shown in Fig. 1, each active node has six active neighboring nodes that can enter a dormant state. Without considering the coverage redundancy between nodes, the detection range of each node is the area of the hexagon with R as its side length, which can be calculated as $1.5\sqrt{3}R^2$. Theoretically, for the area S, the number of nodes required is $2S/3\sqrt{3}R^2$ in the cellular network model.

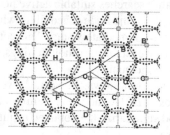

Fig. 1. The update of sensors' status based on the cellular network model.

3.1 Initialize the Neighborhood Location Information

At this stage, the node broadcasts its finding information to neighboring nodes within the scope. For any node i, if its neighboring node set is defined as $N(i) = \{j \in \eta | d(i,j) \leq \sqrt{3}R, i \in \eta, j \neq i\}$, where $d(i,j)$ represents the distances between node i and j, R is the sensing radius of nodes. Each node has five states: Active: the working mode; Sleep: the sleeping mode; Pre-active: the transient state before the active mode; Pre-sleep: the transient state before the sleeping mode; Dead: the node's energy is used up.

3.2   The Update of Status of Sensors Based on the Cellular Network

Based on the cellular network model described above, the new LRHC algorithm divides the monitoring area into multiple cellular. However, the randomly distributed nodes which do not have the location information, may not satisfy the cellular network coverage. To solve the above problem, we use the following steps.

3.2.1   The Random Selection of the Starting Nodes
Firstly, all sensor nodes are in sleep status. A stochastic node is selected as an active node to send messages to neighboring nodes. As can be seen in Fig. 1, ideally, after the division, each cellular within the monitoring area has the characteristics of the cellular network model.

3.2.2   Iterative Traversal
After an active node is selected, the relatively optimal neighboring node is selected as the active neighboring node. All the neighboring nodes update the status, location information until all nodes have updated their information.

3.3   The Checking and Repairment of the Coverage Holes

Theorem. When the side length of the triangle is not greater than the radius of the sensing nodes multiplied by $\sqrt{3}$, then, the three nodes of triangle vertex fully cover the area.

Proof. In Fig. 2, if the side length of the $\triangle ABC$ is $\sqrt{3}R$ (R represents the sensing radius of a node), the area of the $\triangle ABC$ is fully covered by nodes A, B and C. If AB = AC = R, when the length of BC decreases (see the $\triangle ADC$), it is easy to know DO < AO = R (O is the crossover point of three circles), then the circle with D as the center and R as the radius must cover node O. So the area of $\triangle ADC$ is fully covered with the triangle vertex of three nodes A, D and C. Similarly, if there are two or three sides are less than $\sqrt{3}R$, the area of $\triangle ABC$ is fully covered with the triangle vertex of three nodes.

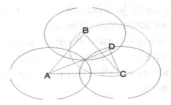

Fig. 2. An example of the triangle coverage.

Lemma. When the side lengths of the triangle are less than $\sqrt{3}R$, the nodes inside the area of triangle can be in the sleep status, and the distances between the sleep nodes and the vertices of triangle are less than $\sqrt{3}R$. It means that when a node has three active neighboring nodes which are not overlapped, and the distances to the three vertex nodes are less than $\sqrt{3}R$, then the node can go to sleep.

As shown in Fig. 2, When the radius of node sensing is R, the side length of the equilateral $\triangle COB$ is $\sqrt{3}R$, then any node inside the $\triangle COB$ with the distances to three active vertex nodes are less than $\sqrt{3}R$, such nodes inside the area of $\triangle COB$ do not need to wake up sleeping nodes to check and repair. If there is no node within a small area C, while there is node in the area O' (the side $DO' > \sqrt{3}R$ of the $\triangle DOO'$), then the area of $\triangle DOO'$ must have some coverage holes, and need to wake up sleeping nodes to check and repair the coverage holes.

After steps 3.1 and 3.2, check the active nodes near the sleeping node. If in the range of the round area which uses the sleeping or pre-sleeping node as the center and $\sqrt{3}R$ as the radius, there are less than three active neighboring nodes, then the sleeping or pre-sleeping node enters the pre-active state. For the node that is in the pre-active state, after a random delay time t_w, check the area of the pre-active node (using pre-active node as the circle center and $\sqrt{3}R$ as the radius), if the active neighboring nodes are less than three, the node will be in the active status, otherwise it maintains the sleep status (Fig. 3).

3.4   The Node Scheduling

This section describes the procedure of scheduling. At beginning, assuming all nodes are in the sleep mode:

1. Randomly select a starting point in the monitoring area, based on the information of its neighbors to find the best suitable nodes (see ②) (satisfy the cellular network model distribution) and update the states of traversed nodes using the procedure described in Sect. 3.2., Start from the new active points, traverse all nodes and repeat the above procedure.
2. Active node sends the sleep information to its neighboring nodes that are in pre-sleeping state. If the number of the sleep information received by the pre-sleeping node is not less than 3, then the node enters the sleeping state (see ⑤) otherwise enters the pre-active mode (see ③).
3. Each pre-active node randomly selects a rollback time t_w, and sends the sleep request to its active or pre-active neighboring nodes. If the number of received reply message is greater than or equal to 3 (see Sect. 3.3), then it enters a pre-sleep state (see ④), otherwise enters an active state (see ①).
4. The active node sends the sleep information to its neighbors that are in pre-sleeping state. If the number of received sleep information of the current node is greater than or equal to 3, then the node enters the sleeping state directly (see ⑦), otherwise it enters an active mode (see ⑥).

Based on the characteristics of the cellular network described in Sect. 3.4, the above four steps reduce the mutual interference among nodes and optimize the network coverage quality (Fig. 4).

```
Process Accept Voting( )
{
    //n : The numbers of neighboring nodes are active;
    //totalVot: The numbers of neighboring nodes are
    active or pre-active of the current //node; //S: The
    set of neighbors; //Length: The number of neighbors;
    //S[i].state : The i-th state of the neighboring///
    node of the current //node; c.state : The current
    node's state; //T: A maximum number of delay; //t1:
    the Random delay time t1<T;
    totalVot =0;
    for (i=0; i< length; i++)
        {if (S[i].state = = Working) totalVot+= 1;}
    if (totalVot≤3) {
        c.state = pre-Working ;
        delay t1; // random delay t1
        totalVot =0;
    }
    else  c.state= pre-Sleep;
    //after Running out of T
    for (j=0; j< t; j++) {
        if (j==t1) {
            for (i=0; i< length; i++)
                if (S[i].Mode = = Working)
                    totalVot+= 1;
        }
    }
    if (totalVot≤3)   c.state = Working;
    else  c.state= pre-Sleep;
}
```

Fig. 3. The pseudo code of the detection of the pre-sleep node to its neighboring nodes

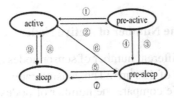

Fig. 4. A node state transition diagram in LRHC

4   The Experimental Results and Analysis

Assuming that the monitoring area is deployed with random sensor nodes, the monitoring scope of any node i satisfies: the round area whose radius is R and the center is r, denoted as $S(R_i)$. The neighboring nodes of any node i meets the following: $N(i) = \left\{ j \in \eta | d(i,j) \le \sqrt{3}R, i \in \eta, j \ne i \right\}$ ∘ η is the node set within the monitoring area. $d(i,j)$ is the distance between node i and node j. Without using GPS, Beidou system or other positioning method to obtain the location information, the selection of active nodes depends on the communication between neighboring nodes.

We evaluate the performance of LRHC algorithm compared with two algorithms TCA and ECONS in the literature in this section.

We use Matlab as the simulation tool. We apply the energy model in [13], the energy consumption of the radio of communication, sleep and reception (idle) are 20:4:0.01. The life time is 550–650 s for the idle (pre-sleep and pre-active) node. In the area of $150^2 \mathrm{m}^2$, nodes are randomly deployed with the sensing range of 10 meters, and the communication range of a node is $10\sqrt{3}$ meters, the dormant time is 2 seconds. As defined in [20], there are two different states include the idle and sleep states, while when the node is dormant means that it is sleeping.

4.1   The Comparison of Network Life Time

In the first group of experiments, we deploy the same number of nodes N (200, 400, 500 and 1000, respectively) in the $150^2 \mathrm{m}^2$ area, the same sensing radius (10 m), and the same coverage quality requirement (95 %) are set in the experiments. The comparison of network life time after the scheduling of LRHC, compared with TCAI and ECONS are shown in Fig. 5. Figure 5(a) shows that the LRHC algorithm can obtain a longer life time than that of TCAI and ECONS. And its death time of the first dead node is later than the TCAI and ECONS. With the growing number of nodes deployed, the performance of LRHC becomes even better compared with other two algorithm s. After the node selection of step 3.1 and 3.2, LRHC can obtain a high quality of coverage (QOC). It demonstrates that using the cellular network model LRHC can achieve a higher coverage rate with few nodes to prolong the network life time.

From Fig. 6 we can see that, with different coverage quality requirements, the LRHC algorithm always has slower increase of death nodes than those of TCAI and ECONS in terms of the network life time.

4.2   The Comparison of the Number of Active Nodes

In this experiment section, different number of sensor nodes are deployed, i.e. 200, 400, 500 and 1000, in the region of $150^2 \mathrm{m}^2$. The sensing radius is 10 m, and the required coverage quality is 95 %. We compare the number of nodes that is needed by LRHC, TCAI and ECONS. Each algorithm was tested 20 times for each network size.

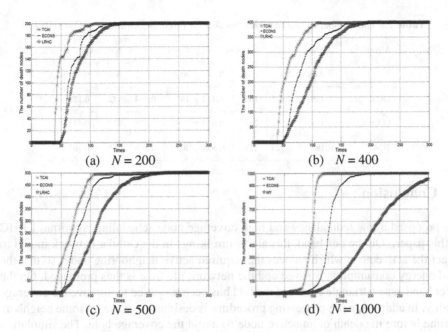

(a) $N = 200$ (b) $N = 400$

(c) $N = 500$ (d) $N = 1000$

Fig. 5. The comparison of network life time ($R = 10$, QOC $= 0.95$).

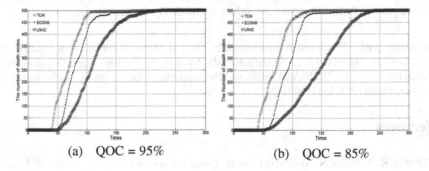

(a) QOC $= 95\%$ (b) QOC $= 85\%$

Fig. 6. The network's survival situation when $R = 10$ and $N = 500$.

Table 1 shows that the number of active nodes needed by LRHC is significantly less than that by ECONS and TCAI. The reason is that LRHC only needs to schedule a small amount of nodes to reach a higher level of coverage by using the cellular network model and the schedule strategies described in Sect. 3. It also shows that the growth of active nodes needed by LRHC is obviously less than that of ECONS and TCAI.

Table 1. The number of active nodes needed for three algorithms (QOC = 0.95)

Algorithms	$N = 200$		$N = 400$		$N = 500$		$N = 1000$	
	Avg.	%	Avg.	%	Avg.	%	Avg.	%
LRHC	**125**	**0.625**	**165**	**0.412**	**167**	**0.334**	**172**	**0.172**
ECONS	141	0.705	247	0.618	289	0.578	493	0.493
TCAI	185	0.925	247	0.855	403	0.806	705	0.705

5   Conclusion

We proposed a low redundancy and high coverage node scheduling algorithm LRHC in this paper,. On the one hand, this algorithm brings in the cellular network model to select the active node which reduces the required active neighboring nodes so that the total energy consumption is saved and the network life time is thus prolonged. On the other hand, a new triangle coverage method has been proposed to improve the coverage quality. In addition, a pre-processing procedure is designed to wake up some neighbors in time before the death of an active node to avoid the coverage hole. The simulation experiments demonstrate that the proposed LRHC can obtain a high coverage rate with a relatively less nodes compared with other two algorithms in the literature. In our future work, we plan to further improve the selection method of active nodes.

Acknowledgment. This research is supported by Natural Science Foundation of China (NSFC project No. 61202289 and 61272396), the national science and technology supporting plan project of Hunan Province (No. 2012BAD35B06), and the supporting plan for young teachers in Hunan University, China (Ref. 531107021137).

References

1. Te Witt, R., Vaessen, N., Melles, D.C., et al.: Good performance of the SpectraCellRA system for typing of methicillin-resistant Staphylococcus aureus isolates. J. Clin. Microbiol. **51**(5), 1434–1438 (2013)
2. Yong, P.J.A., Koh, C.H., Shim, W.S.N.: Endothelial microparticles: missing link in endothelial dysfunction? Eur. J. Prev. Cardiol. **20**(3), 496–512 (2013)
3. L'hadi, I., Marwa, R., Yassine, S.A.: An energy-efficient WSN-based traffic safety system. In: 5th International Conference on Information and Communication Systems (ICICS), pp. 1–6. IEEE (2014)
4. Gupta, H.P., Rao, S.V., Venkatesh, T.: Sleep scheduling for partial coverage in heterogeneous wireless sensor networks. In: 2013 Fifth International Conference on Communication Systems and Networks (COMSNETS), pp. 1–10. IEEE (2013)
5. Wang, L., Da Xu, L., Bi, Z., et al.: Data cleaning for RFID and WSN integration. IEEE Trans. J. Industr. Inf. **10**(1), 408–418 (2014)
6. Potdar, V., Atif, S., Elizabeth, C.: Wireless sensor networks: a survey. In: International Conference, pp. 636–641. IEEE (2009)

7. Navarro, M., Tyler, W., Davis, Y.L., Xu, L.: ASWP: a long-term WSN deployment for environmental monitoring. In: Proceedings of the 12th International Conference on Information Processing in Sensor Networks, pp. 351–352. ACM (2013)

8. Alemdar, H., Ersoy, C.: Wireless sensor networks for healthcare: a survey. Comput. Netw. 54(15), 2688–2710 (2010)

9. Zeng, B., Yabo, D., Jie, H., Dongming, L.: An energy-efficient TDMA scheduling for data collection in wireless sensor networks. In: 2013 IEEE/CIC International Conference on Communications in China (ICCC), pp. 633–638. IEEE (2013)

10. Diongue, D., Thiare, O.: A New Sentinel Approach for Energy Efficient and Hole Aware Wireless Sensor Networks. arXiv preprint arXiv (2013)

11. Ruiz-Garcia, L., Lunadei, L.: The role of RFID in agriculture: applications, limitations and challenges. J. Comput. Electron. Agric. 79(1), 42–50 (2011)

12. Wang, L., Xiao, Y.: A survey of energy-efficient schedulingm in sesor networks. Mob. Netw. Appl. 11(5), 723–740 (2006)

13. Tian, D., Nicolas, D.G.: A coverage-preserving node scheduling scheme for large wireless sensor networks. In: Proceedings of the 1st ACM International Workshop on Wireless Sensor Networks and Applications, pp. 32–41. ACM (2002)

14. Zhang, H., Hou, J.C.: Maintaining sensing coverage and connectivity in large sensor networks. Ad Hoc Sens. Wirel. Netw. (AHSWN) 1(1–2), 89–124 (2005)

15. Zhan, J., Yongzhong, S., Jingsong, Y.: Design and implementation of logistics vehicle monitoring system based on the SaaS model. In: 2012 Fifth International Conference on Business Intelligence and Financial Engineering (BIFE), pp. 524–526. IEEE (2012)

16. Wang, Y.: Topology control for wireless sensor networks. In: Li, Y., Thai, M.T., Wu, W. (eds.) Wireless Sensor Networks and Applications, pp. 113–147. Springer, New York (2008)

17. Molina, G., Alba, E.: Location discovery in wireless sensor networks using metaheuristics. J. Appl. Soft Comput. 11(1), 1223–1240 (2011)

18. Chizari, H., et al.: Local coverage measurement algorithm in GPS-free wireless sensor networks. Ad Hoc Netw. 23, 1–17 (2014)

19. Wu, K., Gao, Y., Li, F., Xiao, Y.: Lightweight deployment-aware scheduling for wireless sensor networks. ACM/Kluwer Mob. Netw. Appl. (MONET) 10(6), 837–852 (2005)

20. Lu, X., Cheng, L.: Energy-efficient coverage optimized node scheduling algorithm for sensor layer in internet of things. J. Appl. Res. Comput. 5, 043 (2013)

21. Fan, G., Zhang, C.: A new metric for modeling the uneven sleeping problem in coordinated sensor node scheduling. Int. J. Distrib. Sens. Netw. 2013, 8 (2013)

Compressive Spectrum Sensing Based on Sparse Sub-band Basis in Wireless Sensor Network

Yu Wang[(✉)], Jincheng Zhang, Quan Wang, Fangxu Lv, and Kewei Chen

Air and Missile Defense College, AFEU, Shaanxi Xi'an, China
{nfswy1990,zjc6011,lvfangxu1988}@163.com, wangquan628@126.com,
1286198251@qq.com

Abstract. An approach based on Sparse Sub-band Basis (SSB) for compressive spectrum sensing in Wireless Sensor Network (WSN) is presented in this paper, considering the unsatisfactory accuracy and complex calculation of the traditional ones. It is proved that the SSB matches not only the orthogonality and completeness of the basis, but also the Restricted Isometry Property (RIP) in reconstructing the signal. The simulation results show that the reconstruction based on SSB can detect the accurate location and amplitude of spectrum occupancy, and is more robust than traditional edge detection method. Additionally, this approach has higher compression ratio and less calculation, which is suitable for nodes in WSN.

Keywords: Wireless sensor network · Spectrum sensing · Compressive sensing · Sparse sub-band basis

1 Introduction

The spectrum scarcity problem has increasingly aroused people's attention in recent years. The Cognitive Radio (CR) [1] was found to be an efficient way of solving this problem and improving the spectrum utilization. Since the usage of spectrum is considered to be sparse at any given time and spatial region [2], the CRs can exploit frequency bands to identify the idle spectral holes and use these unoccupied bands to communicate. However, spectrum sensing also faces considerable technical challenges, for example wireless fading and high sampling rate. Using WSN for spectrum sensing, with its own distributed nature, can effectively overcome the influence of fading channel and shadow effect [3]. Then the technique of Compressed Sensing (CS) [4] and the Analog to Information Converter (AIC) [5] was proposed, which promoted the realization of compressed spectrum sensing in WSN.

Aiming at the sensing accuracy, an approach using wavelet edge detection to get the location of occupied channel was introduced [6]. To improve the performance with low Signal Noise Ratio (SNR), an approach using wavelet de-noising to smooth over the recovered edges was implemented [7]. All these methods were based on an assumption that the signal was sparse in frequency domain, which was comprised of frequency points one by one. However, finite frequency points, which we use in Discrete Fourier Transform (DFT), cannot accurately depict the signal in nature. In spectral analysis we always

© Springer-Verlag Berlin Heidelberg 2015
L. Sun et al. (Eds): CWSN 2014, CCIS 501, pp. 52–58, 2015.
DOI: 10.1007/978-3-662-46981-1_5

divide the interested spectrum into several non-overlapping narrowband sub-bands. Following this idea, we directly choose the non-overlapping sub-band as the sparse basis in the frequency domain to represent the signal.

2   An Overview of Compressive Spectrum Sensing

Signals in time domain do not generally reveal their characteristic information, thus it is routine to look for their frequency representation. Assume a signal $x \in R^{N \times 1}$ that has a sparse representation in some domains, such as Fourier Transform, Wavelet, or Discrete Cosine Transform (DCT) [8]. So it can be represented in

$$x = \sum_{i=1}^{N} \theta_i \psi_i \tag{1}$$

where Ψ_i is the orthonormal basis in relevant domain. The advantage of an orthonormal basis is that the coefficients θ_i can be calculated by $\theta_i = \langle x, \Psi_i \rangle = \langle \Psi_i^T x \rangle$. The equation can be written in

$$x = \Psi \theta \tag{2}$$

The $N \times 1$ vector θ is a sparse vector. It is said that θ is K sparse if it has at most K non-zero (and large enough) entries with $K \ll N$ [4]. The sparsity of signal is fatal for WSN, since it can obviously reduce the measurements and the traffic, which will increase the service life of the WSN.

It was shown that signal x can be recovered using non-adaptive linear projection measurements on to an $M \times N$ sampling matrix Φ [4], which is incoherent with Ψ. The measurement vector y can be written as

$$y = \Phi x \tag{3}$$

It was proved that the sparse vector θ can be recovered by solving the following $l_1 - norm$ minimization problem.

$$\hat{\theta} = \arg \min \|\theta\|_1 \tag{4}$$

One of the preconditions is that M needs to be at least $C \cdot \mu^2(A) \cdot K \cdot logN$ for accurate recovery [4], where A is the sensing matrix $A = \Phi \Psi$. At the same time, the RIP of A can guarantee a unique solution, with high probability. The mutual coherence parameter $\mu(\Phi, \Psi)$ is defined as a measurement of the incoherence between the compressive sampling matrix Φ and sparse basis matrix Ψ [9].

$$\mu(\Phi, \Psi) = \max_{1 \leq i,j \leq N} \left| < \varphi_i, \psi_j > \right| = \max_{1 \leq i,j \leq N} |A(i,j)| \tag{5}$$

With the range $\mu(\Phi, \Psi) \in \left[1/\sqrt{N}, 1 \right]$, the lower number equates to higher accuracy in signal reconstruction.

3   Reconstruction with Different Basis

3.1   Spectrum Sensing Based on Discrete Frequency Points

CS worked on the assumption that a signal can be represented as a finite weighted sum of basic functions [4]. It is supposed that the spectrum sensing signal is sparse in frequency domain and we conventionally use DFT to represent the analog signal in frequency domain. Hence an estimate of the target spectrum is made, using a wavelet edge detector along the resulting Power Spectrum Density (PSD). This process was described in [10]. The detector gives the edge spectrum. It can be calculated by a first-order $2N \times 2N$ difference matrix Γ, then the sparse vector can be got as

$$\theta = (\Gamma F W) r_x \tag{6}$$

where F is a $2N \times 2N$ DFT matrix, W is a transform matrix in wavelet edge detection, r_x is the relevant autocorrelation vector of signal x and θ is the sparse vector indicated the occupancy. The link between r_y, autocorrelation vector of measurement y, and θ can be described as

$$r_y = \Phi r_x = \Phi (\Gamma F W)^{-1} \theta = \Phi \Psi \theta \tag{7}$$

Now we can solve the edge detection in signal reconstruction as an $l_1 -$ norm optimization problem of θ.

We evaluate the performance of this method by using db5 as wavelet basic function to make wavelet edge detection. The wavelet scale is 3 and the M/N ratio is 40 %. Firstly, we simulate the performance with different spectrum occupation, as depicted in Fig. 1. In Fig. 1(a), the edge of the occupied segment has sharp edge. With 1-scale, we can accurately get the location. But in real, the edge is slowly changed as showed in Fig. 1(b). Then we extend the scale, as depicted in the Fig. 1(b), but this method still cannot discriminate the accurate location. With on the same setting in Fig. 1(a), we lower the SNR as showed in Fig. 1(c). The result shows that this method cannot give the accurate location completely. In the progress of this simulation, we also found this method has complex computation for reconstruction, which was not suitable for the WSN, whose computation capacity is limited.

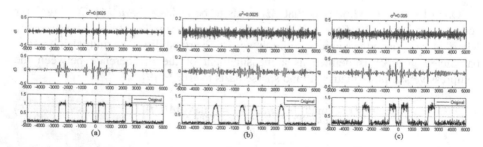

Fig. 1.   The location got by wavelet edge detection

3.2 Spectrum Sensing Based on SSB

Conventionally we use discrete frequency points as the sparse basis, and the sparse vector based on this basis to represent the analog signal. But the real spectrum occupancy cannot be described accurately by finite frequency points as we discuss above. When we use frequency points as the sparse basis, the distance between adjoining points represents its distinguishability. If we want to describe the usage of the spectrum as accurate as we can, there must be lots of frequency points, and the sparse vector will not be sparse any more. From the simulation above, we know that the performance of this method will decrease with relatively low SNR. Whereas, when we make the model to analysis the spectrum, we always divide the spectrum into non-overlapping sub-bands. This inspired us to use the non-overlapping sub-band in frequency domain as the sparse basis.

All CRs in the network should avoid transmitting at any occupied sub-channels, and share the vacant bands among themselves. Based on this point, the spectrum sensing task is simplified to spectrum detection. The target spectrum is composed of several channels and each channel is partitioned to narrower sub-bands. That is to say the spectrum is divided into n sub-bands $b_1, b_2, \cdots, b_n$ and the total bandwidth is $B = \sum_{i=1}^{n} b_i$. We choose the sub-bands as the sparse basis. Since these sub-bands are continued non-overlapping bands, it is easy to prove that this basis is an orthonormal basis. It means that the basis vectors $\{b_i\}_{i=1}^{n}$ satisfying

$$\langle b_i, b_j \rangle = \delta_{ij} = \begin{cases} 1, & i = j \\ 0, & i \neq j \end{cases} \tag{8}$$

As an orthonormal basis, the transform coefficients θ_i can be calculated as

$$\theta_i = \langle x, F^{-1}(b_i) \rangle \tag{9}$$

where the $F^{-1}(b_i)$ means the inverse Fourier transform. So the signal in time domain can be described as

$$x = \Psi_b \theta \tag{10}$$

The $\Psi_b = \{\varphi_i = F^{-1}(b_i)\}_{i=1}^{n}$ is the sparse sub-band basis presented in time domain. And the compressive spectrum sensing progress can be rewritten as

$$y = \Phi x = \Phi \Psi_b \theta \tag{11}$$

In frequency domain, the occupation of target spectrum can be linearly described as

$$F(f) \approx \sum_{i=1}^{N} \theta_i b_i \tag{12}$$

Representing based on this basis can overcome the drawback in using frequency points as basis. Since the occupation of sub-band is what we care about, the coefficient

θ_i represents the usage of each sub-band. Each sub-band basis can be regarded as the translation of gate function.

$$b_i = g_\tau(f - f_i) \tag{13}$$

The τ represents the width of each sub-band. As $\tau \to 0$, the sum of non-overlapping sub-band basis changes to continuous spectral representing.

$$\lim_{\tau \to 0} \sum_{i=1}^{N} \theta_i b_i \to F(f) \tag{14}$$

The partition of sub-band depends on many factors such as:

- Width of interested spectrum
- Distinguishability
- Number of distributed sensor node
- Sampling rate of AIC chip.

Another thing we must consider in choosing basis is that the basis should satisfy the RIP. In process of recovering signal, measurement vector y and sensing matrix $A = \Phi\Psi_b$ are used to reconstruct the sparse vector θ, and the matric A must satisfy the RIP. In simulation, we select the Low Density Parity Check (LDPC) matric [11] as the sampling matrix to check out the coherence parameter $\mu(\Phi, \Psi_b)$ with sparse sub-band basis. The results display $\mu < 0.28$, which satisfies the condition of accurate reconstruction [9].

4   Simulation Results

In this section, we perform numerical simulations to illustrate the performance of the proposed sub-band basis. In all of our simulations, we consider a wideband target spectrum with a bandwidth [20,500] MHz and divide it into 96 sub-bands with same bandwidth. The AIC output in one sampling period is 1000, i.e. $N = 1000$. According to the inequality $M > C \cdot \mu^2(A) \cdot K \cdot logN$, we select $M = 130$ as the row number of sampling matrix, so the M/N ratio is 13 %. The Additive White Gaussian Noise (AWGN) $\sigma_{p,w}^2$ range is 0.0025 ~ 0.05, and the SNR range is 8 dB ~ 15 dB with corresponding. The performance can be shown as Fig. 2.

In the simulations, the occupied segments are composed of window functions with different shape. We sample in the time domain to get the $N \times 1$ vector x, and then compress it with sampling matrix Φ to get the $M \times 1$ vector y. After this process, we use the measurement vector y and the sensing matric $A = \Phi\Psi_b$ to get the sparse representation vector θ. Firstly we select the gate function as the basic function, whose edge is sharp, to simulate the usage of spectrum. In Fig. 2(a) and (d), with SNR $\sigma_{p,w}^2 = 0.0025$ and $\sigma_{p,w}^2 = 0.05$ respectively, we can find that the results indicate the accurate location and approximate altitude. Then we select the Hamming window function, whose edge is slowly changed, to simulate with same SNR as above. As show in Fig. 2(b) and (e), the coefficients can still point out the accurate

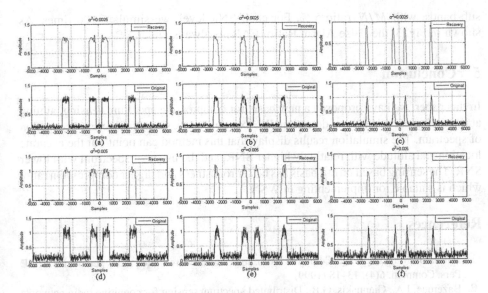

Fig. 2. The results of spectrum sensing based on SSB with different SNR and usage

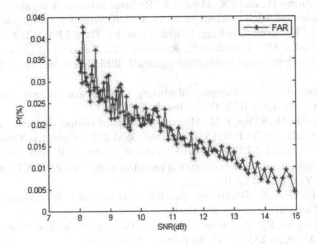

Fig. 3. Change of false alarm ratio versus SNR

location with high SNR, and can point out the major part of occupation with low SNR. Lastly we select the Kaiser window function, whose shape is spike, to simulate. According to Fig. 2(c), this method is still effective. However in Fig. 2(f), the sub-bands with lower energy cannot be detected. It is due to the iterate stop threshold in the searching progress of reconstruction.

Finally, we evaluate the sub-band basis by simulating the false alarm ratio of spectrum detection versus different SNRs. In the simulation, we select the gate function to simulate the occupied channel, and 20 sub-bands are occupied of 90 sub-bands, with M/N ratio 5 %. For each SNR level, we simulate 100 times. As shown in Fig. 3, the False Alarm Ratio (FAR) is always under 5 %.

5 Conclusion

In this paper, we have proposed a new basis for compressive spectrum sensing, aiming at improving the accuracy of detection. We examine our basis with different occupation of spectrum. The simulation results display that this method can point out the accurate location and altitude with relatively higher SNR, and the usage of spectrum with lower SNR. The sensing based on our basis has better robustness and higher compression ratio, which is suitable for implementing in WSN.

References

1. Mitola, J., Maguire, G.Q.: Cognitive radio: making software radios more personal. J. IEEE Pers. Commun. **6**(4), 13–18 (1999)
2. Bazerque, J.A., Giannakis, G.B.: Distributed spectrum sensing for cognitive radio networks by exploiting sparsity. J. IEEE Trans. Sign. Proces. **58**(3), 1847–1862 (2009)
3. Granelli, F., Zhang, H., Zhou, X., Marano, S.: Research advances in cognitive ultra wideband radio and their application to sensor networks. J. Mob. Netw. Appl. **11**(4), 487–499 (2006)
4. Donoho, D.L.: Compressed sensing. J. IEEE Trans. Inf. Theo. **52**(4), 1289–1306 (2006)
5. Tropp, A., Laska, J.N., Duarte, M.F., Romberg, J.K., Baraniuk, R.G.: Beyond Nyquist: efficient sampling of sparse bandlimited signals. J. IEEE Trans. Inf. Theo. **56**(1), 520–544 (2010)
6. Tian, Z., Giannakis, G.B.: Compressed sensing for wideband cognitive radios. In: IEEE ICASSP, pp. 1357–1360. IEEE Press, Honolulu (2007)
7. Yu, Z., Sebastian, H., Sadler, B.M.: Mixed-signal parallel compressed sensing and reception for cognitive radio. In: IEEE ICASSP, pp. 3861–3864. IEEE Press, Las Vegas (2008)
8. Amaro, J.P., Ferreira, F.J.T.E., Cortesao, R., Vinagre, N., Bras, R.P.: Low cost wireless sensor network for in-field operation monitoring of induction motors. In: IEEE ICIT, pp. 1044–1049. IEEE Press, Vi a del Mar (2010)
9. Donoho, D.L., Huo, X.: Uncertainty principles and ideal atomic decomposition. J. IEEE Trans. Inf. Theor. **47**(7), 2845–2862 (2001)
10. Polo, Y.L., Ying W., Pandharipande, A., Leus, G.: Compressive wide-band spectrum sensing. In: IEEE ICASSP, pp.2337–2340. IEEE Press, Taipei (2009)
11. Sun, X., Zhou, Z., Shi, L., Zou, W.: A novel compressed collaborative sensing scheme using LDPC technique. In: CHINACOM ICST, pp. 959–963. IEEE Press, Harbin (2011)

Maintaining Coverage Node Scheduling Algorithm in Wireless Sensor Network

KaiGuo Qian[1,2], ShiKai Shen[2,3,4(✉)], ZuCheng Dai[1], and Ren Duan[5]

[1] Department of Physics Science and Technology, Kunming University, Kunming, China
{qiankaiguo,958524088}@qq.com
[2] Kunming IOT & Ubiquitous Engineering Center, Kunming, China
kmssk2000@sina.com
[3] School of Information and Technology, Kunming University, Kunming, China
[4] Future University, Hakodate, Japan
[5] School of Information, Yunnan University of Finance and Economics, Kunming, China
402602@qq.com

Abstract. Scheduling the redundant nodes to sleep is an effective technology to sufficiently prolong the life circle of wireless sensor network on the premise of meeting the coverage quality. According to position distribution of the neighboring nodes, a node scheduling algorithm of wireless sensor network is proposed on the basis of the necessary condition that a node becomes a redundant one and whether the complementary neighboring nodes meet the circle cover. The new algorithm reduces the computational complexity. Simulation results show that the new algorithm is effective to schedule the redundant node to sleep for energy-saving. It predicates nearly 26 % nodes to sleep when the perception radius is 10 meters and coverage rate is unchanged. It identifies more than 50 % nodes to sleep with 15 meters radius.

Keywords: Wireless sensor network · Internal-neighbor node · Redundant node · Coverage performance

1 Introduction

Wireless sensor networks [1] is a monitoring networks composed by a large number of micro computer equipment which is randomly deployed to task area through wireless self-composition. Wireless sensor networks can be applied in military invasion, environmental monitoring, industrial data collection, health monitoring, smart home and precision agriculture. The coverage control [2] is often described as a standard in monitoring the QoS (quality of service) of the wireless sensor network, which is the basis of other networking technologies such as routing protocols and positioning design. In special applications or the inaccessible areas, dense (density up to 20 node/m3) and large-scale deployment is commonly applied in the deployment of the sensor network nodes to ensure the performance of the network coverage [3], but which leads to data redundancy, conflict between the packets and reduce network throughput. On the other hand, the wireless sensor node is provided by the battery, which makes it difficult to replace or recharge the energy.

© Springer-Verlag Berlin Heidelberg 2015
L. Sun et al. (Eds.): CWSN 2014, CCIS 501, pp. 59–68, 2015.
DOI: 10.1007/978-3-662-46981-1_6

The energy consumption of the node determines the lifetime of the wireless sensor network, thus, the design of the sensor network coverage control must provide the maximum network life cycle under the premise of ensuring the quality of coverage.

In the application of the high-density and randomly-deployed wireless sensor network, redundant nodes whose coverage area is completely covered by the neighboring nodes are often turned off to reduce the node density of the local area, while extending the life cycle of the network through node scheduling. VSGCA [4] identifies the redundant node by virtual Meshing, that is, the sense coverage of each node is divided into a virtual grid. It is identified as a redundant node when its grid is covered by the neighboring node. TIAN [5] proposed the Off-duty eligibility rule to determine the redundant nodes, which calculates the covering relations between nodes according to the location of the nodes or the angle of the signal. Based on probability analysis, NDNS [6] (non-uniform distribution node scheduling) system identifies the redundancy of the node according to the distance between nodes and their neighboring ones. Based on numbers of the neighboring nodes, Gao [7] analyzes the redundant node coverage probability model, points out when there are 11 neighboring nodes, the probability of the node becoming a redundant node is over 90 %. AEKYU [8] uses sponsored sector and the effective angle to determine whether a node is redundant ones or not. HUANG [9] considers the coverage circumference of each sensor node, then determines whether a given circumference of the sensor node is completely covered by the neighbor nodes. If the circumference of a node is completely covered, the node becomes a redundant node. Based on the circumference covering, LIU X [10] proposes that in the premise of ensuring the coverage of network, the lifetime of the network can be improved by putting the redundant nodes in dormancy. Based on greedy node scheduling algorithm, ERGS [11] uses the position relationship between the nodes and residual energy to determine whether the node is dormant. Reference [12] proposes an algorithm that ordinary node competes to determine whether it is dormant, and which is necessarily managed by high capacity nodes. EBNDNS [13] determines whether a node is dormant by depending on the distance between the sensor nodes, the way is simple, but the conclusion is insufficient, causing coverage gap. ECHS and EDHS [14] designed a heuristic algorithm based on energy-aware to complete node scheduling. Based on residual energy and signal strength, EECDS [15] selects the backbone nodes to constitute coverage sets to save energy, those algorithms [4–7] depend on accurate position information of neighboring nodes, in which calculation are more complicated. The judgments of circumference coverage [8–10] are insufficient. When taking the neighbor nodes within a radius of perception only in consideration, the criteria are stricter, and the redundant nodes are usually judge as backbone ones, causing inaccurate judgments. When considering neighbor nodes within perception radius of two times, the criteria are less strict, and the backbone nodes are often regarded as the redundant ones, causing false judgments. Algorithms in [11–15] are based on heuristic designing ideas, proposing that the residual energy of the sensor network nodes can be used to form the working set of nodes, but the calculation is complicated. According to the position relationship between neighboring nodes, this paper proposes the necessary conditions that node becomes redundant ones, and combining the judgments based on complement of partly radius angle, which reduces the computational complexity and further solves the inaccurate and false judgment problems caused by the inadequate judgment conditions of the circumference covering algorithm.

2 System Model and Problem Description

2.1 Network Model

Generally, wireless sensor networks can be abstracted as an undirected graph $G = (V, E)$, $V = \{s_1, s_2, \ldots, s_i, \ldots, s_n\}$ is the set of nodes in wireless sensor networks. $E = \{e_1, e_2, \ldots, e_j, \ldots e_m\}$ is the set of edges that can communicate with each other between the nodes, $e_j = (u, v)$ represents the link by which node u and v can transmit data directly. The sensing radius of sensor node is r, communication radius is R, when the network covers the task area, it requires the mutual communication between nodes, and there is no isolated node. All nodes have positioning capability and obstacles in the monitoring area are not considered in the research.

2.2 Coverage Model

Definition 1: The Euclidean Distance of sensor node $S(x_s, y_s)$ and $P(x_p, y_p)$ is shown as Eq. 1.

$$disp(s, p) = \sqrt{(x_s - x_p)^2 + (y_s - y_p)^2} \tag{1}$$

Definition 2: If any point within a certain area is not covered by any sensor node, then this area is called blind zone.

Definition 3: The coordinate of sensor node S in two-dimensional plane R^2 is (x, y), then the coverage area of node S is a circular region called as the coverage circle with its center of point(x, y) and its sensor radius is r, which shows as Eq. 2.

$$ca\,(s) = \{p | p \in R^2, Dist(s, p) \leq r\} \tag{2}$$

Definition 4: The coverage model is described as Eq. 3.

$$p(s, q) = \begin{cases} 1, & if\ dist(s, q) \leq r \\ 0, & otherwise \end{cases} \tag{3}$$

3 Maintaining Coverage Node Scheduling Algorithm

3.1 Related Concepts

Definition 5: Neighbor Node. The neighboring node of the any node s_i refers to the node S_j whose distance from s_i is less than the communication radius R. It is described as Eq. 4.

$$N\,(s_i) = \{s_j | dist\,(s_i, s_j) \leq R\} \tag{4}$$

Definition 6:   Redundant Node. When the coverage circle of the node S_i is covered by the coverage circle of the neighbor node set $N(S_i)$, then the node S_i is a redundant node. It is described as Eq. 5.

$$ca\left(s_i\right) \subseteq \bigcup_{j \in N(s_i)} ca(s_j) \tag{5}$$

Definition 7:   Inter-neighbor Node: The inter-neighbor node of the node S_i refers to the node set constituted of the node S_j whose distance from S_i is less than the sensor radius r. It is described as Eq. 6.

$$N_{s_j \to s_i}(s_i) = \{s_j | dsit(s_j, s_i) \le r\} \tag{6}$$

Definition 8:   Outer-neighbor Node: The outer-neighbor node of the nodes S_i refers to node set constituted of the node S_j whose distance from S_i is larger than r, smaller than R. It is described as Eq. 7.

$$N_{\overline{s_j \to s_i}}(s_i) = \{s_j | r < dsit(s_j, s_i) \le R\} = \overline{N_{s_j \to s_i}(s_i)} \tag{7}$$

Definition 9:   Coverage Sponsor Region: The coverage sponsor region of S_j to S_i refers to the part that the covering circle of node S_i is covered by the covering circle of S_j. It is shown in Fig. 1. The sponsor region is described as Eq. 8.

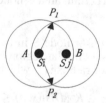

Fig. 1. The coverage sponsor region of neighbor node S_j to S_i

$$\theta_{s_j \to s_i}(s_j) = p_1 S_i p_2 = 2a \cos(\frac{dist(s_j, s_i)}{R}) \tag{8}$$

Theorem 1: The necessary condition that the node S_i becomes redundant node is that there must be at least one node is distributed in the coverage circle of S_i.

Proving: (contradiction proving), Suppose the node S_i is a redundant node, and there is no any inter-neighboring node S_j which located in its covering circle, that is all the neighboring nodes are outer-neighbor nodes, which meets to the condition: $r < dsit(s_j, s_i) \le R$. Dot Si meets the condition: $s_i \notin ca(s_j)$, that is point S_i is not covered by its any neighbor node S_j. If no neighboring node S_j covers point S_i, then the set of the neighbor nodes doesn't cover circle point S_i, it is described as Eq. 9.

$$s_i \notin \bigcup_{j \in N_{\overline{s_j \to s_i}}(s_i) = N(s_i)} ca(s_j) \tag{9}$$

It doesn't meet to the criteria in Eq. 5. Therefore the assumption is false, and the theorem is proved to be true.

3.2   The Basic Steps of Node Scheduling Algorithm

The operation of new algorithm is broken up into rounds, where each round traverses every sensor node ascended by the node ID numbers. When traversing to the sensor node S_i, It judges itself whether in working state or sleep by four steps of inter-neighbor node discovery, neighbor node discovery, redundant node determination and node scheduling. It is shown in Fig. 2.

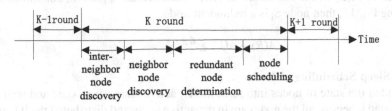

Fig. 2.   Operation steps of node scheduling

The step of inter-neighbor node discovery is to detect if there is inter-neighbor node in the covering circle of node S_i. Neighbor node discovery is to collect the information of the neighbor nodes in the premise of detecting inter-neighbor nodes. Redundant node determination is to judge if node S_i applies to dormant conditions. Node scheduling is to complete state transition.

3.2.1   Inter-neighbor Node Discovery

The processes of inter-neighbor node discovery are: (1) node Si broadcasts query message within scope of circle with radius r. (2) The node which receives message makes response that includes the node number ID and their positions. (3) Node S_i counts the response message, and calculates the sponsor circle angle $\theta_{s_j \to s_i}(s_j)$ of the inter-neighbor node according to formula 8. It is concluded that $\theta_{s_j \to s_i}(s_j) \geq 2\pi/3$. If node S_i gets no response message, it means node S_i has no inter-neighbor node. According to theorem 1, node S_i doesn't apply to the condition of the redundant node, then node S_i will quit the process of the dormant scheduling immediately. It plays a key role in reducing the complexity of the algorithm.

3.2.2   Neighbor Node Discovery

If node S_i detects the inter-neighboring node S_j, it will get in the process of detecting the neighbor node discovery, the processes are: (1) node S_i broadcasts query message within scope of circle with radius R. (2) Node S_k that received message makes response that include ID number of the node and its position. (3) According to the received position information, node S_i makes sure whether S_k located in the sector area of the sponsored circle angles of $\theta_{s_j \to s_i}(s_j)$, if it locates in this area, then node S_k is neglected, or S_k will be recorded in the complementary set of Sector(S_j). It is described as Eq. 10.

$$\overline{Sector\,(s_j)} = \left\{ s_k | s_k \notin Sector\,(\theta_{j \to i}) \right\} \tag{10}$$

3.2.3   Redundant Node Judgment

It traverses all the nodes of the set of $\overline{Sector\,(s_j)}$, and marks the circle angles with S_i as A(L) and A(R). It is ascended as the A(L) order. If there is no intermission from the minimum of A(L) to the maximum of A(R), meanwhile, applies to conditions of the following Eq. 11, then node S_i is a redundant node.

$$A(R) - A(L) \geq {}^{4\pi}/_3 \tag{11}$$

3.2.4   Sleep Scheduling of Node

It is divided the state of nodes into three kinds: active state, sleep state and wait state. When round k begins, all the nodes are in the active state, and distributed the ID number randomly. The steps of the sleep scheduling of node are:

Step 1: If the traversed present nodes leave to solve problems, It is still in active state, and if there is nothing to do, it get into step 2.

Step 2: running stated in 3.2.1 to detect an inter-neighboring node, if there is no such one, node S_i keep active state and quit from the process of sleep node scheduling to traverse the next node. Otherwise, node S_i calculates $\theta_{s_j \to s_i}(s_j)$ and $\sec ter(\theta_{s_j \to s_i})$, then get into step 3.

Step 3: Detecting neighboring nodes with means stated in 3.2.2 to obtain set of the $\overline{Sector\,(s_j)}$. If it is equivalent to ϕ, then node S_i keeps in active state and traverse the next node, Otherwise, it get into step 4.

Step 4: Judging the redundant node according to state in 3.2.3, if it is a redundant node, node S_i transfer into sleep state. Otherwise, node S_i keeps active state.

Step 5: After the sleep stage over, nodes S_i turns into wait state to get in the next dormant scheduling.

4   Performance Evaluation

4.1   Performance Analysis

It supposes n sensor nodes distributed in the task area A, then the probability that there is no inter-neighboring node in the covering circle of node S_i is shown as Eq. 12.

$$p_r(s_i) = \begin{pmatrix} n-1 \\ n-2 \end{pmatrix} (\frac{A-\pi r^2}{A})^{n-2}(\frac{\pi r^2}{A})$$

$$= (n-1)(\frac{\pi r^2}{A})(1-\frac{\pi r^2}{A})^{n-2} \approx (n-1)(\frac{\pi r^2}{A}) \tag{12}$$

If there is no inter-neighboring node detected when the algorithm traverses, node S_i quits the present redundant node scheduling process. Therefore, the algorithm quits the running of redundant node scheduling as the probability $p_r(s_i)$, In the comparison, the circle coverage algorithm performs all the steps of the process of redundant node scheduling. When the algorithm detects that node S_i has an inter-neighboring node, it is necessary to judge the coverage within two times of the sensor radius r, and the probability that node S_i has k neighboring node is shown in Eq. 13.

$$p_{2r}(s_i) = \begin{pmatrix} n-1 \\ k \end{pmatrix} (\frac{\pi(2r)^2}{A})^k(\frac{A-\pi(2r)^2}{A})^{n-1-k} \tag{13}$$

The average neighboring nodes number is calculated as Eq. 14.

$$z = \sum_{k=0}^{n-1} kp_{2r}(k) = \sum_{k=0}^{n-1} \begin{pmatrix} n-1 \\ k \end{pmatrix} (\frac{\pi(2r)^2}{A})^k(\frac{A-\pi(2r)^2}{A})^{n-1-k}$$

$$= (n-1)\frac{\pi(2r)^2}{A} \tag{14}$$

What necessary is only to calculate the coverage that neighboring nodes in area $\overline{Sector}(s_j)$ covers the circle of node S_i. The average neighboring nodes number is shown as the Eq. 15.

$$z = 2(n-1)\frac{\pi(2r)^2}{3A} \tag{15}$$

Z is the average executing frequency of the algorithm to judge the redundant nodes of step 4. In a contrast, the circle coverage algorithm is $(n-1)\frac{\pi(2r)^2}{A}$. Therefore, compared to circle coverage algorithm, the new algorithm reduces one third performance frequency in Step 4. Performance in Step 4 itself is very complicated, since it is necessary for every node to count two angles that overlaps the circle of node S_i, and it must ascends order and judges intermission.

4.2 Simulation Experiment

4.2.1 Coverage Rate

Coverage rate refers to the ratio of the covering area of the working nodes and the task area A. In MATLAB R2012a, with task area A = 100 m*100 m, sensor nodes are deployed with different numbers and different radius of perception as 5 m, 10 m, 15 m. Coverage rate that before and after the new algorithm running is shown as Fig. 3.

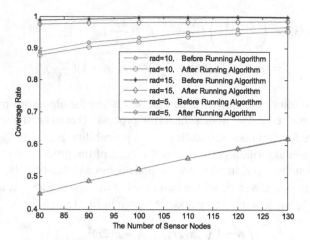

Fig. 3. Experiment results of the coverage rate

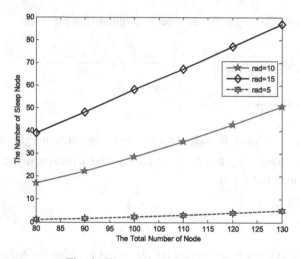

Fig. 4. The number of sleep nodes

4.2.2 The Number of Sleep Nodes

We deploy different number of sensor nodes and set the sensor radius r as 5 m, 10 m and 15 m, then the number of sleep nodes is shown as Fig. 4. The result combined with Figs. 3 and 4 shows that the coverage rate increases with more nodes are deployed regardless of the algorithm to perform or not. After the running of the algorithm, when the sensor radius is 5, the sleep nodes is little, and the coverage rate almost doesn't change, and when the sensor radius be comes 10, the sleep nodes are about 25 %, the coverage rate decreases about 0.1 %, and when the sensor radius comes to 15, the sleep nodes are about 50 %, the coverage rate decreases about 0.1 %. These data show that on the premise of full coverage, the algorithm proposed in the paper can effectively schedule nodes to the sleep state as well as reduce energy consumption and prolong lifetime of the network.

5 Conclusion

Coverage control is the basic problem of the sensor network. The important requirement of designing coverage control is to reduce energy consumption to prolong lifetime of the network. We analyze the necessary condition that node becomes redundant nodes is the existence of at least one inter-neighbor node. The neighboring node covers at least 1/3 area for this node, and the rest areas are determined according to the circle covering. It greatly reduces calculating complexity, and reduces energy consumption by putting the redundant nodes in sleep state. On the premise of keeping coverage, the performance analysis and simulation show that the proposed algorithm can reduce the calculating complexity of judging the redundant nodes, and it also can judge the redundant nodes accurately, which puts those nodes into sleep state to reduce energy consumption and prolong lifetime of the network.

Acknowledgement. This research was supported by Natural Science Foundation of Yunnan (2011FZ176), China. The authors thank the anonymous reviewers whose comments have significantly improved the quality of this article.

References

1. Ren, F.Y., Huang, H.N., Lin, C.: Wireless sensor network. J. Softw. **14**(7), 1282–1291 (2003)
2. Tao, D., Sun, Y., Cheng, H.J.: Worst_case coverage detection and repair algorithm for video sensor networks. Acta Electronica Sin. **37**(10), 2284–2290 (2009). (In Chinese)
3. Shih, E., Cho, S., Ickes, N.: Physical layer driven protocol and algorithm design for energy-efficient wireless sensor networks. In: Proceedings of the 7th Annual International Conference on Mobile Computing and Networking, pp. 272–287. ACM Press, Rome (2001)
4. Liu, Y., Suo, L., Sun, D., Wanga, A.: Virtual square grid-based coverage algorithm of redundant node for wireless sensor network. J. Netw. Comput. Appl. **36**(5), 811–817 (2013)
5. Tian, D., Georganas, N.: A coverage-preserving node scheduling scheme for large wireless sensor networks. In: Proceedings of the 1st ACM International Workshop on Wireless Sensor Networks and Applications, pp. 32–41. ACM Press, Atlanta (2002)
6. Fan, G.J., Sun, L.J., Wang, H.P.: Non-uniform distribution node scheme in wireless sensor networks. J. Commun. **32**(1), 10–17 (2011). (In Chinese)
7. Gao, Y., Wu, K., Li, F.: Analysis on the redundancy of wireless sensor networks. In: Proceedings of the 2nd ACM International Conference on Wireless Sensor Networks and Applications, pp. 108–114. ACM Press, San Diego (2003)
8. Aekyu, C., Gilsoo, K., Taekyoung, K., et al.: A distributed node scheduling protocol considering sensing coverage in wireless sensor networks. In: IEEE 66th Vehicular Technology Conference, pp. 352–356. IEEE Computer Society, Baltimore (2007)
9. Huang, C.F., Tseng, Y.C.: The Coverage Problem in a Wireless Sensor Network, pp. 115–121. ACM Press, New York (2003)
10. Liu, X., Zhang, J., Wang, X.: SCCP: self-adjusting of circle coverage protocol in wireless sensor network. Appl. Res. Comput. **27**(4), 1407–1409 (2010). (In Chinese)

11. Singaram, M., Finney, S., Sathish, K.N., Chandraprasad, V.: Energy efficient self-scheduling algorithm for wireless sensor networks. Int. J. Sci. Technol. Res. **3**(1), 44–78 (2014)
12. Fatemeh, M.K., Ahmad, K.: Coverage problem in heterogeneous wireless sensor networks. Eur. Sci. J. **27**(9), 81–96 (2013)
13. Ma, S.S., Qian, J.S.: Energy balanced non-uniform distribution node scheduling algorithm for wireless sensor networks. Appl. Math. Inf. Sci. **8**(4), 1997–2003 (2014)
14. Hong, J.C., Guo, R.L.: Service-oriented node scheduling schemes with energy efficiency in wireless sensor networks. Distrib. Sens. Netw. **12**, 1155–1165 (2014)
15. Sajjad, R., Hassaan, K.Q., Syed, A.K.: An energy efficient topology control algorithm for connected area coverage in wireless sensor networks. J. Netw. Comput. Appl. **35**(4), 597–605 (2012)

An Adaptive Channel Sensing Approach and its Analysis Based on Hierarchical Colored Petri Net in Distributed Cognitive Radio Networks

Guangsheng Feng[1]([⊠]), Qian Zhao[2], Huiqiang Wang[1],
Hongwu Lv[1], and Junyu Lin[1]

[1] College of Computer Science and Technology,
Harbin Engineering University, Harbin 150001, China
{fengguangsheng,wanghuiqiang,lvhongwu,linjunyu}@hrbeu.edu.cn
[2] School of Computer and Information Engineering,
Harbin University of Commerce, Harbin 150028, China
zhaoqian@hrbcu.edu.cn

Abstract. In distributed Cognitive Radio Networks (CRNs), the high collision rate among the communication network nodes has attracted lots of attentions. In this paper, we first investigate the related model in our previous work and focus on the case that the number of Cognitive Radios (CRs) is more than that of the available channels. Then, we employ hierarchical colored petri net (HCPN) to analyze this model, which includes an adaptive sensing threshold for available channels, a sensing and accessing strategy. Last, we conduct extensive simulations to compare the performance of our approach with others that have closely been attended recently. Simulation results show that the proposed scheme achieves an outstanding performance on channel utilization in the case of heavy channel workload.

Keywords: Cognitive Radio Networks · Spectrum sense · Channel selection · Hierarchical colored petri net

1 Introduction

The new technologies of Cognitive Radio Networks (CRNs), built on the platform of Cognitive Radio (CR), have been designed to alleviate the dilemma of spectrum scarcity [1–5], in which primary users (PUs) have exclusive rights to transmit over the licensed channels whenever necessary. However, the secondary users (SUs) or CR nodes must perform spectrum sensing to attain transmission opportunities under the premise of protecting PUs communication. In a distributed CRN, each CR node must be equipped with a proper mechanism to avoid collisions and to evacuate the occupied channels whenever some PUs reclaim them. To solve the open problem, centralized and decentralized approaches are two typical branches.

© Springer-Verlag Berlin Heidelberg 2015
L. Sun et al. (Eds.): CWSN 2014, CCIS 501, pp. 69–83, 2015.
DOI: 10.1007/978-3-662-46981-1_7

In centralized one, a coordinator is required to schedule all CRs sensing and transmission activities, such as in [3,6]. The work in [3] is established on an assumption that CRs and PUs can cooperate with each other, where each CR reports its channel sensing results to the centralized Dynamic Spectrum Access (DSA) base station. Therefore, the overall throughput will be maximized through scheduling each CRs transmission opportunity. In consideration of DSA unknowing all the operational parameters of PUs, it proposes a sequential channel sensing order based on estimated traffic. However, all CR devices may not be managed by the same service provider in actual application scenarios, and hence it is impossible to attain an optimal scheduling strategy with several different coordinators. The work in [6] considers the statistical features of channel availabilities for a long period and attains an optimal sensing sequential order by its specific coordinator, which is only suitable for two CRs existed. If there are lots of CRs desiring to communicate, a heavy workload on channels will definitely deteriorate the network performance due to massive collisions among CRs.

Sensing channel with a distributed manner is another branch in the scenario of CRNs. A distributed learning approach is investigated in the work [7,8], where an adaptive random selection strategy on orthogonal channels is employed. Although its implementation is simple, the collision probability is quite high. Using sequential channel order to hunt for spectrum opportunities has become a hot issue [9], in which a CR probes multiple channels one by one with an elaborated order. In the work [10,11], a low load approach is proposed to sense channels sequentially jointed with transmission optimization, where the priori knowledge of licensed channels is not necessary but requires perfect bandwidth and data rate. Another sequential channel sensing strategy [12] requires all CRs to sense channels based on a specific descending order, and the priori knowledge of PUs is not requited either. However, this approach is only suitable for OFDM surroundings, and also requires all channel gains in advance. In order to reach optimal energy efficiency, the work [13] is focused on the access strategies and sensing order simultaneously, and the theory of stochastic sequential decision-making process is employed to formulate this problem. Besides, the long-term statistical features, the short-term diverse features [14], and the fast channel sharing [15] are taken into account. Recently, an adaptive sequential sensing strategy is proposed in Khans work [5]. It allows two or more autonomous CRs to observe the channels for spectrum opportunities sequentially. The key of this work is the strategy for choosing channel order with false alarms. However, this approach may achieve a better performance only when the CRs quantity is no more than the available channels.

Different from existing work, we propose a novel sequential order strategy for sensing multiple channels in distributed CRNs jointing Khans work and random access, but the two work have essential differences. On the basis of our previous work [16], we pay more attention on the sequential channel sensing strategy without a centralized coordinator under the case of heavy channel workload, i.e., more CRs but fewer available channels. The remainder of the paper is organized as follows. In Sect. 2, we design a distributed system model, including the system process mechanism, the stop condition of sensing, the threshold of available channels required to sense, and the collision avoidance approach. In Sect. 3, we employ HCPN to analyze its performance. In Sect. 4, we evaluate our proposed design at different channel workloads through numerical experiments. Finally, Sect. 5 concludes the paper.

2 An Adaptive Channels Sensing Model in Distributed CRNs

2.1 System Model

In a distributed CRN, M CRs and N licensed channels are coexisted, which are denoted as $\mathbf{CR} = \{CR_1, CR_2, \cdots, CR_M\}$ and $\mathbf{C} = \{C_1, C_2, \cdots, C_N\}$ respectively. If some channels are idle and sensed simultaneously by some CRs, they could transmit over those channels. In this case, if a PU reclaims one of the channels occupied by some CR, it will be evacuated by the related CR at once, which is consistent with the basic principle of Cognitive Radio. Given that all PUs and CRs employ the same time-slot system, a CR maybe have experienced i sensing sub-slots when k, the sensing threshold of available channels, idle channels are found. In other words, each CR is required to find k idle channels and then makes a decision on whether to transmit or sense continually. The maximum of sensing duration is an allowable sensing interval, and the sensing process will be stopped and stay quiet if there is no any idle channel found until this upper bound. A PUs communication activity starts only in the beginning of a time slot and last to its end when a PUs transmission is completed.

Similar to Khans approach, all channels are organized as a form of Latin Square:

$$\mathbf{CS} = \begin{bmatrix} C_1, & C_2, & \cdots, & C_{N-1}, & C_N \\ C_2, & C_3, & \cdots, & C_N, & C_1 \\ \vdots & \vdots & \ddots & \vdots & \vdots \\ C_N, & C_1, & \cdots & C_{N-2}, & C_{N-1} \end{bmatrix} \tag{1}$$

In matrix $\mathbf{CS}$, there are N^2 elements and row CS_i $(i = 1, 2, \cdots, N)$ stands for a sequential channel order whose elements are consisted of CS_{ij} $(i = 1, 2, \cdots, N)$. All CRs maintain their own sensing probabilities for CS_i i.e., $P^{(CS)} = \{p_i^{(CS)}\}$, which the CR senses sequential channel order CS_i according to the probability. At the beginning, each CR will select some CS_i according to the probability $p_i^{(CS)} - 1/N_{CS} = 1/N$. With the process going, the $p_i^{(CS)}$ will be updated according to its transmission and collision states, the objective of which is to lower the sensing probability to crowded channel orders. Note that the specific adaptive updating approach for $p_i^{(CS)}$ will be elaborated in next section.

In this model, one CR can make a decision on communication over some idle channels only when k available channels are found. If two or more CRs are crowded at the same sequential channel order, it is necessary to sensing more available channels before making a transmission decision. Otherwise, a smaller number of available channels can help make a transmission decision. The more detail about this model can be found in our previous work [16].

2.2 Stopping Condition and Sensing Threshold for Available Channels

We mainly concern the distributed approach for sequential channel sensing and there is no possibility of cooperative communications among CRs as well as PUs. Suppose that the sensing threshold for available channel is k and then a CR successively sense the sequential channel order CS_i i.e., $\{CS_{i1}, CS_{i2}, \cdots, CS_{im}\}$, based on its sensing probability $p_i^{(CS)}$ until k available channels found. Afterwards, the CR makes a decision on whether to transmit or sense continuously. Here, we do not consider the traditional stopping condition that once an idle channel is found, the process will be turned to transmission from channel sensing. In the case of heavy channel load, two or more CRs are crowded at the same sequential channel order which therefore causes serious collisions. If we continuously sense until k available channels (at least one) being found, each CR on this channel order will have an opportunity to choose a different channel C_j to transmit according to its access probability $p_{CH}(CS_i, C_j)$. As discussed above, the value of k is sensitive to collision probability. If it is too small, more collisions will be caused. On the contrary, the overall sensing time will be increased and the transmission time is shortened correspondingly.

$p_i^{(CS)}$ is the foregoing sensing probability that a CR attends at sequential channel order CS_i, which is estimated according to its transmission status: success or not on CS_i. Therefore, a smaller $p_i^{(CS)}$ stands for a higher collision probability on CS_i. On this basis, the threshold k could be estimated as follows:

$$k = \min\{\lfloor 1 \setminus p_i^{(CS)} \rfloor, C_a\} \tag{2}$$

where C_a is the total quantity of available channels. Therefore, k's value stands for the crowded level of the current channel order. If k equals 1, our approach is similar to Khans. In conclusion, the stop condition of sensing channel is that k available channels have been found by the current CR.

It is frequent that collision events happen due to different CRs contending spectrum opportunity as well as short of coordinated mechanism among CRs. If two or more CRs are crowded at the same sequential channel order, each CR may attain similar sensing results and they surely collide with each other even the idle channels being found. In this case, all the transmission data will be corrupted. To solve the problems, we propose a dynamic collision avoidance mechanism in this paper.

Suppose that a CR senses on sequential channel order CS_i, and will not take transmission activity before k available channels being found. If the specific quantity channels are found, the CR will randomly make a choice to transmit or to sense continuously. If continuous sensing is selected, the similar decision will be made in next sensing round. In other words, once k available channels are found, the CR faces two choices:

(1) Selecting channel C_j to transmit based on $p_{CH}(CS_i, C_j)$ that denotes the probability of selecting channel C_j:

$$p_{CH}(CS_i, C_j) = 2 \times r_j/(1+k) \times k \qquad (3)$$

where r_j is the index number of channel C_j in current available channel set. As shown in (3), the last available channel in sensing result set has the highest access probability. Let $r(r = 1, 2, \cdots, k)$ denotes the index number in available set, and I_r is the subscript of some channel, i.e., $C_{I_r} \in \mathbf{C}$. Therefore, C_{I_k} is the last element and $p_{CH}(CS_i, C_j) = 2 \times k/(1+k) \times k = 2/(1+k)$. To sum up, the access probability of each element in the available set is sensitive to its index number in this set as well as the total quantity k.

(2) Continuing to sense at the current sequential channel order CS_i.

If it is the first choice, the following two cases maybe happen.

Case 1: If there is no collision during the transmission interval over C_j, this transmission is successful. In this case, the sensing probability CS_j with first item C_j is increased correspondingly:

$$\begin{cases} p_j^{(CS)} = p_j^{(CS)'} + \sigma_j \\ p_{k \neq j}^{(CS)} = ((1 - p_j^{(CS)})/ \sum\limits_{q \neq j} p_{q \neq j}^{(CS)'}) \times p_{k \neq j}^{(CS)}, if\ p_j^{(CS)'} + \sigma_j < 1 \end{cases} \qquad (4)$$

where $p_j^{(CS)'}$ is the sensing probability of CS_j at the last slot and $\sigma_j \geq 0$ denotes the augmentation of sensing probability to CS_j at this slot. The value of σ_j should meet the requirement $\lceil 1/p_j \rceil - \lceil 1/p_j' \rceil \geq K^{(CS_j)}$, which means that the sensing threshold of available channels should be increased by $K^{(CS_j)}$ such that the hit rate of channel C_j will be raised correspondingly. In this updating process, if $p_j^{(CS)'} + \sigma_j \geq 1$ happens, the sensing probability to CS_j is set to 1 and others are set to 0, i.e., $p_{k \neq j}^{(CS)} = 0$.

Case 2: If the ACK is not received correctly, a collision may happen on channel C_j probably. In this case, the sensing probability to channel order CS_j will be decreased and other sensing probabilities will be increased:

$$\begin{cases} p_j^{(CS)} = p_j^{(CS)'} - \sigma_j \\ p_{k \neq j}^{(CS)} = ((1 - p_j^{(CS)})/ \sum\limits_{q \neq j} p_{q \neq j}^{(CS)'}) \times p_{k \neq j}^{(CS)'}, s.t., p_j^{(CS)'} - \sigma_j \geq 0 \end{cases} \qquad (5)$$

Similarly, the value of $\sigma_j \geq 0$ should meet the requirement $\lceil 1/p_j' \rceil - \lceil 1/p_j \rceil \geq K^{(CS_j)}$ such that the hit rate of CS_j as well as C_j will be decreased. If there is a contradictory between the two inequalities $p_j^{(CS)'} - \sigma_j \geq 0$ and $\lceil 1/p_j' \rceil - \lceil 1/p_j \rceil \geq K^{(CS_j)}$, the former one should be guaranteed first.

In case 1, a CR possibly continues to sense at the current sequential channel order CS_i. It starts to sense from the first element of CS_i in next sensing round, but those channels being found busy in the first sensing round will be omitted.

Similarly, the process will transfer to transmission or selection decision when k available channels are found. When the whole time of sensing rounds reaches to the maximum of sensing duration, the sensing process will be stopped at once.

3   State Analysis Based on Hierarchical Colored Petri Net

In order to verify the proposed models performance, we employ Hierarchical Colored Petrified Net (HCPN) to design and analysis, which makes it possible to examine the proposed approach at different abstraction levels. Because different CRs quantity will generated different markings distributions, the markings in every place are omitted in our HCPN but the *colset* types are given in Fig. 1. Meanwhile, input and output markings are labeled on the arc between places and transitions.

---
1. colset INT = int;
2. colset CHAN = product INT*INT;
3. colset CHLIST = list INT;
4. colset GCLOCK = product INT*INT;

Fig. 1. *colset* in proposed model

3.1   The Top-Level Module

In this top-level module of the HCPN, the notations for places and transitions are summarized as in Table 1.

Table 1. The notations for places and transitions in top level of HCPN

Places and their descriptions	
Global Clock	All CRs and PUs employ the same time system that is *Global Clock*
Sync	*Sync* is the condition and the related substitution transition *Initialize* will be fired when *Sync* is satisfied
Channels	All channels belong to the *colset* type CHAN, i.e., a two-tuple where the first item is channel number and the second is its state
Unm	Place *Unm* is the total number of CRs
U	Place *U* denotes that a CR is ready for a new transmission
Receive	Place *Receive* denotes the received packets
Transitions and substitution transitions	
Initialize	The substitution transition is used to initialize all CRs and channels at the beginning of each transmission slot
Handler	All CRs use the substitution transition to sense and transmit

Figure 2 shows the top-level module, where the red places are commonly used in all CRs activities. The substitution transition is denoted by red rectangular-double-line boxes, and there is a rectangular substitution tag adjacent to each of substitution transitions, such as *Initialize* and *Handler*. The name in this tag is pointed to a sub-module, and thus it is relevant to a substitution transition. In other words, the substitution transition could be described in detail by the related sub-module. This process is similar to a procedure call in main function. Here each CR has its own substitution transition *Handler*, where its sensing, decision, and transmission can be handled. The quantity of CRs could be easily extended because all CRs have the same handling structure.

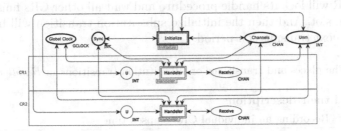

Fig. 2. The top-level module (Color figure online)

In the beginning of each transmission slot, each CR calibrates its local clock to the *Global Clock* which can guarantee all the CRs have the same time system, and also all the channels are be evacuated for next transmission slot, as shown in Fig. 3. The sensing slot is equal to time duration that the CR finishes a time sensing, which is the same for all CRs. The place *Sync* denotes the difference between the *Unm* and the quantity of CRs finishing this *Handler* procedure, and therefore the substitution transition will be fired when *Sync* is decreased to zero. Moreover, the place *Receive* has a *colset* type product INT*INT, i.e., a two-tuple (*bad, ok*), which denote the corrupted and correct packets.

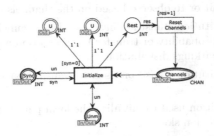

Fig. 3. The *Initialize* module in top

3.2 The *Handler* Substitution Transition and its Lower-level Transitions

The *Handler* substitution transition in top-level module is shown in Fig. 4, where the substitution transitions *Sense*, *Decide*, *Process* and *Transmit* constitute a mainly cognitive cycle. The places and transitions or substitution transitions are summarized as follows (Table 2).

The main body of *Handler* substitution transition is used to complete a cognitive cycle that is from the first substitution transition *Sense* to the last one *Transmission* orderly controlled by place *Lock* and *B*, such as Fig. 4 shown, where this cycle will be repeated until the end of transmission slot. At that time, the CR will lock its handle procedure and wait all other CRs finishing this transmission slot. And then the initialize substitution transition will be fired to prepare for next transmission period.

Table 2. The places and transitions or substitution transitions in *Handler* module

Places and their descriptions	
Local Clock	Recording an individual CRs elapsed time
A1 and *A2*	Denoting the available channels found by the CR
DT	Indicating the decision result between observation or transmission
Sch	Denoting the selected channels for transmission
B and *Lock*	Control mechanisms that guarantee the transitions *Sense*, *Decide*, *Process* and *Transmit* are fired in the order of cognitive cycle
Uk	Controlling the sensing threshold discussed in Sect. 2
Od	Storing the next channel required to sense according the sensing order
Ret	Storing the condition that can fire transition *Re* to initialize the local parameters for the next transmission slot
Transitions and substitution transitions	
Sense	The substitution transition used to find available channels by a CR
Decide	The substitution transition used to make a decision on whether to transmit or to observe based on the channels crowded state
Process	The substitution transition used to select channels to transmit based on its probability or transfer to observation according to place *DT*s markings distribution
Transmit	The substitution transition used to transmit packets over the selected channel
Re	The transition used to initialize the local parameters for the next transmission slot
Reset	The transition related to *Sync* and update the value of *Sync*

As shown in Fig. 5, the substitution transition *Sense* will be fired and the CR will search the available channels according its sensing order and until the sensing threshold is reached that is specified by place *Uk*, where the sensing

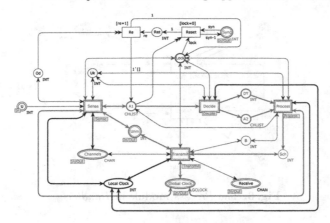

Fig. 4. The *Handler* module in top

order is guaranteed by transition *Order*. Note that the value specific by place *Uk* is a variable that would be updated in every transmission slot based on the channel crowded state. Transition *Sense* could be fired only in the case of function *checkse()* evaluated to true, where variables *chl* is the list of available channels that have been found, List.length *chl* < *k* and *gt* = *t* guarantee the local time is the same with the global one and the current quantity of available channels found by the CR has not reached the sensing threshold *k*. If *Sensing* transition is fired, place A1 will be updated by function *seta1()*. Note that if the current sensing slot is the last one in the current transmission slot, the *Lock* will be reset by *setlock()*, so that the procedure could go into *Initialize* substitution transmission and prepare for the next transmission round.

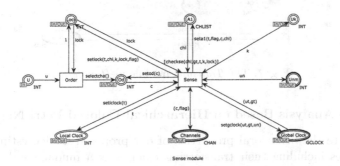

Fig. 5. The *Sense* module in *Handler*

Then, the CR will go into the substitution transition *Decide* to make a decision on whether to transmit or observe continually. If the choice is to observe, the CR will continue to sense from the first available channel in A1 until the available channels reached to the sensing threshold. Otherwise, it is required to select an available channel to transmit by the current CR, which could be completed by function *select()* such as Fig. 6 shown.

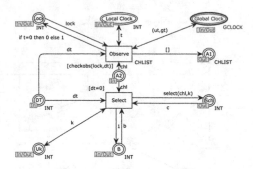

Fig. 6. The *Process* module in *Handler*

In the *Transmit* module as Fig. 7 shown, place *Receive* is used to record the packets that may be correct or incorrect depending on collision during this transmission. If one of other CRs transmits over the same channel, there is a collision happening, which results in a bad packet recorded in the place *Receive*. In this case, the sensing probability and access probability will be decreased correspondingly.

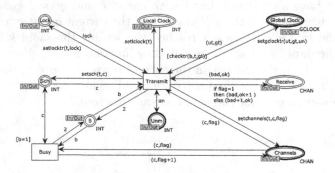

Fig. 7. The *Transmit* module in *Handler*

3.3 State Analysis Based on Hierarchical Colored Petri Net

To investigate the behavioral properties of our proposed model, estimating all system states including their transferring changes is a fundamental way. In a HCPN model, all the states could be described by means of directed graph, in which the nodes are related to the reachable marking set, and the arcs are related to the occurring binding elements correspondingly. Thus, the behavior properties of our model could be verified through state-space analysis.

Random distribution functions, infinite time, and infinite receive capacity are used in our model for making decisions on the next procedure, which leads to a marking that cannot be uniquely determined by the binding of the transition's variables. Thus, our model is nondeterministic and non-terminated, which will have varying effects on the nondeterministic behavior in the model. In order to handle these problems, we use ten sense slots as a period and next transmission round will start from zero. Then the place Receive is replaced by a sink node and once a packet arrived, it will be absorbed immediately. The sense probability and access probability are remained and 300 s is the termination condition for analyzing the state space. The analysis result is shown in Table 3, which is generated automatically by CPN tools 4.0.

Table 3. The state space at different CR numbers

CR, CH	State Space	State Arcs	SCC Graph	SCC Arcs	Dead Transition
2,5	65539	132638	29937	59217	None
3,5	33764	54522	33764	54522	None
4,5	42471	76328	42471	76328	None
5,5	28772	54169	28772	54169	None
6,5	31450	58713	31450	58713	None
7,5	33791	70086	33791	70086	None

Under different CR numbers, Table 3 gives the statistical information of state space. For the proposed model, there are 65539 nodes (states) and 132638 arcs when there are 2 CRs and 5 channels. With the number increasing of CRs, the state space in decreased dramatically, such as 3, 4, 5, and 6 CRs, which means that our model has an outstanding performance at heavy channel workload. This phenomenon is verified by the later simulations. SCC (Strongly Connected Components) graph is also counted. We note that the nodes in SCC graph are fewer than that in the state space, which means that non-trivial SCCs are existed. In other words, this procedure related to this model could not be terminated automatically.

4 Experiments and Analysis

In order to verify the performance and compare with other typical approaches, some numerical experiments has been conducted in this section, where the mainly parameters in our experiment are similar to Khans approach. The channel busy probability Pu is set 0.0, 0.1, 0.3 and 0.5, such that we can check the performance of different approaches at different channel workloads. The total channel quantity is 10 and the quantity of CRs are various from 2 to 20. The performance of channel utilization can be inferred from the wasted ratio of transmission slot, including collision interval and idle interval. Moreover, we set 50 transmission slots in each time experiment and total 10 experiments are conducted. Thus, we have attained 100 times experimental data. Meanwhile, we set 11 sub-slots as transmission duration, i.e., if a CR has sensed the last item in current sequential order, there is only one sub-slot for transmission. The experimental results are shown in Figs. 8, 9, 10, 11 and 12.

Figures 8 and 9 are the comparison between our approach and Khans. Khans approach has an excellent performance under the case that there is a light work-load with a fewer CRs on the channels, where the wasted ration of transmission is no more than 20 %. While the CR quantity is more than 10, the wasted ratio is soaring. Even all the channel are not occupied by PUs, i.e., $Pu = 0.0$, the wasted ratio reaches 60 % with 20 CRs. But in the case of $Pu = 0.5$, the wasted ratio is about 33 % in Khans approach. Figure 6 shows the experimental result of our approach. It is obvious that the proposed approach has a better overall performance compared with Khans, and the wasted ratio is constrained about 10 % at different probabilities of Pus. Only when the CR quantity is 2 or 3, the performance is not superior to Khans.

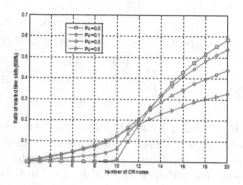

Fig. 8. Khans method at different busy probability of channels

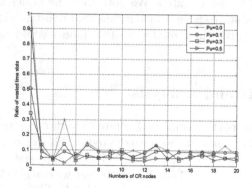

Fig. 9. The proposed method at different Pus with various CR quantities

Figure 10 shows the comparison at the channel busy probability $Pu = 0.1$. Only when the CR quantity is less than channel quantity, Khans method has a better performance. After that, this approach has an intolerable increasing on channel wasted ratio. On the contrary, our approach remains a comparative stable wasted ration about 10 %, only when the CR quantity is 2 or 3, the performance is poor, which is verified by the state space analysis in Sect. 3.

In the case of heavy channel workload, our proposed approach will be a quite effective complement to Khans approach. The Random LS approach [14] has the lowest performance compared with others.

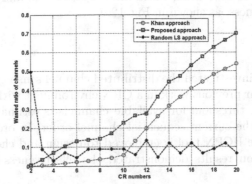

Fig. 10. The wasted ratio comparison between different approaches

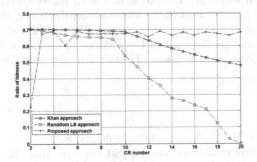

Fig. 11. Comparison of throughput

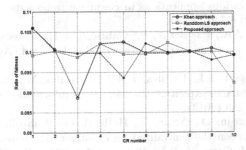

Fig. 12. The comparison in transmission ratio of different CR nodes

Figure 11 shows the throughput comparison of those three approaches. Our proposed approach has an almost 70 % throughput when the CRs number is more than 3. In contrast to this, the throughput in other two approaches decline dramatically when the CRs number exceeds 10, i.e., the quantity of channels. When only two CRs exist, our proposed approach has a little poor performance.

When there are 10 CRs, each CR could attain an almost equitable transmission chance about 10 % in all those three approaches, and all of them have achieved a well fairness, as shown in Fig. 12.

5   Conclusion

In this paper, we reinvestigated the distributed channel sensing strategy that we have proposed in our previous work in a CRN environment with heavy workload channels. A sensing threshold for available channels is estimated based on the crowded degree of the current sequential channel order. In order to implement this mechanism, the HCPN tool is employed to design and check our proposed approach. Simulation results demonstrated the effectiveness of our proposed approach.

Acknowledgments. This work was supported in part by the Research Fund for the Doctoral Program of Higher Education of China under Grant 20122304130002, the Natural Science Foundation in China under Grant 61370212, the Natural Science Foundation of Heilongjiang Province under Grant ZD 201102 and F201037, the Fundamental Research Fund for the Central Universities under Grant HEUCFZ1213 and HEUCF100601, and Postdoctoral Science Foundation of Heilongjiang Province under Grant LBH-210204.

References

1. Akyildiz, I.F., Lee, W.-Y., Vuran, M.C., Mohanty, S.: A survey on spectrum management in cognitive radio networks. IEEE Commun. Mag. **46**, 40–48 (2008)
2. Liang, Y.-C., Zeng, Y., Peh, E.C., Hoang, A.T.: Sensing-throughput tradeoff for cognitive radio networks. IEEE Trans. Wireless Commun. **7**, 1326–1337 (2008)
3. Huang, J., Zhou, H., Chen, Y., Chen, B., Zhu, X., Kong, R.: Optimal channel sensing order for various applications in cognitive radio networks. Wireless Pers. Commun. **71**, 1721–1740 (2013)
4. Liu, C.-H., Tran, J.A., Pawelczak, P., Cabric, D.: Traffic-aware channel sensing order in dynamic spectrum access networks. IEEE J. Sel. Areas Commun. **31**, 2312–2323 (2013)
5. Khan, Z., Lehtomaki, J.J., DaSilva, L.A., Latva-aho, M.: Autonomous sensing order selection strategies exploiting channel access information. IEEE Trans. Mob. Comput. **12**, 274–288 (2013)
6. Salami, G., Durowoju, O., Attar, A., Holland, O., Tafazolli, R., Aghvami, H.: A comparison between the centralized and distributed approaches for spectrum management. IEEE Commun. Surv. Tutorials **13**, 274–290 (2011)
7. Fan, R., Jiang, H.: Channel sensing-order setting in cognitive radio networks: a two-user case. IEEE Trans. Veh. Technol. **58**, 4997–5008 (2009)
8. Anandkumar, A., Michael, N., Tang, A.: Opportunistic spectrum access with multiple users: learning under competition. In: The 29th IEEE Conference on Computer Communications (INFOCOM 2010), pp. 1–9. IEEE Communications Society (2010)

9. Anandkumar, A., Michael, N., Tang, A.K., Swami, A.: Distributed algorithms for learning and cognitive medium access with logarithmic regret. IEEE J. Sel. Areas Commun. **29**, 731–745 (2011)

10. Theis, N.C., Thomas, R.W., DaSilva, L.A.: Rendezvous for cognitive radios. IEEE Trans. Mob. Comput. **10**, 216–227 (2011)

11. Jiang, H., Lai, L., Fan, R., Poor, H.V.: Optimal selection of channel sensing order in cognitive radio. IEEE Trans. Wireless Commun. **8**, 297–307 (2009)

12. Chang, N.B., Liu, M.: Competitive analysis of opportunistic spectrum access strategies. In: The 27th IEEE Conference on Computer Communications (INFOCOM 2008), pp. 2207–2215. IEEE Communications Society (2008)

13. Cheng, H.T., Zhuang, W.: Simple channel sensing order in cognitive radio networks. IEEE J. Sel. Areas Commun. **29**, 676–688 (2011)

14. Pei, Y., Liang, Y.-C., Teh, K.C., Li, K.H.: Energy-efficient design of sequential channel sensing in cognitive radio networks: optimal sensing strategy, power allocation, and sensing order. IEEE J. Sel. Areas Commun. **29**, 1648–1659 (2011)

15. Li, B., Yang, P., Wang, J., Wu, Q., Tang, S., Li, X., Liu, Y.: Almost optimal dynamically-ordered channel sensing and accessing for cognitive networks. IEEE Trans. Mob. Comput., 1–14 (2013)

16. Feng, G., Wang, H., Zhao, Q., Lv, H.: An adaptive channel sensing approach based on sequential order in distributed cognitive radio networks. In: Hsu, C.-H., Shi, X., Salapura, V. (eds.) NPC 2014. LNCS, vol. 8707, pp. 395–408. Springer, Heidelberg (2014)

BEE OS: Supporting Batch Execution with a Preemptive Real-Time Kernel

Shuo Cai[1,2], Xiaotong Zhang[1(✉)], Fuqiang Ma[1], Yunfei Song[3],
and Liang Chen[3]

[1] Department of Computer and Communication Engineering,
University of Science and Technology, Beijing, People's Republic of China
caishuo99@gmail.com, zxt@ustb.edu.cn, mafuqiang639@sina.com
[2] Air China Limited, Beijing, China
[3] Lehigh University, Bethlehem, USA
yus210@lehigh.edu, Cheng@cse.lehigh.edu

Abstract. Modern wireless sensor networks require operating system with real-time, low-power, multi-tasking features, in order to quickly deal with matters of wireless sensor nodes. Event-driven systems and multi-threaded systems are two major operating systems used by wireless sensor networks (WSN). To take advantage of salient features of both types, based on μC/OS-II and WSN characteristics, we have designed a tiny and hybrid embedded operating system, BEE OS, which integrates a preemptive real-time kernel supporting batch execution. Besides BEE has a real-time, low-power and multi-tasking feature. We propose a multi-task management scheme with multi-priority queues and analyze its timeliness performance based on a round-robin theoretical model, which leads to our novel design of the preemptive task scheduling algorithm to optimize the average waiting-time of all tasks. Finally, an adaptive method is introduced into BEE OS in order to avoid task starvation. Our experimental results show the overhead and performance comparisons among BEE OS, μC/OS-II, and TinyOS. Compared with μC/OS-II, the RAM and Flash of BEE OS are about two-fold down, and the task response time achieved by BEE OS is approximately a quarter of those by TinyOS and μC/OS-II. BEE operating system can be widely applied to relatively fixed tasks in industrial environments, with low power consumption and preemptive real-time characteristics.

Keywords: Wireless sensor network · Operating system · Preemptive scheduling · Batch execution

1 Introduction

While designing an OS for WSN, it is crucial to pay attention to the concrete WSN applications which will be applied to and the features of WSNs. There are primarily three aspects of WSNs to consider. First, sensor nodes are limited in power, computational capacities and memory. The low power consumption is

© Springer-Verlag Berlin Heidelberg 2015
L. Sun et al. (Eds.): CWSN 2014, CCIS 501, pp. 84–96, 2015.
DOI: 10.1007/978-3-662-46981-1_8

one of the most important constraints on sensor nodes which carry limited and generally irreplaceable power sources [1]. Furthermore, sensor nodes are prone to failures, and the topology of a sensor network changes very frequently. Thus, OSs should have features of robustness, fault-tolerance and scalability. Finally, an OS for WSNs must provide scheduling algorithms that accommodate the application requirements [2].

Multi-threaded operating systems, which can meet the needs of time-critical tasks by means of task preemption, can achieve better timeliness than event-driven operating systems, while the event-driven model is more energy efficient. The event-driven approach is suitable for extremely resource constrained sensor nodes and can build energy efficient sensor networks as it requires little memory and processing resources such as TinyOS [3] and SOS [4].

In this paper, we present a survey of embedded operating systems and scheduling algorithms proposed for wireless sensor networks. Our aim is to provide an embedded operating system for WSNs, which has advantages of both models mentioned above. After the analysis on the requirements of the industrial applications in WSNs and constraints of TinyOS1and μC/OS-II, we propose a BEE OS that adopts a preemptive real-time kernel, which is equipped with multi-priority queues and round-robin features, to increase system responsiveness without introducing too much memory overhead. It supports the batch execution which mainly focuses on the industrial multi-task management by means of these scheduling strategies and also has positive characteristics of the event-driven model. Therefore, it is a hybrid embedded operating system for WSNs, especially for industrial wireless applications. The remainder of the paper is organized as follows. Section 2 shows the related work. Section 3 describes in detail our novel OS in terms of the architecture, multi-task management and so on. Sections 4 evaluates this operating system. Section 5 makes a conclusion of this paper and discusses the directions for future work.

2   Related Work

Our motes are all based on one classic real-time embedded operating system μC/OS-II which is more suitable for industrial environments under comparison with other widely-used operating systems. However, there are also some deadly deficiencies in μC/OS-II which cannot meet our requirements to monitor industrial phenomena. Therefore, we do some work and experiments on the current-used operating system μC/OS-II in the same way as did researchers towards TinyOS. However, μC/OS-III is improved in functions. μC/OS-III manages an unlimited number of application tasks, constrained only by a processors access to memory. μC/OS-III also supports an unlimited number of priority levels (typically configured for between 8 and 256 different priority levels). μC/OS-III allows for unlimited tasks, semaphores, mutexes, event flags, message queues, timers and memory partitions. The user allocates all kernel objects at run time. μC/OS-III provides features to allow stack growth of tasks to be monitored. While task size is not limited, they need to have a minimum size based on the CPU used.

Fig. 1. The developing environment and hardware platforms.

All application-oriented operating systems have some unique characteristics towards the specific applications. Considering that μC/OS-II is a widely-used open source embedded operating system and we have used μC/OS-II as the operating system of almost our motes which are applied to industrial environments, so it is necessary to modify μC/OS-II scheduling strategies and communication modes to better handle resource allocation efficiently in an industrial background after analyzing the industrial characteristics and requirements. Therefore, the main trend of designing an embedded operating system is to optimize the performance and overhead of some classical operating systems by analyzing the characteristics of specific applications and WSNs. We believe that this modified operating system will be the most suitable OS for this kind of application.

3   Overview of BEE OS

3.1   Multi-task Management

However, there exist some severe constraints in μC/OS-II. One of limitations in μC/OS-II is that each priority is assigned to only one task, which means this scheduling strategy only applied to schedule tasks with entirely different importance. Furthermore, μC/OS-II has some other limitations in terms of memory overhead. It has two 8-bit variables, OSRdyGrp and OSRdyTbl, to calculate the highest priority through a 16 * 16 table named OSUnMapTbl while scheduling tasks. These tables mentioned above occupy too much memory space. Last but not least, it is emphasized that the μC/OS-II scheduler adopts a static priority based assignment strategy which must make sure each task priority in advance. In this situation, tasks with lower priorities have to wait an unacceptable long period of time because tasks queued in front of them have a long processing duration. After that, μC/OS-II which uses preemptive real-time kernel and manages the number of tasks unrestricted is improved. Obviously, compared to tick management of μC/OS-II, μC/OS-III uses a specialized task clock ticks to deal with clock ticks, that can greatly reduce the execution time of the interrupt service routine. However, the more clock tick interrupt frequency in μC/OS-II, the more frequent the clock tick interrupt and the higher accuracy of the system delay, the higher processing ability requires. Therefore, μC/OS-II will lead to an increase in power consumption and is still not able to meet the low power requirements of industrial production.

Currently, a wireless sensor network is made up of many sensor nodes, most of which have very limited energy and resources, so sensor nodes require the operating system to be as small as possible. Moreover, with regard to the industrial environment our motes will be applied to, it has a large batch of identical tasks, which need to be assigned the same priorities. All these requirements cannot be satisfied in the μC/OS-II. Therefore, BEE OS is born with the multi-priority queues and the round-robin scheduling strategies to support the batch processing.

Multi-priority Queues. Similar tasks in μC/OS-II must have different priorities; however, it leads to unequal phenomenon among tasks while assigning resources. Actually, we suggest that there should be 64 priorities in the μC/OS-II, which wastes too much memory. As for features of the industrial environment, there are not many various tasks. Thus, BEE OS decreases the number of priorities to 16. The number of priorities depends on the specific application the BEE OS is applied to. Hence, it is very flexible to adjust the number of priorities in BEE OS according to the needs of the specific environment. We also add two pointers which are OSPSNext and OSPSPrev stored in the task control block (TCB) to achieve the multi-priority queues based scheduling. Because of the introduction of the multi-priority queues, each priority can be assigned to many tasks which are organized as a link through pointers OSPSNext and OSPSPrev described in Fig. 2. The overall scheduling strategy is a priority based and in each priority queue, the scheduling rule is First In, First Out (FIFO).

Round-Robin Theory Model in IWSNs. After adopting the multi-priority queues, it is necessary to add a round-robin strategy into BEE OS so that tasks with the same priority have an equal right to compete for the resources. In particular, there are some tasks with such a long lifetime in one priority queue that tasks behind it fail to gain resources to run. The kernel schedules tasks according to their priorities and each task has a fixed execution time-slice to run. If a task cannot complete before the set time deadline, it will be put at the end of its priority queue and wait to be scheduled again. Tasks whose execution time is equal to or lower than the execution time-slice assigned need not to be scheduled again. Two variables are given in the TCB structure, OSPSLen and OSPSCurLen, this is illustrated in Fig. 2. OSPSLen stores the execution time-slice assigned and OSPSCurLen records the rest execution time of the task.

In order to analyze the round-robin method accurately, we have estimated the execution time of many kinds of tasks implemented on the motes showed in Fig. 1 in the industrial wireless sensor networks. The execution time and the waiting-time of each task are measured by *cycle per task* (CPT) and the statistical data is presented in the Table 1.

There are a batch of tasks to execute in the Fig. 3 to illustrate the round-robin method. Assume this batch of tasks consists of four tasks, which are Time-Out, ASSOCIATE_request, NEI_info_request and NEI_info_response according to Table 1. Suppose TimeOut, NEI_info_request and NEI_info_response are in the

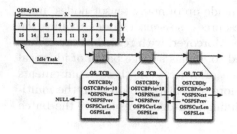

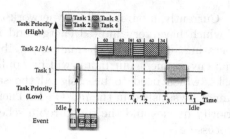

Fig. 2. The block diagram of multi-priority queues in BEEOS.

Fig. 3. The task processing strategy in the 103-154-9 example.

Table 1. The Execution Time of Tasks in the IWSNs.

Task	The execution time	Task description
ACK	2	The time of sending ACK after the receiver gets the data packet
TimeOut	103	The time of waiting ACK after the sender transmits the data packet
ASSOCIATE_request	156	Synchronization request
NEI_info_request	154	Neighbor information report request
NEI_info_response	9	Neighbor information report acknowledgement

same priority queue, whose required execution time are 103 CPT, 154 CPT and 9 CPT respectively, so this example is named as *103-154-9*. Define the execution time-slice of this priority queue is 60 cycles. The priority of ASSOCIATE_request is lower than them, so they can interrupt ASSOCIATE_request and execute sequentially according to whose event is fired first. In this case, the sequence is TimeOut, NEI_info_request and NEI_info_response. NEI_info_response will be finished in 9 CPT, while TimeOut and NEI_info_request are unable to finish in 60 cycles, which requires that they are divided into several parts. After finishing TimeOut and NEI_info_request in their first 60-cycle and NEI_info_response in its 9 CPT, the remaining 43-cycle TimeOut can be executed till completion. Then, there is only task NEI_info_request to run. Finally, the kernel will continue to reschedule ASSOCIATE_request to process for its lowest priority among all the tasks.

The average waiting-time is one of standard index to evaluate the performance of operating systems. The kernel assigns a fixed execution time-slice to each task according to its priority in order to minimize the total mean waiting-time. Before presenting the theoretical model developed in this paper, we introduce the concept of *waiting-time* for a task. If the execution time-slice of a task is greater than or equals to the required execution time of such task, which means the task can be finished in one execution time-slice, then the waiting-time is the whole time used by the tasks queued before this task. The definition of waiting-time is a little complicated if the execution time-slice of a task is less than this task's required execution time. The task has to be divided into several parts, some of which are needed to be arranged to the end of the queue due to the FIFO rule, since it cannot be finished in one execution time-slice. In such case, we define the waiting-time of the task is the average of all the waiting-times of the small divided parts of the task.

Let us refer to the *103-154-9* example mentioned above to explain the concept of waiting-time. After the analysis of the *103-154-9* previously, as the calculation approach given in the definition of waiting-time, we obtain the waiting-times of the three tasks are $(0 + 129)/2 = 64.5$ CPT, $(60 + 172 + 232)/3 = 154.67$ CPT and 120 CPT, respectively.

We now return to propose the theoretical model used in our paper. Assume there are r priority queues, and there are n_i tasks in i-th priority queue. For sake of simplicity, we introduce index set is $\mathcal{I}_r = \{1, 2...r\}$, thus the priority queues index set is $\mathcal{I}_r$ and the i-th priority queue index set is $\mathcal{I}_{n_i} = \{1, 2, ..., n_i\}$ where $i \in \mathcal{I}_r$. Let the j-th task in i-th priority queue denoted by a_{ij}, where $i \in \mathcal{I}_r, j \in \mathcal{I}_{n_i}$, and the waiting-time of the task a_{ij} denoted by $\mathcal{W}(a_{ij})$. Without loss of generality, we also let a_{ij} denote the required execution time for task a_{ij}. The aim of an operation system is to optimize the limited resources, which is, in other words in this paper, minimizing the average of the waiting-times of all tasks executed in the processors with different priorities requirements. This is mathematically formulated as follows:

$$\min_{i \in \mathcal{I}_r, j \in \mathcal{I}_{n_i}} \frac{\sum_i \sum_j \mathcal{W}(a_{ij})}{\sum_i n_i} \tag{1}$$

One may claim that it is optimal, i.e. minimize the average waiting-time, to set the execution time-slice sufficiently large such that all tasks can be finished in one execution time-slice. This, however, is an incorrect conclusion, to which we present the counterexample *103-154-9* mentioned above to demonstrate. If the execution time-slice is sufficiently large, e.g. more than 154 cycles, then the waiting-times for the three tasks are 0 CPT, 103 CPT and 257 CPT, respectively, which yields the average waiting-time is 120 CPT. Now we choose the execution time-slice be 60 cycles that causes the first and the second task be divided. In such case, it is not difficult to obtain the waiting-times of the three tasks are 64.5 CPT, 154.67 CPT and 120 CPT, respectively, which yields the average waiting-time is 113.06 CPT. Thus, it is better if the execution time-slice is not chosen sufficiently large in this example.

We continue to build the constraints in the model. Let the execution time-slice for i-th priority queue denoted by $x_i, i \in \mathcal{I}_r$. Since there may be some tasks whose required execution time is greater than the execution time-slice, we divide all queues with a same priority into some small pieces shown as follows:

$$
\begin{array}{c}
\begin{array}{c} a_{i1} \\ a_{i2} \\ \vdots \\ a_{in_i} \end{array} \Rightarrow
\begin{array}{cccc}
m_{i11} & m_{i21} & \ldots & m_{in_i1} \\
m_{i12} & m_{i22} & \ldots & m_{in_i2} \\
\ldots & \ldots & \ldots & \ldots \\
m_{i1p_i} & m_{i2p_i} & \ldots & m_{in_ip_i}
\end{array}
\end{array} \tag{2}
$$

$$
\Rightarrow
\begin{array}{cccc}
w_{i11} & w_{i21} & \ldots & w_{in_i1} \\
w_{i12} & w_{i22} & \ldots & w_{in_i2} \\
\ldots & \ldots & \ldots & \ldots \\
w_{i1p_i} & w_{i2p_i} & \ldots & w_{in_ip_i}
\end{array}
$$

where $p_i = \max_{j \in \mathcal{I}_{n_i}} [\frac{a_{ij}}{x_i}] + 1$, $[\cdot]$ is the Gaussian function for a real number, the j-th column in the second matrix contains all the small pieces of a_{ij}, and the w_{ijk} is the accumulated waiting-time for the small task m_{ijk}, which are defined in the following three equations.

$$
a_{ij} = \sum_{k \in \mathcal{I}_{p_i}} m_{ijk}, \tag{3}
$$

$$
m_{ijk} = \begin{cases} x_i, & \text{if } a_{ij} \geq kx_i; \\ \max\{a_{ij} - (k-1)x_i, 0\}, & \text{if } a_{ij} < kx_i. \end{cases} \tag{4}
$$

$$
w_{ijk} = \begin{cases} \displaystyle\sum_{q \in \mathcal{I}_{n_i}} \sum_{s \in \mathcal{I}_{k-1}} m_{isq} + \sum_{u \in \mathcal{I}_{j-1}} m_{iuk}, & \text{if } m_{ijk} \neq 0; \\ 0, & \text{if } m_{ijk} = 0. \end{cases} \tag{5}
$$

where $i \in \mathcal{I}_r, j \in \mathcal{I}_{n_i}$ and $k \in \mathcal{I}_{p_i}$. Although m_{ijk} and w_{ijk} above are variables, they are also functions of x_i, which deduces that x_i is determined implies that m_{ijk} and w_{ijk} are determined as well. Thus, it is done if we figure out the value of the execution time-slice x_i. Furthermore, we introduce the constants for simplicity sake, $F_i, i \in \mathcal{I}_r$, to represent all required execution time of the tasks with the i-th priority queues.

$$
F_i = \sum_{j \in \mathcal{I}_{n_i}} a_{ij}, \quad i \in \mathcal{I}_r, \tag{6}
$$

Now we can present the formula of the waiting-time for task $a_{ij}, i \in \mathcal{I}_r, j \in \mathcal{I}_{n_i}$. The waiting-time of the task in a lower priority queues should include all required execution time for the tasks in a higher priority queues, since the task in higher priority queues is executed before the task in lower priority queues.

$$
\mathcal{W}(a_{ij}) = \sum_{s \in \mathcal{I}_{i-1}} F_i + \frac{1}{n_{ij}} \sum_{u \in \mathcal{I}_{n_{ij}}} w_{iju}, \tag{7}
$$

where $n_{ij} = [\frac{a_{ij}}{x_i}] + 1$. Finally, as the consideration in real world, the values of execution time-slice x_i we can choose should have lower and upper bounds. The lower bound can be the smallest time clock in a computer, while the upper bound can be any numbers that human being assigns for any purposes.

$$
y_i \leq x_i \leq z_i, i \in \mathcal{I}_r. \tag{8}
$$

The overall theoretical model with the variables x_i, the value of execution time-slice, in this paper is summarized below by combining of the equations from (1) to (11).

$$\min \quad \frac{\sum_{i\in\mathcal{I}_r}\sum_{j\in\mathcal{I}_{n_i}}\mathcal{W}(a_{ij})}{\sum_{i\in\mathcal{I}_r}n_i}$$

$$\text{s.t.} \quad a_{ij} = \sum_{k\in\mathcal{I}_{p_i}} m_{ijk},$$

$$m_{ijk} = \begin{cases} x_i, & \text{if } a_{ij} \geq kx_i; \\ \max\{a_{ij}-(k-1)x_i, 0\}, & \text{if } a_{ij} < kx_i. \end{cases}$$

$$w_{ijk} = \begin{cases} \sum_{q\in\mathcal{I}_{n_i}}\sum_{s\in\mathcal{I}_{k-1}} m_{iqs} + \sum_{u\in\mathcal{I}_{j-1}} m_{iuk}, & \text{if } m_{ijk} \neq 0; \\ 0, & \text{if } m_{ijk} = 0. \end{cases} \qquad (9)$$

$$F_i = \sum_{j\in\mathcal{I}_{n_i}} a_{ij},$$

$$\mathcal{W}(a_{ij}) = \sum_{i\in\mathcal{I}_{i-1}} F_i + \frac{1}{n_{ij}}\sum_{u\in\mathcal{I}_{n_{ij}}} w_{iju},$$

$$y_i \leq x_i \leq z_i,$$

$$\text{where } i \in \mathcal{I}_r, j \in \mathcal{I}_{n_i}, k \in \mathcal{I}_{p_i}, \text{ and } n_{ij} = [\frac{a_{ij}}{x_i}] + 1.$$

This model can be actually reformulated into a linear programming problem by applying the M-approach, which eliminate the effects of max-function and categories of m_{ijk} and w_{ijk}. We are not presenting the details about that technique here.

Without loss of generality, we tested the relationship of the mean waiting-time, the number of context switches and the length of execution time-slice in the example of *103-154-9* according to the theoretical model. Moreover, in order to prove our analysis, we estimated the 3-task and the 5-task cases mentioned in Table 1. The simulation result is demonstrated in and Fig. 4, which proves that the mean waiting-time and the length of execution time-slice have an approximately linear relationship. Therefore, regardless of the other constraints in designing OSs, the smaller the execution time-slice is, the higher the efficiency of OSs' task responsiveness is. Moreover, the number of context switch is inversely proportional to the length of execution time-slice. The larger the number of context switch is, the higher overhead of resources. Thus, we should make a compromise between the average waiting-time and the number of context switches.

Adaptive Method. By analyzing Fig. 3, we can find a deadly limitation that if there are too many tasks with the same priorities or tasks have a long execution time like task NEI_info_request, tasks with lower priorities have to wait a considerably long time such as task ASSOCIATE_request. Therefore, we adopt an

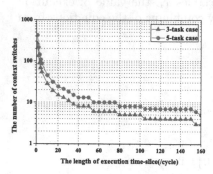

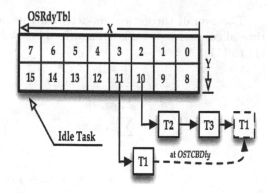

Fig. 4. The relationship between the length of execution time-slice and the number of context switches.

Fig. 5. The adaptive method in BEE OS.

adaptive method to promise tasks with lower priorities to execute timely. The basic conception is to assign a fixed waiting time-slice to tasks, which is stored in the variable OSTCBDly. If the time a task waits to execute overweigh the value of OSTCBDly, the priority of the task will increase one level and the task will be queued at the end of updated priority queue. OSTCBDly is defined in the TCB which has been showed in Fig. 3. In Fig. 5, task 2 and task 3 have the same priority No.10, and the priority of task 1 is No.11 that is lower than No.10. Therefore, task 1 will not execute until task 2 and task 3 complete. The worst case is task 2 and task 3 execute alternatively all the time, which results in task starvation. Task 1 fails to gain the processor resources for an unbearable long period of time. After adopting this kind of method, the priority of task 1 can rise one level, which equals to the priority of task 2 and task 3, and task 1 will be queued behind task 2 and task 3 when OSTCBDly subtract to zero. Such an adaptive method can ensure the timeliness of time-critical tasks in the different multi-priority queues, while rotary-time scheduling method is for the tasks in the same priority queue.

3.2   Algorithm Analysis

Algorithm 1 shows the processing of multi-task management in BEE OS. The kernel will continuously check the ReadyTable which stores the ready tasks. If there are tasks in the ready state, the kernel can find the task with the highest priority and schedule it, or it is supposed to run the idle task. OSPSCurLen records the rest execution time-slice of a task. Hence, when the OSPSCurLen is zero, the task will be put at the end of its priority queue. And once the OSTCBDly that stores the maximum unaccepted waiting time-slice is decreased to zero, the corresponding task priority will increase one level. Interruptions could signal a sensor activity or the arrival of a network packet, and the corresponding task will then process the sensor reading or handle the incoming data

---

Algorithm 1. The Pseudo Code of Multi-Task Management in BEE OS

Require:
  Set $ReadyTable = \phi$;
Ensure:
1: **while** $ReadyTable \neq \phi$ **do**
2:     **for all** $Tasks \in ReadyTable$ **do**
3:         Find the task with the highest priority and execute;
4:         **if** $OSPSCurLen = 0$ **then**
5:             Put the task at the end of its own queue;
6:         **else**
7:             Run the task to completion;
8:         **end if**
9:         **while** $OSTCBDly_i = 0$ **do**
10:            /*increase the currently task priority one level*/
11:            $OSTCBPrio_i \leftarrow OSTCBPrio_i - 1$;
12:        **end while**
13:        **while** Any interrupts is happened **do**
14:            **if** TIMER interrupt **then**
15:                $OSPSCurLen \leftarrow OSPSCurLen - 1$;
16:                $OSTCBDly_i \leftarrow OSTCBDly_i - 1$;
17:            **else**
18:                **if** The kernel is sleeping **then**
19:                    Wake up the kernel;
20:                    $ReadyTable \leftarrow ReadyTable \cup Task$;
21:                **else**
22:                    $ReadyTable \leftarrow ReadyTable \cup Task$;
23:                **end if**
24:            **end if**
25:        **end while**
26:    **end for**
27: **end while**
28: Run the idle task;

---

packet. Any interruptions are able to wake up the kernel from the sleep state, and add the related task into the ReadyTable. If it is a TIMER interruption, two variables, OSPSCurLen and OSTCBDly will subtract one automatically.

4   Evaluation

The performance of the BEE OS is indicated in terms of three respects that are timeliness, data memory (RAM) and program memory (Flash). These performance indicators are evaluated among TinyOS, μC/OS-II and BEE OS. In order to compare these operating systems better and more clearly, we adopt the application multi-task which is composed of several processes which are sensing or blinking every certain period of time (Fig. 6). The simulation tool is Avrora [5].

Figure 7 illustrates that compared with the RAM of TinyOS, the BEE OS increases by 19.2 % and decreases by 51.9 % in comparison with μC/OS-II. By

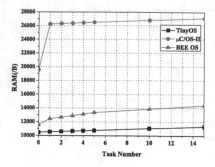
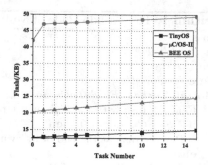

Fig. 6. The relationship between data memory (RAM) and task number.

Fig. 7. The relationship between program memory (Flash) and task number.

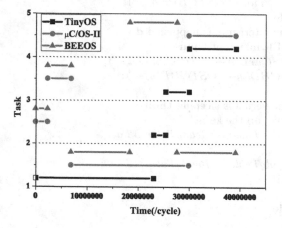

Fig. 8. The scheduling map of four tasks with Three priorities in BEE OS.

analyzing the program memory in Fig. 7, BEE OS is 60.3 % larger than that of TinyOS, while the Flash of BEE OS is about two-fold down in contrast with μC/OS-II. The memory stamp has a linear relationship with the number of tasks in three operating systems.

Despite the memory footprint of BEE OS being larger than TinyOS, it is more timely on the multi-task management. Figure 8 presents the simulation testing the scheduling strategies of three operating systems, which are TinyOS, μC/OS-II and BEE OS based on the processor ATmega128 and CC2420 radio transceiver. The evaluation includes 4 tasks, and rows from bottom to top in Fig. 8 represent task 1, task 2, task 3 and task 4 respectively. Task 2 is assigned the highest level of priority for trigger messages, task 3 has a priority level lower than task 2 for time-sync control packets, and others have the lowest priority level for sensor data packets. Moreover, task 1 is executed firstly, and then task 2, task 3 and task 4. Considering the FIFO rule in TinyOS, tasks will be executed according to whose packet or event arrives first. Despite the sensor data packets of task 1 arrive first, tasks accessing the medium in μC/OS-II and BEE OS are depended on the priority level of each task. Therefore, task 2 will execute first, then task 3 and finally task 1 and task 4. However, the big difference between μC/OS-II and BEE OS is the round-robin method used in the BEE OS. Task 1 executes for about 11,521,468 CPU cycles which is its assigned execution time-slice, and it is interrupted by task 4. This case is advantageous to some tasks in the same priority queue in which the currently running task has an unaccepted execution time. For an illustration, task 4 in μC/OS-II has to wait about 29,955,429 CPU cycles to execute, while in BEE OS, the waiting-time is only 18,433,962 CPU cycles, which is about 60 % of μC/OS-II.

5 Conclusions

As shown in the paper, it is possible to transplant the embedded operating system BEE OS into industrial wireless sensor networks to support batch execution without introducing much more overheads used in multi-threaded systems. If the assigned priority level of each task is depending on the arrival sequence of corresponding packet or event while doing the interruption management and the priority level of each task is completely different, the scheduling strategies of BEE OS is the same as TinyOS. BEE OS is compatible with μC/OS-II when every task has a unique priority. The established event-driven processing concepts can be in parallel with the multi-thread management, which adopts round-robin and multi-level priority queues based scheduling strategies. Moreover, adaptive method is added to this operating system in order to improve the responsiveness of tasks. This system is more capable of fitting both sensor network design goals of energy and timeliness than TinyOS and μC/OS-II, and provides more choices for researchers on WSN and its operating systems.

There is also much future work to consider: (1) The scope of applications. This paper describes that the performance of BEE OS that is applied in the Multi-task applications. After that, BEE OS will be applied to large-scale applications in the future. (2) Energy efficient. The trade-off between energy efficiency and timeliness in all the applications will be the focus of our research. (3) Comprehensive comparison. It is necessary to compare BEE OS with TinyOS 2.x and other operating systems to analyze the performance and overhead further.

Acknowledgements. The paper is sponsored by the National Natural Science Foundation of China (No. 61173150, 61273071), National High Technology Research and Development Program of China (863 Program) (No. 2011AA0401, 2014AA041801).

References

1. Anastasi, G., Conti, M., Francesco, M.D., Passarella, A.: Energy conservation in wireless sensor networks: a survey. Ad Hoc Netw. **7**(3), 537–568 (2009)
2. Farooq, M.O., Kunz, T.: Operating systems for wireless sensor networks: a survey. Sensors **11**(6), 5900–5930 (2011)

3. Levis, P., et al.: TinyOS: an operating system for sensor networks ambient intelligence. In: Weber, W., Rabaey, J.M., Aarts, E. (eds.) Ambient Intelligence, Chapter 7, pp. 115–148. Springer, Heidelberg (2005)
4. Han, C.C., Kumar, R., Shea, R., Kohler, E., Srivastava, M.; A dynamic operating system for sensor nodes. In: Proceedings of the 3rd International Conference on Mobile Systems, Applications, and Services, MobiSys 2005, pp. 163–176. ACM, New York (2005)
5. Avrora. http://docs.tinyos.net/tinywiki/index.php/Avrora

Step Cycle Detection of Human Gait Based on Inertial Sensor Signal

Yundong Xuan[✉], Yingfei Sun, Zhibei Huang, Zhan Zhao,
Zhen Fang, Lianying Ji, and Moli Zhang

University of Chinese Academy of Science,
No.19A Yuquan Road, Beijing, China
{xuanyundong,yfsun,zhphuang,jilianying}@ucas.ac.cn

Abstract. As a biologic character Human gait is very important for
identity recognized, health evaluation, medical monitoring. Gait cycle is
one of the most basic parameters in gait analysis. We can easily calculate
the gait uniformity, gait symmetry, gait continuity and other parameters
based on this parameter. Especially for many of diseases estimation,
such as Parkinsons disease, to get the phase synchronization, the precise
time of every step event must be determined. We can simply get gait
counts from traditional pedometer, but we can not get the precise step
interval. In this paper, based on Pan-Tompkins algorithm used in ECG
(electrocardiogram) signal, we develop one method using peak detection
based on feet acceleration and angular velocity. Experimental results
show the method has high precision and less error.

Keywords: Gait detection · Inertia sensor · Gait cycle

1 Introduction

Walking is one of humanity's most basic daily activities, and lots of research
on walking is also research on gait. Gait as a biometric, has important applications in the identity recognized, health evaluation, medical monitoring and
other fields. Currently, there are two categories on the method of gait research.
One is the traditional method based on image processing [1–3], with complexity
algorithm, higher equipment requirements for hardware and software resources,
high costs and larger size of the device. The other method is based on inertial sensors. This method uses miniaturized, high-precision MEMS sensors, with
low-power, low-cost, small size, and portable. More importantly this method is
almost unaffected by the surrounding environment, on the whole better than the
image-based methods, and therefore have a good prospect.

Gait cycle is an important parameter in gait analysis. Based on gait cycle,
gait uniformity, gait symmetry, gait continuity and other parameters can be
easily calculated. Especially when some diseases (Parkinson's disease, Hunting-
ton's disease [4], etc.) to assess, the exact time period between each step can
be used as a standard to judge the severity of a particular disease. It is difficult

© Springer-Verlag Berlin Heidelberg 2015
L. Sun et al. (Eds.): CWSN 2014, CCIS 501, pp. 97–104, 2015.
DOI: 10.1007/978-3-662-46981-1_9

for the traditional commercial pedometer to do this, it can only be given simple steps, and thus give the average gait cycle. D. Gafurov et al. gives several simple methods to calculate gait cycles, but these methods do not give the results automatically in real time [5]. Based inertial sensors to determine the gait cycle, mostly only use acceleration signal in the time domain and frequency domain analysis. D.M. Karantonis et al. find out the feature extraction of the acceleration signal in the time domain, give a multi-class classification algorithm based on binary tree, to achieve recognition of people's various sports state [6–8]. Based on gait acceleration Moe-Nilssen R. et al. use non-partial autocorrelation features extracted method to get gait cycle parameters, by analyzing these parameters to assess the symmetry of gait [9–11].

N. Ravi et al. according to the three-dimensional acceleration sensor, extract the mean value, standard deviation value, energy value and other characteristics to achieve recognition of the motion state [12]. Lingxiao et al. introduce the theory of compressed sensing, sparse representation into human activities analysis and give one method of action recognition based on compressed sensing [13].

When ECG signal analysis, in order to determine the various parameters of the ECG, you must first find out the exact location of QRS wave group. One more classic algorithm is Pan-Tompkins algorithm that can identify the peak point R of QRS wave group in real time, and as the reference point when analysis of the ECG signal. The inertial signal (acceleration, angular velocity, etc.) of feet is similar to the ECG signal with 15 Hz bandwidth. And as the ECG signal, there are also similar QRS wave group. So it is possible to find the extreme point of the inertial signal using Pan-Tompkins algorithm accurately at each step, and further calculate the gait cycle. In this paper, we use Pan-Tompkins algorithm to respectively process the acceleration and angular velocity signal of the feet, after the normalized operation, fuse the results, and calculate the maximum value point sequence. Gait cycle can be derived based on the maximum value point sequence.

2 Mathematical Model

Real-time ECG signal R-wave detection algorithm is proposed by Pan and Tompkins [14, 15]. The Pan-Tompkins algorithm includes a series of filters, including band-pass filters, differentiator, square operation, sliding window average, and adaptive threshold detection. The process is shown in Fig. 1:

2.1 Band-Pass Filter

In the Pan-Tompkins algorithm, band-pass filter is composed of a low-pass filter and a high pass filter. Low-pass filter is used to eliminate high-frequency

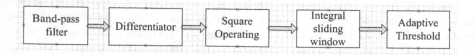

Fig. 1. Mathematical model of Pan-Tompkins algorithm

interference (e.g. around $50\,HZ$ frequency interference). High-pass filter is used to eliminate baseline drift of the ECG signal. Usually, the transfer function for such a low pass filter is

$$H_{LP}(z) = \frac{1 - z^{-6}}{1 - z^{-1}} = 1 + z^{-1} + z^{-2} + \cdots + z^{-5} \tag{1}$$

The cutoff frequency of approximately $15\,Hz$. It's current magnification is $(\omega = 0, z = 1)$

$$H_{LP}(z = 1) = 1 + z^{-1} + z^{-2} + \cdots + z^{-5}\big|_{z=1} = 6 \tag{2}$$

Usually the low pass filter is cascade of the above formula. So the transfer function of the low-pass filter is

$$H_{LP}(z) = \frac{1}{32}\left(\frac{1 - z^{-6}}{1 - z^{-1}}\right)^2 = \frac{1}{32}\frac{1 - 2z^{-6} + z^{-12}}{1 - 2z^{-1} + z^{-2}} \tag{3}$$

The difference function is

$$y[n] = 2y[n-1] - y[n-2] + \frac{1}{32}\left(x[n] - 2x[n-6] + x[n-12]\right) \tag{4}$$

where x[n] is input, y[n] is output. The transfer function of the High-pass filter is

$$H_{HP}(z) = z^{-16} - \frac{1}{32}H_{LP}(z) \tag{5}$$

The difference function of the High-pass filter is

$$z(n) = x[n-16] - \frac{1}{32}\left(y[n-1] + x[n] - x[n-32]\right) \tag{6}$$

2.2 Differentiator

In the Pan-Tompkins algorithm, the differentiator is used to enhance the high frequency ECG R-wave, and suppress the low frequency P-wave and T-wave. In the gait signal the differentiator is used to enhance the differential signal peak, and the suppress the low-frequency interference signal. We use a five points differentiator. The Z transformation function is

$$H_{dif}(z) = \frac{1}{10}\left(2 + z^{-1} - z^{-3} - 2z^{-4}\right) \tag{7}$$

where the magnification is 0.1, can be approximately $1/8$. So the differential function is

$$y(n) = \frac{1}{8}\left(2x[n] + x[n-1] - x[n-3] - 2x[n-4]\right) \tag{8}$$

where x[n] is input, y[n] is output.

2.3   Square Operating

The peak can be more obvious after squared. The difference function is

$$y[n] = (x[n])^2 \tag{9}$$

where x[n] is input, y[n] is output.

2.4   Integral Sliding Window

In order to get a smooth waveform area, requires the sliding window calculus average. The difference function is

$$y(n) = \frac{1}{N}\left(x[n] + x[n-1] + \cdots + x[n-(N-1)]\right) \tag{10}$$

where x[n] is input, y[n] is output. N is the window width, When the ECG signal the value is determined by Equation

$$N \cong f_s * 0.15\,(sec) \tag{11}$$

where f_s is the sampling frequency, 0.15 s is the average width of the ECG QRS wave.

2.5   Adaptive Threshold

After the above operation, to find a suitable threshold to determine the extreme points, and generally the threshold is 0.5 times the maximum points after sliding window.

3   Algorithm Improvement and Implementation

Since the maximum value of the acceleration and angular velocity is much greater than the gait stationary value when the person is walking. And the problems of baseline drift can be ignored, so removing the high-pass filter when gait analysis, using the low-pass filter instead of band-pass filters of the Pan-Tompkins algorithm.

Due to acceleration and gyroscope mounted on the soles, based on the mounting position of the acceleration and gyroscope, the x-axis direction of the acceleration is the forward direction of foot, and the y-axis direction of the gyroscope is the direction of rotation around the knee of the foot. The waveform width of the acceleration and angular velocity is about 0.5 s. So the sampling frequency is 20 Hz and the sliding window width N = 10.

On the basis of the original algorithm, we use the Pan-Tompkins algorithm processing the acceleration signal and gyroscope signal respectively, and then use the accelerometer, gyroscope signal processed to assess the gait cycle. Since the acceleration value and angular velocity values vary widely, in order to get valuable data, it needs to be normalized. And data fusion using the following function 12:

$$Y(n) = \sum_{n=1}^{M} \frac{A_n}{A_1 + A_2 + \cdots + A_M} X(n) \qquad (12)$$

When data fusion according to the formula 12, use M = 2, since the acceleration is the Quadratic differential of displacement. And the angular velocity is the differential of angular displacement of. So acceleration signal is more intense than the angular velocity signal. And corresponding to the acceleration signal A1 = 0.4, corresponding to the angular velocity A2 = 0.6. In the adaptive computing the threshold is 0.5 times of the maximum points. Algorithm flow diagram is as follows (Fig. 2).

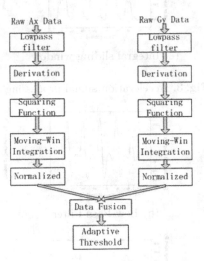

Fig. 2. Algorithm flow diagram

4   Results and Analysis

After the above operations, the results of each step as follows, where Fig. 3 shows the acceleration sensitive axis x-axis processing, and Fig. 4 is the y-axis gyro sensitive axis of the processing.(the mounting position of the sensor determines the X-axis acceleration and gyroscope Y axis is the sensitive axis).

After the adaptive threshold calculation time series of the extreme points can be got A_n, we define a periodic sequence T_n, According to Eq. 13 gait cycle of each step can be accurately determined.

$$T_n = (A_{n+1} - A_n) * T_s = (A_{n+1} - A_n)/f_s \qquad (13)$$

where T_s is the sampling period of gait signal, and the sampling frequency is f_s. Referring to the University of California at Berkeley's Yang offered wearable motion sensor identification database (Wearable Action Recognition Database,

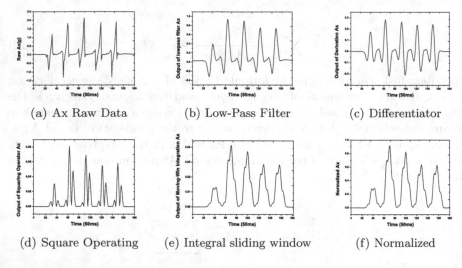

(a) Ax Raw Data   (b) Low-Pass Filter   (c) Differentiator

(d) Square Operating   (e) Integral sliding window   (f) Normalized

Fig. 3. Acceleration signal processing

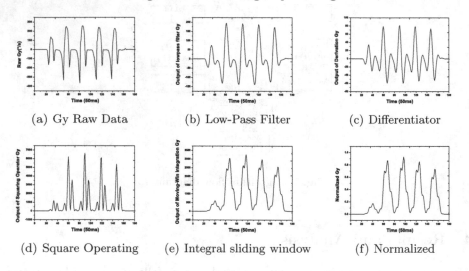

(a) Gy Raw Data   (b) Low-Pass Filter   (c) Differentiator

(d) Square Operating   (e) Integral sliding window   (f) Normalized

Fig. 4. Angular velocity signal processing

WARD) [16], T_s is taken as 50 ms. By Eq. 13, the sampling period determines the rate of each of the gait cycle. So in order to get higher resolution, we need to improve the sampling frequency of the gait signal, and reduce the sampling time of the gait signal. To test the anti-jamming capability of the algorithm, we simulate the case of patients suffering from Parkinson's disease. The results show that the algorithm can identify a number of steps, and find out the pole position. Based on the pole position the accuracy of gait cycle can reach 0.05 s (Fig. 5).

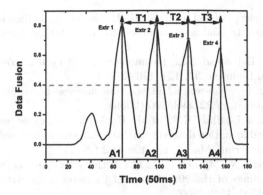

Fig. 5. Result of data fusion

5   Conclusion

Based on ECG signal Pan-Tompkins algorithm, we use data fusion algorithm to process and analyse gait signal. Focuses on the use of Pan-Tompkins algorithm to process the acceleration signal and angular velocity signal of the foot. Then we fuse the two normalized data and determine the extreme points by peak detection, and accurate calculation of the gait cycle based on the extreme points. Experimental results show that the gait recognition algorithm based on Pan-Tompkins has good results. Calculated by the extreme points of the gait cycle information can be done millisecond accuracy. Verification of this method is achieved by simulation of abnormal gait. To further verify the validity of the method, the next step will be directly through the specific gait populations.

References

1. Shi, C., Tian-jun, M., Wan-hong, H.: A multi-layer windows method of moments for gait recognition. J. Electron. Inf. Technol. **31**, 116–119 (2009)
2. Yi, L., Dong, M., Li, F., et al.: Gait recognition method based on hybrid feature in infrared image. Comput. Eng. **37**, 1–3 (2011)
3. Qi, Y., Ding-yu, X.: Gait recognition based on two-scale dynamic bayesian network and more information fusion. J. Electron. Inf. Technol. **34**, 1148–1153 (2012)
4. Dalton, A., Khalil, H., Busse, M., et al.: Analysis of gait and balance through a single triaxial accelerometer in presymptomatic and symptomatic huntingtons disease. Gait Posture **37**, 49–54 (2013)
5. Gafurov, D.: Performance and security analysis of gait-based user authentication[D]. Ph.D. dissertation, University of Oslo (2008)
6. Yue-xiang, L., Yan, L., Tao, Y., et al.: Multiple classifier based walking pattern recognizing algorithm using acceleration signal. Acta Electronica Sinica **37**, 1794–1798 (2009)
7. Karantonis, D.M., Narayanan, M.R., Mathie, M., et al.: Implementation of a real-time human movement classifier using a triaxial accelerometer for ambulatory monitoring. IEEE Trans. Inf Technol. Biomed. **10**, 156–167 (2006)

8. Mathie, M.J., Celer, B.G., Lovell Nigel, H., et al.: Classification of basic daily movements using a triaxial accelerometer. Med. Biol. Eng. Comput. **42**, 679–687 (2004)
9. Moe Nilssen, R., Helbostad, J.L.: Estimation of gait cycle characteristics of trunk accelerometry. J. Biomech. **37**, 121–126 (2004)
10. Rong, L., Huang, L., Shao-wei, L., et al.: Gait analysis based on gait acceleration. Chin. J. Sens. Actuators **22**, 893–896 (2009)
11. Yang, C.C., Hsu, Y.L., Shih, K.S., et al.: Real-time gait cycle parameters recognition using a wearable motion detector. In: 2011 International Conference on System Science and Engineering, Macao, pp. 498–502 (2011)
12. Ravi, N., Dandekar, N., Mysore, P., et al.: Activity recognition from accelerometer data. In: Proceedings of the 20th Notional Conference on Artificial Intelligence. Pittsburgh, pp. 1541–1546 (2005)
13. Ling, X., Ren-fa, L., Juan, L.: Recognition of human activity based on compressed sensing in bady sensor networks. J. Electron. Inf. Technol. **35**, 119–125 (2013)
14. Pan, J., Tompkins, W.: A real-time QRS detection algorithm. IEEE Trans. Biomed. Eng. **32**, 230–236 (1985)
15. Hamilton, P.S., Tompkins, W.J.: Quantitative investigation of QRS detection rules using the MIT/BIH arrhythmia database. IEEE Trans. Biomed. Eng. **33**, 1157–1165 (1986)
16. Yang, Y., Jafari, R., Shankar, S., et al.: Distributed recognition of human actions using wearable motion sensor networks. J. Ambient Intell. Smart Environ. **1**, 1–5 (2009)

Research on Anti-interference Algorithm for Indoor RSSI Measuring

Jun Guo[1(✉)], Weiwei Zhang[2], Cangsong Zhang[1], Xunli Fan[1], and Lei Wang[1]

[1] Department of Computer Science, Northwest University, Xi'an, China
guojun@nwu.edu.cn, 597988635@qq.com
[2] Department of Computer Science, Xi'an Siyuan University, Xi'an, China
weiweidongting@sohu.com

Abstract. High accuracy RSSI data gathering is still a great challenge in indoor environment because the measuring procedure is prone to being interfered by barriers or random walking people. This paper thus focused on anti-interference algorithm to improve the RSSI data accuracy. The interference factors concerned with RSSI value measuring process are analyzed firstly. And then the characteristics of different interference sources are discussed in detail. Two kinds of algorithm are proposed to cope with two kinds of interference sources. One is clustering algorithm, which is used to eliminate the burst interference. The other is filter algorithm, which is used to minimize the random noise. Algorithms are tested on Zigbee platform. Experimental results indicate that the proposed approaches could obviously improve the RSSI accuracy.

Keywords: RSSI · Anti-interference · Clustering algorithm · Filter algorithm

1 Introduction

RSSI (Received Signal Strength Indication) is an important parameter in wireless sensor networks, which plays a crucial role in node range measuring, node position and performance estimation [1]. As an instance of node range measuring, there are four kinds of approaches now: TOA (Time of Arrival), TDOA (Time Difference of Arrival), AOA (Angle of Arrival), and RSSI [2–6]. But indoor environment is often interfered by barriers or random walking people, which cause the radio signal reflection and diffraction. The radio signal propagates in multipath. So TOA, TDOA and AOA cannot work well in indoor environment. Usually, RSSI is the first candidate for indoor node range measuring [7].

In fact, RSSI value indicates the quality of the communication link in wireless networks. The radio communication is very complex in indoor wireless networks. Nonlinear time varying interference will seriously affect the quality of communication channel, which is introduced by multipath radio propagation and moving objects reflection. The worse radio communication performance gives rise to big error about RSSI [8].

This work is supported by Ministry of Science and Technology, P.R. China. (2013BAK01B05), Educational Commission of Shaanxi Province, China (No. 11JK1062).

© Springer-Verlag Berlin Heidelberg 2015
L. Sun et al. (Eds.): CWSN 2014, CCIS 501, pp. 105–113, 2015.
DOI: 10.1007/978-3-662-46981-1_10

Reference [9] has analyzed the factor related with the RSSI accuracy through experiments. The technique for eliminating interference is proposed in [9]. Reference [10] improves the parameter in RSSI measuring model and proposed a parameter self adaption model to improve the accuracy of RSSI.

Different from above methods, we focus on anti-interference algorithm according to data process technology. Firstly, we study the two factors which mainly affect the RSSI measuring accuracy. One is burst interference, another is random noise. And then a cluster algorithm is adopted to cope with burst interference, while a digital filter algorithm is adopted to cope with random noise. Finally, the algorithms are tested on Zigbee platform and we conclude the paper.

2   Algorithm for Burst Interference

2.1   The Feature of Burst Interference

In indoor environments, some unexpected events of the wireless network coverage area, such as personnel random walk, sudden changes of environmental facilities, wireless signal transient interference, will greatly impact the measurement of RSSI values [11]. These disturbances will eventually cause a large measurement error in the measured data. Excluding interference data through data processing technology, is an effective means to improve the measurement accuracy. To do this, you need to analyze characteristics of interference data in order to design a highly effective anti-interference algorithm.

There are many kinds of burst interference, the random walk people is the most common one and higher-frequency interference event. In order to determine characteristic of this kind of burst interference, we designed two groups of comparative experiments: in first group of experiments, the RSSI value of target node and the reference node is measured without burst interference. In second group of experiments, some burst interference sources were added to the experiments. All experiments were performed in an indoor environment. In each group of experiments, we test the range of target node at 1 m, 2 m, 3 m, 4 m, and 5 m from the reference node. We use walking staff to simulate the burst interference in the experiments and measure the RSSI value between the target node and a reference node. Statistical results of several experiments are shown in Fig. 1.

As can be seen from the experimental data in Fig. 1, burst interference seriously impact the RSSI value. Without the burst interference, RSSI value is relatively stable. Experimental data are more focused and RSSI measured value is close to the theoretical RSSI value at each communication distance. In case there is a sudden disturbance, RSSI measurement values are scattered. Some of the data which is impacted by unexpected disturbances are significantly deviate from normal values. From the statistics view, the RSSI data affected by the burst interference are outliers, which are far away from the normal range. Compared to the normal observation data, outlier data hold larger error value, while the proportion is small. During the statistical calculations, the outlier data will inevitably reduce the RSSI value statistical measurement accuracy. Therefore, in order to ensure the measurement result is not affected by outliers and improve RSSI measurement accuracy, outliers must be removed prior to the statistical measurement.

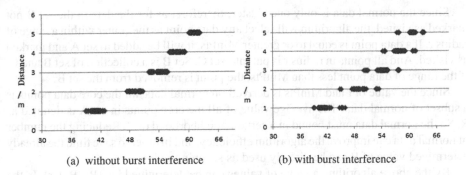

(a) without burst interference   (b) with burst interference

Fig. 1. RSSI measurement data comparison

2.2 Burst Interference Remedy

The key of clearing the outlier is how to detect them. The existing outlier detection methods mostly based on statistical detection algorithm, distance detection algorithm, the density detection algorithm, the depth detection algorithm and offset detection algorithm and so on. Since the theoretical basis for these algorithms is different, the degree of difficulty and complexity of these algorithms are different. Currently, the common method to remove outliers is clustering algorithm [11, 12]. Clustering algorithm is a classic algorithm in data mining and applied to the data processing field in recent years. Compared with the previous outlier removal algorithm, clustering algorithm is more simple and efficient. But the clustering algorithm is originally designed for characterized classification, not for excluding outliers. Therefore, the algorithm should be modified in our application.

The basic idea of clustering algorithm is the same, but there are many improvements in different applications. In the RSSI data processing, clustering algorithm can find out core data, determine the range of normal data and achieve the purpose of removing abnormal data. Therefore, the key of the problem is to find the core data in the normal data set, but for the abnormal data set clustering is not necessary. By analyzing the collected RSSI data, it can be found that abnormal data occupied ratio is about 15 %– 20 %. That is to say, in a period of time the ratio of normal RSSI data is least 80 %, and normal data is only one cluster. Therefore, DBSCAN (Density-Based Spatial Clustering of Application with Noise, DBSCAN) is a more suitable one, which is also a representative clustering algorithm [13].

DBSCAN algorithm needs to get two key parameters: scanning radius r and minimum contain points MinPts. Combined with the available experimental data, this paper modified some of the algorithm parameters. MinPts value is set as less than half the normal data, i.e., 0.4n. Through analyzing experimental data of sudden disturbance on the RSSI value, it can be drawn that the average different value between maximum and minimum data is 1.736 at all observation points. So MinPts is set to 0.45.

After determining the value of r and MinPts, q is selected as an arbitrary point of the center of radius r, if any data is equal to or greater than MinPts, the data is recorded as the core point, meanwhile creating the cluster of core q, the q recorded as visited and put into the set A. All data points in the cluster put into set B, denoted by {q1, q2, q3, ...}. The data point of less than MinPts is discarded.

Since the normal data is only one cluster, therefore, as for the data in the set B not marked as visited, the algorithm will select any data point as the center within a range of radius r. If a data point is equal to or greater MinPts, it will be added to set A and marked as visited. And all points in radius r is put into set C. Set B is a collection of set B and C. If the range of data point less than MinPts, the point is removed from the set B.

Since the value of r and MinPts is derived on normal data, all the core data points is a subset of normal data. The average value of all the core points in set A is denoted as R. So the normal data must bound in a certain neighborhood of R. Reducing the number of normal data can improve the algorithm efficiency, and in order to save time the already determined value of R can be directly used as scanning radius r.

By the above algorithm, a range of values can be determined i.e. (Rr, R + r). In the environment with sudden disturbance, when the target node receives the RSSI value from the reference nodes, algorithm will determine whether the data is in (Rr, R + r). If the received data is within this range, it is considered that the data is normal data, not subject to sudden disturbances, and vice versa, it is considered that the data affected by unexpected interference.

Using the above algorithm, we cluster the data in Fig. 1(b) and get the results shown in Fig. 2. As can be seen from the data in Fig. 2, after clustering algorithm processing the data is close to the data in Fig. 1(a) in the case of non-burst interference. Through DBSCAN algorithm processing, there were not outliers of RSSI data at 1 m–5 m with sudden disturbances. Compared with non-interference RSSI value, the RSSI measurements average error is eliminates to 0.87. Therefore, the improved DBSCAN algorithm can effectively clusters normal data, eliminate the impact of unexpected personnel walking disturbances, reducing the measurement error.

3   Filtering Algorithm to Eliminate Random Noise

3.1   Random Interference on RSSI Measurements

Since the wireless signal is impacted by multipath, random noise, signal reflection, diffraction in the propagation process, as well as the self-noise measurement system and A/D quantization noise [12]. The target node received the RSSI values inevitably contain random error. Random errors in different environments have different mechanisms. In order to quantitatively analyze random error of RSSI data in indoor environment, we conducted a set of experiments. The distance from the target node and the reference node is 3 m in experiments. The change of RSSI value is measured within 60 s, and the measured RSSI values are compared with the theoretical value. The experimental data are shown in Fig. 3.

As can be seen from the experimental results, random noise exists in the RSSI measurement process, the measurement values fluctuate within a small range of the theoretical values, the error magnitude and direction is random. Speaking of the target node and the reference node at 3 m, the theoretical RSSI value is 54.36, while the maximum under the influence of random errors RSSI measurement data is 57.16, the minimum is 52.21, the average of this set of measurements was 54.52. So the average error value is 0.16. The variance of the set of measurements is 2.36.

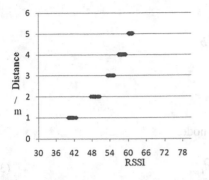
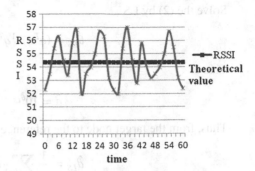

Fig. 2. RSSI eliminating burst interference   **Fig. 3.** RSSI with random interference

The actual distribution of measured values is more uniform, generally a normal distribution. The deviation from the theoretical value is smaller and, the actual average value of the measurement series is very close to the theoretical value.

3.2 Filtering Technology to Eliminate Random Noise

Effective way to eliminate random noise is filtered. Digital filtering algorithm is easy to achieve with low cost. Existing filtering algorithms have different adaptability. In this paper, least squares estimation filter and limiter arithmetic mean filtering algorithm are used to eliminate the effects of random interference for RSSI values measurement. The performance of the two filtering algorithms is compared.

Least Squares Estimation Filter. Least squares estimation filter (LSEF) can clear zero mean and normally distributed random noise [16]. Therefore, LSEF is more suitable for RSSI measurement data filtering.

Known that the target node may received a plurality of RSSI data from reference node in a period of time, the number of received RSSI data is assumed m. According to the RSSI measurement model, RSSI absolute value can be listed in the following equations:

$$\begin{cases} RSSI_1 = 10n \log d_1 + A \\ RSSI_2 = 10n \log d_2 + A \\ \quad\vdots \\ RSSI_m = 10n \log d_m + A \end{cases} \tag{1}$$

Define $q = 10n$, $\theta = [\log d_1, \log d_2, \cdots, \log d_m]^T$,
$b = [(RSSI_1 - A), (RSSI_2 - A), \cdots, (RSSI_m - A)]^T$

Then the Eq. (1) can be written as:

$$q\,\theta = b \tag{2}$$

Solve the (2) by LS

$$\hat{\theta}_{LS} = (q^T q)^{-1} q^T b$$

That is

$$\hat{d} = 10^{\hat{\theta}_{LS}}$$

Thus, from the target node to the reference node:

$$\hat{d}_{LS} = \frac{1}{m} \sum_{i=1}^{m} \hat{d}_i \qquad (3)$$

$$RSSI = A - 10n \log d \qquad (4)$$

Where $\hat{d}_i$ is the i-th element of the vector, $i = 1, 2, \ldots, m$. Will $\hat{d}_{LS}$ be substituted into the formula (4), the RSSI value can be realized on least squares estimation filtering.

To achieve the best filter results, least squares estimation filter will achieve this by increasing the amount of data. Because the method includes matrix operations, algorithm will cause a great waste of time and space when the amount of data increasing. Considering clustering algorithms have eliminated most large pulse interference caused by sudden disturbances, therefore, filtered data is relatively flat, the deviation is lesser. Select the part of the data in this context can be reached filtering purposes, thereby avoiding inefficiencies caused by excessive amount of data. Based on this idea, this paper makes some improvements of LSEF for the issues of the amount of data increasing. (A) Within a time t, n RSSI measurement data are counted and record by its serial number. (B) Select a parameters m, m is a positive integer, take the measured RSSI value modulo m, and if the result is zero, then the RSSI values are stored in a queue of size N. If the queue is full, stop the measurement. (C) Use least square estimate filtering algorithm on the queue of N samples stored data.

Limiting and Arithmetic Mean Filtering Method. Another commonly used filtering algorithm is limiting [16, 17], the method for limiting filtering combined with the arithmetic mean filter and arithmetic average filtering method. Limiting filtering method can effectively overcome the glitches caused by accidental factors. Many physical quantity changes at a certain range, to determine the maximum allowable deviation of two samples (set A) is based on experience. Each time a new value is detected and judged by the difference between the value and the last value. If this difference value is greater than the previous value of A, then this value is invalid and should abandoned. Although limiting filtering method can effectively overcome glitches due to accidental factors, but it cannot suppress periodic disturbances. Therefore it needs to combine with arithmetic mean filtering. Arithmetic mean filtering method is continuous take N samples arithmetic mean value, the mathematical expression is $\bar{y} = \sum_{i=1}^{N} y_i / N$, where, $\bar{y}$ is the arithmetic mean value of N samples. y_i is the i-th sample value.

Arithmetic mean filtering method is suitable for signal generally has a random interference. These signals usually have a mean value, signal fluctuations up and down near a certain value. The smoothing of signal depends entirely on the number N for arithmetic average filtering method. When N is large, the smooth degree is high, when N is small, low degree of smoothness. All in all, this method makes up for the inadequacies of the single limiting filtering method.

Denoted measured RSSI value within time t by a vector, and then calculate the arithmetic average value. Namely, $\overline{rssi} = \sum_{k=1}^{n} rssi_k / n$.

Experimental Data Analysis. To analyze the effectiveness of the proposed algorithm in the indoor environment, we use Zigbee platform for the experiment. The RSSI values with random interference are measured in the range of 1 m–5 m. Each measurement records all RSSI data within 60 s, denoted by vector $rssi_a$. The above two filtering algorithms are used to processing the measured RSSI values respectively. Combining the theoretical calculation of the error distribution of RSSI values, unfiltered RSSI measurement values were compared with the results shown in Table 1.

Table 1. Measurement error (before and after filtering)

	Unfiltered	LSEF	LAMF
1 m	1.25	0.21	0.13
1.5 m	1.73	0.2	0.12
2 m	1.12	0.19	0.12
2.5 m	0.83	0.2	0.11
3 m	1.52	0.19	0.12
3.5 m	1.61	0.18	0.13
4 m	1.92	0.19	0.15
4.5 m	2.31	0.2	0.16
5 m	1.82	0.21	0.15

As can be seen from the experimental data, the RSSI value through filtering algorithm eliminates random noise significantly and the error to theoretical RSSI value reduced a lot. The theoretical RSSI value at 3 m is 54.36, maximum error of measured RSSI values at nine observation points without wave filter is 2.31, the minimum error is 0.83, and the average error is 1.57. After least squares filtering algorithm, the maximum error of RSSI measurement value is 0.21, the minimum error is 0.18, and the average error is 0.197. After limiting arithmetic average filtering algorithm processing, the maximum error RSSI is 0.16, the minimum error is 0.11, and the average error is 0.132. Seen, these two filtering algorithms greatly improves the accuracy of the measurement data, reduces data fluctuation caused by random interference. The experimental results indicate that filtering algorithm significantly eliminate random error of RSSI and improve the measurement accuracy. Limiter arithmetic average filtering algorithm is better than least squares filtering algorithm.

4   Conclusion

As for RSSI measurement values vulnerable to environmental interference, this paper proposes a method to improve measurement accuracy of RSSI value. The approach uses an improved density-based clustering algorithm to exclude outliers caused by burst interference, while applying filtering algorithm to eliminate the effects of random interference. Through experiments on Zigbee platform, the feasibility of the proposed anti-interference algorithm is verified. The experimental results show that the anti-interference algorithm employed in the measurement of RSSI in indoor environment significantly improves RSSI measurement accuracy. Compared with the conventional method, the proposed approach is suitable for accurate measurement of RSSI in indoor environment.

References

1. Li, J., Gao, H.: Progress in wireless sensor networks. Comput. Res. Dev. **45**(1), 1–15 (2008)
2. Yu, P., Dan, W.: Summary of wireless sensor network positioning technology. J. Electron. Measur. Instrum. **25**(5), 389–399 (2011)
3. Yanliang, J., Yong, X., Yong, Z.: RSSI-based indoor positioning analysis of WSN nodes. J. Shanghai Univ. **18**, 5 (2012)
4. Martin-Escalona, I., Barcelo-Arroyo, F.: Impact of geometry on the accuracy of the passive-TDOA algorithm. In: IEEE 19th International Symposium on Personal, Indoor and Mobile Radio Communications, 2008, PIMRC 2008, pp. 1–6. IEEE (2008)
5. Brida, P., Machaj, J., Benikovsky, J., et al.: A new complex angle of arrival location method for ad hoc networks. In: 2010 7th Workshop on Positioning Navigation and Communication (WPNC), pp. 284–290. IEEE (2010)
6. Girod, L., Bychkovskiy, V., Elson, J., et al.: Locating tiny sensors in time and space: a case study. In: 2002 IEEE International Conference on Computer Design: VLSI in Computers and Processors, 2002, Proceedings, pp. 214–219. IEEE (2002)
7. Fang, Z., Zhao, Z., Guo, P.: Range analyze based on RSSI. Sens. Technol. **11**, 2526–2530 (2008)
8. Bahl, P., Padmanabhan, V.N.: RADAR. an in-building RF-based user location and tracking system. In: INFOCOM 2000, Nineteenth Annual Joint Conference of the IEEE Computer and Communications Societies, Proceedings IEEE, vol. 2, 775–784 (2000)
9. Savvides, A., Park, H., Srivastava, M.B.: The bits and flops of the n-hop multilateration primitive for node localization problems. In: Proceedings of the 1st ACM International Workshop on Wireless Sensor Networks and Applications, pp. 112–121. ACM (2002)
10. Xu, J., Liu, W., Lang, F., Zhang, Y., Wang, C.: Distance measurement model based on RSSI in WSN. Wirel. Sens. Netw. **2**, 606–611 (2010)
11. Xue, A., Ju, S., He, W., Chen, W.: Local outlier mining algorithm. Comput. J. **30**(8) (2007)

12. Li, B., Qiu, T.: RF signal noise elimination and inhibition studies. Dalian University of Technology, Master's thesis (2009)
13. Han, J., Kamber, M., et al.: Data Mining Concepts and Techniques. Machinery Industry Press, Beijing (2007)
14. Ester, M., Kriegel, H.P., Sander, J., et al.: A density-based algorithm for discovering clusters in large spatial databases with noise. In: KDD 1996, pp. 226–231 (1996)
15. Niculescu, D.S.: Forwarding and positioning problems in ad hoc networks. The State University of New Jersey, Rutgers (2004)
16. Lai, X.: Recursive least squares FIR digital filter design algorithm. Sig. Process. 15(3), 260–264 (1999)
17. Zhu, H., Wang, F., Yao, Z.: Microcontroller-based digital filtering algorithm analysis and implementation. Qiqihar Univ. 24(6), 53–54 (2008)

Channel Estimation Algorithm Based on Compressed Sensing for Underwater Acoustic OFDM Communication System

Zhiqiang Zou[1,2,3](✉), Siyu Lu[1,2,3], Shu Shen[1,2,3],
Ruchuan Wang[1,2,3], and Xiangyu Lin[1,2,3]

[1] College of Computer, Nanjing University of Posts and Telecommunications,
Xin Mofan Road No. 66, Nanjing 210003, China
[2] Jiangsu High Technology Research Key Laboratory for Wireless Sensor Networks,
Xin Mofan Road No. 66, Nanjing 210003, China
[3] Department of Geography, University of Wisconsin-Madison,
Madison, WI 53706, USA
{zouzq,shens,wangrc}@njupt.edu.cn,
lusiyu90@163.com, 289466360@qq.com

Abstract. According to underwater acoustic orthogonal frequency division multiplexing communication system, an underwater acoustic channel estimation algorithm based on compressed sensing is proposed in this paper, by making use of the natural sparse features of the underwater acoustic. The samples of the channel frequency response are obtained by inserting the two-dimensional pilot symbols according to linear interpolation with the channel-sensing on the basis of existing underwater acoustic OFDM communication system. And then a complete dictionary is designed. Finally, the underwater acoustic channel estimation is completed by using the compressive sampling matching pursuit algorithm. The simulation results show that the estimation accuracy of our algorithm is better than the conventional underwater acoustic estimation algorithm with lower computational complexity and higher stability at the same time. Therefore, our algorithm can be applied to practical underwater acoustic OFDM communication system preferably.

Keywords: Underwater acoustic communication · Channel estimation · OFDM · Compressed sensing · Complete dictionary

1 Introduction

Underwater acoustic channel has many features such as the complexity of environment, multi-path effect, limited available bandwidth, Doppler shift, channel

Z. Zou—Please note that this project is supported by the National Natural Science Foundation of China (No. 61170065, 61373137, 61100199, and 61401221), Natural Science Foundation of Jiangsu Province (No. BK2012436 and BK20141429), Scientific and Technological Support Project (Society) of Jiangsu Province (No. BE2014718 and BE2013666), and NJUPT Natural Science Foundation (No. NY213157 and NY213037).

© Springer-Verlag Berlin Heidelberg 2015
L. Sun et al. (Eds.): CWSN 2014, CCIS 501, pp. 114–124, 2015.
DOI: 10.1007/978-3-662-46981-1_11

attenuation, and the background noise of the marine environment. Together with these factors' influence on the receivers, it leads to the low quality of Underwater Acoustic Communication (UWAC). These severely restrict the application of UWAC [1–3].

Orthogonal frequency-division multiplexing (OFDM) can resist frequency selective fading so that it is an effective, high-speed transmission technology. The multi-carrier communication technology based on OFDM has following advantages: (1) the ability of anti-multi-path; (2) high utilization of bandwidth; (3) high efficiency of communication; (4) easy to realize the channel equalization and so on, it is suited for the application in UWAC. However, this technology also has many challenges: (1) the effect of Doppler frequency shift; (2) the long delay of channel propagation which leads to the significant inefficiency to OFDM system transmission. In response to these shortcomings, accurate and efficient channel estimation is a good solution.

In [4], for the effects of the Doppler shift, it designed a scheme employing orthogonal signal basis of the chirp type corresponding to the fractional Fourier transform signal basis which improved the communication rate. The scheme in [5], chose a basis expansion model, but with the growing of time-varying, the accuracy of channel estimation decreases while the complexity of channel estimation increases. Reference [6] put forward an improved method joint with carrier frequency offset estimation, channel estimation and high precision symbol timing synchronous based on scattered pilot, while the performance of channel estimation will reduce under large synchronization error. In [7], the authors studied the least-squares (LS) in channel estimation, then evaluated a trend estimation technique based on the empirical modal decomposition (EMD) method applied to the LS estimate of the channel impulse response. This method has achieved good effects. But, these studies did not adequately take the sparse of underwater acoustic channel into account, and the sparse signals can be effectively used in compressive sensing(CS) theory [8]. Putting the CS theory into underwater acoustic channel estimation can improve the accuracy and efficiency of estimation results [1,9,10]. In [1], the authors proposed underwater acoustic channel estimation method based on sparse reconstruction by using homology algorithm, Gauss-Markov model and the recursive least squares method, which optimized the location of the pilot and improve the channel estimation performance. In addition, channel estimation method proposed in the paper [9] is a method of tracking signal based on CS-by-block with the better estimation accuracy error while the channel estimation efficiency is reduced due to the operation of the tracking approach block by block.

This paper proposes a novel underwater channel estimation algorithm, which makes use of the natural sparse characteristic of underwater channel. The method adopts the underwater acoustic OFDM communication system and is combined with the compressed sensing theory. The method uses the underwater acoustic OFDM communication system model, inserts the two-dimensional pilot through the linear interpolation method, constructs the corresponding complete dictionary with a channel perception channel frequency response sampling values, and fulfills the channel estimation for underwater acoustic OFDM communication system by using the compressed sampling matching pursuit algorithm.

2   Underwater Acoustic OFDM Communication System

In the underwater acoustic OFDM communication system, the transmitter splits
the original input signal into N sub-signals, modulates sub-signals into mutually
orthogonal sub-carriers, and then the transmitting terminal superposes the sub-
carriers. Meanwhile to recover the sub-signal, the receiving terminal mixes and
integrates the sub-carriers with the transmitter signals, and then recovers the
signals by utilizing parallel-serial conversion and demodulation. The underwater
acoustic OFDM communication system diagram is shown in Fig. 1.

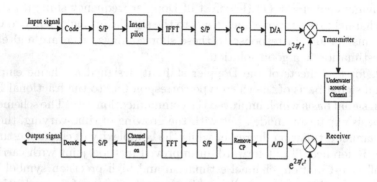

Fig. 1. Underwater acoustic OFDM communication system diagram.

Based on the underwater acoustic OFDM communication system with transmission path of time-varying [11], we estimate the underwater acoustic channel,
wherein the impulse response of the system is expressed as follows:

$$h(\tau, t) = \sum_{n=0}^{N-1} h_n(t) \delta(\tau - \tau_n(t)) \tag{1}$$

where N be the multi-path channel number, $h_n(t)$ be complex gain of nth path
at time t, and $\tau_n(t)$ represents the time delay of nth path at time t, $0 \le \tau_n(t) \le$
$\tau_{\max}$, in which $\tau_{\max}$ is the possible maximum relative delay. We assume that
the symbol period of acoustic OFDM is far less than the coherence time of
the channel, then $h(\tau, t)$ can be considered to be time-invariant approximately
within the same OFDM symbol period. We sample the system according to the
OFDM system sampling period T_s ($T_s = T/K$, T is the signal duration, and
K is the total number of carriers), thus we can obtain the channel model under
discrete-time as follows:

$$h(n) = \sum_{i=0}^{L-1} h_i \delta(n - i) \tag{2}$$

In Formula (2), we round the value of $\tau_{\max}/T_S$ as the channel length L under
the discrete time. Since underwater acoustic signal is typically sparse signal, as

a significant feature of sparse, $h = [h_0, h_1, h_2, \cdots, h_{L-1}]$ contains only a very small number of non-zero elements. Using compressed sensing theory can effectively take advantage of this sparse underwater acoustic signals characteristic to estimate the underwater acoustic channel.

3   Compressed Sensing Theory

A signal can be projected into a low dimensional space using the sampling matrix, and relatively accurately reconstruct the original signal from a small number of projection values, as long as it is sparse or compressible in the corresponding transform domain, according to the compressed sensing theory.

Let an $N \times 1$-dimensional column vector can represent a discrete-time signal $\mathbf{x}$,

$$\mathbf{y} = \mathbf{\Phi x} + \mathbf{v} = \mathbf{\Phi D u} + \mathbf{v} \tag{3}$$

where, as an observation vector, $\mathbf{y} \in \mathbf{R}^M$ has M elements, each element of which is a measurement value of $\mathbf{x}$; $\mathbf{\Phi}$ is a $M \times N$ dimensional measurement matrix; $\mathbf{v}$ is a vector of noise signal; $\mathbf{D}$ is a complete dictionary; sparse signal $\mathbf{x}$ is represented as $\mathbf{u}$, if $\mathbf{u} \in \mathbf{R}^N$ only has k nonzero elements, when $k << N$, $\mathbf{x}$ is compressible signal, $\mathbf{u}$ is the N-dimensional k- sparse vector. As for the underwater acoustic OFDM communication system in this paper, we combine with discrete-time channel model in formula (2), construct complete dictionary $\mathbf{D}$, establish appropriate observation matrix $\mathbf{\Phi}$, and then we get the output signal $\mathbf{y}$, finally restore the original signal based recovery algorithms.

4   Channel Estimation Algorithm Based on CS
for Underwater Acoustic OFDM Communication

The channel estimation based on CS for underwater acoustic OFDM communication system adopts the linear interpolation. Two-dimensional pilot symbols are inserted in the time and frequency domains, respectively, which can obtain the sample values of frequency response based on the channel sensing. And then, the corresponding complete dictionary is constructed. Finally, the channel estimation for underwater acoustic OFDM communication system is completed by adopting the compressive sampling matching pursuit algorithm. Because the position of the pilot directly determines the recovery performance of the matrix, the reasonable pilot insertion will benefit the signal recovery. In summary, the analysis of pilot insertion and channel sensing will be completed firstly, then construct the complete dictionary. At last, the channel estimation based on CoSaMP recovery algorithm for underwater acoustic OFDM communication is completed.

4.1   Pilot Interpolation

In this paper, two different kinds of pilot symbols, including frequency domain and time domain, are used to make the two-dimensional interpolation [11].

Linear interpolation on the frequency domain is considered first, the formula corresponds to

$$H\left(f,l\right) = H\left(n\Delta_F + \varepsilon_F, l\right) = \left(1 - \frac{\varepsilon_F}{\Delta_F}\right) H\left(n, l/\Delta_T\right)$$

$$+ \frac{\varepsilon_F}{\Delta_F} H_F\left(n+1, l/\Delta_T\right)\left(\forall l \in h\right) \tag{4}$$

where $H\left(f, l\right)$ is the complete response of channel, H_F is the response of channel, Δ_T is the interpolation interval of the pilot of time domain, and Δ_F is the interpolation interval of the pilot of frequency domain, $0 \leq \varepsilon_F \leq \Delta_F$, $n\Delta_F \leq f \leq (n+1)\Delta_F$.

According to (4), all of the channel response of subcarrier would be gotten from the pilot OFDM symbols, and the linear interpolation is made on its time domain, the corresponding formula is as follows:

$$H\left(f,l\right) = H\left(f, m\Delta_T + \varepsilon_T\right) = \left(1 - \frac{\varepsilon_T}{\Delta_T}\right) H\left(f, m\Delta_T\right) + \frac{\varepsilon_T}{\Delta_T} H\left(f, (m+1)\Delta_T\right)$$
$$\tag{5}$$

where $0 \leq \varepsilon_T \leq \Delta_T$, $m\Delta_T \leq l \leq (m+1)\Delta_T$.

4.2   Channel Sensing

The number of pilot subcarrier of the underwater acoustic OFDM communication system is P. The K point Discrete Fourier Transform (DFT) is used on the transmitter of the system. The maximum of system path delay would be less than the length of symbol cyclic prefix, and after the Fast Fourier Transform (FFT), the received signal $\mathbf{Y}$ of the $K \times 1$ dimension sampling vector can be represented:

$$\mathbf{Y} = \mathbf{XH} + \mathbf{G} = \mathbf{XWh} + \mathbf{G} \tag{6}$$

where $\mathbf{X} = diag\left(\mathbf{X}\left(1\right), \mathbf{X}\left(2\right), \cdots, \mathbf{X}\left(K\right)\right)$ is a $K \times K$ dimension matrix, $\mathbf{X}\left(K\right)$ is the signal vector mapped from the pilot signal and the user data, $\mathbf{H}$ is a $K \times 1$ dimension matrix, corresponding to the frequency domain response of channel, $\mathbf{G}$ is a $K \times 1$ matrix, corresponding to additional white Gaussian noise, $\mathbf{W}$ is a $K \times L$ dimension matrix of the DFT transformation, and L is the length of channel of the discrete time in (2), $\mathbf{h}$ is a $L \times 1$ dimension matrix, corresponding to the underwater acoustic signal.

P pilot position is chosen from the K subcarrier, corresponding to a $P \times K$ dimension matrix $\mathbf{Q}$. The pilot signal from the receiving end of the system is given by

$$\mathbf{Y_P} = \mathbf{X_P W_P h} + \mathbf{G_P} \tag{7}$$

where $\mathbf{Y}_P$, $\mathbf{X}_P$, $\mathbf{W}_P$ are the known signals on the receiving end of the system. $\mathbf{Y}_P$ is a $P \times 1$ dimension matrix, $\mathbf{Y_P} = \mathbf{QY}$, $\mathbf{X}_P$ is a $P \times P$ dimension matrix, $\mathbf{X_P} = \mathbf{QXQ'}$, $\mathbf{W}_P$ is a $P \times L$ dimension matrix, $\mathbf{W_P} = \mathbf{QW}$, and $\mathbf{G}_P$ is a $P \times 1$ dimension matrix, $\mathbf{G_P} = \mathbf{QG}$. In this paper, the CS reconstruction algorithm is used to get the underwater acoustic vector signal $\mathbf{h}$, a $L \times 1$ vector, from (8):

$$\mathbf{H} = \mathbf{Wh} \tag{8}$$

4.3   The Structure of the Complete Dictionary

In this paper, based on the method in the reference [12], the over complete dictionary can be constructed as follows:

$$\mathbf{D} = \left[d(0)\, d\left(\frac{1}{\beta T}\right) \cdots d\left(T + \max(\phi_1, \phi_2)\right) \right] \qquad (9)$$

In the above formula, we put $\beta = 4$, the coefficient β reflects accuracy of the complete dictionary. There are N atoms in the dictionary. At a time, there are L carriers in underwater acoustic OFDM communication system. This article selects M carriers randomly to transmit pilot signal, the channel frequency $\mathbf{H}$ response can be described by using formula (10):

$$\mathbf{H} = \mathbf{D}\mathbf{A_k} \qquad (10)$$

Among them, $\mathbf{D}$ is the order of the complete dictionary, $\mathbf{A}_K$ is a column with contains $2L$ nonzero elements $\{a_{-L}, \cdots, a_j, \cdots, a_{L-1}\}$, and $-L \leq j < L$, a_j is the channel attenuation. Because a_j is sparse, so there is only a small number of nonzero values. $\mathbf{Y}$ can be solved by combining (6), (7), (8), (9) and (10):

$$\mathbf{Y} = [\mathbf{X}(1), \mathbf{X}(2), \cdots, \mathbf{X}(K)] \times \begin{pmatrix} \mathbf{D} & & & \\ & \mathbf{D} & & \\ & & \ddots & \\ & & & \mathbf{D} \end{pmatrix} \begin{pmatrix} \mathbf{A}_1 \\ \mathbf{A}_2 \\ \vdots \\ \mathbf{A}_K \end{pmatrix} + \mathbf{G} \qquad (11)$$

where $\mathbf{Y}$, $\{\mathbf{X}(1), \mathbf{X}(2), \mathbf{X}(3), \cdots, \mathbf{X}(K)\}$ and $\mathbf{D}$ are the known conditions. This paper recovers sparse vector $\{\mathbf{A}_1, \mathbf{A}_2, \mathbf{A}_3, \cdots, \mathbf{A}_K\}$ from signal $\mathbf{Y}$ by using the recovery algorithms for sparse signal recovery [13].

4.4   Channel Estimation Algorithm Based on CoSaMP for UWAC

In the channel estimation for underwater acoustic OFDM communication system, different recovery algorithms have different errors and bit error rate. Currently, there are some common recovery algorithms, such as: MP algorithm[[14], OMP algorithm [15,16] and CoSaMP algorithm [17]. In this paper, we will focus on the use of the CoSaMP algorithm to realize the channel estimation for underwater acoustic OFDM communication system.

In this paper, the channel perception model of underwater acoustic OFDM system, uses Gaussian matrix that meets the restricted isometry property as the measurement matrix $\mathbf{\Phi}$. If the sparse degree of the signal $\mathbf{h}$ is k, we can regard vector $\mathbf{u} = \mathbf{\Phi}^*\mathbf{\Phi}\mathbf{h}$ as the proxy of it. Then the largest component k in vector $\mathbf{u}$ corresponds to the biggest component k in the signal $\mathbf{h}$. The basic idea of underwater acoustic channel estimation algorithm based on CoSaMP is to use an iterative approach to approximate the target signal first, to consider the newly introduced residual signal, and to update data samples iteratively to structure residual signal proxy. Among them, the number of CoSaMPs iteration is related to the sparse degree. The advantage is that it guarantees a certain degree of precision and stability, but its operation efficiency is slightly lower than the OMP algorithm. Important elements of the signal are obtained by the signal proxy and they provide the prerequisite for the next iteration. The specific operation steps are shown below:

Initialization:
Iteration $i = 0$, residuals $\mathbf{r_0} = \mathbf{y}$, Sparse vector $\mathbf{h_0} = \mathbf{0}$
Input:
measurement matrix $\mathbf{\Phi}$, received signal $\mathbf{Y}$, signal sparsity k
Output:
Recovered signal $\mathbf{h}$
Process:

step 1: Generate equivalent signal $\mathbf{u} = \mathbf{\Phi}^*\mathbf{y}$ and decide the greatest component of the signal: $\Omega = \sup(\mathbf{u_k})$;
step 2: Update and merge components: $\Omega_i = \Omega \cup \sup(\mathbf{u_{i-1}})$;
step 3: Get the collection of components by the Least Squares:

$$\bar{\mathbf{h}} = \underset{\tilde{\mathbf{h}}:\sup(\tilde{\mathbf{h}})=\Omega_i}{\arg\min} \left\| \mathbf{\Phi}\tilde{\mathbf{h}} - \mathbf{y} \right\|$$

step 4: Optimal estimate of sparsity by $\tilde{\mathbf{h}}$, and update new value $\mathbf{h_i} = \left(\bar{\mathbf{h}}\right)^v$;
step 5: Updated samples: $\mathbf{r} = \mathbf{y} - \mathbf{\Phi}\mathbf{h_i}$;
step 6: $i + +$, if $i \leq k - 1$, then go to setp1,or do setp7;
step 7: Output recovered signal $\hat{\mathbf{h}} = \mathbf{h_k}$.

5   Simulation and Performance Analysis

In order to analyze the performance of the proposed channel estimation algorithms for UWAC, comparative tests of the following five kinds of algorithms are taken. The mentioned algorithms are CoSaMP algorithm [17], BP algorithm, OMP algorithm [16], LS algorithm based on MP structured, and traditional LS algorithm. And a comprehensive comparative analysis are undertaken to estimate the performance of the algorithms. The evaluation indicators are: (1) normalized mean square error (NMSE), (2) the bit error rate(BER), (3) complexity of the algorithm, (4) stability, etc. The simulation parameters are shown in Table 1.

Figure 2 shows the comparison chart of normalized MSE with noise ratio (SNR) of the five channel estimation algorithms. Experimental results show that when underwater acoustic OFDM communication system channel estimation is taken, CoSaMP algorithm has the Minimum error, BP algorithm and OMP algorithm take second place with a good estimation error, but the estimation error of LS algorithm based on MP structured and traditional LS algorithm are large. And with the increasing of underwater acoustic channel SNR, the advantage of CoSaMP algorithm is more obvious. And when the value of underwater acoustic channel SNR is 30dB, the NMSE value of CoSaMP algorithms is smaller

Table 1. The simulation parameters.

Parameters	Value
Channel length (L)	50
Channel bandwidth/kHz	4
Cyclic prefix length	16
Pilot number	36
Pilot number	512
The guard interval/ms	18
Carrier frequency/kHz	13
Carrier modulation	QPSK

than the BP algorithm nearly 3dB, smaller than the OMP algorithm nearly 4dB, smaller than the traditional LS algorithm about 15dB. In addition, when observing the normalized MSE trend, its easy to find that the normalized MSE values of CoSaMP, BP and OMP algorithms are getting smaller with the increase of underwater acoustic channel SNR, and CoSaMP algorithm has the most obvious downward trend and the most accuracy channel estimation, at the same time the channel estimation normalized MSE curves of LS algorithm based on MP structured and traditional LS algorithm become flat and horizontal.

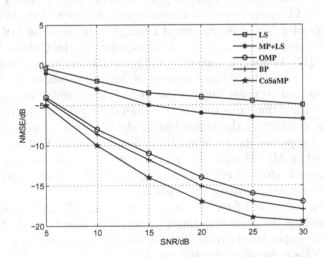

Fig. 2. The normalized MSE comparison of channel estimation algorithms.

Figure 3 is the BER curves of underwater acoustic OFDM communication system under different underwater acoustic channel estimation methods. By analyzing this figure, it is obvious that with the increasing of SNR, CoSaMP algorithms error rate is the lowest, BP algorithm and OMP algorithm are following, and the error rates of traditional LS algorithm and LS MP structured

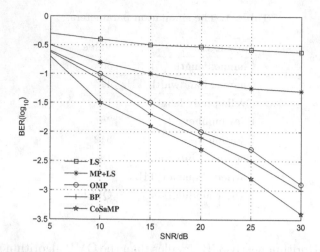

Fig. 3. The BER comparison of 5 channel estimation algorithms.

algorithm are very high. Although BP algorithm and OMP algorithms have shown a good performance, but compared with CoSaMP algorithm, the overall performance of the CoSaMP algorithm is the best.

Considering the algorithm complexity, the complexity of traditional LS algorithm is $O(P^3)$, where P is the inserted pilot number. OMP recovery algorithms complexity is $O(Lk^2)$, where L and k respectively represent the channel length and channel sparsity. The complexities of LS algorithm based on MP structured and BP algorithm are between them, the complexity of the CoSaMP algorithm is $O(L\log^2 L)$ [17]. When the same data set is used, considering from the experimental running time (the average results of 40 experiments), CoSaMP algorithm is not optimal (running time is less than 0.15 s), which is slightly slower than the OMP algorithm (run time is less than 0.05 s). From the point of view of the running stability of the algorithm, under the same conditions, running through several experiments, we found that the traditional LS algorithm and LS algorithm based on MP structured cross failed recovery occasionally during the underwater acoustic channel estimation process, but CoSaMP algorithm, OMP and BP algorithms are relatively more stable.

In summary, considering from the recovery accuracy, BER, the algorithm complexity and stability, the channel estimation algorithm based CoSaMP for UWAC proposed in the paper is relatively optimal though its algorithm complexity is slightly high. This is because the channel estimation algorithm based CoSaMP fully takes the advantage of the sparsity of underwater acoustic channel.

6   Conclusion

This paper proposed a novel channel estimation algorithm that makes use of the natural sparse characteristic of underwater acoustic channel. The algorithm adopts the underwater acoustic OFDM communication system and combines with the compressed sensing theory. At the meantime, by inserting the pilot symbols in both time and frequency domains using linear interpolation, this method can make the influence of Doppler frequency shift equivalent to attenuation and construct a reasonable complete dictionary, which can describe the frequency response of the channel. At last, the estimation of underwater acoustic channel is completed by adopting CoSaMP recovery algorithm. The experimental results show that the algorithm is feasible and effective. Compared with other algorithms, it can obtain higher estimation accuracy and improve the overall performance of OFDM communication system channel estimation with lower complexity and higher stability so that it has a good prospect for practical application. However, our algorithm is only completed in the simulation environment and needs to be integrated into the study of underwater acoustic wireless sensors in the future.

References

1. Qi, C., Wang, X., Wu, L.: Underwater acoustic channel estimation based on sparse recovery algorithms. IET Sig. Process. **5**(8), 739–747 (2011)
2. Etter, P.C.: Underwater Acoustic Modeling and Simulation. Spon Press, New York (2003)
3. Yin, J., Hui, J., Cai, P., Guo, L.: Application of fractional fourier transform in long range deep-water acoustic. Communication **35**(8), 1499–1504 (2007)
4. Wang, Y., Chen, Y., Yin, J., Cai, P., Zhang, Y.: Research on orthogonal multicarrier underwater acoustic communication system based on factional Fourier transform. J. Commun. **33**(8), 162–170 (2012)
5. Qu, F., Yang, L.: Basis expansion model for underwater acoustic channels. In: OCEANS 2008, pp. 1–7. IEEE (2008)
6. Chang, J., Wang, H., Shen, X.: Joint method of synchronization and channel estimation in OFDM underwater acoustic communication. Comput. Eng. Appl. **43**(11), 122–124 (2007)
7. Kaddouri, S., Beaujean, P.P.J., Bouvet, P.J.: Least square and trended doppler estimation in fading channel for high-frequency underwater acoustic communications. IEEE J. Oceanic Eng. **39**(1), 1–10 (2014)
8. Donoho, D.L.: Compressed sensing. IEEE Trans. Inf. Theory **52**(4), 1289–1306 (2006)
9. Guo, S., He, Z., Jiang, W.: Channel estimation based on compressed sensing in high-speed underwater acoustic communication. In: 2013 9th International Conference on Information, Communications and Signal Processing (ICICS), pp. 1–5. IEEE (2013)
10. Berger, C.R., Zhou, S., Preisig, J.C.: Sparse channel estimation for multicarrier underwater acoustic communication: from subspace methods to compressed sensing. IEEE Trans. Sig. Process. **58**(3), 1708–1721 (2010)
11. Yin, J.: The Principle and Signal Processing Technique of Underwater Acoustic Communication. National Defence Industry Press, Beijing (2011)
12. Huanan, Y., Guo, S.: Channel estimation algorithm based on compressed sensing in MIMO-OFDM underwater acoustic communication. Syst. Eng. Electron. **34**(6), 1252–1257 (2012)

13. Cands, E.J., Wakin, M.B.: An introduction to compressive sampling. IEEE Sig. Process. Mag. **25**(2), 21–30 (2008)
14. Kang, T., Iltis, R.A.: Matching pursuits channel estimation for an underwater acoustic OFDM modem. Acoustics. In: IEEE International Conference on Speech and Signal Processing, ICASSP 2008, pp. 5296–5299. IEEE (2008)
15. Tropp, J.A.: Greed is good: algorithmic results for sparse approximation. IEEE Trans. Inf. Theory **50**(10), 2231–2242 (2004)
16. Tropp, J.A., Gilbert, A.C.: Signal recovery from random measurements via orthogonal matching pursuit. IEEE Trans. Inf. Theory **53**(12), 4655–4666 (2007)
17. Needell, D., Tropp, J.A.: CoSaMP: iterative signal recovery from incomplete and inaccurate samples. Appl. Comput. Harmonic Anal. **26**(3), 301–321 (2007)

Semi-Stochastic Topology Control with Application to Mobile Robot Team of Leader-Following Formation

Yanjun Hu[1], Lei Zhang[1], Li Gao[2]($\boxtimes$), and Enjie Ding[1]

[1] IoT Perception Mine Research Center, China University of Mining and Technology, Xuzhou 221008, China
[2] School of Electrical Engineering and Automation, Jiangsu Normal University, Xuzhou 221116, China
gaoli@jsnu.edu.cn

Abstract. Scouting emergence situation in underground is a danger mission. It is a good choice that a robot team of leader-following formation is used in underground situation surveillance. This paper proposes how to control the robot team. A model of following robot is built in cyber-physical perspective. Based on this model, a semi-stochastic topology control algorithm, which is a tight conjoining of communications and mobility control, is proposed. Using the distance between the following-robot and leader-robot as the basis of next-hop chosen probability, this algorithm combines the advantages of random transmission model of point-to-point and the direction transmission model of end-to-end. The algorithm also balances the link connection redundancy and average end-to-end delay. The topology and movement control parameters are solvers of a convex optimum problem. Experiments demonstrate that the topology control can ensure the communication throughput while robot team succeeds in moving to the assigned points.

Keywords: Cyber-physical systems · Stochastic topology control · Convex optimization · Dual decomposition

1 Introduction

Deploying a robot team with sensors to detect the hazardous areas or post-disaster situations in coal mine, can reduce the casualties caused by secondary disasters. The wireless communication mode is used by robots since the hard environment of underground of coal mine. Therefore, network topology control and movement control are necessary for the robot team in order to complete the exploring task. Network topology control is used to guarantee the reliability of data transmission, and movement control is required to ensure the robot arrives at the assigned position.

The network topology control is an effective method to achieve reliability of data transmission [1,2]. Topology control algorithms of network, such as literatures [3–5], are proposed based on method, immunity and reliability constraints.

© Springer-Verlag Berlin Heidelberg 2015
L. Sun et al. (Eds.): CWSN 2014, CCIS 501, pp. 125–134, 2015.
DOI: 10.1007/978-3-662-46981-1_12

However, the algorithms did not take the mobility of communication nodes into consideration. Literature [6] discussed the topology control for mobile nodes. But the emphasis of the literature is how to eliminate the effect of movement to topology control, and the paper unrealized the synchronization of topology and movement. The control and path planning of robot with communication constraints studied in [7]. However, it only confirms the connection established between the nodes without considering the quality of communication. In fact, the movement of the robot and the ability of the communications among the robots influence each other. A control method combing the topology and mobility controls on robots is needed. Cyber-Physical System (CPS) [8,9] provides a possible solution. Such as, [10–12] gave movement control algorithms with the framework of CPS. And, the features of these algorithms are put the mobile control firstly and none-redundant communication links. Therefore, those algorithms are unsatisfied the requirements in the scenario of scouting emergence situation in underground. The primary task of the robot team is to transmit the detected information to monitoring center in the scenario. If the robots can arrive at the assigned positions but fail to transmit data, the robots movements are nonsense.

This paper proposes a network topology control algorithm, which confirms data transmission priorities and redundant communication link while controlling the robots movement, on robot team of leader-following formation in the perception of the CPS.

2   System Architecture and Models

2.1   Control Model of Leader Robot

To accomplish the scout the dangerous area of coal mine, a robot team is designed as a leader-following system in. And the roles of robots and operators are previously set. In the robot team, the robot with sensors and camera is the leader robot whose task is to scout the surroundings and collect information. The other robots, named following robots, are used as the data transmission node. In the security zones, people or intelligent decision algorithm will monitor the robot team.

The leader robot tries its best to reach the designated location and detect the environmental information. Thus, its mathematical model can be expressed as a optimum problem

$$\min \|l_0(t) - l^{\text{goal}}\|$$
$$\text{s.t. } \dot{l}_0 = f(l_0(t), I) \tag{1}$$

where $l_0(t) \in \mathbb{R}^2$ is a variable denoted the position of the leader robot, $l_0^{\text{goal}} \in \mathbb{R}^2$ is the target position of the leader robot; $f(l_0, I)$ is the abstract control algorithm on movement. I is a indicator function of communication status. If the leader robot can not communicate with any following robots, $f(l_0(t), I) = 0$, otherwise $f(l_0(t), I) = 1$.

We focus on the topology and movement control of the following robot, because (a) the movement of the leader robot is almost not affected by the following robots, (b) there are mass algorithms can be used to control the leader.

2.2 Control Model of the Following Robots

An architecture diagram of the following robots control is shown in Fig. 1. The concurrent network topology and node mobility control reflects the CPS character- the integration of computing, communications, control. Based on the current positions of the robots and communication model for the coal mine, the control realizes the network topology control (cyber) and the mobility control (physical), while it is restrained by requirements of throughput and position.

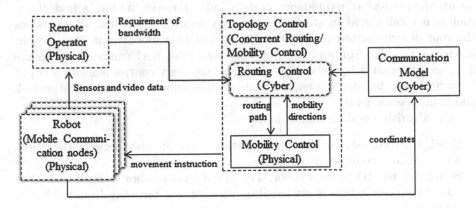

Fig. 1. System architecture of mobile robot teams control.

To precise, the following robots have two requirements. (a) During the movement, the network should be formed. And, the network topology should guarantee the throughput of each robot high enough to make sure the transmission of data and video signal well. (b) The following robots should follow the leader.

An abstract model of the following robots can be described by the nonlinear optimal control model shown as Eq. 2. We assumes that the following robots constitutes a two-dimensional vector graphic $G = (S, A)$. A is the arc set in the vector graphic, $S = \{s_j\}$ is the set of robots. The control model of the following robots is

$$
\begin{cases}
\max\limits_{s_i \in S} \ \sum_i \Pr(\rho_i(t) \geqslant \rho_i^{\min}) \\
\min\limits_{s_i \in S} \ \sum_i \|l_i(t) - l_i^{\text{goal}}\|
\end{cases}
\tag{2}
$$
$$
\text{s.t. } \ l(t) = l(0) + \int_0^t \frac{dl(t)}{dt} du
$$

where l is a set whose elements $l_i(t), i = 1, \cdots$ is the position coordinates of i-th robot s_i, l_i^{goal} is the goal position coordinates of s_i; $\rho_i(l_i)$ stands for measure of communication reliability which is related to the current position; ρ_i^{min} represents the minimum throughput of the s_i, τ_{ij} is the packet error rate from s_i to s_j. The two target function represent the network reliability requirements of the robot team and movement requirement respectively.

3 Semi-stochastic Topology Control Algorithm

3.1 Algorithm Description

The idea of stochastic topology control algorithm is that the target node is chosen randomly [13,14] when the communication node is transmitting packet. Therefore, compared with the deterministic routing algorithm, all neighbor nodes are the potential next-hop nodes in stochastic topology control algorithm, which means the existent of redundancy of data link. However, finding a best global rout is not calculated in stochastic topology control algorithm, which means the rout of transmitted packet may be not the best global rout. As a result, stochastic topology control algorithm may have poor performance, such as the data transmission delay. The semi-stochastic topology control algorithm is put forward. It can balance the requirements of redundancy of communication link and transmission delay.

The algorithm is described as follows:

– Step1: Use received signal strength to estimate the distance between the robots which are also communication nodes.
– Step2: Set the ID to each robot. The ID of leader robot is fixed as 0. The IDs of following robots is set based on the distance far away from the leader robot.
– Step3: Solve the (2) in following robots. The solution has two results which are the direction of movement and the transmission probabilities of the neighbor node.
– Step4: Move robots or transmit data base on the solutions. Especially, hen the data need to be transmitted, the robot will chose randomly a neighbor in a set whose ID is greater (or less) than sender's.

We can learn from the above description that the packet transmission is random from the perspective of point-to-point communication. However, from the perspective of end-to-end communication, packet transmission is directional. Therefore, we name this algorithm for semi-random algorithm.

The following part will specifically address the mathematical model and distributed implementation of step 3 of the algorithm.

3.2 Communication Error Model in Point-to-point Communication

According to the two-dimensional Poisson summation formula, the ray mode of underground electromagnetic can be converted into waveguide mode. Compared with the analytical expression characteristic pattern to determine the strength of each wave excitation mode, the incentive intensity of each transmission mode, denoted as $E_{0_{mn}}$ [15], was obtained.

$$E_{0_{mn}} = \frac{4E_0\pi \sin\left(\frac{m\pi}{\omega} + \varphi_x\right)\cos\left(\frac{n\pi}{h} + \varphi_y\right)}{wh\sqrt{1 - \left(\frac{m\pi}{wk_0}\right)^2 - \left(\frac{n\pi}{hk_0}\right)^2}}. \tag{3}$$

Based on (3), a complete power transmission formula [16] was established

$$P_r = P_t G_t G_r \left[\frac{1}{E_0}\sum_{m,n} E_{0_{mn}} \sin\left(\frac{m\pi}{\omega} + \varphi_x\right)\cos\left(\frac{n\pi}{h} + \varphi_y\right) e^{-k_{zmn}z}\right]. \tag{4}$$

where E_0 represents field strength at the transmitting antenna; P_t is instead of input power of transmission antenna; G_t and G_r mean the antenna emission and receive gain, respectively. If m is odd, $\varphi_x = 0$; if m is even, $\varphi_x = \pi/2$. And, the $\varphi_y = 0$ when n is odd, the $\varphi_y = \pi/2$ when n is even.

Consequently, we can calculate the packet error rate τ_{ij} between the i-th and j-th robot, if the locations of two robots is known.

$$\tau_{i,j} = \text{erfc}\left(\sqrt{\frac{kP_r}{P_{N_0}}}\right) \tag{5}$$

where $\text{erfc}(x)$ is the complementary error function, k is a constant parameter related with wireless communication encoding, P_{N_0} means channel noise inter-city. And, the probability R_{ij} that a packet sent by the i-th robot is correctly decoded by the j-th robot is obtained

$$R_{i,j} = 1 - \tau_{i,j}. \tag{6}$$

3.3   Optimal Model and Solution

Let μ_i denote the maximum communication rate of each robot in MAC layer. ρ_i is defined as the data throughout of the i-th robot with the routing parameter T whose elements $T_{i,j}$ means the probability that the j-th robot is chosen to receive the packet send by the i-th robot. N_i and N_i' represent the set of robots whose ID is greater or less than the i-th robot ID, respectively. The ρ_i is defined

$$\begin{aligned}\rho_i &= \text{outgoing packets - incoming packets}\\ &= \sum_{j\in N_i}\mu_i R_{i,j}T_{i,j} - \sum_{k\in N_i'}\mu_k R_{k,i}T_{k,i}.\end{aligned} \tag{7}$$

We introduce $\bar{\rho}_i$ and $\tilde{\rho}_i$ as the mean and variance of ρ_i, respectively.

Using the definitions of τ_{ij}, (2) becomes

$$\begin{cases}\max\limits_{s_i\in S} & \sum_i \Pr(\rho_i(t) \geq \rho_i^{\min})\\ \min\limits_{s_i\in S} & \sum_i \|l_i(t) - l_i^{\text{goal}}\|\end{cases}$$

$$\text{s.t. } l(t) = l(0) + \int_0^t \frac{dl(t)}{dt}du$$
$$\rho_i(t) = \sum_{j\in N_i}\mu_i R_{i,j}T_{i,j} - \sum_{k\in N_i'}\mu_k R_{k,i}T_{k,i} \quad \forall i. \tag{8}$$

In practical applications, it is invalid that the following robot fails to construct network to transmit the data to monitoring center. According to the different importance of two targets, we can transforms (8) into

$$\max_{s_i \in S} \sum_i \Pr(\rho_i(t) \geqslant \rho_i^{\min}) - \omega \sum_i \|l_i(t) - l^{\text{goal}}\|$$

$$\text{s.t. } l(t) = l(0) + \int_0^t \frac{dl(t)}{dt} du \tag{9}$$

$$\rho_i(t) = \sum_{j \in N_i} \mu_i R_{i,j} T_{i,j} - \sum_{k \in N_i'} \mu_k R_{k,i} T_{k,i} \quad \forall i.$$

Furthermore, we use the slack variable Δ to make the (9) solvable. Thus, (9) becomes

$$\max_{s_i \in S} \sum_i \Pr(\rho_i(t) \geqslant \rho_i^{\min}) - \omega \sum_i \|l_i(t) - l^{\text{goal}}\| > \Delta$$

$$\text{s.t. } l(t) = l(0) + \int_0^t \frac{dl(t)}{dt} du \tag{10}$$

$$\rho_i(t) = \sum_{j \in N_i} \mu_i R_{i,j} T_{i,j} - \sum_{k \in N_i'} \mu_k R_{k,i} T_{k,i} \quad \forall i.$$

Let $\varepsilon = \Delta + \omega \sum_i \|l_i(t) - l^{\text{goal}}\|$, we can invoke Chebyshev inequality to claim that $\Pr(\rho_i(t) \geqslant d_i^{\min}) > \varepsilon$ is a sufficient condition for satisfying $(\bar{\rho}_i(t) - d_i^{\min})/\sqrt{1/\varepsilon}$. Finally, we obtain model

$$\max_{s_i \in S} \sum_i \frac{\bar{\rho}_i(t) - d_i^{\min}}{\sqrt{\tilde{\rho}_i(t)}} - \sqrt{\frac{1}{\Delta + \omega \sum_i \|l_i(t) - l^{\text{goal}}\|}}$$

$$\text{s.t. } l(t) = l(0) + \int_0^t \frac{dl(t)}{dt} du \tag{11}$$

$$\rho_i(t) = \sum_{j \in N_i} \mu_i R_{i,j} T_{i,j} - \sum_{k \in N_i'} \mu_k R_{k,i} T_{k,i} \quad \forall i.$$

Since the Chebyshev inequality and Constraints are both convexity [17], the optimization model shown in (11) is a convex optimization problem satisfied Slater constraints qualification. According to convexity, we may implement a distributed algorithm based on dual decomposition theory [18].

3.4   Convergence of Algorithm

The leader-following consensus can be achieved if the following robots are linked to their leader together via their neighbors frequently enough as the system evolves [19]. According to (1), if the communication between the following robot and the leader robot is not established, we can get $f(l_0, I) = 0$. In other words, during the movement, the leader robot must communication with a following robot. At the same time, when $\tau_{ij} > 0$, $T_{i,j} > 0$, which is guaranteed by the constraints of the following robot model. Therefore, the robot team that uses this algorithm has leader-following consensus.

4   Experiments

4.1   Feasibility Experiments

One leader robot and two following robots are used to form a robot team in this simulation. Experiments are done by assuming that every robot in this robot team has the same speed and communication ability. In addition, Zigbee protocol is used in the communication between the robots. The maximum communication distance is limited to 20 m [20]; The minimum communication throughput is 0.2. The leader robot will move to destination in the direction of gradient descent. The coordinate of monitoring people is (0, 0). The coordinate of specified destination is (0, 10).

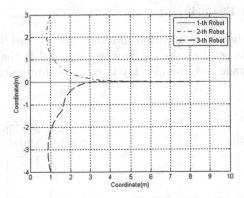

Fig. 2. Experimental movement traces of robots.

The movement traces of robots are shown in Fig. 2. The leader robot moves to specified destination in the direction of gradient descent directly. In the initial time, the distance between the 1-th robot and the leader robot is short. Based on the objective function, the shift direction of 1-th is the direction of the optimal communication throughout. At the same time, the 2-th robot travels to the leader robot in the initial shift. When the 2-th robot is close to the leader robot, its direction will be the direction of optimal network communication throughout. At last, the system will be steady.

Figure 3 is a partial result topology control that is communication random routing probability of 1-th robot, 2 Cth robot and 3-th robot. In the initial stage (0–5 s), the two following robots are communication nodes, which can be replaced by each other for the leader robot. The rout probabilities of the two robots are very close. With the change of position of the robot team, the rout probabilities will change corresponding. It can be seen between 5 s and 20 s in Fig. 3. After 20 s phase, robot topology and the relative position are in a stable state, routing probability is characterized by a steady state.

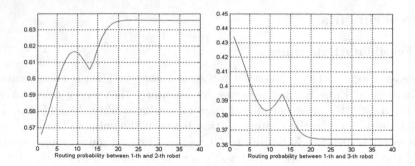

Fig. 3. Experimental result of topology control.

4.2   Performance Experiment

In order to balance the communication link redundancy and delay performance, this algorithm adopts semi-random algorithm. Figure 4 is the simulation result of comparison of average end-to-end delay in case of communication node failure.

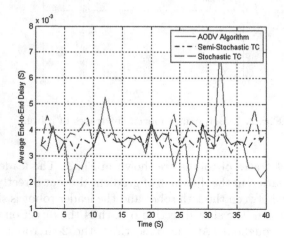

Fig. 4. Experimental result of topology control.

The experiment compared AODV algorithm and random topology control algorithm. When the node failed, AODV algorithm restarted to look for the best rout, which increased the delay. At other stages, the delay performance of AODV algorithm is better than others. In Fig. 4, semi-random topology control algorithm is prior than random topology control algorithm during the whole time. However, when the node failed, the delay performance of semi-random topology control algorithm is similar with the random topology control algorithm.

Though, there are only three robots in our experiment, we can inferred reasonably the following results: with the increase number of communication nodes, semi-random topology control algorithm performs better, when the rate of node failure is high.

5 Conclusions

This paper studies topology control model and algorithm of the leader-following robot team which is used for coal mine disaster detection. A nonlinear optimization model is set up to satisfy the requirements of data transmission priority. The optimal model ensures the maximum probability of communication throughout and the robot moves to the specified location under constraint condition. The distributed of this algorithm is realized by dual decomposition theory. Based on the random of point-to-point communication and orientation of end-to-end communication, this algorithm can balance communication link redundancy and network delay. Model presented in this paper has the versatility. Specific topology control algorithm depends on the bandwidth constraint function, underground wireless communication model and robot path planning method.

Acknowledgments. This work was supported by a grant from the National Science and Technology Support Program of China (No.2012BAH27B04, No.2013 BAK06B05).

References

1. Santi, P.: Topology control in wireless ad hoc and sensor networks. ACM Comput. Surv. (CSUR). **37**(2), 164–194 (2005)
2. Zhang, X., Lu, S.L., Chen, G.H.: Topology control for wireless sensor networks. J. Softw. **18**(4), 943–954 (2007)
3. Li, X.H., Zhang, D.F., Chen, W.B.: An energy efficient topology control protocol for ad hoc networks utilizing randomized beamforming. Chin. J. Comput. **34**(7), 1342–1350 (2011)
4. Dong, W., Xiao-liLi, C., Xiao-hong, L.: Research on the interference- optimized topology control algorithms in ad hoc networks. J. Yunnan Univ. Nationalities (Natural Sciences Edition) **20**(5), 372–380 (2011)
5. Wei-zhan, B.X.D.F.H.: Optimization methods of topology control with reliability constraints in wireless mesh network. J. Electron. Inf. Technol. **35**(1), 159–165 (2013)
6. Nishiyama, H., Ngo, T., Ansari, N.: On minimizing the impact of mobility on topology control in mobile ad hoc networks. IEEE Trans. Wireless Commun. **11**(3), 1158–1166 (2012)
7. Ghaffarkhah, A., Mostofi, Y.: Communication-aware motion planning in mobile networks. IEEE Trans. Autom. Control. **56**(10), 2478–2485 (2011)
8. Jiefeng, H.: Cyber-physical systems. Commun. CCF **6**(1), 25–29 (2010)
9. Jingrong, W., Muqing, W., Jingfang, S.: Cyber-physical system. Acta Automatica Sinica **38**(4), 507–517 (2012)
10. Zavlanos, M.M., Ribeiro, A., Pappas, G.J.: Mobility and routing control in networks of robots. In: 49th IEEE Conference on Decision and Control (CDC), pp. 7545–7550. IEEE Press, New York (2010)

11. Fink, J., Ribeiro, A., Kumar, V.: Robust control for mobility and wireless communication in cyberc physical systems with application to robot teams. Proc. IEEE **100**(1), 164–178 (2012)
12. Chun, I., Park, J., Kim, W.: Self-adaptive system development method for smart control systems in CPS. In: 16th International Conference on Advanced Communication Technology (ICACT), pp. 635–639. IEEE Press, New York (2014)
13. Ribeiro, A., Sidiropoulos, N., Giannakis, G.B.: Optimal distributed stochastic routing algorithms for wireless multihop networks. IEEE Trans. Wirel. Commun. **7**(11), 4261–4272 (2008)
14. Sarkar, S., Datta, R.: A game theoretic model for stochastic routing in self-organized MANETs. In: 2013 IEEE Wireless Communications and Networking (WCNC), pp. 1962–1967. IEEE Press, New York (2013)
15. Sun, Z., Akyildiz, I.F.: Channel modeling and analysis for wireless networks in underground mines and road tunnels. IEEE Trans. Commun. **58**(6), 1758–1768 (2010)
16. Huo, Y., Fengxue, L., Zhao, X.: Effect of antenna location on radiation field distribution in coal mine tunnels. J. Chin. Coal Soc. **38**(4), 715–720 (2013)
17. Bertsimas, D., Popescu, I.: Optimal inequalities in probability theory: a convex optimization approach. SIAM J. Optim. **15**(3), 780–804 (2005)
18. Palomar, D.P., Chiang, M.: A tutorial on decomposition methods for network utility maximization. IEEE J. Sel. Areas Commun. **24**(8), 1439–1451 (2006)
19. Jadbabaie, A., Lin, J., Morse, A.S.: Coordination of groups of mobile autonomous agents using nearest neighbor rules. IEEE Trans. Autom. Control. **48**(6), 988–1001 (2003)
20. Hargrave, C.O., Ralston, J.C., Hainsworth, D.W.: Optimizing wireless LAN for longwall coal mine automation. IEEE Trans. Ind. Appl. **43**(1), 111–117 (2007)

Positioning and Location-Based Services in Wireless Sensor Networks

Cellular Iterative Position Method
with Gaussian Noise

Qinli An[1,2(✉)], Jianfeng Chen[1], and Zhonghai Yin[2]

[1] College of Marine, Northwestern Polytechnical University,
Xi'an 710072, China
an_qinli@126.com, chenjf@nwpu.edu.cn
[2] College of Science, Air Force Engineering University,
Xi'an 710051, China
yinzhonghai2005@yahoo.com.cn

Abstract. On the assumption that the errors obey same gaussian noise for every sensor in the base station network, maximum likelihood estimation iterative algorithm is presented for localizing a target using angle of arrival measurements. It is shown that the RMSs and means of error between maximum likelihood estimation iterative algorithm is much less than that of least squares estimation algorithm by simulation experiments.

Keywords: Angle of arrival · Gaussian noise · Cellular position · Base station

1 Introduction

In the United States, Federal Communications Commission (FCC) rules cellular service to provide subscriber position information within a given precision [1]. Various methods with own relative advantages are presented in the open document [2–5].

In the article, the measurement of AOA with gaussian noise is assumed. An iterative method of MLE is presented and compared with LSE using simulation experiments of various parameters.

2 Least Squares Estimation (LSE)

Each AOA measurement is described as

$$\hat{\theta}_i - \theta_i = \Delta\theta_i (i = 1, \cdots, n) \tag{1}$$

$$\Delta\theta_i \sim N(0, \sigma^2)(i = 1, \cdots, n)$$

$$\tan\theta_i = \frac{y - y_i}{x - x_i}(i = 1, \cdots, n)$$

© Springer-Verlag Berlin Heidelberg 2015
L. Sun et al. (Eds.): CWSN 2014, CCIS 501, pp. 137–143, 2015.
DOI: 10.1007/978-3-662-46981-1_13

Adapted as

$$x \sin \theta_i - y \cos \theta_i = x_i \sin \theta_i - y_i \cos \theta_i (i = 1, \cdots, n) \qquad (2)$$

Where $\hat{\theta}_i$ and θ_i are measured AOA and real AOA of base station i, the coordinates of base station i and target are (x_i, y_i) and (x, y) respectively.

According to Eq. (2), the LSE of target position [6] are

$$\begin{pmatrix} x \\ y \end{pmatrix} = (A_L^T A)^{-1} A_L^T b_L \qquad (3)$$

where

$$A_L = \begin{bmatrix} \sin \hat{\theta}_1 & -\cos \hat{\theta}_1 \\ \vdots & \vdots \\ \sin \hat{\theta}_i & -\cos \hat{\theta}_i \\ \vdots & \vdots \\ \sin \hat{\theta}_n & -\cos \hat{\theta}_n \end{bmatrix}, \; b_L = \begin{pmatrix} x_1 \sin \hat{\theta}_1 - y_1 \cos \hat{\theta}_1 \\ \vdots \\ x_i \sin \hat{\theta}_i - y_i \cos \hat{\theta}_i \\ \vdots \\ x_n \sin \hat{\theta}_n - y_n \cos \hat{\theta}_n \end{pmatrix}$$

3   Maximum Likelihood Estimation (MLE)

Assumed that the AOA measurements have the same gaussian noise for every sensor in the base station network, The MLE cost function of target's coordinate is given as

$$L(x, y; \sigma, \hat{\theta}_1, \cdots, \hat{\theta}_n) = \prod_{i=1}^{n} \frac{1}{\sqrt{2\pi}\sigma} \exp\left[-\frac{1}{2\sigma^2}(\hat{\theta}_i - \theta_i)^2 \right]$$

$$\ln L = -\frac{n}{2}\ln(2\pi) - \frac{n}{2}\ln \sigma^2 - \frac{1}{2\sigma^2}\sum_{i=1}^{n}(\hat{\theta}_i - \theta_i)^2$$

$$= -\frac{n}{2}\ln(2\pi) - \frac{n}{2}\ln \sigma^2 - \frac{1}{2\sigma^2}\sum_{i=1}^{n}(\hat{\theta}_i - \arg\tan\frac{y - y_i}{x - x_i})^2$$

Maximum of $\ln L$ is the minimum of

$$\sum_{i=1}^{n} \Delta\theta_i^2 = \sum_{i=1}^{n}(\hat{\theta}_i - \arg\tan\frac{y - y_i}{x - x_i})^2$$

The tangent of Eq. (1) is given by

$$\tan \Delta\theta_i = \frac{\tan \hat{\theta}_i - \frac{y - y_i}{x - x_i}}{1 + \frac{y - y_i}{x - x_i}\tan \hat{\theta}_i} (i = 1, \cdots, n)$$

The equation above is multiplied by $1 + \frac{y-y_i}{x-x_i} \tan \hat{\theta}_i$, i.e.

$$\tan \hat{\theta}_i - \frac{y-y_i}{x-x_i} = \tan \Delta\theta_i (1 + \frac{y-y_i}{x-x_i} \tan \hat{\theta}_i) \ (i = 1, \cdots, n)$$

The equation above is multiplied by $(x - x_i) \cos \hat{\theta}_i$, i.e.

$$(y - y_i)(\cos \hat{\theta}_i + \tan \Delta\theta_i \sin \hat{\theta}_i)$$

$$+(x - x_i)(-\sin \hat{\theta}_i + \tan \Delta\theta_i \cos \hat{\theta}_i) = 0 \ (i = 1, \cdots, n)$$

When $\Delta\theta_i$ is very small, substituting $\Delta\theta_i$ for $\tan \Delta\theta_i$, optimization model is obtained as follows.

$$\min \sum_{i=1}^{n} \Delta\theta_i^2$$

s.t.

$$(y - y_i)(\cos \hat{\theta}_i + \Delta\theta_i \sin \hat{\theta}_i)$$

$$+(x - x_i)(-\sin \hat{\theta}_i + \Delta\theta_i \cos \hat{\theta}_i) = 0 \ (i = 1, \cdots, n) \tag{4}$$

4 Iterative Method for MLE

The solving of MLE is difficult for a nonlinear optimization process. So the iterative method of MLE is presented.

Adapt (4) as

$$(y - y_i) \cos \hat{\theta}_i + (y - y_i)\Delta\theta_i \sin \hat{\theta}_i$$

$$-(x - x_i) \sin \hat{\theta}_i + (x - x_i)\Delta\theta_i \cos \hat{\theta}_i = 0 \ (i = 1, \cdots, n) \tag{5}$$

Approximate (5) as

$$(y - y_i) \cos \hat{\theta}_i + (y_p - y_i)\Delta\theta_i \sin \hat{\theta}_i$$

$$-(x - x_i) \sin \hat{\theta}_i + (x_p - x_i)\Delta\theta_i \cos \hat{\theta}_i = 0 (i = 1, \cdots, n)$$

Target initial coordinate is presented by $p = \begin{pmatrix} x_p \\ y_p \end{pmatrix} = (A_L^T A)^{-1} A_L^T b_L$. A new LSE is obtained.

$$\min \sum_{i=1}^{n} \Delta\theta_i^2$$

$$\frac{x\sin\hat{\theta}_i - y\cos\hat{\theta}_i}{(x_p - x_i)\cos\hat{\theta}_i + (y_p - y_i)\sin\hat{\theta}_i} - \frac{x_i\sin\hat{\theta}_i - y_i\cos\hat{\theta}_i}{(x_p - x_i)\cos\hat{\theta}_i + (y_p - y_i)\sin\hat{\theta}_i}$$
$$= \Delta\theta_i (i = 1, \cdots, n)$$

LSE is obtained as

$$\begin{bmatrix} x \\ y \end{bmatrix} = \left(A_p^T A_p\right)^{-1} A_p^T b_p$$

Where

$$A_p = \begin{bmatrix} \dfrac{\sin\hat{\theta}_1}{(x_p-x_1)\cos\hat{\theta}_1+(y_p-y_1)\sin\hat{\theta}_1} & \dfrac{-\cos\hat{\theta}_1}{(x_p-x_1)\cos\hat{\theta}_1+(y_p-y_1)\sin\hat{\theta}_1} \\ \vdots & \vdots \\ \dfrac{\sin\hat{\theta}_i}{(x_p-x_i)\cos\hat{\theta}_i+(y_p-y_i)\sin\hat{\theta}_i} & \dfrac{-\cos\hat{\theta}_i}{(x_p-x_i)\cos\hat{\theta}_i+(y_p-y_i)\sin\hat{\theta}_i} \\ \vdots & \vdots \\ \dfrac{\sin\hat{\theta}_n}{(x_p-x_n)\cos\hat{\theta}_n+(y_p-y_n)\sin\hat{\theta}_n} & \dfrac{-\cos\hat{\theta}_n}{(x_p-x_n)\cos\hat{\theta}_n+(y_p-y_n)\sin\hat{\theta}_n} \end{bmatrix} \tag{6}$$

$$b_p = \begin{bmatrix} \dfrac{x_1\sin\hat{\theta}_1-y_1\cos\hat{\theta}_1}{(x_p-x_1)\cos\hat{\theta}_1+(y_p-y_1)\sin\hat{\theta}_1} \\ \vdots \\ \dfrac{x_i\sin\hat{\theta}_i-y_i\cos\hat{\theta}_i}{(x_p-x_i)\cos\hat{\theta}_i+(y_p-y_i)\sin\hat{\theta}_i} \\ \vdots \\ \dfrac{x_n\sin\hat{\theta}_n-y_n\cos\hat{\theta}_n}{(x_p-x_n)\cos\hat{\theta}_n+(y_p-y_n)\sin\hat{\theta}_n} \end{bmatrix} \tag{7}$$

Assume that the obtained solution is $\begin{bmatrix} x_p \\ y_p \end{bmatrix}$, the new A_p, b_p is obtained through substituting $\begin{bmatrix} x_p \\ y_p \end{bmatrix}$ into (6) and (7). LSE is obtained again. So the iterative process of MLE is obtained as

Input: $p = \begin{pmatrix} x_p \\ y_p \end{pmatrix} = \left(A_L^T A_L\right)^{-1} A_L^T b_L$, A_p, b_p, error limit $\varepsilon > 0$;

Output: coordinate of target $p = \begin{pmatrix} x_p \\ y_p \end{pmatrix}$.

(1) If $\left\| p - (A_p^T A_p)^{-1} A_p^T b_p \right\| < \varepsilon$, stop and output $p = (A_p^T A_p)^{-1} A_p^T b_p$; otherwise, goto (2).

(2) Let $p = (A_p^T A_p)^{-1} A_p^T b_p$, goto (1).

5 Simulation Experiment

The simulation experiment is done for the validity of the method above. The base station coordinates and target coordinates are assumed as $(0,0)$, $(0,R)$, $(0,-R)$, $(R\cos(\pi/6), R\sin(\pi/6))$, $(R\cos(\pi/6), -R\sin(\pi/6))$, $(-R\cos(\pi/6), -R\sin(\pi/6))$, $(-R\cos(\pi/6), R\sin(\pi/6))$ and $(\frac{R}{2}\cos\frac{k\pi}{30}, \frac{R}{3}\sin\frac{k\pi}{30})$ $(k = 0, \cdots, 59)$ in Fig. 1. Given that $\varepsilon = 0.001$, $R = 1$, $\Delta\theta_i \sim N(0, (\frac{k\pi}{540})^2)(3\sigma = \frac{k\pi}{180}, k = 1, \cdots, 10)$. The target coordinates and various gaussian noise above is simulated 100 times. It is shown in Figs. 2 and 3 that The means and RMSs of the error between iterative algorithm of MLE is much less than LSE Algorithm.

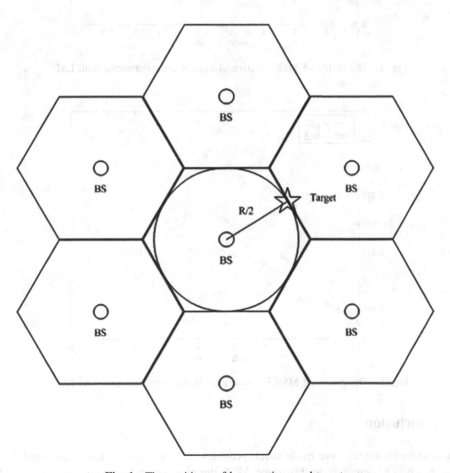

Fig. 1. The positions of base stations and targets

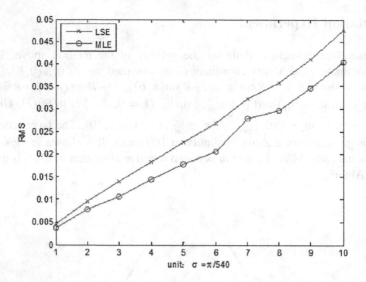

Fig. 2. The RMSs of MSE iterative algorithm error compared with LSE

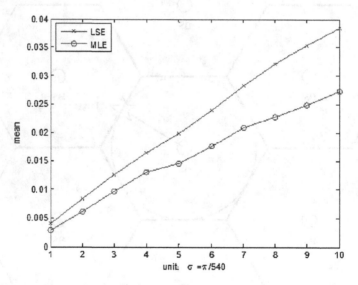

Fig. 3. The means of MSE iterative algorithm error compared with LSE

6 Conclusion

Position technologies have made much progress, but no methods have displayed that they reach FCC demands. In this paper, MLE iterative method is given. The RMSs and means of the error between iterative algorithm of MLE is much less than LSE algorithm as shown in Figs. 2 and 3. From result above, the method provide the high accuracy for cellular position than LSE method.

References

1. FCC Wireless 911 Requirements. http://www.fcc.gov/e911/
2. Botteron, C., Host-Madsen, A., Fattouche, M.: Effects of system and environment parameters on the performance of network-based mobile station position estimators. IEEE Trans. Veh. Technol. 53(1), 163–180 (2004)
3. Gustafsson, F., Gunnarsson, F.: Mobile positioning using wireless networks. IEEE Signal Process. Mag. 22(4), 41–53 (2005)
4. Spirito, M.A.: On the accuracy of cellular mobile station location. IEEE Trans. Veh. Technol. 50(3), 674–685 (2001)
5. Hellebrandt, M., Mathar, R.: Location tracking of mobiles in cellular radio networks. IEEE Trans. Veh. Technol. 48(5), 1558–1562 (1999)
6. Sayed, A.H., Tarighat, A., Khajehnouri, N.: Network-based wireless location. IEEE Signal Process. Mag. 22(4), 24–40 (2005)

Research on Improved DV-Hop Localization Algorithm Based on RSSI and Feedback Mechanism

Fei Liu[1,2(✉)] and Guang-zeng Feng[2]

[1] College of Telecommunications and Information Engineering, Nanjing University of Post and Telecommunications, Nanjing 210003, China
[2] College of Mechanical Engineering, Guizhou University, Guiyang 550025, China
981890733@qq.com

Abstract. The average hop distance is chosen from the nearest beacon in DV-Hop, and it can't reflect the real status of the whole network, and this will promote the average localization error. In this paper, we propose one improved DV-Hop algorithm based on RSSI and feedback mechanism which called RFDV-Hop. It can be divided into two phases. First, it uses the RSSI for replacing the hops in DV-Hop to calculate the preliminary location of unknown node, second, it uses the distance difference between the real location embedded into beacons and the estimated location calculated from DV-Hop as the adjustment factor, and calculates the real location of unknown node by calculating the distances between unknown node and beacons, and also the adjustment factor. The simulations show that RFDV-Hop can reduce the average localization effectively and keep the localization algorithm stable.

Keywords: Wireless sensor network · Localization · DV-Hop · RSSI · Localization feedback

1 Introduction

Nowadays, Wireless sensor network (WSN) is the ideal solution for many applications, such as wireless data transmission, self organization of network management, environment sensing, multi-hops routing, low power consumption, etc. Based on the embedded sensors, WSN can achieve the environmental information easily, including temperature and humidity, light intensity, speed/acceleration, chemical gas concentration. Most of applications binding with location can be more useful. So, the research of localization is one key topic for WSN [1, 2].

In WSN, the localization refers to the process unknown node achieves the estimating location by using algorithms. The unknown node gets help from beacons which embedded precise location, or angles, interior clock, antenna, and others, to estimate exact location.

GPS (Global Positioning System) is the most widely used position system. GPS can get accurate location by communicating with satellites. In many fields, GPS meets the real time and the accuracy well. But, it is hard to be applied in WSN because of cost, effect, size, etc. In the indoor environment, GPS signal will be weak, wrong, and loss in indoor environment, and this results in the error of localization.

© Springer-Verlag Berlin Heidelberg 2015
L. Sun et al. (Eds.): CWSN 2014, CCIS 501, pp. 144–154, 2015.
DOI: 10.1007/978-3-662-46981-1_14

The localization methods can be divided into two categories according the distance measurement, one is range based algorithm, and the other is the range free algorithm.

Range based localization algorithms have the characteristics of high localization accuracy, but they often need to upgrade the WSN nodes for distance measuring modules, and this will increase the system cost, power consumption, and reduce the lifetime of network. So range based localization algorithms are often used in special cases, or small scale of WSN, etc. [3].

Range free localization algorithms can't get high localization accuracy as range based localization algorithms do, but they have advantages in many aspects, including simple network layout, low cost of construction, easy maintenance. Range free localization algorithms are fit for large scale WSN. The system is isotropy in the good connectivity conditions, and this will increase the localization accuracy.

DV-Hop [4], centroid [5], APIT [6], and MDS-MAP [7], are representative range free localization algorithms.

2 DV-Hop Basics

DV-Hop is one distributed localization algorithm. DV-Hop has characteristics of simple calculation, low communication cost, etc. DV-Hop can fulfill localization even if the proportion of beacon of WSN is quite low. Because the distance measurement is replaced by the total count of hops, the WSN node can be simple and low cost. DV-Hop meets most requests of range free localization algorithm and are widely used in many applications.

2.1 DV-Hop Algorithm

The DV-Hop mainly includes the following three stages:

(1) Calculate average hop-size for distance calculation

After initialization of WSN, beacons broadcast self location following the distance-vector protocol. Nodes analyze the received messages and do the following actions: if message comes from the same beacon and has the larger count of hops, then ignore this message; if not, node will add one to hop count and forward the message to neighbors.

Most of node build the minimum hop count information table after time slice is over.

According to the formula 1, Each beacon counts the average hop-size:

$$C_i = \frac{\sum\limits_{j \neq i} \sqrt{(x_i - x_j)^2 + (y_i - y_j)^2}}{\sum\limits_{j \neq i} h_{ij}} \tag{1}$$

where C_i is the average hop-size for beacon i, (xi, yi) is the coordinate of beacon i, (xj, yj) is the coordinate of beacon j, h_{ij} is the total count of hops between i and j, j = 1, ..., n, and $i \neq j$, n is the total of beacons. The numerator of formula is the sum of distances between beacon i and other beacons, and the denominator is the sum of minimum hops between beacon i and other beacons.

(2) Estimate the distance between unknown node and beacons

After beacons broadcast average hop-size to WSN, unknown node chooses the hop-size from the nearest beacon as its average hop-size, and calculate the distances between unknown node and beacons, as shown in Fig. 1:

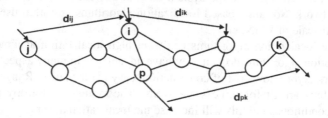

Fig. 1. The diagram of DV-Hop algorithm

Set i, j, k, as the name of beacons, p is the unknown node, and d is the distance between nodes.

As Fig. 1 shows, j and k are far from p, so p chooses hop-size of i as it's hop-size, that is $C_p = C_i$.

We can calculate distances between p and other beacons by hop-size of p times the count of hops. So, the distances between p and i, j, k are:

$$C_i \times h_{pi} \ , \quad C_i \times h_{pj} \ , \quad C_i \times h_{pk}$$

(3) Calculate the location of unknown node

According to the distances from stage 2, and the precise location of beacons, DV-Hop calculates the location of unknown node by using maximum likelihood.

2.2 Shortcomings of DV-Hop

DV-Hop has some shortcomings and mainly concentrated in three areas: first, the localization accuracy is easily influenced by the proportion of beacons, the network layout, and the location of beacons; second, using the hop-size from the nearest beacon can't represent the real status of whole WSN; third, the maximum likelihood is easy to bring some error into calculation and reduce the localization accuracy when the nodes near the boundary are taken into account.

Many algorithms proposed the improved scheme of DV-Hop, such as using expected hop-size to replace the calculated hop-size [8]; analyzing the influence of beacon's neighbors on hop-size [9]; adding weigh settings for hop-size and using new multilateral localization formula [10]; using average hop count instead of the minimum hop count, and replacing average hop-size with node communicating radius [11, 12]; dividing the WSN with Voronoi diagram, reducing the space for DV-Hop broadcasting and the computational complexity [13].

In literature [8], it calculates the expected distance to replace the hop-size by using the parameters of local network. It can reduce the localization error. But, it requires the details of network for calculating, and it will increase the localization error when the network is in sparse arrangement or the layout of network is irregular. In literature [9], the minimum hop count can't represent the status of network well, it adds the neighbors of beacons as the parameters for hop-size calculating, and it also reduces the communication radius for the low nodes density environment. It shows that the RSSI can be mo effective as the distance measurement. But, the cost of calculation may increase rapidly when the node density raises, and this will result in the traffic jam and the lower the efficiency of localization. In literature [10], it uses the measured value and the fitted value to compose the residuals. Using the residuals, it obtains the weights for each group, and calculates the degree of correlation between unknown node and beacons. Finally, it adds the weights and the degree of correlation into maximum likelihood calculating to get the precise location of unknown node. It is simple and efficient, but the result of localization is volatile when the strict strategy of distance measurement and the beacons classification pattern is given. In literature [11, 12], they adjust the minimum hop counts and the hop-size respectively from beacons and the unknown node. They use the average hop counts of local area to replace the minimum hop counts, and use the communication of node and the average connectivity degree to calculate the average hop-size. They can increase the localization accuracy, but they can't be applied into irregular network because of high computational complexity, the mathematical model based on experience data. In literature [13], it uses the predefined grading system for classify the nodes, and use the Voronoi diagram to divide the network. After doing these actions, the nodes and beacons can be divided into several units. In each unit, the beacons broadcast within the unit, and this reduces the amount of the communication greatly. Using the Voronoi diagram, it figures out the precise minimum hop counts and increases the localization accuracy. But, the parameters of minimum hop counts and the hop-size are rely on the grading system. If the grading system is not suit for the network, or the network is irregular, the localization accuracy can be instable.

From analysis described above, the improved algorithms focus on the areas: adding more information of network into localization, such as [8, 9]; reducing the complexity of network, such as [11–13]; improving the multilateral localization method, such as [10]; reforming the hop-size, such as [8–12]. These algorithms can increase the localization accuracy, but some shortcomings are also brought out, such as more communication cost, more complexity of network arrangement, and higher power consumption of nodes, etc.

Based on the DV-Hop, we improve one localization algorithm which has ability of self stabilization and fits the status of the real network well. Considering the distance in DV-Hop is the result of the hop counts multiplied by hop-size, the hop-size among neighbors must similar to the average hop-size. But, this assumption is hard to be applied into applications when the WSN nodes are random arranged. So, we use the RSSI to improve the distance calculation method, and build feedback channels between unknown node and beacons which embedded precise location. These feedback channels can reduce the localization error dramatically, and promote the ability of self stabilization for different network layout.

3   Improved Localization Algorithm RFDV-Hop

In this paper, we improve one DV-Hop based localization algorithm with RSSI and feedback mechanism RFDV-Hop (RSSI and Feedback Mechanism Based DV-Hop). RFDV-Hop can use the RSSI and the feedback of location bias to increase the localization accuracy.

RFDV-Hop can be divided two stages. First, it uses the RSSI to replace the hop counts, and calculates the estimated location of unknown node; Second, it builds one feedback channel between beacon and unknown node. The unknown node uses the bias which is the difference between real location and estimated location of beacon as adjustment factor, and adds this adjustment factor into maximum likelihood calculation to get the optimized location.

3.1   RFDV-Hop with RSSI Reformed

The ranging methods based on hop counts, in sparse network, are easy to occur distance deviation. Adding RSSI into distance calculation will greatly eliminate the distance deviation which is the result that the hop counts can't represent the real status of network well. The value of RSSI can be easily obtained through the common chips, such as CC2430, CEL2410.

Adding RSSI as the replacement of hop counts into distance calculation needs to know the signal attenuation model first. We choose log-normal distribution model in RFDV-Hop. Comparing with other signal propagation model, the log-normal distribution model is more versatility, and can be applied to both indoor and outdoor environments. Log-normal distribution model also provides a set of setup parameters for adjustment, as shown in formula 2 [15]:

$$PL(d) = \overline{PL}(d_0) + 10\eta \lg(\frac{d}{d_0}) + X\sigma \tag{2}$$

where $PL(d)$ is the path loss while distance is d, $\overline{PL}(d_0)$ is the path loss while d_0 is 1 m, η is the path loss index, $X\sigma$ is gauss random distribution function while the mean is 0.

To more accurately using RSSI to calculate the distance between unknown node and beacons, RFDV-Hop uses the following two measures, that is RSSI value for each receiving node and the average of all RSSI over the routing route called RSSI_avg.

Beacons broadcast their location messages which can be unknown node used for distance calculating. The format of message is {IDB, (Xi, Yi), Hops, RSSI_pre, RSSI_total}, where IDB is the id of beacon, (Xi, Yi) is the location of beacon i, Hops are the hop counts which is the sum of beacons that the message has been passed over, RSSI_pre is the signal intensity of receiving message coming from neighbors, RSSI_total is the sum of all RSSI_pre.

So, we can get the RSSI_avg, as shown in formula 3:

$$RSSI\_avg = RSSI\_total/Hops \tag{3}$$

RSSI can be stronger when the nodes get closer, unless it gets weaker. Based on this, we set W_R as the weight for distance calculating, as shown in formula 4:

$$W_{Rj} = \varepsilon \times \frac{RSSI\_avg}{RSSI\_pre} \tag{4}$$

where W_{Rj} is the weight for beacon j which is in the routing route, ε is the weight adjusting factor, and set $\varepsilon=1$ for simplicity.

Using RSSI to replace hop counts for distance calculating, as shown in formula 5:

$$d_{Bi} = \sum_{j=1}^{i} (W_{Rj} \times C_{Bi}) \tag{5}$$

where d_{Bi} is the distance between beacon i and unknown node, C_{Bi} is the average hop-size from beacon i to unknown node.

We can use the maximum likelihood to calculate the estimate location of unknown node based on the distances between unknown node and each beacon.

3.2 RFDV-Hop with Feedback Mechanism

In RFDV-Hop, unknown node uses the DV-Hop reformed by RSSI to obtain the estimate location, builds new message with location and hop-size in the format {C, (X, Y), ID}, and broadcasts to beacons. As to the unknown node, C is the hop-size, (X, Y) is the estimate location, ID is the node number. After beacons receive message from unknown node, beacons perform lookup operation in routing table, find the minimum hop corresponding ID, regard the unknown node as beacon, and use the reformed DV-Hop to calculate the estimate location of themselves. Beacons set the difference between the embedded precise location and the estimate location as the adjustment factor $P(\triangle X, \triangle Y)$, construct new message {$(\triangle X, \triangle Y)$, IDB}, and feedback to unknown node. Finally, the unknown node adds P into reformed DV-Hop and calculates the optimized location of unknown node.

Adding P into multilateral localization formula, as shown in formula 6 and 7, where d is the result of distance reformed by RSSI.

$$\begin{cases} A_1x + B_1y = d_1^2 - d_n^2 + C_1 + D_1 \\ \quad\quad\quad\vdots \\ A_{n-1}x + B_{n-1}y = d_{n-1}^2 - d_n^2 + C_{n-1} + D_{n-1} \end{cases} \tag{6}$$

$$\begin{aligned} A_i &= (2\Delta x_i - 2\Delta x_n + 2x_n - 2x_i), \\ B_i &= (2\Delta y_i - 2\Delta y_n + 2y_n - 2y_i) \\ C_i &= -[(x_i^2 - x_n^2 - 2x_i\Delta x_i + 2x_n\Delta x_n + \Delta x_i^2 - \Delta x_n^2)] \\ D_i &= -[(y_i^2 - y_n^2 - 2y_i\Delta y_i + 2y_n\Delta y_n + \Delta y_i^2 - \Delta y_n^2)] \end{aligned} \tag{7}$$

where i = 1,2, ..., n − 1.

Constructing $JX = K$ matrix, as shown in formula 8:

$$J = \begin{bmatrix} A_1 & B_1 \\ \vdots & \vdots \\ A_{n-1} & B_{n-1} \end{bmatrix},$$

$$K = \begin{bmatrix} d_1^2 - d_n^2 + C_1 + D_1 \\ \vdots \\ d_{n-1}^2 - d_n^2 + C_{n-1} + D_{n-1} \end{bmatrix}, X = \begin{bmatrix} x \\ y \end{bmatrix} \tag{8}$$

Finally, we can get the location of unknown node by using the least square method to solve the matrix in formula 8, as shown in formula 9:

$$X^T = (J^T J)^{-1} J^T K \tag{9}$$

3.3   Implementation

RFDV-Hop is mainly divided into following three stages:

(1) Unknown node uses RSSI to replace the hop counts in DV-Hop, calculates the estimate location, and broadcasts it in the format {C, (X, Y), ID}.
(2) Regarding unknown node as one beacon, beacons use the average hop-size C and the reformed DV-Hop by RSSI to calculate estimate location of themselves.
(3) Beacons set the difference between the embedded precise location and the estimate location as the adjustment factor P, and feedback to the unknown node.
(4) Unknown node adds the adjustment P into the reformed DV-Hop by RSSI, and gets the optimized location.

4   Simulation and Analysis

We use MATLAB as RFDV-Hop simulation platform. Simulations focus on average localization error. Two representative environment are chosen for simulations: network nodes are random arranged in square area and the network is isotropy; network nodes are random arranged in C-shaped area and the network is anisotropy. The comparison of algorithms performance focus on RFDV-Hop, DV-Hop, and literature [10]. Because literature [10] has no special requirements for network and weight settings, it is ideal target for simulation comparison.

Referring to literature [10], we set the simulation settings, as shown in Table 1:

The definition of average localization error is the ratio of the difference between estimate location and real location and communication radius of nodes. The definition is shown as formula 10:

$$E = \frac{\sum\limits_{i=1}^{N} \sqrt{(x_{ri} - x_i)^2 + (y_{ri} - y_i)^2}}{N \times R} \times 100\% \tag{10}$$

where E is the average localization error, N is the total number of nodes, (x_{ri}, y_{ri}) is the real location of unknown node, (x_i, y_i) is the estimate of unknown node.

Table 1. The parameters of simulation

Parameters	Descriptions
Network	100 m × 100 m square area
Layout	Uniform distribution
Communication radius (R)	20m
Node type	Homogeneous
Total numbers of nodes (N)	100
Platform	MATLAB 2010B
Numbers of simulation	100

Experiments I: The influence of the total number of beacons on localization error in square network. The result is shown in Fig. 2:

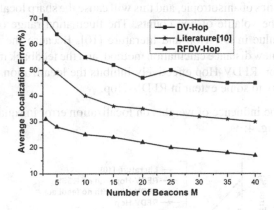

Fig. 2. The comparison of localization error in square area

As Fig. 2 shows, in square network, RFDV-Hop obtains higher localization accuracy than DV-Hop and literature [10]. The average localization error of RFDV-Hop is less than the results of other algorithms over 20 units. While the total number of beacons is shall, such as only 3–5 beacons are available, RFDV-Hop can still keep good localization accuracy. The reason for this result is the beacons use the adjustment factor P as the feedback for localization, and this reduces the possibilities of distance deviation. When the total number of beacons has been increased to 15, the localization errors of all the three algorithms start to level off, and the localization error of RFDV-Hop is the smallest.

Experiments II: The influence of the total number of beacons on localization error in C-shaped network. The result is shown in Fig. 3:

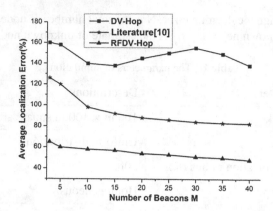

Fig. 3. The comparison of localization error in C-shaped area

The network of the simulation is changed into C-chaped network, and the other parameters are unchanged.

As Fig. 3 shows, in C-shaped network, all the three algorithms have more than 40 units increase of localization error, and this is mainly because the DV-Hop and related algorithms in irregular network, such as C-shaped network, X-shaped network, have obvious characteristics of anisotropic, and this will cause the sharp localization accuracy drops because of the volatile of hop counts. The fluctuation range of RFDV-Hop is smaller than the value in DV-Hop and literature [10]. Because the new hop counts reformed by RSSI, new distance calculation method, and the feedback mechanism based on adjustment factor, RFDV-Hop effectively inhibits the localization error. But, there will be a small delay to some extent in RFDV-Hop.

Experiments III: The influence of weights on localization error in square network. The result is shown in Fig. 4:

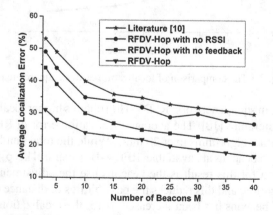

Fig. 4. The comparison of weights influence of FDV-Hop

The settings of simulation is same as experiment I.

As Fig. 4 shows, in square network, because of the hop-size reformed by RSSI and the adjustment factor, RFDV-Hop has the smaller localization error than the value of literature [10]. When RFDV-Hop lacks the adjustment factor and the RSSI reformation respectively, the localization error rises successively. This is mainly because RSSI has reduced the localization error results from hop-size at the localization estimation period. In addition, comparing with the ability of adjustment factor's feedback regulation, the impact of RSSI for localization error is much bigger. We can see that the RFDV-Hop containing RSSI reformation function only, will obtain much smaller localization error than the RFDV-Hop containing adjustment factor only. But, in irregular network, such as C-shaped or X-shaped network, the feedback mechanism based on adjustment factor will have the great role in stability of algorithm.

5 Conclusion

In this paper, based on the analysis of the localization error of DV-Hop and its related algorithms results from the nearest hop-size, we promote one improved algorithm with feedback function. It reforms the distance calculation model in DV-Hop with RSSI signal, defines the bias which is the difference between real location and estimated location of beacon as adjustment factor, and adds this adjustment factor into maximum likelihood method for calculating the optimized location of unknown node. Simulations show that RFDV-Hop obtains less localization error, smaller variation range of localization error, the faster convergence speed, and better robustness in both square and C-shaped network than DV-Hop and literature [10]. In future work, we are ready to reduce the localization error results from maximum likelihood, and use fuzzy strategy or support vector or particle swam optimization to promote the adaptive ability and intelligence of RFDV-Hop.

Acknowledgements. The work was supported by National Major Scientific and Technological Special Project under Grant No. 2012ZX03003011-005, 2011ZX03005-004-003.

References

1. Akyildiz, I., Su, W., Sankarasubramaniam, Y., et al.: A survey on sensor network. IEEE Commun. Mag. **40**(8), 102–144 (2002)
2. Niclescu, D., Americ, N.L.: Communication paradigms for sensor networks. IEEE Commun. Mag. **43**(3), 116–122 (2005)
3. Boukerche, A., Oliveira, H.A., Nakamura, E.F.: Localization systems for wireless sensor network. IEEE Wirel. Commun. **14**(6), 6–12 (2007)
4. Niculescu, D., Nath, B.: DV based positioning in ad hoc networks. J. Telecommun. Syst. **22**(14), 267–280 (2003)
5. Laurendau, C., Barbeau M.: Centroid localization of uncooperative nodes in wireless sensor networks using a relative span weighting method. EURASIP J. Wirel. Commun. Netw. Spec. Issue Wirel. Netw. Algorithm Syst. Appl. 1–10 (2010)

6. Chiti, F., Pierucci, L.: APIT: a bit of improvement for applications in critical scenarios. In: 6th International Wireless Communications and Mobile Computing Conference, Caen rance (Suppl), pp. 794–798 (2010)
7. Shang, Y., Ruml, W., Zhang, Y., et al.: Localization from mere connectivity. In: Proceedings of the 4th ACM International Symposium on Mobile Ad Hoc Networking & Computing. Annapolis, pp. 201–212. ACM Press (2003)
8. Yun, W., Xiao-dong, W., De-min, W., et al.: Range free localization using expected hop progress in wireless sensor networks. IEEE Trans. Parallel Distrib. Syst. **20**(10), 1540–1552 (2009)
9. Ma, D., Er, M.J., Wang, B.: Analysis of hop-count-based source-to-destination distance estimation in wireless sensor networks with application in localization. IEEE Trans. Veh. Technol. **59**(6), 2998–3011 (2010)
10. Shu, X., Yun-zhou, Z., Zhi-jia, X., et al.: An improved DV-Hop localization algorithm using residual weight in wireless sensor network. J. Comput. Inf. Syst. **8**(15), 6357–6364 (2012)
11. Nagpal, R.: Organizing a global coordinate system from local information on an amorphous computer. Technical Report AI Memo No. 1666, MIT Artificial Intelligence Laboratory (1999)
12. Nagpal, R., Shrobe, H., Bachrach, J.: Organizing a global coordinate system from local information on an ad hoc sensor network. In: Proceeding of Workshop on Information Processing in Sensor Networks, pp. 333–348, April 2003
13. Boukerche, A., Oliveira, H.A.B.F., Nakamura, E.F., Loureiro, A.A.F.: DV-Loc: a scalable localization protocol using Voronoi diagrams for wireless sensor networks. DV-Loc: a scalable localization protocol using Voronoi diagrams for wireless sensor networks. IEEE Wirel. Commun. **16**(2), 50–55 (2009)
14. Jiuqiang, X., Liu, W., Lang, F., Zhang, Y., et al.: Distance measurement model based on RSSI in WSN. Wirel. Sens. Netw. **2**, 606–611 (2010)
15. Ghasemi, A., Elvino, S.: Asymptotic performance of collaborative spectrum sensing under correlated log- normal shadowing. Commun. Lett. **11**(1), 34–36 (2007)

A Three-Dimensional Localization Algorithm Based on DV-Hop in Wireless Sensor Networks

Hua Yang[1,2(✉)], Min Wu[1,2], Chao Sha[1,2], and Ru-chuan Wang[1,2]

[1] College of Computer, Nanjing University of Posts and Telecommunications,
Nanjing 210003, Jiangsu, China
{youngmanhua,wuyuchen_2usa}@163.com
[2] Jiangsu Key Laboratory for Wireless Sensor Networks, Nanjing 210003, Jiangsu, China
{wumin,wangrc}@njupt.edu.cn

Abstract. Aiming at localization algorithms in 3D space which has some problems such as high complexity, large power consumption, long delay and so on, a 3D localization algorithm was proposed which combines DV-Hop with cube shell intersection method. This algorithm improves the DV-Hop in a special situation to get the unknown nodes' initial positions and employs the Cube Radius scale to get the final position. The theoretical analysis shows this algorithm has low complexity. Compared with 3D-DV-Hop, the location accuracy and fraction of coverage of this algorithm were improved obviously.

Keywords: Wireless Sensor Networks (WSNs) · 3D space · Localization · Radius scale

1 Introduction

Localization is a fundamental technology in wireless networks, while it's a precondition of most applications. Many algorithms are proposed which can be divided into two categories, named Range-based algorithm and Range-free algorithm [1]. Both of them have a few typical algorithms. For the range-based one, the typical algorithms are the TOA, AOA and RSSI while the APIT and DV-Hop algorithms are the classical range-free algorithms. Each of both algorithms has their respective advantages and disadvantages. Range-based algorithms have been more accurate but need extra hardware to support and have a high computational complexity. On the contrary, range-free algorithms have lower hardware requirements and lower power consumption with a low accuracy correspondingly. In recent years, more attention was paid to the range-free algorithms because of its low power consumption.

With the deepening of the research, WSNs (Wireless Sensor Networks) are applied into 3D (three-dimensional) space. Many 3D localization algorithms were proposed such as LandScape-3D [2], Bounding Cube [3], the improved IAPIT-3D [4], Constrained-3D [5]. At present, to ensure the accuracy of the node position, 3D localization algorithms have some general problems, such as the high complexity of calculation, the big delay

© Springer-Verlag Berlin Heidelberg 2015
L. Sun et al. (Eds.): CWSN 2014, CCIS 501, pp. 155–163, 2015.
DOI: 10.1007/978-3-662-46981-1_15

of network response or need extra assist device. All of these shortcomings make the proposed algorithms hard to adapt to the actual application scenario.

Therefore, in this paper, we are focused on these issues in large-scale positioning model and propose an improved DV-Hop arithmetic called DV-Hop-Cube. Our contributions are threefold. First, we established a large–scale positioning model. Most of 3D localization algorithms did not give a positioning model so that the algorithms can be used in anywhere without pertinence. However, application scenario has a great influence on the positioning. In our model, the sensor nodes do not obey uniform distribution but a Gaussian distribution which can reduce the deployment of nodes. Second, shortcomings of DV-Hop are that its inaccurate one-hop-distance and its long network convergence time. Depending on the model, we modified the method to reduce the convergence time, and let the one-hop-distance more precise for our model. Third, to decrease the computation complexity and improve the positioning coverage rate, Cubes intersection method was added to our DV-Hop-Cube algorithm.

The rest of paper is organized as five parts. Section 2 introduces our positioning model. The improved algorithm for one-hop-distance is presented at Sect. 3. In Sect. 3 we add the Cube intersection algorithm. Section 4 gives the simulation results and discusses the performance of the algorithm. In the concluding section, Sect. 5 is our conclusion.

2 Establishment of Positioning Model

Assuming that the nodes are widely deployment, there will always be some are the key monitoring areas, we called them Hot Regions. In these areas, more useful information will be got and the occurrence of the events generally follows the same distribution. Because of the events occurred in these Hot Regions are independent and identically distributed, the probability of the events in line with the central-limit theorem. The total of events lives up to Gaussian distribution [6]. The probability of each event is displayed in Fig. 1. So we establish a positioning model according to the probability distribution.

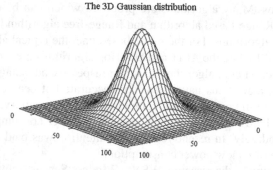

Fig. 1. The event probability model in Hot Regions

Assuming a given cube as deployment region of sensor nodes, to establish a 3D space coordinates system with the help of the location of beacons. Here we call the coordinate system as Outside Coordinate System. The whole region will be split into much more small cubes. Each of these cube's location is doubtless, and we can figure out the center of each small cube. Figure 2 is a planform of Outside Coordinate System in xoy plane where the dotted lines are the isoline of probability distribution.

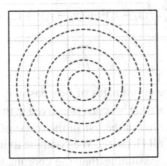

Fig. 2. Planform of Outside Coordinate System

3   Improvement of DV-HOP

There are two types of nodes in WSNs, one is the beacons that can get an accurate location with the assistant device such as GPS, the other is the unknown nodes that they should interact with other beacons and determine their location ultimately. Our algorithm extends DV-Hop algorithm to 3D space firstly. Aiming at the more complex transfer environment, larger number of nodes and the characteristics of the node distribution model, we add some constraints on the information interaction between nodes.

In the positioning model presented above, DV-Hop has a few drawbacks such as the inaccurate one-hop-distance and the big positioning delay which lead to the big error. Limit the scope of hop is a way to improve the accuracy of one-hop-distance when nodes are non-uniform distributed but Gaussian distributed. Moreover, with the scope of hop narrowed, the time delay of the algorithm will be brought under control. In addition, algorithm introduces a parameter α to balance the incomplete Gaussian distribution. The concrete implementation steps are as follows.

Step1. Initialize the networks. Nodes allocated randomly and un-uniformly in the 3D space. However, in the Hot Regions, nodes obey Gaussian distribution approximately in order to the center of Hot Regions at the center. Unknown nodes broadcast locates request information including hop count information need transferred by unknown nodes, transmit timestamp and so on.

Step2. After receiving the request information, beacons broadcast their location information packets to their neighbor nodes, such as hop count that the initial value is zero, the ID of the anchor node. Nodes in network neglect larger number from their same neighbors and plus one to hop count then retransmit to other nodes.

Step3. When hop count achieved to N, unknown nodes will check whether the number of beacons achieved to 4 or more. If achieved, the hop counts number and beacons location information will be stored in a list. Each beacon in the list repeats Step2 to seek more beacons within N-hop-count scope where N should be only a little number.

In the scope of N-hop-count, nodes relatively distributed uniformly. Therefore, take average Hopsize as one-hop-distance of the unknown nodes which can be calculated by the following formula:

$$HopSize_i = \frac{\sum_{j \neq i} \sqrt{(x_i - x_j)^2 + (y_i - y_j)^2 + (z_i - z_j)^2}}{\sum_{j \neq i} h_{ij}} \tag{1}$$

(x_i, y_i, z_i), (x_j, y_j, z_j) are the coordinates of beacons v_i, v_j, h_{ij} is hop count between v_i and v_j $(j \neq i)$. Among them, v_i are the beacons preserved in the list and v_j are the neighbor beacons of the beacons preserved in the list in the scope of N-Hop-count. Eventually, the Hopsize is the average of all $HopSize_i$. We continue to improve DV-Hop algorithm in the model of distribution. Assuming that the coordinate of Hot Region center is (x_0, y_0, z_0). From the preserved beacons we can get the nearest node k to point (x_0, y_0, z_0) and the distance r between them. Eventually we obtain one-hop -distance estimation equations as following shows:

$$Hopsize = \alpha HopSize_k + (1 - \alpha) HopSize_l, \ (l \in \Omega, l \neq k) \tag{2}$$

Parameter α is a control-parameter whose optimal value will be determined by experiment.

Step4. If the number of beacons in the list is less than 4 but more than 1, we can get unknown nodes' Hopsize to estimate all the distances between unknown nodes and their beacons. By cube scaling intersection method, we can get gravity coordinate of the inter-action region as the unknown nodes' location. While the number of beacons in the list is less than 2, the unknown node should be marked as a node can't be located. Figure 3 shows the information interaction process of distance estimation among all nodes.

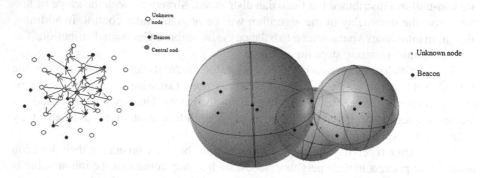

Fig. 3. The process of localization

Before using the method, an Outside Coordinate System should be established that is an auxiliary system used as location reference. It is built outside of the actual coordinate system, so we call it Outside Coordinate System. Beacons' locations can be easily got from GPS. We can obtain the coordinate unit based on beacons' locations. After that,

Outside Coordinate System could be established quickly. Figure 4 shows the cube inter-action method based on Outside Coordinate System.

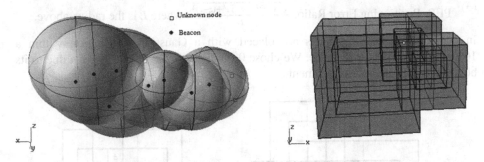

Fig. 4. The establishment of Outside Coordinate System

The distance d_i between unknown node and anchor v_i can be easily got according to the Hopsize. The coordinate of unknown node (x, y, z) can be figured out by the Least Square Method.

However, in the calculation of Hopsize, we chose the beacon in the list to stand for all the beacons which may cause some error. To solve this problem, we introduce cube interaction method to decrease the error. In Fig. 4, anchor is the center of the cube. If the estimated distance between the unknown node and anchor is accurate enough, the location of unknown node should he inside the interaction region. To build these beacon-centered cubes, the scaling radius should be determined firstly. Assuming the inner-side-length and outer-side-length of cube$_i$ whose center is v_i are l_i^{in} and l_i^{out} correspondingly and distance between the unknown node and v_i is R_i. Formulas for the scaling radius are as follows:

$$l_{in}^i = 2 \times (R_i - usR_i) \qquad (3)$$

$$l_{out}^i = 2 \times (R_i + usR_i) \qquad (4)$$

$$s = \max \left\{ Hopsize_i \mid i \in \Omega \right\} - \min \left\{ Hopsize_i \mid i \in \Omega \right\} \qquad (5)$$

Where u is a parameter is able to be discussed in the following simulation. The projections of Fig. 4 on xoy plane and yoz plane are shown as the following Fig. 5. Vertex positions of these intersecting cubes are easy to obtain from the figure. After that, the position of orthocenter can be easily calculated which defined as (x', y', z').

4   Simulation and Analysis of Algorithm

DV-Hop-Cube is improved mainly aiming at location accuracy and positioning coverage rate in the MATLAB environment. Before analysis, some concepts should be defined as follows:

(1) Network density, the average number of beacons in N-hop-count in the network.
(2) Node communication radius L.
(3) PER, Positioning Error Ratio, $\frac{\sqrt{(x-\bar{x})^2+(y-\bar{y})^2+(z-\bar{z})^2}}{L}$, where L is the radius above.

In our experiments, the nodes are placed with a Gaussian distribution within a 100 m × 100 m × 100 m space. We chose 0.05 as the value of parameter u due to its best performance in our experiments.

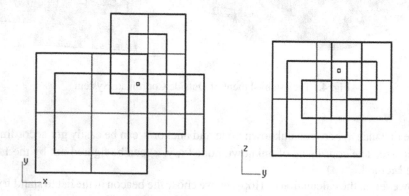

Fig. 5. The projection of a cube interaction region on xoy plane and yoz plane

Figure 6 shows α's impact on positioning accuracy represented by PER. In the graph, N was set as 3 and we chose three values of network density respectively 10 %, 20 % and 30 %. When α ranges from 0 to 1, PER grows from tall to small, then the opposite. When α is 0.4, algorithm achieved the highest positioning accuracy. We introduce α to weighting the beacon beside the unknown node, when network density is low relatively which will make the one-hop-distance more accurate. On the contrary, if network density is quite high, α does the opposite.

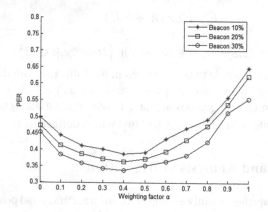

Fig. 6. Parameter α's impart on algorithm's accuracy

Next, we discuss the effects of N on the positioning accuracy. The selection of experimental parameters is as follows: network density is 20 %, $\alpha = 0.4$, $L = 20$ m. As Fig. 7 shows, we can get some results: When N = 2, PER is higher and unstable but it decreases with the beacon density increases. It is because that number of beacons in the list is small which cause the one-hop-distance not so accurate. When N = 4, the PER is lower. While with the increase of network density, the PER increases. Because that when beacon density is high, one-hop-distance is inaccurate because of averaging of more beacons. When N = 3, the number of beacons in the list is just an appropriate value. The positioning accuracy is high and changes stably.

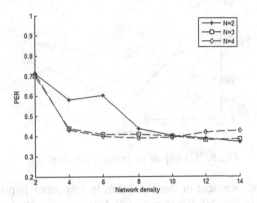

Fig. 7. The impact of N on positioning accuracy

We compared the DV-Hop-Cube with 3D-DV-Hop when network density is 10 % and 20 %. The result is shown in Fig. 8. In this graph, the positioning accuracy of DV-Hop-Cube is much higher than that of 3D-DV-Hop both when network density is 10 % and 20 %. Especially when network density is 10 %, DV-Hop-Cube is much superior to 3D-DV-Hop because of its more excellent computing method for one-hop-distance.

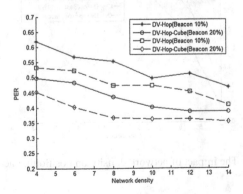

Fig. 8. Network density's impact on positioning accuracy

Communication radius is another influence factor of positioning accuracy. Its impact on positioning accuracy is shown in Fig. 9. From the graph, we know that when beacon density is quite low, the longer of communication radius the better of positioning accuracy within a certain range. Once surpass a specified threshold, the effect of it on positioning accuracy is opposite. While, beacon density is high, to increase communication radius makes little difference.

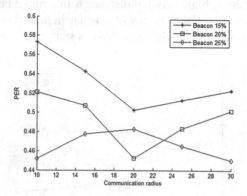

Fig. 9. L's impact on positioning accuracy

Another large improvement of the algorithm in this paper is positioning coverage rate which is shown in Fig. 10. When network density is low, the number of neighbor beacons will decrease rapidly. Many unknown nodes in 3D-DV-Hop algorithm can't be located. Under the circumstances, DV-Hop-Cube has a great advantage for it needs two neighbor beacons only. DV-Hop-Cube is greater than 3D-DV-Hop in this aspect.

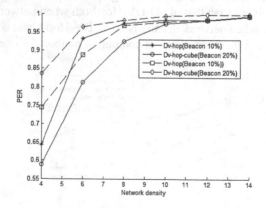

Fig. 10. The impact of network density on positioning accuracy

5   Conclusion

Through theoretical analysis and the validation of simulation experience above, it's proved that the proposed DV-Hop-Cube localization algorithm in this paper has better accuracy and higher positioning coverage rate. On account of the hop limit, it will have lower traffic and computing complexity which deserved to study in future work.

Acknowledgments. This work is supported by the National Natural Science Foundation of China (No. 61202355, 61373138), Jiangsu Province natural science foundation of China (No. BK2012436), Jiangsu province science and technology support plan (industrial) project (No. BE2012183), The national postdoctoral fund (No. 2013M531394), The specialized research fund for the doctoral program of higher education (No. 20123223120006), The science and technology innovation plan in university of Jiangsu (No. CXLX13_467). In addition, we wish to thank the anonymous reviewers for their insightful and constructive suggestions.

References

1. Sing, P., Agrawal, S.: Node localization in wireless sensor networks using the M5P tree and SMOreg Algorithms. J. Comput. Intell. Commun. Netw. (CICN) **5**, 104–108 (2013)
2. Zhang, L., Zhou, X., Cheng, Q.: Landscape-3D: a robust Localization scheme for sensor networks over complex 3D. In: 31st IEEE Conference on Local Computer Networks New York, pp. 239–246. IEEE Press, New York (2006)
3. Yang, S., Bo, Z., Kun, W., Hui, C.: DB: A Developed 3D positioning algorithm in WSN based on DV-Hop and bounding cube. J. Comput. Manag. (CAMAN) **10**, 1–4 (2011)
4. Liu, L., Zhang, H., Shu, J., Chen, Y.: A RSSI-weighted refinement method of IAPIT-3D. J. Comput. Sci. Netw. Technol. (ICCSNT) **3**, 1973–1977 (2011)
5. Liang, J., Shao, J., Xu, Y., Tan, J., Davis, B.T., Bergstrom, P.: Sensor networks localization in constrained 3-D spaces. In: 3rd 2006 IEEE International Conference, pp. 49–54. IEEE Press(2006)
6. Yang, G.: Central limit theorem and its application in statistical analysis. J. Stat. Inf. Forum **15**, 13–15 (2000)
7. Liu, S., Zheng, Y., Zhong, Z., Li, Y., Fan, X.: Improved DV-Hop algorithm for high accuracy and low energy consumption. J. Comput. Sci. Autom. Eng. (CSAE) **3**, 349–353 (2012)
8. Yang, P., Wu, W., Moniri, M.: Efficient object localization using sparsely distributed passive RFID tags. J. Comput. Sci. Autom. Eng. (CSAE) **60**, 5914–5924 (2013)
9. Shen, H., Ding, Z., Zhao, C.: Multiple source localization in wireless sensor networks based on time of arrival measurement. J. Signal Process. **62**, 1938–1949 (2014)
10. Ren, Y., Yu, N., Guo, X., Wan, J.: Cube-scan based three-dimensional localization for large-scale underwater wireless sensor networks. In: SysCon 2012 - 2012 IEEE International Systems Conference, pp. 186–191. IEEE Press (2012)
11. Wu, Q., Xu, P., Zhang, S., Chu, H.: A distributed localization algorithm based on random diffusion in WSN. J. Trust Secur. Priv. Comput. Commun. **12**, 1774–1777 (2013)
12. Han, G., Qian, A., Li, X.: Performance evaluation of localization algorithms in large-scale underwater sensor networks. J. Comm. Netw. Chin. (CHINACOM) **8**, 14–16 (2013)
13. Liu, Z., Li, G., Liu, X.: Monte-Carlo mobile node localization algorithms based on least squares method. J. Sens. Technol. **25**(4), 541–544 (2012)
14. Cui, H., Wang, Y., Lv, J.: Monte-Carlo mobile node localization algorithms based on least squares method. J. Sens. Technol. **25**(4), 541–544 (2012)
15. Zhou, S., Huang, B., Zeng, Z., Zhou, M., Zhan, J.: New type of hot spot cluster centered positioning algorithm and its application. J. Commun. **33**(5), 124–137 (2012)
16. Cui, H., Wang, Y., Guo, Q.: Muti-mobile-beacon assisted distributed node localization scheme. J. Commun. **33**(3), 103–110 (2012)

RI-MDS: Multidimensional Scaling Iterative Localization Algorithm Using RSSI in Wireless Sensor Networks

Chunyu Miao, Guoyong Dai, Keji Mao, Yidong Li, and Qingzhang Chen[✉]

College of Computer Science and Technology, Zhejiang University of Technology,
Hangzhou, China
cymiao@zjnu.cn, daiguoyong@gmail.com, {kjmao,ydli}@zjut.edu.cn,
qzchen@zjnu.edu.cn

Abstract. To improve the feasibility and the convenience of localization methods for wireless sensor networks, a localization algorithm RI-MDS (RSSI-based Iterative-Multidimensional Scaling) is proposed. The RI-MDS method is centralized, and mainly focuses on improving localization accuracy. It collects RSSI vectors as ranging basis, and combines the metric-MDS method and the nonmetric MDS method to accomplish the relative localization. Then it uses the maximum likelihood method in affine transformation to transform the relative coordinates to absolute ones. Our method has no need for additional equipment on the WSN nodes. Simulation and field experiments show that the average localization error and the localization error ratio of the RI-MDS method is relatively lower, thus it is more feasible.

Keywords: Wireless sensor networks · Node localization · Multidimensional scaling

1 Introduction

Wireless sensor networks (WSNs) are very important for the IOT (internet of things). They are ad hoc networks via wireless communication and consist of a large number of smart nodes [1]. WSNs are widely used in applications such as medical, military and environment surveillance. We deploy WSNs for information perception, collection and management, and send information to the observer. Usually, the sensor nodes are deployed randomly and the location of the nodes cannot be known. But in many applications, the positions of the sensor nodes must be estimated first. As a result, the sensor localization is one of the important research tasks.

Due to the high cost and high energy consumption, it's impossible to use a GPS (Global Positioning System) on every sensor node. In general, we get the positions of sensor nodes by indirect estimation. Localization techniques for sensor nodes can be classified into range-based techniques and range-free techniques [2]. Range-based techniques estimate location by the received signal strength indicator (RSSI) [3], the time of arrival (TOA) [4] and the angel of arrival (AOA) [5] etc.. They perform localization via geometric calculation. The range-based method using RSSI is the most feasible and suitable due to the hardware overhead and the energy saving. But, range-based localization methods

© Springer-Verlag Berlin Heidelberg 2015
L. Sun et al. (Eds.): CWSN 2014, CCIS 501, pp. 164–175, 2015.
DOI: 10.1007/978-3-662-46981-1_16

suffer from physical limitation and measurement error. Range-free localization methods do not use additional devices. So, range-free localization methods estimate the positions according to the network connectivity, and the localization output is an extent with considerable error. According to the difference of localization reference, the localization algorithm can be classified into absolute positioning scheme and relative positioning scheme. The former produces global standard coordinate, and the latter produces local relative coordinate. Each method has its own pros and cons. The multidimensional scaling (MDS) localization method can fulfill the both two schemes according to the configuration of network.

The MDS algorithms also can be classified into metric MDS and nonmetric MDS (NMDS) according to if it needs ranging or not [6]. The diversity matrix of metric MDS method comes from ranging, and the data are accurate comparatively. So it can reflect the similarity and the diversity of the entity quantitatively. While the nonmetric MDS has no special demand on the distance between nodes. Usually, the nonmetric MDS can gain a good performance only if the similarity or diversity of the node distance satisfies monotone increasing or monotone decreasing. It is found that the MDS localization methods always have significant error. The nonmetric MDS can get the approximate optimal solution via iterations, so it has higher tolerance to error. But, the localization accuracy of nonmetric MDS greatly depends on initial configuration.

In this paper, we proposed a new type of MDS localization method – RSSI-based MDS (RI-MDS) method. It combines the metric MDS scheme with the nonmetric MDS scheme. The initial position coordinates are calculated via metric MDS method, and construct the relative position relationship via iterative nonmetric MDS. Then we transform the relative localization coordinates to the absolute localization coordinates using mathematical method. With the rational cooperation of these two kinds of MDS methods, the localization accuracy was improved. In addition, our RI-MDS needs no special device equipped. Extensive simulation experiments and field experiments show that the performance and the practicability of RI-MDS method are good. The main contributions can be summarized as follows: (1) Improving the localization accuracy by combining the metric MDS method and the nonmetric MDS method, (2) improving the robustness by introducing the Maximum Likelihood Estimation (MLE) method to the affine transformation process.

The rest of this paper is organized as follows. A brief introduction to the state of art of the MDS localization methods is presented in Sect. 2. In Sect. 3, the details of our RI-MDS method is given. Performance analysis of our RI-MDS algorithm is provided in Sect. 4, and conclusions are drawn in Sect. 5.

2   Related Work

The MDS technology is widely used in psychometrics and psychophysics. It itself is a data analysis method on a group of data structures which represent distances using geometric figure. It is first applied in localization of wireless sensor networks by Yi Shang et al. [7], that is, we called their method as classical MDS algorithm (MDS-MAP). Latter, Yi Shang et al. improved the MDS-MAP in [8]. The MDS localization method has strong robustness and higher accuracy even in sparse network. Lots of MDS-like WSNs localization methods have been proposed in [9–11]. There are two ways to improve it (1) to develop new MDS methods based on distribute computation, (2) to improve the localization accuracy of the MDS method. In view of that the MDS method has a high computational time complexity, [12, 13] use the distributed MDS methods. They divided the whole network to several cluster. In each cluster, the head node fulfills the MDS method to work out the node local positions, and converts the local position coordinates to the global position coordinates by using the coordinates of some communal nodes. The distributed MDS method increases the network overhead and cause accumulative errors, although it can relieve the computation pressure. In this paper, we focus on how to improve the localization accuracy of centralized MDS method. In [14], Alon Amar et al. divide the sensor nodes to two groups according to the connectivity. Then they adopted MDS method in the group with the higher connectivity, and extended the localization process to another group by the least square method. The error accumulation makes the localization accuracy should be improved. Di Ma et al. [15] showed that the distance of nodes can be estimated by the hop counts which can be represented by a real number. However, the improvement of localization accuracy is trivial. Other researchers applied the rang-based MDS algorithm using the mobile anchor nodes [16]. Although the redundancy of dissimilarity matrix is increased, the anchor node with mobility is necessary, and the design of mobile path is thus complex. A linear WLS-based weighted MDS estimating method is proposed in [17], which can get an accuracy closed to Cramer–Rao Lower Bound (CRLB) for sufficiently small noise conditions, and it is modified to operate in partially connected WSN scenarios. Literature [18] estimates the distance of un-direct communicate nodes using the shortest possible theoretical distance instead of Dijkstra algorithm. Although it improves the dissimilarity matrix accuracy to some extent, but the improvement of localization accuracy is limited because of the lack of the subsequent error eliminate process. The most important research issues relating to centralized MDS method are how to generate the relative coordinates which can really reflect the monotonous relationship of nodes, and how to eliminate the error produced in the previous step.

3   RI-MDS Localization Algorithm

3.1   The Basic Idea of RI-MDS

The range-free MDS methods take advantage of the relationship in which the distances and the diversities of nodes are monotonous. It improves localization accuracy via iterative computation. Range-free methods have the great tolerance to the measurement error via iterative calculations. But the localization accuracy of the range-free MDS methods can be influenced largely by initial configuration. The value of RSSI suffers the impact of environment, but we can acquire the relatively actual initial location information of nodes by simplicity treatment. The impact of environment can be eliminated in some degree via iterative calculation of NMDS. The localization error also can be further eliminated in the coordinate translation process by introducing Maximum Likelihood Estimation (MLE).

According to the analysis mentioned above, we proposed the RI-MDS localization method which adopted the RSSI values to construct the dissimilarity matrix and utilized the NMDS method to calculate the relative coordinates. Sensor nodes collect the RSSI values t times to form the distance vector, and transmit the distance vectors to the sink node. Sink node constructs the dissimilarity matrix using the distance vectors. By combining metric-MDS method with the nonmetric MDS method, Sink node acquires the relative coordinates of sensor nodes, and then, the relative coordinates are transformed to the absolute coordinates. The algorithm flow of RI-MDS is depicted in Fig. 1.

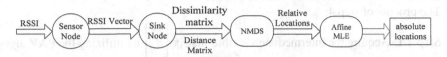

Fig. 1. Algorithm flow chart of RI-MDS

3.2 Algorithm Design and Description

The description of RI-MDS algorithm as follows:

Algorithm Input: RSSI distance vectors of nodes.
Algorithm Output: the absolute location coordinates of nodes.

The steps of RI-MDS algorithm:
Step 1: Sensor nodes collect the pairwise RSSI values for t times to form the distance vector, and transmit these distance vector to sink node.
Step 2: Sink node calculates the average RSSI, and acquires the ranging values according to the formula (1). The dissimilarity matrix $[p_{ij}]$ was constructed based on the ranging values.

$$d = 10^{\frac{Rssi-E}{10n}} \tag{1}$$

Where d denotes distance, E and n are constant which are related to the antenna gain and environment. The ranging value is influenced by the environment factor E greatly, but it can be degraded by the subsequent NMDS iterations.
Step 3: According to the known distance information, the average distance of single hop Dave can be acquired. Distances of nodes which can't communicate directly are estimated by the shortest path algorithm, then, the integrity of $[p_{ij}]$ is provided by adding these distances. Calculating the relative coordinate X^0 by using the classical MDS algorithm on the dissimilarity matrix $[p_{ij}]$ acquired in step 2. We can get the distance matrix $[d_{ij}^k]$ based on X^0.
Step 4: Calculate the relative position coordinate X^r of each node via nonmetric MDS algorithm.
Step 5: Select several anchor nodes (more than 3 non-collinear nodes in two-dimension space, and more than 4 un-coplanar nodes in three-dimension space). Convert the

relative coordinate X^r of every node to the absolute one by utilizing the affine transform based the absolute coordinates of these anchor nodes.

The step 4 is a key step; it adopted nonmetric MDS method to compute the coordinates of nodes iteratively such that the STRESS is satisfied. The detailed description as follows:

Input of step 4: the threshold value ε of the stress coefficient, and the initial position coordinate X^0 acquired in step 3.

Output of step 4: the relative position coordinates X^r of each node.

Initialization: initialize the iterations K as 0.

The process of step 4:

Step 4.1: Acquire the intermediate variable matrix $\left[\hat{d}_{ij}^k\right]$ by utilizing the PAV algorithm [19] on $\left[d_{ij}^k\right]$ and dissimilarity matrix $[p_{ij}]$ acquired in step 3. The value of $\hat{d}_{ij}^k$ must satisfied following conditions for any nodes a, b, c, and d, where $p_{ab} < p_{cd}$.

if $d_{ab}^k < d_{cd}^k$, then $\hat{d}_{ab}^k = d_{ab}^k$, $\hat{d}_{cd}^k = d_{cd}^k$.

If $d_{ab}^k \geq d_{cd}^k$, then $\hat{d}_{ab}^k = \hat{d}_{cd}^k = \frac{1}{2}\left(d_{ab}^k + d_{cd}^k\right)$.

Step 4.2: The iterations counter $K = K + 1$, calculate the new coordinate X_k of each node by utilizing the steepest descent method as formula (2).

$$X_i^k = X_i^{k-1} + \frac{a}{n-1} \sum_{i \neq j} \left(1 - \frac{\hat{d}_{ij}^{k-1}}{d_{ij}^{k-1}}\right)\left(X_j^{k-1} - X_i^{k-1}\right) \tag{2}$$

Where n stands for the number of nodes, a represents the iteration increment of the steepest descent method. Properly speaking, the value of a should be recalculated in every iteration. But, what the value of a can influence is not the result of algorithm but is the convergence. So we adopted $a = 0.2$ [20].

Step 4.3: Recalculate the pairwise distance information of nodes to update the distance matrix $\left[d_{ij}^k\right]$.

Step 4.4: Calculate the STRESS coefficient via formula (3), if the *STRESS* > ε, then go to step 4.2, otherwise, the step 4 is finished.

$$STRESS' = \sqrt{\frac{\sum_{i=0,j=0,i \neq j}^{n}\left(\hat{d}_{ij} - d_{ij}\right)^2}{\sum_{i=0,j=0,i \neq j}^{n} d_{ij}^2}} \tag{3}$$

The last step of the RI-MDS is coordinate transformation. Assumed (x_1, y_1), $(x_2, y_2) \cdots (x_m, y_m)$ is the relative position coordinates of m nodes, the corresponding absolute localization coordinates is (x'_1, y'_1), $(x'_2, y'_2) \cdots (x'_m, y'_m)$. The coordinate transformation matrix is acquired as formula (4) by applying mirror operation (optional), zoom operation, rotation and translation by sequence:

$$\begin{bmatrix} x'_m \\ y'_m \\ 1 \end{bmatrix} = \begin{bmatrix} \lambda \cos \theta & \pm \lambda \sin \theta & b_x \\ \lambda \sin \theta & \mp \lambda \cos \theta & b_y \\ 0 & 0 & 1 \end{bmatrix} \cdot \begin{bmatrix} x_m \\ y_m \\ 1 \end{bmatrix} \tag{4}$$

Where θ stands for the angle that coordinate axis rotates counter-clockwise around the origin, bx and by are movement distances of origin on the X axis and Y axis, respectively.

Apply the relative coordinates and the absolute coordinates of m nodes into formula (4), we get:

$$\begin{cases} x'_1 = \lambda \cos \theta x_1 \pm \lambda \sin \theta x_1 + b_x \\ x'_2 = \lambda \cos \theta x_2 \pm \lambda \sin \theta x_2 + b_x \\ \quad \vdots \\ x'_m = \lambda \cos \theta x_m \pm \lambda \sin \theta x_m + b_x \end{cases} \tag{5}$$

and

$$\begin{cases} y'_1 = \lambda \cos \theta y_1 \mp \lambda \sin \theta y_1 + b_y \\ y'_2 = \lambda \cos \theta y_2 \mp \lambda \sin \theta y_2 + b_y \\ \quad \vdots \\ y'_m = \lambda \cos \theta y_m \mp \lambda \sin \theta y_m + b_y \end{cases} \tag{6}$$

Acquire the estimated values of arguments $\lambda \sin \theta$, $\lambda \cos \theta$, b_x and b_y by applying the MLE method on (5) and (6). These values are in the sense of least mean square error. And we get the linear transformation equation:

$$\begin{cases} x' = \lambda \cos \theta x \pm \lambda \sin \theta y + b_x \\ y' = \lambda \sin \theta x \mp \lambda \cos \theta y + b_y \end{cases} \tag{7}$$

Acquire the absolute coordinates of the other n-m nodes via Applying (7) successively.

3.3 Algorithm Time Complexity Analysis

RI-MDS method has seven main steps as mentioned above, covered the Dijkstra shortest path algorithm, classical MDS method, nonmetric MDS method, affine transformation and coordinate transformation et.. Due to the RSSI information can be acquired easily, The RI-MDS method can be fulfilled conveniently. The time complexity analysis of these steps as follows:

The time complexity of Dijkstra shortest path algorithm is $O(n^2)$.

The time complexity of metric MDS is $O(n^2)$.

The time complexity of the nonmetric MDS is $O(n^4)$. This step is the most time consumption step, but in line with the variation of the stress coefficient, the number of iterations changed too. So, the RI-MDS has great flexibility.

The time complexity of affine transformation is $O(m^3)$, where m is the number of nodes that needed transformation.

The time complexity of the coordinate transformation is $O(n - m)$.

4 Experiments Analysis

4.1 Simulation Environment

To verify the effectiveness and the performance of RI-MDS, simulation experiments are conducted. Due to so many matrix calculations in MDS algorithm, the MATLAB simulator is suitable. For the performance comparison under different nodes deployments, we adopt two kinds of nodes deployments, the random deployment and grid deployment are tested respectively. In the grid deployment, the nodes are not set at the cross of the gird line preciously but with small deviation to the grid cross.

4.2 Wireless Propagation Model

The classical wireless propagation model with random interference is employed to simulate the RSSI variation. The model mentioned above is described as follows:

$$P(d)[dBm] = P(d_0)[dBm] - 10n\log(\frac{d}{d_0}) + X_\sigma \tag{8}$$

Where d stands for the distance between a couple of nodes, and d0 is the reference distance, n denotes the path-loss exponent, which can be from 2 to 4 generally. *P(d0)* represents the received signal strength where the distance of sender and receiver is d0, *P(d)* stands for the same meaning when the nodes distance is d. X_σ is the Gaussian white noise, which can be generated by Gaussian random function where the average value is 0 and the variance is σ. By utilizing above model, we can simulate the RSSI values where the nodes distance is given.

4.3 Simulation Experiment Design and Evaluation Indicators

The most commonly used indicators are the average localization error (ALE) and the localization error ratio (LER), these two indicators are given:

$$ALE = \frac{\sum_{i=1}^{n} \sqrt{\left(\left|x_i' - x_i\right|\right)^2}}{n} \tag{9}$$

$$LER = \frac{ALE}{r} \times 100\% \tag{10}$$

Where n denotes the number of nodes, X_i' represents the measuring coordinate of node i, X_i denotes the real coordinate of node i, and r stands the communication radius.

There are two parts in our experiment:

1. Performance comparison of the proposed algorithm under the random deployment and the grid deployment with different average connectivity. In the random deployment, 200 nodes are randomly scattered in an area of 1000*1000 unites, and the number of nodes in grid scene is depend on the grid unit length. Given the length of grid unit is 50 units. The network connectivity is adjusted by changing the communication radius. Furthermore, the number of beacons is 4.
2. LER comparison of the proposed RI-MDS method with the Improved MDS (IMDS) algorithm in [18] under two deployments with different connectivity. There are still 4 beacons and 200 nodes randomly scattered in the area of 1000*1000 units. The network connectivity is adjusted by changing the communication radius.

4.4   Simulation Result and Analysis

Simulation results (Fig. 1) suggest that along with the network average connectivity increased, the LER of the RI-MDS algorithm decline under both of these two deployments. And, the LER of the RI-MDS under grid deployment is better than under random deployment, especially in the low connectivity.

By analyzing the principle of RI-MDS algorithm, we know that there have regular distribution characteristics in the grid deployment. And, the diversities of nodes are mainly reflected in connectivity. As well as the connectivity of nodes are stable and enough. Hence the diversity of nodes is similar in redundancy, and the localization accuracy is relative mean. So we draw the conclusion mentioned above.

Furthermore, the localization accuracy of civil GPS system is about 10 m. While most of wireless sensor nodes have a communication radius about from 30 m to 50 m, the localization algorithm can be regard as practicable only when the LER is less than 25 %. The LER get the practicability when the network average connectivity is 8 and 14 under the two deployments as we can see in Fig. 1.

The results of second simulation experiment are shown in Figs. 2 and 3 respectively. We can draw a conclusion from the Figs. 2 and 3 that the LER of the RI-MDS method is 5 %–10 %, which is lower than the IMDS algorithm regardless of what deployment is used. We can also note that the LER decline trend of the IMDS is slow down when the network average connectivity increased to more than 16. However, the LER of RI-MDS method is declining along with the connectivity increasing in the same situation. The feature mentioned above became more obvious under the grid deployment.

4.5   Field Experiment and Analysis

The field experiments are fulfilled on the GAINSJ hardware platform. The sensor nodes of GAINSJ adopt the ZigBee integrated solution of Jennic Company, and support the IEEE802.15.4 protocol.

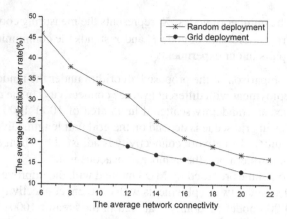

Fig. 2. Performance comparison of localization error of RI-MDS in different deployment

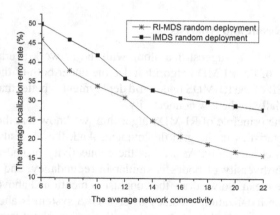

Fig. 3. Average network connectivity versus average localization error rate in random deployment scenario

The experiment scene (Fig. 4) is a rectangular area witch edge length is 12 m, and covered by small square gridding with 60 cm edge length. From N1 to N9 denote the position of 9 sensor nodes respectively. All of the nodes have the same configuration, and run the same program that pre-write by Flash Programmer.

The field experiment repeats 10 times and the number of beacon nodes is 4. We adopt the absolute localization error of every time to make comparison. The LER, maximum localization error and the minimum localization error are shown in Fig. 5.

The field experiment of [20] is based on the same hardware platform and the same scene, the typical value of LER in [20] is ranged from 2 m to 6 m, while the LER ranged from 1.5 m to 4 m when using the RI-MDS method. By comparison, it shows that the RI-MDS method has a better performance and higher localization accuracy (Fig. 6).

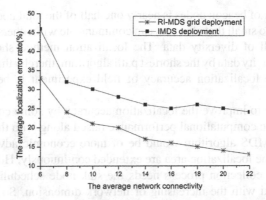

Fig. 4. Average network connectivity versus average localization error rate in gird deployment

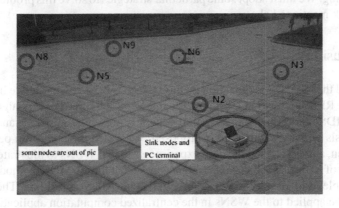

Fig. 5. Field experiment scenario

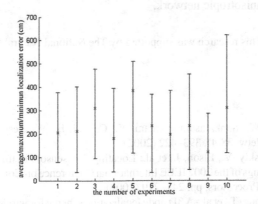

Fig. 6. The localization error of RI-MDS method

By comparing the experimental data, if we convert the average localization accuracy of field experiment to the LER value, the value is better than the LER in simulation.

Because the number of beacon nodes is nearly one-half of the total node numbers. And, the network size is so small that all nodes can communicate with others, thus the dissimilarity matrix is full of diversity data. The localization method should not have to supplement the diversity data by the shortest path algorithm, thereby the introduced error is reduced. So, the localization accuracy of field experiment is better than that in simulation.

So, it is feasible to improve the localization accuracy by some computational cost sacrificed, due to the computational performance raised along with the hardware price declining. The RI-MDS algorithm would be of more economic advantage when the network scale and the localization area are extended continuously. However, the localization information collection process needs the sink node scheduling, and the time complexity is raised with the increasing of network dimension. So the node energy consumption and the algorithm feasibility have to meet the challenge with the network scale increasing. We must adopt some particular strategies to solve this problem in large-scale network mentioned above.

5   Conclusion

We proposed the RI-MDS localization method which is based on hardware information ranging. The RI-MDS method takes full advantage of both metric MDS algorithm and nonmetric MDS algorithm. The algorithm design is presented in detail, and the theoretical analysis of RI-MDS method is proposed. We tested the algorithm performance via simulation, and performed the field experiments in real WSNs to illustrate the actual performance of RI-MDS. All the experiments prove that the RI-MDS method is feasible and practicable, and its performance is better than IMDS algorithm. The RI-MDS method can be applied to the WSNs in the centralized computation applications. In the future, we are going to develop the cluster-based RI-MDS method to meet the demand of high accuracy in anisotropic network.

Acknowledgments.   This research was supported by The National Natural Science Foundation of China (61379023).

References

1. Akyildiz, F., Su, W., Sankarasubramaniam, Y., Cayirci, E.: Wireless sensor networks: a survey. Comput. Netw. **38**(4), 393–422 (2002)
2. Girod, L., Bychovskiy, V., Elson, J., et al.: Locating tiny sensors in time and space: a case study. In: Proceedings of the 2002 IEEE International Conference on Computer Design: VLSI in Computers and Processors, pp. 241–219 (2002)
3. Shi, Q., Huo, H., Fang, T., et al.: A 3D node localization scheme for wireless sensor networks. IEICE Electron. **6**(3), 167–172 (2009)
4. Niculescu, D., Nath, B.: Ad hoc positioning system (APS) using AOA. In: Proceedings of the 22nd Annual Joint Conference of the IEEE Computer and Communication Societies (INFOCOM 2003), vol. 3, pp. 1734–1743 (2003)

5. Wu, G., Wang, S., Wang, B., et al.: A novel range-free localization based on regulated neighborhood distance for wireless ad hoc and sensor networks. Comput. Netw. **56**, 3581–3593 (2012)
6. France, S.L., Carroll, J.D.: Two-way multidimensional scaling: a review. IEEE Trans. Syst. Man Cybern.—part C Appl. Rev. **41**(5), 644–661 (2011)
7. Shang, Y., Ruml, W., Zhang, Y., et al.: Localization from mere connectivity. In: Proceedings of ACM MobiHoc, Annapolis, MD, NY, pp. 201–212 (2003)
8. Shang, Y., Ruml, W.: Improved MDS-based localization. In: Twenty-Third Annual Joint Conference on IEEE Computer and Communications Societies (INFOCOM 2004), vol. 4, pp. 2640–2651 (2004)
9. Latsoudas, G., Sidiropoulos, N.D.: A fast and effective multidimensional scaling approach for node localization in wireless sensor networks. IEEE Trans. Signal Process. **55**(10), 5121–5127 (2007)
10. Wei, H., Wan, Q., Chen, Z., et al.: A novel weighted multidimensional scaling analysis for time-of-arrival-based mobile location. IEEE Trans. Signal Process. **55**(4), 1511–1524 (2008)
11. Stone, K., Camp, T.: A survey of distance-based wireless sensor network localization techniques. Int. J. Pervasive Comput. Commun. **8**(2), 158–184 (2012)
12. Shon, M., Jo, M., Choo, H.: An interactive cluster-based MDS localization scheme for multimedia information in wireless sensor networks. Comput. Commun. **35**, 1921–1929 (2012)
13. Ding, Y., Du, L., Yang, T., et al.: Distributed localization algorithm for wireless sensor network based on multidimensional scaling and the shortest path distance correction. Trans. Tianjin Univ. **15**, 237–244 (2009)
14. Amar, A., Wang, Y., Leus, G.: Extending the classical multidimensional scaling algorithm given partial pairwise distance measurements. IEEE Signal Process. Lett. **17**(5), 473–476 (2010)
15. Ma, D., Er, M.J., Wang, B.: Range-free wireless sensor networks localization based on hop-count quantization. Telecommun. Syst. **50**(3), 199–213 (2012)
16. Kim, E., Lee, S., Kim, C., et al.: Mobile beacon-based 3D-localization with multidimensional scaling in large sensor networks. IEEE Commun. Lett. **14**(7), 647–649 (2010)
17. Chan, F., So, H.C.: Efficient weighted multidimensional scaling for wireless sensor network localization. IEEE Trans. Signal Process. **57**(11), 4548–4553 (2009)
18. Stojkoska, B.R., Kirandziska, V.: Improved MDS-based algorithm for nodes localization in wireless sensor networks. In: EuroCon, pp. 608–612 (2013)
19. Kruskal, J.B.: Multidimensional scaling by optimizing goodness of fit to a nonmetric hypothesis. Psychometrika **29**(1), 1–27 (1964)
20. Peng, X., Li, R., Luo, J.: Nonmetric MDS-based Localization Algorithm in Wireless Sensor Networks. Comput. Sci. **35**(10), 219–223 (2008). (in Chinese with English abstract)

Study on Tree-Based Clustering MDS Algorithm for Nodes Localization in WSNs

Guoyong Dai[1,2], Chunyu Miao[1], Yidong Li[1], Keji Mao[1], and Qingzhang Chen[1(✉)]

[1] College of Computer Science and Technology,
Zhejiang University of Technology, Hangzhou 310023, China
qzchen@zjut.edu.cn
[2] College of Information Science and Technology,
Zhejiang Shuren University, Hangzhou 310014, China

Abstract. Localization of sensors nodes is a key and fundamental issue in WSNs due to random deployment. In this paper, we propose a tree based clustering (TBC) multidimensional scaling algorithm for wireless sensor networks with the purpose of overcoming the shortage of classical MDS algorithms in its localization accuracy and computing complexity. Clustering is adopted to degrade the problem scale in our approach and a moderate number of common nodes between clusters are kept during clustering. Inner cluster local coordinates are calculated and then mapped into global coordinates according the tree structure formed by clustering. The simulations on MATLAB are conducted and the results show that the proposed algorithm has better localization coverage and higher accuracy than the traditional MDS based algorithms.

Keywords: WSN · Multidimensional scaling · Clustering · Tree

1 Introduction

Wireless sensor networks (WSNs) have attracted a great deal of research interests due to their potential applications in military, environmental monitoring, medical care, etc. [1–4]. Especially with the blossom of the Internet of Things (IOT) and cloud computing in recent years, WSNs have been fundamental infrastructures of IOT and cloud computing for data gathering. The initial locations of sensor nodes are uncertain since nodes are randomly scattered in many application scenarios [2, 4–6]. Besides, many subsequent environmental factors (such as winds, streams etc.) may make the locations of nodes change after deployment. Locations of sensor nodes are uncontrollable to some extent. However, data unassociated with its position may make no sense in many applications. Equipping all the sensor nodes with a global positioning system (GPS) is a direct but not available way since its considerable costs. Therefore localization of sensor nodes in WSNs is one of the most critical and fundamental tasks.

Supported by the National Natural Science Foundation of China under Grant No. 61379023.

L. Sun et al. (Eds.): CWSN 2014, CCIS 501, pp. 176–186, 2015.
DOI: 10.1007/978-3-662-46981-1_17

Localization algorithms in WSNs can be classified as centralized algorithms and distributed algorithms. The centralized approaches, which use a powerful node (sink node) to calculate the position of each node, are disadvantageous due to the computational limitation of sensor nodes. Multi-dimensional Scaling (MDS) is a typical centralized algorithm. However, the centralized algorithms may not be available in large scale WSNs owing to the heavy computation and communication cost. A MDS-based distributed approach is proposed in this paper which employs the concept of clustering to degrade the problem scale. Our contributions are: (1) we devised a competitive mechanism to carry out the cluster heads in which the nodes' capability of recruiting members is used as the main competitive factor. So that very small clusters with only very few nodes can be avoided. (2) In our approach, cluster numbers and overlaps between clusters are well controlled and a tree structure is formed to help mapping to global coordinates from local coordinates in cluster.

The rest of the paper is organized as follows. Section 2 discusses the related works. Section 3 describes the proposed tree-based clustering MDS algorithm in detail. Section 4 provides the simulation and result analysis. Finally, Sect. 5 concludes the paper.

2 Related Works

Current localization approaches can be categorized as range-based and range-free [2, 4, 7, 8]. Range estimation hardware is employed to estimate the distance between sensor nodes and key techniques such as received signal strength indicator (RSSI), angle of arrival (AOA), time of arrival (TOA) and time difference of arrival (TDOA) are used in range-based schemes. Range-free algorithms use the connectivity of sensor nodes to estimate their positions. Distance vector (DV) hop, centroid system, and approximate point in triangulation (APIT) are typical range-free algorithms. Y. Liu and Z. Yang have made great effort to the localization and localizability problem in WSN and have proposed many effective localization methods, such as confidence based iterative localization [9], mobile beacon based non-iterative localization [10], component based localization in sparse wireless networks [11], etc.

MDS, which has its origins in psychometrics and psychophysics [4] and views similarities between data as distances, is now employed in localization approaches in WSNs. MDS-MAP [12] is the first MDS-based localization method proposed in 2003 by Shang Yi et al. The connectivity information is used to compute the shortest path between all pairs of nodes in order to approximate the missing entries of the distance matrix in this method. Then if a sufficient number of anchor nodes are known, the absolute coordinates of all nodes can be determined. Since the shortest path distance is not the true Euclidean distance, MDS-MAP does not work well in case of irregularly-shaped WSNs. Shang Yi et al. developed another distributed method called MDS-MAP(P) in 2004 [13]. It build a local map for each node and its neighbors, then merge these maps together to get a global map. However the precision of MDS-MAP(P) in range-free mode is still to be improved.

Inspired from these classical algorithms, many other derived algorithms based on MDS are proposed. R. Iyengar and B. Sikdar proposed a scalable and distributed localization scheme for WSNs [14]. The idea of clustering is adopted in this scheme for the coordinates formation wherein a small subset of the nodes, then the local relative coordinates are used to establish the coordinate system for the whole network. The cluster head is randomly chosen in this scheme. The heavy communication caused by excessive clusters and repetitive computation cause by excessive overlaps between clusters may lead to overhead costs for sensor nodes. A range-based weighted MDS algorithm is proposed in reference [15], which can be operated in partially connected WSNs. CMDS [16] is also proposed to improve the accuracy and computational complexity of classical MDS method by using k-hop clustering. The value of k is not clearly introduced. However, it may affect the performance of this algorithm. IMDS [17] improves MDS by distance matrix refinement in order to decrease distance matrix error in classical MDS. Though the accuracy is improved, the computational complexity is still remained.

3 The TBC-MDS Approach

The principle idea of this method is the divide and rule strategy by which a large scale WSN is divided into several small clusters. Then the MDS based localization algorithm is applied in each cluster to calculate the local coordinates which will be mapped into global coordinates. The whole localization procedure can be illustrated by three phases: clustering phase, inner-cluster localization phase and global coordinates mapping phase.

3.1 Tree-Based Clustering and Inner-Cluster Localization

Here we define some states for the sensor nodes during the clustering phase.

- CH (Cluster Head): Obviously, it means a sensor node in this state is a cluster header. Only the root node is initiated to this state.
- NM (Non-Member): It means a sensor node in this state hasn't join in any cluster ever. All nodes except the root node are initiated to this state.
- CM (Cluster Member): It means a sensor node in this state is a member of a specific cluster.
- BN (Border Node): It means a sensor node in this state has joint in more than two different clusters.
- CHC (Cluster Head Candidate): It means a sensor node in this state is qualified for competing to be a cluster head. In another word, it is a candidate for cluster head.
- END: Simply it means the ending.

These states can be transited under certain condition. The procedures of state transition are shown in Fig. 1. Each number in Fig. 1 represents a transition from one state to another. Init1() and Init2() are two initialization procedures. All the procedures will be described in pseudo code and some symbols are explained in Table 1.

Init1() is an initialization for a cluster head and Init2() is an initialization for a non-member node.

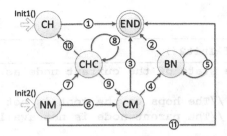

Fig. 1. State transition diagram during the clustering phase

Table 1. Identifiers in the pseudo codes

Symbols	Explanations
State	A variable to save the current state for the node, its value can be CH, NM, CM, BN, CHC, FAIL
Hop	A variable to save the number of hops from the current node to the root
Parent	A variable to save the parent node in the tree structure
CH[]	A variable to save the cluster heads for the current node
NB[]	A variable to save the neighbors for the current node
P_CH[]	A variable to save the candidate for parent node
b	A parameter for head competing, implicate the number of members that the current node can recruit if it is a cluster head
B[]	A variable to save the neighbors' b parameters
Timer1	The primary timer which is started when initiating the algorithm and the algorithm will be force to quit when time is up
Timer2	The timer for receiving messages which is started when a message is received
Recruit	It is a message name with the structure of (Recruit, u, Hop, Mu[]), where Recruit is a tag, u is the ID of sender, Hop is the value of the variable Hop and Mu[] is the set of neighbor nodes. This message is always sent by a cluster head to notify its neighbors to join in the cluster
Relay	It is a message name with the structure of (Relay, u, Hop, Mu[]), where Reply is a tag, other parameters is a direct copy from the Recruit message it received. This message is always sent by a node who received a Recruit message. If a non-member node receives a Replay message, value of P_CH[] should be updated and decide if to compete for cluster head
UpdateB	It is a message name with the structure of (UpdateB, u, bu), where UpdateB is a tag, u is the ID of sender and bu is the value of the variable b. A node broadcast this message to its neighbors to notify its value of the variable b

- Init1

Pseudo code of Init1()

```
1   State=CH;  //Set the state of the current node as CH
2   Hop=0;
3   //Set the current node itself as its parent node
    Parent=&this;
```

- Init2

Pseudo code of Init2()

1   // Set the state of the current node as NM
      State=NM;

2   Hop=-1;   //The hops to the root is not available
3   Parent=0; //The parent node is not available
4   CH[]=∅;
5   NB[]=∅;
6   P_CH[]=∅;
7   b=0;
8   B[]=∅;
9   Timer1=T1;
10   Timer2=-1;

The following transition procedures are presented in the order of first executed in the clustering algorithm.

- Transition ①

Pseudo code of Transition ①
1   IF(State==CH)
2   IF(NB[]==∅)
//Neighbor discovering
3   NB[]=Find_My_Neighbor();
4   END IF
5   Mu[]=NB[];

6   //Build a *Recruit* Message
      Send_Msg=(Recruit,u,Hop,Mu[]);

7   Send_Msg.send(); //Send the *Recruit* Message
8   EXIT(); //Go to the state of END
9   END IF

- Transition ⑥ or ⑨

Pseudo code of Transition ⑥ or ⑨
1   IF(Received_Msg==(Recruit,u,Hop,Mu[]) &&   (State==NM||CHC))
2   CH[]←u; //Put u into the set CH[]
3   State=CM;
4   Send_Msg=(Relay,u,Hop,Mu[]);
5   Send_Msg.send();
6   END IF

- Transition ⑦ is a stringent conditional procedure, which means the state of current node won't change if not all these conditions are satisfied.

```
Pseudo code of Transition ⑦
1    IF(Received_Msg==(Relay,u,Hop,Mu[]) && (State==NM))
2      IF(NB[]==∅)
3        NB[]=Find_My_Neighbor(); //Neighbor discovering
4      END IF
5      IF(NB[] Mu[]>=3)
6        P_CH[] ← [1];
7        State=CHC;
8      END IF
9      IF(P_CH[] !=∅)
10       Parent=the node in P_CH[] with the minimum Hop
     value;
11       Hop=P_CH[Parent]+1;
12       b=(NB[]-(NB[] Mu[])).size; //b is the number of
     nodes in NB[] but not in Mu[]
13       Send_Msg=(UpdateB,v,b);  //v is the ID of current
     node
14       Send_Msg.send();
15     END IF
16   END IF
```

- Transition ⑧ is a reflexive procedure which will not change the state of the current node.

```
Pseudo code of Transition ⑧
1    IF(Received_Msg==(Relay,u,Hop,Mu[]) && (State==CHC))
2      execute Line 2 to Line 14 in Transition ⑦;
3    ELSE IF(Received_Msg==(UpdateB,u,b) &&
     (State==CHC||NM))
4      B[] ← {u,b};
5    END IF
```

- Transition ⑩

```
Pseudo code of Transition ⑩
1    IF(State==CHC && Timer2 time`s up && b>max(B[].b))

2      State=CH;
3    END IF
```

- Transition ④ or ⑤

```
Pseudo code of Transition ④ or ⑤
1   IF(Received_Msg==(Recruit,u,Hop,Mu[]))&&(State==CM||BN)
    )
2       CH[]←u;
3       State=BN;
4       Send_Msg=(Relay,u,Hop,Mu[]);
5       Send_Msg.send();
6   END IF
```

- Transition ② or ③

```
Pseudo code of Transition ② or ③
1   IF(Timer2 is up && (State==CM||BN))
2       EXIT();
3   END IF
```

- Transition ⑪

```
Pseudo code of Transition ⑪
1   IF(Timer1 is up)
2       IF(State==NM)
3           State=FAIL; //Set the state of current node as
            FAIL
4       END IF
5       EXIT();
6   END IF
```

The whole clustering algorithm can be explained as follows:

(1) A sensor node in the center of the WSN, which may have many neighbors, should be manually chosen as the root node.
(2) Once the root node is identified, it is initiated as a cluster head. Find_My_Neighber() and Recruit() functions are executed sequentially by the root to discover its neighbors and to recruit cluster members.
(3) A node joins in the cluster once received a Recruit message and sends a Relay message to its neighbors. If a node is already a member of a cluster when it receives a new Recruit message, it is then a border node.
(4) Find_My_Neighber() function is executed when a node receives a Relay message to discover its neighbor nodes. The intersection of its neighbors and the neighbors of the cluster head indicated in the Relay messages are carried out. If the elements in the intersection are more than three, the head is recognized as a parent candidate and the current node itself turns into a head candidate.

(5) The head candidate choose the node with the minimum hops to the root from P_CH[] as its parent and calculate its potential cluster member count which will be delivered to other head candidates in an UpdateB message.

(6) One node with the maximum value of b will make itself as a cluster head when Timer2 is up. And then send a Recruit message to recruit members.

(7) All the above operations will be repeated until Timer1 is up.

After the clustering phase is accomplished, the classical MDS method [8] is applied to in each cluster to carry out the local coordinates.

3.2 Clusters Merging Phase

The local coordinates of each sensor node in cluster are mapped into global coordinates by traversing the tree in the depth-first order. Border nodes, which have more than one local coordinates, play as the intermediary in the mapping process. The affine transformation details are described as follows.

Suppose there are m nodes with their local coordinates (x_1, y_1), (x_2, y_2), ..., (x_m, y_m), and their corresponding global coordinates are (x_1', y_1'), (x_2', y_2'), ..., (x_m', y_m'). The global coordinates (x_m', y_m') can be carried out by Formula (1).

$$\begin{bmatrix} x_m' \\ y_m' \\ 1 \end{bmatrix} = \begin{bmatrix} \lambda \cos\theta & \pm\lambda\sin\theta & b_x \\ \lambda\sin\theta & \mp\lambda\cos\theta & b_y \\ 0 & 0 & 1 \end{bmatrix} \cdot \begin{bmatrix} x_m \\ y_m \\ 1 \end{bmatrix} \tag{1}$$

In order to get the parameters λ, θ, b_x and b_y, the coordinates of the m nodes should be substituted into Formula (1). Then we get the equation set (2) and (3).

$$\begin{cases} x_1' = \lambda\cos\theta x_1 \pm \lambda\sin\theta x_1 + b_x \\ x_2' = \lambda\cos\theta x_2 \pm \lambda\sin\theta x_2 + b_x \\ \qquad\vdots \\ x_m' = \lambda\cos\theta x_m \pm \lambda\sin\theta x_m + b_x \end{cases} \tag{2}$$

$$\begin{cases} y_1' = \lambda\cos\theta y_1 \mp \lambda\sin\theta y_1 + b_y \\ y_2' = \lambda\cos\theta y_2 \mp \lambda\sin\theta y_2 + b_y \\ \qquad\vdots \\ y_m' = \lambda\cos\theta y_m \mp \lambda\sin\theta y_m + b_y \end{cases} \tag{3}$$

MLE (Maximum Likelihood Estimation) is applied to get the value of these parameters in the sense of MMSE (Minimum Mean Square Error) and finally we get the following linear equations in Formula (4).

$$\begin{cases} x' = \lambda\cos\theta x \pm \lambda\sin\theta y + b_x \\ y' = \lambda\sin\theta x \mp \lambda\cos\theta y + b_y \end{cases} \tag{4}$$

4 Simulation and Discussion

4.1 Simulation Setting

Computer simulations on Matlab are conducted to evaluate the performance of the proposed approach. We consider that there are 200 sensor nodes randomly deployed in a square of 1000 m × 1000 m. The communication range of each sensor node is variable, and different degrees of connectivity are simulated by setting different communication ranges of sensor nodes.

4.2 Evaluation Criteria

The average positioning error ratio (APER) and positioning coverage ratio (PCR) are mainly considered to evaluate the performance of our approach.

APER is defined in Formula (5), where n is the total number of sensor nodes, r is the communication range of sensor nodes, (x_i', y_i') and (x_i, y_i) are the localization result and true coordinates respectively.

$$APER = \frac{\sum_{i=1}^{n} \sqrt{(x_i' - x_i)^2 + (y_i' - y_i)^2}}{nr} \times 100\% \qquad (5)$$

PCR is defined in Formula (6), where N_P is the number of positioned nodes and n is the total number of sensor nodes. Higher PRC means strong capability of localization.

$$PCR = \frac{N_P}{n} \times 100\% \qquad (6)$$

4.3 Results and Discussion

Our proposed TBC-MDS algorithm is compared with SDGPSN [11] algorithm in PCR with different average connectivity degree of nodes (Fig. 2). The result shows that PCR increases as the connectivity degree increases. The PCR of TBC-MDS is more than 90 % in case of the average connectivity degree reached 12, while the PCR of SDGPSN is only 60 %. When the average connectivity degree reached 14, only one node is not positioned with the TBC-MDS algorithm, the PCR of which is much higher than SDGPSN algorithm. But when the average connectivity degree is more than 18, the PCR of the two algorithms tend to be closer.

By analyzing the clustering procedure of the two algorithms, it is known that clustering mechanism in SDGPSN is randomly head election which may lead to uneven distribution of clusters and the number of border nodes is uncontrollable. Even isolated clusters or isolated nodes may exist. That will further result in unavailability of mapping local coordinates into global. Therefore some nodes cannot be positioned with SDGPSN. Conversely, the clustering procedure is much more controllable in out

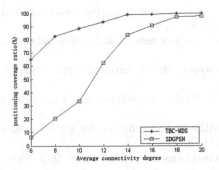   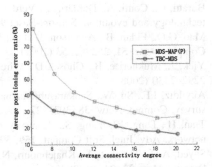

Fig. 2. PCR in different connectivity degrees   **Fig. 3.** APER comparison of different algorithms

scheme. It is ensured that there are enough border nodes unless there are isolated nodes which are not connectable to the root node because of the constraints of communication range. That is why the PCR of our approach is higher than SDGPSN.

The APER accuracy comparison of the well-known MDS-MAP(P) and the proposed TBC-MDS is shown in Fig. 3. Obviously, it can be seen that both of the two algorithms have lower average positioning error ratio when the connectivity degree increases. But on the whole, our algorithm has a higher accuracy than MDS-MAP(P), especially in low connectivity degree cases.

5 Conclusion and Future Work

A tree based clustering MDS algorithm for node localization in WSN is devised in this paper. The inner-cluster local coordinates are carried out by applying traditional MDS method after clusters are formed and then mapped into global coordinates. The simulation results show that TBC-MDS has a high positioning coverage ratio and low average positioning error ratio. It works better than classical MDS methods especially in low connectivity scenarios or sparse networks. As it is a distributed algorithm with high coverage and accuracy, it can be applied in large scale WSNs.

As the sensor nodes are battery-operated, the energy is highly limited. The energy consumption of localization algorithms is crucial though it is not addressed in this paper. As a future work, we will do some further research on energy consumption of node localization.

References

1. Viani, F., Rocca, P., Oliveri, G., Trinchero, D.: A.: Massa, Localization, tracking, and imaging of targets in wireless sensor networks: an invited review. Radio Sci. **46**, 1–12 (2011)
2. Cheng, L., Wu, C.D., Zhang, Y.Z., Wu, H., Li, M.X., Maple, C.: A survey of localization in wireless sensor network. Int. J. Distrib. Sens. Netw. **2012**, 1–12 (2012)

3. Buratti, C., Conti, A., Dardari, D., Verdone, R.: An overview on wireless sensor networks technology and evolution. Sensors-Basel **9**, 6869–6896 (2009)

4. Mao, G.Q., Fidan, B., Anderson, B.D.O.: Wireless sensor network localization techniques. Comput. Netw. **51**, 2529–2553 (2007)

5. Yick, J., Mukherjee, B., Ghosal, D.: Wireless sensor network survey. Comput. Netw. **52**, 2292–2330 (2008)

6. Akyildiz, I.F., Su, W., Sankarasubramaniam, Y., Cayirci, E.: Wireless sensor networks: a survey. Comput. Netw. **38**, 393–422 (2002)

7. Tian, H., Ding, Y., Yang, S.: A survey on MDS-Based localization for wireless sensor network. Adv. Intel. Soft Comput. **159**, 399–403 (2012)

8. Sayed, A.H., Tarighat, A., Khajehnouri, N.: Network-based wireless location. IEEE Signal Process. Mag. **22**, 24–40 (2005)

9. Yang, Z., Liu, Y.: Quality of trilateration: confidence-based iterative localization. IEEE Trans. Parallel Distrib. Syst. **21**, 631–640 (2010)

10. He, Y., Liu, Y., Shen, X., Mo, L., Dai, G.: Noninteractive localization of wireless camera sensors with mobile beacon. IEEE Trans. Mob. Comput. **12**, 333–345 (2013)

11. Wang, X., Luo, J., Liu, Y., Li, S., Dong, D.: Component-based localization in sparse wireless networks. IEEE/ACM Trans. Netw. (ToN) **19**, 540–548 (2011)

12. Shang, Y., Ruml, W., Zhang, Y., Fromherz, M.: Localization from mere connectivity. In: The 4th ACM International Symposium on Mobile Ad Hoc Networking & Computing, pp. 201–212. ACM, New York (2003)

13. Shang, Y., Ruml, W., Zhang, Y., Fromherz, M.: Localization from connectivity in sensor networks. IEEE Trans. Parallel Distrb. Syst. **15**, 961–974 (2004)

14. Iyengar, R., Sikdar, B.: Scalable and distributed GPS free positioning for sensor networks. In: IEEE International Conference on Communications 2003, pp. 338–342. IEEE Communications Society, Anchorage (2003)

15. Chan, F.K.W., So, H.C.: Efficient weighted multidimensional scaling for wireless sensor network localization. IEEE Trans. Signal Process. **57**, 4548–4553 (2009)

16. Shon, M., Jo, M., Choo, H.: An interactive cluster-based MDS localization scheme for multimedia information in wireless sensor networks. Comput. Commun. **35**, 1921–1929 (2012)

17. Stojkoska, B., Kirandziska, V.: Improved MDS-based algorithm for nodes localization in wireless sensor networks. In: EUROCON 2013, pp. 608–613. IEEE, Zagreb (2013)

Theoretical and Experimental Analysis of WiFi Location Fingerprint Sampling Period

Qin Wu, Hao Lin, and Jiuzhen Liang[✉]

Department of Computer Science, Jiangnan University,
Jiangsu, Wuxi 214122, China
jzliang@jiangnan.edu.cn

Abstract. Indoor positioning with smartphones is of great importance for a lot of applications and has attracted many researchers' interests these years. Received Signal Strength (RSS) fingerprinting has been considered as an efficient method for indoor positioning. Numerous systems have been developed based on it. Location fingerprint sampling is the first step of the RSS fingerprinting method. Slow sampling speed will delay the positioning speed and will reduce the accuracy if the tracking object is moving. Theoretically, the sampling period is about one fingerprint per second. However, our experiments on some Android phones/pads show that it may even take more than 10 s to sample a fingerprint occasionally. By analyzing the Android WiFi scanning framework, it is easy to find which part of the fingerprint sampling process costs more time. After theoretically analysis and experimental measurement, we provide some suggestions on how to improve sampling speed on some practical WiFi positioning system architectures. To contribute to the research community of WiFi positioning, we make all our measurement codes and our data sets available as open source.

Keywords: Indoor positioning · WiFi · Location fingerprint · Sampling period · Android

1 Introduction

Indoor positioning with smartphones is critical for many applications. In many environment (e.g. airport terminals, conferences, shopping malls), indoor positioning of mobile phones helps users to realize indoor navigation or find friends. Hospitals can use it to take care of patients. Businesses need it to analyze customers' group behaviour [1].

There are many methods for indoor positioning. And these methods can be roughly classified into three categories: ranging based TOA/TDOA (Time of Arrival/Time Differential of Arrival) [2], Radio Frequency (RF) Fingerprinting [3,4], and Inertial Sensor based dead-reckoning [5]. WiFi Received Signal Strength (RSS) Fingerprinting belongs to RF Fingerprinting. It is one of the most outstanding indoor positioning methods. It depends on the WiFi RSS of smartphones. Current work on WiFi RSS Fingerprinting mainly focuses on design

© Springer-Verlag Berlin Heidelberg 2015
L. Sun et al. (Eds.): CWSN 2014, CCIS 501, pp. 187–197, 2015.
DOI: 10.1007/978-3-662-46981-1_18

and implementation of WiFi based positioning systems [4,6], cutting down the workload of WiFi site surveys [7], and improving the robustness of indoor positioning [8,9].

The procedure of RSS Fingerprinting can be divided into two stages: offline stage and online stage. During the *offline* stage, a site survey is performed in the location area. The collected location coordinates/labels and their correlation RSS from nearby Access Points (APs) are saved into a database (also called Radiomap). During the *online* stage, a location positioning technique uses the currently observed RSS and previously collected information to calculate the estimated location.

The **fingerprint sampling** is the first step for both offline stage and online stage. It is often overlooked by many researchers. In this paper, the WiFi RSS Fingerprint sampling speed procedure is analyzed theoretically based on IEEE 802.11 scanning scheme. And we did many experiments to measure the sampling speed with different android phones/pads. Based on the theoretically analysis and experimental measurements, fingerprint sampling selection strategies are proposed for different indoor positioning system architectures. In order to contribute to the WiFi positioning research community, we make all our data and codes available as open source.

The rest of the paper is organized as follows. Section 2 introduces the IEEE 802.11 channel scanning mechanism, which is the theoretical foundation of WiFi fingerprint sampling. In Sect. 3, Android WiFi scanning framework is introduced and some experimental observations are presented. Some WiFi fingerprint sampling strategies on different WiFi positioning system architectures are proposed in Sect. 4. And conclusions are made in Sect. 5.

2 IEEE 802.11 Channel Scanning

Two scanning methods are defined in the IEEE 802.11 [10]: *passive scanning* and *active scanning*, which are depend on the *ScanType* parameter of the MLME-SCAN.request primitive. In the following, we discuss these two methods in details and calculate the sampling period via theoretical analysis.

2.1 Passive Scanning

In the passive scanning (as shown in Fig. 1(a)), the Station(STA) switches to a candidate channel and waits for a periodical Beacon from any AP on that channel to announce its presence. Since the time span of beacons generated by different AP is independent, the STA must therefore wait for a full period on each channel. Thus,

$$t_{passive} = N_{channel} \cdot T_{beacon} \tag{1}$$

where $t_{passive}$ is the total time for a round of passive scanning, $N_{channel}$ is the number of channels used by the passive scanning, $N_{channel}$ is less than or equal to the total number of channels used in a country. For example, there are 13 channels available for usage in the 802.11 2.4 GHz WiFi frequency range in China.

With all the 13 channels to be scanned and a beacon period of 102.4 ms, it will take roughly 1.33 s (we do not consider the channel switch time at this moment) for a sampling period. The passive scanning scheme assumes that the target is at a fixed location during the sampling period. However, in real application, the target is usually moving. Suppose a person walks at a speed 2 m/s and starts from the origin, then the distance that person walked is $2\,m/s \times 1.33\,s = 2.66\,m$ after one sampling period. One may find that the sampling result is actually a blur line in the interval $[0\,m, 2.66\,m]$ of the walking distance. We call it motion blur. On the other hand, if fingerprints from several sampling periods are collected and their average is used to determine the location of an AP, then slow fingerprint sampling speed will influence the result badly.

2.2 Active Scanning

In the active scanning (Fig. 1(b)), the STA will do the following procedure, when it receives a MLME-SCAN.request primitive whose *ScanType* parameter is set as ACTIVE.

1. Wait until the *ProbeDelay* time has expired or a PHYRxStart.indication primitive has been received.
2. Contenting the media to send out the *ProbeRequest* frame.
3. Starting a *ProbeTimer*.
4. If the STA didn't receive any frame before the *ProbeTimer* reaches *MinChannelTime*, then the STA scans the next channel. Otherwise, the STA has to wait until the *ProbeTimer* reaches *MaxChannelTime*, then scans the next channel.

To determine the active scanning period, there are five parameters: *ProbeDelay*, *media contention time*, *MinChannelTime*, *MaxChannelTime*, and *channel switching time*. The default value of *ProbeDelay* is negligible (<1 ms) [11,12]. And on lightly loaded networks, the value of *media contention time* is also negligibly small. The settings of *MinChannelTime* and *MaxChannelTime* have attracted many research's attentions [13,14]. The *MinChannelTime* is recommended to be set as 6–7 ms, and *MaxChannelTime* is recommended to be set as 10–15 ms by [13]. The last parameter, *channel switching time*, is dependent of 802.11 cards.

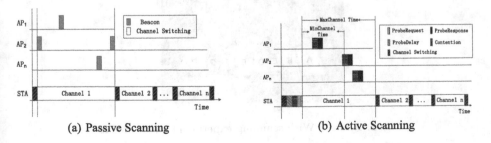

(a) Passive Scanning   (b) Active Scanning

Fig. 1. Two types of scanning

For example, it is around 2.9 ms for cards with Intel chipsets, 4.8 ms for cards with Atheros chipsets [15] and 19 ms for cards with Intersil Prism2 chipsets [11]. Thus, the idealized bound of active scanning is calculated as

$$N_{channel} \cdot T_{min} \leq t_{active} \leq N_{channel} \cdot T_{max} \tag{2}$$

where $N_{channel}$ is the number of channels used to do active scanning, T_{min} is MinChannelTime, T_{max} is MaxChannelTime, t_{active} is the sampling period for active scanning. If taking the hardware dependent channel switching time into account, we should plus $(N_{channel} - 1) \cdot T_{switch}$, where T_{switch} is the channel switching time. Since the smallest channel switching time of the above three chipsets is 2.9 ms, MinChannelTime is 6 ms and there are 13 channels, then the total time of active scanning for each round is $13 \times 6 + 12 \times 2.9 = 112.8$ ms. If the MaxChannelTime is set to be 15 ms and the Intersil Prisms chipsets (whose channel switching time is 19 ms) is used, then the upper bound of the active scanning is $13 \times 15 + 12 \times 19 = 423$ ms.

A measurement conducted by [11] shows that, active scanning fired by Intersil Prism2-based 802.11b NICs (Network Interface Cards) takes around 350 to 400 ms (based on a firmware initiated scan), and Atheros 5212-based NICs takes roughly 500 ms (via a Windows XP driver-controlled scan).

3   WiFi Scanning on Android

3.1   Scanning Speed Measurements on Android

Last section shows the theoretically analysis of WiFi scanning and some measurement results on computers. But there is little work discussing the experimental measurement results based on popular Android phones/pads. So we conducted WiFi scanning experiments on 8 different android phones/pads. Figure 2 shows the phones/pads used in the experiments. The models and corresponding android OS (Operating System) versions of the phones/pads (marked as 'A' - 'H' in Fig. 2) are listed in Table 1.

Fig. 2. Android WiFi scanning experiment environment

Table 1. Phone/Pads' models and OS versions

Phone	Model	Android version
A	SAMSUNG GT-P6800	4.0.4
B	HUAWEI C8650+	2.3.6
C	HUAWEI C8812	4.0.3
D	HTC ONE X	4.0.4
E	SAMSUNG GT-N7108	4.1.1
F	COOLPAD 5860	2.3.5
G	MEIZU M9	2.3.5
H	GOOGLE NEXUS 7	4.2.1

The easiest and most stable way to let the Android phones/pads to do scanning is using Android SDK API. Firstly, the WifiManager.startScan() is called to fire a SCAN event, and the BroadcastReceiver.onReceive() is overridden to receive the SCAN_RESULTS_AVAILABLE_EVENT. When the SCAN_RESULTS_AVAIL-ABLE_EVENT is received, it means a round of scanning is done (this also means that we have sampled one fingerprint). Then the scan result is saved in a file. Right after it, another WifiManager.startScan() is fired and the procedure is repeated. The procedure is shown in Fig. 3.

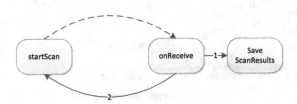

Fig. 3. SDK API scan procedure

We set AP generating beacons at channel 6, and used the 8 phones/pads to run the scan procedure about five minutes. Then we calculated the fingerprint sampling period by the difference the staring time of two successive WifiMan-ager.startScan(). The results, which are shown in Fig. 4, are amazing. From Fig. 4, one may find that Phone A, C, F, G took over 10 s to sample a fingerprint occasion-ally. For Phone F, we sampled 103 times, and there were 12 times that the sampling period of Phone F was greater than 10 s, so the percentage of sampling period over 10 s is $12/103 \times 100\,\% = 11.7\,\%$. We also find that phone G is interesting, its finger-print sampling time alternates between 0 s and 0.6 s. We guess it is because that, when the phone calls WifiManager.startScan(), the under layer started scan and immediately returned a SCAN_RESULTS_AVAILABLE_EVENT, which should not occur logically. And after hardware finished the scan, it reportd another

SCAN_RESULTS_AVAILABLE_EVENT, which eventually caused the SCAN_RESULTS_AVAILABLE_EVENT to be reported twice. Phone B also comes to our attention as it used less than 0 s to sampling a fingerprint, we guess it was caused by the background scanning and message queue mechanism. The scanning time on Phone E and Phone H is stable, but 1.59 s and 0.87 s is a little larger than the sampling period by theoretical analysis, which is around 400 ms to 500 ms (we also used a PC to monitor the phones/pads' Probe Request frames to confirm their active scanning periods in another separate experiment).

Is the difference caused by the Android OS? Can we go over the WiFi scanning framework on the android platform to improve the scanning speed? Is the program still stable in that case? In the next subsection, we dig into details of the Android based WiFi scanning framework, and find the keys to these questions.

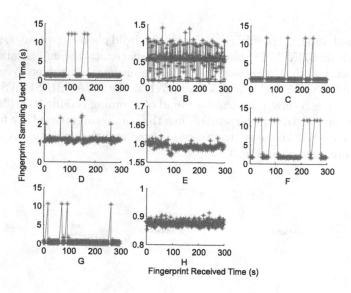

Fig. 4. Scan time by using SDK API

3.2   WiFi Scanning Workflow on Android Platform

The Android WiFi Scanning Framework can be divided into the following parts: SDK API, Android Framework, JNI Layer, HAL Layer, wpa_supplicant and network device driver. Figure 5 shows the more detailed partitions graphically. WifiMonitor.MonitorThread.run, eloop_run and inter layer socket communication represent time delays. In order to calculate these time delays, the most efficient way is to record the time right before and right after them. As presented in previous section, we already recorded SDK API time, here we also recorded the scan starting time at *wpa_supplicant_ctrl_iface_process()*, where a branch matches the "SCAN" event, we recorded the time in *if (os_strcmp(buf, "SCAN") == 0){...}*. And we also record the receive time below the *case NL80211_CMD _NEW_SCAN_RESULTS: ...* in *do_process_drv_event()* method.

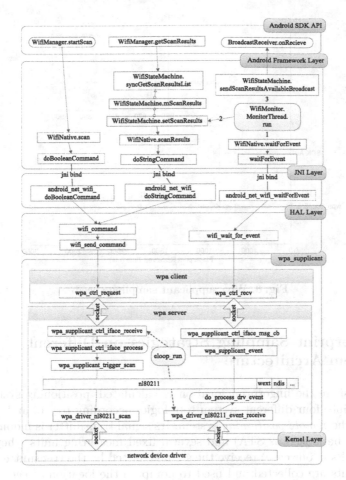

Fig. 5. Android WiFi scanning architecture

We conducted this experiment on Phone H, and the results are shown in Fig. 6. In the upper right corner of Fig. 6, one may find that the time used by all layers above the wpa_supplicant server is about 25 ms. We also calculated the average fingerprint sampling time, which is 841.7 ms.

Our experimental results show that it is hard to make the android OS scan faster even use the bottom layer. All the previous discussion is based on the general application scenarios, that is, STA samples the fingerprint and all channels have to be scanned. However, in some special scenarios, we can change WiFi location system frameworks and fingerprint sampling strategies to improve the sampling speed. We discuss fingerprint sampling strategies at different system frameworks in next section.

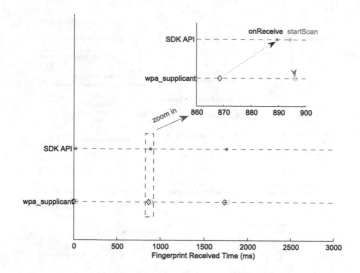

Fig. 6. Wpa_supplicant sampling speed

4 Fingerprint Sampling Strategies on Different System Architecture

Based on where the fingerprint location is calculated, positioning systems can be divided into four different system topologies according to [16] and [17]. The first one is the *remote positioning* system. Its signal transmitter is mobile (in our case, it can be looked as STA) and several fixed measuring units (they can be looked as APs in our case) receive the signal emitted by the transmitter. All the measurements are collected and used to compute the location of the transmitter at a central station. The second one is *self-positioning*. The measuring unit receives signals from several geographically distributed transmitters, and determine its position based on these measurements. The third one is *indirect remote positioning*, where the self-positioning measuring unit sends the position measusment to a remote side via a data link. Conversely, if the position measument is transmitted from a remote positioning system to a mobile unit using a data link, it is called *indirect self-positioning*, which is the fourth system topology. All these four topologies are shown in Fig. 7.

Based on whether we have full control on APs, we add two classification criteria: AP channel setting permission and AP fingerprint sampling permission. AP channel setting permission is that we have the right to set the APs in the location service area work at specific channels. If APs can report the RSS sampling from STA (AP can measure the RSS of STA's ProbeRequst frame) and we have the right to collect these information to the Master Station, then we say that we have the AP fingerprint sampling permission. Actually, the remote positioning system and indirect self-positioning system implicitly need the AP fingerprint sampling permission. Generally, We should not assume that we have

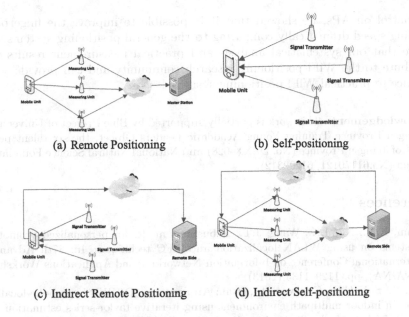

(a) Remote Positioning   (b) Self-positioning

(c) Indirect Remote Positioning   (d) Indirect Self-positioning

Fig. 7. Four different location system topologies

any permission to APs and we have to conduct the scanning procedure on every channel one after another.

If we have the permission to set the AP working channel, then we can set all APs in less than the max number of available channels defined by each country. For example, we can just use 3 non-overlap (actually they may still be a little overlap) channels: 1, 6, 11, to cover the location service area. In that circumstance, We can just scan 3 channels, and the scanning time will be less than $3 \cdot T_{max} + 2 \cdot T_{switch}$ in active scanning mode, and $3 \cdot T_{beacon} + 2 \cdot T_{switch}$ in passive scanning.

If we have the AP sampling permission, what will happen? The STA can dwell on each channel 0 second. Eventually, we need only $(N_{channel} - 1) \cdot T_{switch}$ seconds to scan all channels. If we also have the AP working channel set permission at the same time, we need only $2 \cdot T_{switch}$ seconds to scan 3 channels.

5   Conclusion

In this paper, we studied the WiFi fingerprint sampling problem. We theoretically analyzed the fingerprint sampling procedure, and calculated the fingerprint sampling speed. The Fingerprint sampling experiments were done on 8 phones/pads with Android SDK API. All our source codes and data are available as open source. We believe more measurements should be conducted on different phones/pads. In order to explore whether WiFi location fingerprint can be sampled more quickly, we analyzed the Android WiFi sampling framework and measured the fingerprint sampling speed at different layers. If we have full control on APs, we showed that it is possible to improve the fingerprint sampling speed dramatically comparing to the general positioning systems. We believe that our systematical analysis and practical measurement results will contribute to the WiFi positioning research community and can provide some reference to practical WiFi positioning system design.

Acknowledgement. This work is partially supported by Blue Project of Universities in Jiangsu Province Training Young Academic Leaders Object, the six talent peaks project of Jiangsu Province (No. DZXX-028) and National Natural Science Foundation of China (No.61170121, 61202312).

References

1. Lam, K.Y., Ng, J.K., Wang, J.T.: A business model for personalized promotion systems on using WLAN localization and NFC techniques. In: 27th Advanced International Conference on Information Networking and Applications Workshops (WAINA), pp. 1129–1134 (2013)
2. Qi, Y., Soh, C.B., Gunawan, E., et al.: An accurate 3D UWB hyperbolic localization in indoor multipath environment using iterative taylor-series estimation. In: IEEE 77th Vehicular Technology Conference (VTC Spring), pp. 1–5 (2013)
3. Bahl, P., Padmanabhan, V.N.: RADAR: an in-building rf-based user location and tracking system. In: Proceedings of IEEE INFOCOM, pp. 775–784 (2000)
4. Youssef, M., Agrawala, A.K.: The horus wlan location determination system. In: Proceedings of ACM MobiSys, pp. 205–218 (2005)
5. Wang, H., Sen, S., Elgohary, A., et al.: No need to war-drive: unsupervised indoor localization. In: Proceedings of ACM MobiSys, pp. 197–210 (2012)
6. Laoudias, C., Constantinou, G., Constantinides, M., et al.: The airplace indoor positioning platform for android smartphones. In: IEEE 13th International Conference on Mobile Data Management (MDM), pp. 312–315 (2012)
7. Yang, Z., Wu, C., Liu, Y.: Locating in fingerprint space: wireless indoor localization with little human intervention. In: Proceedings of ACM MOBICOM, pp. 269–280 (2012)
8. Fang, S.-H., Lin, T.-N.: A dynamic system approach for radio location fingerprinting in wireless local area networks. IEEE Trans. Commun. **58**(4), 1020–1025 (2010)
9. Laoudias, C., Constantinou, G., Constantinides, M., Nicolaou, S., Zeinalipour-Yazti, D., Panayiotou, C.G.: An online sequential extreme learning machine approach to wifi based indoor positioning. In: IEEE World Forum on Internet of Things (2014)
10. IEEE Computer Society LAN/MAN Standards Committee. Ieee standard for information technology: Part 11: Wireless lan medium access control (MAC) and physical layer (PHY) specifications (2012)
11. Ramani, I., Savage, S.: Syncscan: practical fast handoff for 802.11 infrastructure networks. In: Proceedings of IEEE INFOCOM, pp. 675–684 (2005)
12. Almulla, M., Wang, Y., Boukerche, A., et al.: A fast location-based handoff scheme for vehicular networks. In: IEEE International Conference on Communications (ICC), pp. 1464–1468 (2013)
13. Mishra, A., Shin, M., Arbaugh, W.A.: An empirical analysis of the ieee 802.11 MAC layer handoff process. ACM SIGCOMM Comput. Commun. Rev. **33**(2), 93–102 (2003)

14. Montavont, N., Arcia-Moret, A., Castignani, G.: On the selection of scanning parameters in IEEE 802.11 networks. In: IEEE 24th International Symposium on Personal Indoor and Mobile Radio Communications (PIMRC), pp. 2137–2141 (2013)
15. Chen, X., Qiao, D.: Hand: Fast handoff with null dwell time for ieee 802.11 networks. In: Proceedings of IEEE INFOCOM, pp. 1–9 (2010)
16. Liu, H., Darabi, H., Banerjee, P.P., et al.: Survey of wireless indoor positioning techniques and systems. IEEE Trans. Syst. Man Cybern. **37**(6), 1067–1080 (2007)
17. Drane, C., Macnaughtan, M., Scott, C.: Positioning GSM telephones. IEEE Commun. Mag. **36**(4), 46–54 (1998)

Node Localization Based on Optimized Genetic Algorithm in Wireless Sensor Networks

Zhiqiang Zou[1,2]($\boxtimes$), Yinbo Lan[1,2], Shu Shen[1,2], and Ruchuan Wang[1,2]

[1] College of Computer, Nanjing University of Posts and Telecommunications,
Nanjing 210003, Jiangsu, China
[2] Jiangsu High Technology Research Key Laboratory for Wireless Sensor Networks,
Nanjing 210003, Jiangsu, China
{zouzq,shens,wangrc}@njupt.edu.cn
lanyinbo0906@163.com

Abstract. In this paper, based on an optimized genetic algorithm for node localization, a new localization algorithm is proposed by combining genetic algorithm with GPS positioning technology. The first step of the algorithm is to get the precise position of the anchor node using GPS and the part of unknown position nodes by combining with the optimized genetic algorithm. The second step is to locate other nodes by using these unknown nodes as anchor nodes. The above two steps are implemented by the following modules: the module of establishing initial population of genetic algorithm for the nodes randomly distributed in the monitoring region, the module of computing fitness value and coefficient of variation, the module of selecting optimal individual by simulating the evolutionary mechanism. Based on these modules, we optimize the whole node localization process in Wireless Sensor Networks. The experimental results demonstrate that our algorithm is efficient to locate the unknown node under the outdoor environment with the low proportion of the anchor nodes. In addition, it has the high positioning accuracy at the low cost of energy as well as the wide application.

Keywords: Wireless Sensor Networks (WSNs) · Genetic Algorithm (GA) · Node localization · Global Position System (GPS)

1 Introduction

With the rapid development of industrialization, human living environment is deteriorating and the water environment also has been destroyed. Decline of water quality and people's increasing requirements on quality of life level make people pay a growing attention on water quality monitoring.

Z. Zou—is an Associate Professor at the College of Computers, Nanjing University of Posts and Telecommunications. This project is supported by the National Natural Science Foundation of China No.61401221, Jiangsu province science and technology plan project No.BE2014718, and a Nanjing University of Posts and Telecommunication research project No.NY213037.

© Springer-Verlag Berlin Heidelberg 2015
L. Sun et al. (Eds.): CWSN 2014, CCIS 501, pp. 198–207, 2015.
DOI: 10.1007/978-3-662-46981-1_19

Wireless Sensor Networks (WSNs) [1] is Ad Hoc Networks which is composed by lots of wireless sensor nodes deployed in the monitoring region and formed by the radio communication. Its purpose is to perceive, gather, transmit and process information which is needed to be perceived in network coverage area, and sent to the terminal equipment for those who need to have an observation. If the sensor nodes gather or perceive data without knowing the specific location information, the result is meaningless, so the sensor node localization technology [2] is one of the key technologies in wireless sensor networks. Common localization algorithm for wireless sensor networks can be divided into range-based localization algorithm and range-free localization algorithm. Range-based localization algorithm [3] (such as RSSI, TOA and TDOA) needs to measure the distance or angle between nodes during the process of locating, this localization algorithm has a higher requirement on hardware and can be greatly influenced by the measurement environment. Range-free localization algorithm [4] does not need to measure the distance or angle between nodes during the locating process, but to achieve node localization with the estimation of the distance between the nodes (such as Amorphous localization algorithm, Dv Hop algorithm), this kind of localization algorithm has low hardware cost and low power consumption, but has a greatly localization accuracy. Existing wireless sensor network localization algorithm mostly estimate the unknown node position in the whole network on the basis of the anchor nodes which location have been known.

By comparison, range-free localization algorithm is more suitable for theoretical research, while range-based localization algorithm has a more practical use. Although binding of GPS positioning device at each node will make the system positioning has a high accuracy, but also greatly increase the cost, and can not be widely used for localization of sensor nodes. If using traditional localization algorithm, then the positioning accuracy is not high and not suitable for harsh outdoor environments. To solve these problems, this paper presents a localization algorithm which combine GPS with improved genetic algorithm, in the first step, using GPS to get an accurate location of anchor nodes and combine traditional range-based localization algorithm to get part of the unknown node location, in the second step, use these unknown nodes as anchor nodes to locate other nodes. The algorithm is equipped with GPS devices on the anchor node, with a relatively small proportion of anchor nodes, can greatly improve the positioning accuracy fewer costs, and has low requirements on density of the anchor node. Therefore, our algorithm is suitable for low-density anchor nodes in the open air wireless sensor networks.

2 The Principle of Genetic Algorithm

Genetic Algorithm [5] (GA) is a new random search and optimization algorithm which is developed rapidly in recent years, and the basic idea is based on Darwin's theory of evolution and Mendel's genetics. The algorithm was created by Professor Holland and his students at University of Michigan in 1975. GA is a global and efficient search method, it is a stochastic optimization method developed through imitating the evolutionary mechanism of nature. GA can automatically acquire and accumulate knowledge about the search space during research, and adaptively control the search process in order to achieve the optimal solution. There are main steps as follows:

(1) Build the Initial State: The initial population is randomly selected from the solution, these solutions will be compared to a chromosome or gene, the population was called the first generation, it is not the same with symbolic artificial intelligence system in which the initial state of the problem has been given.
(2) Reproduction: Those chromosomes with higher fitness values are more likely to produce offspring (The mutation also occurrs after the offspring). Offspring is the product of their parents, and is formed by the junction of genes from their parents, which process is called a "hybrid".
(3) Fitness of Evaluation: This means to specify a fitness value for every fitness solution (chromosomes) according to the actual proximity degree of problem solving (in order to approximate the answer to the question). Don't confuse these solutions and the answer to the question, they can be understood as to get an answer and the system may need to use.
(4) Calculation of Fitness: Each individual's degree of adaptation to the environment is called fitness. To reflect adaptation of chromosome, we introduced function that can measure each chromosome in question which is called fitness function.

3   Node Localization Algorithm based on Optimized Genetic

Literature [6] presents a wireless sensor network node localization algorithm based on genetic algorithm. The algorithm establishes location optimization model based on the parameters of localization of unknown node, and uses genetic algorithms to get parameters of positioning optimization model through the analysis of measuring the distance between unknown nodes and a small amount of anchor nodes. Algorithm is divided into two stages, in the first stage, the anchor nodes broadcast their location information, and after the unknown node receives the information, The unknown node will save and broadcast it. Through this method, we can obtain a part of the unknown node position. In the second stage, it will optimize the operation. Each unknown node broadcasts its location information, and then the unknown node combines with genetic algorithm to optimize their position by making use of the location information from other nodes and distance between it and the other nodes. This algorithm has the following problems: (1) the initial position of the anchor node is unclear; (2) many unknown node operation is repeated in the first stage and the second stage. So that excessive communication consumes energy of nodes which is not conducive to energy conservation. Because each nodes relies on its own to carry limited battery powercell loss should be reduced as much as possible. Based on these problems, this paper made a further improvement on the aspects of location accuracy and came up with Node Localization based on Optimized Genetic Algorithm in WSNs, called NL_OGA, which uses the lower energy consumption advantage of ZigBee and improves the precision at the same time. It is divided into two stages: node localization based on the trilateral localization algorithm and node localization based on NL_OGA localization algorithm.

3.1 Node Localization Based on the Trilateral Localization Algorithm

After deploying wireless sensor nodes within a specified area randomly, the wireless sensor nodes start sending and receiving devices. Assuming the unknown node is A_j, the coordinates of A_j is (x_j, y_j), anchor node is B_i (x_i, y_i), there are M anchor nodes and N unknown nodes in the system. Node communication radius of each node is R and its the same circle with wireless propagation model. If the distance between two nodes is smaller than R, then it shows that the two node is connected. According to the preset cycle, anchor nodes (with GPS devices) broadcast positioning information, including the current location information. After the unknown node within the communication range receives the anchor node position information, it will save this information and use it to calculate its own position. When receives more than three anchor nodes position coordinate information, it can calculate its own position according to trilateral localization algorithm. Specific steps are as follows:

(1) The anchor node B_i measures the distance to the unknown node A_j, assmujing this distance is d_i, then sends the coordinates and the distance information in a frame format to unpositioning node.
(2) After unpositioning node receives the message anchor node sent, it will record the coordinate and distance. If unknown nodes A_j can communicate with three anchor nodes B_i (i = 1,2,3), then A_j is in the intersection of three circles which centers are B_i.

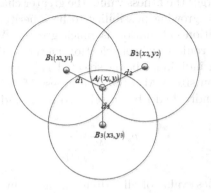

Fig. 1. The unknown node and anchor node communication diagram

(3) Using trilateral localization algorithm to calculate the location of unknown node A_j is (x,y), For the q anchor nodes communicating with unknown node A_j, the distance of anchor node $(x_1,y_1),...,(x_q,y_q)$ and unknown node are respectively $d_1,...,d_q$, then the location of the unknown node is gotten by solving the following equation.

$$\begin{cases} \sqrt{(x-x_1)^2 + (y-y_1)^2} = d_1 \\ \quad \cdots \\ \sqrt{(x-x_q)^2 + (y-y_q)^2} = d_q \end{cases} \tag{1}$$

Due to environmental or hardware factors, distance measurements in practical applications always exists an error, therefore the essence of positioning operation is to minimize the value of function (2), that is to get the minimum point of the function (Fig. 1).

$$f(x,y) = \sum_{i=1}^{M} \left(\sqrt{(x-x_i)^2 + (y-y_i)^2} - d_i \right)^2 \tag{2}$$

3.2   Node Localization Based on NL_OGA Algorithm

Only positioning part of the unknown nodes in the first stage, the position coordinates of other unknown nodes cant be obtained because the number of communicating with anchor nodes are less than 3. At this stage, the location of unknown nodes in the first stage is regarded as using the concept of genetic algorithm through the following steps and then we can complete the positioning of nodes in the system when unknown nodes participate in the locating of remain unknown nodes. Thus, we propose the node localization algorithm based on NL_OGA localization. The details are as follows:

(1) The nodes that are randomly distributed in the monitoring area is regarded as the initial population, then calculating the fitness value of each anchor node, the larger the fitness value, the greater chance of being selected, thus there will be a growing possibility to be inherited, that is the chance to involved in position calculation is much greater. We select individuals based on fitness of roulette wheel selection method. The basic idea is: the probability of each individual being selected is proportional to its fitness, assuming population size is $M = 100$, the fitness of individual i is f(i), then the probability of individual i being selected is p_i, and p_i can be expressed as:

$$p_i = \frac{f(i)}{\sum_{i=1}^{M} f(i)} \tag{3}$$

Calculating the fitness value of all individuals according to function (3) and sorting them in order of descending.
(2) Having got the fitness value of all individuals in the first step, deleting smaller individual fitness in the population, and being replaced by the best individual, and putting it into positioning procedure.

(3) Because of the influence of test environment, the individuals in the population mutate at a certain mutation probability, taking a random number $\alpha \in [0, 1]$ for the coefficient of variation.

(4) Population initialization is to set the evolutionary algebraic calculator $t = 0$, setting the maximum number of T and iteration until $t = T$, i.e, that is the iteration number reaches a predetermined number of times that is the optimal solution of the population.

4   Verification and Analysis of Simulation Experiments

To test the performance of the algorithm, we conducted a series of simulation experiments, under MATLAB7.0. We compared an optimization algorithm which is based on dv-distance algorithm [7] with our improved genetic algorithm proposed in this paper.

In the region of 100 m*100 m randomly tossed 100 sensor nodes to form a wireless sensor network. Nodes can calculate the distance between nodes and nodes within the communication range by measuring the value of RSSI. Communication ability of anchor nodes and unknown nodes are the same, so assuming the communication radius of node is 30 m. Definition of average positioning error is:

$$Error = \frac{\sum_{i=1}^{N} \sqrt{(x_r - x_t)^2 + (y_r - y_t)^2}}{N} \tag{4}$$

N is the number of unknown nodes, (x_r, y_r), (x_t, y_t) are real coordinates and estimated coordinates of unknown nodes respectively.

Figures 2 and 3 are the location result figure when the anchor node proportion is 10 % and the node communication radius is 30 m. It is divided into the first (Fig. 2) and the second stage (Fig. 3) positioning effect chart. In these figures,

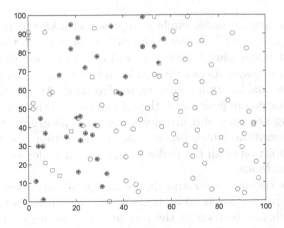

Fig. 2. The first stage positioning effect chart

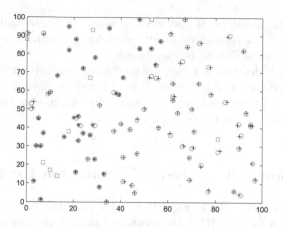

Fig. 3. The second stage positioning effect chart

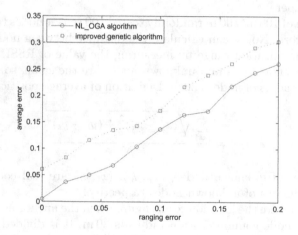

Fig. 4. The ranging error and average error diagram

square represents anchor node, circle o represents unknown nodes randomly tossed in the area, asterisk * indicates the estimated position that can be positioned in the first stage, plus + means he estimated position that can be positioned in the second stage. As can be seen from the graph, estimated position is very close to the actual location according to algorithm. Almost all nodes in system in the second step are positioned, thus it can be seen that the algorithm has higher positioning accuracy and broader coverage. The graph shows the effectiveness of the algorithm, which proves that the algorithm is still can effective to complete the position of all the nodes in the system under lower anchor node proportion circumstance.

Figure 4 is the distance error and the average localization error graph when the anchor node proportion is 20 %, because this algorithm is based on range localization, which can be seen as the ranging error is bigger, the positioning error becomes larger too. Compared with the positioning algorithm based on

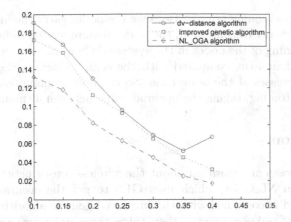

Fig. 5. Anchor node proportion and average positioning error graph

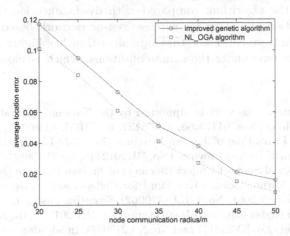

Fig. 6. Node communication radius and average location error graph

general genetic algorithm and dv-distance algorithm [7], positioning accuracy of the algorithm in this paper optimized is higher.

Figure 5 is a graph about anchor node proportion and average positioning. From the chart we can see that the relationship between the anchor node proportion and average positioning error. Compared with the localization of genetic algorithm and the classical algorithm DV-Distance, we can see the positioning accuracy of the algorithm in this paper is higher.

Figure 6 is a node communication radius and average location error graph when the anchor node proportion is 20 %. This graph shows that the value change of node communication radius has an influence on average positioning error. Compared with the literature [6], the node in this paper mainly has the lower battery energy consumption by reducing the repeated computation. When the number of anchor node is certain, the larger the node communication radius is, the smaller the positioning error is. Because the nodes carry the limited battery, considering the energy consumption, the node communication radius of 40 m can meet the positioning of the nodes in the system. When the node communication radius is more than 40 m, compared with the error reduction, the node energy consumption increases at the same time. So the node communication radius is not suitable for too big, taking the optimal value between 40 m and 45 m.

5   Conclusion

This paper proposes an algorithm about the wireless sensor network node positioning based on NL_OGA, which uses GPS to get the accurate position of anchor node, and is combined with the improved genetic algorithm to get part of the position of unknown nodes, then takes these unknown nodes as anchor nodes to participating in locating other nodes. The simulation results verify the effectiveness of the algorithm, compared with dv-distance location algorithm and self-localization algorithm for wireless sensor network based on Improved Genetic Algorithm, we can know that our algorithm has higher accuracy, and lower energy consume under the same conditions, which is more feasible and effective.

Acknowledgments. This work is supported by the National Natural Science Foundation of P. R. China (Nos. 61170065, 61373137, 61171053, 61103195, 61203217), Six Industries Talent Peaks Plan of Jiangsu Province (No. 2013-DZXX-014), the Natural Science Foundation of Jiangsu Province (No. BK2012436, No. BK20141429), The Scientific and Technological Support Project (Society) of Jiangsu Province (No. BE2014718, No. BE2013666), Natural Science Key Fund for Colleges and Universities in Jiangsu Province (No. 11KJA520001, No. 12KJA520002), Scientific Research & Industry Promotion Project for Higher Education Institutions (No. JHB2012-7), the NJUPT Natural Science Foundation (No. NY213157 and No. NY213037). In addition, we are grateful to the anonymous reviewers for their insightful and constructive suggestions.

References

1. Sun, L.: Wireless Sensor Network. Tsinghua University, Beijing (2005)
2. Li, J.Z., Gao, H.: Advances in wireless sensor networks. Res. Dev. Comput. **45**(1), 1–15 (2008)
3. Bulusu, N., Heidemann, J., Estrin, D.: GPS-less lowcost outdoor localization for very small devices. IEEE Pers. Commun. **7**(5), 28–34 (2000)
4. Fang, L., Du, W.L., Ning, P.: A beacon-less location discovery scheme for wireless sensor networks. In: Proceedings of the IEEEINFOCOM 2005, pp. 161–171. IEEE Press (2005)
5. Holland, J.H.: Adaptation in Natural and Artificial Systems: An Introductory Analysis with Applications to Biology, Control, and Artificial Intelligence. University of Michigan, Ann Arbor (1975)

6. Zhang, L., Duan, L.L., Qian, Z.J.: WSN node localization technology based on genetic algorithm. Comput. Eng. **36**(10), 85–87 (2010)
7. Nicolescud, D., Nath, B.: Ad-Hoc positioning systems. In: IEEE Global Communications Conference Report, SanAntonio, TX, USA, vol. 5(10), pp. 2926–2931 (2001)

TACO: A Traceback Algorithm Based on Ant Colony Optimization for Geomagnetic Positioning

Hui Li[1(✉)], Haiyong Luo[1], Fang Zhao[2], and Xinrong Li[3]

[1] Institute of Computing Technology, Chinese Academy of Sciences,
Beijing, China
{lihui2010,yhluo}@ict.ac.cn
[2] Beijing University of Posts and Telecommunications, Beijing, China
zfsse@bupt.edu.cn
[3] University of North Texas, Denton, USA
xinrong.li@unt.edu

Abstract. Magnetic field fluctuations in modern buildings can derive from both natural and man-made sources, which typically include steel, reinforced concrete structures, and electric power systems, etc. Since the anomalies of the magnetic field inside the building are nearly static and have sufficient local variability, this provides a unique magnetic clue which could be utilized for global self-localization. In this research, we propose TACO, an algorithm that uses Ant Colony Optimization (ACO) and Multi-Position TraceBack Algorithm (MTA) to solve one dimensional magnetic data localization problem. TACO employs a set of novel techniques to resolve ambiguity in locations: ACO is used to generate candidate locations and MTA to make full use of both historical positions and users moving direction information. The evaluation results show that TACO could achieve high localization accuracy, when appropriate previous position information is provided.

Keywords: Geomagnetic positioning · Ant colony optimization · Traceback algorithm · Indoor localization

1 Introduction

In the past few years indoor positioning has already attracted increasing interests from both research and industrial sectors. With the advent of the latest generation smart phones, it is widely expected that the demand for location

This work was supported in part by the National Natural Science Foundation of China (61374214), the Major Projects of Ministry of Industry and Information Technology (2014ZX03006003-002), the National High Technology Research and Development Program of China (2013AA12A201) and Taiyuan-Zhongguancun Cooperation special Project (130104).

L. Sun et al. (Eds.): CWSN 2014, CCIS 501, pp. 208–222, 2015.
DOI: 10.1007/978-3-662-46981-1_20

based services inside buildings (indoor location services) will increase, which in turn requires mass market indoor localization technologies.

WiFi is one of the most popular techniques in indoor localization. Even though the WiFi infrastructures are being widely deployed with the rapid development of communication industry, there are still many indoor environments that remain beyond the WiFi coverage. So in this research, we focus on indoor localization techniques that do not require specialized infrastructure support. The inspiration of a potential solution to this problem comes from some animals.

Evidence suggests that animals utilize the Earths magnetic field for navigation [1,2], orientation detection [3], and even position estimation. Some animals, such as spiny lobsters, can not only detect the direction of the Earths magnetic field, but also sense their relative true position relative to their destination [1]. Such observations indicate that these animals are capable of deriving positional information from local clues that arise from the local anomalies of the Earths magnetic field.

Static and extremely low-frequency (ELF) magnetic fields in modern buildings arise from both natural and man-made sources, such as electric power systems, electric and electronic appliances, and industrial devices [4]. Steel and reinforced concrete structures of buildings bring distortions in the ambient magnetic field [5–7]. It is argued here that each building has its own unique magnetic field. If the anomalies of the geomagnetic field have sufficient variability, it is possible to utilize the geomagnetic field in the problem domain of indoor localization.

In this research, we focus on improving the accuracy of indoor localization by using geomagnetic filed and its unique characteristics in modern buildings.

2 Related Work

The research on indoor localization using geomagnetic field has attracted great interest in the past ten years. And Suksakulchai is one of the pioneers in this field. In his research, ambient magnetic field is utilized for self-localization [8]. Suksakulchai used deviations of compass headings to provide distinctive location signatures for place recognition. The local properties of the magnetic field are used as observations to provide a spatially changing physical quantity, assuming a non-uniform magnetic vector field. Dellaert and Thrun proposed a MCL technique in [9,10], which is used to estimate the position of the localization target (robot or human), given the observations of the magnetic field and the approximate dynamics of the target. Furthermore, Janne Haverinen's experiments reported in [11] suggest that the ambient magnetic field may remain sufficiently stable for longer periods of time, providing support for self-localization techniques utilizing the local deviations of the field. Additionally, Etienne Le Grand exposes a 2D mapping technique to produce magnetic maps and he applies this technique to show the stability of the magnetic disturbances in time [12]. While in Blankenbachs research in [13,14], artificial quasi static magnetic field based on Direct Current magnetic is applied to indoor positioning, which shows no multipath effects and has excellent characteristics for penetrating various obstacles. But this strategy needs to take consideration of additional interference fields (e.g. Earths magnetic field, electrical disturbances) and infrastructure pre-deployment.

In our study, we propose a localization system based on Earths magnetic field. With this system, a number of users carrying smart phones walk around in the indoor space of interest in normal course (e.g., stroll through a mall), with each user traversing a subset of the paths in the space. We assume no knowledge of where within the space a user walks or even the starting point of the users walk. In this system, user's step could be detected, and the suggested position is provided for user after every 5 steps. In each positioning, multiple candidate locations would be computed based on ant colony optimization algorithm. And the position demonstrated to user is computed by the trace-back algorithm which employs historical position information.

3   TACO Algorithm

One of the most difficult issues in geomagnetic localization is to calculate the ground truth location by only one-dimensional magnetic data. This study not only introduces ant colony optimization to accelerate global search, but also proposes multi-position TraceBack algorithm to make full use of history travel information.

3.1   Ant Colony Optimization

The ant colony optimization algorithm (ACO) is a probabilistic and heuristic technique for solving computational problems [15,16]. In the natural world, ants (initially) wander randomly and laying down pheromone trails while moving. They would not return to their colony until they find the food. If other ants find such a path, they are not likely to keep travelling at random, but to follow the trail instead, and reinforce it if they eventually find the food. The idea of the ant colony algorithm is to mimic this behavior with "simulated ants" walking around the graphical problem path.

Considering the advantage of ACO in distributed mechanism and probabilistic model, we apply it to search candidate locations, using magnetic data comparison. Figure 2 shows the main procedure of ACO at each time positioning. At first, it scatters the ants on each path randomly, and sets the pheromone on the path to a constant value. Before the ant start to move, it will sense both the density of pheromone and the similarity between training and observation magnetic data on its optional neighbor path, which decides the probability of ant moving direction. The higher density and similarity of the optional neighbor path, the more probable ant is going to moving toward. The step length of an ant should be the same with that of the user. After the ant moves a step, the observed and training magnetic data on that piece of path would be collected and compared with each other. Similarity of these two pieces of data is turned into pheromone density. If the similarity is higher, the pheromone is denser.

After all of the ants finish one step moving, the pheromone on the whole path is updated. Assuming the ant is intelligent enough to remember and communicate, it could remember several candidate locations where the training magnetic data has more similarity with observed magnetic data and share its knowledge with other ants they have met each other on the way. So the most possible candidate locations could be spread and shared among ants. Ants will continue to move around, until a certain percent of ants own the same memory of candidate locations. The detail of those procedures is demonstrated below.

1. Initialization
   - The number of ants is initialized to N.
   - Ants are scattered on each path randomly.
   - Initialize the dense of pheromone on each path to $1/M$, M is the number of total location nodes (the minimum unit of positioning). Let it be the Min Max Ant System, in order to reach the convergence condition faster. Set the min and max dense of pheromone $1/M$ and 1 respectively.
2. Determining ants moving direction
   - Each ant owns a neighbor area which is the area circle around the ant and takes its step length for radius.
   - The density of pheromone and the likelihood of magnetic data matching similarity on its neighbor path determined the moving direction of ant k.
   - Assuming ant k could move toward a direction with J possibilities at time t. Let the sensed pheromone density on direction i be $\tau_i^{k\alpha}(t)$, and let the likelihood of magnetic data matching similarity on direction i be $\mu_i^{k\beta}(t)$, α and β are constants. So the probability of ant k moving toward direction i at time t is $P_i^k(t)$.

$$P_i^k(t) = \frac{\tau_i^{k\alpha}(t)\mu_i^{k\beta}(t)}{\sum_{i=1}^{J} \tau_i^{k\alpha}(t)\mu_i^{k\beta}(t)} \tag{1}$$

3. Estimating ants Step length
   - The step length of ant is the distance that user walks through between two positions.
   - While user moving, the number of steps could be detected by using acceleration sensor [17–19], and the step length could also be estimated [20,21]. So the moving distance L' of the user between two positioning point could be obtained.
   - The step length of ant is $L = L' + \delta$. Stochastic disturbance δ is introduced to make compensation for estimation error.
4. Updating density of pheromone
   - Pheromone is a clue that leads ants to find their destination more quickly. And it is spread on the path by ants, according to the similarity between observed and training magnetic data.
   - Every time the ant moves, new pheromone is produced. After all the ants finish one step moving, the density of pheromone on the whole path would be updated.

- In this paper, reciprocal transformation function f is used to transform magnetic data similarity to density of ant pheromone, shown in Fig. 1. In function 2, S represents the similarity computed by waveform-based DTW algorithm which is introduced in Sect. 3.3.

$$f = \frac{1}{S} \tag{2}$$

- If ant k moves in direction i at time t, then the density of pheromone on the path where ant k pass by at time $t+1$ is updated to $\tau_i^k(t+1)$. ρ is the volatilization rate of pheromone. Q is a constant value. $f_i(t+1)$ is the density of pheromone converted from magnetic data similarity on direction i at time $t+1$.

$$\tau_i^k(t+1) = (1 - \rho)\tau_i^k(t) + \Delta\tau^k(t+1) \tag{3}$$

$$\Delta\tau^k(t+1) = Qf_i(t+1) \tag{4}$$

$$f_i(t+1) = \frac{1}{S_i(t+1)} \tag{5}$$

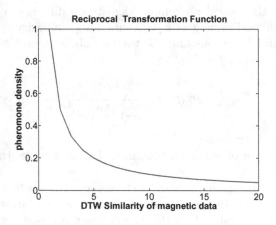

Fig. 1. Reciprocal transformation function.

5. Updating ants memory
   - Assuming ant is intelligent enough to remember and share information with others.
   - An ant could remember K places with the highest similarity between observation and training magnetic data.
   - At initialization, the K places are set to empty for each ant.

- After ant i finishes one step moving, it will compute the similarity of magnetic data on this pieces of path and compare with its K places in memory. If the new place owns higher similarity, update the ants memory K_i.
- When a group of ants come across at one place, they get the chance to exchange their information and update their memory to the most common similar K_{common} places.

6. Ending condition
- If $p\%$ of ants owns the same memory, the algorithm stops. Otherwise, the ant will continue to move on.

7. Get multiple candidate positions
- After completing one iteration, the K places that the majority of ants own in memory are considered as the candidate positions. Those contiguous candidate places will be merged into one place which takes the mean position of them.
- Assuming the number of the final candidate positions is M.

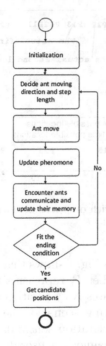

Fig. 2. Reciprocal transformation function.

3.2   Multi-position TraceBack Algorithm

Multi-position traceback algorithm (MTA) is responsible for determining the final position within these candidate positions selected by ant colony optimization (ACO).

In locating scenario, the user walks from one place to another with successive steps, which means the distance of contiguous localization should have accordance with the users step length which could be estimated by acceleration sensor. The further the user walks, the more precise the route will be predicted through historical positions, basing on distance correlation among contiguous localization. Furthermore, the user moving direction is also valuable information that could narrow down selection range and improve accuracy of localization. So MTA is a dynamic programming algorithm which uses historical multi-position and moving direction to produce more reasonable locating result. Figure 3 shows a localization scenario with one possible location. Green-triangle and pink-square represent the first time and second time candidate locations respectively after applying ACO algorithm. Two red circles are the actual places. Considering both distance correlation and direction influence among candidate positions, only path (P13→P22) will be selected. Because not only the direction but also the distance between P13 and P22 is the best match with users actual moving steps.

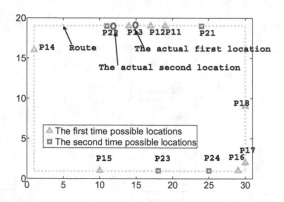

Fig. 3. A positioning scenario with one possible location (Color figure online).

MTA Mathematic Model. As Fig. 4 shows that each time locating ACO will produce M candidate positions. Let P_i represents the set of the i-th time candidate positions where $P_{i,j}$ indicates No j position at the i-th locating scenario. From the i-th to $(i+1)$-th locating scenario, the users actual moving length $L'_{i,i+1}$ could be estimated by acceleration sensor data, and the moving direction $\overrightarrow{\alpha}_{i,i+1}$ could be obtained from magnetic sensor data.

In this paper, we only consider last J historical localization information by using sliding window technique, which means the window size is J. The MTA applied dynamic programming ideas to pick a most feasible route from last J historical candidate positions.

The MTA model includes the following parts.

1. Gathering the last J-1 candidate positions set $(P_{K-J+1}, ..., P_K)$ at the k-th locating.

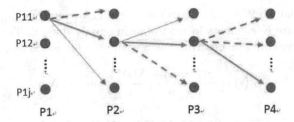

Fig. 4. MTA mathematic model.

2. Compute the distance $l_{i,j}^{i+1,m}$ between neighbor candidate positions. Where $l_{i,j}^{i+1,m}$ indicates the distance between position $P_{i,j}$ and its neighbor $P_{i+1,m}$. Then calculate the difference between $\Delta l_{i,j}^{i+1,m}$ and $l_{i,j}^{i+1,m}$ estimated actual moving length $L'_{i,i+1}$ Where,

$$\Delta l_{i,j}^{i+1,m} = l_{i,j}^{i+1,m} - L'_{i,i+1} \tag{6}$$

3. Furthermore, let $\overrightarrow{\beta}_{i,j}^{i+1,m}$ represent the direction from $P_{i,j}$ to $P_{i+1,m}$. Then, the angle between $\overrightarrow{\beta}_{i,j}^{i+1,m}$ and $\overrightarrow{\alpha}_{i,i+1}$ is $\Delta\theta_{i,j}^{i+1,m}$, where,

$$\Delta\theta_{i,j}^{i+1,m} = arcos(\overrightarrow{\beta}_{i,j}^{i+1,m}, \overrightarrow{\alpha}_{i,i+1}) \tag{7}$$

4. Assuming that, the tolerant direction error estimated by magnetic sensor is δ, then the difference angle needs to satisfy this equation: $\Delta\theta_{i,j}^{i+1,m} < \delta$.
5. Apply dynamic programming ideas to excavate the most feasible route to get the minimum ΔL.

$$\Delta L = min(\sum_{i=k-p+1}^{k} \Delta l_{i,j}^{i+1,m}) \tag{8}$$

$$L(n) = \begin{cases} min(\Delta l_{1,j}^{2,m}) & n = 1, \Delta\theta_{1,j}^{2,m} < \delta \\ min(L(n-1) + \Delta l_{n-1,j}^{n,m}) & n > 1, \Delta\theta_{n-1,j}^{n,m} < \delta \end{cases} \tag{9}$$

3.3 Waveform-Based DTW Matching Algorithm

William and Shibuhisas research in [22,24] proves that the strength of magnetic data in the same route will keep steady with time changes. While in analyzing characteristic of indoor magnetic data collected by smartphone, we found an interesting phenomenon. The strength of magnetic data that we gather from smartphone will jump to a higher value but still keep the same waveform sometime, showed in Fig. 5. It occurs occasionally, which is probably because the hardware in smartphone is uncorrected.

Traditional DTW algorithm cant handle data offset [23]. So we propose a waveform-based DTW algorithm which extracts the slope of original curve and applies traditional DTW algorithm to compute the waveform similarity. Assuming that, there are N elements in a sample magnetic data S. The slope of this sample data curve could be described as S', where S'(i) is the i-th number of S'.

$$S'(i) = \frac{S(i+m) - S(i)}{m}(i+m) \leq N \tag{10}$$

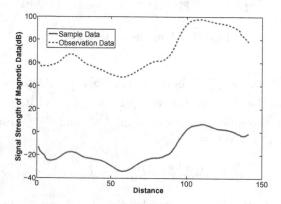

Fig. 5. Magnetic data without slope extraction.

As shown in Fig. 6, after extraction of slope from magnetic data curve, the similarity of new curve which represents the similarity of waveform could be computed by DTW algorithm efficiently.

Figure 7 demonstrates the difference of localization error among three matching algorithms on a single road length of 45 m. The reformed waveform-based DTW achieves the highest accuracy. In cosine matching algorithm, the length of two comparing data must be the same; however, observation and sample data can hardly reach the same length because of the diversity of users walking speed. But DTW algorithm could tolerate those differences.

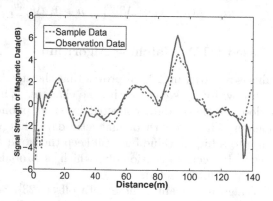

Fig. 6. Slope data of magnetic data curve.

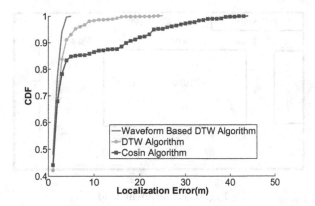

Fig. 7. Localization error based on matching algorithm.

4   Evaluation

4.1   Sampling Strategy

As previously mentioned in Sect. 3.1, users walking speed could be quite different. So it is the first problem that should be solved before sampling. In this research, we introduce a convenient sampling strategy based on mark points. First of all, mark points are scattered over all routes and the connections between adjacent mark points should cover the whole routes with a suitable distance, as Fig. 8 shows.

We just need to click a mark button on the sampling software while coming across the mark point on sampling. Thus the sample data and actual position could have a more precise correspondent relationship.

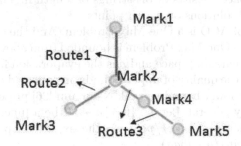

Fig. 8. Sampling strategy based on mark point.

4.2   Experiment Setup

We evaluate the performance of TACO experimentally in a large office building, with a $60\,m \times 15\,m$ floor plan, as shown in Fig. 9. The experiment field has 4 routes, 150 m in total length. Ten mark points have been deployed in this field. For this experiment, we used Huawei Honor smart phone, with 25 Hz sampling

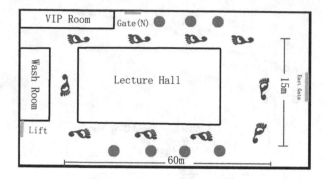

Fig. 9. Experiment field.

rate. Few sampling magnetic data is required. In this paper, we just sampled 3 times on each route. All simulations are run in Matlab 7.5.0 on a PC platform with a 1.70 GHz Pentium (R) 4 CPU and 1G RAM.

4.3   Computing Complexity Analysis

The Computing Complexity of TACO is consisted of ACO algorithm and MTA.

Computing Complexity of ACO. The following theorem has already been proven by Gutjahr and Sebastian [25] with a more general parameterization for the pheromone borders. They present a proof for MMAS*(Min Max Ant System) using the simplified presentation of the fitness-level method [26] restricted to pseudo-Boolean optimization. The goal is to maximize a function $f : \{0, 1\}n \rightarrow R$, i.e., the search space consists of bit strings of length n. These bit strings are synonymously called solutions or search points.

Our application of ACO is a One-Max Problem. And the expected optimization time of MMAS on One-Max Problem is bounded from above by $O((nlogn)/\rho)$ [29]. N is size of the searching space and ρ is the evaporation factor, $0 < \rho < 1$.

In order to judge the quality of upper bounds on expected optimization times it is helpful to aim at lower bounds. Frank Neumann [26] presents a lower bound that is weak but very general. Let $f : \{0, 1\}n \rightarrow R$ be a function with a unique global optimum. Choosing $\rho = 1/poly(n)$, the expected optimization time of MMAS on f is $\Omega((logn)/\rho - logn)$.

Computing Complexity of MTA. The main part of MTA is dynamic programming algorithm which exhibits optimal substructure if an optimal solution solution to the problem contain within it optimal solution solution to subproblems. As we have seen in the recursive solution to the problem that same subproblem is computed again and again. The time bound of recursive solution is $\Omega(2^n)$. If we compute these overlapping problems only once and store their value for further use, the time bound can reach to $O(n^2)$.

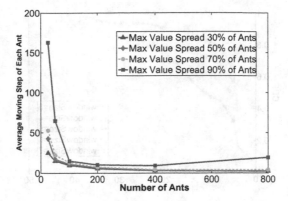

Fig. 10. Relationship between information spreading speed and number of ants.

4.4   Searching Efficiency of ACO Algorithm

Furthermore, we use experiments to demonstrate the relationship between the efficiency of ACO algorithm and the number of ants, where the efficiency is measured by the number of ants moving step and the time taken during a search case. Since Sect. 3.1 has mentioned that top k max values will be scattered among ants when they come across with each other. Figures 10 and 11 demonstrate the difference of max value propagation range from 30 % to 90 %. In this simulation, the number of ants is increased from 25 to 800; both moving step and time taking are considered.

Figure 10 shows that the average moving step of ants has a quick decline when the number of ant is less than 100, and then a slower decrease is coming after with the increase of ant. But the decrease will change to increase after the number of ant hits its threshold. For 90 % spreading situation, the threshold is around 400 ants. The time of computation performance demonstrates the similar tendency as the number of ant increases as shown in Fig. 11.

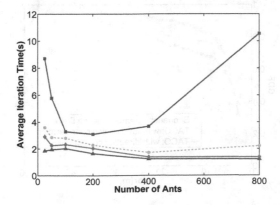

Fig. 11. Relationship between computing overhead and number of ants.

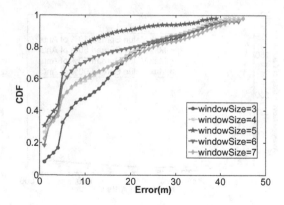

Fig. 12. Positioning error under different window size.

Since the following localization simulation required to find the top k max values, 50 % of spread range is enough. And 400 of ants will be selected, which can achieve the fewest moving step and computing time overhead.

4.5   Localization Error

Figure 12 depicts the positioning error under different window size of MTA, where the window size represents the number of historical localization results employed. As seen from Fig. 12, the localization performance first improves as window size increases from 3 to 5, but then decreases when window size increases from 5 to 7. There is little historical information contribute to localization result when window size is small. But when it increases, the historical information could also be overloaded because there are few candidate locations to describe the historical moving trend. As seen from Fig. 13, three algorithms are evaluated. Global sequential

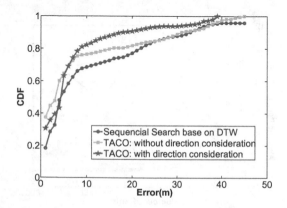

Fig. 13. Positioning error with different algorithm.

search based on DTW is an algorithm completely relied on magnetic data matching, which can hardly achieve satisfactory accuracy. In TACO, taking consideration of users walking direction is an important factor that can highly improve the positioning performance, as it showed in Fig. 13.

5   Conclusion

In this research, we propose TACO, an algorithm that uses ant colony optimization and multi-position TraceBack strategy to solve one dimensional magnetic data localization problem. A key contribution of TACO is that a person could be localized with just a magnetic sensing smartphone in indoor environment without any other application-specific infrastructure. TACO employs a set of novel techniques to resolve ambiguity in location, using ACO to generate candidate locations and MTA to make full use of both historical position information and users moving direction. In the performance evaluation, we proposed a mark node based sampling strategy and explored the search efficiency of ACO. Finally, the simulation on a large office floor shows that TACO could achieve higher positioning accuracy when historical position information is appropriately considered.

References

1. Larry, C.B., Kenneth, J.L.: True navigation and magnetic maps in spiny lobsters. Nature **421**(6918), 60–63 (2003)
2. Robert, J.G., Lauren, E.F., Robert, J.G.: Human cryptochrome exhibits light-dependent magnetosensitivity. Nat. Commun. **2**, 356–362 (2011)
3. Treiber, C.D., Salzer, M.C.: Clusters of iron-rich cells in the upper beak of pigeons are macrophages not magneto sensitive neurons. Nature **484**(7394), 367–370 (2012)
4. Burnett, J., Yaping, P.D.: Mitigation of extremely low frequency magnetic fields from electrical installations in high-rise buildings. Build. Environ. **37**(8), 769–775 (2002)
5. Odawara, S., Haraguchi, Y., Muramatsu, K., Yamazaki, K., Hirosato, S.: Magnetic field analyses of architectural components using homogenization technique. IEEE Trans. Magn. **46**(8), 3313–3316 (2010)
6. Bao, G.C., Ming, D.L.: Quantitative analyses of magnetic field distributions for buildings of steel structure. In: 6th International Conference of ICEF (Electromagnetic Field Problems and Applications), pp. 1–4, Dalian (2012)
7. Paolinelli, D.C., Cunha, D., Cota, A.B.: Study of the simultaneous effects of the hot band grain size and cold rolling reduction on the structure and magnetic properties of nonoriented 3% si steel. IEEE Trans. Magn. **48**(4), 1401–1404 (2012)
8. Suksakulchai, S., Thongchai, S., Wilkes, D.M., Kawamura, K.: Mobile robot localization using an electronic compass for corridor environment. In: International Conference on Systems, Man, and Cybernetics. pp, 3354–3359, Nashville (2000)
9. Dellaert, F., Fox, D., Burgard, W., Thrun, S.: Monte carlo localization for mobile robots. In: International Conference on Robotics and Automation, pp, 1322–1328, Detroit (1999)
10. Thrun, S., Burgard, W., Fox, D.: Probabilistic robotics. Commun. of the ACM - Robots: Intell. Versatility Adaptively **45**(3), 52–57 (2002)

11. Haverinen, J., Kemppainen, A.: A global self-localization technique utilizing local anomalies of the ambient magnetic field. In: IEEE International Conference on Robotics and Automation, pp, 3142–3147, Kobe (2009)

12. Grand, E.L., Thrun, S.: 3-Axis magnetic field mapping and fusion for indoor localization. In: IEEE International Conference on Multisensor Fusion and Integration for Intelligent Systems (MFI), pp, 358–364, Hamburg (2012)

13. Blankenbach, J., Norrdine, A.: Position estimation using artificial generated magnetic fields. In: International Conference on Indoor Positioning and Indoor Navigation (IPIN), pp. 1–5, Zurich (2010)

14. Blankenbach, J., Norrdine, A., Hellmers H.: A robust and precise 3D indoor positioning system for harsh environments. In: International Conference on Indoor Positioning and Indoor Navigation (IPIN), pp, 1–8, Sydney (2012)

15. Yuan, X.M., Zhi, Y.W.: Grid Task scheduling based on chaotic ant colony optimization algorithm. In: 2nd International Conference on Computer Science and Network Technology, pp. 469–472, Changchun (2012)

16. Ping, J.Z., Gang, J.L., Wen, X.G.: Research of path planning for mobile robot based on improved ant colony optimization algorithm. In: 2nd International Conference on Advanced Computer Control, pp. 241–245, Shenyang (2010)

17. Fang, L., Antsaklis, P.J., Montestruque, L.A., McMickell, M.B.: Design of a wireless assisted pedestrian dead reckoning system the navmote experience. IEEE Trans. Instrum. Meas. **54**(6), 2342–2358 (2005)

18. Anshul, R., Chintalapudi, K.K., Padmanabhan, V.N., Rijurekha, S.: Zee: zero-effort crowdsourcing for indoor localization. In: 18th Annual International Conference on Mobile Computing and Networking (MOBICOM), pp. 293–304, Istanbul (2012)

19. Weimann, F., Abwerzger, G., Wellenhof, B.H.: A pedestrian navigation system for urban and indoor environments. In: 20th International Technical Meeting of the Satellite Division of the Institute of Navigation, pp. 1380–1389, Fort Worth (2007)

20. Robert, W.L., Judd, T.: Dead Reckoning Navigation System Using Accelerometer to Measure Foot Impacts. US Patent No. 5583776 (1996)

21. Fan, L., Shui, Z.C., Zhong, D.G., Gong, J., Xing, L.C., Feng, Z.: A reliable and accurate indoor localization method using phone inertial sensors. In: 14th ACM Conference on Ubiquitous Computing, pp. 421–430, Pittsburgh (2012)

22. Storms, W., Shockley, J., Raquet, J.: Magnetic field navigation in an indoor environment. In: Ubiquitous Positioning Indoor Navigation and Location Based Service (UPINLBS) Conference, pp. 1–10, Kirkkonummi (2010)

23. Shibuhisa, N., Sato, J., Takahashi, T., Ide, I., Murase, H., Kojima, Y., Takahashi, A.: Accurate vehicle localization using DTW between range data map and laser scanner data sequences. In: Intelligent Vehicles Symposium Conference, pp. 975–980, Istanbul (2007)

24. Fan, J.X., Mike, L., Fei, C.K., Ben, Z., Hsu, J., Jie, L., Bin, C., Feng, Z.: Design and evaluation of a wireless magnetic-based proximity detection platform for indoor applications. In: 11th International Conference on Information Processing in Sensor Networks, pp, 221–232, Beijing (2012)

25. Gutjahr, W.J.: First steps to the runtime complexity analysis of ant colony optimization. Comput. Oper. Res. **35**(9), 2711–2727 (2008)

26. Neumann, F., Sudholt, D., Witt, C.: Computational complexity of ant colony optimization and its hybridization. Innovations Swarm Intell. **248**, 91–120 (2009)

Localization Algorithm in Wireless Sensor Networks Based on Multi-objective Particle Swarm Optimization

Ziwen Sun[✉], Xinyu Wang, Li Tao, and Zhiping Zhou

School of Internet of Things Engineering, Jiangnan University,
Lihu Rd. 1800, Wuxi 214122, China
{sunziwen,zzp}@jiangnan.edu.cn, garywxy@126.com, TaoLi.jnu@gmail.com

Abstract. Based on multi-objective particle swarm optimization, a localization algorithm is proposed to solve the multi-objective optimization localization issues in wireless sensor networks. The multi-objective functions consist of the space distance constraint and the geometric topology constraint. The optimal solution is found by multi-objective particle swarm optimization algorithm. Dynamic method is adopted to maintain the archive in order to limit the size of archive, and the global optimum is obtained according to the proportion of selection. The simulation results show considerable improvements in terms of localization accuracy and convergence rate while keeping limited archive size by using both global optimal selection operator and dynamic maintaining archive method.

Keywords: Wireless sensor networks · Localization · Multi-objective particle swarm optimization

1 Introduction

The research on localization issues is important to the practical application of wireless sensor networks (WSN) technology. Modern WSN applications pose increasingly complex and stringent performance requirements on localization in terms of accuracy. However, the localization methods by using traditional ranging technologies, such as Received Signal Strength Indication (RSSI), exist drawback of low accuracy. Thus the intelligent algorithms have been used to solve the problems of localization [1–3]. Among these methods, the Particle Swarm Optimization (PSO) algorithm is concerned by many researchers for its fast convergence rate and simple implementation. For example, the PSO localization algorithm based on log-barrier constraint function could accelerate the convergence speed and save energy [4], the PSO localization adopting crossover operator and mutation operator could avoid premature convergence [5], and the PSO localization algorithm based on quantum mechanics could enhance the global convergence and improve the accuracy [6].

© Springer-Verlag Berlin Heidelberg 2015
L. Sun et al. (Eds.): CWSN 2014, CCIS 501, pp. 223–232, 2015.
DOI: 10.1007/978-3-662-46981-1_21

The above methods imitate the estimating coordinates of unknown nodes by using particles of PSO, which take the space distance constraint as fitness function and obtain the global optimal solution as the final location. However, it always happens that the localization results meet the space distance constraint without meeting the geometric topology constraint because of ranging errors in solving the practical issues. Therefore, localization issues can be described as a multi-objective model rather than simply described as a single-objective model. A multi-objective model was adopted and the optimal solution was resolved through the genetic algorithm [7]. However, the method in [7] has some problems: the estimation accuracy is affected by the selection and mutation operators and the convergence rate is slow, and also the nodes storage space has to be increased due to limitless of the archive being used for the storage of Pareto optimal solutions.

The Multi-objective PSO has been studied to resolve optimal issues. An multi-objective multi leader PSO was used handling the extra objective by constraint handling method [8]. A bare-bones PSO was combined with sensitivity-based clustering to solve Multi-objective reliability redundancy allocation problems [9]. Multi-objective PSO algorithm was used to optimize parameters of Stirling engine with more effective than genetic algorithms [10]. A local search operator based on attraction was introduced to speed up the convergence [11]. PSO was combined with charge system search to select the global best particle from a set of Pareto-optimal solutions to solve the convergence and diversity of solutions in Multi-objective swarm optimization problem [12]. Based on decomposition, the multi-swarm Multi-objective PSO could solve the problems of local optimum solution, the convergence and accuracy of Pareto solution set [13].

To address the issues of slow convergence and limitless archive in reference [7], based on Multi-objective PSO, a novel method Multi-objective Particle Swarm Optimization Localization Algorithm (MOPSOLA) for WSN localization is proposed in this paper. Combined with the theory of Pareto optimality, MOPSOLA constructs a multi-objective model with both the space distance constraint and the geometric topology constraint as multi-objective functions. Archive is set a maximum capacity to save the storage space for storing the Pareto optimal solutions and dynamically maintained. The global optimum is obtained according to the proportion of selection. The simulation results approve the algorithm can effectively find the multi-objective optimal solutions and achieve both the better convergence speed and positioning accuracy.

2   Multi-objective Localization Model

The coordinates of unknown nodes need to meet both the space distance constraint and geometric topology constraint. The purpose of meeting the space distance constraint is to make the estimating coordinates closer to the real value, and meanwhile the purpose of meeting the geometric topology constraint is to make the network topology unique to avoid forming a topological structure which is not in conformity with the actual situation.

Assuming that n nodes are deployed in two-dimensional space Z^2 of WSN, including m anchor nodes with $m < n$ and $n - m$ unknown nodes. To the two nodes i and j, which are in the communication radius of each other, the inter-node ranging distance d_{ij} can be obtained by RSSI ranging technology. The ranging distance is donated by formula (1):

$$d_{ij} = r_{ij} + e_{ij}. \tag{1}$$

Where $r_{ij} = \sqrt{(x_i - x_j)^2 + (y_i - y_j)^2}$ is the actual distance between inter-node i and j, e_{ij} is the ranging errors of RSSI which follows a zero mean Gaussian distribution with variance σ^2 [7].

The neighbor set N_i and the complement set $\overline{N}_i$ of node i are defined as formula (2) and (3):

$$N_i = \{j \in 1, \ldots, n, j \neq i : r_{ij} \leq R\}. \tag{2}$$

$$\overline{N}_i = \{j \in 1, \ldots, n, j \neq i : r_{ij} > R\}. \tag{3}$$

Where R is the communication radius of node i.

Assuming $(\hat{x}_i, \hat{y}_i)$ is the estimate coordinate of unknown node $i, i = m + 1, \ldots, n$, thus the objective function of space distance constraint is denoted by formula (4):

$$f_1 = \sum_{i=m+1}^{n} \left(\sum_{j \in N_i} \left(\hat{d}_{ij} - d_{ij} \right)^2 \right). \tag{4}$$

Where $\hat{d}_{ij}$ is the estimated distance between nodes i and j, denoted by formula (5):

$$\hat{d}_{ij} = \begin{cases} \sqrt{(\hat{x}_i - x_j)^2 + (\hat{y}_i - y_j)^2} & \text{if } j \text{ is an anchor} \\ \sqrt{(\hat{x}_i - \hat{x}_j)^2 + (\hat{y}_i - \hat{y}_j)^2} & \text{otherwise}. \end{cases} \tag{5}$$

The objective function of geometric topology constraint is denoted by formula (6):

$$f_2 = \sum_{i=m+1}^{n} \left(\sum_{j \in N_i} \delta_{ij} + \sum_{j \in \overline{N}_i} (1 - \delta_{ij}) \right). \tag{6}$$

Where δ_{ij} is denoted by formula (7):

$$\delta_{ij} = \begin{cases} 1 & \text{if } \hat{d}_{ij} > R \\ 0 & \text{otherwise}. \end{cases} \tag{7}$$

The estimating coordinates of the unknown nodes are the optimum solutions for the multi-objective optimization issues, which can be obtained by decreasing both the value of objective function f_1 and f_2 through multi-objective PSO algorithm at the same time during processing of localization.

3   MOPSOLA

3.1   Mathematical Description of MOPSOLA

The optimal solution of multi-objective optimization issues is called Pareto optimal solution [14] as well. Multi-objective optimization issues with u-dimensional decision vectors and v objectives are denoted as formula (8):

$$\min y = F(x) = (f_1(x), f_2(x), \ldots, f_v(x))$$
$$\text{s.t.} x \in [L, U].$$
(8)

Where $x = (x_1, x_2, \ldots x_u) \in X \subset R^u$ is u-dimensional particle and $y = (y_1, y_2, \ldots y_v) \in Y \subset R^v$ is v-dimensional objective variable $(v = 2)$, Y is v-dimensional objective space, L and U are lower and upper bound constraint of particle range respectively. The set consist of every particle which meets the constraint forms the decision space feasible set Ω as $\Omega = \{x \in R^u | x \in [L, U]\}$.

Obtaining the multi-objective Pareto optimal solution is the ultimate goal of building a multi-objective optimal model for localization issues, which meets both space distance constraint and geometric topology constraint. For two feasible solutions x_a $x_b \in \Omega$ in the process of PSO, if $\forall i = 1, 2, \ldots, v, f_i(x_b) \leq f_i(x_a) \land \exists j = 1, 2, \ldots, v, f_j(x_b) < f_j(x_a)$, then call x_b dominate x_a, denoted as $x_b \prec x_a$, and keep x_b as optimization results. The purpose of optimization is to find Pareto optimal solution x^*, denoted as $\neg \exists x \in \Omega : x \prec x^*$. Save all of the Pareto optimal solution into an archive to obtain the set of Pareto optimal solution S: $S = \{x \in \Omega | \neg \exists x' \in \Omega, f_j(x') \leq f_j(x), (j = 1, 2, \ldots, v)\}$. Obtain the value of f_1 and f_2 through the image of Pareto optimal solution set in objective space, called Pareto front F : $F = \{F(x^*) = (f_1(x^*), f_2(x^*), \ldots, f_v(x^*)) | x^* \in S\}$.

Therefore the main essence of MOPSOLA can be descripted as determining the dominant relationship according to the decision space feasible set Ω and Pareto front F, saving Pareto optimal solution set S, and updating the position and velocity of multi-objective PSO.

3.2   Realization of MOPSOLA

Overall Framework. Shown as Fig. 1, multi-objective PSO algorithm framework includes some key operators such as archive maintenance, global optimum selection, and the position and velocity update etc. The population needs to rely on archive saving Pareto optimal solutions during the iterative process and selecting the global optimum from these solutions, which is the key issue that the multi-objective PSO is different from traditional single objective localization. Therefore, the localization issue is modeled as multi-objective optimization model in this article, and two operators, both the dynamic maintenance operator for archive and global optimum selection operator based on proportion of selection, are designed to be suitable for limited energy and poor computing power of WSN nodes.

In archive maintenance operator, the maximum capacity of archive is set as ArcMax and the archive is dynamically updated according to the density

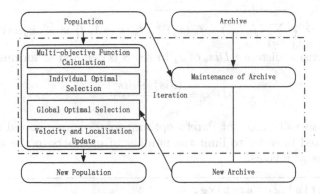

Fig. 1. Overall framework of multi-objective PSO

distance in objective space of Pareto optimal solution in order to save the storage space. In global optimum selection operator, the proportion of selection is set for each Pareto optimal solution based on intensive distance and a global optimum for each particle is selected by proportion of selection. The position and velocity update operator is similar to the traditional single objective PSO as formula (9) and (10):

$$v_{ab}(k+1) = \omega v_{ab}(k) + c_1 r_1 (p_{ab} - h_{ab}(k)) + c_2 r_2 (pg_b - h_{ab}(k)). \qquad (9)$$

$$h_{ab}(k+1) = h_{ab}(k) + v_{ab}(k+1). \qquad (10)$$

Archive Maintenance Operator. Multi-objective PSO algorithm does not produce the unique solution but a set of Pareto optimal solutions at the end of each iteration, thus an archive is used to save these Pareto optimal solutions, and the members in the archive become the final solution set when the iteration stops. As the storage space of node is limited, a method is adopted to limit the members in an archive by deleting some of members when the maximum capacity is reached, as a result, a space will be left the solutions going to enter into the archive.

However, due to non-dominated property of Pareto optimal solutions, namely there is no difference between the solutions, a concept of intensive distance is introduced to evaluate the solution quality. Generally, the point in sparse area which has bigger intensive distance is better than the point in intensive area in the objective space [15]. The concept of intensive distance is presented as: Suppose set S is the set of Pareto optimal solutions in archive, $x_i \in S$ is a Pareto optimal solution, two kinds of distance are evaluated firstly which are the minimum distance dis_i^1 and second minimum distance dis_i^2 between x_i and other Pareto optimal solutions in the archive, the dis_i^1 and dis_i^2 are denoted as formula (11):

$$
\begin{aligned}
dis_i^1 &= \min \left\{ dis_{i,j} \, | x_i \in S, j \neq i \right\} \\
dis_i^2 &= \min \left\{ dis_{i,j} \, | dis_{i,j} > dis_i^1, x_i \in S, j \neq i \right\}.
\end{aligned} \qquad (11)
$$

Where $dis_{i,j} = \sqrt{\sum\limits_{k=1}^{2} (f_k(x_i) - f_k(x_j))^2}$, f_k $(k = 1, 2)$ is a objective function.

Then the intensive distance Dis_i of x_i in set S is denoted as formula (12):

$$Dis_i = \frac{(dis_i^1 + dis_i^2)}{2}. \tag{12}$$

The intensive distances of Pareto optimal solutions are sorted and smaller ones are deleted in order to limit the number of members in the archive. The pseudo code is as follow:

```
Initialize archive;
WHILE Receive feasible solution DO
   TempArc=archive ∪ feasible solution;
   Delete repetitive solution in TempArc;
   FOR Every member in TempArc DO
      IF dominated
            Delete;
      END
   END
   IF number of TempArc ≤ ArcMax
         archive=TempArc;
   ELSE
         Compute Dis of TempArc;
         Descending sort of TempArc;
         archive= ArcMax members in TempArc;
   END
END
```

It is ensured that the members in the archive can be limited in the maximum capacity by the archive maintenance operator, which avoids the non-dominated solutions increasing infinitely to reduce the efficiency along with the evolution. At the same time, the most intense individual is deleted, and the uniform distribution of Pareto front is ensured by saving lots of scattered individuals.

Global Optimum Selection Operator. In traditional single objective PSO algorithm, it is tolerable to use the optimal solution with best fitness as the global optimum $gbest$ because $gbest$ of every particle is the same. However, in multi-objective PSO the population generates more than one non-dominated $gbest$ leading difference among some particle global optimums, which results to necessarily choose the appropriate global optimum.

Based on the conception of intensive distance, the method adopts proportion of selection to select global optimum for each particle. The concept of proportion of selection is presented as: suppose that the number of Pareto optimal solutions in the archive of current iteration is c with $c \leq$ ArcMax, a proportion of selection ξ_i is generated for each Pareto optimal solution according to the formula (13):

$$\xi_i = \frac{Dis_i}{\sum\limits_{k=1}^{c} Dis_k}, \ i = 1, \ldots, c. \tag{13}$$

Formula (13) presents that the larger intensive distance a Pareto optimal solution has, the bigger proportion of selection it has, and therefore it has a bigger proportion to be selected as the global optimum. The pseudo code is as follow:

```
WHILE t ≤ t_max  DO
    FOR Every member of archive DO
        Compute Dis;
        Compute ξ_i;
    END
    FOR Every particle DO
        Using roulette wheel to choose
        gbest according to ξ_i;
    END
END
```

4   Simulations and Analysis

The simulation platform is Matlab 2010b. 100 nodes are randomly deployed and anchor nodes are randomly generated from these nodes in $100\,\mathrm{m} \times 100\,\mathrm{m}$ area. RSSI ranging error e_{ij} follows Gaussian distribution with a zero mean and variance σ^2, $\sigma^2 = \beta^2 r_{ij}^2$, $\beta = 0.1$. The population of the multi-objective PSO is 100, ArcMax is 50, the communication radius of nodes is $R = 25\,\mathrm{m}$.

The Pareto front formed by space distance constraint and the geometric topology constraint is shown as Fig. 2. Every node on the Pareto front plan corresponds to a Pareto optimal solution in the decision space. Under the condition of 20 % ratio of anchor nodes, a Pareto optimal solution consists of a vector with estimated coordinates corresponding to 80 unknown nodes. In Fig. 2, the value of f_1 is from 0.92 to 0.98 and f_2 is from 30 to 95.

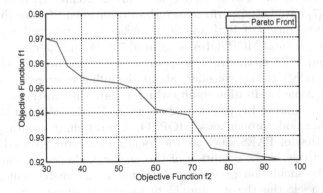

Fig. 2. The pareto front of f_1 and f_2

Figure 3 shows three pair comparisons of objective function f_2 values between the MOPSOLA and traditional PSO localization algorithm. The three data sets of objective function f_2 are 140, 150 and 155 in PSO and 47, 66 and 68 in MOP-SOLA respectively. It can be observed that the values are reduced in MOPSOLA by 66%, 56%, and 56% compared with the traditional PSO respectively. The reason about this phenomenon is because that the essential meaning of f_2 is the times of inaccuracy localization not meeting the geometric topology constraint during the process of localization. The simulation result proves that the performance of MOPSOLA is better in correcting inaccuracy geometric topology compared with the traditional PSO.

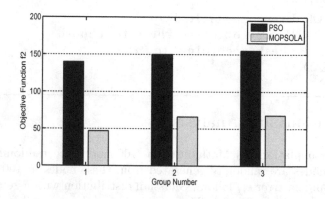

Fig. 3. The comparison of f_2 between MOPSOLA and PSO

Simulation results are also shown in Table 1 for the relationship between anchor node proportion and positioning error, in condition of communication radius of 25 m and ranging error of 20%. The simulation results in Table 1 shows the node positioning error decreases with the increasing of the anchor node proportion. This is because the increase of anchor nodes among the neighbor of unknown nodes cause positioning accuracy improved. In the condition of same anchor nodes ratio, MOPSOLA and Pareto Archive Evolutionary Strategy (PAES) [7] have better performance than traditional PSO localization algorithm. In the condition of 10% and 20% anchor node proportion respectively, the positioning error of MOPSOLA is reduced 7.09% and 7.39% compared with the traditional PSO method. These results show that because the model of multi-objective localization considers about the influence of geometric topology constraint f_2, some localization results which violate the constraint will be modified to further improve the positioning accuracy. Furthermore, in the condition of same anchor node proportions, MOPSOLA positioning accuracy is slightly higher than that of PAES, such as the localization error reduced 0.95% and 0.88% respectively in the condition of the anchor node proportion being 10% and 25%. The simulation results prove that dynamic maintenance of archive combined with selecting the optimum by proportion of selection can obtain closer result to the real localization and improve the positioning accuracy.

Table 1. The relationship between anchor node proportion and localization error

Anchor nodes	Proportion	5%	10%	15%	20%	25%	30%
Localization error	PSO	22.57%	20.33%	19.19%	18.94%	17.17%	16.77%
	PAES	16.47%	14.19%	12.88%	12.10%	11.87%	11.02%
	MOPSOLA	15.57%	13.24%	12.17%	11.55%	10.99%	10.54%

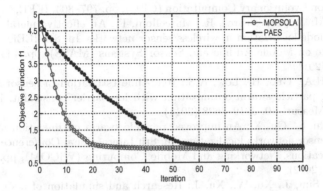

Fig. 4. The comparison of convergence rate between MOPSOLA and PAES

Figure 4 is the comparison of objective function f_1 about the convergence rate between MOPSOLA and PAES. MOPSOLA and PAES starts to convergence at the 20th iteration and 60th respectively. The result shows that MOPSOLA retains more outstanding individuals to accelerate the algorithm convergence by avoiding the affection of selection and mutation operation on the next generation and adopting dynamic maintenance of archive combined with selecting the optimum by proportion of selection.

5   Conclusions

MOPSOLA adopts multi-objective localization with objective functions consisting of space distance constraint and geometric topology constraint, and solves optimal solutions by adopting both the dynamic maintenance operator for archive and global optimal selection operator based on proportion of selection. Compared with traditional PSO localization algorithm, MOPSOLA can improve the localization accuracy and decrease the convergence rate. Compared with similar multi-objective localization algorithm PAES, the convergence rate is greatly enhanced but the localization accuracy is slightly increased. Under the premise of ensuring position accuracy, how to further improve the convergence rate and reduce the energy consumption will be the next research emphasis.

Acknowledgments. This work is supported by the National Natural Science Foundation of China under Grant No. 61373126, the Natural Science Foundation of Jiangsu Province of China under Grant No. BK20131107 and the State Scholarship Fund by China Scholarship Council.

References

1. Kulkarni, R.V., Förster, A., Venayagamoorthy, G.K.: Computational intelligence in wireless sensor networks: a survey. IEEE Commun. Surv. Tutorials **13**, 68–96 (2011)
2. Assis, A.F., Vieira, L.F.M., Rodrigues, M.T.R., Pappa, G.L.: A genetic algorithm for the minimum cost localization problem in wireless sensor networks. In: IEEE Congress on Evolutionary Computation (CEC), pp. 797–804. IEEE, Cancun (2013)
3. Vecchio, M., López-Valcarce, R., Marcelloni, F.: An effective metaheuristic approach to node localization in wireless sensor networks. In: 8th IEEE International Conference on Mobile Ad-hoc and Sensor Systems (MASS), pp. 143–145. IEEE, Valencia (2011)
4. Nguyen, H.A., Guo, H., Low, K.S.: Real-time estimation of sensor node's position using particle swarm optimization with log-barrier constraint. IEEE Trans. Instrum. Measur. **60**, 3619–3628 (2011)
5. Hu, X., Shi, S., Gu, X.: An improved particle swarm optimization algorithm for wireless sensor networks localization. In: 8th International Conference on Wireless Communications. Networking and Mobile Computing (WiCOM), pp. 1–4. IEEE, Shanghai (2012)
6. Gong, L., Sun, J., Xu, W., Xu, J.: Research and simulation of node localization in WSN based on quantum particle swarm optimization. In: 11th International Symposium on Distributed Computing and Applications to Business. Engineering and Science (DCABES), pp. 144–148. IEEE, Guilin (2012)
7. Vecchio, M., López-Valcarce, R., Marcelloni, F.: A two-objective evolutionary approach based on topological constraints for node localization in wireless sensor networks. Appl. Soft Comput. J. **12**, 1891–1901 (2012)
8. Shokrian, M., High, K.A.: Application of a multi objective multi-leader particle swarm optimization algorithm on NLP and MINLP problems. Comput. Chem. Eng. **60**, 57–75 (2014)
9. Zhang, E., Wu, Y., Chen, Q.: A practical approach for solving multi-objective reliability redundancy allocation problems using extended bare-bones particle swarm optimization. Reliab. Eng. Syst. Saf. **127**, 65–76 (2014)
10. Duan, C., Wang, X., Shu, S., Jing, C., Chang, H.: Thermodynamic design of Stirling engine using multi-objective particle swarm optimization algorithm. Energy Convers. Manage. **84**, 88–96 (2014)
11. Kaveh, A., Laknejadi, K.: A novel hybrid charge system search and particle swarm optimization method for multi-objective optimization. Expert Syst. Appl. **38**, 15475–15488 (2011)
12. Peng, H., Li, R., Cao, L.L., Li, L.X.: Multiple swarms multi-objective particle swarm optimization based on decomposition. Procedia Eng. **15**, 3371–3375 (2011)
13. Wei, J., Zhang, M.: Attraction based PSO with sphere search for dynamic constrained multi-objective optimization problems. In: Genetic and Evolutionary Computation Conference (GECCO), pp. 77–78. IEEE, Dublin (2011)
14. Gong, M.G., Jiao, L.C., Yang, D.D., Ma, W.P.: Research on evolutionary multi-objective optimization algorithms. J. Softw. **20**, 271–289 (2009)
15. Li, W., Zhang, X.: An improved multi-objective particle swarm optimization algorithm based on pareto. Comput. Simul. **27**, 96–99 (2010)

2-D Adaptive Beamforming with Multiple Bi-Direction Optimization Based on Data Matrix and Application in Interferences Localization

Weike Nie[1]($\boxtimes$), Dazheng Feng[2], Dingyi Fang[1],
and Xiaojiang Chen[1]

[1] School of Information Science and Technology, Northwest University, Xi'an, China
weikenie@163.com
[2] National Key Lab of Radar Signal Processing, Xidian University, Xi'an, China

Abstract. Based on data matrix, a novel algorithm termed multiple bi-direction optimization (MBDO) is proposed to implement two-dimension (2-D) adaptive beamforming and interference sources localization. The main contribution of MBDO is to process the long weight vector. We decomposed the long weight vector into two short weight vectors. MBDO is used to compute the two short weight vectors by data matrix to finish beamforming. Moreover, the inverse of high dimension correlation matrix is replaced by low dimension data matrix. Theoretical analysis and simulations are provided to demonstrate the significant reduction in computational complexity and the improvement in performance compared with the well-known LCMV beamforming in most cases.

Keywords: Sensor array signal processing · Data domain · Interference location · MBDO algorithm

1 Introduction

Adaptive beamforming is a classical problem encountered in radar, sonar and wireless communications [1]. The key of adaptive beamforming is to find a weight vector which can maintains signal and suppress interference and noise, hence the output signal to interference plus noise ratio (SINR) can be improved. The weight vector of well-known linearly constrained minimum variance (LCMV) beamformer [2–4] is computed by the inverse of correlation matrix, i.e. $\mathbf{w}_{LCMV} = f(\hat{\mathbf{R}}^{-1})$. In 2-D application, the plane array should be used to implement the spatial beam, and the array sensors commonly much more than 1-D scenario, which results in a much longer received data vector and corresponding high dimension correlation matrix. In order to obtain a better correlation matrix estimation, the LCMV suffers from a huge snapshots requirement, and the inverse of high dimension correlation matrix calculation needs large computational burden.

To overcome the above drawbacks, the high dimension weight vector can be divided into two short weight vectors named forward and backward weight respectively. An iterative optimization algorithm was provided to compute the

© Springer-Verlag Berlin Heidelberg 2015
L. Sun et al. (Eds.): CWSN 2014, CCIS 501, pp. 233–242, 2015.
DOI: 10.1007/978-3-662-46981-1_22

short weight vectors. Each iteration includes forward and backward processing to compute the corresponding forward and backward weights. After convergence of the iterative algorithm, the high dimension weight needed for 2-D beamforming can be obtained by kronecker product of the two short weight vectors. As noted previously, we called our proposed as multiple bi-direction optimization method (MBDO).

It should be noted that the MBDO computes the forward and backward weight through received data matrix other than correlation matrix in LCMV algorithm. Obviously the dimension of data matrix in 2-D beamforming is much lower than the dimension of correlation matrix, we can obtain a better estimation of data matrix than correlation matrix in the case of finite sampling, hence our MBDO shows a better performance in smaller snapshots. Moreover, the inverse of the high dimension correlation matrix is avoided by using the data matrix, the computational complexity of MBDO is remarkably reduced. We analyzed the convergence performance of the proposed MBDO, compared it with LCMV in the beampattern, the output SINR and the performance within pointing error.

2   Array Model and 2D Lcmv Beamforming

Consider a rectangular antenna array with M row and N column sensors spaced on the XOY plane. Let the m row n column element received data at snapshot t is $x_{m,n}(t)$, received data matrix can be written as a M row and N column matrix

$$\mathbf{X}(t) = [x_{m,n}(t)] \quad m\ (n) = 1, 2, \cdots, M\ (N) \tag{1}$$

Let the corresponding weigh matrix is

$$\mathbf{W} = [w_{m,n}] \quad m\ (n) = 1, 2, \cdots, M\ (N) \tag{2}$$

Column stacking $\mathbf{X}(t)$ forms data vector $\mathbf{x}(t) = vec[\mathbf{X}(t)]$, column stacking $\mathbf{W}$ forms weigh vector $\mathbf{w} = vec(\mathbf{W})$. Let $\hat{\mathbf{R}} = E[\mathbf{x}\mathbf{x}^H]$, the 2D LCMV beamforming solves the following optimization problem

$$\begin{cases} \min(\mathbf{w}^H \hat{\mathbf{R}} \mathbf{w}) \\ s.t.\ \mathbf{w}^H \mathbf{a}(\Theta, \Phi) = 1 \end{cases} \tag{3}$$

where $\mathbf{a}(\Theta, \Phi)$ represents the steering vector of desired signal with azimuth and elevation angle are Θ and Φ. The LCMV weight can be derived as

$$\mathbf{w}_{LCMV} = \frac{\hat{\mathbf{R}}^{-1}\mathbf{a}(\Theta, \Phi)}{\mathbf{a}^H(\Theta, \Phi)\hat{\mathbf{R}}^{-1}\mathbf{a}(\Theta, \Phi)} \tag{4}$$

It is clear that $\mathbf{w}_{LCMV}$ is a $MN \times 1$ high dimension vector especially in 2D beamforming. Meanwhile, the $\mathbf{w}_{LCMV}$ is obtained from the inverse of $MN \times MN$ high dimension correlation matrix $\hat{\mathbf{R}}$. In order to obtain a accurate $\hat{\mathbf{R}}$ estimation to ensure the performance, a plenty of snapshots are needed. In most practical applications, it is hard to have a plenty of snapshots because of time and computation consumption.

3   Proposed Multiple Bi-Direction Optimization Method

Let $M \times 1$ vector $\mathbf{w}_{xm}$ and $N \times 1$ vector $\mathbf{w}_{yn}$ as forward and backward weight vector respectively, The weigh vector of 2-D beamforming can be expressed [5] as $\mathbf{w} = \mathbf{w}_{yn} \otimes \mathbf{w}_{xm}$. The output of beamformer is

$$\mathbf{w}^H \mathbf{x}(t) = \sum_{m=1}^{M} \sum_{n=1}^{N} w_{m,n}^* x_{m,n}(t) = \mathbf{w}_{xm}^H \mathbf{X}(t) \mathbf{w}_{yn}^* \tag{5}$$

The output average power of beamformer is

$$\bar{P} = \frac{1}{T} \sum_{t=1}^{T} \left| \mathbf{w}_{xm}^H \mathbf{X}(t) \mathbf{w}_{yn}^* \right|^2 = E \left| \mathbf{w}_{xm}^H \mathbf{X}(t) \mathbf{w}_{yn}^* \right|^2 \tag{6}$$

With the property of kronecker product [8], a new cost function can be constructed as

$$\begin{cases} \min\limits_{\mathbf{w}_{xm}, \mathbf{w}_{yn}} J = E \left| \mathbf{w}_{xm}^H \mathbf{X}(t) \mathbf{w}_{yn}^* \right|^2 \\ s.t. \ \mathbf{w}_{yn}^H \mathbf{a}_{yn} = 1 \quad and \quad \mathbf{w}_{xm}^H \mathbf{a}_{xm} = 1 \end{cases} \tag{7}$$

Using Lagrange multiplier method, we transform (7) to a unconstrained optimization problem as

$$\begin{aligned} \min\limits_{\mathbf{w}_{xm}, \mathbf{w}_{yn}, \lambda_1, \lambda_2} & J(\mathbf{w}_{xm}, \mathbf{w}_{yn}; \lambda_1, \lambda_2) \\ = & E\{ tr[\mathbf{w}_{xm}^H \mathbf{X}(t) \mathbf{w}_{yn}^* \mathbf{w}_{yn}^T \mathbf{X}^H(t) \mathbf{w}_{xm}] \} \\ & + \lambda_1 (\mathbf{w}_{yn}^H \mathbf{a}_{yn} - 1) + \lambda_2 (\mathbf{w}_{xm}^H \mathbf{a}_{xm} - 1) \end{aligned} \tag{8}$$

where tr represent the trace of a matrix. According the ideas in [6]–[7], we now proposed a MBDO method to solve the function (8). It is a iterative method, each iteration includes forward and backward optimization. In the forward optimization, we fixed $\mathbf{w}_{yn}$, Differentiating (8) with respect to $\mathbf{w}_{xm}^H$ and let $\partial J / \partial \mathbf{w}_{xm}^H = 0$ yields

$$\mathbf{w}_{xm} = -\lambda_2 \{ E[\mathbf{X}(t) \mathbf{w}_{yn}^* \mathbf{w}_{yn}^T \mathbf{X}^H(t)] \}^{-1} \mathbf{a}_{xm} \tag{9}$$

From $\mathbf{w}_{xm}^H \mathbf{a}_{xm} = 1$ in (7) easily know $\mathbf{w}_{xm} \mathbf{a}_{xm}^H = 1$, substituting (9) in $\mathbf{w}_{xm} \mathbf{a}_{xm}^H = 1$, the λ_2 can be derived as

$$\lambda_2 = \frac{-1}{\mathbf{a}_{xm}^H \{ E[\mathbf{X}(t) \mathbf{w}_{yn}^* \mathbf{w}_{yn}^T \mathbf{X}^H(t)] \}^{-1} \mathbf{a}_{xm}} \tag{10}$$

Then substituting λ_2 in (9) yields the expression of forward weight

$$\mathbf{w}_{xm} = \frac{\{ E[(\mathbf{X}(t) \mathbf{w}_{yn}^*)(\mathbf{X}(t) \mathbf{w}_{yn}^*)^H] \}^{-1} \mathbf{a}_{xm}}{\mathbf{a}_{xm}^H \{ E[(\mathbf{X}(t) \mathbf{w}_{yn}^*)(\mathbf{X}(t) \mathbf{w}_{yn}^*)^H] \}^{-1} \mathbf{a}_{xm}} \tag{11}$$

In the backward optimization, we fixed $\mathbf{w}_{xm}$, Differentiating (8) with respect to $(\mathbf{w}_{yn}^*)^H$ and let $\partial J / \partial (\mathbf{w}_{yn}^*)^H = 0$ yields

$$\mathbf{w}_{yn}^* = -\lambda_1 E[\mathbf{X}^H(t) \mathbf{w}_{xm} \mathbf{w}_{xm}^H \mathbf{X}(t)]^{-1} \mathbf{a}_{yn}^* \tag{12}$$

From the $\mathbf{w}_{yn}^{H}\mathbf{a}_{yn} = 1$ in (7) easily know $\mathbf{a}_{yn}^{T}\mathbf{w}_{yn}^{*} = 1$, substituting (12) in $\mathbf{a}_{yn}^{T}\mathbf{w}_{yn}^{*} = 1$, the λ_1 can be derived as

$$\lambda_1 = \frac{-1}{\mathbf{a}_{yn}^{T}\{E[\mathbf{X}^{H}(t)\mathbf{w}_{xm}\mathbf{w}_{xm}^{H}\mathbf{X}(t)]\}^{-1}\mathbf{a}_{yn}^{*}} \tag{13}$$

Then substituting λ_1 in (12) yields the expression of backward weight

$$\mathbf{w}_{yn}^{*} = \frac{\{E[(\mathbf{X}^{H}(t)\mathbf{w}_{xm})(\mathbf{X}^{H}(t)\mathbf{w}_{xm})^{H}]\}^{-1}\mathbf{a}_{yn}^{*}}{\mathbf{a}_{yn}^{T}\{E[(\mathbf{X}^{H}(t)\mathbf{w}_{xm})(\mathbf{X}^{H}(t)\mathbf{w}_{xm})^{H}]\}^{-1}\mathbf{a}_{yn}^{*}} \tag{14}$$

Once the algorithm has been convergent, the weight vector of proposed MBDO method can be derived as $\mathbf{w}_{MBDO} = \mathbf{w}_{yn} \otimes \mathbf{w}_{xm}$.

4   Computational Complexity Analysis

We carefully compute the multiplication and division number (MDN) required by classical LCMV and proposed MBDO. Assume the snapshots is κ, in the forward computation of MBDO, computs $\widehat{\mathbf{R}} = E[\mathbf{X}_{\mathbf{w}}(\mathbf{X}_{\mathbf{w}})^{H}]$ takes $\kappa(MN + M^2) + 1$ MDN, computs $\widehat{\mathbf{R}}^{-1}$ takes $2M^3/3$ MDN [8], computs $\mathbf{f}_1 = \widehat{\mathbf{R}}^{-1}\mathbf{a}_{xm}$ takes M^2 MDN, computs $g = \mathbf{a}_{xm}^{H}\widehat{\mathbf{R}}^{-1}\mathbf{a}_{xm}$ takes $M^2 + M$ MDN, computs $\mathbf{w}_{xm} = \mathbf{f}_1/g$ takes M MDN. In the backward computation of MBDO, computs $\tilde{\mathbf{R}} = E[\tilde{\mathbf{X}}_{\mathbf{w}}(\tilde{\mathbf{X}}_{\mathbf{w}})^{H}]$ takes $\kappa(MN + N^2) + 1$ MDN, computs $\tilde{\mathbf{R}}^{-1}$ takes $2N^3/3$ MDN, computs $\tilde{\mathbf{f}}_1 = \tilde{\mathbf{R}}^{-1}\mathbf{a}_{yn}^{*}$ takes N^2 MDN, computs $\tilde{g} = \mathbf{a}_{yn}^{T}\tilde{\mathbf{R}}^{-1}\mathbf{a}_{yn}^{*}$ takes $N^2 + N$ MDN, computs $\mathbf{w}_{yn}^{*} = \tilde{\mathbf{f}}_1/\tilde{g}$ takes $\eta_5 = N$ MDN. Let c_n represent the iteration number needed by convergence, the computation complexity of MBDO is

$$\eta_M = c_n[2(M^3 + N^3)/3 + 2(M^2 + N^2) + \kappa(M + N)^2 + 2(M + N) + 1] \tag{15}$$

For LCMV algorithm, computs $\hat{\mathbf{R}}$ takes $\kappa(MN)^2 + 1$ MDN, computs $\hat{\mathbf{R}}^{-1}$ takes $2(MN)^3/3$ MDN, computs $\hat{\mathbf{R}}^{-1}\mathbf{a}(\Theta, \Phi)$ takes $(MN)^2$ MDN, computs $\mathbf{a}^{H}(\Theta, \Phi)$ $\hat{\mathbf{R}}^{-1} \times \mathbf{a}(\Theta, \Phi)$ takes $(MN)^2 + MN$ MDN, the computation complexity of LCMV is

$$\eta_L = 2(MN)^3/3 + (\kappa + 2)(MN)^2 + MN + 1 \tag{16}$$

Obviously, with the increasing of array elements, η_L will rise faster because the major parts of the polynomial is MN.

5   Simulation Results

Simulations are given to compare the performance of the provided MBDO and the well-known LCMV with optimal performance. For these simulations, a rectangular antenna array with $M = 11$ row and $N = 9$ column sensors is assumed and the signal is corrupted by additive Gaussian noise, two interference sources

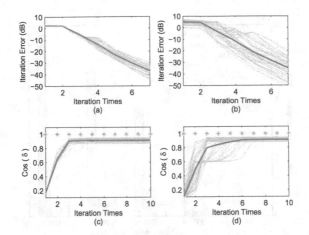

Fig. 1. Convergence performance of the proposed MBDO

with plane wavefronts and the directions of $(20°, 20°)$ and $(70°, 70°)$, there are two interference and the INR are always INR $= 20$ dB. The results have been averaged over 50 Monte Carlo runs.

In Fig. 1, we analyzed the convergence performance of the proposed MBDO. Let SNR $= -10$ dB, interference to noise ratio INR $= 20$ dB, the number of training snapshots is 1000. It is necessary to evaluate the Iteration Error (IE) which is defined by

$$IE = 10 \log_{10} \|(\mathbf{w}_{xm})_T - (\mathbf{w}_{xm})_L\|_F \quad (dB) \tag{17}$$

where $(\mathbf{w}_{xm})_T$ and $(\mathbf{w}_{xm})_L$ represent the weight computed this time and last time respectively, $\|\|_F$ represents Frobenius norm. Figure 1(a) shows the IE with the vector $\mathbf{w}_{yn}$ as a suitable initial value, the nth element of $\mathbf{w}_{yn}$ is $e^{j\frac{2\pi}{\lambda} y_{n-1} \sin\Theta \sin\Phi}$ $n = 1, 2, \cdots, N$. Figure 1(b) shows the IE with random initialization randn(N+1, 1)+j*randn(N+1, 1). The light-colored thin lines are the IE of each time and dark thick line is the average. we find the average performance is similar and think the traditional IE definition in (17) can not completely reflects the convergence circumstances, because a weak iterative algorithm or a inferior initialization will also deduce the computation results of the two adjacent IE very close, i.e. small Iteration Error. Furthermore, we compared the cosine angle of iteration weigh and theory weigh as

$$\cos(\delta) = \frac{\mathbf{w}_{MBDO}^H \mathbf{w}_{theo}}{\|\mathbf{w}_{MBDO}\|_F \|\mathbf{w}_{theo}\|_F} \tag{18}$$

where $\mathbf{w}_{theo} = \frac{\mathbf{R}_{theo}^{-1} \mathbf{a}(\Theta, \Phi)}{\mathbf{a}^H(\Theta, \Phi) \mathbf{R}_{theo}^{-1} \mathbf{a}(\Theta, \Phi)}$, $\mathbf{R}_{theo}$ is the correlation matrix in theory of received signal. Figure 1(c) and (d) show the $\cos(\delta)$ will rapid converge to 1 in average three times and seven iteration times with suitable initial value and random initialization respectively. Now, we can substitute $c_n = 3$, $c_n = 7$,

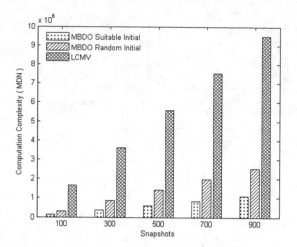

Fig. 2. Computation complexity versus snapshots

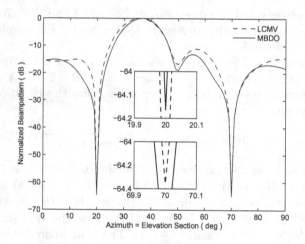

Fig. 3. Beampatterns of the proposed and LCMV beamformers

$M = 11$, $N = 9$ to (15) and (16), the computation complexity can be intuitively shows in Fig. 2.

Figure 3 shows the beampatterns of our proposed beamformer and the LCMV algorithm. The plane wave signal is assumed in this example, and is impinging on the array from $(\Theta, \Phi) = (35°, 35°)$ with SNR $= -5$ dB, In order to observe the beampatterns more clearly, without loss of generality, we let the azimuth and elevation angles are equal for signal and interferences, hence we can observe the 2D beampatterns in the section of equal azimuth and elevation angles instead of observation the 3D beampatterns which is usually inconvenient for analysis. From Fig. 3 and the partial enlargements, it can be seen both methods show the similar pattern behavior.

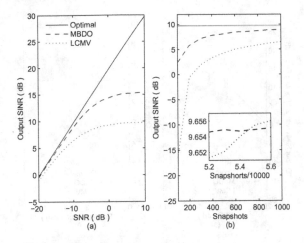

Fig. 4. Output SINR versus SNR and snapshots

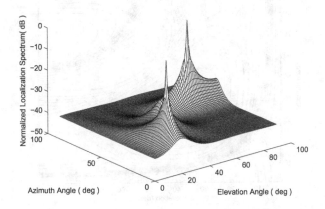

Fig. 5. Normlized localization spectrum of two interferences

Figure 4 shows the output SINR versus SNR and snapshots. In Fig. 4(a), the number of training snapshots is 1000. In Fig. 4(b), we fix the SNR $= -10$ dB. Figure 4 demonstrates the proposed MBDO has a obvious improvement in output SINR compared with LCMV. Specially, the output SINR of LCMV will be better than our MBDO because it is a closed-form solution while our MBDO is a iteration solution, but this case can only be completed in a huge snapshots, we find the snapshots usually between 53000 to 55000 (see subplot in Fig. 4(b)) which is too much for ordinary application.

Figure 5 shows the normlized localization spectrum of two interferences, the two interferences come from $(15°, 20°)$ and $(60°, 70°)$, interference to noise ratio INR $= 20$ dB, the number of training snapshots is 1000. The figure demonstrates

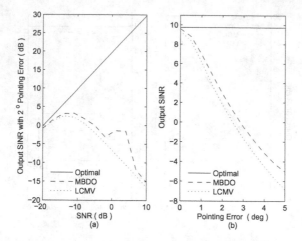

Fig. 6. Output SINR versus SNR and snapshots

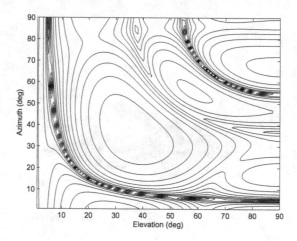

Fig. 7. Contour plot of the proposed algorithm

that the localiztion spectrum are sharp and hence the the proposed method possess a high resolution.

In Fig. 6, a case of pointing error is considered under fixed snapshots of 10000. In Fig. 6(a) the presumed and actual signal have a 2° mismatch, in Fig. 6(b) the mismatch vary from 2° to 5° and the SNR =−10 dB. we can see the output SINR loss of MBDO is slower than LCMV algorithm.

Figures 7 and 8 show the contour plots of proposed and LCMV algorithm respectively. the two interferences come from (15°, 20°) and (60°, 70°), we assumed the desired signal is impinging on the array from $(\Theta, \Phi) = (35°, 35°)$ with SNR = −10 dB, interference to noise ratio INR = 20 dB. From the contour plots, it can be seen clearly that the desired signal is maintained and the interferences can be suppressed deeply.

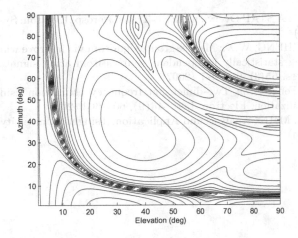

Fig. 8. Contour plot of the LCMV algorithm

6   Conclusions

Based on data domain, an iteration algorithm with good convergence termed MBDO is proposed for beamforming. Compared with the well-known LCMV method, it has an obvious advantage in computation complexity especially in large amount of array element or snapshots cases, both methods show similar pattern behavior. MBDO has better output SINR performance versus SNR and pointing error. In ordinary snapshot ranges, the output SINR of MBDO is closer to the optimal performance.

Acknowledgment. This paper was supported by the National Natural Science Foundation of China (61373177, 61272461, 61170218), the Natural Science Foundation of Shaanxi Province (2013JM8008) and the Scientific Research Plan of Education Department of Shaanxi Province (11JK0903).

References

1. Du, L., Li, J., Stoica, P.: Fully automatic computation of diagonal loading levels for robust adaptive beamforming. IEEE Trans. Aerosp. Electron. Syst. **46**(1), 449–458 (2010)
2. Buckley, K.M.: Spatial spectral filtering with linearly constrained minimum variance beamformers. IEEE Trans. Acoust. Speech, Signal Process. **35**(3), 249–266 (1987)
3. Van Veen, B.: Beamforming: a versatile approach to spatial filtering. IEEE Acoust. Speech, Signal Process. Mag. **5**(2), 4–24 (1988)
4. Bertrand, A., Szurley, J., Ruckebusch, P., Moerman, I., Moonen, M.: Efficient calculation of sensors utility and sensor removal in wireless sensor networks for adaptive signal estimation and beamforming. IEEE Trans. Signal Process. **60**(11), 5857–5869 (2012)

5. Melvin, W.L.: A STAP Overview. IEEE Trans. Aerosp. Electron. Syst. Mag. **19**(1), 19–35 (2004)
6. Feng, D.Z., ZHENG, W.X.: Matrix-group algorithm via improve whitening process for extracting statistically independent sources from array signals. IEEE Trans. Signal Process. **55**(3), 962–977 (2007)
7. Nie, W.K., Feng, D.Z.: Two-dimension frequency estimation using non-unitary joint diagonalization. Electron. Lett. **44**(9), 603–604 (2008)
8. Zhang, X.D.: Matrix Analysis and Application. Tsinghua University and Springer, Beijing (2004)

Heterogeneous Data Fusion Model
for Passive Object Localization

Tianzhang Xing, Binbin Xie, Liqiong Chang, Xiaojiang Chen[✉],
and Dingyi Fang

School of Information Science and Technology,
Northwest University, Xian 710127, China
{xtz,xjchen,dyf}@nwu.edu.cn, {xiebinbin001,changliqiong}@gmail.com

Abstract. The passive object localization problemPOLPaims to detect the location of the target. This task requires the target does not have any device to receive signal or transfer. The sensor fusion model for localization is more popular, such as the Kalman Filter(KF). In this paper, an novel fusion model based on the KF is used in fusing some parameters, like the RSSI(Receive Signal Strength Index), infrared data and ultrasound data, which are come from the measurements. The proposed fusion model can promote the accuracy of localization, and provides the higher available of localization. The simulation result have proved that the proposed methods is adequate to the passive localization, compared with other traditional methods, the localization accuracy is greatly improved.

Keywords: Wireless sensor network · Passive object localization · Kalman filter · RSSI · Infrared

1 Introduction

Wireless Sensor Network (WSNs) is a kind of network that consisted of a great quantity of static or mobile sensor nodes in the way of self-organization and multi-hop [1]. Many researchers and industries are looking to address the localization problem with the deployment of Radio-Frequency (RF) based devices/ systems. These systems may not be applicable in some scenarios. For instance, in case of the intrusion detection, it is impossible to pre-install the tracking devices on the intruders. Similarly, in the wild animal monitoring, it is hard to attach any device to the animal body. So, the Passive object localization (POL) has been of a great interest in both the academia and industry, and becoming most necessary to some application, service and manage in various fields, related the localization [2,3].

The POL does not ask the target to have any device for signal receiving or transmitting [4]. This limitation bring the great challenge for localization. We should estimate the location from fluctuating value of RSSI (Received Signal Strength Indication) caused by the target. The accuracy has been affected. In this paper, the fusion model is used for fusing the heterogenous data, including the

© Springer-Verlag Berlin Heidelberg 2015
L. Sun et al. (Eds.): CWSN 2014, CCIS 501, pp. 243–251, 2015.
DOI: 10.1007/978-3-662-46981-1_23

RSSI, infrared data and ultrasound data. Except the usual location information of the heterogenous data sources, for the accuracy improving, the pre-deployment information are used in the fusion, too. That can restraint the measurements data to be in the expect range.

The rest of this paper is organized as follows. Section 2 introduces the related work; Sect. 3 analyses the heterogeneous data fusion model; Sect. 4 give the performance evaluation. Section 5 concludes this paper and presents some discussions about the future work.

2   Related Work

In this section, we summarize the most relevant existing researches on the POL. Zhang et al. [5,6] proposed a real time, accurate and scalable system (RASS) to perform POL. They divided the tracking field into grids, and used the support vector regression model to locate the object in each area. Based on the original classic LANDMARC [7], Liu has completed the research and design the fingerprint method for passive location systems [8–10]. Wilson et al. [11] proposed the Radio Tomographic Imaging (RTI) technique, which uses the redundancy introduced by sensor arrays surrounding the monitored area to visualize the target-induced RSS fluctuations. Sigg et al. [12] identified the features obtained on the Radio Frequency Channel to detect the activities of non-actively transmitting subjects, and they showed that a detected activity can also be localized within an area of less than 1 m radius. A single data type is common characteristics of these studies mentioned above. As known as, the WSN including multiple sensor, how to effective use the hierarchical multiple sensor data for the POL, it is our focused on. Based on the hierarchical data fusion method, we propose a hierarchical multiple sensor data fusion model, in view of the outdoors passive target detection and localization problem.

3   Ranging Models

3.1   Signal Transmission Model

In wireless communication systems, radio waves usually spread in an irregular and non-monolithic environment. If we want to estimate the channel loss, the obstacles on the propagation path need to be considered, such as the topography, buildings, trees, telegraph poles. RSSI will not only be affected by the link environment, the voltage of the transceiver, the direction of antenna and other conditions will also have a huge impact. In theoretical study, these conditions are treated as constants. When wireless signal is propagating in free space, RSSI is consistent with the normal distribution with the distance, it is calculated as follows:

$$PL(dB) = 10 \log \frac{P_t}{P_r} = -10 \log \left[\frac{G_t G_r \lambda^2}{(4\pi)^2 d^2} \right] \tag{1}$$

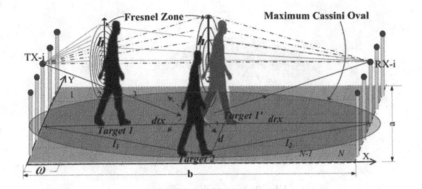

Fig. 1. Signal transmission model.

where $PL(dB)$ denotes the path loss, that is, signal attenuation, defined as the difference between effective transmit power and receive power. P_t denotes transmit power, P_r denotes receive power. G_t denotes transmit antenna gain, G_r denotes receive antenna gain. λ denotes the wireless signal wavelength in meters; d denotes the distance between the transmitter and the receiver in meters.

When the target into the monitoring area, the $PL(db)$ will change. It is because the diffraction gain and the scattering gain, as shown in Fig. 1. We can calculate the distance between the target and sensor, based on the RSSI measured.

Diffraction model:

$$D\,(dB) = 20 \log\left| \frac{1+j}{2} \int\limits_{v}^{\infty} \exp\exp\left(\frac{-j\pi t^2}{2} dt \right) \right| \tag{2}$$

Scattering model:

$$S\,(dB) = 10 \log \frac{P_t G_t G_r \lambda^2 \sigma}{4\pi^3 l_1^2 l_2^2} \tag{3}$$

3.2 Infrared Ranging Model

Every object has a certain temperature energy rely on the electromagnetic radiation. The total flow rate and the radiation wavelength are rely on its temperature T and the radiant emissivity. The radiant emissivity is wthin the range $[0..1]$ and draws the talent of a the emit radiation in equivalence to a flawless emitter at a certain temperature, it is blackbody defined in the Physics. The wavelength decides the emissivity, as shown in Fig. 2. However, in some situations, the wavelength range is limited, as the [16] constants. The triadic relation between the λ, T, and M_λ is defined as:

$$M_\lambda = \frac{\varepsilon(\lambda) \cdot C_1}{\lambda^5 (e^{C_2/\lambda T} - 1)} \tag{4}$$

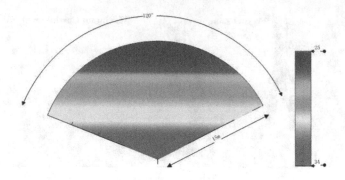

Fig. 2. Infrared ranging.

where $C_1 = 3.74 \cdot 10^{-12}\,W/cm^2$ and $C_2 = 1.44\,cmK$, the λ is wavelength, the T is temperature, the M_λ is radiant existence.

The relationship between the radiant existence and the irradiance is shown as:

$$\frac{\varepsilon M_\lambda A}{\pi} = Ee \cdot d^2 \tag{5}$$

3.3 Ultrasonic Ranging Model

There are several methods of ultrasonic distance measurement, such as phase assay, acoustic amplitude value test and transit-time method, etc. Among them, the transit-time method is the most widely used and its basic idea is using ultrasound to calculate the distance between the sensors and targets. It has three parts specificly. First, The ultrasonic wave is inspired by the pulse signal from the ultrasonic sensors and is transmitted to the targets by the medium, thus the reflective wave will be producted. Second, The reflective wave return to the receving sensor by the sound transmission medium, then the acoustic signals is transformed into electrical signals by sensors. Last but not least, The system records the ultrasonic transmission time from transmitting to receiving, and calculates the distance between the sensors and targets according to the speed of ultrasonic wave in the medium. The formula is shown as follows:

$$s = \frac{CT}{2} \tag{6}$$

where s is the distance on measure and C is the speed of ultrasonic wave in the sound transmission medium, and T is the ultrasonic transmission time from transmitting to receiving.

In this paper, the simulation experiment adopts two ultrasonic sensors, one is using for receiving ultrasonic wave and the other one is for transmitting. The whole experiment use the air as the transmission medium. The ultrasonic ranging principle is shown in Fig. 3.

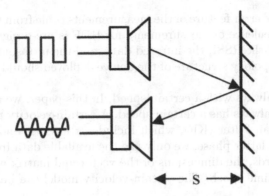

Fig. 3. Ultrasonic ranging.

4   Heterogeneous Data Fusion Model

In this section, we will describe the HDF, which is the model for fusing heterogenous data. The state vector S_i is the most important for HDF, as playing the important role in the SM(Statstic Model) and RSE(Recursive State Estimation)[13–15]. The uncertain state vector S_i could not be obtained by the measuring. We only through the operation for the measurements to get it. At the beginning, we can define some parameters, such as the initial state S_0, the noises which including the measurement noises and process noises. The noises are always stochastic in usual. The Bayesian framework have two phases: forecast and modification. In the forecast phase, the current state has been updated relayed on the antecedent state and the other parameters of the system. While, in the modification phase, the forecast has been refreshed wit new data which come from the measurement. The Bayesian framework including the measure model and dynamic model should be displaced respectively as:

$$A_i = G_i + s_i + \xi_i, \tag{7}$$

$$s_{i+1} = U_i S_i + s_i + \eta_i, \tag{8}$$

where, the A_i denotes the vector of measurement, the S_i denotes state vector which need to be solved, the G_i denotes the matrix of measurement, the U_i denotes the matrix of state transition, ξ_i and η_i are the measure noise and process noise vector with known, respectively. Typically, $\xi_i \sim N(0, R_i)$, where R_i is the covariance matrix of measurement. Similarly, $\eta_i \sim N(0, Q_i)$, where Q_i is the covariance matrix of process. In general assumption, the noises ξ_i and η_i are independent of each other.

For creating the measure model, we should know the three questions: (i) Which available measurement can be used. (ii) What kind of relationship exist in the position and the data come from the measure work. (iii) How the reference system can be used for the localization [16]. Moreover, the other important question should be ensured, that is the error feature of the measurements come from the the deployed sensors. The provenience of measurements for HDF is pre-designed Radio-Map, which is consist of the RSSI, the infrared data, and the ultrasound data. On the other hand, the topology structure of the device deployed should derive direction restrictions.

The target is always with a certain speed. In this paper, we assume that the target monitored always has a certain speed. A certain-velocity model is applied used in the Kalman Filter (KF), which includes a forecast and a modification phase. During the latter phase, we only use the available data from the measure work. In other words, the dimensions of the vector and matrix will not constant in the particular time epoch. The certain-velocity model can be presented as:

$$X_{i+1} = X_i + \dot{X}_i \Delta t + \eta_1, \tag{9}$$

$$Y_{i+1} = Y_i + \dot{Y}_i \Delta t + \eta_2, \tag{10}$$

$$\dot{X}_{i+1} = \dot{X}_i + \eta_3, \tag{11}$$

$$\dot{Y}_{i+1} = \dot{Y}_i + \eta_4, \tag{12}$$

where, i is the current time, X_i is the coordinate in x direction, Y_i is the coordinate in y direction, $\dot{X}_i$ is the speed in x direction, $\dot{Y}_i$ is the speed in y direction.

Thus, the KF should be described as the three steps:

Initialization:

$$s_0; V(s_0) = P_0, \tag{13}$$

Measurement model:

$$A_i = G_i + s_i + \xi_i; V(\xi_i) = Q_i, \tag{14}$$

Dynamic model:

$$s_{i+1} = U_i s_i + \eta_i; V(\eta_i) = R_i, \tag{15}$$

In Eqs. (13) and (15), $V(\alpha)$ is the covariance of the vector α. The state model includes the time consumption information for the status. The measurement model discourses the data come from the measure to the status. In the beginning of the KF, the covariance and estimate of the initial state will be defined, respectively. They can be denoted by P_0 and $\hat{s}_0$, and represented as:

$$\hat{s}'_{i+1} = U_i s_i; P'_{i+1} = U_i P_i U_i^T, \tag{16}$$

At the t_{i+1}, the covariance and estimate can be denoted as:

$$\hat{s}_i + 1 = \hat{s}'_{i+1} + K_i(A_{i+1} - G_i \hat{s}'_{i+1}); \quad P_{i+1} = (I - K_{i+1} G_{i+1}) P'_{i+1}, \tag{17}$$

where the K_{i+1} is the gain of KF, it can be defined as:

$$K_{i+1} = P'_{i+1} G_{i+1}^T (G_{i+1} P'_{i+1} G_{i+1}^T + R_{i+1})^{-1}, \tag{18}$$

The s of the KF can be defined as:

$$s_i = [X \quad Y \quad \dot{X} \quad \dot{Y}]_i^T, \tag{19}$$

(X, Y) is the target's position at time i, with the velocity vector $(\dot{X}, \dot{Y})$, the matrix of state transition U and the matrix of process noise Q are expressed as:

$$U_i = \begin{bmatrix} 1 & 0 & \Delta t & 0 \\ 0 & 1 & 0 & \Delta t \\ 0 & 0 & 1 & 0 \\ 0 & 0 & 0 & 1 \end{bmatrix}, \tag{20}$$

$$Q_i = \int_0^{\Delta t} U_i(r) q q^T U_i(r)^T dr, \tag{21}$$

Here, the q is the vector, which reflect the spectral densities. The matrix of process noise Q_i, it can be denoted as:

$$Q_i = \begin{bmatrix} q_1 \frac{\Delta t^4}{4} & 0 & q_1 \frac{\Delta t^3}{2} & 0 \\ 0 & q_2 \frac{\Delta t^4}{4} & 0 & q_2 \frac{\Delta t^3}{2} \\ q_1 \frac{\Delta t^3}{2} & 0 & q_1 \Delta t^2 & 0 \\ 0 & q_2 \frac{\Delta t^3}{2} & 0 & q_2 \Delta t^2 \end{bmatrix}, \tag{22}$$

In (17), A is the measurement vector, G is the designed matrix. They are represented as

$$A_i = \begin{bmatrix} X_{rssi} \\ Y_{rssi} \\ X_{inf} \\ Y_{inf} \\ X_{ult} \\ Y_{ult} \end{bmatrix}; \quad G_i = \begin{bmatrix} 1 & 0 & 0 & 0 \\ 0 & 1 & 0 & 0 \\ 1 & 0 & 0 & 0 \\ 0 & 1 & 0 & 0 \\ 0 & 0 & 1 & 0 \\ 0 & 0 & 0 & 1 \end{bmatrix}, \tag{23}$$

The measurement covariance matrix R_i is defined as:

$$R_i = diag(\sigma^2_{X_{rssi}}, \sigma^2_{Y_{rssi}}, \sigma^2_{X_{inf}}, \sigma^2_{Y_{inf}}, \sigma^2_{X_{ult}}, \sigma^2_{Y_{ult}}), \tag{24}$$

5   Performance Evaluation

5.1   Simulation Setup

We conducted simulations using a square area with $10 * 10 \, m^2$. On each slide, there are two groups sensor, ever group includes the RSSI sensor, infrared sensor and ultrasound sensor. We take the single target in this area at the different location. The HDF will locate the target position, and compare to the location result from the single data type location process. In all, we had nine simulations in total.

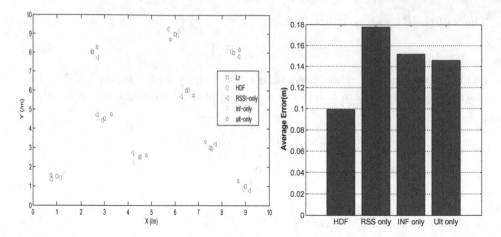

Fig. 4. Localization results.

Fig. 5. Average error of localization results.

5.2 Simulation Result

The localization simulation results is shown in Fig. 1. We also calculate the average error of the localization results, it is shown in Fig. 2.

As the Fig. 4 shown, the target real location, and the localization results of the HDF, the RSSI-only, the infrared-only and the ultrasound-only are presented in one picture. It can clearly be observed that the HDF is better than other methods. As seen in Fig. 5, the average error calculated provides that the best solutions in terms of position accuracy is HDF.

6   Conclusion

Fusing the heterogeneous data for localization is not an unimportant work, especially when the error distribution of the measure work is uncertain. This paper brought a preliminary insight into the novel method with fusing RSSIinfrared data and ultrasound data for POL. The simulation results show that the localization results and the accuracy can be significantly improved. In future work, we will research the noise variance of measure work, and take it into the KF. On the experiment, we need take more testing in the real environment, and expand our data sets.

Acknowledgement. This research was supported in part by China NSFC Grants (61170218 and 61272461), the National Key Technology R & D Program (2013BAK01 B02), Department of Education research project of Shaanxi province, China (2013JK1126, 2013JK1127), and the Natural Science Foundation of Northwest University (12NW05).

References

1. Park, J., Curtis, D., Teller, S., Ledlie, J.: Implications of device diversity for organic localization. In: 30th IEEE International Conference on Computer Communications, pp. 3182–3190. IEEE Press, Shanghai (2011)
2. Pei, L., Chen, R., Chen, Y., Leppäkoski, H., Perttula, A.: Indoor/Outdoor seamless positioning technologies integrated on smart phone. In: 1st International Conference on Advances in Satellite and Space Communications, pp. 141–145. IEEE Press, Colmar (2009)
3. Pei, L., Liu, J., Guinness, R., Chen, Y., Kuusniemi, H., Chen, R.: Using LS-SVM based motion recognition for smartphone indoor wireless positioning. Sensors 12(5), 6155–6175 (2012)
4. Youssef, M., Mah, M., Agrawala, A.: Challenges: device-free passivelocalization for wireless environments. In: 13th Annual ACM International Conference on Mobile Computing and Networking, pp. 222–229. ACM Press, Montreal (2007)
5. Zhang, D., Liu, Y., Ni, L.M.: RASS: a real-time, accurate and scalable system for tracking transceiver-free objects. In: 19th IEEE International Conference on Pervasive Computing and Communications, pp. 197–204. IEEE Press, Missouri (2011)
6. Zhang, D., Ni, L.M.: Dynamic clustering for tracking multiple transceiver-free objects. In: 17th International Conference on Pervasive Computing and Communications, pp. 1–8. IEEE Press, Texas (2009)
7. Ni, L.M., Liu, Y., Lau, Y.C., Patil, A.P.: LANDMARC: indoor location sensing using active RFID. Wirel. Netw. 10(6), 701–710 (2004)
8. Liu, Y., Chen, L., Pei, J., Chen, Q., Zhao, Y.: Mining frequent trajectory patterns for activity monitoring using radio frequency tag arrays. In: 15th IEEE International Conference on Pervasive Computing and Communications, pp. 37–46. IEEE Press, New York (2007)
9. Yang, Z., Liu, Y.: Understanding node localizability of wireless ad-hoc networks. IEEE Trans. Mob. Comput. 11(8), 1240–1260 (2012)
10. Yang, Z., Wu, C., Liu, Y.: Locating in fingerprint space: wireless indoor localization with little human intervention. In: 18th International Conference on Mobile Computing and Networking, pp. 22–26. ACM Press, Istanbul (2012)
11. Wilson, J., Patwari, N.: Radio tomographic imaging in wireless networks. IEEE Trans. Mob. Comput. 9(5), 621–632 (2010)
12. Sigg, S., Scholz, M., Shi, S., Ji, Y., Beigl, M.: RF-sensing of activities from non-cooperative subjects in device-free recognition systems using ambient and local signals. IEEE Trans. Mob. Comput. 13(4), 907–920 (2013)
13. Roos, T., Myllymaki, P., Tirri, H.: A statistical modeling approach to location estimation. IEEE Trans. Mob. Comput. 1(1), 59–69 (2002)
14. Sirola, N.: Mathematical methods for personal positioning and navigation. Ph.D. Dissertation, Tampere University of Technology, August 2007. Available: http://webhotel.tut.fi/library/tutdiss/pdf/sirola.pdf [Online]
15. Figueiras, J., Frattasi, S.: Mobile Positioning and Tracking: From Conventional to Cooperative Techniques. John Wiley & Sons Ltd, Manhattan (2010)
16. Aggarwal, P., Syed, Z., Noureldin, A., El-Sheimy, N.: MEMS-Based Integrated Navigation. Artech House Inc, Massachusetts (2010)

A Self-Localization Scheme with Grid-Based Anchor Selection in Wireless Sensor Networks

Wei Wang[1,2], Haoshan Shi[1], Pengyu Huang[3(✉)], Fuping Wu[4],
Dingyi Fang[2], Xiaojiang Chen[2], and Yun Xiao[2]

[1] School of Electronics and Information, Northwestern Polytechnical University, Xi'an, China
shilaoshi@nwpu.edu.cn
[2] School of Information and Technology, Northwest University, Xi'an, China
{wwang,dyf,xjchen,yxiao}@nwu.edu.cn
[3] School of Telecommunication and Engineering, Xidian University, Xi'an, China
pyhuang@mail.xidian.edu.cn
[4] School of Physics and Optoelectronic Engineering, Xidian University, Xi'an, China
Fpwu@xidian.edu.cn

Abstract. Self-Localization is one of the key technologies in the wireless sensor network (WSN). The traditional self-localization algorithms can provide a reasonable positioning accuracy only in a uniform and dense network, while for a non-uniform network, the performance is not acceptable. In this paper, we presented a novel grid-based linear least squares (LLS) self-localization algorithm. The proposed algorithm uses the grid method to screen the anchors based on the distribution characteristic of a non-uniform network. Furthermore, by taking into consideration the quasi-uniform distribution of anchors in the area we select suitable anchors to assist the localization. Simulation results demonstrate that the proposed algorithm can greatly enhance the localization accuracy of the anonymous nodes and impose less computation burden compared to traditional trilateration and multilateration.

Keywords: WSN · Self-localization · Grid · LLS

1 Introduction

Wireless Sensor Networks (WSN) is a kind of multi-hop and self-organizing networks, which is constituted by a mount of low-cost micro sensor nodes. These nodes are deployed in a monitoring area to perform collaboration sensing, collect and process the information of the objects in the area, and send the messages to observers [1].

For many implementations, only when the sensor node gets the location of itself then it can tell the observers where the accident happens. So obtaining the location of the sensor node is one of the most basic functions of the sensor networks. Base on if we need to measure the distance between the nodes, we can classify the algorithm to Range-based and Range-free. As comparing the kind of Range-based algorithm, Range-free algorithm has advantages of lower cost of hardware, lower power consumption and more powerful in noise resistance. At the same time the structure of the hardware is simple.

© Springer-Verlag Berlin Heidelberg 2015
L. Sun et al. (Eds.): CWSN 2014, CCIS 501, pp. 252–262, 2015.
DOI: 10.1007/978-3-662-46981-1_24

Though the precision of Range-free algorithms is low, but for most part of implementation it's enough. Some research indicates that even though the location error is nearly 40 % of the communication distance in non-uniform networks. The error still only have a few influence on the precision of the routing algorithms and the object pursuit. Anyhow the consequent of the range-free localization can be invoked as the original iterate value of more precise range-based algorithms. There are numerous classical Range-free localization algorithms as DV-Hop, convex programming, MDS-MAP and DHL and so on. In this paper, we mainly study how to promote the precision of Range-free localization algorithm.

Generally Range-free algorithm can be divided into three steps [4]:

1. Estimate the distance between sensor node and sink node;
2. Calculate the localization of the sensor node with trilateration localization algorithm;
3. Optimize the result we get in the last step with iterative method.

So these three steps were always where we can start to promote the precision of Range-free localization algorithm. When we promote the precision with the proceeding of the loop, the distance error will decrease but at the same time it results in amount of traffic and computations. For it's hard to predict the number of loops, the uncertainty of the result will increase. For these reasons, it's restricted to use loops in practice [5]. Another way is to increase range precision as we can get more accurate estimation of the distance between nodes and anchors. Some research achievements have appeared in this field. As in literature [2], it is studying on non-uniformly distributed WSN, based on the number of the hops to anchor, the network was divided into three areas, CR (Concentric Ring), CG (Centrifugal Gradient), DG (Distorted Gradient). In each area, different method was used to reduce the error of the distance estimate. Literature [6] thinks as in two-dimensional random distribution networks we cannot use the normal Gaussian probability density function to estimate the distance between sensor nodes and anchors. And the author proposes a biggest distance estimate method base on the greedy algorithm. Literature [7] studies on the expected number of hops in different WSN which has different parameters. Base on these analysis, authors deduced the mathematical expression of the hops, and in this method greatly enhances the estimation precision of the distance between the sensors to the anchors.

From these descriptions, we can see most of the research focus on the effect of estimate the distance between sensor and anchor to the performance of localization. When we get the estimated value of the distance in generally, Trilateration-localization or Multilateral-localization method will be used to estimate the position of the unknown node. In this process, few studies have addressed how to improve the performance of Trilateration-localization or Multilateral-localization algorithm. From the theory of Trilateration-localization, we can see it have advantages of simple computation. On the other side, in this method the information from more anchors will not be used, so it is difficult to promote the precision of the localization. But if we use more anchors' information to promote the precision of localization more computing resources will be required. In order to solve the above problems, Ref. [3] indicates that the error of the distance estimate will increase with the increase of the number of hops. Reference [8] explained we can promote the precision by deleting some anchors which have large errors. Reference [9] shows that the precision of unknown nodes position is affected by spatial distribution of the involved anchors. The more uniformity of the anchors distributed, the more accurate that result will be. The simulation result of Ref. [10] also shows that the uniform distribution of the anchors can greatly improve the positioning performance.

This paper proposed a grid-based linear least squares (LLS) Self-localization algorithm. This algorithm fully considers the character of the non-uniformity networks, and uses the grid method to screen the anchors. We delete those anchors which have bigger error and bad distribution, at the same time, choose the appropriate anchors to make the distribution of the anchors to be more evenly in this algorithm. Simulation results show our improved localization method is more precise, more adaptability and has lower computational cost, compare to the traditional trilateration and multilaterally.

2   Grid-Based Linear Least Squares (LLS) Self-Localization Algorithm

References [3, 8–10] show multilateration have higher location accuracy for involve more anchors in positioning method, and use least squares estimation method to decrease the influence of the errors. But as the number of the anchors increased, they need higher-bandwidth to send data and more computation and more energy. And in Range-free localization algorithm, the error of the distance estimate will increase with the increase of the hops. Therefore use more anchors in localization means we must choose more further anchors which have more distance estimated errors. These errors will influence the accuracy of the positioning. As we known, the uniformity of the anchors distribution has a very important effect on the precision of position.

In summarizing, the numbers and distribution of the anchors are the key elements to improve the precision of node self-localization. Therefore, if we can use a filter to the anchors that involved in localization delete the anchors with bigger errors and bad distribution. Then we can promote the precision of localization, at the same time decrease the calculation and energy. This is helpful to prolong the life-time of WSN node.

In view of this idea, we propose a grid-based linear least squares (LLS) Self-localization algorithm. This algorithm still estimates the distance base on the number of hops, so we don't need to change the hardware structure of the sensor nodes and the transport process. There should be minimal impact on existing systems. On this basis, we first delete the anchors which number of the hops to unknown nodes is larger than threshold T0, reducing the probability to involve larger errors. In addition, the correlations of the anchors will increase with the decrease of the distance. But over-correlation is not conducive to promoting the location accuracy, even can seriously interfere in some conditions. We define the positions of the unknown nodes. So we use the grid method to delete the over-correlation anchors. At last, in the remaining anchors, we select well-distributed anchors base on the grid location of the node to determine the location of the unknown node with LLS.

In this paper, we call the nodes need to be localized as unknown node. Nodes which know the location of themselves, and can help the unknown nodes to be localized as anchor nodes. Neighbor nodes are the nodes involved in a node's communication range. Current node means the node is being localized.

This algorithm is divided into 5 steps:

- Make sure the distance between unknown node and anchors.
- Make up grid and initial screening of anchors.
- Get the location base on grid of the unknown node.
- Generate a collection of the anchors which have even distribution to current node.
- LLS localization.

Step 1: Estimate the distance between the unknown nodes to anchors. There are many algorithms to get the distance between the unknown nodes and anchors, but for comparison's sake, we use distance estimate method of DV-Hop in every algorithm. In DV-Hop, distance is estimated base on the estimate of the number of the hops, as showed in Formula 1.

$$HopSize_i = \frac{\sum\limits_{j \neq i} \sqrt{(x_i - x_j)^2 + (y_i - y_j)^2}}{\sum\limits_{j \neq i} h_j} \tag{1}$$

In the Formula 1, $(x_i, y_i), (x_j, y_j)$ is the location coordinates of anchor i and j, h_j is the number of the hops between i and j ($j \neq i$), $HopSize_i$ is average distance of each hop to anchor i, and it will be broadcast to whole networks. While unknown node gets the nearest anchors' $HopSize$, it will calculate the actual distance to the anchor base on the even hops have got.

Step 2: Set up the grid and filter the anchors. For the unknown node, after getting the information of the anchors, it can make sure the number of the hop from the anchors to the unknown node. Then we can delete the anchors which the number of hops is bigger than threshold T_0, to decrease the probability of greater errors involved in localization proceeding. After deleting the anchors we can determine the distribution of the remainder anchors by their coordinates. We set x_{min}, x_{max}, y_{min}, y_{max} as the minimum and maximum X and Y coordinate of the remainder anchors, and set R as the communication range of the node. Then $[x_{min}, x_{max}]$, $[y_{min}, y_{max}]$ is the distribution range of the anchors to the X and Y axes. To facilitate the use of the grid, we just the start position of it. At first, calculate the remainder of the distribution range of the anchors to the X and Y axes to R.

$$\begin{cases} x_{residue} = \mod((x_{max} - x_{min}), R) \\ y_{residue} = \mod((y_{max} - y_{min}), R) \end{cases} \tag{2}$$

Then equally split the difference between the R and the remainder to both sides of the distributed region of the anchors.

$$\begin{cases} X_{min} = x_{min} - (R - x_{residue})/2 \\ X_{max} = x_{max} + (R - x_{residue})/2 \end{cases} \quad \begin{cases} Y_{min} = y_{min} - (R - y_{residue})/2 \\ Y_{max} = y_{max} + (R - y_{residue})/2 \end{cases} \tag{3}$$

At last, we use $[X_{min}, X_{max}], [Y_{min}, Y_{max}]$ as the region of the grid, R as the interval to set up the grid system, as showed in Fig. 1(a).

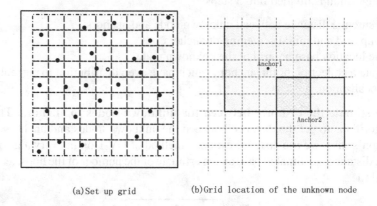

(a) Set up grid   (b) Grid location of the unknown node

Fig. 1. Set up the grid and get the grid location of the unknown node

We can see every unit of the grid is a square with each side of length R. And as we know, if there are too many anchors in a unit, the accuracy of localization will be affected. So in this condition, we choose the anchor with minimum hops to the unknown node as the delegate anchor of the unit, and if more than one anchor have the minimum hops we choose the delegate anchor randomly.

Step3: Determine the grid location of the unknown node. After setting up the grid and initial anchor screening, we need to determine the grid location of the unknown node. Then we can choose the appropriate anchors to form evenly distribution. In this paper, we use Min-Max localization algorithm for reference and calculate the Min-Max range of every anchor base on the number of hops from the anchor to the unknown node. Then choose a grid unit randomly among the overlapping area of every anchor's Min-Max range as the grid location of current unknown node. The main points of this proceeding are showed in Fig. 1(b).

Step 4: Generate the collection of evenly distributed anchors. Now we choose the evenly distributed anchors from the anchor collection centered in the unknown node. Here we use the conception of template.

As showed in Fig. 2, we first generate a square grid template with each side of length $(2T_0 + 1) \times R$ and 8 partitions. Then adjust the position of the template, make the grid unit of the unknown node to be the center unit of the template. With the template, every anchor can get its partition. Then the question is how to choose the adequate anchors in every partition, which is nearly uniform distribution. Here we have 4 steps to perform.

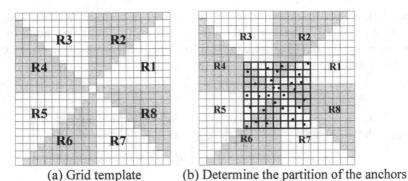

(a) Grid template   (b) Determine the partition of the anchors

Fig. 2. Determine the location of the anchors by grid template

We set parameter T as the minimum number of the anchors been chosen to location proceeding.

1. Count the number of anchors in every partition, set the minimum number as $R8_{min}$. If $R8_{min} \times 8 \geq T_1$, we'll choose $R8_{min}$ relatively small hops anchors in every partition, and stop the screening proceeding. Else skip to step 2.
2. Count the minimum number of anchors in the set as Set1: {R1, R3, R5, R7} and Set2: {R2, R4, R6, R8}, recorded as $R4\_1_{min1}$, $R4\_1_{min2}$.
   - While $R4\_1_{min1} \geq R4\_1_{min2}$:
     - If $R4\_1_{min2} \times 4 \geq T_1$ choose the nodes which hop number less than $R4\_1_{min2}$ in every area of Set2 and end screening.
     - Else if $R4\_1_{min1} \times 4 \geq T_1$ choose the nodes which hop number less than $R4\_1_{min1}$ in every area of Set1 and end screening.
   - While $R4\_1_{min2} > R4\_1_{min1}$:
     - If $R4\_1_{min2} \times 4 \geq T_1$ choose the nodes which hop number less than $R4\_1_{min2}$ in every area of Set2 and end screening.
     - Else if $R4\_1_{min1} \times 4 \geq T_1$ choose the nodes which hop number less than $R4\_1_{min1}$ in every area of Set1 and end screening.
3. Redistribute the set as Set3: {R1, R2, R5, R6} and Set2: {R3, R4, R7, R8}, screen anchors with Step2. If this condition is not met, access Step4.
4. Choose T2 anchors with minimum hops from original anchor set directly.

Step5: locating the unknown node by the linear least square method. While the unknown node gets the location information from three or more than three anchors, we can process location method to calculate the position of the node. The location algorithm which only needs the information of three anchors is Trilateration. Else if the algorithm needs more than three anchors, we call it as Multilateration, and Trilateration is an exception of Multilateration.

According to the requirements for the application environment of the Range-free localization algorithm, LLS algorithm is usually been used to calculate the location coordinates of the unknown node. The proceeding of the algorithm is described below. Set the coordinates of the unknown node as $X(x,y)$, and the anchors as $L_1(x_1,y_1),\cdots,L_k(x_k,y_k)$, the distance from the unknown node to the anchors are $r_1, r_2, \cdots, r_k$. Then we can establish linear equations base on the estimate distance and known quantity as follow.

$$AX = b \qquad (4)$$

$$A = (-2) \times \begin{bmatrix} x_1 - x_k & y_1 - y_k \\ x_2 - x_k & y_2 - y_k \\ \vdots & \vdots \\ x_{k-1} - x_k & y_{k-1} - y_k \end{bmatrix} \quad X = \begin{bmatrix} x \\ y \end{bmatrix} \quad b = \begin{bmatrix} r_1^2 - r_k^2 - x_1^2 + x_k^2 - y_1^2 + y_k^2 \\ r_2^2 - r_k^2 - x_2^2 + x_k^2 - y_2^2 + y_k^2 \\ \vdots \\ r_{k-1}^2 - r_k^2 - x_{k-1}^2 + x_k^2 - y_{k-1}^2 + y_k^2 \end{bmatrix}$$

For the existent of distant estimate error, a detailed linear model can be described as:

$$AX + N = b \qquad (5)$$

Among the equation, N is distance error vector of $k - 1$ dimensional. We can get the minimum position estimate value of the unknown node:

$$\hat{x}_{LS} = (A^T A)^{-1} A^T b \qquad (6)$$

3   Simulation

In this paper, we divide the simulation scenes into two kinds as uniform scene (Scene 1) and non-uniform scene (Scene 2, 3, 4). In our simulations, 500 sensors were deployed in a 2D field (500*500), and the sensor's communication range is 50 m. Anchors were randomly selected, and we assumed every node can received messages from every anchor. The screening thresholds were set as $T_0 = 10, T_1 = 15, T_2 = 8$.

Scene 1: The sensors are distributed randomly.
Scene 2: As showed in Fig. 3, the number of the node in Region are $1{:}3{:}1{:}3 = DR_I{:}DR_{II}{:}DR_{III}{:}DR_{IV}$.

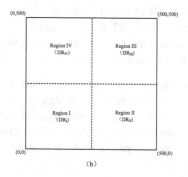

(b)

Fig. 3.   Simulation scene

Scene 3: the number of the node in Region is $1:5:1:5 = DR_I:DR_{II}:DR_{III}:DR_{IV}$.

Scene 4: the number of the node in Region is $1:7:1:7 = DR_I:DR_{II}:DR_{III}:DR_{IV}$.

3.1 Analyses

Definition: Normalization position error δ_p is the percentage of the Euclidean distance between the estimate coordinate (x_e, y_e) and the real coordinate (x_r, y_r) of the unknown node to the node's communication range R.

$$\delta_p = \frac{\sqrt{(x_e - x_r)^2 + (y_e - y_r)^2}}{R} \times 100\% \tag{7}$$

For comparison, localization algorithm base on grid screening will be abbreviated to LLS+GRID.

Figure 4 showed the performance difference between these three localization algorithms in non-uniform scenes.

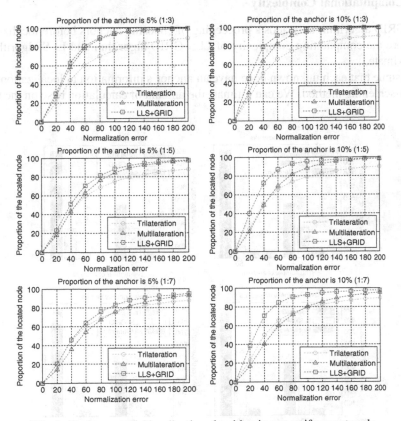

Fig. 4. Performance of localization algorithm in non-uniform network

The simulations reveal that no matter how the heterogeneity degree is, the LLS-GRID algorithm is better than Trilateration and Multilateration. We can focus on the number of the node which can be located with different algorithms and see it as the key performance indicator. While the percentage of the anchor is 10 % and P is 40 %, heterogeneity degree is 1:3, the number with LLS-GRID algorithm is 14.76 % more than Multilateration, and it's 14.76 % and 29.47 % more than Multilateration while the heterogeneity degree is 1:5 and 1:7.

According to the simulation results, the performance of Multilateration algorithm is unstable with the increase of heterogeneity degree of the network, even worth than Trilateration algorithm if the network is more uneven. But LLS+GRID algorithm is more resilient to this condition. While the percentage of the anchor is 10 % and P is 40 %, as the heterogeneity degree of the network increase from 1:3 and 1:7, the location precision of LLS+GRID algorithm decrease 8.43 %, but to Multilateration it's 23.14 % decreasing. Therefore we can see LLS+GRID algorithm has more adaptability to the environment.

3.2 Computational Complexity

LLS-GRID algorithm only adds a proceeding of choosing anchors before localization, therefore the computation complexity of LLS-GRID algorithm and LLS algorithm is approximate.

Assume that each unknown node have an anchor's information to localization after anchor screening method. We can estimate the amount of calculation base on the times

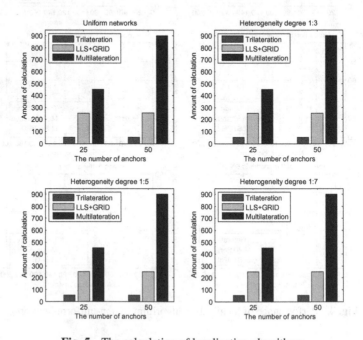

Fig. 5. The calculation of localization algorithms

of multiplication and addition in formula 6. Since most of the hardware can do multiplication and addition in a single instruction, so we can consider multiplication and addition as the same calculation, then formula (6) needs about 18n times calculation.

As showed in Fig. 5, the calculation of LLS-GRID algorithm can be got through simulation. From the Fig. 5, we can see the calculation of Trilateration is the same no matter in which scene, for it only uses the three nearest anchor's information in localization. Similarly, the calculation of Multilateration algorithm is the biggest for it needs every anchor's information in localization. To LLS-GRID algorithm, the calculation is slightly increased than Trilateration, but it's significantly decreased than Multilateration. As the percentage of the anchor is 5 % and 10 % the calculation of LLS-GRID is 44 % and 72 % smaller than Multilateration. And a notable feature of the calculation of LLS-GRID algorithm is it's very stable for every node and every scene, whether in even network or uneven network. In a word, with LLS-GRID algorithm the accuracy of localization was improved while the amount of calculation was reduced.

4   Conclusion

This paper proposes a novel grid-based linear least squares (LLS) self-localization algorithm base on analyze and simulates normal Range-free self-localization algorithm in WSN. The result of simulation indicates that the algorithm proposed effectively solved the problem of low precision of Trilateration and the large computation of Multilateration. This algorithm does not require changing the structure of hardware and the proceeding of algorithm. The precision is much greater than Trilateration and Multilateration. Meanwhile, the calculation of the algorithm is equivalent to 30 %–40 % of Multilateration, but it's more stable than Multilateration. So this grid-based LLS algorithm can greatly extend the application range of Range-free localization method.

Acknowledgement.   This research was supported by the foundation of Northwest University ND14041, and the National Natural Science Foundation of China 61373177.

References

1. Sun, L., Li, J.: Wireless Sensor Network, p. 135. Tsinghua University Press, Beijing (2005)
2. Xiao, Q., Xiao, B., Cao, J., Wang, J.: Multi-hop range-free localization in anisotropic wireless sensor networks: a pattern-driven scheme. IEEE Trans. Mob. Comput. **9**(11), 1592–1607 (2010)
3. Wong, S.Y., Lim, J.G., Rao, S.V., Seah, W.K.G.: Density-Aware Hop-Count Location (DHL) in wireless sensor networks with variable density. In: Proceedings of IEEE Wireless Communications and Networking Conference, vol. 3, pp. 1848–1853, March 2005
4. Koen, L., Niels, R.: Distributed localization in wireless sensor networks: a quantitative comparison. Comput. Netw. **43**(4), 499–518 (2003)
5. Wang, F., Shi, L., Ren, F.: Self-localization systems and algorithms for wireless sensor networks. J. Softw. **16**(5), 857–868 (2005)
6. Vural, S., Ekici, E.: On multi-hop distances in wireless sensor networks with random node location. IEEE Trans. Mob. Comput. **9**(4), 540–552 (2010)

7. Wang, Y., Wang, X., Wang, D., Agrawal, D.P.: Range-free localization using expected hop progression wireless sensor networks. IEEE Trans. Parallel Distrib. Syst. **20**(10), 1540–1552 (2009)
8. Garg, R., Varna, A.L., Wu, M.: An efficient gradient descent approach to secure localization in resource constrained wireless sensor networks. IEEE Trans. Inf. Forensics Secur. **7**(2), 717–730 (2012)
9. Zheng, Y., Wang, L., Sun, Z., et al.: A long range DV-hop localization algorithm with placement strategy in wireless sensor networks. In: Proceedings of the 4th International Conference on Wireless Communications Networking and Mobile Computing, pp. 4090–4094. IEEE, Avignon (2008)
10. Myint, T.Z., Lynn, N., Ohtsuki, T.: Range-free localization algorithm using local expected hop length in wireless sensor networks. In: Proceedings of International Symposture on Communications and Information Technologies, Tokyo, pp. 356–361 (2010)

A PLLS-PKF Method for Target Tracking of DOA Measurement Sensor Networks

Yiwei Huang[1], Wei Xie[1], Xiaoqing Hu[1], Ming Bao[1(✉)], Zhi Wang[2], and Luyang Guan[1]

[1] Institute of Acoustics, Chinese Academy of Science, Beijing 100190, China
{timathyhuang,auxqhu}@gmail.com,
{xiewei,baoming,guanluyang}@mail.ioa.ac.cn
[2] Department of Control Science and Engineering, Zhejiang University, Zhejiang 310027, China
wangzhi@iipc.zju.edu.cn

Abstract. In this paper, we propose a novel tracking algorithm that adopts both Pseudo-linear least square method and Pseudo-linear Kalman Filtering (PLLS-PKF) for target tracking using bearing only sensor networks. The conventional Pseudo-linear Kalman Filtering (PKF) is one of the practice tracking methods in this situation. Limited by the data accuracy, the outputs of PKF tend to be unstable by incorporating signal data with large error. Using PLLS localization to yield one step iteration updating process, the modified method can help to improve the estimation accuracy. Both numerical simulations and real experiment are conducted to illustrate that the PLLS-PKF method can provide better tracking performance compared with the conventional PKF method.

Keywords: Target tracking · DOA measurement · PKF · Sensor networks

1 Introduction

Target tracking is an important application for Wireless Sensor Networks (WSNs) in environment monitoring, military and transportation fields [1]. For most purposes distance information is very important on target tracking. However, not all kinds of sensors can provide distance measurements for their principles or simply economic reasons. As a special case bearing only sensor networks consisting of such sensors which could measure the directions of arrival (DOA) data of targets, has attracted much attention. For instance the passive acoustic microphone array which could capture the direction of acoustic source by beamforming or other technologies [2] and bearing only data from single array could not conduct the initialization of a tracking progress. Particular algorithms are designed to convey the target tracking by building the bearing only sensor networks and calculating useful data without using other kinds of information [3].

The popular implement of tracking a moving target is a kind of online adaptive filtering. The Kalman filtering (KF) [4] is widely used in target tracking area and proved to be one of the most effective adaptive filtering methods for linear systems. However, the DOA sensor networks are typically non-linear systems and KF can't be put into use directly. Thus its variants, for instance, Pseudo-linear Kalman filter (PKF) [5], Extended Kalman filter (EKF) [6] and Unscented Kalman filter (UKF) [7] are presented to solve

L. Sun et al. (Eds.): CWSN 2014, CCIS 501, pp. 263–272, 2015.
DOI: 10.1007/978-3-662-46981-1_25

tracking problem in bearing-only measurements situation. Particle Filter (PF) is also used in recent literatures [8]. However, the performance of PF is restricted by the accuracy of the motion model used and the real-time property would be sacrificed with a huge amount of particles for getting ideal tracking results. Both UKF and EKF for this case are sensitive to the prediction errors, since the angle measurement function is piecewise function in practical bearing-only tracking applications. Utilizing trigonometric function to create pseudo-linear relationship between target state and observation, PKF is simple but can avoid this problem. However, Limited by the data accuracy, the outputs of the conventional PKF method tends to be unstable by incorporating signal data with large error. In this paper, we actually iterate the DOA measurement in one sampling period by inserting a localization process using pseudo-linear least square method in PKF, and it contributes to improve the performance and stability compared with the conventional PKF.

In Sect. 2, the target tracking modes, the DOA measurement model in sensor networks and pseudo-linear least square (PLLS) estimation method are introduced. In Sect. 3, the conventional PKF method is reviewed and the modified PLLS-PKF method is given. In Sect. 4, the numerical simulation and real experiment results are conducted. Some conclusions are given in Sect. 5.

2   Target Tracking Model of Bearing Only Sensor Networks

2.1   Target Motion Model

The mathematic motion model we used is mentioned in this section. In general, motion models for tracking are described as the functions of time to represent the state evolutions with time and they follow the basic form named state-space model which represents the new motion state and observation state depended with the history motion states until the current. Unlike continuous time situation models, the discrete time models are used in a lot of applications of digital systems. The common equations of discrete time situation are described as follows [9]:

$$\begin{cases} x_{k+1} = f_k(x_k, u_k, \omega_k) \\ z_k = h_k(x_k) + v_k \end{cases} \tag{1}$$

where x_k, z_k and u_k are the current target state, observation, and control input vectors at the discrete time t_k. ω_k, v_k are the process and measurement noises.

CV (Constant velocity) model is a basic model for maneuvering target tracking that runs steadily in most cases and it assumes that the velocities hold steady in sampling time and the accelerations are Gaussian noises. Take two-dimensional Cartesian coordinates for instance, the state of a moving point could be described with the position and velocity along x- and y-axes. Denoted the state vector by $x = \begin{bmatrix} x & \dot{x} & y & \dot{y} \end{bmatrix}^T$, the state updating equation in discrete time state-space model is as follows:

$$x_{k+1} = \begin{bmatrix} 1 & T & 0 & 0 \\ 0 & 1 & 0 & 0 \\ 0 & 0 & 1 & T \\ 0 & 0 & 0 & 1 \end{bmatrix} x_k + \begin{bmatrix} T \\ T^2/2 \\ T \\ T^2/2 \end{bmatrix} \omega_k \qquad (2)$$

where T represents the sampling time of the discrete time system.

2.2 DOA Measurement Model

The distance information can be estimated and the targets can be successfully tracked by using several DOA sensors [11]. A sketch of DOA measurement sensor networks is shown in Fig. 1. We assume sensor S_i is the i-th sensor of a DOA measurement sensor network system, the position of the target can be given as

$$\begin{cases} x_t = x_i + \tilde{r}_i \cos \tilde{\theta}_i \\ y_t = y_i + \tilde{r}_i \sin \tilde{\theta}_i \end{cases} \qquad (3)$$

where x_t and y_t are the position coordinates of the target t in the fixed Cartesian reference frame (x, y), and x_i, y_i are the position of S_i, $\tilde{r}_i$, $\tilde{\theta}_i$ are the true distance and angle values of S_i with respect to the target.

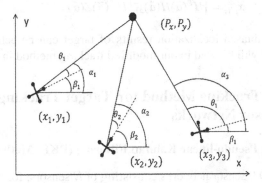

Fig. 1. DOA measurement in sensor networks

However, the observation angles of sensors can't be used directly in array algorithms unless they have been adjusted with the heading angles of the sensors with respect to the fixed Cartesian reference frame. In Fig. 1 β is the heading angle of the sensor with respect to x-coordinate, θ is the observation angle of the sensor with respect to its heading, $\alpha = \theta + \beta$ represents the true value of angle in the fixed Cartesian reference frame for each sensor's observation.

2.3 Pseudo-linear Least Square (PLLS) Estimation Method

In general, target tracking requires the target's location information in the initialization process. Under ideal condition, two sensors can provide enough information as shown in Fig. 1. However, measuring errors are unavoidable in reality. PLLS method can make full use of all these measurements and give estimations of the target location [12].

Consider a sensor network consisting of N DOA sensors, for the *i-th* sensor, from the relationship equation set (3) we can eliminate variable r and then we get an equation

$$x_t \sin \alpha_i - y_t \cos \alpha_i = x_i \sin \alpha_i - y_i \cos \alpha_i; i = 1, 2, \ldots, N \tag{4}$$

Set a virtual observation vector of the *i-th* sensor as

$$z_i(\alpha_i) = x_i \sin \alpha_i - y_i \cos \alpha_i; i = 1, 2, \ldots, N \tag{5}$$

The observation matrix of the sensor network system is

$$Z = [z_1^T \quad z_2^T \quad .. \quad z_N^T]^T \tag{6}$$

Accordingly we define a matrix and a vector:

$$H(\vec{\alpha}) = \begin{bmatrix} h_1 & h_2 & \cdots & h_N \end{bmatrix}^T; h_i = [\sin \alpha_i - \cos \alpha_i]^T \tag{7}$$

The relationship $Z(\vec{\alpha}) = H(\vec{\alpha}) [x_t \quad y_t]^T$ exists and the closed form solution of the least square method can be obtained:

$$\bar{x}_{plls} = [H^T(\vec{\alpha})H(\vec{\alpha})]^{-1}H^T(\vec{\alpha})Z(\vec{\alpha}) \tag{8}$$

From (6)–(9) unbiased localization results of target can be achieved. The PLLS localization method will be used in our modified tracking method in the Sect. 3.

3 PLLS-PKF Tracking Method for Target Tracking of DOA Sensor Networks

3.1 Conventional Pseudo-linear Kalman Filtering (PKF) Method

Considering the DOA sensor networks consisting of N sensors, for the *i-th* sensor, the calibrated observation contaminated by noises at the current sampling time is expressed as follows:

$$\alpha_{m,i}(k) = \alpha_i(k) + v_i(k) \tag{9}$$

where $\alpha_{m,i}(k)$ is the measurement value, $\alpha_i(k)$ is the true value, $v_i(k)$ is a Gaussian observation noise.

Replacing the angle $\alpha_i(k)$ in Eq. (10) with $\alpha_{m,i}(k) - v_i(k)$ and ignoring the second order small-quantities, we can get a new equation as follows:

$$x_i(k) \sin \alpha_{m,i}(k) - y_i(k) \cos \alpha_{m,i}(k) = x_T(k) \sin \alpha_{m,i}(k) - y_T(k) \cos \alpha_{m,i}(k) + \hat{r}_i v(k); \tag{10}$$

Define a virtual pseudo-linear observation quantity matrix, its corresponding observation transition matrix yields

$$Z = [z_1^T \quad z_2^T \quad .. \quad z_N^T]^T, z_i(k) = x_i(k) \sin \alpha_{m,i}(k) - y_i(k) \cos \alpha_{m,i}(k); \qquad (11)$$

$$H_K(\vec{\alpha}) = \begin{bmatrix} h_1 & h_2 & \cdots & h_N \end{bmatrix}^T ; h_i = \begin{bmatrix} \sin \alpha_{m,i}(k) & 0 & -\cos \alpha_{m,i}(k) & 0 \end{bmatrix}^T \qquad (12)$$

The pseudo-linear Observation equation has

$$Z(k) = H_K(k)x(k) + \eta(k) \qquad (13)$$

where $(k) = \begin{bmatrix} r_1(k)v_i(k) & r_2(k)v_2(k) & \cdots & r_N(k)v_N(k) \end{bmatrix}^T$, $r_i(k)$ is the distance value of the *i-th* sensor with respect to the target, which can be calculated by the position components of the predictive state. Note that the matrix H_k is not equal to the matrix H in PLLS as the state variable $x(k)$ contains velocity information here.

Since the new observation Eq. (14) is linear in form, it can be used in Kalman Filter to predict target states directly.

3.2   The Modified PLLS-PKF Method

On account of the elements in the pseudo-linear observation $z(k)$ are coupling, the covariance matrix used in PKF is an approximate value. Hence, the tracking results of the conventional PKF method tend to be unstable by incorporating signal data with large error. We suppose a modified PKF method which uses the PLLS location results as feedback in the update process to provide more accurate outputs than the conventional PKF method. The flow diagram of this method is showed in Fig. 2. In this new method, a PLLS localization progress is inserted before creating the visual pseudo-linear observation. We assume that the localization output $X_p(x_p, y_p)$ equals to the real position component (x_t, y_t) of the state vector $x(k)$.

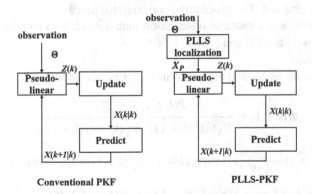

Fig. 2. Structure of the conventional PKF and PLLS-PKF

In order to use the angles observed twice, we rewrite an equation with angle information as follows:

$$[x_p(k) - x_T(k)] \sin \alpha_m(k) - [y_p(k) - y_T(k)] \cos \alpha_m(k) = \hat{r}v(k) \tag{14}$$

Since (15) is familiar to (11), we redefine the visual pseudo-linear observation and the observation equations are as follows:

$$Z_p = \left[z_{p_1}^{\ T} \ z_{p_2}^{\ T} \ .. \ z_{p_N}^{\ T} \right]^T, \quad z_{pi}(k) = x_p(k) \sin \alpha_{m_i}(k) - y_p(k) \cos \alpha_{m_i}(k); \tag{15}$$

$$Z_p(k) = H_K(k)x(k) + \eta(k) \tag{16}$$

where $x_T(k)$, $y_T(k)$ are the outputs of the PLLS localization progress, $\eta(k)$ is the visual noises vector as same as $\eta(k)$ in (14).

We take CV model for instance to introduce how the PLLS-PKF works. The complete PLLS-PKF algorithm contains three steps as follows:

1. State prediction process.
   Using the equation from state-space model to predict the state of the next state

$$\hat{x}(k+1/k) = E\left\{x(k+1)/Z^k\right\} = F_{cv}x(k/k) \tag{17}$$

$$P(k+1/k) = F_{cv}P(k/k)F_{cv}^T + R(k+1) \tag{18}$$

$$R(k+1) = G_{cv}R_\omega G_{cv}^T \tag{19}$$

where F_{cv} and G_{cv} are the state transition matrix and state noise matrix in CV model (referring to (4)). $R(k + 1)$ is the system error covariance matrix; $R_\omega = \text{diag} \begin{bmatrix} \sigma_x^2 & \sigma_y^2 \end{bmatrix}$ is the covariance matrix of the acceleration noise.

2. Localization process
   Conduct a PLLS localization process to give the estimation (x_p, y_p) when new DOA observation received. The procedure is referred to (6)–(9).
   Then create the $k + 1$ moment observation matrix $H_K(k + 1)$ and the visual observation $Z_p(k + 1)$ by (13) and (16).

3. Update process
   Update the state vector and the covariance matrix as follows:

$$K(k+1) = \frac{P(k+1/k)H_K^T(k)}{H_K(k)P(k+1/k)H_K^T(k) + Q(k+1)} \tag{20}$$

$$\hat{x}(k+1/k+1) = F_{cv}\hat{x}(k/k) + K(k+1)\left[Z_p(k+1) - H_K(k)\hat{x}(k+1/k)\right] \tag{21}$$

$$P(k+1/k+1) = P(k+1/k) - K(k+1)H_K(k+1)P(k+1/k) \tag{22}$$

$$Q_\eta(k) = \text{diag} \begin{bmatrix} r_1^2 Q_{v1}(k) & \cdots & r_i^2 Q_{vi}(k) & \cdots & r_N^2 Q_{vN} \end{bmatrix} \tag{23}$$

where $Q_{vi}(k)$ is the variance of $v(k)$, $r_{is}(k)$ is the distance value of the *i-th* sensor with respect to the target which can be calculate by the localization results and the position information of sensors.

It's not hard to see that the virtual observation in PLLS and PKF follow the similar form. DOA measurements are used twice in PLlS-PKF method as the PLLS results are iterated in PKF. In essence, the modified method is an application of iterated Kalman filter.

4 Numerical Simulation and Real Experiment Results

4.1 Numerical Simulation

In this section we build a simulation environment to test the performance of the two methods. The motion trail of the target is randomly generated based on CV model. The DOA measurements are calculated by inverse computation.

The conditions of the simulation are set as follows: number of sensors is set as 4 and the locations of sensors are set as [0, 0], [0, 200], [200, 0], [200, 200] (the units are in meters). The original position of the target is set as [5, 100]. The original speeds $v_x = 4$ *m/s* and $v_y = -2$ *m/s*. The standard deviation of the Gaussian noise of acceleration is 0.7 m/s^2. The observation noise is set to be white noises with 2° standard deviations. The simple period is 1 s and the total simulation time is 50 s. Both PKF method and PLLS-PKF method need two steps to initialization.

Figure 3 is the tracking results of the two methods and Fig. 4 is their mean square error. From Fig. 3 it is not hard to see that the results of the PLLS-PKF (the blue triangle points) are closer to the real path (the black line) than the conventional PKF results (the red diamond points). Figure 4 shows that the tracking error of the PLLS-PKF method

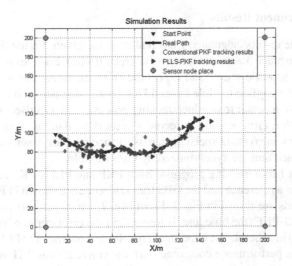

Fig. 3. Simulation result of PKF and PLLS-PKF (Color figure online)

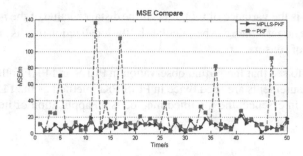

Fig. 4. MSE of PKF and PLLS-PKF in simulation (Color figure online)

Fig. 5. Test plant (Acoustic array sensor and the target) (Color figure online)

is obviously smaller than the tracking error of the conventional PKF method. The simulation shows that the PLLS-PKF method can improve the tracking performance.

4.2 Real Experiment Results

In this section the results calculated from real data are given. Figure 5 is the photo of our test plant. We place 3 acoustic arrays (the green frame). Each array has 19 acoustic sensors to detect acoustic source and export the DOA measurement with 5° maximum error in 1 km and a ZigBee module to send DOA data once per second. A computer is set as the data fusion center to conduct tracking process with a ZigBee receiver. A delta wing aircraft with a GPS module to record the location data as well as time data as reference data flew in constant speed up across the acoustic array sensor networks. The system time of each unit are synchronized by GPS module.

We conduct a 1 min tracking progress. Both PKF and PLLS-PKF results as well as the EKF results as a reference and the GPS trail reference are shown in Fig. 6. The MSE of the two methods are shown in Fig. 7. From Fig. 7, we can clearly find that the error curve of the PLLS-PKF (the blue line) is lower than the error curve of the conventional PKF (the red line) in general. The experiment results demonstrate the PLLS-PKF method can provide better performance compared with the conventional PKF method.

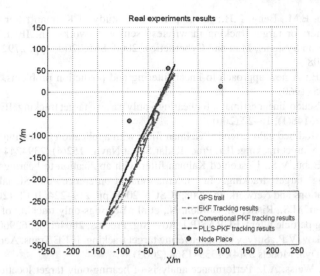

Fig. 6. Real experiment result of EKF, PKF and PLLS-PKF (Color figure online)

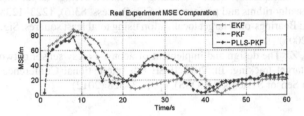

Fig. 7. MSE of EKF, PKF and PLLS-PKF in real experiment (Color figure online)

5   Conclusion

In this paper, a modified PKF tracking method using PLLS target localization for DOA measurement sensor networks is proposed. The PLLS-PKF method takes two steps: using PLLS to give target location estimation and taking the localization result into the updating progress. The one step iteration of the bearing only observation can improve the tracking performance and reduce error to a certain extent. Both numerical simulation and real experiment test demonstrate the nice tracking performance of the new method.

References

1. Akyildiz, I.F., Su, W., Sankarasubramaniam, Y., et al.: Wireless sensor networks: a survey. Comput. Netw. **38**(4), 393–422 (2002)
2. Hawkes, M., Nehorai, A.: Acoustic vector-sensor beamforming and Capon direction estimation. IEEE Trans. Sig. Process. **46**(9), 2291–2304 (1998)

3. Di, M., Joo, E.M., Beng, L.H.: A comprehensive study of Kalman filter and extended Kalman filter for target tracking in wireless sensor networks. In: IEEE International Conference on Systems, Man and Cybernetics, 2008, SMC 2008, pp. 2792–2797. IEEE, October 2008

4. Kalman, R.E.: A new approach to linear filtering and prediction problems. J. Basic Eng. **82**(1), 35–45 (1960)

5. Rao, S.K.: Pseudo-linear estimator for bearings-only passive target tracking. IEE Proc.-Radar Sonar Navig. **148**(1), 16–22 (2001)

6. Rao, S.K.: Modified gain extended Kalman filter with application to bearings-only passive manoeuvring target tracking. IEE Proc.-Radar Sonar Navig. **152**(4), 239–244 (2005)

7. Rao, S.K., Babu, V.S.: Unscented Kalman filter with application to bearings-only passive manoeuvring target tracking. In: International Conference on Signal Processing, Communications and Networking, 2008, ICSCN 2008, pp. 219–224. IEEE (2008)

8. Arulampalam, M.S., Ristic, B., Gordon, N., et al.: Bearings-only tracking of manoeuvring targets using particle filters. EURASIP J. Adv. Sig. Process. **2004**(15), 562960 (2004)

9. Li, X.R., Jilkov, V.P.: Survey of maneuvering target tracking. IEEE Trans. Aerosp. Electron. Syst. Part I Dyn. Models **39**(4), 1333–1364 (2003)

10. Gavish, M., Weiss, A.J.: Performance analysis of bearing-only target location algorithms. IEEE Trans. Aerosp. Electron. Syst. **28**(3), 817–828 (1992)

11. Ristic, B., Arulampalam, M.S.: Tracking a manoeuvring target using angle-only measurements: algorithms and performance. Sig. Process. **83**(6), 1223–1238 (2003)

12. Doğançay, K.: Bearings-only target localization using total least squares. Sig. Process. **85**(9), 1695–1710 (2005)

13. Li, Y., Wang, Z.: The design and implement of acoustic array sensor network platform for online multi-target tracking. In: 2012 IEEE 8th International Conference on Distributed Computing in Sensor Systems (DCOSS), pp. 323–328 (2012)

Security and Privacy

Distributed Fault Diagnosis of Wireless Sensor Network

Xu Huang[✉]

School of Information Engineering, Shandong Ying Cai University,
No. 2 Yingcai Road, High-Tech Zone,
Jinan 250014, Shandong, People's Republic of China
huangxu0813@163.com

Abstract. This paper considers a novel distribute fault diagnosis mechanism for wireless sensor network (WSN). Do not need additional agents, the built-in and self-organization diagnosis mechanism can monitor each node and identify fault nodes in real-time. Faulty sensor nodes are identified based on comparisons between neighboring nodes, and the testing node dissemination the status (testing result) to other neighbors, so the whole node detection is implemented. As the diagnosis is operated periodic and triggered, it can reduce energy consumption and traffic. We also proposed a new method to improve fault diagnosis rate in different average node degree. Large number of experiments demonstrate the effectiveness of this method.

Keywords: Wireless sensor network (WSN) · Distribute · Fault diagnosis · Fault detection · Average node degree

1 Introduction

With advances in hardware and wireless network technology, low cost, low power consumption and multiple functions of the sensor device is in actual use provides. Wireless Sensor Network (WSN) is a large number of sensor nodes across the geographic area transmission. The main applications of wireless sensor networks include environmental monitoring, security surveillance, manufacturing and industrial automation [1].

The sensor nodes of wireless sensor network is too fragile, so it easy to fault. Because of bad environment and limited power supply, sensor nodes may not be able to perform the correct operation. In addition, the connection between the sensor nodes is facing the severe environment and it is easy to cause a temporary or permanent failure. On the other hand, based on packet switching network communication between sensor nodes, node failure will seriously affect the network performance. It is necessary to provide a diagnostic test operation mechanism of sensor network, it can monitor and maintain the network system, and on the basis of the mechanism of the formation is the result of diagnosis of the system state.

Supported by the 2013 Shandong province science and technology development plan (No. 2013 GGB01257) and the Colleges and Universities in Shandong Province Scientific Research Plan (No. J13LN55) and 2013 Ji'nan science and technology development plan (No. 201303217).

L. Sun et al. (Eds.): CWSN 2014, CCIS 501, pp. 275–283, 2015.
DOI: 10.1007/978-3-662-46981-1_26

In this paper, we consider a novel fault diagnosis mechanism for WSN. The diagnosis mechanism is regularly launched to monitor every node and identify fault node in real-time. Do not need additional agents, the built-in and self-organization diagnosis mechanism can monitor each node and identify fault node in real-time. As the diagnosis is operated periodic and triggered, it can reduce energy consumption and traffic. We also present a method to improve fault diagnosis rate in different average node degree for WSN. Extensive experiments demonstrate the effectiveness of the proposed method.

The rest of this paper is organized as follows. Section 2 presents related work. Section 3 describes the fault model. In Sect. 4, we describe the diagnosis protocol in detail. Section 5 shows the results of our experiments, and we compare the relationship between the network nodes distribution of density and the node failure rate. Finally, we conclude the paper in Sect. 6.

2   Related Works

Many studies have focused on the diagnosis mechanism, conventional or wireless networks [1, 3–9]. In [10], the authors propose a diagnostic mechanism, with the same degree of topological structure of the system. In [5], the authors propose a mechanism, any connection systems. In [11], the authors present a shared structures of diagnosis method specialized for systems. For these studies, however, WSN is still faced with many challenges [12]. For Wireless sensor network, only a handful of proposed diagnosis mechanism, it can be divided into two categories: active and passive approach.

The active approaches embed debugging agents into each node. The agents monitor the status of the wireless sensor nodes and report to the sink node periodically. Zhao [13] think that wireless network resources and application activities are important for WSN. They put forward a method to scan the residual energy and monitor status information link loss rate and packet number. Sympathy [14] collect status information includes a routing table, from each sensor node and the flow of information, testing and commissioning of wireless sensor network may fail. Failure analysis is based on state information and network anomalies. However, due to the positive method need to constantly monitor and report the status of various types for each sensor node, they introduced a large number of additional computing operations to cover wireless sensor network sensor node and traffic.

The passive approach PAD [15] is presented for efficiency. Using a packet marking algorithm, network topology are analyzed by PAD. Based on the analysis and observations on, PAD introduction of probabilistic reasoning model, used to detect the failed node. However, relying on continuous flow analysis, pad is not suitable for those who are not continuous communication applications.

3   Node Fault Model

3.1   Network Model

Wireless sensor network each node can be in one of two states: a fault or no fault. Fault is permanent, that is the fault node failure is retained until it is repaired or replaced.

Faults are static, i.e. the fault diagnosis process does not generate a new fault [16]. It can be either hard faults or soft faults. When a node hard fault occurs, it can't communicate with other nodes. In WSN, nodes can be hard failure may be due to its crash or because the battery is depleted. Soft fault is subtle, because the soft accused continues to communicate with other nodes of WSN nodes, though changed the specification.

In wireless sensor network fault diagnosis, the node soft faults detection is mainly aimed. There n sensors are assumed randomly deployed in the area be interested and all sensor nodes have a common transmission range. The region is considered to be complete coverage of sensor nodes. As shown in Fig. 1, the sign of all the sensors of the rectangular area covered. In the darkness of the figures represent the sensor fault, white is a good sensor. Likely to occur in the region shown in Fig failure. All sensor faults in the region.

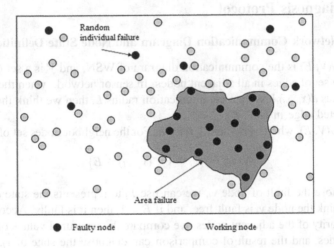

Fig. 1. Sensor nodes randomly deployed over an area

We define $\tilde{p}$ is the sensor network node failure probability (including software and hardware failures), then the number of fault node in sensor network is $n\tilde{p}$. We define the soft failure probability of all the failed nodes is r, so the number is $n\tilde{p}r$. Therefore, the total number of valid node in network for fault diagnosis is $n(1 - \tilde{p}) + n\tilde{p}r$.

Then define the new fault probability is

$$p = \frac{n\tilde{p}r}{n(1 - \tilde{p}) + n\tilde{p}r} = \frac{\tilde{p}r}{1 - \tilde{p} + \tilde{p}r} \tag{1}$$

as an important parameter in study of fault diagnosis algorithm.

In a fixed communication distance wireless sensor networks, the network average node degree d is another important parameter which this paper study fault diagnosis. The average node degree of network is that the average number of neighbors a node has, and it is depends on node distribution density of the network and the effective number of nodes n.

3.2   Data Model

In wireless sensor network, there having a spatial similarity between the node and its neighbors. That is means the measured values is same or similar between the fault free nodes and its neighbors in the network. Therefore, we can use the sensor data which the neighbors measured to diagnose the state of the current node. We define the node v_i and v_j are failure-free neighbors, then x_i and x_j are their corresponding measured values, so the two nodes should satisfy:

$$|x_i - x_j \leq \xi|$$ (2)

Where $0 \leq \xi \leq 1$, and the threshold ξ depending on the different applications.

4   The Diagnosis Protocol

4.1   The Network Communication Diagram and Node State Definition

We define $G(V, E)$ is the communication diagram of WSN, and V is a set of all sensor nodes; E is a set of edges in all adjacent nodes. In sensor network, when the distance of adjacent nodes $d(x_i, x_j)$ less than communication radius L, then we think the two nodes have connected edge in $G(V, E)$.

For the $G(V, E)$, where $v_i \in V$ and $1 \leq i \leq n$. For the neighbor nodes set of v_i, we have

$$N(v_i) = \{v_j \in V : (v_i, v_j) \in E\}$$ (3)

To diagnose the fault of node v_i, we can use F_i to represents the state of v_i. When $F_i = 0$, we think the node v_i is fault-free, and if $F_i = 1$, then it is faulty. According to the spatial similarity of the adjacent nodes, we compare the measured values of v_i to all its neighbor nodes, and the result of comparison can diagnose the state of v_i. Given two adjacent nodes $(v_i, v_j) \in E$, $v_j \in N(v_i)$ we define $C(v_i, v_j)$ is the comparison function of the node v_i and its all neighbors, abbreviated as C_{ij}, we have:

$$C_{ij} = C(v_i, v_j) = \begin{cases} 0 & if \ |x_i - x_j \leq \xi| \\ 1 & otherwise \end{cases}$$ (4)

When the node v_i and its neighbor is similar to the result of comparison, return the result of 0, otherwise it return 1. We use C_i to describe the number of $C_{ij} = 0$ in the neighbors of v_i, and there is $0 \leq |C_i| \leq |N(v_i)|$. C_i is also describe the similar degree of node v_i and its neighbors. If $|C_i| \geq \theta$ (θ is the threshold value), we can diagnose the node v_i is fault-free, and set $F_i = 0$.

4.2   Node Fault Diagnosis Algorithm

The fault diagnosis algorithm contains two procedures, namely the threshold test and the fault-free node state diffusion. In the first stage, we set a threshold value θ, and threshold test for each sensor node v_i. When the $|C_i| \geq \theta$, then set the $F_i = 0$; Else when $|C_i| < \theta$, it is said that the node have not pass the threshold test, then without any operation and quit the threshold test. In the second stage, for the fault-free node v_i which had passed the threshold test, if their neighbor node v_j and its $C_{ji} = C_{ij}$, then set the $F_i = 0$, we do this process repeatedly until the node status spread to all the neighbors. The node fault diagnosis algorithm is summarized in the following:

Algorithm

Step 1: Each detected sensor v_i to generate its neighbor set $N(v_i)$, initialize $F_i = 0$ and initialize the threshold θ.

Step 2: For $j = 1$ to $|N(v_i)|$ {Calculate the return value of $C_{ij} = C(v_i, v_j)$; }

   Statistical the value of C_i;

   If$(|C_i| \geq \theta)$ { $F_i = 0$;

   For $j = 1$ to $|N(v_i)|$

   {If $(C_{ji} = C_{ij} = 0)$ $F_j = 0$;}}

Step 3: For the remaining unprocessed nodes $v_r = v - \{v_i | v_i \in v, F = 0\}$

   For each v_k in v_r

   If$(C_{ki} = C_{ik} = 0$, $F_i = 0$ and $F_k = 1)$

   $\{F_k = 0$; Spread $F_k = 0$ to its neighbors ;}

Step 4: Flag all $F_i = 0$ nodes for fault node;

5   Experimental Evaluations

We evaluate the performance of our diagnosis algorithm numerically. For simulation we used GloMoSim as the tool. An example of simulation scenario 1024 random deployment of sensor nodes in an area the size of the 32×32 units as shown in Fig. 2. The measurement parameter x_i is considered to be temperature. We set the values of x_i as good and faulty with ranges as follows, "Good" = 21–23 °C and "Faulty" as 37–40 °C. Also spread range was selected to ensure that the sensor in the simulation run the average number of neighbors. In step 1 of the algorithm, a threshold value θ and the average node degree d are needed to determine the testing value.

Faulty sensor diagnosis accuracy (FSDA) and false alarm rate (FAR) are used to assess the performance of the two indicators of our algorithm. FSDA diagnosis is defined as the ratio of the total number of field failures of the number of sensors sensor failure. FAR is the total number of faulty diagnosis of non-faulty sensors ratio of the number of non-fault sensor. For simulation, we analyses the change of FSDA and FAR in the different average node degree d, then we also analyses the influence of θ and d to FSDA, FAR.

In the process of the simulation, the sensors are random selected with the probability of fault (p) of 0.05, 0.10, 0.15, 0.20, and 0.25 respectively under d for each sensor. Average node degree d is chosen to be 7, 10, 15, and 20 respectively.

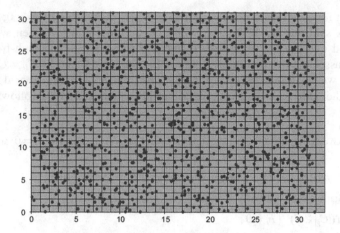

Fig. 2. The 32 × 32 region with 1024 sensors randomly deployed in it

False positive rate and the diagnostic accuracy of Figs. 3 and 4 shows a faulty sensor of a different average node degree d of the probability of a sensor failure. In Fig. 3, the diagnostic accuracy of the neighbor and the neighbor's 10 7, when the probability of failure increases decreases. However, the fault diagnosis accuracy rate remains at about 25 % to about 97 % is wrong sensor. There has not been diagnosed as having a few failures faulty sensor, because the result of random deployed sensor network in a handful of neighboring sensors. When the average value of the number of neighbors is greater than 15, the fault diagnosis is very high, and almost all of the failure of the sensor may be a sensor, even in a high probability of failure diagnosis.

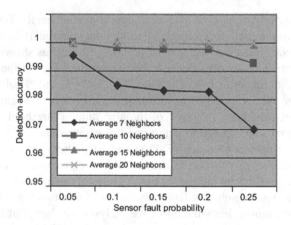

Fig. 3. Fault sensor diagnosis accuracy

In Fig. 4, 7 neighbors and 10 neighbors, the higher the probability of failure, the higher the rate of false positives. This is because a large number of faulty sensor test good sensor is possible failures, these good diagnosis of a faulty sensor is a sensor. For neighbors 15 and 20, the false positive rate is as low as 0.

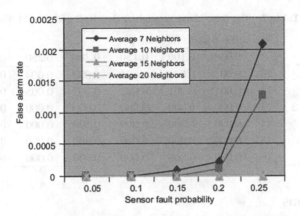

Fig. 4. False alarm rate in faulty sensor diagnosis

In the experiment, in order to analyze the impact on the threshold value θ and the diagnosis performance of the network average node degree d, we change the average node degree of the network respectively. The average node degree d is chosen to be approximate 10.3 and 14.8 respectively under different threshold values θ, then analysis the FSDA and FAR.

In Tables 1 and 2, when the average node degree d is relatively high, the node failure detection has reached high FSDA and FAR. With d increases, the range of choice of the threshold value θ is also increased. For example, in the average node degree $d \approx 14.8$, threshold θ can choose 13, 14, 15, 16 of any one, and makes fault diagnosis to achieve better effect. Therefore, when the average node degree is high, the influence of node failure rate to FSDA and FAR is a little, and FAR can always control in very low range; For the FSDA, we can adjust the threshold θ to achieve the best value, the experimental results show that, when $\theta \approx d$ it is the most ideal results.

Table 1. The fault sensor diagnosis accuracy when d ≈ 10.3 and d ≈ 14.8

d	θ	The node failure rate p					
		0.050	0.100	0.150	0.200	0.250	0.300
$d \approx 10.3$	10	1.000	1.000	1.000	0.998	0.993	0.960
	11	1.000	1.000	1.000	0.999	0.996	0.984
$d \approx 14.8$	13	1.000	1.000	1.000	0.998	0.992	0.910
	14	1.000	1.000	1.000	1.000	0.996	0.934
	15	1.000	1.000	1.000	1.000	1.000	0.995
	16	1.000	1.000	1.000	1.000	1.000	0.996

Overall, our localized fault diagnosis algorithm achieves high diagnosis accuracy and low false alarm rate even with a large set of faulty sensors.

Table 2. The false alarm rate when d ≈ 10.3 and d ≈ 14.8

d	θ	The node failure rate p					
		0.050	0.100	0.150	0.200	0.250	0.300
d ≈ 10.3	10	0.001	0.001	0.001	0.002	0.004	0.007
	11	0.001	0.001	0.002	0.003	0.005	0.008
d ≈ 14.8	13	0.000	0.000	0.000	0.000	0.000	0.000
	14	0.000	0.000	0.000	0.000	0.000	0.000
	15	0.000	0.000	0.000	0.000	0.000	0.001
	16	0.000	0.000	0.000	0.000	0.000	0.002

6 Conclusions

We put forward a distributed localized sensor fault detection algorithm, each sensor identify their identity is "good" or "faulty", claimed by its neighbor and then support or restore as they evaluate the behavior of the node.

Finally, the algorithm is tested using the simulation of an example of the case where there is a different number in the same area of the faulty sensor. Our simulation results show that, FSDA more than 96 % even though 25.3 % of node failure. FAR is the very accurate, when the probability of failure of the sensor is low. And we also analyzed the network average node degree, threshold value and the relationship between the node failure rates. Simulation results support and prove that our algorithm can have higher fault detection accuracy and low false alarm rate and a number of defects of sensor networks.

At this time there may be issues related to scalability and overhead due to exchange of information between neighbors. However, the aim of this work was to detect errors of sensors that "faulty" in the distributed environment. This success is promising, we want to extend it, and look at its performance in a very large deployment. The further working is to find the event edge by partially, using the algorithm proposed on developing an algorithm in this paper. Future work should include the implementation of the algorithms on GloMoSim sensor network simulators.

7 Conflict of Interests

The authors declare that there is no conflict of interests regarding the publication of this article.

References

1. You, Z., Zhao, X., Wan, H., Hung, W.N.N., Wang, Y.: A novel fault diagnosis mechanism for wireless sensor networks. Math. Comput. Model. **54**, 330–343 (2011)
2. Cruller, D., Estrin, D., Srivastava, M.: Over view of sensor networks. Comput. Netw. **37**, 41–49 (2004)

3. Chandra, R., Padmanabhan, V., Zhang, M.: WiFi profiler: cooperative diagnosis in wireless LANs. In: Proceedings of the 4th International Conference on Mobile Systems, Applications and Services, pp. 205–219. ACM (2006)
4. Zhao, Y., Chen, Y., Bindel, D.: Towards unbiased end-to-end network diagnosis. IEEE/ACM Trans. Netw. **17**, 1724–1737 (2009)
5. Tang, Y., Song, X.: Diagnosis of parallel computers with arbitrary connectivity. IEEE Trans. Comput. **48**, 757–761 (1999)
6. Song, X., Hung, W., Mishchenko, A., Chrzanowska-Jeske, M., Kennings, A., Coppola, A.: Board-level multi-terminal net assignment for the partial cross-bar architecture. IEEE Trans. Very Large Scale Integr. VLSI Syst. **11**, 511–551 (2003)
7. Song, X., Tang, Q., Zhou, D., Wang, Y.: Wire space estimation and routability analysis. IEEE Trans. Comput. Aided Des. Integr. Circ. Syst. **19**, 624–628 (2000)
8. Cao, Y., Xu, D., Guan, J., Zhang, H.: Cross-layer retransmission approach for efficient VoD transfer over multi-homed wireless networks. Int. J. Digit. Content Technol. Appl. AICIT **6** (23), 98–109 (2012)
9. Cui, C., Yang, Y., Li, X.: Research on congestion in wireless networks based on cross-layer design. Adv. Inf. Sci. Serv. Sci. AICIT **4**(20), 552–561 (2012)
10. Tang, Q., Song, X., Wang, Y.: Diagnosis of clustered faults for identical degree topologies. IEEE Trans. Comput. Aided Des. Integr. Circ. Syst. **18**, 1192–1201 (1999)
11. Lu, X., Li, J., Seo, C.: Probabilistic diagnosis of clustered faults for shared structures. Math. Comput. Model. **49**, 623–634 (2009)
12. Paradis, L., Han, Q.: A survey of fault management in wireless sensor networks. J. Netw. Syst. Manage. **15**, 171–190 (2007)
13. Zhao, Y., Govindan, R., Estrin, D.: Residual energy scan for monitoring sensor networks. In: Proceedings of IEEE Wireless Communications and Networking Conference, WCNC 2002, pp. 169–172 (2002)
14. Ramanathan, N., Chang, K., Kapur, R., Girod, L., Kohler, E., Estrin, D.: Sympathy for the sensor network debugger. In: Proceedings of the 3rd International Conference on Embedded Networked Sensor Systems, pp. 55–267. ACM (2005)
15. Liu, K., Li, M., Liu, Y., Li, M., Guo, Z., Hong, F.: Passive diagnosis for wireless sensor networks. In: Proceedings of the 6th ACM Conference on Embedded Network Sensor Systems, pp. 113–126. ACM (2011)
16. Chessa, S., Santi, P.: Comparison-based system level fault diagnosis in ad hoc networks. In: Proceedings of the 20th IEEE on Reliable Distributed Systems, pp. 568–576. IEEE Press (2001)

Privacy Protection Model for Location-Based Service in Mobile Ad Hoc Networks

Lili Zhang[✉], Chenming Li, Jie Shen, and Qiaomei Luo

College of Computer and Information Engineering, Hohai University, Nanjing, China
lilzhang@hhu.edu.cn

Abstract. Nowadays, Mobile ad hoc Network has been applied in the real life. Like Vehicular ad hoc Network, it can provide plenty of location-based services. But it also brings the privacy protection simultaneously. And there are some conflicts between the privacy protection and the high-quality service. Hence, in this paper, we will propose one privacy protection model including two parts, location anonymous algorithm and nearest neighbor query algorithm. The location anonymous algorithm is to protect the location of the user based on the Grid model, and the nearest neighbor query algorithm is to improve the quality of the service. So our model can achieve the tradeoff between the privacy protection and the quality of the service. Finally, the simulation shows that the algorithm we proposed is better than the Casper algorithm on the success rate of anonymous area constructing, and our algorithm can adapt the node mobility as well. The nearest neighbor query algorithm is good on reducing the query area and query error.

Keywords: Vehicular ad hoc network · Location-based service · Privacy protection · Nearest-neighboring query

1 Introduction

With the development of VANET, it's possible to obtain individual precise location anytime and anywhere, which promoted the generation of the new application, location-based services [1] (LBS, the location-based service). Generally, the system structure of the location-based services is as shown in Fig. 1. In the VANET, LBS can provide some kinds of information and related service for the user or others and the services to different users have the following categories basically:

- To find nearby convenience service. LBS can provide the interested location of the service for each vehicle users with its surrounding, such as restaurants, hotels, entertainment places, etc.;
- Emergency service. When a user is in danger, even if the user don't know their place, VANET can periodically send message information to find the location of the user;
- Social networking service. LBS can provide users around vehicles, and the users can use self-organizing network to organize their LAN to chat, play games or other entertainment.

© Springer-Verlag Berlin Heidelberg 2015
L. Sun et al. (Eds.): CWSN 2014, CCIS 501, pp. 284–292, 2015.
DOI: 10.1007/978-3-662-46981-1_27

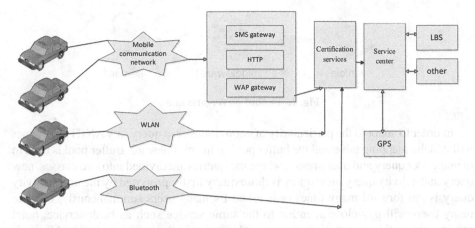

Fig. 1. LBS system diagram

Because the user must provide their location information before they apply the location-based service, this would lead the user's location information to be used illegally or to be threatened. Therefore, privacy protection problem is becoming one of research hot topic in VANET.

2 Related Work

At present, the k-anonymity methods was used widely to solve the privacy protection of LBS. k-anonymity was proposed by Sweeney [2] to apply in the relational database; and it was generalized in [3] to apply in the privacy protection, and named k - anonymous model. This model is good to protect the user's privacy, but the service quality decreased. Because the server does not know the location of the user, and can only find all members within the region as a result. In [4, 5], the authors proposed the time-to-confusion mechanism in order to get the tradeoff between privacy protection and the quality of service, it allows LBS server to get the user's identity information. In order to get the anonymous region, Casper scheme [6] uses the incomplete pyramid data structure to decompose city region into H layers. However, the cost of this algorithm in position updating is larger.

LBS needs not only to protect the user's location privacy, but also to provide users the accurate and efficient service. In this paper, we will give one model including two parts, part A is to protect the user's privacy, and the part B is to guarantee the quality of the service. By far, the most commonly used method to guarantee the quality of the service is the range nearest-neighbor query [7–9], which can find the service result of closest the target.

3 Center Server Structure

Like most of the existing work, we use the center server structure [10–14], which include center server, the user(vehicle), and the trusted third party middleware, as shown in Fig. 2.

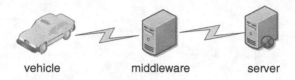

vehicle   middleware   server

Fig. 2. Central server structure

In order to adapt to the particularity of anonymous area query in VANET, this paper will add the mapping table and the buffer pool in the middleware. Buffer pool is used to manage user query and query result, where the queries are divided into two classes, new query and activity query, new query is those query firstly proposed by the user, activity query is put forward many times or is asked by many users simultaneously, because many users will pay close attention to the same service such as bank service, hotel service, etc. In this case, activity query can be stored in the buffer pool of middleware, when there are request, just directly sending the stored result from the buffer pool to user, thus avoiding the frequent query on the service providers at the same request, then we can improve the query efficiency by this method, and reduce the burden of service providers. Mapping table is a drawing of the matching of the position of the user and mesh network of its corresponding grid, in preparation for anonymous search algorithm.

4   Algorithm

4.1   Part A- Location Anonymous Algorithm

Grid Model. Grid model is to divide the large area the vehicle located into small grids with the same size and the size can be defined by the system on demand. There are two aspects in each grid, the unit grid of the identity and vehicle number, defined as (CID, N). If one vehicle's location changes, leaving or entering into a new grid, the vehicle will send update location information to the center server of middleware, maintenance of the grid information is the duty of the middleware. When vehicle location updates, mapping the vehicle's position to the current network, this is finished by the mapping table. In addition, we need start one hash table, each vehicles should be registered in the form of $(VID, CID, V, angle, Last)$, as shown in Fig. 3. VID is the vehicle ID and CID is the temporary ID of the grid, V and $angle$ are the moving speed and direction of the vehicle, $Last$ records the CID of last LBS query. When the vehicle's location changes, the middleware will receive location updates in the form of (CID, x, y), where x, y is the latest vehicle location coordinates. Using hash functions $h(x, y)$ to obtain the new CID of vehicles in the grid, and then compared to old CID. If they are equal, do not update. If not, update the information of vehicle in the grid. The table on the left in Fig. 3 is the information table of the vehicles, and the right is the network structure.

Anonymous Region Generation. Generally, the privacy protection is proposed based on Grid model, but, in this paper, the different between our algorithm and the previous work is we do not use proxy node, the details as follows.

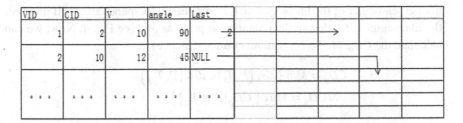

VID	CID	V	angle	Last						
1	2	10	90	2						
2	10	12	45	NULL						
...	...	...	...	...						

Fig. 3. Vehicle information mapping

(1) Firstly the middleware checks the vehicle in the grid and the others around this grid to guarantee they must be within the scope of the grid, if the location of some vehicle changes, then update the hash table. Grid *ID* can be updated by calculating the vehicle's position, and the position of the vehicle can be calculated by the speed of vehicle and the time difference between these two times, the path of the vehicle between these two times.

(2) Check the value of *Last* that vehicle's registration in the hash table, if it is not empty, the *Last* query vehicles are anonymous area. Then check whether the vehicle is still in the anonymous area, if yes, check the privacy requirements, if the total number of vehicles in the grid is no less than k, and the area of the grid size is no less than A_{min}, return the anonymous area, or (3).

(3) To observe the adjacent grid of the current grid from four directions, select the grid with most vehicles and combined it with the current grid into one, if the combined grid meets the demand of privacy protection, the anonymous area can be returned as an anonymous area, or to (4).

(4) Repeat (1)–(3) until get the anonymous area.

In the algorithm, k can be set on demand by the users, and we first update the position of the vehicle due to improve the quality of the query service.

4.2 Part B-The Grid-Based Range Nearest-Neighbor Algorithm

The main idea of algorithm is based on the Grid model and the range nearest-neighbor algorithm, so we can named as G-RNN algorithm. Our goal is to calculate a RQR (Result of the Query Region) such that RQR as small as possible and including the nearest target of each point in C. So query result is the set of all nearest targets in RQR. The key of this algorithm is how to calculate the RQR as small as possible, we will get that by applying the range nearest-neighbor algorithm on the point, line, and surface.

(1) Point

For each point, get the nearest targets in anonymous area C by the point nearest-neighbor query algorithm. If the target T is the nearest target of a point P, the distance between P and T is called dominating distance, called P is dominated by T.

(2) Line

Calculate the edge control rectangular of each edge in C. If the nearest targets of the nodes V_i and V_j are not same, denoted as T_i, T_j respectively, and we draw the midperpendicular of the line segment T_iT_j, the the midperpendicular will intersect the line segment E_{ij}, denote the intersection point as M_{ij}, see Fig. 4. Now, we can calculate the CD_p, MCD_{ij} (maximum control distance).

$$CD_p = Min\left\{dist\left(P, T_i\right), dist\left(P, T_j\right)\right\}$$
$$MCD_{ij} = Max\left\{CD_p|P \in E_{ij}\right)\right\}$$

After that, we can extend the edge E_{ij}, and get the edge control rectangular.

If the nearest targets of the nodes V_i and V_j are same, denoted as T, then we can calculate MCD_{ij}.

$$MCD_{ij} = Max\left\{dist\left(V_i, T_i\right), dist\left(V_j, T_j\right)\right\}$$

(3) Surface

We can get the RQR of C is the convex hull of the union of C and edge control rectangular. Figure 5 shows the key step to get RQR.

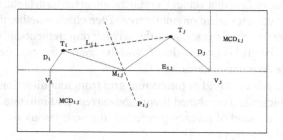

Fig. 4. Rectangular side control

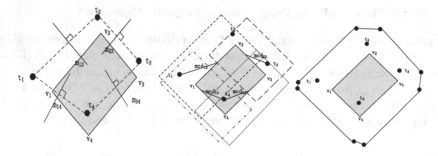

Fig. 5. RQR calculating key process

5   Experimental Results and Analysis

We get our experiment result on one real city urban scenario. We will compares the Casper algorithm and Grid model from three aspects: success rate of anonymous area construction and query error. Success rate of anonymous area construction:

$$S = \frac{U + u\_come - u\_leave}{k} \times 100\%$$

Where U represents the number of vehicles in this area before data update. u_come and u_leave represent the latest update on number of vehicles that entering in and leaving the area, respectively. Set $A_{min} = 2$ and $k = 5$, Figs. 6 and 7 shows the comparison of the two algorithms with different node density.

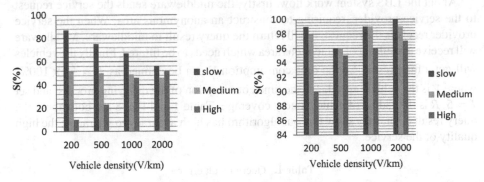

Fig. 6. Vehicle density *vs* S(left is the result of Casper, right is the result of Grid model)

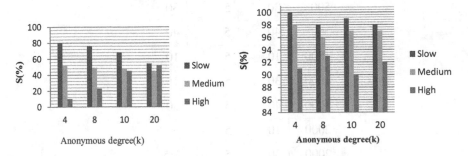

Fig. 7. Anonymous degree *vs* S (left is the result of Casper, right is the result of Grid model)

According to Casper, as can be seen from the left one in Fig. 6, when the vehicle is under high speed, S is lower than 60 %. And it reduces obviously as the node density of anonymous area vehicles drops. While the vehicle is under medium speed, the vehicle density influences a little on S, normally at 50 %. When the vehicle is under high speed, it means the vehicle is on the highway and cars around must be under high speed which forms an unstable environment for Casper. Data in Casper can' t be updated in time. When the anonymous area is to be built, all data in the system is out of date and thus leads to the lower S.

Compared the result about the Capser algorithm and the Grid model in Fig. 6, Grid model improves a lot no matter under high speed, medium speed or low speed. Under high speed, when the node density is very low, S of Casper is only 10 % while S of Grid reaches 90 %. It clearly shows Grid model has higher efficient and more stable.

Figure 7 shows the anonymous success rate of regional tectonic of Grid model with the different anonymous degree, and we can see that the S will reduce when the anonymous degree is 4, 8, and 10 with the speed reduced, but it is not the same when the anonymous degree is 20. It shows us the vehicle speed will lost its effect on S when the anonymous degree is enough.

About the LBS system work flow, firstly, the middleware sends the service request to the service provider, requiring to construct an anonymous area. When the service provider receives the request, it will return the query result to middleware. Middleware will receive a result set of anonymous area which needs to be filtered. Finally the vehicles will get a final result. So the time consumption E can be defined as $E = \frac{VT}{R} \times 100\%$, where V is the vehicle speed, T is the time consumption of the querying process, and set $T = 5$, R is the radius of vehicle query coverage. Table 1 and Fig. 8 are both about the query result error, they show that our algorithm has high accuracy to guarantee the high quality of the service.

Table 1. Query result error

$R(m)$	$V(m/s)$	$T(s)$	$E(\%)$
500	10	5	20
500	30	5	30
500	40	5	40
1000	10	5	10
1000	30	5	15
1000	40	5	20
2000	10	5	5
2000	30	5	7.5
2000	40	5	10

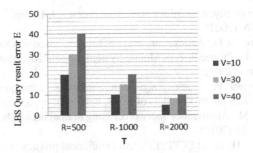

Fig. 8. Query result error of our algorithm

6 Conclusion

This paper proposed one privacy protection model, which can protect the privacy of the user when gives the user high quality location-based service. Nowadays, the privacy protection is becoming one of key important research field [15], we will focus on the light algorithm in the future wok.

References

1. Mokbel, M.F.: Privacy in location-based services: start-of-the-art and research directions. In: Proceedings of 8th International Conference on Mobile Data Management (MDM 2007), Mannheim, p. 228 (2007)
2. Sweeney, L.: K-anonymity: a model for protecting privacy. Int. J. Uncertainty Fuzziness Knowl. Syst. **10**(5), 557–570 (2002)
3. Gruteser, M., Grunwal, D.: Anonymous usage of location based services through spatial and temporal cloaking. In: Proceedings of International Conference on Mobile Systems, Applications, and Services, pp. 163–168 (2003)
4. Hoh, B., Gruteser, M., Xiong, H., et al.: Preserving privacy in gps traces via uncertainty aware path cloaking. In: Proceedings of the 14th ACM Conference on Computer and Communications Security, pp. 161–171 (2007)
5. Hoh, B., Gruteser, M., Xiong, H., et al.: Achieving guaranteed anonymity in GPS traces via uncertainty-aware path cloaking. IEEE Trans. Mob. Comput. **9**(8), 1089–1107 (2010)
6. Kianzad, V., Shuvra, S.: CASPER: an integrated energy-driven approach for task graph scheduling on distributed embedded systems. In: Proceedings of the 16th IEEE International Conference on Application-Specific Systems, Architecture Processors, pp. 191–197 (2005)
7. Tao, Y., Papadias, D., Shen, Q.: Continuous nearest neighbor search. In: Proceedings of the 28th International Conference on Very Large Data Bases, pp. 287–298 (2002)
8. Hu, H., Lee, D.L.: Range nearest-neighbor query. IEEE TKDE **18**(1), 78–91 (2006)
9. Chow, C.-Y., Mokbel, M.F., Naps, J., Nath, S.: Approximate evaluation of range nearest neighbor queries with quality guarantee. In: Mamoulis, N., Seidl, T., Pedersen, T.B., Torp, K., Assent, I. (eds.) SSTD 2009. LNCS, vol. 5644, pp. 283–301. Springer, Heidelberg (2009)
10. Barkhuus, L., Dey, A.: Location-based services for mobile telephony: a study of users 's privacy concerns. In: Proceedings of Interact, pp. 709–712. IOS, Zurich (2003)

11. Sweeney, L.: k-anonymity: a model for protecting privacy. J. Uncertainty Fuzziness Knowl. Syst. **10**(5), 557–570 (2002)
12. Gruteser, M., Grunwald, D.: Anonymous usage of location based services through spatial and temporal cloaking. In: Proceedings of Mobile Systems, Application and Services, pp. 31–42. ACM, San Francisco (2003)
13. Kido, H., Yanagisawa Y.: A anonymous communication technique using dummies for location-based services. In: Proceedings of ICPS, Santorini, pp. 88–97 (2005)
14. Kyriakos, M., Yiu, M.: Anonymous query processing in road networks. IEEE Trans. Knowl. Data Eng. **22**(1), 2–15 (2010)
15. Lu, R., Lin, X., Zhu, H., et al.: ECPP: Efficient conditional privacy preservation protocol for secure vehicular communications. In: Proceedings of INFOCOM 2008, pp. 1229–1237 (2008)

Trust Model Based on D-S Evidence Theory in Wireless Sensor Networks

Kai Yang[✉], Shuguang Liu, and Junwei Shen

Department of Electronics Technology, Engineering University of CAPF,
Xi'an, Shaanxi, China
{sydeny-001,liushuguang,jwshen}@163.com

Abstract. The existing trust model cannot solve malicious nodes in wireless sensor networks quickly and effectively, and counter-intuitive results may appear when combining evidence, so a trust model based on improved D-S evidence theory is proposed. According to Jousselme's distance, this trust model defines evidence variance to modify the evidence before combination, and then combines these evidences according to Dempster combination rule. Simulation results show that this model can find and isolate malicious nodes quickly and accurately, suppress nodes collusion and improve network performance. Compared with other existing trust models, this model has more security, robustness and accuracy.

Keywords: Trust model · Dempster-Shafer evidence theory · Evidence variance · Trust evaluation

1 Introduction

Wireless Sensor Networks (WSNs) is profoundly influenced by surrounding environment and variety attacks in traditional networks, and sensor nodes are easily captured by adversaries. Encryption authentication and other schemes [1] cannot solve this problem completely. So, it is necessary to use all kinds of tools from different fields, such as social scientific filed, statistic and other fields, with cryptology theory to solve various threats in networks, for example blackhole attack, sybil attack, and DoS attack.

The survival of WSNs is dependent on the cooperative of sensors, so it is an absolutely necessarily method to evaluate trustworthy and an effective way to strength network security to build trust relationship among sensors.

Dempster-Shafer (D-S) evidence theory [2] is a powerful tool to deal with uncertainty, which has the ability of expressing imprecise and uncertainty. It can deal with randomcity and subjective uncertainty in trust evaluation. According to accumulating evidence, it can reduce hypothesis sets without transcendental distribution and provide powerful method to express and deal with trust uncertainty. So, aimed at the problems mentioned-above, a trust evaluation model based on Dempster-Shafer evidence theory is proposed in this paper, without any central or distributed infrastructure.

The organization of the rest paper is organized as follows. In Sect. 2, the related work is described; Dempster-Shafer evidence theory is introduced in Sect. 3; an improved D-S evidence theory based trust model in WSNSs is proposed in Sect. 4;

© Springer-Verlag Berlin Heidelberg 2015
L. Sun et al. (Eds.): CWSN 2014, CCIS 501, pp. 293–301, 2015.
DOI: 10.1007/978-3-662-46981-1_28

Sect. 5 simulates the proposed trust model in Sect. 4 and makes analysis of the simulation results; finally, Sect. 6 concludes the paper.

2 Related Work

Trust-based and reputation-based models in WSNs have attracted more and more attentions in recent years.

ATRM [3] is a trust and reputation management scheme based on agent in WSNSs. In this scheme, trust and reputation management is operated with title costs in local area, such as additional message and time delay. However, mobile agents are roaming in this network and operating in remote nodes, so they must be started by trust entities. Chen et al. [4] present a trust model based on agent in WSNs, which uses a scheme named watchdog to monitor neighbors' behaviors and announce all the evaluations. Sensor can get those evaluations from agent sensors, they observe the nodes ahead and compute and broadcast their evaluations. The DRBTS (Distributed Reputation-based Beacon Trust System) presented in [5] is a scheme based on reputation. This scheme uses Beacon Nodes (BNs) to observe nodes then sensors can select the trusted nodes according to an election scheme. Nevertheless, so as to trust the information from BNs, sensors have to obtain enough support from more than half neighbors. [1] proposes a bio-inspired trust and reputation based model named BTRM-WSN, which can provide a most trustworthy path for certain services. Each node contains pheromone tracks leading to each neighbor nodes. CONFIDANT [6] extends reactive routings with the reputation based system, realizes the isolation of abnormal nodes. Every sensor observes their one-hop node's behaviors. Both trust relationship and routing decisions are all depended on the behaviors of other sensors. [7] proposes a scheme called SORI to embolden packet forwarding and punish no-cooperation behaviors. This scheme uses the objective metric to qualify node's reputation. Also, this scheme guarantees the security of propagation of reputation according to an authentication scheme based on one-way hash chain. Both Watchdog and Pathrater [8] are the extension versions of DSR.

However, not all the known work consider the capacity of process, storage and communication. Some depend on the watchdog scheme with or without multi-agent systems. To resolve these problems, it is a necessity to develop novel trust models different from the existed models. Based on the research on WSNs and the in-depth understanding of DRBTS, BTRM-WSN and CONFIDANT, this paper proposes a novel trust model which strengthens nodes cooperation based on behaviors.

3 Dempster-Shafer Evidence Theory

Dempster-Shafer evidence theory (D-S) can represent and process uncertainty information more effectively than probability theory. It can implement evidence convergence without the prior information and is one fundamental theory and important method of decision-making level in the field of information fusion.

Suppose that X is a set consisting of N hypotheses which are mutually exclusive and exhaustive, and then X is named the frame of discernment. The power set of X is represent by $P(X)$, which consists of 2^N elements that are all the possible subsets of X, that is to say, $P(X) = \{\varphi, \{A_1\}, \ldots, \{A_2\}, \{A_1, A_2\}, \{A_1, A_3\}, \ldots, X\}$, where φ denotes the empty set. In this paper, X = {T,–T}, where T and –T denotes one node trusts and distrusts the other node in WSNSs respectively. The power set of X is $P(X) = \{\varphi, \{T\}, \{-T\}, \{T,-T\}\}$.

Definition 1 (Basic Probability Assignment, BPA). For the frame of discernment X, function $m(A) : p(\theta) \rightarrow [0, 1]$ is named Basic Probability Assignment (BPA), if it satisfies: (1) $\sum\limits_{A \subseteq P(\theta)} m(A) = 1$; (2) $m(\varphi) = 0$.

Definition 2 (Belief Function). For the frame of discernment X, m is X's BPA, A is a set in X, so the belief function of A is defined as $Bel(A) : p(\theta) \rightarrow [0, 1]$, if it satisfies: (1) $Bel(A) = \sum\limits_{B \subseteq A} m(B)$; (2) $\forall A \subseteq P(\theta)$. It denotes the total belief in A.

Definition 3 (Plausibility Function). For the frame of discernment X, m is a BPA in X, A is a set in X, so the plausibility function of A is defined as $Pl(A) : p(\theta) \rightarrow [0, 1]$, if it satisfies: (1) $Pl(A) = \sum\limits_{B \cap A \neq 0} m(B)$; (2) $\forall A \subseteq P(\theta)$. It can also be stated by $Pl(A) = 1 - Bel(\neg A)$ where $\neg A$ is the complement of A.

Definition 4 (Dempster Combination Rule). Suppose that there are two mutually exclusive and exhaustive BPAs m_1 and m_2 on the same frame of discernment, $m(A)$, the result of the two BPAs by the Dempster combination rule, satisfies the following conditions:

$$\begin{cases} m(A) = m_1(A) \oplus m_2(A) = \dfrac{\sum\limits_{X \cap Y = A} m_1(X)m_2(Y)}{1 - K} \\ K = \sum\limits_{X \cap Y = \varphi} m_1(X)m_2(Y) \\ m(\varphi) = 0 \end{cases} \tag{1}$$

where K is a normalization constant, named conflict coefficient, it presents the degree of conflict between two different BPAs.

4 A Trust Model Based on Dempster-Shafer Evidence Theory

The historical interaction information among nodes in WSNs is the basis of trustworthy evaluation. When there is direct interaction information among nodes, the trustworthy can be evaluated by the direct interaction, and trust in this case is named Direct Trust (DT); when there are no direct interaction information, trustworthy evaluation depends on others' recommendation, and trust in this case is named Indirect Trust (IT). So, in the frame of discernment X = {T,–T}, it is necessary to computer both DT and IT, that is to say, the combined trust CT.

Meanwhile, the trustworthy need to be updated as the time goes on, so the computation of trustworthy must be carried out in the time domain. In this paper, we set a constant period δ, and compute CT according to the new interaction records after a period, then obtain the new trustworthy.

4.1 Direct Trust

During the evaluation of direct trust, we evaluate the reliability of an arbitrary node through packets forwarding successfully. Based on direct interaction history, nodes compute the direct trust to other nodes. In this paper, T_{ij} denotes the total interaction times between node i and node j, S_{ij} denotes the successful interaction times between i and j, and F_{ij} denotes the failed interaction times. For node i, the direct trust to node j is denoted as $DT_{ij} = <DT_{ij}(\{T\}), DT_{ij}(\{-T\}), DT_{ij}(\{T,-T\})> = <S_{ij}/T_{ij}, F_{ij}/T_{ij}, (T_{ij}-S_{ij}-F_{ij})/T_{ij}>$ during the period.

4.2 Indirect Trust

When there are no history interaction records between i and j or the history interaction records between i and j are not enough to determine whether j is trust or not, i needs to inquire the third party nodes for their recommendation to j, then they send their direct trusts to j as recommendation value to i. Using Dempster combination rule, we combine the recommendation values and obtain the indirect trust IT_{ij}. Considering the constraints in WSNSs, this paper only considers the recommendation from the next hop neighbors when computing IT_{ij}.

However, counter-intuitive results may appear when combining evidence using Dempster combination rule, which results in the trust deviation [9, 10].

Suppose that node i receives N recommendations about node j, the nth ($n = 1, ..., N$) recommendation is $DT_{nj} = <0.1, 0.9, 0>$, that is to say, all the N recommendations are the same. Using Dempster combination rule, we can know that the conflict coefficient K is 0 and the combined indirect trust is $IT_{ij} = <1-0.9^N, 0.9^N, 0>$. When N is 20, $IT_{ij} = <0.878, 0.122, 0>$, this shows that although all the 20 recommenders consider the dependability of node j is 0.1, the calculated trustworthy of j by Dempster combination rule is up to 0.878, which apparently results in the trust deviation. The reason of trust deviation lies in the fact that Dempster combination rule does not satisfy idempotent property and the convergence speed is too fast [11]. To avoid these problems, the combination of evidences is amended in this paper.

Firstly, this paper defines evidence variance according to Jousselme's distance [12]. Suppose that there are k evidences, and their BPAs are $m_i(i = 1, ..., k)$ respectively, then the variance of the k evidence is defined as follows

$$VAR_k = \sqrt{(\sum_{i=1}^{k} d^2(m_i, \overline{m}))/k} \qquad (2)$$

where, $\overline{m} = (\sum_{i=1}^{k} m_i)/k$ denotes the average evidence. Since evidence obtaining is ordered, therefore, when the ith evidence is obtained, this paper updates the indirect trust as follows.

```
Algorithm 1
code for update evidence mi
m₁=m₁; // update m₁
m₂=m₁*1/2+m₂*1/2; //更新m₂
for (i=3; i<k+1; i++)
{
    α=exp(- ε *VARᵢ); // ε is a constant
    β=exp(- ε *VARᵢ₋₁);
    mᵢ=mᵢ*α/(α+β)+mᵢ₋₁*β/(α+β); //amend
the new eivdence
}
```

From Algorithm 1, when the recommended evidences include evidences from malicious nodes, the variance of evidences increases, indicating that the deviation between the new evidence and other evidences is larger. Therefore, the new evidence should be inhibited to weaken its effect on the ultimate synthesis of trust. This algorithm can effectively reduce the impact of malicious nodes, and significantly improve the safety and the overall network performance.

After amendment by Algorithm 1, node i gets the indirect trust of node j using Dempster combination rule.

4.3   Combined Trust

After getting the direct trust DT_{ij} and the indirect trust IT_{ij}, node i gets the combined trust $CT_{ij} = DT_{ij} \oplus IT_{ij}$ according to Dempster combination rule.

5   Simulation and Analysis

5.1   Simulation Settings

We model the proposed trust model and simulate it to verify its effectiveness in this paper. The results are the average values of 10 different running. Simulations are operated in an area of 1000m*1000m in which there are 300 nodes deployed randomly; each node is equipped with a single 802.11 interface and an omni-directional antenna. In the simulation, each node randomly selects one of its neighbors and requests service every 5 s. The simulation time is 900 s and the routing protocol is AODV [13]. Table 1 lists partial parameters of our simulation.

Table 1. Simulation parameters

Parameters	Values
Simulation tool	OPNET 14.5
Area	1000 m*1000 m
Routing protocol	AODV
MAC protocol	IEEE 802.11
Total number of wireless nodes	300
Transmission power	0.5w
Simulation time	900 s
Size of packet	512 Byte
Period δ	5 s
ε	2.0

5.2   Evaluation Metrics

In order to qualify the proposed scheme, some trust evaluation metrics are defined as follows.

(1) End-to-end Packet Forwarding Ratio (*EPFR*). *EPFR* is the ratio of the amount of packets accepted by the destination nodes to the amount transmitted by the source node. It is obtained by the following equation:

$$EPFR = \frac{\sum_{i=1}^{k} RECV_i}{\sum_{i=1}^{n} SEND_i}, 0 \leq k \leq n \tag{3}$$

where $RECV_i$ and $SEND_i$ denotes the numbers of the ith node receiving packets and sending packets respectively. k is the successful times of receiving, and n denotes the total sending times.

(2) Average Energy Consume (AEC). A critical criteria of designing trust models in WSNSs is energy consume. So as to investigate the energy consume of the proposed trust model, this paper defines the following AEC

$$AEC = \frac{\sum_{i=1}^{k} consume_i}{\sum_{i=1}^{n} send_i + recv_i + \tau} \tag{4}$$

where $send_i$ and $recv_i$ denotes the energy consume of sending or receiving message of the ith sensor node, respectively. $consume_i$ is the energy consume of computing the trustworthiness. τ is the other energy consume.

(3) Detection Probability (DP). DP demonstrates the ability of the model handling the untrusted recommended information from the third parties.

5.3   Performance Analysis

5.3.1   EPFR

During the simulations, some sensors are malicious and other sensors are normal. The ratio of malicious nodes is between 10 % and 60 %, while other sensor nodes in the network are all good. Comparison of AODV with and without trust model on EPFR is shown in Fig. 1.

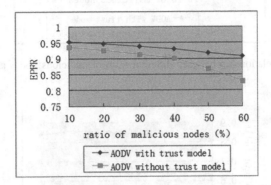

Fig. 1. Relationship between different ratio of malicious nodes and EPFR

As shown in Fig. 1, as the number of malicious nodes increases, both protocols decrease. After the ratio of malicious nodes increases to 50 %, both EPFR decrease more obviously. Compared with the original AODV, the EPFR of the AODV with the proposed trust model in this paper declines gently. It is because that the proposed trust model in this paper can choose the most reliable nodes for routing so as to avoid selecting untrusted nodes to forward messages, which ensures the stability of EPFR to some extent.

5.3.2   AEC

During routings, nodes consume some energy for forwarding, calculating the trust-worthy. Comparison of AEC with different ratios of malicious nodes is shown in Fig. 2. As shown in Fig. 2, with the increase of malicious nodes, both AECs of the two schemes decrease. Since malicious nodes do not take part in the discovery process of AODV, or malicious nodes do not forward message, so the AECs of malicious nodes are smaller than other normal nodes. Figure 2 demonstrates that the proposed model can isolate malicious nodes effectively and reduce the energy consume of normal nodes significantly.

5.3.3   DP

DP demonstrates the ability of the model handling the untrusted recommended information from the third parties. As shown in Fig. 3, the performance of BTRM-WSN is better than DRBTS. This is because BTRM-WSN can better deal with the untrusted recommendations from the third parties. The proposed model is better than the other

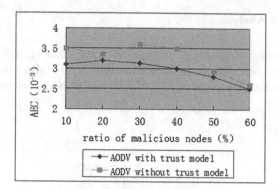

Fig. 2. Relationship between different ratio of malicious nodes and AEC

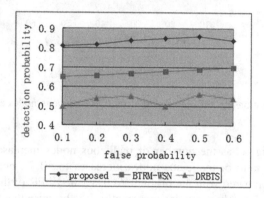

Fig. 3. Relationship between false probability and detection probability

two models. It is mainly because that the trust model in this paper considers the possible errors when evaluating trustworthy, such as trust deviation and counter-intuitive results. It can suppress collusion of malicious nodes to some extent. As a result, the proposed trust model has better performance on DP.

6   Conclusion

The existing trust model cannot handle malicious nodes in WSNs quickly and effectively, and counter-intuitive results may appear when combining evidence. Therefore, based on improved D-S evidence theory, a new trust model is proposed. By defining evidence variance, this trust model modifies the evidences before combination, and then combines these evidences according to Dempster combination rule, which avoids the emergency of counter-intuitive results and inhibits the collusion of malicious nodes to some extent. Finally, simulation results show this model has more security, robustness and accuracy, compared with two existing trust models.

Next, we will further improve the proposed trust model, combine with data privacy and better algorithms of data convergence, and research more practical and effective trust model in WSNs.

Acknowledgments. This work was supported by the Natural Science Foundation of Shaanxi Province (2014JQ8301) and National Natural Science Foundation of China (61402530).

References

1. Marmol, G., Perez, M.: Providing trust in wireless sensor networks using a bioinspired technique. Telecommun. Syst. **46**(2), 163–180 (2010)
2. Shafer, G.: A Mathematical Theory of Evidence. Princeton University Press, Princeton, USA (1976)
3. Boukercha, A., Xua, L.: EL-Khatibb, K.: Trust-based security for wireless ad hoc and sensor networks. Comput. Commun. **30**(12), 2413–2427 (2007)
4. Chen, H. G., Wu, H. F., Zhou, X., Gao, C. S.: Agent-based trust model in wireless sensor networks. In: Proceeding of the Eighth ACIS International Conference on Software Engineering, Artificial Intelligence, Networking and Parallel/Distributed Computing, pp. 119–124 (2007)
5. Srinivasan, A., Teitelbaum, J. and Wu, J.: DRBTS: Distributed reputation-based beacon trust system. In: Proceedings of 2nd IEEE International Symposium on Dependable, Autonomic and Secure Computing (DASC'06), pp. 277–283 (2006)
6. Buchegger, S., Boudec, J. Y. L.: Performance analysis of the confidant protocol. In: Proceedings of MobiHoc'02: Proceedings of the 3rd ACM International Symposium on Mobile Ad-hoc Networking and Computing, pp. 226–236, ACM, New York, NY, USA (2002)
7. He, Q., Wu, D., Khosla, P.: Sori: A secure and objective reputation-based incentive scheme for ad-hoc networks. In: Proceedings of 2004. Wireless Communications and Networking Conference, vol. **2**, No. 23, pp. 825–830 (2004)
8. Zhong, S., Chen, J., Yang, Y.: Sprite: a simple, cheat-proof, credit-based system for mobile ad-hoc networks. In: Proceedings of INFOCOM 2003, Twenty- Second Annual Joint Conference of the IEEE Computer and Communications Societies, pp. 1987–1997 (2003)
9. Zadehl, A.: A simple view of the Dempster-Shafer theory of evidence and its implication for the rule of combination. AI Mag. **7**, 85–90 (1986)
10. Zhang, L., Liu, J.W., Wang, R.C., Wang, H.Y.: Trust evaluation model based on improved D-S evidence theory. J. Commun. **34**(7), 167–173 (2013)
11. Han, D.Q., Han, C.Z., Deng, Y., Yang, Y.: Weighted combination of conflicting evidence based on evidence variance. ACTA ELECTRONICA AINICA **39**(3A), 153–157 (2011)
12. Jousselme, A.L., Grenier, D., Bosse, E.: A new distance between two bodies of evidence. Inf. Fusion **2**(2), 91–101 (2001)
13. Perkins, C., Belding, R.E., Das, S.: Ad-hoc On-Demanding Distance Vector (AODV) Routing, IETF RFC 3591 (2003)

Layered Negotiation-Based Self-protection for Wireless Sensor Networks

Wenzhe Zhang[✉]

Provincial Key Laboratory for Computer Information Processing Technology,
Soochow University, Suzhou 215006, China
wzzhang@suda.edu.cn

Abstract. Wireless sensor networks may be destroyed by targets in field surveillance. Self-protection technology focuses on using sensor nodes to protect themselves so as to resist attacks. Selecting protecting nodes has been proved to be a NP-complete problem. In this paper, we propose a new distributed layered negotiation based approximation algorithm to find a protecting set using local topology information. Experimental result manifests the feasibility and efficiency of our algorithms proposed.

Keywords: Self-protection · Layered negotiation · Dominator · Dominatee · Connector

1 Introduction

Wireless Sensor Networks (WSNs) are made up of many sensor nodes which are deployed in a sensory field. These nodes compose ad hoc network after they get the topology information, and begin with all kinds of work such as detecting, monitoring, computing and transmitting [1, 2]. As one of the main applications, field surveillance use WSNs to monitor a field and find possible targets. Usually this kind of work may be executed under hostile circumstance and sensor nodes may be destroyed physically by targets, e.g. enemies in the battle field. The sensor node may lose function because of its physical attack, and also it is fragile to limited energy [3]. So it is necessary to give WSN certain level of protection or fault tolerance. In WSNs, the best candidate to provide protection is the sensor nodes, that is called as *self-protection*, i.e. selecting a set of sensor nodes to be active to protect the whole network. WSNs are self-protected if and only if at any moment, for any sensor node, there are at least one active sensors that can monitor it. For example, Fig. 1 shows a WSN is self-protected by active nodes (in black color). Every node in Fig. 1 can be protected by at least one active neighbor. The active sensor nodes consume more energy than ordinary ones because they can't sleep, so the number of active nodes should be as small as possible. Once the active node find that some node is damaged, it need to report an urgent message to the sink as soon as possible. In order to balance the energy consumption of the whole network, there should be several active sets work in turns during the lifetime of the network [4].

© Springer-Verlag Berlin Heidelberg 2015
L. Sun et al. (Eds.): CWSN 2014, CCIS 501, pp. 302–310, 2015.
DOI: 10.1007/978-3-662-46981-1_29

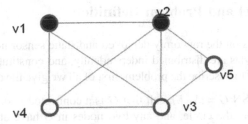

Fig. 1. A self-protected WSN

The remainder of this paper is organized as follows: related work is presented in Sect. 2. In Sect. 3, we introduce the formal definition of self-protection problem and the system model. A new self-protection algorithm based on local information is presented in Sect. 4. Section 5 shows the simulation results of our algorithm. Finally we conclude the work in our paper in Sect. 6.

2 Related Work

D. Wang first proposes the formal definition of self-protection and proves it NP-complete to find the minimum self-protection set [5]. D. Wang presents two distributed algorithms in which each sensor activate itself. But the sensors need to be synchronized, and pre-set with a probability before deployment. Besides, the node density need to be estimated.

Y. Wang proposes the concept of p-self-protection for WSNs and provides both a set of centralized and distributed algorithms [6]. The centralized algorithm generates p MISs (Maximal Independent Sets) in p round. Every MIS can cover the network separately, so p MISs can provide p-protection. The distributed algorithm is based on the centralized algorithm, but the nodes need using the information of itself and its neighbors' to decide its round and state.

J. Cheng proposes a distributed algorithm for self-protection using minimum dominating set [7]. Based on local topology information, they select sensor nodes as active ones which can dominating most neighbors. The algorithm can select the minimum set for self-protection and is scalable for WSN, whereas the efficiency of the algorithm need to be improved. J. Cheng conducts a set of local optimum protection for sensor networks, but the method is locally optimal, not globally.

Harutyunyan studies minimum 2-connected distance-k p-dominating set in wireless sensor networks [8], but the proposed algorithm is centralized. D. Dong proposes edge self-monitoring algorithm for wireless sensor networks [9], but ignores the important role of sink node – collecting urgent message from fragile nodes.

In summary, the literatures above never mention the important feature of protection - the average number of hops from protecting nodes to the sink. In field surveillance, we usually need to report an urgent message to the sink as soon as possible. Therefore, the average hops of any urgent message to the sink is as little as may be. In this paper, we start from the layered sensor network and propose a distributed approximation algorithm based on negotiation to acquire the minimum protecting set.

3   System Model and Problem Definition

In this paper we focus on the randomly-deployed and static sensor network. Suppose the position of sensor nodes are distributed independently, and constitute a connected undirected graph. In order to describe the problem, first of all we give the definition as follows.

Definition 1. Set WSN $G = (V, E)$, call that G is a connected undirected graph, if and only if: G is free from the circle, and any two nodes in G have at most one edge up.

Definition 2. If p and q are two nodes in WSN G, namely $p, q \in V$, if there exists an edge in G connecting from p to q, call that the node q is with neighbor p, namely $q \in N$ *(p)*, and vice versa.

Definition 3. If p is a node in G and p is active, all neighbor nodes of p can be protected by p, call that $N(p)$ is *1*-hop dominated.

Definition 4. The subset $S \subseteq V$ is the dominating set of graph G, if and only if: for every node $p \in V$ then there exist $q \in S$ and q is an adjacent node of p. Subset S is called a dominating set, and the node in S is called *Dominator node*. Subset $\{V\text{-}S\}$ is called the dominated set, and the node in $\{V\text{-}S\}$ is called *Dominatee node*.

To solve the problem of self-protection, we need to acquire the Minimum Connected Dominating Set (MCDS). In this paper, we start from the sink node and acquire MCDS based on local information. For simplicity, we make the following assumptions:

- Network topology is connected. Because for unconnected network, complete protection is impossible;
- Each node can identify itself with a unique ID, and inform its neighbors by one hop communication.

4   Layered-Negotiation Based Protection

Similar to the minimum cover set problem, minimum 1-self-protection problem has been proved to be NP complete. In this section, we propose a new approximate algorithm for connected dominating set in wireless sensor network. Firstly, sink node stimulate the limited flooding algorithm and divide WSN into several layers. We find the fact that in the minimum dominating set in graph theory, if the distance between every two dominating nodes is three, the dominating set is minimum. Secondly, we obtain the minimum dominating set based on local topology information. Finally, adding some connecting nodes, we achieve the sink-centered minimum connected dominating set of any WSN.

4.1   WSN Topology Layering

We use limited flooding algorithm to mark the layer of any node. At first, the sink node marks itself layer 0 and broadcasts to its neighbors layering packet, in which layer count LC is included. If receiving layering packet, sensor node add one to layer count and compare the new layer count with its own layer number. If the new layer count is smaller than layer number, or the node is never layered, the sensor node marks itself layer with the layer count and forward the layering packet with the layer count. In this way, wireless sensor network is divided into a hierarchy network layered from sink with 0, 1, 2…

4.2 MDS Based on Layered Negotiation

Based on the layered topology, we select dominating node starting from the sink node. The sink node is spontaneous dominating node. In randomly-deployed sensor network, sensor node is deployed randomly and the density of sensor node is random too.

In the sink-centered layered network, if the middle layer of every three layers is dominating, all nodes of network is dominated. And part of dominating nodes is redundancy. So we can reduce the dominating set through negotiation method.

According to the function, we can divide the sensor nodes into four types: dominator, dominatee, semi-dominator and semi-dominatee nodes as shown in Sect. 3. We define the state of the corresponding nodes as dominating, dominated, semi-dominating and semi-dominated states respectively. Taking into account the network's initial state, all nodes are in the primal state. Therefore, sensor nodes have five states, namely, the primal state, the dominated state, the dominating state, semi-dominating state and semi-dominated state.

In order to achieve distributed node selection algorithm, each node needs to communicate and negotiate its state with others. So we design message to informing their states. The message is transmitted in only one hop, i.e. any node only receives, never forwards. There are five kinds of state messages:

Dominating (n): noting node n is dominating, i.e. a dominator;
Dominated (n): noting node n is dominated, i.e. a dominatee;
Semi-dominating (n): noting node n is semi-dominating, i.e. a semi-dominator;
Semi-dominated (n): noting node n is semi-dominated, i.e. a semi-dominatee;
Request-dominating (n): noting node n is not dominated, i.e. a primal node.

There are five kinds of nodes, and node status should change accordingly when receiving state messages. Detailed state transition diagram is shown in Fig. 2.

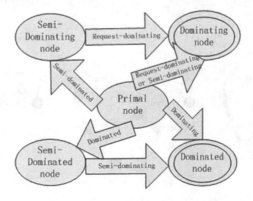

Fig. 2. State transmission diagram

At the beginning of the algorithm, all nodes except sink are initialized as primal state. Sink node is the dominating node and stimulate the negotiation process by sending state message to neighbors. Neighbors transmit its state and negotiate with other layers as shown in Algorithm 1.

```
ALGORITHM 1. Layered Negotiation for MDS
Start: state (Sink) = dominator, broadcasts Dominating
(Sink);
For any node Nᵢ and Nⱼ, Nᵢ∈Neighbor (Nⱼ)
1.    state(Nⱼ)=primal, if receives Dominating(Nᵢ),then mark
state(Nⱼ)=dominatee, broadcasts Dominated(Nⱼ)
2.    state(Nⱼ)=primal, if receives Dominated(Nᵢ), then mark
state(Nⱼ)= semi-dominatee, broadcasts semi-dominated(Nⱼ)
3.    state(Nⱼ)=primal, if receives semi-dominated(Nᵢ), and
number of semi-dominated != Max of Neighbor(Nⱼ) then mark
state(Nⱼ)= semi-dominator, broadcasts semi-dominating(Nⱼ),
else mark state(Nⱼ) = dominator, broadcasts dominating(Nⱼ)
4.    Any node Nⱼ, if receives Semi-dominating (Nᵢ), then
mark state (Nⱼ) = dominatee, and send Request-dominating
(Nⱼ) to Nᵢ
5.    State (Nⱼ)=semi-dominator, if receives request-
dominating(Ni), then mark state(Nⱼ)=dominator
6.    Any node Nⱼ, if never receives any state message, then
mark state (Nⱼ) =dominating
```

For example, wireless sensor network is deployed as shown in Fig. 3. Sink node *a* is the inherent dominating node (in black color) and broadcasts the Dominating message after layering procedure. Nodes *b, c, d* and *e* are dominated nodes (in gray color) and send Dominated message. Nodes *f, g, h, j, k* and *n* become Semi-dominated

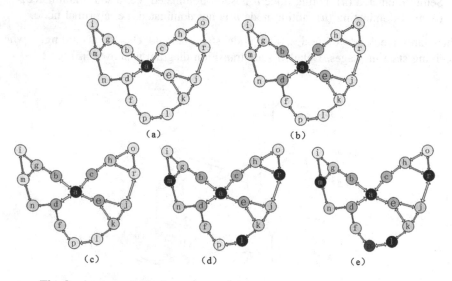

Fig. 3. An example for layered negotiation procedure (Color figure online)

when the receive the Dominated message. Finally, Nodes m, r, l and p become semi-dominating nodes when the receive the Semi-dominated message. node p and l both are probably selected as dominating node. After negotiation between p and l as shown in Algorithm 1, l is selected as dominating node and p fail to be chosen.

4.3 Connection of MDS

In Sect. 4.2, we get a minimum dominating set through algorithm 1. In this section, we select least connecting nodes which can connect all dominating nodes and realize a sink-centered minimum connected dominating set finally. The connecting nodes selected are called connector. In the minimum dominating set from algorithm 1, the hops of any two dominating nodes is not more than 3, therefore we can send request connecting message starting from sink and confirm the connecting path between two layers according to the request connecting message. Request connecting message includes node ID and layer number of transmitting node. The lifetime of every request connecting message is 3. Connector selection algorithm is shown as follows in Algorithm 2.

```
ALGORITHM 2. Connector Selection for MCDS
Start:
1.  state (Sink) = dominator, broadcasts Request-
connecting (Sink);
2.  For any node Nj, if receives Request-connecting (Ni)
and Request-connecting (Nk), and layer-number (Ni) = lay-
er-number (Nk) then delete Request-Connecting (Ni or k),
else
a)  if layer-number(Nj)> layer-number(Ni) and layer-
number(Nj)> layer-number(Nk) then
i.  if lifetime of request-connect(Ni or k) = 1, broad-
casts request-connect(Ni or k)
ii. if lifetime of request-connect (Ni or k) = 0, send
acknowledge(Nj) to Ni or k and broadcasts request-
connecting(Nj)
iii. For node Nk, if receives acknowledge (Nj), mark
state (Nk) = connector
b)  if layer-number(Nj)<= layer-number(Ni or k) then delete
Request-Connecting(Ni or k)
```

5   Experimental Result and Performance Analysis

In order to gain a deeper understanding of the layer-based negotiation algorithm, we have performed a wide range of simulations and case-studies. In this section, we present several interesting results and discuss their implications. The main simulation platform consists of a standalone C++ package. The visualization and user interface elements are currently implemented using Visual C++ libraries. Network Simulator (NS2) and

CrossBow® MICAZ sensor nodes are also used to verify the sensing models and the qualitative performance of the negotiation model in a realistic environment. The sensor field in all experiments is defined as a square of 500 × 500 wide and N sensor nodes deployed in the field. In our algorithm, the transmission range of sensor nodes are the same radius R. All experiments are performed on randomly deployed sensors.

As shown in Fig. 4, when the radius R is set 100, the number of dominators increases when N grows, and the curve becomes smooth when N grows up to 200 or so. This phenomenon can be explained by the fact that most part of the sensory field is filled when N is large enough.

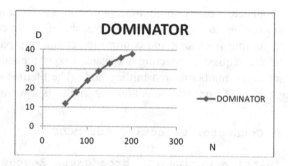

Fig. 4. Size of MDS vs. sensor density

The size of MCDS in algorithms is shown as in Fig. 5. From Fig. 5, we can conclude that the size of MCDS (including dominators and connectors) of all algorithms is nearly one third of N. Besides, the number of connectors changes little when sensor density varies.

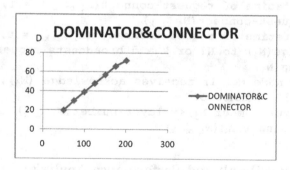

Fig. 5. Size of MCDS vs. sensor density

In the experiment, we calculate the MDS and MCDS with different algorithms respectively. We present a comparison in Fig. 6, which is the mean of 10 independent trials. From Fig. 6, we can see that the performance of our algorithm presented is better than LOP [7]. When the sensor density is sparse, the size of MDS increases quickly and when the sensor deployment is dense, few nodes are added into MDS. This can be

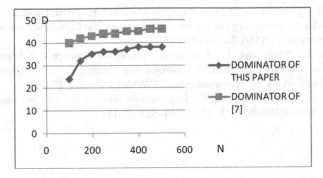

Fig. 6. Size of MDS vs. sensor density

explained by the fact that one dominator can dominates more nodes when sensors is denser.

6 Conclusion

In this paper, we investigate the typical algorithm of MCDS for self-protection of wireless sensor networks. Based on layered negotiation, we firstly acquire a minimum dominating set. Secondly, we select some nodes from dominated nodes and mark the MCDS as protecting nodes. The algorithm is suitable for self-protection in wireless sensor networks. The algorithm is distributed and scalable. Simulation manifests that the algorithm can calculate a better self-protection set. In the near future, we will make more effort to study other interesting behaviors.

Acknowledgment. This work is supported in part by the National Science Foundation of China (No. 61070169) and Natural Science Research Plan of Jiangsu Province College (No. 10KJB 520017).

References

1. Raymond, D.R., Midkiff, S.F.: Denial-of-service in wireless sensor networks: attacks and defenses. IEEE Pervasive Comput. **7**(1), 74–81 (2008)
2. Akyildiz, I.F., Su, W., Sankarasubramaniam, Y., Cayirci, E.: Wireless sensor networks: a survey. Comput. Netw. **38**(4), 393–422 (2002)
3. Chin, T., Clouqueur, T., Ramanathan, P., Saluja, K.K.: Vulnerability of surveillance networks to faults. Int. J. Distrib. Sens. Netw. **3**, 289–311 (2006)
4. Ma, J., Lou, W., Wu, Y., Li, M.: Energy efficient TDMA sleep scheduling in wireless sensor networks. In: IEEE INFOCOM 2009, pp. 630–638
5. Wang, D., Zhang, Q., Liu, J.: Self-protection for wireless sensor networks. In: Proceedings of 26th IEEE Inter national Conference on Distributed Computing Systems (ICDCS) (2006)
6. Wang, Y., Li, X., Zhang, Q.: Efficient algorithms for the p-self-protection problem in static wireless sensor networks. IEEE Trans. Parallel Distrib. Syst. **19**(10), 1426–1438 (2008)

7. Cheng, J., Zhang, W., Yang, J.: Local optimum algorithms for self-protection in wireless sensor networks. In: Proceedings of the 5th IEEE International Conference on Mobile Ad-hoc and Sensor Networks (MSN), December 2009
8. Harutyunyan, L., Narayanan, L.: Minimum 2-connected distance-k p-dominating set in wireless sensor networks. In: IEEE 8th International Conference on Wireless and Mobile Computing, Networking and Communications (WiMob), pp. 1–6 (2012)
9. Dong, D., Liao, X., Liu, Y., Shen, C.: Edge self-monitoring for wireless sensor networks. IEEE Trans. Parallel Distrib. Syst. 22(3), 514–527 (2011)

An Experimental Analysis on the Behavior and Influence of the Selfish Sensor Nodes on Node Scheduling in Wireless Sensor Networks

Gaojuan Fan[✉] and Yuan Liu

School of Computer and Information Engineering, Henan University, Kaifeng 475004, China
fangaojuan@henu.edu.cn

Abstract. Sensor nodes are often densely deployed in Wireless Sensor Networks (WSN) applications, due to the constraints such as computing and processing capabilities, energy supply, etc. Node scheduling mechanisms can greatly prolong network lifetime, through reasonable scheduling of the work/sleep states of the coordinated nodes, and the handling of communication interference in the work state and the data transmission redundancy. However, for saving energy, there are inevitably a part of the nodes that are selfish in the monitoring applications. Based on the characteristics of node scheduling, we discover three types of selfish nodes in node scheduling. Through experimental simulations, we analyze the influence of the selfish nodes on the coverage and energy of their neighbors, and on the network performance, measured in terms of network coverage, network lifetime and the balancedness of energy consumption. Experimental results show that, selfish nodes can breach the coordination among the nodes, violate the goal of node scheduling and reduce network lifetime. By analyzing the behavior and impact of the selfish nodes, this work provides important experimental evidence for the detection and punishment of selfish nodes.

Keywords: Wireless sensor network · Node scheduling · Selfish node · Network performance

1 Introduction

A Wireless Sensor Network (WSN) is typically composed of a large number of tiny, low-powered sensor nodes equipped with data processing, sensing, and communication capabilities. WSNs have been extensively used in a variety of domains, including environmental observation, military monitoring, health-care, and commercial applications. Coordinated node scheduling plays a critical role in energy saving and network-lifetime maximization in WSNs, it exploits the redundancy of sensor nodes to minimize the number of active nodes while preserving some properties of the network [1, 2].

The problem of sensor scheduling has been extensively addressed in the literature. Gao et al. [3] analyzed the lower and upper bounds of complete node redundancy and proposed to compute the redundancy probability using the number of neighbors within the sensing area. Lightweight Deployment-Aware Scheduling (LDAS) [5] is an

© Springer-Verlag Berlin Heidelberg 2015
L. Sun et al. (Eds.): CWSN 2014, CCIS 501, pp. 311–317, 2015.
DOI: 10.1007/978-3-662-46981-1_30

improvement of [4]; a number of nodes will be closed when the number of nearby working nodes reaches the threshold. Besides being location free, this new method can guarantee the network connectivity.

All the above methods require the sensor nodes to be densely deployed. They prolong the network lifetime through adjusting the states of the sensor nodes, while still assuring the network monitoring performance. However, they have not considered the selfish behaviors of the sensor nodes in node scheduling, in which the selfish nodes will not process or forward the data received to save their own energy. The selfish behaviors of the sensor nodes will greatly influence the fairness in scheduling the sensor nodes and weaken the network performance.

A great many recent research efforts have been focused on the selfish behaviors of the sensor nodes. In [6], the authors analyzed the influence of the selfish intermediate nodes on the network fairness and proposed a tolerance-based credibility measure to detect selfish nodes. The authors in [7] analyzed the hitchhiking behaviors in WSNs and showed that many sensor nodes only want the service provided by others, but are reluctant to contribute to other nodes. The work in [8] researched the selfish behaviors of the selfish nodes and presented a balanced strategy under incomplete information. The authors in [9] analyzed the influence of the selfish nodes on the network performance. They designed an intrusion detection system with detection and punishment parts.

This work studies the selfish behaviors of the sensor nodes and provides an experimental analysis of different selfish behaviors and their influence on the states of the neighboring nodes and the overall network monitoring performance.

2   Network Model

In Lightweight Deployment-Aware Scheduling (LDAS) [5], a number of nodes will be closed when the number of nearby working nodes reaches the threshold. Besides being location free, this new method can guarantee the network connectivity. The constraints of this method are: the senor nodes should be uniformly distributed and each node can get the number of its neighbors. As shown in Fig. 1, there are three steps in LDAS: (1) neighbors discovery; (2) redundancy detection; (3) node scheduling. In (1), they collect the information of the neighbor nodes such as the number of nodes; in (2), they calculate the probability that a sensor node can be covered by its neighbors detected in (1) and determine whether the node should be switched to sleep state, or be in the monitoring state. In (3), the states of the nodes will switch between working and sleeping modes, depending on their conditions. It will also handle the energy-consumption influence of the selfish nodes on their neighbors.

3   The Selfish Behavior of Nodes Scheduling

Definition 1. The selfish nodes in node scheduling in resource-constrained wireless sensor network (WSN) refer to the nodes that reject the data forward requests made by other nodes for the purpose of saving their own energy, and refuse waking up and fast sleep in different node status.

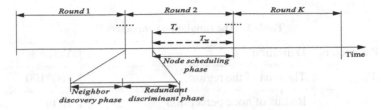

Fig. 1. The three steps in node scheduling

According to the characteristics of node scheduling and the selfish nodes, the selfish nodes in node scheduling basically have the following three types of selfish behaviors

(1) Behavior of not forwarding data: Such selfish nodes would forward data that they collect to neighbor nodes, but refuse to forward the data obtained from their neighbor nodes.
(2) Excessive sleep behavior: After being in a sleep state after checking the coverage redundancy, the selfish nodes don't follow the pre-set sleep time, but increase their sleep time without permission.
(3) Behavior of seizing sleep: In order to avoid coverage holes caused by the adjacent nodes entering a sleep state at the same time, in the node scheduling algorithms, nodes will send Backoff news before entering a sleep state, to notify the neighbors that they will enter into the sleep state. The nodes receiving the Backoff messages will recheck their own states. In order to be able to obtain a priority of sleep, the selfish nodes will ignore the Backoff messages sent from their neighbor nodes from package to take over the sleep opportunity.

4   Analysis of the Influence of Selfish Behavior to Neighbor Nodes

4.1   Parameter Settings

In order to illustrate the influence of selfish nodes in the network, we use MATLAB as a experiment platform for simulation of LDAS algorithm, analyzing mainly from the impact effect on the neighbor node and the network performance. This section mainly analyzes the effect on the neighbor node, including the cover effect and energy of neighbor nodes. The simulation parameters are shown in Table 1.

4.2   Coverage Affects of Selfish Behaviors on Neighbor Nodes

Figure 2 shows the monitoring area of 100 m*100 m randomly deployed with 100 nodes, 10 selfish nodes randomly distributed in the network. Among them: "o" means ordinary nodes, "." means selfish nodes, "*" denotes selfish nodes of an example analysis in this section, and the ID of the node is 40.

Table 1. The simulation parameters

Parameters	Definition	Value
A	The area of the region	100*100
r	Radius of node perception	15 m
n	Nodes in a region	100
θ	Redundant coverage	90 %
E_0	Initial energy of nodes	1 J
E_{sleep}	A dormant state node energy consumption	0.000001 J
E_{work}	Active node energy consumption	0.002 J
E_i	Free, selfish state energy consumption	0.004 J
$N_{selfish}$	Selfish number of node	30
$sleeptime$	Sleep time	10 s
$lsleeptime$	Long sleep time	15 s
$activetime$	Activity time	3 s
CT_{time}	Data processing time	1 s

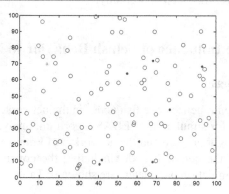

Fig. 2. Network deployment

Figure 3 shows the selfish node of size 40 changing over time to neighbor's coverage. In the graph "o" represent active neighbor nodes, "+" denotes dormant neighbor nodes, "." means the failure neighbor node due to energy consumption. Figure 3(a) is the situation of neighbor nodes' coverage of selfish node as the network running 500 s, we can find that, the existence of selfish nodes has not been much impact on network operation, coverage redundant nodes can be selected by nodes according to the scheduling algorithm, due to the node of energy consumption and death has not been all in network. Figure 3(b) is a state situation of selfish node neighbor with the network running 1000 s, we can see that, the number of its neighbor entering into a dormant stat decrease with time because of the selfish node. Figure 3(c) is a state situation of selfish node neighbor with the network running 1500 s, because of the existence of selfish nodes, four failure nodes exist due to the help for part of its neighbor nodes forward data work. And Fig. 3(d) is a state situation of selfish node neighbor with the network running 2000 s, its neighbor nodes are all invalidated. It can be concluded from the Fig. 3, the existence of selfish nodes will have affect on the neighbor node coverage, but the node deployment of no uniformity and boundary effect will impact the coverage of neighbor nodes.

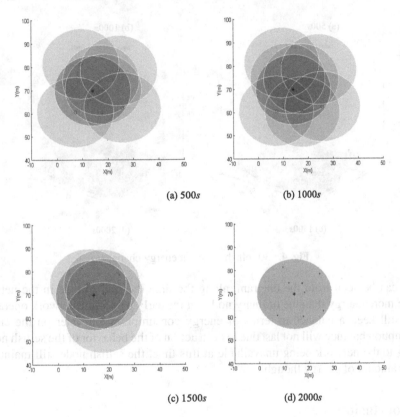

(a) 500*s*

(b) 1000*s*

(c) 1500*s*

(d) 2000*s*

Fig. 3. The number of 40 node to neighbors coverage changes over time

4.3   Selfish Behavior to Cut Energy Consumption

Figure 4 gives the network in the presence of 30 selfish nodes, the network in the 500 s and 1000 s, 1500 s and 2000 s when the entire network energy consumption.

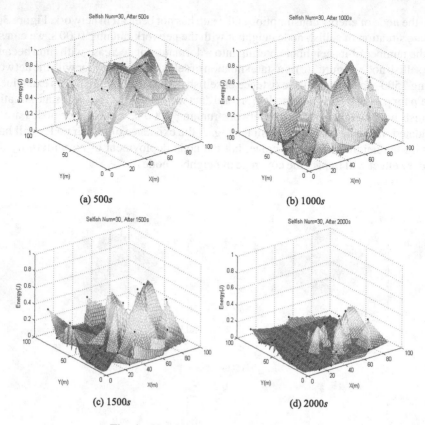

Fig. 4. 30 selfish node cut energy changes

As can be seen from the diagram, along the time the selfish node in the network reserve more energy than the ordinary node. In the early part of the network operation, it can still keep a balance in terms of energy consumption, but later on the energy consumption balance will not last due to destruction of the behavior of the selfish nodes, leading to the network being unavailable at this time, the selfish node still maintain a certain amount of energy though.

5 Conclusion

In this paper, we experimentally analyze the selfish behavior of sensor nodes in node scheduling in WSNs. Experimental results show that the selfish behaviors of the nodes can seriously affect the whole network performance, even result in the network paralysis, thus the monitoring performance cannot be guaranteed. This experimental study has very important reference value for network security monitoring applications. Future work will be directed towards analyzing the influence of the selfish nodes on the other well-known node scheduling algorithms.

Acknowledgments. This work is supported by the National Natural Science Foundation of China under Grants no. 61300215, Key Scientific and Technological Project of Henan Province under Grant no. 122102210053, and Jiangsu High Technology Research Key Laboratory for Wireless Sensor Networks under Grants no. BM2010577. © Springer-Verlag Berlin Heidelberg 2011.

References

1. Li-ling, H., Yu-wei, H., Chun-cheng, L.: Temporal coverage mechanism for distinct quality of monitoring in wireless mobile sensor networks[J]. Ad Hoc Netw. **21**, 97–108 (2014)
2. Watfa, M.K., Al, H.H., Salmens, S.: A novel solution to the energy hole problem in sensor networks[J]. J. Netw. Comput. Appl. **36**(2), 949–958 (2013)
3. Gao-juan, F., Li-juan, S., Ru-chuan, W., et al.: Non-uniform distribution node scheduling scheme in wireless sensor networks[J]. J. Commun. **32**(3), 10–17 (2011)
4. Wu, K., Gao, Y., Li, F. et al.: Analysis on the redundancy of wireless sensor networks. In: Proceedings of the 2nd ACM International Conference on Wireless Sensor Networks and Applications[C], pp. 108–114. ACM Press, San Diego (2003)
5. Kui, W., Yong, G., Fu-lu, L., et al.: Light-weight deployment-aware scheduling for wireless sensor networks[J]. Mob. Netw. Appl. **10**(6), 837–852 (2005)
6. Luo, J., Pan, C.: Selfish behavior detection and confine mechanism in wireless sensor network[J]. J. Comput. Res. Dev. **48**(Suppl.), 75–79 (2011)
7. Yi-Jiao, Yu., Hai, J.: A survey on overcoming free riding in peer- to-peer networks[J]. Chin. J. Comput. **31**(1), 1–15 (2008)
8. Inaltekin, H.: Random access games: selfish nodes with incomplete information[C]. In: IEEE Military Communications Conference (MILCOM), pp. 1–6 (2007)
9. Bo, C., Jian-Lin, M., Ning, G., Guan-Hua, Q.: An incentive detection mechanism for cooperation of nodes selfish behavior in wireless sensor networks[C]. In: Control and Decision Conference (CCDC), pp. 4021–4024 (2013)

Wireless Communication Systems and Protocols

A MAC Protocol for Data Gathering in Linear Wireless Sensor Network Based on Selective Relay Nodes

Guoyong Dai[1,2], Chunyu Miao[1], Kai Wang[1], and Qingzhang Chen[1(✉)]

[1] College of Computer Science and Technology, Zhejiang University of Technology,
Hangzhou 310023, China
qzchen@zjut.edu.cn
[2] College of Information Science and Technology, Zhejiang Shuren University,
Hangzhou 310014, China

Abstract. Medium access control (MAC) protocol is very important for energy efficiency in WSN. Different from mesh WSN, linear WSN has specific features of long and narrow. An energy efficient MAC protocol is proposed for data gathering in linear WSN in this paper. In this protocol, the energy consumption factor and residual energy balance factor are defined and combined together to form a comprehensive energy consumption impact factor. In order to enhance the performance, specific nodes with small energy consumption impact factor are chosen as relay nodes when a source node transmits data to the sink. A gradient schedule mechanism is used to schedule the sleep/wakeup states of nodes in each data collection cycle. Simulation experiments are conducted and the results show that SLDMAC provides better energy efficiency and long lifetime than the other two protocols with acceptable delay.

Keywords: Linear WSN · MAC protocol · Low-energy consumption · Relay nodes

1 Introduction

WSN (Wireless Sensor Network) is the key infrastructure of the Internet of Things, which can be applied in environment monitoring, city traffic monitoring and control, urban infrastructure monitoring, etc. [1–3]. WSNs are composed of a large number of self-organized sensor nodes which have the ability of wireless communication and computing. Since WSNs are usually deployed in unattended and wild environment, it is not convenient to change battery when it is used out. So energy consumption is a hot topic for researchers in the area of WSN.

MAC protocol, is the fundament of the communication among sensor nodes, which ensures that there aren't any two nodes interfering with each other's transmission so that successful operation of the network is ensured [4, 5]. An energy efficient MAC protocol can reduce energy consumption of nodes so that can prolong the lifetime of the whole sensor network. Many energy efficient MAC protocols have been proposed for WSN, including S-MAC [5], T-MAC [6], DMAC [7] etc. These protocols are designed similar to the MAC protocols in traditional wireless networks. Although some of these have

© Springer-Verlag Berlin Heidelberg 2015
L. Sun et al. (Eds.): CWSN 2014, CCIS 501, pp. 321–331, 2015.
DOI: 10.1007/978-3-662-46981-1_31

taken the features of data transmissions in WSNs, most of them are based on random deployment rather than a specific topology. In fact, linear topology is commonly used in many WSN applications [8–10], such as power line monitoring, street lights monitoring and so on. In such scenario, the monitoring area is usually long and narrow and can be considered as linear. Compared to traditional WSN, there usually exits more hops when data transmit from the sensor nodes to the sink in linear WSN. But there is few MAC protocol proposed to adapt to the characteristics of linear WSN.

In order to improve the energy efficiency and prolong the network life time, we designed a relay node based MAC protocol for linear WSN called SLDMAC. Our contributions are: (1) based on the linear topology, the sensor nodes are constructed as a data gathering chain and the layer concept is employed into our scheme; (2) during the relay nodes selection, we take the energy consumption factor and residual energy balance factor into consideration; (3) we designed a gradient schedule mechanism to schedule the sleep/wakeup states of the nodes to avoid idle listening.

The rest of this paper is organized as follows. In Sect. 2, some related works are presented, Sect. 3 describes the proposed SLDMAC protocol in detail. Some experiments are conducted and analyzed in Sect. 4, and Sect. 5 concludes the paper.

2   Related Works

There are already many literatures on design and implementation of MAC protocols for WSN [11, 12]. Most of these researches focus on reducing energy consumption and prolong network lifetime [5, 6, 13]. LIU et al. [14] proposed an asynchronous protocol CMAC which avoid the cost for synchronization. CMAC make the network runs in low duty cycle mode when there is no data traffic. All the forwarding nodes will be waked up by anycast until there is data need to be sent and then converge to the optimal routing. DMAC [7] is a tree based WSN data collection protocol. The layer of node in the tree is used to schedule the sleep/wakeup states of nodes. Data transmit from the leaves to the root of the tree. However it does not take the variation of network traffic into consideration. Y.Z. Zhao et al. [15] developed a protocol called ASMAC with self-adaptive schedule. Nodes are activated according to the current data traffic. That is to say, nodes are stay at sleep mode to save energy while there is little traffic on the network. H. Oh et al. [16] designed a TDMA-based MAC protocol for timely and reliable delivery in dynamic WSN. This protocol addresses the problem of load un-balancing between the nodes near the sink and the other nodes. X.Y. Wang et al. [17] proposed a cooperative MAC protocol for WSN called NCAC-MAC which use neighboring nodes to relay the overhearing information to deal with the channel fading. Network coding is employed to the cooperative retransmission process to reduce the redundancy and conserve energy.

All these existing MAC protocols are designed to save energy and prolong network life-time. However, they are all based on randomly deployed irregular topology. There are still few specific energy efficient MAC protocol devised for linear topology. So we focus on energy efficient MAC protocol for linear wireless sensor network.

3   Relay Nodes Based Data Gathering MAC Protocol: SLDMAC

3.1   Network Model

As Fig. 1 shows, a linear wireless sensor network consists of n sensor nodes in a linear topology where the sink node is on one end of the line. The sensor nodes set is presented as $V = \{v_1, v_2, \ldots, v_{n-1}, v_n\}$ and S is the sink node. $d_{i,j}$ is the distance between any two nodes v_i and v_j. We assume that all the nodes are homogeneous and are manually precisely installed rather than randomly scatted.

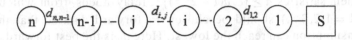

Fig. 1. Network model of linear WSN

A commonly used energy consumption model is employed in which the energy consumption of node i when it transmits l bits data to node j can be computed by formula (1), and the energy consumption of node j can be computed by formula (2).

$$E_{tx\_i} = l(c_1 + ad_{i,j}^{\alpha}) \tag{1}$$

$$E_{r\_j} = lc_2 \tag{2}$$

Here c_1 is the energy per bit consumed in the transmitter circuit, c_2 is the energy per bit consumed by the receiver circuit, a accounts for the energy dissipated in the transmit amplifier, α is the path loss exponent (typically ranges between 2 and 6). Let $c = c_1 + c_2$, then the total energy consumption is:

$$E = l(c + ad_{i,j}^{\alpha}) \tag{3}$$

Considering that node A send data to node D (the distance between node A and D is d), if $d \geq \left(c/a(1 - 2^{1-\alpha})\right)^{\frac{1}{\alpha}}$, then there must exists a relay node B between node A and D that it will consume lower energy. More generally, in this case, we can get the approach with the lowest energy consumption. Suppose that data transferred from node A to D will be forwarded by $n - 1$ relay nodes, the path of data transfer can be cut into n segments and the length of each segment is denoted as $x_1, x_2, \ldots, x_n$. Then the energy consumption of this case can be represented by formula (4).

$$f(x_1, x_2 \ldots x_n) = a \sum_{i=1}^{n} x_i^{\alpha} + nc, \; where \; \sum_{i=1}^{n} x_i = d \tag{4}$$

By applying Lagrange multiplier, we can know the function f get its minimum value when $x_1 = x_2 = \ldots x_n = \frac{d}{n}$. In other words, if the distances between each pair of neighbors (including node A, node D and all the relay nodes) are equal, we can get the minimum energy consumption. Substituting $x_1 = x_2 = \ldots x_n = \frac{d}{n}$ into formula (4), we have

$$f(x_1, x_2 \ldots x_n) = ad^\alpha n^{1-\alpha} + nc = k(n) \tag{5}$$

Let $\frac{dk(n)}{dn} = 0$, when $n = \frac{d}{(c/a(\alpha-1))^{1/\alpha}} = n_0$, f get its minimum value and $d_0 = \frac{d}{n_0} = (c/a(\alpha - 1))^{1/\alpha}$.

Given the above, if node A transmit data to node D and the distance between them satisfies $d \geq \left(c/a(1 - 2^{1-\alpha})\right)^{\frac{1}{\alpha}}$, relay nodes from which to node A is $kd_0(k = 1, 2, 3 \ldots)$ should be chosen to forward data so that the whole energy consumption can reach the lowest. Here d_0 is the best forward distance.

3.2 The Main Idea

According to the linear topology, all the sensed data are sent to the sink, so the direction of data transmission is always from one end which is far from the sink to the other end. Data transmission in linear WSN can be recognized as data gathering in a chain. All the nodes which need to send data constitute a linear data gathering chain. Therefore, the sensor nodes can be divided in to several layers from downstream to upstream. In each round of data gathering, we can schedule the sleep/wakeup state of each node according to its layer so that each node who have data to send will wait until data from downstream arrives, then combines and sends the received data and raw data together. Those who have no data to send only need to stay in sleep state. However if the distance between adjacent nodes is too long, it would cost too much energy. Based on this idea, we devised an algorithm to choose relay nodes which are then add into the data gathering chain to forward data.

We divide the whole duty cycle T into three phases (see Fig. 2):

(1) **Request phase**: It is composed of several time slots which are pre-assigned to each sensor node. Sensors who has data to send should send a request to the sink node within its own time slot. If one node need to send information, it always stays in sleep mode until its own time slot arrives and then a 1-bit request is sent to the sink in a single hop way. The sink node can know which node has data to be sent according to the request it receives and therefore it is set as a transmitter. In this way, the transmitter collection Vs can be retrieved by the sink node.

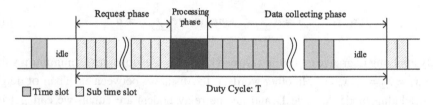

Fig. 2. Three phases in SLDMAC

(2) **Processing phase**: The tasks in this phase are working out the relay nodes and schedule the sleep/wakeup states for the nodes in Vs by the sink in centralized way.

(3) **Data collecting phase**: In this phase, all the nodes in Vs with all the relay nodes together constitute a data gathering chain. Then, the sink node schedule the sleep/ wakeup state for all the nodes on the chain to collecting sensed information. As there may be some nodes have no information to send, there may exist some idle time at the end of this phase. During the idle time all the nodes are in the state of sleep.

3.3 Relay Nodes Selecting

It may lead to energy over consumption of the chosen relay nodes so that the lifetime of the relay nodes may be bottleneck of the network. On the other hand, the physical distance between adjacent nodes may not be equal to d_0. For these reasons, we devised an algorithm for selecting relay nodes with the consideration of energy consumption and energy balance among sensor nodes.

We first analyze the impact of energy consumption by selecting different relay nodes. In the case of Node A sending data to Node D, if it is necessary to choose a relay node R, then R must be within the distance of $2d_0$. Suppose the distance between R and A is x, we can carry out the additional energy consumption ΔE compared to the case of d_0.

(1) If $x < d_0$, when R received data from node A, R then choose the next relay node with the best distance d_0. In such case, ΔE comes from the transmission between R and the next relay node with the distance of $d_0 - x$. ΔE can be calculated by Eq. (6).

$$\Delta E = E_x + E_{d_0-x} - E_{d_0} = a(x^\alpha + (d_0 - x)^\alpha - d_0^\alpha) + c \tag{6}$$

(2) If $d_0 < x < 2d_0$, similarly ΔE comes from the transmission between R and the next relay node with the distance of $2d_0 - x$ ΔE can be calculated by Eq. (7).

$$\Delta E = E_x + E_{2d_0-x} - 2E_{d_0} = a(x^\alpha + (2d_0 - x)^\alpha - 2d_0^\alpha) \tag{7}$$

Suppose that there are k nodes in the range of $2d_0$ from node A. Their residual energy is denoted as $E_1, E_2 \dots E_k$ respectively (see Fig. 3) and E_0 is the residual energy of node A.

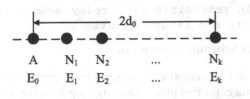

Fig. 3. A case of nodes' residual energy

We define the residual energy balance factor ϕ as:

$$\phi = \frac{\sum\limits_{i=0}^{k} (E_i - E_a)^2}{k + 1}, \; where \; E_a = \frac{\sum\limits_{j=0}^{k} E_j}{k + 1} \tag{8}$$

A smaller ϕ indicates that the residual energy of each node is close to the average one Ea. That is to say it is a balance state. According to the previous analysis, we also define the residual energy impact factor as:

$$\delta = \Delta E^2 \tag{9}$$

A comprehensive impact factor ε is defined by formula (10) which combines the energy balance factor ϕ and the residual energy impact factor δ together.

$$\varepsilon = \phi + \delta = \frac{\sum_{i=0}^{k}(E_i - E_a)^2}{k+1} + \Delta E^2 \tag{10}$$

A node who has data to send will always choose a relay node with the minimum ε among its neighbors within the distance of 0 to 2 d_0. For example, in the case of Fig. 3, when node A choose a node u as a relay node, the residual energy of these nodes can be updated as $E_0 - E_t, E_1, E_2 \ldots (E_u - E_r - E_{d0}) \ldots E_k$. Here, E_t is energy consumption of transmission, E_r is energy consumption of receiving data and E_{d0} is the energy consumption of forwarding data with the distance of d_0. Then ϕ_u, δ_u and ε_u can be calculated and we can get k different value of ε, then the node with the minimum ε will be selected as the relay node. The next relay node can be found in the same way.

```
Step 1. Initialization. Set Vr = null and Vss = Vs.
Step 2. Choose a node pair (Vss_iVss_j) from Vss which
hasn´t been chosen before. If there is no such pair, quit
the algorithm.
Step 3. If |Vss_iVss_j|<dt, then these two node can communi-
cate directly, no relay node is need. Return to Step 2.
Step 4. If d_t <|Vss_iVss_j|<2d_0, then only one relay node is
need, find the node with the minimum ε to be the relay
node and return to Step 2.
Step 5. If |Vss_iVss_j|>2d_0, pick out the node with the min-
imum ε among the nodes within the distance of 2d_0 from
Vss_i, which is recognized as a relay node R, then add
node R into Vss and return to Step 2.
```

3.4 Gradient Nodes Schedule Mechanism

All the nodes in Vs and Vr composed a linear data gathering chain, they need to be wakeup during the data collecting phase. Data moving from the most far away node to the sink through relay nodes. We use the concept of layer to represent the relationship between nodes. The most adjacent node of the sink is defined as the first layer. Therefore, we set Layer 2, Layer 3… Layer N to each node in the chain accordingly.

The data collection procedure always start from the highest level layer. Then once nodes of other layers received data from a higher layer, they put the data into the received packet and send it to the next node on the chain. Nodes on the chain are waked up only when in their turn for sending data. We note the transmitting and receiving time of each node as T. Obviously, it can be divided into receiving time RX and transmitting time TX, $T = RX + TX$. During RX, it receives data from a node of higher layer while during TX it then send packets which mix the received data and current sensed data together to a node of lower layer. For any two adjacent nodes of layer i and layer $_{i-1}$, their receiving and transmitting time T_i and T_{i-1} is successive. Specifically, TX_i and RX_{i-1} are absolutely overlapped. We set TX and RX as long as the time of full load data transmitting so that all data can be transmitted in a single TX. The gradient nodes schedule mechanism is shown in Fig. 4. In a data gathering chain, the node with highest layer is first scheduled into wakeup state. Then other nodes are scheduled in turns according their layers. Once the transmitting is completed, the node is scheduled into sleep state to save energy.

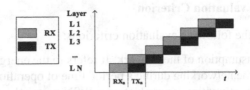

Fig. 4. Gradient nodes schedule

4 Experiment and Analysis

4.1 Experimental Setting

Our experiments are conducted on MATLAB platform. Sensor nodes are deployed in linear topology in the length of 500 m. There are N (4–20) nodes and the distance between adjacent nodes is 500/Nm. Suppose all the nodes can communicate with each other directly. The basic parameters of wireless communication and their values in our experiments are shown Table 1. Further, the initial energy of a sensor nodes is 0.1 J and the time of transmitting full load data is $Tu = 10$ ms. The length of data to be send is $L = 300$ bits.

The experiments are event driven. We define data arrival time as the time between the current data transmission and the previous one. Data arrival follows Poisson distribution and the waiting time in Poisson events stream follows negative exponential distribution which is defined by formula (11).

$$f(x) = \begin{cases} \lambda e^{-\lambda x} & x > 0 \\ 0 & x < 0 \end{cases} \tag{11}$$

λ is a positive constant which indicates the number of a certain event occurs within the unit time.

Table 1. Parameters and their values in our experiments

Parameters	Value
c_1	50 nJ/bit
c_2	50 nJ/bit
α	2
a	10 pJ/bit/m_2
d_0	100 m

4.2 Performance Evaluation Criterion

We mainly consider the following evaluation criterions:

(1) Total energy consumption of the network. It refers to the energy consumed by the sensor nodes in the networking during a period time of operation. It is a main indicator of energy consumption for evaluating a WSN protocol.
(2) Network lifetime. It refers to the time duration that start from the network boot up until the first node's death (run out of energy). It reflects not only energy consumption but also the energy balance between nodes. Since the network works periodically, we user working cycles to describe network lifetime.

4.3 Results and Analysis

Experiments are conducted to compare SLDMAC with DMAC and LDMAC (LDMAC is similar to SLDMAC but without choosing relay nodes). We first evaluate the performance of the three protocols with increasing number of nodes. The experiments run 400 cycles and the number of nodes varies from 4 to 20. Without loss of generality, we set $\lambda = 0.3$ (which means data arrives in 3 cycles) to adapt a normal data traffic.

Figure 5(a) shows the variation of energy consumption with the increasing number of nodes. We can see clearly that SLDMAC consumes less energy than LDMAC no matter how many nodes there are in the network. It's a reasonable result because SLDMAC always choose proper relay nodes to forward data to save energy. Compared to DMAC, SLDMAC also consumes less energy. On the one hand, the data gathering chain in DMAC is composed of all the nodes in the network so that those who with higher layer than the source node need to keep listening which cost much energy. However, in SLDMAC, nodes with no data to send are not included in the data gathering chain unless they are chosen as relay nodes so that they do not need to keep listening.

Figure 5(b) shows the variation of lifetime with the increasing number of nodes. The line of SLDMAC is more stable than other two and it indicates that the number of sensor nodes has little impact on SLDMAC. Further, it always has longer lifetime than the other two protocols. That is because SLDMAC take both nodes' energy consumption and residual energy balance into consideration while DMAC do not

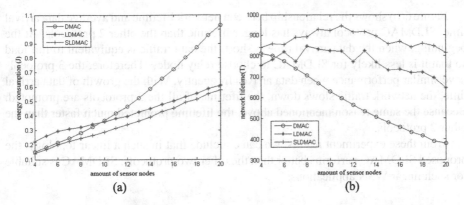

Fig. 5. (a). Relationship between energy consumption and number of nodes; (b). Relationship between lifetime and number of nodes

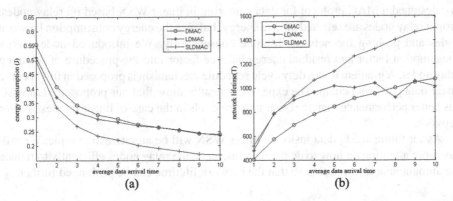

Fig. 6. (a) Relationship between energy consumption and average data arrival time; (b) Relationship between lifetime and average data arrival time

choose relay nodes at all. Therefore, the most adjacent node of sink may run out energy first and become a bottleneck of the network. Lifetime of LDMAC is shorter than DMAC when the number of nodes is small but longer than DMAC when the number of nodes increases. Lifetime of DMAC drops rapidly with the increasing of nodes.

Another experiment is conducted to show the performance of the three protocols with the variation of the average data arrival time. The average data arrival time is denoted by $1/\lambda$. Let $1/\lambda$ be 1, 2, 3….10 so that λ varies from 1 to 0.1 unevenly. Here the length of network is still 500 m and the best forward distance d_0 is 100 m. We deploy 10 nodes uniformly in this experiment.

Figure 6(a) shows the relationship between energy consumption and average data arrival time with the network running 400 cycles. It is understandable that all the 3 protocols' energy consumption reduces while the data arrival time grows because the total data traffic become lower. However, in SLDMAC the reduction is much more significant. If the number of nodes who have data to send is decreasing, it is more likely to choose relay nodes to save energy while the other two protocol still cost much energy.

Figure 6(b) shows the relationship between network lifetime and average data arrival time. SLDMAC protocol always has longer lifetime than the other 2 protocols. At the beginning, when the data arrival time is short, the data traffic is equivalent to full load so that it is less likely for SLDMAC to choose relay nodes. Therefore, the 3 protocols have similar performance when data arrives frequently. With the growth of data arrival time, the network traffic slows down, the lifetime of all the 3 protocols are promoted. Because the same reason mentioned above, the lifetime promoted much faster than the other 2 protocols.

From these experiment results, we can conclude that in such a linear topology, the proposed SLDMAC performs better than the other two protocols. SLDMAC is suitable for such linear WSN applications.

5   Conclusion

We designed a MAC protocol for data gathering in linear WSN based on relay nodes. Proper relay nodes are selected to save energy, balance the energy consumption between nodes and prolong the network lifetime consequently. We introduced node energy consumption factor and residual energy balance factor into the procedure of selecting relay nodes. A gradient nodes duty cycle schedule mechanism is proposed in this specific linear data gathering chain. The experiment results show that our proposed SLDMAC has better performance than the other two protocols in the case of linear wireless sensor network.

As for future work, data fusion in linear WSN will be an interesting topic. We will pay more attention on how to do the data fusion on the relay nodes efficiently to reduce the amount data transmission so that the network lifetime can be prolonged further.

References

1. Buratti, C., Conti, A., Dardari, D., Verdone, R.: An overview on wireless sensor networks technology and evolution. Sens. Basel **9**, 6869–6896 (2009)
2. Yick, J., Mukherjee, B., Ghosal, D.: Wireless sensor network survey. Comput. Netw. **52**, 2292–2330 (2008)
3. Wang, B., Lim, H.B., Ma, D.: A survey of movement strategies for improving network coverage in wireless sensor networks. Comput. Commun. **32**, 1427–1436 (2009)
4. Ye, W., Heidemann, J., Estrin, D.: An energy-efficient MAC protocol for wireless sensor networks. In: INFOCOM 2002. Twenty-First Annual Joint Conference of the IEEE Computer and Communications Societies. Proceedings IEEE, IEEE, 2002, pp. 1567–1576 (2002)
5. Wei, Y., Heidemann, J., Estrin, D.: Medium access control with coordinated adaptive sleeping for wireless sensor networks. Netw. IEEE/ACM Trans. **12**, 493–506 (2004)
6. Langendoen, K., Dam, T.V.: An adaptive energy-efficient MAC protocol for wireless sensor networks. In: ACM Sensys (2003)
7. Lu, G., Krishnamachari, B., Raghavendra, C.S.: An adaptive energy-efficient and low-latency MAC for tree-based data gathering in sensor networks. Wirel. Commun. Mob. Comput. **7**, 863–875 (2007)

8. Jawhar, I., Mohamed, N., Shuaib, K., Kesserwan, N.: An efficient framework and networking protocol for linear wireless sensor networks. Ad Hoc Sens. Wirl. Netw. **7**, 3–21 (2009)

9. Jawhar, I., Mohamed, N., Agrawal, D.P.: Linear wireless sensor networks: classification and applications. J. Netw. Comput. Appl. **34**, 1671–1682 (2011)

10. Zimmerling, M., Dargie, W., Reason, J.M.: Localized power-aware routing in linear wireless sensor networks. In: Proceedings of the 2nd ACM international conference on Context-awareness for self-managing systems, ACM, 2008, pp. 24–33 (2008)

11. Huang, P., Xiao, L., Soltani, S., Mutka, M.W., Xi, N.: The evolution of MAC protocols in wireless sensor networks: a survey. Commun. Surv. Tutorials IEEE **15**, 101–120 (2013)

12. Demirkol, I., Ersoy, C., Alagoz, F.: MAC protocols for wireless sensor networks: a survey. Commun. Mag. IEEE **44**, 115–121 (2006)

13. Yahya, B., Ben-Othman, J.: Towards a classification of energy aware MAC protocols for wireless sensor networks. Wirel. Commun. Mob. Comput. **9**, 1572–1607 (2009)

14. Liu, S., Fan, K.-W., Sinha, P.: CMAC: an energy-efficient MAC layer protocol using convergent packet forwarding for wireless sensor networks. ACM Trans. Sens. Netw. (TOSN) **5**, 29 (2009)

15. Zhao, Y.Z., Ma, M., Miao, C.Y., Nguyen, T.N.: An energy-efficient and low-latency MAC protocol with adaptive scheduling for multi-hop wireless sensor networks. Comput. Commun. **33**, 1452–1461 (2010)

16. Oh, H., Vinh, P.V.: Design and implementation of a mac protocol for timely and reliable delivery of command and data in dynamic wireless sensor networks. Sens. Basel **13**, 13228–13257 (2013)

17. Wang, X.Y., Li, J., Tang, F.L.: Network coding aware cooperative mac protocol for wireless ad hoc networks. IEEE Trans. Parall. Distr. **25**, 167–179 (2014)

A Timing-Sync Algorithm Based on PTP in UWSN Considering Utility and Accuracy

Chi Yuan[⊠]

School of Information, Renmin University of China, Beijing 100872, China
chiyuan@ruc.edu.cn

Abstract. Timing-sync problem in underwater wireless sensor network (UWSN) is difficult to solve due to its underwater nature. The routine timing-sync mechanisms such as GPS, NTP are inapplicable to this particular network (WSN). What's more, most sensors in UWSN have very small volume and have no ways to be armed with enough processing equipments special for synchronization, thus they have limited energy, and all of the timing-sync mechanisms must consider the energy consumed.

On the other hand, accuracy is a necessary condition needed to ensure the UWSN systems work stably. Conventional UWSN timing-sync algorithms rarely consider both the energy consumed and accuracy. Thus, they will cause problems such as network congestion and information loss more easily. This paper proposed a modified algorithm based on Kalman filter which has lesser energy consumed and higher accuracy. It realizes the optimal estimate to clock skew/offset on the premise of ensuring algorithm convergence, and constructs a relational model concerning energy consumed and accuracy. Finally, the experiment results show that the proposed algorithm is superior to the existing algorithms in performance.

Keywords: Underwater wireless networks · Timing-sync · Calman filter

1 Introduction

1.1 Natures of UWSN

Limited Transmission. The physical layer of UWSN has a limited transmission bandwidth and a lower traffic rate [1–3]. Table 1 shows the diverse bandwidths at different communication coverage [4].

Limited Energy. The sensors of UWSN are deployed in underwater environment and cannot be charged via solar power. Also, it's hard to replace them when they were deployed already. What's more, communication via underwater acoustic-channel consumes much higher energy when transmission occurs.

Limited Capability of Operation and Storage. The nodes of UWSN are embedded devices which have low price and low power consumption [5, 6]. Thus they have processors with limited operation capability and memories with limited storage space [7].

© Springer-Verlag Berlin Heidelberg 2015
L. Sun et al. (Eds.): CWSN 2014, CCIS 501, pp. 332–339, 2015.
DOI: 10.1007/978-3-662-46981-1_32

Table 1. The bandwidths in underwater acoustic communication systems

	Distance (Km)	Bandwidth (KHz)
Ultra-long distance	1000	<1
Long distance	10–100	2–5
Middling distance	1–10	≈10
Short distance	0.1–1	20–50
Ultra-short distance	<0.1	>100

Requirements of Timing-Sync. Conventional Timing-sync means make clock\frequency-correction constantly during a short period of time. They rarely consider energy consumed in the process of calculation and communication. Especially, such means will cause problems such as network congestions and information losses more easily in the underwater wireless environment.

1.2   Two Types Timing-Sync Algorithms in UWSN

Energy Preponderated Algorithms. DMTS focus on flexibility and light weight [8], and realize Timing-sync between sensors via evaluation of the synchronous message delay on transmission path. FTSP achieves Timing-sync via single broadcast [9], and compensates the clock drift via linear regression method to reduce the sending times and energy consumed. LTS reduces the system energy consumed by means of reducing synchronization times and the participation times of sensors [10]. Iny-Sync & Mini-Sync are fallen into light weight category [11]. They obtain error-limited estimated value of frequency deviation and phase deviation at the expense of a small amount of calculation.

Accuracy Preponderated Algorithms. RBS realizes Timing-sync between the nodes and eliminates the deviation caused by transmit leg [12]. This algorithm achieves a high-accuracy but also has higher energy consumption. TPSN uses pair-wise synchronization, like PTP (Precision Time Protocol) protocol [13], it includes two phases: to determine levels and realize synchronization. It has high-accuracy and also high energy consumption. PTP was applied to Timing-sync of Zigbee nodes by H. Cho et al. [14]. In PTT, the master clock and the slave clock read timestamps from Media Independent Interface(MII), and then the slave clock carries out time calibration.

2   PTP and Calman Filter

2.1   PTP Used in UWSN

In 2010, A. Manhood proposed that PTP can be applied in WLAN [15]. However, it has limitations to apply in all sorts of application environments of UWSN, because it is designed based on wired network which has a stable network states. It ignores the impacts of asymmetric network delay and the critical packet loss rate. It also requires higher stability of internal clocking and without thinking balance between energy consumption and clock accuracy. So, a new timing-sync algorithm based on PTP architecture in UWSN should be proposed.

2.2 Process of Timing-Sync Based on PTP

Time stamping between the MAC layer and the PHY layer can eliminate ill effects of system thrashing to the synchronization accuracy. The process of master-slave timing-sync is illustrated in Fig. 1. In this process, the slave clock records four time points: t_{m1}, t_{s2}, t_{s3}, t_{m4}, which satisfy the following requirements:

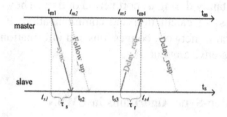

Fig. 1. The process of master-slave timing-sync

$$t_{s2} = t_{m1} + \tau_s + t'_d \tag{1}$$

$$t_{m4} = t_{s3} + \tau_r + t_d \tag{2}$$

Where τ_s denotes the delay of the transmitting path, τ_r denotes the delay of the receiving path.

2.3 Calman Filter

The Process of Calman Filter. Given there is a standard deterministic system which has a deterministic control input $\{u_j\}$. Its state space mode is shown as follows [16].

$$\begin{cases} x_{(k+1)} = A_k x_k + B_k u_k + \Gamma_k \varepsilon_k \\ v_{(k)} = C_k x_k + D_k u_k + \mu_k \end{cases} \tag{3}$$

$$\begin{cases} P_0 = \text{Var}_{x_0} \\ \hat{x}_{0|0} = E_{(x_0)} \\ \hat{x}_{j|j-1} = A_{j-1} \cdot \hat{x}_{j-1|j-1} + B_{j-1} \cdot u_{j-1} \\ P_{j,j-1} = A_{j-1} A_{j-1}^T + \Gamma_{j-1} Q_{j-1} \Gamma_{j-1}^T \\ \hat{x}_{j|j} = \hat{x}_{j-1|j-1} + G_j \left(v_j - D_j u_j - C_j \hat{x}_{j|j-1} \right) \\ G_j = P_{j,j-1} C_j^T \left(C_j P_{j,j-1} C_j^T + R_j \right)^{-1} \\ P_{j,j} = \left(1 - G_k C_j \right) P_{j,j-1} \\ j = 1, 2, \cdots \end{cases} \tag{4}$$

where u_j means the sequences vector with the dimension M. $(1 \leq M \leq n)$.

The Model of Calman Filter. According to the simple model of energy consumption in document [17], we can obtain communication energy consumption during time period T between the arbitrary two codes as follows:

$$C = n * (C_e + \emptyset_{am} \cdot squ(d) + C_e) = C_{tx} + C_{rx} \tag{5}$$

where C_e denotes the energy consumed per frame in the transmission circuits and the reception circuits, $\emptyset_{am}$ denotes the energy consumed per frame in the amplifying circuits. d denotes the transmission distance of the message. If the number of synchronous frame sent in a synchronizing cycle is k, the average number of the synchronous frame sent during the time period T is shown as follows:

$$Num_{ave} = (k * \left(\frac{1}{t_{de}} + t_{in}\right)) * T \tag{6}$$

$$C_j(t) \approx \rho * C_{master}(t) + \emptyset * squ(t) + dev_0 \tag{7}$$

where t_{in} denotes the time period from the end of the synchronization to the beginning of the next synchronization. $C_j(t)$ denotes the clock waiting for being adjusted, $C_{master}(t)$ denotes the master clock, ρ denotes the frequency ratio relative to the master clock. dev_0 denotes the deviation of the slave clock relative to the master clock at the initial time. $\emptyset$ denotes the parameter of the clock-drift caused by the change of temperature or environment. The maximal discrepancy of the slave clock relative to the master clock in the synchronization interval is shown as follows:

$$Max(E(SK)) \geq (t_{de} + t_{in}) * \sqrt[2]{squ(\rho + \theta - 1)} + \sqrt[2]{squ(acc_t)} \tag{8}$$

Where θ denotes the average instability factor of the clock skew during this time period and is determined by $\emptyset$. acc_t denotes the accuracy of the Timing-sync, Max(EXP(SK)) denotes the maximal value of the expected clock skew. According to formulas (6), (7) and (8), inequality can be shown as follows:

$$T \leq C * \left(E(SK) - \sqrt[2]{squ(acc_t)}\right)$$
$$* \left(\frac{1}{k * \sqrt[2]{squ(\rho + \theta - 1)} * (2 * C_e + C_p * squ(d))}\right) \tag{9}$$

In this paper, state variable undetermined is $x_{(j)} = \left[dev_{(j)}, (rel(Sk))_{(j)}\right]^T$, where $dev_{(j)}$ denotes clock offset, $(rel(Sk))_{(j)}$ denotes the relative clock skew and is relative to the instability factor θ and ρ. $Ob = f(t_1, t_2, t_3, t_4)$ is the observed value. Then observation equation and the state equation can be shown according to the synchronizing process above as follows:

$$\mathbf{Va}_{(j)} = \begin{bmatrix} 1 & \mathbf{intv}_{(adj)} \\ 0 & 1 \end{bmatrix} \cdot \mathbf{Va}_{(j-1)} + \mathbf{Sys}(\mathbf{noi}_{(j)}) \tag{10}$$

$$\mathbf{Obs}_{(j)} = (2 * \mathrm{intv}(\mathbf{t}_{res})) * \mathbf{Va}_{(j)} + \mathbf{Obs}(\mathbf{noi}_{(j)}) \tag{11}$$

where $\mathbf{intv}_{(adj)}$ denotes interval of clock adjustment, $\mathrm{intv}(\mathbf{t}_{res})$ denotes the response interval of the slave clock, $\mathbf{Sys}(\mathbf{noi}_{(j)})$ denotes systematic noise, $\mathbf{Obs}(\mathbf{noi}_{(j)})$ denotes measurement noise [18, 19].

3 The Modified Clock-Sync Algorithm

3.1 The Modified Algorithm

The newer algorithm employs cholesky resolution and quick resolution (QR) [20], and it is defined as follows:

Given Tr denotes a lower triangular matrix, P denotes a symmetric positive semi-definite matrix, $\mathbf{P} = (\mathbf{Tr})(\mathbf{Tr}^T)$, Tr is Cholesky factor of P which is marked as Tr = chol (P). QR of a matrix of n*m named B is given as $A^T = QR$, where Q denotes a unitary matrix of n*m (based on $\mathbf{Q}^T\mathbf{Q} = \mathbf{I}$), R denotes a upper triangular matrix of n*n which is defined as qr{B}. This means that if $P = \mathbf{BB}^T$, then $\mathbf{Tr}^T = \mathbf{qr}\{\mathbf{B}\}$, also $\mathbf{P} = (\mathbf{Tr})(\mathbf{Tr}^T)$. Based on the given Initial $\mathbf{Va}_0 = \mathbf{E}((\mathbf{Va})_0)$ and initial value of square root of covariance matrix $\mathcal{S}_0 = \mathbf{chol}(\mathbf{P}_0) = \mathbf{chol}\{\mathbf{E}(\left((\mathbf{Va})_0 - \widehat{(\mathbf{Va})}_0\right)\left((\mathbf{Va})_0 - \widehat{(\mathbf{Va})}_0\right)^T)\}$, the initial value of state is estimated via IEEE1588 algorithm according to the first group data which has been measured. By doing this, the convergence rate is sped up. According to the system model given in formulas (10) and (11), The following table can be given (Table 2):

Thus, the current Kalman gain is $\mathbf{Kg}_j$. Finally, update the value of the state and square root of the covariance matrix according to the current observed value.

$$kg_j = \mathrm{Tr}_{(j|j-1)}\alpha_j \cdot \beta_j \tag{12}$$

Table 2. Derivation

$\mathbf{A}\,\widehat{(\mathbf{Va})}((\mathbf{j}-1|\mathbf{j}-1)$	$\rightarrow$	$\widehat{(\mathbf{Va})}(\mathbf{j}|\mathbf{j}-1)$
$\mathbf{qr}\{[\mathbf{ATr}(\mathbf{j}-1|\mathbf{j}-1)\sqrt{\mathbf{Q}}]\}$	$\rightarrow$	$(\mathbf{Tr})^T(\mathbf{j}|\mathbf{j}-1)$
$\mathbf{H}\widehat{(\mathbf{Va})}(\mathbf{j}|\mathbf{j}-1)$	$\rightarrow$	$\widehat{\mathbf{Obs}}(\mathbf{j}|\mathbf{j}-1)$
$\mathbf{Tr}^T(\mathbf{j}|\mathbf{j}-1)\mathbf{H}^T$	$\rightarrow$	α_j
$(\alpha_j^T \cdot \alpha_j + \mathbf{R})^{-1}$	$\rightarrow$	β_j
$\left(1 + \sqrt{\beta_j R}\right)^{-1}$	$\rightarrow$	γ_j

$$(\textbf{Va})_{(j|j-1)} + \textbf{Kg}_j[\textbf{Obs}_j - \widehat{\textbf{Obs}}_{(j|j-1)}] \rightarrow (\textbf{Va})_{(j|j)} \tag{13}$$

$$\text{Tr}_{(j|j-1)} - \gamma_j \bullet \text{kg}_j \bullet \alpha_j^{\text{T}} \rightarrow \text{Tr}_{(j|j)} \tag{14}$$

3.2   Simulated Analysis

This paper simulate wireless environment outdoor with light barrier using the network simulator NS2. Configuration of parameters is set as follows (Table 3):

Table 3. Parameters setting

Communication range	250 m
Bandwidth	20 M
Low-level protocol	802.11
Transport protocol	TCP/UDP
Area and nodes number	300 square meters/21 nodes (randomly)
Simulation time	1000 s
C_e	0.4 mJ/frame
$\emptyset_{am}$	230 mJ/frame/m^2

SRKF adds estimating of clock skew into algorithm compared with PTP, and adjusts intervals of synchronization aiming at all kinds of slave clocks with diverse properties. In Table 4, we list estimated accuracy of clock skew about five nodes and times of the corresponding iterations to achieve the accuracy.

Table 4. Estimated accuracy and times of iterations to achieve the accuracy

Node No.	Accuracy	Relative ratio	Times of iterations
1	7.83×10^{-5}	0.7956 %	4
2	2.54×10^{-5}	0.5235 %	7
3	6.74×10^{-7}	0.06835 %	5
4	1.33×10^{-7}	0.00987 %	6
5	5.62×10^{-8}	0.00056 %	5

Given the system noise is zero mean white Gauss noise. Parameters of energy consumption are respectively. Obviously, as shown in Fig. 2, while the expected accuracy is equal, the energy consumption has a higher value when the communication distance is long or the clock skew is large relative to the master clock.

At the same simulation environment, the modified clock-sync algorithm (SRKF) we proposed has a higher performance relative to PTP algorithm when it comes to estimation accuracy of the clock skew. As shown in Fig. 3, the accuracy is tending towards stability ($\leq 10^{-9}$ s) using many times iterative computations.

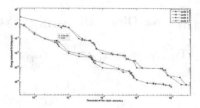

Fig. 2. Relationship between energy consumed and threshold of the accuracy

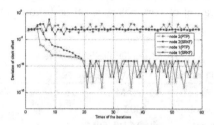

Fig. 3. Comparison of PTP and SRKF

The statistical characteristics of noise are not accurate enough in the model because of the phenomenon such as the asymmetry network delay and retransmission of information lost. Accordingly, there are some fluctuations of the estimated accuracy in Fig. 4. The influences of the blind selection of initial value over the filtering gradually die down and finally disappear. The estimated value tends to be unbiased gradually.

4 Conclusion

This paper defines a clock model according to analysis of the clock property of UWSN at the beginning. Accordingly, a modified clock timing-sync algorithm SRKF is presented to estimate the clock offsets and clock skews in UWSN. Experiment shows, in the same network environment, the modified algorithm SRKF has a higher performance both in the sync-accuracy and the stability than IEEE1588(PTP). Furthermore, the modified algorithm has good adaptability and can satisfy different requirements of accuracy.

Acknowledgment. This paper was supported by the Fundamental Research Funds for the Central Universities, and the Research Funds of Renmin University of China 10XNJ032.

References

1. Pompili, D., Melodia, T., Akyildiz, I.F.: Three-dimensional and two-dimensional deployment analysis for underwater acoustic sensor networks. Ad Hoc Netw. **7**, 778–790 (2009)
2. Indra, G., Taneja, R.: An ECC-time Stamp based mutual authentication and key management scheme for WSNs. In: 27th International Conference on Advanced Information Networking and Applications Workshops, vol. 52, pp. 883–889 (2013)

3. Tan, H.E., Diamant, R., Seah, W.K.G., et al.: A survey of techniques and challenges in underwater localization. J Ocean Eng. **38**, 1663–1676 (2011)
4. Dahl, P.H., Miller, P.H., Cato, P.H., Andrew, R.K.: Underwater ambient noise. Acous. Today **3**, 23–34 (2007)
5. Lorincz, K., Chen, B.R., Challen, G.W., et al.: Mercury: a wearable sensor network platform for high-fidelity motion analysis. In: The 7th ACM International Conference on Embedded Networked Sensor Systems, 2009 pp. 183–196. ACM New York, NY, USA (2009)
6. Li, M., Liu, Y.H.: Underground coal mine monitoring with wireless sensor networks. ACM Trans. Sens. Netw. **5**(2), 99–107 (2009)
7. Karlof, C., Wagner, D.: Secure routing in wireless sensor networks: attacks and countermeasures. Elsevier's AdHoc Netw. J. Appl. Protoc. Spec. Issue Sens. Net. **1**(2), 293–315 (2003)
8. Ping, S.: Delay measurement time synchronization for WSN. Intel Research Berkeley Lab (IRB-TR-03-013) (2003)
9. Maroti, M., Kusy, B., Simon, G., Ledeczi, A.: The flooding time synchronization protocol. In: ACM Second International Conference on Embedded Networked Sensor Systems (SenSys 04), pp. 39–49, Baltimore, MD (2004)
10. Greunen, J., Rabaey, J.: Lightweight time synchronization for sensor networks. In: Proceedings of the 2nd ACM International Conference on WSN and Applications, San Diego, CA (2003)
11. Sichitiu, M.L., Veerarittipahan, C.: Simple, accurate time synchronization for wireless sensor networks. In: Proceedings of the IEEE WCNC, pp. 1266–1273 (2003)
12. Elson, J., Girod, L., Estrin, D.: Fine-grained network time synchronization using reference broadcasts. In: Proceedings of the Fifth Symposium on OSDI 2002, Boston, MA (2002)
13. Ganeriwal, S., Kumar, R., Srivastava, M.B.: Timing-sync protocol for sensor networks. In: proceedings of the 1st international conference on Embedded networked sensor systems pp. 138–149. Los Angeles, CA, USA (2003)
14. Cho, H., Jung, J., Bongrae, C.B., et al.: Precision time synchronization using ieee 1588 for wireless sensor networks. In: Proceedings of the 12th IEEE International Conference on CSE 2009 (2009)
15. Mahmood, A., Gaderer, G., Loschmidt, P.: Clock synchronization in wireless LANs without hardware support. In: Proceedings of the 8th IEEE International WFCS 2010, Nancy, France (2010)
16. Kalman Filtering with Real-Time Applications 4th (ISBN 978-7-302-30907-9)
17. Heinzelman, W., Chandrakasan, A., Balakrishnan, H.: An application-specific protocol architecture for wireless micro sensor networks. IEEE Trans. Wirel. Commun. **10**, 660–670 (2002)
18. Simon, H.: Adaptive Filter Theory. Prentice Hall, New Jersey (2002)
19. Haykin, S.: Kalman Filtering and Neural Networks. John Wiley & Sons, Inc., New York (2001)
20. Van Der Merwe, R., Wan, E.A.: The square-root unscented Kalman filter for state and parameter-estimation. In: 2001 IEEE International Conference on IEEE, vol. 6, pp. 3461–3464 (2001)

Quantum Secure Direct Communication Protocol Based on the Class of Three-Particle W States

Zhengwen Cao[1,2($\boxtimes$)], Xiaoyi Feng[1], Jinye Peng[2], and Li Huifang[1]

[1] School of Electronics and Information, Northwestern Polytechnical University, Xi'an 710072, China
[2] School of Information Science and Technology, Northwest University, Xi'an 710127, China
caozhw@nwu.edu.cn

Abstract. A novel protocol for quantum secure direct communication is proposed using entanglement properties of a class of three-particle W states. Particle sequences are grouped times in particles preparation phase. For intercept-resend attack, security is discussed in detail in particles distribution, the error rate for introduced by eavesdropper is 50 %. Information can be transmitted safely by inserting decoy photons and rearranging order of particles in the information transfer phase, the protocol has the advantage of high security.

Keywords: Quantum secure direct communication · W state · Error rate pacs 03.67.Hk · 03.65.Ud

1 Introduction

Quantum communication is one of most rapid development fields in quantum mechanics today. Quantum secure direct communication (QSDC) is a novel quantum communication, using quantum properties, secret messages are transmitted directly without a key in QSDC. In the future, QSDC has a great potential for relying on quantum mechanics. After Beige et al. put forward the first QSDC protocol in 2002 [1]. In the same year, Bostrom and Felbinge proposed "ping pong" protocol [2]. In 2004, in order to improve the capacity of the "ping pong", Cai and Li designed two new unitary operations [3]. In 2006, Lee et al. suggested QSDC and authentication protocol [4], and some QSDC protocols based on quantum dense code (QDC) [5–7] were presented. In 2011, Gu Bin proposed QSDC in noise channel [8]. In 2012, Huang et al. discussed a QSDC with two robust channel encryption [9], and QSDC with four-qubit cluster states was presented [10,11]. In 2013, Chang et al. proposed a single photon QSDC protocol [12], the cost of the protocol is less than others using entangled qubits. However, the realization of the single photon is still difficult in experiments. With the development of technology, comprehensive application is researched,

© Springer-Verlag Berlin Heidelberg 2015
L. Sun et al. (Eds.): CWSN 2014, CCIS 501, pp. 340–347, 2015.
DOI: 10.1007/978-3-662-46981-1_33

for example, a multiparty controlled bidirectional QSDC with authentication protocol was proposed via entanglement swapping and Einstein-Podolsky-Rosen (EPR) pair [13]. An efficient three-party QSDC based on QDC with EPR pairs was discussed [14].

Because Greenberger-Horne-Zeilinger (GHZ) state has a larger Hilbert space, it can be used for perfect QDC [15] with higher information capacity. Some QSDC protocols based on GHZ states were proposed [16–21]. In 2005, a multi-step QSDC with the multiparticle GHZ state was presented by Wang et al. [16]. In 2008, a novel multiparty QSDC using GHZ states with QDC was proposed by Sun et al. [17]. Chen et al. proposed a novel controlled QSDC protocol with quantum encryption using a partially entangled GHZ state [24]. Recently, they discussed a multiparty quantum secret sharing (QSS) resist attacks [19] and a three-party QSS protocol with a single-particle state [20]. In terms of system implementation, Wang et al. proposed a QSDC scheme via GHZ state in driven cavity QED [21].

W state has stronger robustness against loss of particles than GHZ state [22], that is to say, if one of the particles disappears, the remaining particles are still entangled, which can still be used as a entangled resource. For non-maximally entangled state [23], W state is easier to be prepared. During recent years, some QSDC protocols based on W state have been proposed [24–27]. In these protocols, there are security vulnerabilities, these systems are more complex. This paper proposes a QSDC protocol via a class of three-particle W states, which can improve the security of information transmission and simplify system structure.

2   The QSDC Based on the Class of W States

The QSDC protocol includes particle preparation phase, particle distribution phase and information transfer phase. Alice is sender, Bob is receiver.

2.1   Particle Preparation

Step 1: Alice prepares N groups of the class of three-particle W states as Eq. (1), named $[M_1(A), M_1(B), M_1(C)]$, $[M_2(A), M_2(B), M_2(C)]$, $[M_3(A), M_3(B), M_3(C)]$, ..., $[M_N(A), M_N(B), M_N(C)]$, where the numbers in the subscript are the order number of the groups, A, B and C represent three particles with W states respectively. Alice takes particle A, B and C from N groups separately to form three particle sequences as A-sequence: $[M_1(A), M_2(A), M_3(A), ..., M_N A]$, B-sequence: $[M_1(B), M_2(B), M_3(B), ..., M_N(B)]$ and C-sequence: $[M_1(C), M_2(C), M_3(C), ..., M_N(C)]$.

$$|W\rangle_{ABC} = a|001\rangle + b|010\rangle + \frac{\sqrt{2}}{2}|100\rangle; \tag{1}$$

The coefficients a, b satisfy

$$|a|^2 + |b|^2 = \frac{1}{2}; \qquad (2)$$

Step 2: A-sequence is divided into A_1 and A_2 sequence, A_1 is much longer than A_2, which is used to check eavesdropper (Eve) in quantum channel. Similarly, to get B_1 and B_2, C_1 and C_2.

Step 3: A_2, B_2 and C_2 are randomly inserted to A_1, B_1 and C_1 form new sequence respectively, for example, A_2 is inserted to C_1 to form new C' sequence. The preparation process is shown in Fig. 1.

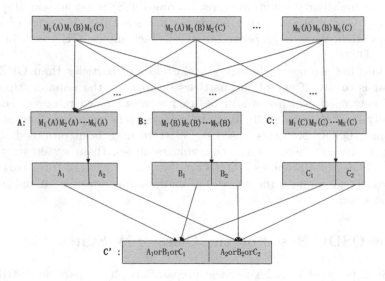

Fig. 1. The preparation process

2.2 Particle Distribution and Channel Security Check

Step 1: Alice sends C' and A_2 particles positions to Bob.

Step 2: Bob picks up and measures A_2 randomly using X-basis or Z-basis as Eqs. (3) and (4), then transmits the measurement results and basis to Alice via classical channel.

$$|0\rangle = \frac{\sqrt{2}}{2}(|+\rangle + |-\rangle); |1\rangle = \frac{\sqrt{2}}{2}(|+\rangle - |-\rangle); \qquad (3)$$

$$|+\rangle = \frac{\sqrt{2}}{2}(|0\rangle + |1\rangle); |-\rangle = \frac{\sqrt{2}}{2}(|0\rangle - |1\rangle); \qquad (4)$$

Step 3: Alice makes joint measurement on B_2 and C_2 using Z-basis or $\{\zeta^{\pm}, \eta^{\pm}\}$-basis according to Bobs information, where

$$\zeta^+ = a|01\rangle + b|10\rangle + \frac{\sqrt{2}}{2}|00\rangle; \zeta^- = a|01\rangle + b|10\rangle - \frac{\sqrt{2}}{2}|00\rangle; \qquad (5)$$

$$\eta^+ = a|10\rangle - b|01\rangle + \frac{\sqrt{2}}{2}|11\rangle; \eta^- = a|10\rangle - b|01\rangle - \frac{\sqrt{2}}{2}|11\rangle; \qquad (6)$$

Step 4: In order to check Eve, Alice and Bob communicates their measurement results via classical channel. If the measurement results and basis completely satisfy correct corresponding relation, there is no Eve. The correct corresponding relation is: If Bob's result is $|1\rangle$ using Z-basis, Alice's result should be $|00\rangle$ using Z-basis with probability $\frac{1}{2}$. If Bob's result is $|+\rangle$ $(|-\rangle)$ using X-basis, Alice's result should be $\zeta^+ (\zeta^-)$ using $\{\zeta^{\pm}, \eta^{\pm}\}$-basis with probability $\frac{1}{2}$. At this time, Bob can trust C_1. Otherwise, communication will be stopped at once and return to particle preparation phase.

2.3   Information Transfer

Step 1: Alice encodes her secret message on particles A_1 and B_1, and $(AB)_1$ $([M_1(A), M_1(B)], [M_2(A), M_2(B)], \ldots, [M_N(A), M_N(B)])$ is formed to particle pairs sequence.

Step 2: After Alice rearranges $(AB)_1$ particles and randomly inserts decoy photons, the outcome sequence is renamed $(AB)_2$, only Alice knows how to finish these operations. Then she sends $(AB)_2$ and decoy photons positions to Bob.

Step 3: Bob receives $(AB)_2$ and selects X-basis or Z-basis to measure the decoy photons, and then he transfers the measurement results and basis to Alice via classical channel to check the security of massage, if passed, they perform next step, otherwise the process will be abandoned.

Step 4: Alice informs the rearrangement order of $(AB)_2$ remaining particles to Bob via classical channel.

Step 5: Bob recovers them and makes joint measurement on A_1, B_1 and C_1 to read Alice's classical message. The QSDC process is completed. The protocol process is shown in Fig. 2.

3   Security Analysis

Quantum teleportation generally can take advantage of W state with probability less than 1. But proper W states and operations can realize perfect quantum teleportation [28]. In this paper, the class of three-particle W states can be written as Eq. (1) [29]. The principle of security check is based on entanglement correlation among particles of W states. Equation (1) can also be rewritten as:

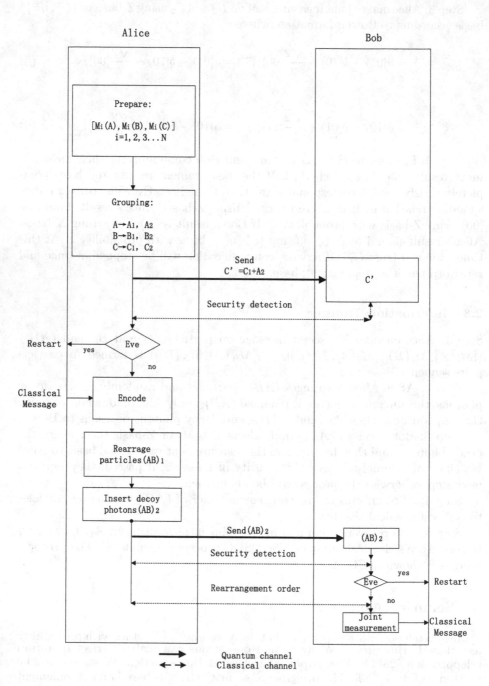

Fig. 2. The protocol process chart

$$|W\rangle_{ABC} = a|001\rangle + b|010\rangle + \frac{\sqrt{2}}{2}|100\rangle$$

$$= \frac{\sqrt{2}}{2}(a|01\rangle + b|10\rangle + \frac{\sqrt{2}}{2}|00\rangle)_{BC}|+\rangle_A + \frac{\sqrt{2}}{2}(a|01\rangle + b|10\rangle - \frac{\sqrt{2}}{2}|00\rangle)_{BC}|-\rangle_A \quad (7)$$

$$= \frac{\sqrt{2}}{2}|\zeta^+\rangle_{BC}|+\rangle_A + \frac{\sqrt{2}}{2}|\zeta^-\rangle_{BC}|-\rangle_A;$$

where $|+\rangle$ and $|-\rangle$ is orthogonal each other. In order to measure particles B and C using complete orthogonal basis, a set of complete orthogonal $\{\zeta^\pm, \eta^\pm\}$-basis in the four-dimensional Hilbert space need be built as Eqs. (5) and (6), $|00\rangle, |01\rangle, |10\rangle$ and $|11\rangle$, can be shown using $\{\zeta^\pm, \eta^\pm\}$-basis:

$$|00\rangle = \frac{\sqrt{2}}{2}(\zeta^+ - \zeta^-); \quad (8)$$

$$|01\rangle = a\zeta^+ + a\zeta^- - b\eta^+ - b\eta^-; \quad (9)$$

$$|10\rangle = b\zeta^+ + b\zeta^- - a\eta^+ - a\eta^-; \quad (10)$$

$$|11\rangle = \frac{\sqrt{2}}{2}(\eta^+ - \eta^-); \quad (11)$$

So there is corresponding relation for Alice and Bob between measurement result and basis, which can be used to security check, In protocol process, Eve can use many kinds of attack to catch secret massage. For example, intercept-resend attack, measure-resend attack and entangled-resend attack. The intercept-resend attack is discussed as follow. In particle distribution phase, suppose Eve intercepts A_2, he prepares his own fake particles (named E_2) with W state and sends it to Bob. Bob measures them randomly using X-basis or Z-basis.

1. Bob gets measurement result $|0\rangle$ using Z-basis. The class of three-particle W states can be rewritten as

$$|W\rangle_{ABC} = |0\rangle_A(a|01\rangle + b|10\rangle)_{BC} + \frac{\sqrt{2}}{2}|1\rangle_A|00\rangle_{BC}; \quad (12)$$

At this time, B_2 and C_2 belong to Alice, fake E_2 belongs to Bob, between E_2 and B,C are not entangled. Alice makes joint measurement on B_2 and C_2. As Eq. (12), the result should be $|01\rangle_{BC}$ or $|10\rangle_{BC}$, if the result is $|00\rangle_{BC}$, Eve must be found because his eavesdropping caused the error. The probability of Eve found is

$$P_{e1} = \langle 00| \bigotimes \left(a|01\rangle + b|10\rangle + \frac{\sqrt{2}}{2}|00\rangle \right) = \frac{1}{2}; \quad (13)$$

2. Bob gets the measurement result $|1\rangle$ using Z-basis. When Alice makes joint measurement on B_2 and C_2, the result should be $|00\rangle_{BC}$, if the result is $|01\rangle_{BC}$

with probability $|a|^2$ or $|10\rangle_{BC}$ with probability $|b|^2$, Eve must be found, the probability of Eve found is

$$P_{e21} = \langle 01| \otimes \left(a|01\rangle + b|10\rangle + \frac{\sqrt{2}}{2}|00\rangle \right) = |a|^2; \tag{14}$$

$$P_{e22} = \langle 10| \otimes \left(a|01\rangle + b|10\rangle + \frac{\sqrt{2}}{2}|00\rangle \right) = |b|^2; \tag{15}$$

$$P_{e2} = P_{e21} + P_{e22} \tag{16}$$
$$= a^2 + b^2$$
$$= \frac{1}{2};$$

3. Bob gets the measurement result $|+\rangle$ using X-basis, the class of three-particle W states can be rewritten as

$$|W\rangle_{ABC} = \frac{\sqrt{2}}{2}|\zeta^+\rangle_{BC}|+\rangle_A + \frac{\sqrt{2}}{2}|\zeta^-\rangle_{BC}|-\rangle_A; \tag{17}$$

As Eq. (17), Alice's result should be ζ^+ using $\{\zeta^\pm, \eta^\pm\}$-basis, the probability of Eve found is

$$P_{e3} = \frac{1}{2}; \tag{18}$$

4. Bob gets the measurement result is $|-\rangle$ using X-basis. Alice's result should be ζ^- using $\{\zeta^\pm, \eta^\pm\}$-basis, the probability of Eve found is

$$P_{e4} = \frac{1}{2}; \tag{19}$$

In summary, the error rate introduced by Eve is

$$P_e = \frac{1}{2} * \frac{1}{2}(P_{e1} + P_{e2}) + \frac{1}{2} * \frac{1}{2}(P_{e3} + P_{e4}) = \frac{1}{2}. \tag{20}$$

When information is transmitted, decoy photons are inserted randomly into $(AB)_1$, and the order of particles is rearranged to resist Eve's attack. The security is discussed in detail in [30].

4   Conclusions

The novel QSDC protocol based on three-particle W states is proposed, and the security of the protocol is discussed in particle distribution phase and information transfer phase. The error rate introduced by Eve is 50 % in intercept-resend attack; it shows the protocol is safe against eavesdropping.

Acknowledgments. This paper was supported by the Natural Science Special Fund of Department of Education in Shaanxi in 2012 (No. 12JK0497) and Natural Fund of Science in Shaanxi in 2013 (No. 2013JM8036).

References

1. Beige, A., Englert, B.G., Kurtsiefer, C., et al.: Acta Phys. Pol. A. **101**, 357 (2002)
2. Bostrom, K., Felbinger, T.: Phys. Rev. Lett. **89**, 187902–1 (2002)
3. Cai, Q.Y., Li, B.W.: Phys. Rev. A **69**, 054301 (2004)
4. Lee, H., Lim, J., Yang, J.H.: Phys. Rev. A. **73**, 042305 (2006)
5. Deng, F.-G., Li, X.-H., Li, C.-Y.: Phys. Scr. **76**, 25–30 (2007)
6. Yan, X.I.A., Shan, S.H.: Phys. Lett. A. **364**, 117 (2007)
7. Liu, Z., Chen, H., Liu, W., Juan, X., Wang, D., Li, Z.: Quantum Inf. Process. **12**, 587–599 (2013)
8. Bin, G., Cheng-yi, Z., Guo-Sheng, C., Yu-Gai, H.: Sci China Ser G-Phys Mech Astron **54**, 942 (2011)
9. Huang, W., Wen, Q.Y., Jia, H.Y., Qin, S.J., Gao, F.: Chin. Phys. B **21**, 100308 (2012)
10. Sun, Z.-W., Du, R.-G., Long, D.-Y.: Int. J. Theor. Phys. **51**, 1946–1952 (2012)
11. Zhang, Q.-N., Li, C.-C., Li, Y.-H., Nie, Y.-Y.: Int. J. Theor. Phys. **52**, 22–27 (2013)
12. Chang, W.-L., Lin, F.-J., Zeng, G.-J., Chou, Y.-H.: Advances in Intelligent Systems and Applications, SIST 21, pp. 195–204 (2013)
13. Yan, C., Shi-Bin, Z., Li-Li, Y., Zhi-Wei, S.: Chin. Phys. Lett. **30**(6), 060301 (2013)
14. Yin, X., Ma, W., Shen, D., Hao, C.: J. Quantum Inf. Sci. **3**, 1–5 (2013)
15. Lee, H.-J., Ahn, D., Hwang, S.W.: Phys. Rev. A. **66**(2), 024304-1–024304-2 (2002)
16. Wang, C., Deng, F.G., Long, G.L.: Opti. Commun. **253**(1), 15–20 (2005)
17. Sun, Y., Wen, Q.Y., Zhu, F.C.: Chin. Phys. Lett. **25**, 828 (2008)
18. Chen, X.B., Wang, T.Y., Du, J.Z., Wen, Q.Y., Zhu, F.C.: Int. J. Quant. Inf. **6**, 543 (2008)
19. Chen, X.B., Yang, S., Su, Y., Yang, Y.X.: Phys. Scr. **86**, 055002 (2012)
20. Chen, X.B., Niu, X.X., Zhou, X.J., Yang, Y.X.: Quantum Inf. Process. **12**, 365 (2013)
21. Wang, B., Xu, S.-H., Meng, Y.-H.: Int. J. Theor. Phys. **52**(11), 3994–3998 (2013)
22. Roos, C.F., Riebe, M., Haffner, H., et al.: Science **304**(5676), 1478–1480 (2004)
23. (De) Sen, A., Sen, U., Wieniak, M.: Phys. Rev. A. **68**(6), 062306/1-7 (2003)
24. Chen, X.B., Wen, Q.Y., Guo, F.Z., Sun, Y., Xu, G., Zhu, F.C.: Int. J. Quantum. Inf. **6**, 899 (2008)
25. Li, D., Ming, X.X., Jun, G.Y., et al.: Commun. Theor. Phys. **52**, 853 (2009)
26. Chiawei, T., Tzonelih, H.: Opt. Commun. **283**, 4397 (2010)
27. Wen, C.Z., Xiaoyi, F., Hong, K.W.: J. Optoelectron. Laser **23**(6), 1152–1158 (2012)
28. Agrawal, P., Pati, A.: Phys. Rev. A. **74**, 062320–1 (2006)
29. MEI, Di.: Dalian University of Technology (2008)
30. Xiao, Q.D., Xing, P.C., Dan, L., et al.: Acta Phys. Sin. **59**, 29 (2010)

High-Throughput, High-Delivery Ratio MAC Protocol for Wireless VOIP Networks

Wei Cao[1], Tao Yang[1], Shuai Zhang[1], Ke Zhao[1], and Bin Cheng[2]([✉])

[1] Third Research Institute of Ministry of Public Security, Shanghai, China
[2] Beijing Institute of Technology, Beijing, China
chengbinpaper@gmail.com

Abstract. Existing duty-cycle MAC protocols for wireless voice-over-IP(VOIP) networks, such as S-MAC, mostly do not consider the influence of inherent traffic distribution characteristic derived from network infrastructure, leading to significant end-to-end delivery latency and poor medium contention handling in data gathering, where multiple data flows generated at sensor nodes converge to the sink. To mitigate these drawbacks, we propose a novel duty-cycle protocol. It adopts a static configuration strategy to configure nodes with un-uniform minimum contention window, in order to optimize application-level medium access fairness, avoiding packet loss and buffer overflow incurred by mismatches between un-uniform payload distribution and node-level fair medium access scheme adopted by current protocols. Our simulation results obtained on ns-2 show that it can better accommodate tree-based data gathering applications, providing high throughput and packet delivery ratio without sacrificing energy efficiency.

Keywords: MAC · Duty cycle · Wireless sensor network · ns-2 · Energy efficiency

1 Introduction

Large-scale WSNs have a wide range of potential applications, such as environmental monitoring and enemy target detection, where some special events may happen. However the limited battery capacity as a bottleneck degrades network performance. So many classic MAC protocols exploit duty cycling to mitigate energy consumption incurred by idle listening. S-MAC as a dedicated MAC protocol for sensor networks is proposed in [1], which primarily introduces a duty cycling mechanism, making sensor nodes periodically turn radio on and off to save energy, however benefits from duty cycling are achieved at the cost of performance degradations in latency and throughput, since relaying data packets from each node to another has to wait until its next downstream node in sleep mode wakes up to receive in the next cycle. T-MAC [2] introduces a dynamic event-driven mechanism to further reduces duty cycle compared to S-MAC, it can perform well under a wide range of traffic load, through setting a short interval at the beginning of listening period to sense special events to detect whether

© Springer-Verlag Berlin Heidelberg 2015
L. Sun et al. (Eds.): CWSN 2014, CCIS 501, pp. 348–354, 2015.
DOI: 10.1007/978-3-662-46981-1_34

there is data to transmit. B-MAC [3], X-MAC [4] WiseMAC [5] and ZMAC [6] abandon the time synchronization mechanism adopted by [1,2], an preamble sampling scheme is proposed to further reduce energy consumption due to idle listening and time synchronization, emulated experiment results show that this approach performs well in low traffic networks. Unfortunately, multi-hop transmission is common in WSNs, leading to the major drawback that every successful multi-hop delivery requires multiple cycles to accomplish, which substantially increasing end-to-end delivery latency. We refer to these protocols with the primitive duty cycling mechanism as S-MAC-like protocols.

Note that S-MAC-like protocols mentioned above, mostly configure nodes with the same-sized CW_{min}(minimum or original contention window). In order to avoid collisions when more than one nodes intend to send data packets in the same cycle, the random backoff mechanism is adopted before real data transmission, that is, when one node with pending data transmits control packets such as RTS/PION/SCH, it must wait for a random time point (randomly select one time slot) during the predefined CW_{min}. To some extent, this random backoff mechanism can well cope with collisions, makes nodes compete for medium equally in order to enhance node-level fairness of shared medium, this can work well in small-scale sensor networks, which means each node is given equal chance to access the shared medium. When collisions happen, CW_{min} will exponentially increases, this can well avoid repeated contention, especially often appears in dense networks. In tree-based data gathering deployment, nodes in different location usually hold un-uniform payloads. As shown in Fig. 1, the payload of B is heavier than A, which means payload is relative to position, and we can easily conclude that the payload is proportional to the distance away from the sink, or the payload is inversely proportional to the value of layer/depth accordingly. Unfortunately, B has the same opportunity as A among above MAC protocols. Under traffic burst condition or as traffic load increases, that even

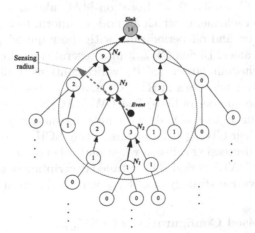

Fig. 1. Un-uniform payload distribution of the tree-based network

chance to access the shared medium makes B suffer buffer overflow and packet loss more often, compared with those with low payload, especially in large-scale dense WSNs.

Motivated by the shortcomings mentioned above, we present the design and evaluation of a new duty-cycle MAC protocol, named Location-MAC, which works on addressing mismatches between payload distribution and node-level fair medium access in data gathering WSNs through a new configuration method of CW_{min}. Different from prior works, Location-MAC can better guarantee application-level fairness at the expense of node-level fairness of medium access.

2 Modeling

Location-MAC focuses on the uplink transmission in the tree-based data gathering WSNs. Figure 1 describes the network model. Moreover some reasonable assumptions are enumerated as follows:

Assumption 1. The deployment of sensor network is static, that is, nodes keep static after being deployed.

Assumption 2. Each node can communicate with other nodes within its communication radius. The whole network is connected, that is, the sink can establishes a valid route to every source node directly or over multiple hops.

3 Location-MAC DESIGN

3.1 Overview

Similar to RMAC [7], each operational cycle is divided into three phases: SYNC, DATA and SLEEP, with their lengths marked as T_{sync}, T_{data} and T_{sleep} respectively. During SYNC, similar to [9] Location-MAC also assumes the existence of a synchronization scheme, in which all nodes conform to a specified schedule to switch between on and off periodically with the required precision through exchanging $Sync$ frames. Divide CW_{min} into several time slots and denote the control packet as scheduling frame (SCH), which contains traditional fields, such as sender and receiver addresses in RTS/CTS, and cross-layer fields (next-hop, destination, and the number of hops) like DW-MAC [8]. At the start of DATA period, once medium is free, a node with pending data must randomly select one timeslot from their CW_{min} before transmitting SCH in order to contend for medium, moreover decreasing collision when multiple nodes try to forward data packets in the same DATA period. The detailed description of the location-based un-uniform configuration strategy of CW_{min} will be shown in the next section.

3.2 Location-Based Configuration of CW_{min}

This problem seriously degrades application-level performances, such as high collision ratio and latency, different from dynamical adjustment of network running parameters or competing for medium on the basis of priority [10,11], a static location-based configuration scheme of CW_{min} to optimize the medium assignment. Our scheme has two calculation steps: Layer-level CW_{min} and Node-level CW_{min}. Before real calculation we give related parameter elucidation, assumes each node's children and layer are known in advance, take node u for example.

Given node u is i hops away from the sink and we denote l_i^u as u's layer. L_i or $L(i)$ denotes the collection of nodes at the layer l_i; C_u is the collection of u's children, and $C_{l(i)}$ stands for the collection of children of l_i or $l(i)$.

Calculation of Layer-Level $CW_{min}^{l_i}$. Node's location is directly related to the medium assignment, and the layer-level CW_{min} provides a reference value to ensure that CW_{min} of current layer is not less than that of its upstream layer. The detailed calculation can be expressed as

$$CW_{min}^{l_{i+1}} = \begin{cases} CW_{min}^0 \times (1 + A_0)^\delta, & i = 0 \\ CW_{min}^{l_i} \times (1 + A_{l(i)})^\delta, & 0 < i < M \end{cases} \tag{1}$$

where CW_{min}^0 and $CW_{min}^{l_i}$ represent the CW_{min} of the sink and the l_i^{th} layer, respectively. The predefined parameter θ depends on the size of the network (refer to the following Theorem 2), which can well avoid long-term failure to seize the medium due to oversized CW_{min}. Seen from the two equations above, the size of $CW_{min}^{l_i}$ is influenced by three factors: $CW_{min}^{l_{i-1}}$, $A_{l(i)}$ and the predefined parameter θ. The difference of CW_{min} between two adjacent layers mainly lies in the average value of their upper layer's children accordingly, and δ as an adjustment factor is calculated by A and the constant θ. Once the network is given with fixed preset parameters, δ's value remains constant.

Calculation of Node-Level CW_{min}. Figure 1 shows the payload distribution of the tree-based network, nodes in the same layer often hold un-uniform payload due to different numbers of sub-nodes. Therefore make the layer-level $CW_{min}^{l_i}$ as a benchmark, then calculate the node-level CW_{min} on basis of the amount of sub-nodes.

Every parent-node holds more chance to occupy the wireless shared medium than its sub-nodes, which is in line with the characteristics of the un-uniform payload distribution, proves this un-uniform configuration scheme on CW_{min} to be effective.

4 Simulation Evaluation

To quantitatively evaluate the performance of Location-MAC, we adopt the popular simulation platform $ns - 2$ to compare Location-MAC against S-MAC and DW-MAC, which can stand for S-MAC-like and R-MAC-like protocols respectively.under a random network scenario. 20 to 200 nodes are randomly deployed in a 1500×1500 m square area. To simulate tree-based converge-cast traffic, we place the sink at the top right corner of the domain.

Location-MAC uses the Random Correlated-Event (RCE) traffic model [8], which well simulates the impulse traffic triggered by spatially-correlated events. Events happen randomly within the grid field, and nodes can generate one unit of data packet in response when one event happen within their sensing range. Table ?? lists the key networking parameters used in our simulation. Although Mica2 radio (CC1000) [11] can support a maximum packet size of 256 bytes, the size of data packet used in our simulations is 50 bytes, which costs a propagation time of 43 ms. Each node's interface queue capacity (Q_{max}) is 1000 bytes. In order to generate comparable results, other parameters are same to those in DW-MAC. Additionally, in order to simulate buffer flow and collision, the maximum hop during one operational cycle is no more than 4 hops. During the contention for medium, large-CW_{min} nodes fail more often than those with small CW_{min}. So Location-MAC introduces a vector called *Failed Times* (FT) to count the number of failures to win the contention, avoiding large-CW_{min} ones waiting for long time to occupy medium, The value of FT vector is determined by node's buffer size, node density and networking scale, however this is not our focus, so the threshhold of FT vector is equal to the *retry limit* presented in S-MAC.

Moreover, to simplify experiments, we neglect the influence of routing traffic, and assume that there is a routing protocol deployed to provide the shortest path between any two nodes. Additionally, we do not consider any synchronization traffic and assume all the nodes have already been synchronized to a common schedule. In all cases the network is always connected, that is, every node can successfully communicate with the sink directly or indirectly. Average results are calculated from 10 runs, each run contains data packets towards the sink triggered by a series of 300 discrete events, and each event occurs randomly between 2 s and 10 s after one another, this can well simulate real applications, sometimes the interval is larger than the length of two cycles, packets generated by an earlier event can reach the sink before the next event is generated, on the contrary, previous packets face the competition of packets generated by following events.

4.1   Throughput

Figure 2 shows curves of throughput. We simulate throughput by adjusting the number of nodes from 20 to 200 m with the interval is 20. When the number of nodes increases, all protocols' throughput increases because the number of generated packets increases. We see that the S-MAC's curve remains flat when the number of nodes is more than 100 in S-MAC. This result can verify that Location-MAC outperforms the DW-MAC and S-MAC-like in throughput, especially in dense networks.

4.2   Packet Delivery Rate

We simulate different packet delivery rate by adjusting the number of nodes from 20 to 200 with the interval is 20. Whenever the value of A is small or big,

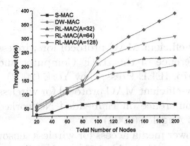

Fig. 2. Throughput at the sink

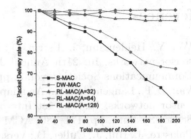

Fig. 3. Packet delivery rate

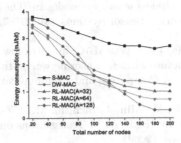

Fig. 4. Energy consumption per bit

Location-MAC can achieve a packet delivery ratio of almost 100 percent, as shown in Fig. 3.

4.3 Energy Consumption

For WSNs are energy-constrained networks, so energy efficiency is always the key hotspot. Figure 4 shows the simulation results of energy consumption. With the increment of number of nodes, all the curves of energy efficiency declines in different degrees. S-MAC consumes more energy than other protocols, due to more energy wasted by collisions and retransmissions when the number of nodes increases.

5 Conclusions

Location-MAC focuses on analyzing and overcoming the mismatches between the fair medium access and the un-uniform payload distribution feature in data gathering WSNs among nodes in different position through analyzing the payload distribution features in data gathering WSNs. Location-MAC proposed a static location-based contention window scheme to optimize chances to contend for the shared wireless medium by un-uniform contention windows.

References

1. Wei, Y., Heidemann, J., Estrin, D.: An energy-efficient MAC protocol for wireless sensor networks. In: 21th Annual Joint Conference of the IEEE Computer and Communications Societies, vol. 3, pp. 1567–1576. IEEE Press, New York (2002)
2. Van, D.T., Langendoen, K.: An adaptive energy-efficient MAC protocol for wireless sensor networks. In: The 1st International Conference on Embedded Networked Sensor Systems, pp. 171–180. ACM Press, Los Angeles (2003)
3. Polastre, J., Hill, J., Culler, D.: Versatile low power media access for wireless sensor networks. In: The 2nd International Conference on Embedded Networked Sensor Systems, pp. 95–107. ACM Press, Maryland (2004)
4. Buettner, M., Yee, G.V., Anderson, E., Han, R.: X-MAC: a short preamble MAC protocol for duty-cycled wireless sensor networks. In: The 4th International Conference on Embedded Networked Sensor Systems, pp. 307–320. ACM Press, Colorado (2006)
5. El-Hoiydi, A., Decotignie, J.-D.: WiseMAC: an ultra low power MAC protocol for the downlink of infrastructure wireless sensor networks. In: The Ninth International Symposium Conference on Computers and Communications, pp. 244–251. IEEE Press (2004)
6. Rhee, I., Warrier, A., Aia, M., Min, J., Sichitiu, M.L.: Z-MAC: a hybrid MAC for wireless VOIP networks. In: IEEE/ACM Transactions on Networking, vol. 16, no. 3, pp. 511–524. IEEE Press (2008)
7. Du, S., Saha, A.K., Johnson, D.B.: RMAC: a routing-enhanced duty-cycle MAC protocol for wireless sensor networks. In: 26th Annual IEEE International Conference on Computer Communications, pp. 1193–1201. IEEE Press, Alaska (2007)
8. Yanjun, S., Du, S., Gurewitz, O., Johnson, D.B.: DW-MAC: a low latency, energy efficient demand-wakeup MAC protocol for wireless sensor networks. In: The 9th ACM International Symposium on Mobile Ad Hoc Networking and Computing, pp. 53–62. IEEE Press, Phoenix (2011)
9. Nguyen, K., Meis, U., Yusheng, J.: An energy efficient, high throughput MAC protocol using packet aggregation. In: GLOBECOM Workshops, pp. 1236–1240. IEEE Press (2007)
10. Hull, B., Jamieson, K., Balakrishnan, H.: Mitigating congestion in wireless sensor networks. In: The 2nd International Conference on Embedded Networked Sensor Systems, pp. 134–147. IEEE Press, Maryland (2004)
11. Warrier, A., Janakiraman, S., Ha, S., Rhee, I.: DiffQ: practical differential backlog congestion control for wireless networks. In: The IEEE Computer and Communications Societies, vol. 3, pp. 262–270. IEEE Press, Rio de Janeiro (2009)

ALPS: Adaptive Linear Prediction for Time Synchronization in Wireless Sensor Networks

Yulong Xing[✉], Yongrui Chen[✉], Hao Sun, Weidong Yi, and Chenghua Duan

University of Chinese Academy of Sciences, Beijing 100049, China
xingyulong11@mails.ucas.ac.cn, chenyr@ucas.ac.cn

Abstract. Clock synchronization is a crucial component in wireless sensor networks (WSN). The estimation of synchronization errors in most of the existing time synchronization algorithms is based on some statistical distribution models. However, these models may not be able to accurately describe the synchronization errors due to the uncertainties in clock drift and message delivery delay in synchronization. Considering that the synchronization errors are highly temporally correlated (short-term correlation), in this paper, we present an Adaptive Linear Prediction Synchronization (ALPS) scheme for WSN. By applying linear prediction on synchronization errors and adaptively adjusting predication coefficients based on the difference between the estimated values and the real values, ALPS enhances synchronization accuracy at a relatively low cost. ALPS has been implemented on the Tmote-sky platform. As experiment results demonstrate, compared with RBS and TPSN, ALPS cuts synchronization cost by almost 50 % while achieving the same accuracy; compared with DMTS, ALPS reduces the average value and the MSE (mean square error) of synchronization errors by 38.3 % and 41 % respectively with the same cost.

Keywords: Wireless sensor networks · Time synchronization · Adaptive linear prediction

1 Introduction

Time synchronization is one of the key middle-ware components in wireless sensor networks (WSN) [1]. Many applications and protocols in WSN rely on time synchronization. In low-duty-cycling protocols, time synchronization is essential to guarantee coordinated wakeup/sleep schedule to save energy. In data aggregation and target tracking, temporal correlation can be utilized to eliminate data redundancy, and data gathering time can be used to identify the sequential relations among data collected by different nodes. In TDMA radio scheduling [2], nodes need time information to identify their active slots so that transmission do not interfere with each other. Time synchronization is also indispensable for many localization and security protocols [3,4].

Many time synchronization algorithms have been proposed in recent years. The early time synchronization algorithms, such as RBS [5], TPSN [2], DMTS [6],

© Springer-Verlag Berlin Heidelberg 2015
L. Sun et al. (Eds.): CWSN 2014, CCIS 501, pp. 355–367, 2015.
DOI: 10.1007/978-3-662-46981-1_35

FTSP [7], are all based on timestamp exchanges, which is intended to offset the uncertainties of message delivery delay to enhance the synchronization accuracy. On-Demand Synchronization (ODS) [4] adaptively adjust the synchronization interval for customized accuracy with minimized communication overhead. Leng, M. presents a synchronization scheme under unknown Gaussian distribution aiming at achieving both low computational complexity and high performance [8]. Leng, M. also models the WSN synchronization under exponential delays as a linear programming problem and solves it with a novel low-complexity estimator [9]. In [10], a Kalman filter is used to estimate both clock offset and skew. An improvement on [10] by adopting an adaptive multi-model mechanism is presented in [11]. Jin, M. and Fang, D. studies how voltage influences the clock skew, and proposes a novel voltage-aware time synchronization (VATS) scheme [12].

Most of the existing synchronization schemes assume that the distribution of clock skew and the delivery delay of synchronization packets follow some statistical models (such as Gaussian distribution model in [4,8,11–13], Exponential distribution model in [9,14,15], and Gamma distribution model in [1]). However, the clock drift and message delivery delay are essentially very random and easily affected by some environment factors (such as temperature and voltage). Therefore, they are not easy to be described accurately by any predetermined model [1,16]. Moreover, some algorithms need to calibrate the clock skew frequently (such as [5,7,11,14]). However, as [4] demonstrates, frequent clock skew calibration will not only increase the computation and communication overhead, but also will increase the synchronization errors due to the miscalculation of the message delivery delay.

Linear Prediction is a mathematical operation where future values of a discrete-time signal are estimated as a linear function of previous samples. In digital signal processing, linear prediction is often called linear predictive coding (LPC), and is widely used in speech coding, digital filter and wireless channel estimation. Considering that synchronization errors are highly temporally correlated (as Fig. 3 shows), in this paper, an Adaptive Linear Prediction Synchronization (ALPS) scheme for WSN is proposed. To the best of our knowledge, this is the first work which applies linear prediction into the time synchronization in WSN.

ALPS predicts clock offset based on its historical values. ALPS does not assume the clock offset to follow any particular statistical distribution or need frequent clock skew calibration. As experimental results demonstrate, ALPS has a better performance than DMTS without increasing synchronization cost; ALPS reduces synchronization cost compared to RBS and TPSN while maintaining the same synchronization accuracy.

2   Motivation

In WSN, each node has an independent local clock. Ideally, the clock should satisfy the equation $C(t) = t$, where t stands for the ideal or reference time. However, due to the influence of voltage, temperature and other environmental factors, the clock will drift away from the ideal time. The clock model is illustrated in Fig. 1. In general, the clock function of node i can be modelled as:

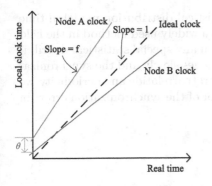

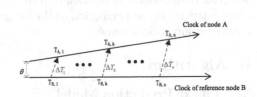

Fig. 1. Clock model of sensor nodes   **Fig. 2.** Synchronization model

$$C_i(t) = \theta + f \cdot t \tag{1}$$

where θ and f are clock offset and clock skew, respectively.

In WSN, offsets exist between clocks of different nodes due to the difference in clock skew and the initial phase. Consider the time synchronization process between node A and node B, where B is the reference node, and A is the node to be synchronized, as illustrated in Fig. 2. Suppose node B sends a message to node A about its clock reading $T_{B,k}$ at node B's local time $T_{B,k}$, and node A receives node B's message at A's local time $T_{A,k}$. Then $T_{A,k}$ and $T_{B,k}$ satisfy the following expression:

$$T_{A,k} = f \cdot T_{B,k} + \theta + \tau \tag{2}$$

where θ and f are the relative clock offset and skew between node A and node B, respectively. τ is the delay of message transmitted from node B to node A.

The goal of time synchronization is to make the clocks of node A and node B the same. In Eq. 2, there are three parameters, f, θ and τ, to be estimated. For f and τ, most of the synchronization schemes first assume that they follow a particular statistical distribution, and then estimate them by some statistical means. For example, the least squares (LS) estimator is applied in [7,16]. In [9,15,17], the parameters are estimated using the maximum likelihood estimator (MLE) and minimum variance unbiased estimator (MVUE), respectively.

However, the delay of the message for synchronization (τ) consists of many components, including send/receive time, access time, transmission/reception time, interrupt time and encoding/decoding time. Among them, the send/receive time, access time and interrupt time are nondeterministic. Although the non-determinacy of the synchronization delay can be reduced by inserting the timestamp at lower layers and appropriate place in the packet [6,7], it can not be eliminated completely. On the other hand, clock skew (f), affected by voltage, temperature and other environment factors [12], exhibits great randomness, and is difficult to be described by any particular statistical model. Moreover, since the randomness of clock skew and synchronization delay are not independent with each other, inappropriate estimation not only can not eliminate the error, but also introduce new errors [4]. Therefore, there are limitations when using a specific statistical distribution model in time synchronization. Linear prediction, however, as a widely used method in the field of random signal estimation, is independent from any special statistical distribution model. Considering that the clock skew changes slowly and the synchronization error samples exhibit high short-term temporal correlation and periodicity, we adopt adaptive linear prediction as the estimator of the synchronization errors in our synchronization scheme.

3 Algorithm

3.1 Linear Prediction Model

The key idea of linear prediction is that if there is temporal correlation between signal samples, we can use past sample values to predict current and future sample values. The sample to be predicted can be closely approximated as a linear combination of past samples. The prediction coefficients are determined by minimizing a certain function of differences between sample values and predicted values.

In the time synchronization model, if we consider the clock offset caused by both clock skew and the synchronization delay as a single variable ΔT_k, $T_{A,k}$ and $T_{B,k}$ satisfy the following expression:

$$T_{A,k} = T_{B,k} + \Delta T_k \tag{3}$$

where ΔT_k is the sum of clock offset caused by clock skew and transmission delay at the Kth synchronization.

In order to examine how the synchronization errors change with time, we implemented several experiments (lasting 24 h, with synchronization interval 2 s, 3 groups) on the Tmote-sky platform. In these experiments, we compensated the clock offset with a fixed value ΔT_k, and recorded all synchronization errors during the testing time. In contiki operating system, the resolution of the clock is 1 tick/30 μs. The synchronization errors over time is shown in Fig. 3, which is similar to [4]. As Fig. 3 demonstrates, in short term (within 30–50 samples), synchronization errors do not vary much (short-term correlation), due to the relatively stable clock skew, where small fluctuations result from rounding in calculation. In long term (interval more than 100–120 samples), synchronization errors become periodical (long-term correlation), due to the effect of varied clock skew.

Considering the patten identified by the above experiment, we can estimate ΔT_k through linear prediction. The basic idea of linear prediction is that ΔT_k can be approximated by its historical values ($\Delta T_{k-1}, \Delta T_{k-2}, \cdots$). We define two symbols: (i) $\hat{\Delta T_k}$, which is the predicted value of ΔT_k; and (ii) e_k, which is the prediction error, i.e. the difference between the real value ΔT_k and the predicted value $\hat{\Delta T_k}$. Then, $\hat{\Delta T_k}$ and e_k can be expressed as:

$$\hat{\Delta T_k} = a_1 \Delta T_{k-1} + \cdots + a_p \Delta T_{k-p} = \sum_{i=1}^{p} a_i \Delta T_{k-i} \tag{4}$$

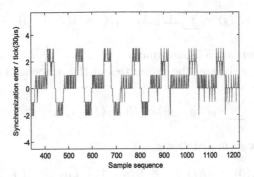

Fig. 3. Synchronization errors over time using a fixed compensation value

$$e_k = \Delta T_k - \hat{\Delta T_k} = \Delta T_k - \sum_{i=1}^{p} a_i \Delta T_{k-i} \tag{5}$$

where $a_i(i = 1, 2, \cdots, p)$ are the prediction coefficients, and p is the prediction order.

3.2 Calculation of the Prediction Coefficient a_i

We use the synchronization Mean Square Error (MSE) to evaluate the synchronization performance. Small MSE indicates high synchronization accuracy [14]. The E_n, which is based on MSE, is defined as follows:

$$E_n = \sum_n e_k^2 = \sum_n \left(\Delta T_k - \hat{\Delta T_k}\right)^2 = \sum_n (\Delta T_k - \sum_{i=1}^{p} a_i \Delta T_{k-i})^2 \tag{6}$$

To minimize E_n, set $\partial E_n / \partial a_i = 0$ $(i = 1, 2, \cdots, p)$, i.e.:

$$\frac{\partial E_n}{\partial a_j} = 2 \sum_n \Delta T_k \Delta T_{k-j} - 2 \sum_{i=1}^{p} a_i \sum_n \Delta T_{k-i} \Delta T_{k-j} = 0 \tag{7}$$

where $j = 1, 2, \cdots, p$.

Equation 7 can be further reduced to the following equation.

$$\sum_n \Delta T_k \Delta T_{k-j} = \sum_{i=1}^{p} a_i \sum_n \Delta T_{k-i} \Delta T_{k-j} \tag{8}$$

Apparently, through solving this equation set, we can obtain all the prediction coefficients $a_i(i = 1, 2, \cdots, p)$ which minimize E_n.

Define $\Phi(i, j)$ and $R(j)$ as follows:

$$\Phi(i, j) = \sum_n \Delta T_{k-i} \Delta T_{k-j}, (i, j = 1, 2, \cdots, p) \tag{9}$$

$$R(j) = \sum_n \Delta T_k \Delta T_{k-j}, (j = 1, 2, \cdots, p) \tag{10}$$

where $R(j)$ is the autocorrelation function of ΔT_k.

Combining Eqs. 8–10 and the properties of the autocorrelation function, we will have:

$$\sum_{i=1}^{p} a_i R(|i - j|) = R(j), (j = 1, 2, \cdots, p) \tag{11}$$

expressed in matrix form as follows:

$$\begin{bmatrix} R(0) & R(1) & \cdots & R(p-1) \\ R(1) & R(0) & \cdots & R(p-2) \\ \vdots & \vdots & \vdots & \vdots \\ R(p-1) & R(p-2) & \cdots & R(0) \end{bmatrix} \begin{bmatrix} a_1 \\ a_2 \\ \vdots \\ a_p \end{bmatrix} = \begin{bmatrix} R(1) \\ R(2) \\ \vdots \\ R(p) \end{bmatrix}$$

The above is called Yule-Walker equations, where the coefficient matrix is a $p \times p$ Toeplitz Matrix in which each descending diagonal from left to right is constant.

We can use Levinson-Durbin recursion algorithm to solve Yule-Walker equations. The Levinson-Durbin recursion algorithm is given as follows [18].

(1) $E_0 = R(0), when\ i = 0$;
(2) Perform recursive calculation with the following formulas:

$$k_i = \frac{R(i) - \sum_{j=1}^{i-1} a_j^{i-1} R(i-j)}{E_{i-1}}, 1 \le i \le p$$

$$a_i^{(i)} = k_i$$

$$a_j^{(i)} = a_j^{i-1} - k_i a_{i-j}^{(i-1)}, 1 \le j \le i-1$$

$$E_i = (1 - k_i^2) E_{i-1}$$

(3) $i = i + 1$. If $i > p$, then go to (4), or return to (2).
(4) The final solution is given as follows:

$$a_j = a_j^{(p)}, 1 \le j \le p$$

3.3   Algorithm Description

ALPS is given as follows. First, a routing tree is established in the network initialization stage, where SINK node acts as its root. SINK node periodically broadcasts synchronization packets, which include timestamp, to the lower levels of the tree. When a child node receives the packet, it extracts the timestamp and calculates the difference (clock offset) between the local clock and the timestamp, and rebroadcasts the synchronization packet only with its own local timestamp.

Table 1. The way to calculate $\hat{\Delta T_k}$

Calculate $\hat{\Delta T_k}$
Inputs: $\Delta T_{k-1}, \Delta T_{k-2}, \cdots, \Delta T_{k-p}$
Output: $\hat{\Delta T_k}$
1: $\Phi(i,j) = f_1(\Delta T_{k-1}, \Delta T_{k-2}, \cdots, \Delta T_{k-p})$
2: $R(j) = f_2(\Delta T_{k-1}, \Delta T_{k-2}, \cdots, \Delta T_{k-p})$
3: $Y - W(P) = f_3(R(j), \Phi(i,j))$
4: $a_1, a_2, \cdots, a_p = f_4(L - D(p))$
5: $\hat{\Delta T_k} = f_5(\Delta T_{k-1}, \Delta T_{k-2}, \cdots, \Delta T_{k-p}, a_1, a_2, \cdots, a_p)$

Then, the child node calculates the prediction coefficients a_i according to previous clock offset samples $\Delta T_{k-1}, \Delta T_{k-2}, \cdots, \Delta T_{k-p}$, as Sect. 3.2 describes. For the first p samples, when estimating ΔT_k ($k = p + 1$), we just set $a_i = 1$ for $i = 1$, and $a_i = 0$ for $i = 2, \cdots, k - 1$. Finally, we substitute a_i ($i = 1, 2, \cdots, p$) and $\Delta T_{k-1}, \Delta T_{k-2}, \cdots, \Delta T_{k-p}$ into Eq. 4 to predict ΔT_k which is further used to calibrate the local clock (Table 1).

ALPS is described as follows:

(1) The child node maintains a FIFO queue which consists of p registers. The previous p clock offset samples are put into the register by the order of $\Delta T_{k-p}, \cdots, \Delta T_{k-2}, \Delta T_{k-1}$;
(2) With Eqs. 9 and 10, $\Phi(i,j)$ and the autocorrelation function $R(j)$ of clock offsets can be calculated;
(3) With $\Phi(i,j)$ and $R(j)$, Yule-Walker equations can be created;
(4) Using Levinson-Durbin iterative algorithm, calculate the prediction coefficients $a_1, a_2, \cdots, a_p$;
(5) Calculate the next clock offset $\hat{\Delta T_k}$ by Eq. 4;
(6) Use $\hat{\Delta T_k}$ for local clock calibration;
(7) When the next synchronization packet arrives, calculate ΔT_k by Eq. 3 according to the node's local time and the timestamp which is extracted from the synchronization packet.
(8) Insert ΔT_k at the end of FIFO queue.

The complexity of ALPS algorithm is analyzed as follows. The most complex part of ALPS is the Levinson-Durbin algorithm. Within the Levinson-Durbin algorithm, the most complicated calculation is resolving the k_i, which requires a nested loop with complexity $O(p^2)$, where p is the prediction order. Therefore, the complexity of the whole ALPS is $O(p^2)$.

4 Performance Evaluation

To evaluate the performance of ALPS, we implemented it in a real test-bed. The hardware platform is Tmote-sky node, which features an msp430 MCU and a cc2420 radio transceiver. Contiki, an open source lightweight embedded operating system, serves as our software platform.

In order to obtain the clock readings of parent nodes and their children nodes at the same time, a pulse signal was sent periodically to these nodes. The nodes recorded and output their clock readings upon receiving the pulse signal. In this way, we could periodically sample the clocks of the synchronization nodes to be tested (Fig. 4).

The experimental scenario is a multi-hop wireless sensor network. The default experiment configuration parameters are given in Table 2.

The experiment is based on tree topology network. Since we are more concerned with the synchronization errors between parent nodes and child nodes, we have only analyzed synchronization performance among parent nodes and their children nodes. The analysis of the synchronization error for the whole network will be in our future work.

Fig. 4. ALPS evaluation with an indoor testbed

Table 2. Experimental configuration

Synchronization model	Master-slave
Number of tests	10
Duration	24 h
Prediction order	3
Number of node pairs	40
Largest hops	7
Synchronization interval	2 s
Skew range	±30 ppm
Synchronization packet length	20 bytes

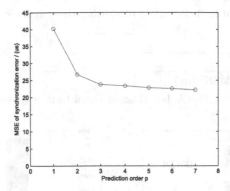

Fig. 5. Relationship between MSE of synchronization errors E_n and prediction order p

4.1   Prediction Order P

From analysis in 3.1 section, we know that synchronization accuracy is highly related to the prediction order p. So we explore the relationship between the MSE E_n and p by experiments. For every value of p within range 1–7, we determine E_n with each test lasting 24 h, and identify the relationship between E_n and p as shown in Fig. 5.

As Fig. 5 demonstrates, E_n declines quickly as p increases when p is small. When $p \geq 3$, the decrease of E_n becomes slow with the increase of p, and gradually becomes trivial. Considering that the limited computing capability of nodes, we have to strike for a balance between the prediction error and the computational complexity. Since E_n changes slightly as p increases when p is greater than 3, and the computational complexity increases as p^2, we set p as 3.

4.2   Comparison Between DMTS and ALPS

We implemented DMTS and ALPS on the Tmote-sky platform. Delay measurement time synchronization (DMTS) is based on the estimation of all delays involved in time synchronization message transfer path, and the delay is calculated by the length and the transmission rate of synchronization packet.

Figure 6 plots the histogram of the synchronization errors of the ALPS and DMTS algorithms, whose results are summarized in Table 3. As shown in Table 3, the average error and the MSE of ALPS decline by 38.3 % and 41 %, respectively, than DMTS. Also, 63 % and 45 % of the synchronization error is no larger than the average error for ALPS and DMTS respectively. This is because DMTS compensates the random synchronization delay with a fixed value, but ALPS takes advantage of short-term correlation of stochastic synchronization errors.

Figure 7 depicts the synchronization errors of ALPS along the timeline for 150 samples (2s per sample). Compared with Fig. 3 (without linear prediction), we can find that in ALPS the variance of errors is smaller, the outliers are less and are more stable.

Table 3. Statistics of synchronization error

	DMTS	ALPS
Average error (μs)	31.34	19.33
Mean Square Error (MSE) (μs)	40.22	23.76
Percentage of time error that is less than or equal to average error	45	63

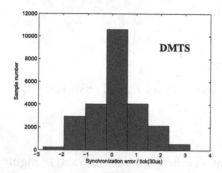 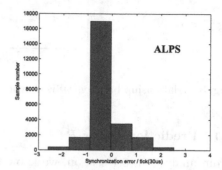

Fig. 6. Histogram of synchronization errors

Through analysis on data of synchronization errors, we can get error distribution falling in different ranges. As demonstrated by Fig. 8, the error distribution of ALPS is more concentrated than DMTS, hence the MSE of ALPS is also smaller than DMTS. 85 % and 70 % of the errors in ALPS and DMTS fall in ±1 tick (30 μs) respectively, almost 100 % of the errors in APLS fall in ±3 tick. This indicates that the distribution of synchronization errors in ALPS is more concentrated, and falls in a smaller range (±1 tick) with a larger probability.

4.3 Synchronization Cost

Since the energy consumption of synchronization mainly arises from the exchanges of synchronization packets (assume the transceiver is turned off when no message is sent or received), we use the number of sending or receiving synchronization packets to approximate the synchronization cost.

Considering the scenario where one reference node and n nodes to be synchronized are within a single broadcast domain, the synchronization costs of different schemes are given in Table 4. In RBS, K denotes the number of reference broadcasts. As K increases, the synchronization error goes down while the energy consumption goes up. According to [2], the average synchronization errors of RBS and TPSN are 29.13 μs and 16.9 μs, respectively. The average synchronization error of ALPS is 19.33 μs, 10 μs smaller than RBS but 2.5 μs greater than TPSN. As Table 4 demonstrates, ALPS has a huge advantage in synchronization cost, which is at least half of both RBS and TPSN. Although ALPS and DMTS share the same synchronization cost, as shown in Table 3,

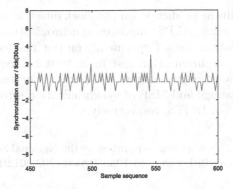

Fig. 7. Synchronization errors of ALPS over time

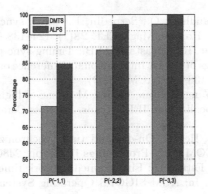

Fig. 8. Distribution of synchronization errors falling into different ranges

Table 4. Comparison of synchronization cost

	ALPS	DMTS	RBS	TPSN
Times of sending	n	n	$K(n+1)$	$2n$
Times of receiving	n	n	$K(n+1)$	$2n$

ALPS has a better performance than DMTS in term of both average and MSE of synchronization error.

In summary, ALPS performs the same with RBS and TPSN in synchronization accuracy with a less cost, and performs better than DMTS at a similar expense. Therefore, when both performance and cost are taken into consideration, APLS performs better than other three synchronization schemes.

5   Conclusion

Considering the high temporal correlation of time synchronization errors, this paper proposes ALPS, a synchronization scheme based on adaptive linear prediction. Through linear prediction on the clock offset, and adaptively adjusting prediction coefficients, ALPS improves synchronization accuracy without increasing synchronization costs. Experiments on the Tmote-sky platform indicate that ALPS cuts synchronization cost by at least half comparing with RBS and TPSN without sacrificing accuracy, and performs better than DMTS with the same cost. The average and MSE of synchronization errors in ALPS decline by 38.3 % and 41 % than DMTS, respectively.

Acknowledgments. This work was supported by the National Science & Technology Pillar Program during the 12th Five-year Plan Period (NO.2012BAJ24B01).

References

1. Yik-Chung, W., Chaudhari, Q., Serpedin, E.: Clock synchronization of wireless sensor networks. Sig. Process. Mag. IEEE **28**(1), 124–138 (2011)
2. Ganeriwal, S., Kumar, R., Srivastava, M.B.: Timing-sync protocol for sensor networks. In: Proceedings of the 1st International Conference on Embedded Networked Sensor Systems, pp. 138–149. ACM (2003)
3. Wang, J., Gao, Q., Wang, H., Yan, Y., Jin, M.: Time-of-flight-based radio tomography for device free localization. IEEE Trans. Wireless Commun. **12**(5), 2355–2365 (2013)
4. Zhong, Z., Chen, P., He, T.: On-demand time synchronization with predictable accuracy. In: INFOCOM, 2011 Proceedings IEEE, pp. 2480–2488. IEEE (2011)
5. Elson, J., Girod, L., Estrin, D.: Fine-grained network time synchronization using reference broadcasts. In: ACM SIGOPS Operating Systems Review, vol. 36(SI), pp. 147–163 (2002)
6. Ping, S.: Delay measurement time synchronization for wireless sensor networks. IRB-TR-03-013, Intel Research Berkeley Lab (2003)
7. Maróti, M., Kusy, B., Simon, G., Lédeczi, Á.: The flooding time synchronization protocol. In: Proceedings of the 2nd International Conference on Embedded Networked Sensor Systems, pp. 39–49. ACM (2004)
8. Leng, M., Yik-Chung, W.: On clock synchronization algorithms for wireless sensor networks under unknown delay. IEEE Trans. Veh. Technol. **59**(1), 182–190 (2010)
9. Leng, M., Yik-Chung, W.: Low-complexity maximum-likelihood estimator for clock synchronization of wireless sensor nodes under exponential delays. IEEE Trans. Signal Process. **59**(10), 4860–4870 (2011)
10. Hamilton, B.R, Ma, X., Zhao, Q., Xu, J.: Aces: adaptive clock estimation and synchronization using kalman filtering. In: Proceedings of the 14th ACM International Conference on Mobile Computing and Networking, pp. 152–162. ACM (2008)
11. Yang, Z., Pan, J., Cai, L.: Adaptive clock skew estimation with interactive multi-model kalman filters for sensor networks. In: 2010 IEEE International Conference on Communications (ICC), pp. 1–5. IEEE (2010)
12. Jin, M., Fang, D., Chen, X., Yang, Z., Liu, C., Xiaoyan, Y.: Voltage-aware time synchronization for wireless sensor networks. Int. J. Distrib. Sens. Netw. **2014**, 13 (2014)
13. Noh, K.-L., Chaudhari, Q.M., Serpedin, E., Suter, B.W.: Novel clock phase offset and skew estimation using two-way timing message exchanges for wireless sensor networks. IEEE Trans. Commun. **55**(4), 766–777 (2007)

14. Leng, M., Wu, Y-C.: On joint synchronization of clock offset and skew for wireless sensor networks under exponential delay. In: Proceedings of the IEEE International Symposium on Circuits and Systems, pp. 461–464. IEEE (2010)
15. Jeske, D.R.: On maximum-likelihood estimation of clock offset. IEEE Trans. Commun. **53**(1), 53–54 (2005)
16. Chen, J., Qing, Y., Zhang, Y., Chen, H.-H., Sun, Y.: Feedback-based clock synchronization in wireless sensor networks: a control theoretic approach. IEEE Trans. Veh. Technol. **59**(6), 2963–2973 (2010)
17. Chaudhari, Q.M., Serpedin, E., Wu, Y-C.: Improved estimation of clock offset in sensor networks. In: IEEE International Conference on Communications, ICC 2009, pp. 1–4. IEEE (2009)
18. Castiglioni, P.: Levinson-durbin algorithm. Encyclopedia of Biostatistics

Routing Algorithm and Transport Protocols in Wireless Sensor Networks

Clustering Routing Protocol Based on Real-Time Constraints in WSNs

Li Ma[✉], Yanan Song, and Dongchao Ma

North China University of Technology, Shijingshan Distrct, Beijing City, China
mali@ncut.edu.cn, connie5@126.com, madongchao@gmail.com

Abstract. In some applications, the requirements for real time data in wireless sensor networks (WSNs) is very high. Thus the interest for real time research is brought. There are many factors affecting the real time of data in WSNs and routing protocol is one of the most important factors. This article proposed a clustering routing protocol based on real-time constraints (CRPRTC) after studying numerous routing protocols of real-time applications. The protocol is designed by combining the priorities of nodes with different types and routing protocols. Through simulation, data transmission delay of CRPRTC is smaller than LEACH protocol, and CRPRTC also can reduce energy consumption and prolong the network's life cycle.

Keywords: WSNs · Real time · Priority · Routing protocol · CRPRTC

1 Introduction

As WSNs are widely applied, real-time scenes often appear, such as fire alarm, real-time control systems, emergency rescue, etc. These applications have high requirements for real-time data. The quality of routing protocols directly affects the data transmission delay, and it becomes a key factor to measure real-time and also the focus of the current study.

LEACH [1] is a low-power adaptive clustering routing protocol but the cluster nodes can only transmit data within a balanced allocation of time slots and the cluster-head communicate directly with the Sink node over one-hop. LEACH-C [2] still did not consider the real-time requirements of the data as well as the occasion of cluster head far from the Sink node. The reference [3] proposed an improved clustering routing algorithm, but it is not applicable for WSNs. TEEN [4] protocol sets soft thresholds and hard thresholds and it is not suitable for wireless sensor networks requiring periodic data collection.

SPEED [5] protocol is a classic soft real-time routing protocol, but it does not prioritize the data packets. As the data rate increases, the real-time of network decreases significantly. The reference [6] is a non-low-power real-time routing protocol, and its drawback is that the data packets have no priority. ARRP [7] is an adaptive real-time routing protocol, without considering the priority of the data packet, and it does not apply to large-scale WSNs with multi-priority and high real-time requirements. The

© Springer-Verlag Berlin Heidelberg 2015
L. Sun et al. (Eds.): CWSN 2014, CCIS 501, pp. 371–379, 2015.
DOI: 10.1007/978-3-662-46981-1_36

reference [8] proposed an opportunistic routing algorithm but its network model is homogeneous, and it really did not take the real-time requirements and priority issues into account.

Due to the characteristics of wireless sensor network, at the situations larger range, large number of nodes, and the energy heterogeneous sensor networks of different types, considering the different real-time requirements of data and energy consumption, a clustering routing protocol based on real-time constraints (CRPRTC) is designed.

2   Network Model

For convenience of discussion, assumptions of WSNs are as follows.

(1)   All of sensor nodes no longer move after deployment in a square region.
(2)   Sink node in a fixed position remotes from the source node S, and the energy of Sink node is not limited.
(3)   The nodes are energy heterogeneous. The initial energy, energy consumption and residual energy are all different.
(4)   Nodes are deployed in line with real-time requirements, and the distance between each node and Sink node is known.
(5)   Sensors monitor different data Types, such as respectively monitoring the temperature and harmful gases. Different priority levels can be set.

The model is shown in Fig. 1.

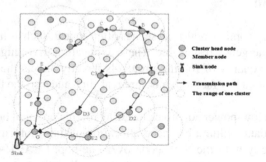

Fig. 1. Network model

In the model, the member nodes in the cluster communicate with the cluster-head node over one-hop. The cluster-head nodes communicate with Sink node through multi-hop and the next hop is optional, for example, the next hop of B can be C, C2 or C3.

3   The Design of the CRPRTC

Based on the above, CRPRTC is designed mainly from clustering algorithm, queue management of cluster-head nodes, route selection among cluster-head nodes.

3.1 The Improved Clustering Algorithm

The clustering algorithm is optimized according to the LEACH algorithm, and improved from cluster head election and stable transmission.

Improved Cluster Head Election. At this stage of the LEACH algorithm, first generate a random real number from 0 to 1 for the nodes never becoming the cluster head. If the random number is less than the threshold T(n) as formula (1) provided by reference [3], the node will become a cluster head in this round.

$$T(n) = \begin{cases} \dfrac{P}{1 - P \cdot \left(r \cdot mod\dfrac{1}{P}\right)} & n \in G \\ 0 & others \end{cases} \tag{1}$$

P is the proportion of cluster head nodes in the network. r is the number of rounds experiencing. G is a set of nodes not becoming the head node in the latest $1/p$ rounds. The improvement is shown as formula (2).

$$T(n) = \begin{cases} \dfrac{P_e}{1 - P_e * \left(r \cdot mod\dfrac{1}{P_e}\right)} & n \in G \cap E_n > E_{T0} \\ 0 & others \end{cases} \tag{2}$$

E_n is the residual energy of node n. E_{T0} stands for threshold of residual energy, and assume the specific value is one third of the initial energy of node. P_e, the optimization of P, is the remaining energy related factors as formula (3).

$$P_e = P * \frac{E_n}{E_{Nave}} \tag{3}$$

E_{Nave} is the average residual energy of all survival nodes. Reality, it is difficult to achieve to know the real-time residual energy of each node, and E_{Nave} is an estimated value calculated according to the number of communication rounds, and this has no effect on the performance of algorithm. The initial total energy of N nodes is E_{Ninit}. The lifetime of the network is T and the network boot time is t. After t, there are formula (4) and (5).

$$E_{Nave} = \frac{1}{N} E_{Ninit} \frac{T - t}{T} \tag{4}$$

$$T = \frac{E_{Ninit}}{E_{each}} \tag{5}$$

E_{each} is the communication energy consumption of each round as formula (6) according to reference [9].

$$E_{each} = 2kNE_{elec} + km_{clu}\varepsilon_{mp}d_{CS_{ink}}{}^4 + kN\varepsilon_{fs}d_{OC}{}^2 \tag{6}$$

$d_{CS_{ink}}$ is the average distance of the cluster head and Sink. d_{OC} is the average distance of the general node and the cluster head.

Improved Stable Transmission in the Cluster. According to the network model, data packets from different sensors have different priority and real-time requirements. Each data collected by each type of sensor need to be also divided into two levels, high priority data over the setting value to alarm and low priority data down the setting value.

(1) According to different node types and the real-time requirements, set multiple priorities mixed communication strategy combining clock-driven and event-driven ways. The clock-driven way is sending a packet every $n\tau$, and the event-driven way is sending a packet every τ. Improvement is as shown in Fig. 2 and the order of priority is S1> S2> S3> S4.

Types of data	Threshold	Relationship of the value of monitoring data and the threshold	The way of driver	Time interval	
Important data	b_{t1}	monitoring data > b_{t1}	Event driver	τ	S1
		monitoring data < b_{t1}	Time driver	$n\tau$	S3
General data	b_{t2}	monitoring data > b_{t2}	Event driver	τ	S2
		monitoring data < b_{t2}	Time driver	$n\tau$	S4

Fig. 2. Other settings of data types, threshold, priority, etc

(2) Improve the TDMA slot allocation mechanism. At the stage of stable transmission, LEACH algorithm uses equilibrium TDMA time slot allocation strategy. Suppose nodes are all marked the best delay threshold at the time of production and the unit of delay is second. Assume the best delay thresholds of important data and general data are t_1 and t_2, and $t_1 < t_2$. The data transmission rate of member nodes is the same as v. Improved TDMA slot assignment process is shown in Fig. 3.

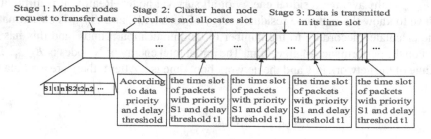

Fig. 3. Improved TDMA slot assignment process

Stage 1: Member nodes request to transfer data.

Member nodes send messages containing data transmission delay and the best priority threshold value, and cluster head node records the number of nodes with the same type and priority. The result recorded by cluster head is shown in Fig. 4.

Priority of data	The transmission delay threshold of data	The number of nodes
S1	t_1	n_1
S2	t_2	n_2
S3	t_1	n_3
S4	t_2	n_4

Fig. 4. The result recorded by cluster head

Stage 2: Cluster head node calculates and allocates slot.

The node with smaller delay threshold gets greater time slot and the proportion relationship is as formula (7). k stands for k node types, here k = 2.

$$pt_j = \frac{t_1 * t_2 \cdots \cdots t_k}{t_j} = \frac{\prod_{i=1}^{i=k} t_i}{t_j} \tag{7}$$

Combined with the number of each type nodes and total duration T of each rotation expected, slot value of each type nodes can be calculated, as shown in formula (8).

$$Tt_j = \frac{T}{pt_1 * N_1 + pt_2 * N_2 + \cdots pt_k * N_k} * pt_j = \frac{T * pt_j}{\sum_{i=1}^{i=k} pt_i * N_i} \tag{8}$$

N_i is the number of each type nodes, and there are only N_1 and N_2 at this time. There are two equations, $N_1 = n_1 + n_3$, $N_2 = n_2 + n_4$.

The transmission time slot of nodes with high priority THt_j is m times as big as the transmission time slot of nodes with low priority TLt_j, as shown in formula (9).

$$THt_j = mTLt_j, \quad m > 1 \tag{9}$$

$$THt_j * n_H + TLt_j * n_L = Tt_j \tag{10}$$

In formula (10), n_H is the number of nodes with high priority, and n_L is the number of nodes with low priority. If j=1, there are $n_H = n_1$, $n_L = n_3$ or $n_H = n_2$, $n_L = n_4$. Then get the transmission time slot of each node in one type of nodes.

3.2   The Queue Management of Cluster-Head Nodes

Each packet needs to be inserted into the corresponding position of the pretest sending queue. Then the high-priority packet will be sent as soon as possible in order to reduce the queuing delay. So the CRPRTC uses scheduling strategy of packet based on priority. The higher the priority of the packet closer to the front of the queue is, the easier the packet is to be sent. In order to prevent the tail packets of the queue waiting forever, the remaining time of packets needs to be subtracted ΔT after every ΔT.

3.3   The Route Selection among Cluster-Head Nodes

The set of neighbor nodes of cluster-head B is located in the circle, whose radius is $R = d_{BR}$, standing for radio radiation distance of B. The next hop candidate node set of B is located in the intersection of two circles, one radius is R, and another is d_{BSink} standing for the Euclidean distance between B and Sink. According to t_{rem} standing for remaining transmission time of B to send data packets and d_{BSink}, the current default transmission rate Sp_{BSink} can be calculated as shown in formula (11).

$$Sp_{BSink} = \frac{d_{BSink}}{t_{rem}} \tag{11}$$

According to the transmission delay t_{BC} of B to the candidate node C and the Euclidean distance d_{CSink} between C and Sink, the actual transmission rate Sp_{BC} of B to C can be calculated as formula (12).

$$Sp_{BC} = \frac{d_{BSink} - d_{CSink}}{t_{BC}} \tag{12}$$

When there is more than one candidate node to satisfy the above conditions, the forwarding fitness of C is shown in formula (13) according to reference [10].

$$\theta_{BC} = \frac{PDR_{BC} * |Sp_{BSink} - Sp_{BC}|}{d_{BSink} - d_{BC}} * \frac{(E_{Crem})^\alpha * (1 - P_{Cerr})^\beta}{E_{T_x}(k, d_{BC}) + E_{R_x}(k, d_{BC})}, \quad \alpha, \ \beta \in (0, 1) \tag{13}$$

PDR_{BC} is packet delivery ratio from B to C. E_{Crem} means the remaining energy of C. P_{Cerr} is packet loss rate. $\alpha \& \beta$ are the relevant parameters. $E_{T_x}(k, d_{BC})$ means the energy consumption of B to send a k-bit message packet to C and $E_{R_x}(k, d_{BC})$ means the energy consumption of C receive a k-bit message packet from B. The implementation process of route selection among cluster-head nodes is shown in Fig. 5.

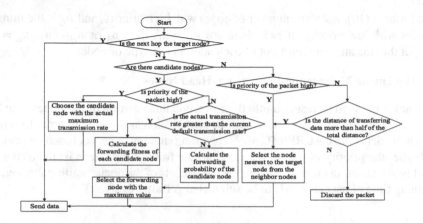

Fig. 5. The implementation process of route selection

4 Experimental Simulation and Analysis

This paper mainly carries on the simulation analysis using NS2 and Mat lab. Figure 6 gives the main parameters of the experimental simulation. It is considered that a packet, 16B, can be transferred completely in the transmission slot. The number of nodes is N, and it is variable or a fixed value, equal to 400. Maximum communication radius is defined as 25m and communication radius is generally less than 25m in CRPRTC.

Routing protocol	LEACH and CRPRTC
MAC layer protocol	802.11b
Wireless transmission model	TwoRayGround
Antenna model	Omnidirectional antenna
Packet Size	16B
Node Bandwidth	250Kb/s
Simulation area /m²	(0,0)-(300,300)
Location of Sink	(0,0)
Node layout	Low-energy nodes are distributed randomly, while high-energy nodes are placed manually
The number of nodes	N
Maximum communication radius	25m
Initial energy	Two kinds, 5J and 10J
Node Type	Two types, A collecting important data and B collecting general data
Packet priority	Four levels, S1,S2,S3,S4

Fig. 6. The parameters of simulation

From Fig. 7, the more the nodes are, the better the effect of reducing the average delay of CRPRTC is. If the number of nodes is less, delay of CRPRTC is greater because CRPRTC increases the computational complexity of cluster. Otherwise, the average delay of CRPRTC is significantly less.

Figure 8 illustrates that the transmission delay of important data is significantly less than that of the general data and the higher the priority of data packet is, the smaller the transmission delay is. Because an important data packet with high priority can be transmitted to the cluster head rapidly in a greater transmission slot and it can be inserted in front of the general packets with low priority and sent preferentially when queuing in the cluster head node.

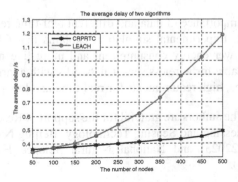

Fig. 7. The average delay

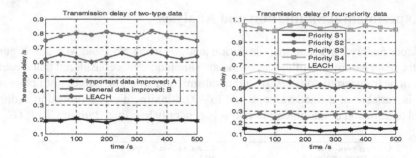

Fig. 8. Transmission delay of data

Figure 9 shows that the energy consumption of CRPRTC is lower than that of LEACH and the number of survival nodes of CRPRTC is more than LEACH. Because the cluster head, elected according to the residual energy, send packets to Sink over multi-hop and nodes collect data in a clock-driven and event-driven combination and send data to the forwarding nodes with more residual energy.

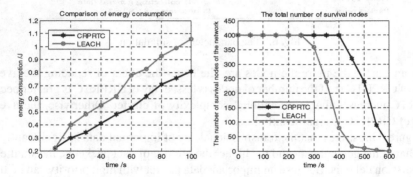

Fig. 9. Energy consumption and survival nodes

5   Conclusion

In this paper, for the importance of data and different real-time requirements for data, CRPRTC is designed. Experimental simulation explains that CRPRTC has smaller transmission delay, lower energy consumption, and more live nodes than LEACH. CRPRTC is more suitable for wireless sensor networks with a large number of nodes, different types of nodes, high requirements for real-time and low power consumption.

Acknowledgments. The authors are grateful for the support of Research Lab of Distributed Information Processing and Sensing Technology, Beijing Natural Science Foundation (4132026, 4122023) and National Natural Science Foundation of China (61300171, 61371143).

References

1. Heinzelman, W., Chandrakasan, A., Balakrishnan, H.: Energy efficient communication protocol for wireless micro sensor networks. J. IEEE Comput. Soc. **16**, 3005–3014 (2007)
2. Heinzelman, W., Chandrakasan, A., Balakrishnan, H.: An application specific protocol architecture for wireless microsensor networks. J. IEEE Trans. Wirel. Commun. **1**(4), 660–670 (2009)
3. Zhang, D.Y., Xu, S.Y., Gao, H.: Research and improvement on LEACH algorithm for internet of things. J. Sichuan Univ. Sci. Eng. (Nat. Sci. Ed.) **25**(2), 35–38 (2012)
4. Manjeshwar, A., Agrawal, D.P.: TEEN: a routing protocol for enhanced efficiency in wireless sensor networks. J. IEEE. **21**(11), 48–53 (2001)
5. Tian, H., Stankovic, J.: SPEED: a stateless protocol for real-time communication in sensor networks. In: 12th IEEE International Conference on Distributed Computing Systems, pp. 181-186. IEEE Computer Society, Rhode Island (2003)
6. Ali, A., Latiff, L.A., Sarijari, M.A., et al.: Real-time routing in wireless sensor networks. In: 28th IEEE International Conference on Distributed Computing Systems Workshops, ICDCS 2008, pp. 114-119 (2008)
7. Wei, Z.C., Yang, S.R.: A kind of adaptive real-time wireless sensor network routing protocol. Chin. J. Sci. Instrum. **32**(12), 237–240 (2011)
8. Ding, N., Tan, G.Z., You, D., Zhang, W.: Opportunistic routing algorithm based on topological time-varying and residual-energy balance in wireless sensor network. J. Electron. Inf. Technol. **35**(3), 715–720 (2013)
9. Mazinani, S.M., Naderi, A., Setoodefar, M. et al.: An energy-efficient real-time routing protocol for differentiated data in wireless sensor networks. In: 17th IEEE International Conference on Engineering of Complex Computer Systems, pp. 302–307. IEEE Press, New York (2012)
10. Ahmed, A.A.: An enhanced real-time routing protocol with load distribution for mobile wireless sensor networks. J. Comput. Netw. **57**(6), 1459–1473 (2013)

Message Forwarding Scheme for Multi-area Opportunistic Network Based on Message Significance

Shaoqing Han, Jian Shu[✉], Na Guo, and Limin Sun

Internet of Things Technology Institute, Nanchang Hangkong University,
Nanchang 330063, China
shaoqinghan@gmail.com, shujian@nchu.edu.cn, naitry@sina.com,
sunlimin@is.iscas.ac.cn

Abstract. In multi-area opportunistic network, the source can not communicate directly with the destination. An efficient low-delay routing algorithm, named message forwarding scheme for multi-area opportunistic network based on message significance (MFSMS) is proposed to solve the issue of long delay. It sorts the node buffer messages based on the level of message significance, and puts them to the message queue. Then it selects the higher forwarding probability node based on probability matrix to exchange message. Through the analysis of experiment results, the algorithm improves message delivery ratio and network resources utilization and decreases the message delay.

Keywords: Multi-area opportunistic network · Message significance · Message queue

1 Introduction

Wireless devices become more and more cheaper. The short distance wireless communicating intelligent devices have been used widely. The mass of solutions are applied to IEEE 802.11, Bluetooth and RFID. The ON (Opportunistic Networks) [1] is developing gradually under those backgrounds. Due to the movement of nodes, sparse nodes and stumbling block such as mountains, buildings, etc., ON does not exist a fully connected path between source and destination. As a result, the protocols of traditional MANET (Mobile Ad hoc Network) could not directly run in such network. In the opportunistic networks, the exchange of message between nodes relies on which one node move into the communication range of another. Despite of longer delay, it is still applied to the remote mountains and severe surroundings for lower cost.

J. Shu—S. Han and J. Shu are with the Internet of Things Technology Institute, Nanchang Hangkong University, Nanchang, 330063, China. N. Guo is with the Unicom Xingye communication technology Co, Beijing, 100005, China. L. Sun is with the State Key Laboratory of Information Security, Institute of Software, The Chinese Academy of Sciences, Beijing, 100190, China.

L. Sun et al. (Eds.): CWSN 2014, CCIS 501, pp. 380–392, 2015.
DOI: 10.1007/978-3-662-46981-1_37

To multi-area opportunistic network which the short wireless communication devices that people carry make up, the movement of people is social and regular. In reality, if people want to go to somewhere, they will choose the shortest path, rather than the classical RW (Random Walk) and RWP (Random Waypoint) model. People tend to live in an interdependent steady area and move together sometimes, which form some different areas. People meet frequently in an area.

The next section describes related work. Then this paper defines multi-area opportunistic network model in Sect. 3. The Sect. 4 presents routing protocol. The experimental results and comparable analysis are given in Sect. 5. The last section summarizes this work and looks far ahead into the future work.

2   Related Work

Most of classical routing protocols implement communications between nodes based on the store-carry-forward pattern. Vahdat and Becker present early the epidemic routing scheme based on the traditional flooding theory [2]. Every node maintains a message vector, nodes exchange the different message when they encounter to achieve message delivery. 2-Hop algorithm has been proposed in [3]. Source copies message to the N encountering nodes, and they forward message to the destination in the movement. Since epidemic routing is easy to cause the network storm, Spyropoulos et al. present SW (Spray and Wait) [4] protocol. SW focuses on controlling the number of message copy to N in network. It divides mainly into two steps. Firstly, source forwards message to the node meets early, and they complete the remaining N-2 copies and stop forwarding when the number of copy reaches N. Secondly, the N nodes forward message until they encounter the destination. The experiments show that this algorithm improves the message delivery ratio and decreases the message delay. Taking into account of the passive waiting step in SW, SF (Spray and Focus) scheme [5] optimizes the second step. It forwards message to the more efficient node. The simulations indicate that performance of SF is better than SW on message delivery ratio and average delay.

Due to the fact that the short distance wireless portable intelligent communicating devices move as people do. Anders Lindren et al. [6] speculate the node encounter probability through analyzing the historical information of nodes move, and use it to improve the performance of routing protocol. Then, PROPHET (Probabilistic Routing Protocol using History of encounters and Transitivity) is presented. Node maintains an encounter probability vector, and updates the encounter probability when two nodes meet. Nodes exchange the different message based on the encounter probability. It could avoid unnecessary message copying. The simulation results show that PROPHET deliveries more messages than epidemic routing and improves the latency. According to the historical information, CSAMT (Connection Status Aware Message Transmission) [7] creates a dynamic temporal graph matrix to estimate the connection status and chooses the overhead, delay, and delivery ratio as the optimizing parameters, based on which select the relay node to forward. The experiments indicate that it improves network overhead. Zhang Zhen-Jing et al. propose CS-DTN (Clustering Social Delay Tolerant

Network) routing protocol [8], which divides nodes into different clusters based on encounter probability. It adopts SW algorithm in cluster and controls the number of message copy. The simulations show that CS-DTN improves the network performance on message delivery ratio, latency and overhead, increases the message delivery ratio and decreases the message delay compared with PROPHET.

The movement of nodes has social attribute in community-based opportunistic network. Niu Jianwei, Sun Limin et al. present CMTS (Message Transmission Scheme for Community-based Opportunistic Network) [9] that divides nodes into some communities based on WNA (Newmans Weighted Network Analysis), which communicate with the active node. During the movement of nodes, nodes choose the active node as relay. The simulation results show that the message delivery ratio of CMTS is superior to SW protocol. Niu Jianwei et al. propose PreS scheme [10] which establishes an adaptive Markov mobile model according to the process of nodes move. It forwards message to the node has higher probability to reach the destination. The simulations indicate that it improves overhead of network. A cross regional model is presented by Jiang Haitao et al. [11]. The network is divided into some vertical and horizontal areas that communicate with the messenger. As the number of delivered message is less in vehicular opportunistic networks, Cai Qingsong, Niu Jianwei, Liu chang propose ACS (Adaptive Copy and Spread) protocol [12] that forwards message based on dynamic parameters of buses and controls the number of message copy and deletes the delivered message. The simulations indicate that it improves the performance in the message delivery ratio, message delay and overhead. A city village model is raised by Li Yun et al. [13]. The network is combined of city and village that transfer message through scheduling path of ferry. The experiments show that message delay of the algorithm is shorter than the message delay of transferring message by area node. Liu Yahong et al. [14] present a parameter of the social relation strength, based on which the protocol divides dynamically the network into some communities. The protocol forwards message through the node with higher social relation strength and controls the number of message copy. The simulations show that network performance is better than PROPHET and SW.

To the point how to improve the efficiency of message transmission, this paper proposes MFSMS protocol that sorts node buffer messages according to the message significance, based on which node forwards message.

3   Multi-area Opportunistic Network Model

3.1   Network Model

In reality, people often live in a relative fixed area such as college that students shuttle, or stay among dormitory, canteen, library and teaching buildings. Similarly, teachers go back and forth among different campuses, home and supermarkets. Students and teachers move regularly among those gathering place, so MFSMS could conjecture the probability where they will move in the next moment according to their habits and customs information. It can be used to

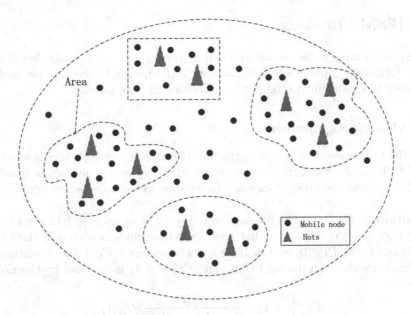

Fig. 1. Multi-area opportunistic network model

transfer message. This paper abstracts similar living areas as network model in Fig. 1. Mobile node is the portable wireless communicating devices. Active node is the node go back and forth among different areas. Hot is the place mobile nodes move frequently to. Different areas transfer message through the active node that go back and forth among different areas.

Definition 1. The multi-area opportunistic network can be described as a directed graph, $G = (V, A, H)$, where V is the network nodes set, $V = \{v_1, v_2, \cdots, v_n\}(n > 1)$, A is the area set, $A = \{a_1, a_2, \cdots, a_c\}(c > 1)$, H is the hot set, $H = \{h_1, h_2, \cdots, h_d\}(d \geq 2c)$. To $\forall v_n$, $\exists!a_c$ let $v_n \in a_c$. To $\forall h_d$, $\exists!a_c$ let $h_d \in a_c$.

3.2 Model Hypothesis

In order to make multi-area opportunistic network model more realistic, the paper gives the following hypothesis.

- Every area have two hot at least.
- Message is transmitted by one hop or multiple hop.
- Mobile node can send any message to other nodes.
- It takes the shortest path mobile mode in area and among areas.
- Mobile node leaves and returns its area by a certain probability.
- Mobile node will randomly stay a moment when it moves to a place.
- Mobile node will randomly choose one area as destination when it leaves its area.

4   MFSMS Routing

MFSMS sorts node buffer messages based on the level of the message significance before forwarding, and selects the node with the higher forwarding probability according to forwarding probability matrix to exchange message.

4.1   Message Significance

With the transmission of message, the number of new message copy is less than the old. To make the new message reach the destination as far as possible, MFSMS controls the order of message forwarding based on message significance.

Definition 2. $Pr_i^m(t)$ is the message significance of message m to node i in the time t slot, $p_{ij}(t)$ is the probability that node i encounters node j in the t time slot. When $t = 0$, $Pr_0^m(0) = 1.0$. If node i encounters node j and transmission happens between them during t time slot, $Pr_j^m(t + 1)$ is updated by the Eq. 1.

$$Pr_j^m(t+1) = \frac{p_{ij}(t)}{1 - (1 - p_{ij}(t))^2} Pr_i^m(t) \tag{1}$$

Every message owns a message significance value. If the value of message is higher, it will be superior to other messages. This paper initializes message significance to Pr_0 when nodes generate message. When message m has been forwarded from node i to node j, this protocol will calculate message significance value by the Eq. 1.

The first equation shows that message significance value of message m will go down when m is forwarded between node i and node j. In other words, the message significance will reduce when the amount of message copy increase. Message significance will be calculated by the first equation when forwarding happens between nodes.

4.2   Update Forward Probability Matrix

This paper assumes there exists N nodes, every node maintain a forwarding probability matrix $P(N \times N)$ about the t time slot. $p_{ij}(t)$ is the probability that node i encounters node j in the t time slot.

At the beginning of t_0 the $p_{ij}(t)$ is initialized to $P_0(P_0 \in [0,1])$. The $p_{ij}(t)$ of the next time slot depends on whether node i met node j in the last time slot. If node i met node j, the protocol will update the $p_{ij}(t)$ by the Eq. 2.

$$p_{ij}(t+1) = p_{ij}(t) + (1 - p_{ij}(t)) \times \theta \tag{2}$$

where θ is the impact factor of encounter probability ($\theta \in (0,1)$), $p_{ij}(t)$ is the probability that node i meet node j in the time slot. The Eq. 2 infers that if node i met node i in the time slot t, the probability node i encounters node j will go up. During the time slot t, if node i didn't meet node j, it would calculate the $p_{ij}(t)$ by Eq. 3.

$$p_{ij}(t+1) = p_{ij}(t) \times \varepsilon \qquad (3)$$

where $\varepsilon \in (0,1)$ is the impact factor. The equation indicates that if node i didn't encounter node j in the last time slot, the p_{ij} would be smaller than before. It updates the p_{ij} by the Eq. 4 when node i met node j and node j encountered node k, but node i didn't encounter node k in the time slot t. Where $\delta \in (0,1)$ is the impact factor.

$$p_{ik}(t+1) = p_{ik}(t) + (1 - p_{ik}(t)) \times p_{ij}(t) \times P_{jk}(t) \times \delta \qquad (4)$$

4.3 Forwarding Algorithm

In multi-area opportunistic network, there does not exist a complete path among nodes, so message is stored in node buffer when node is temporarily unavailable to others. Whether node forwards message m of the sorting message queue or not is depended on the following algorithm when nodes encounter each other. This paper assumes that every node has a sorting message queue Q. Q_i is the sorting message queue of node i. It will run the algorithm 1 if node i encounters node j in the time slot t.

Algorithm 1. Message forwarding algorithm

```
Node_ID(Input)
{Assuming node i encounters node j in the time slot t.}
    var
      Node_ID: i,j;
    Begin
      Calculate_Encounter_Probability(i,j);
      Update_Matrix(i,j);
        IF !Compare_Queue(i,j)
          Exchange_Message(i,j);
          Calculate_Message_Significance(i,j);
          Update_Message_Significance(i,j);
          Sort_Message_Queue(i,j);
    End
```

If nodes encounter each other, the algorithm updates firstly probabilistic matrix and message significance. Then it sorts node buffer message based on message significance in descending order, and puts them to message queue. It chooses the node with the higher forwarding probability to forward message according to the message queue. In the period of forwarding, if node buffer has not enough room, it will delete the message that TTL is zero. Then, if it is still not enough when message queue has not the message whose TTL is zero, the algorithm will delete the tail message until it could store the message m. If transmission happens between nodes, it calculates message significance by formula 1, and updates message significance.

5   Simulation Results

5.1   Simulation Environment

To evaluate the performance of MFSMS, this paper adopts opportunistic Network simulation ONE (Opportunistic Network Environment), which can simulate real network environment based on the discrete simulation engine. It realizes many functions such as nodes move, communicating, routing, message handle, observing real time simulation through GUI. ONE integrates classical routing protocols and move model in opportunistic networks. This paper initializes P_0 to 0.75, time slot to 30 s. The hots in every area is defined as POI (Point of Interest) of PROPHET default configuration file. The probability that node leaves its area and back uses the first table in [6]. The Table 1 shows the impact factors of encounter probability.

Due to the encounter probability based on whether nodes met each other, let the network run about 1000 s. The detailed parameters of simulation environment are setted as the Table 2.

5.2   Result Analysis

In the section, it would like to compare the performance of MFSMS with Random/FIFO Mode of PROPHET on message delivery ratio, network resources

Table 1. Impact Factor

Parameter	Value
θ	0.75
ε	0.25
δ	0.98

Table 2. Main Simulation Parameters

Parameter	Value
SimulationTime (s)	43200
WorldSize (width, highth:m)	4500, 3400
Number of community	4
Number of in node	126
TransmitSpeedLow (kB/s)	250
TransmitSpeedHigh (M/s)	10
MessageTtlDefault (s)	300
Message size (kB)	500–1000
Mininum speed (m/s)	0.5
Maximum speed (m/s)	13.9

Table 3. Different buffer sizes vs the impact of message delay

Buffer(M)\Protocols	PROTPHT FIFO	MFSMW	PROPHET Random
5	4158.8360	4060.7504	3932.6741
10	4350.6163	4155.0539	4220.3850
15	4484.7434	4440.4061	4502.9437
20	4768.2443	4858.2812	4693.6769
25	4961.3888	5088.6732	4901.3285
30	5174.4810	5092.7641	5096.4502
35	5300.4638	5326.1729	5377.0123
40	5652.2791	5512.9237	5537.8031
45	5714.6070	5715.0651	5617.1201
50	5821.3949	5810.1534	5834.1610
100	6152.1043	6073.2216	6091.5373

utilization and the message delay. The message delivery ratio means that the percentage of message that has reached the destination to the number of message that network has created. This paper evaluates network resource utilization from the point of overhead. Message delay is the average time of message that has arrived at the destination.

5.2.1 Different Buffer Size vs The Impact of Message Delay

In the scenario, communication range is 10 m and TTL is 300 s. The Table 3 shows that the buffer size impacts message average delay. It is easy to see that as the buffer size increases, so does the message average delay, which is caused by the method of calculating the message average delay. With the increasing of the buffer space, the message is delivered in the original buffer space could be still delivered, and other messages would be stored more longer than before, so affecting the message average delay. Looking at the Table 3, it could be found that the average delay of MFSMS is slightly shorter than PROPHET FIFO mode on some buffer size. It is reasonable that MFSMS forwards message according to message queue. The algorithm sorts node buffer message based on message significance, and puts them to message queue. New message has a high message significance value, it could preferentially be forwarded. The old messages that creates many copies will be postponed. As can be seen there, the PROPHET Random mode is better than other two protocols. The reason is that it does not deal with node buffer message, hence, it saves much network energy.

5.2.2 Different Communication Range vs The Impact of Message Delay

The experiment is done in the scenario, buffer size is 10 M, message TTL is 300 s. The Table 4 depicts the message delay of PROPHET FIFO/Random mode and

Table 4. Different communication ranges vs the impact of message delay

Range(m)\Protocols	PROTPHT FIFO	MFSMW	PROPHET Random
5	5811.7934	5659.0410	5692.9396
10	4350.6163	4155.0539	4220.385
15	3249.5103	3216.7033	3188.7109
20	2618.8920	2691.0811	2705.3657
25	2398.7321	2372.1222	2391.8323
30	2145.1231	2102.7613	2131.7673
35	2049.4832	2009.2037	2087.0769
40	1960.3375	1936.8244	1897.3246
45	1930.2375	1940.1905	1847.6985
50	1831.1197	1863.8401	1898.5359
100	1421.9005	1402.0086	1404.2531

MFSMS in different communication ranges. It is easy to see there, as the communication range of node increases, the message delay decreases. The reason is that with the increasing of communication range, the probability node encounter other nodes including the destination will increase, so it decreases the message delay. As can be seen there, the message delay of MFSMS is slightly shorter than PROPHET FIFO mode when the communication range of node less than 40 m, but the two protocols have the almost the same message delay when the communication range of node is greater than 40 m. It is because that the increasing of communication range has an effect on message delay, which offsets the advantages of MFSMS message queue mode.

5.2.3   Different TTL vs The Impact of Protocol Performance

The section analyses the performance of PROPHET FIFO/Random mode and MFSMS in message delivery ratio, network resource utilization and message delay in the scenario that node buffer size is 20M and communication range is 10 m, 25 m.

The Fig. 2 depicts message delivery ratio of PROPHET FIFO/Random mode and MFSMS in different message TTLs. It shows that MFSMS is nearly same to PROPHET FIFO mode on message delivery ratio when TTL is less than 3 h. However, as message TTL increases, it is easy to find that message delivery ratio of MFSMS is greater than PROPHET FIFO mode in the Fig. 2a. The reason is that MFSMS forwards message based on message significance. As a result, the new message is prior to the message that has many copies, which avoids the happening of unnecessary copy, so it decreases message delay and improves message delivery ratio. The less superiority can be seen in the Fig. 2b. The reason is that as communication range increases, the probability node encounter others will go up, meanwhile, the number of message in buffer will increase. As a result

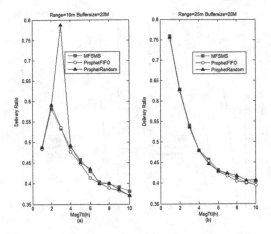

Fig. 2. Different TTLs vs the impact of message delivery ratio

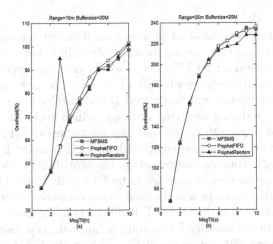

Fig. 3. Different TTLs vs the impact of network overhead

the scheme of sorting node buffer message will consume more network resources. It can been seen that delivery ratio of Fig. 2b is greater than Fig. 2a. It is because that with the increasing of communication range, the probability node encounter others will go up, and the number of message in buffer will increase. The scheme of sorting node buffer message based on message significance is benefited to delivery ratio. Figure 2 shows that the PROPHET Random mode is better than MFSMS. It is because that Random mode does nothing to node buffer message. As can been seen from Fig. 2, the Random mode runs unsteadily, especially TTL is 3 h in the Fig. 2a. It is easy to see that message delivery ratio decreases with the increasing of message TTL from the Fig. 2. The reason is that when message TTL increases, message will stay more longer in network, which will consume more network resources.

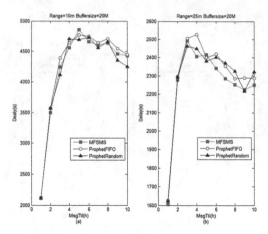

Fig. 4. Different TTLs vs the impact of message delay

The Fig. 3 depicts overhead of protocol on different message TTLs. From Fig. 3a, it is easy to see that the overhead of MFSMS is lower than PROPHET FIFO mode. The reason is that MFSMS forwards message based message significance and deletes firstly message whose TTL is zero. Then, the message with the lowest message significance will be deleted if node buffer has not enough room to store the message during receiving message, which avoid the transmission of worthless message. Figure 3b shows that the advantage of MFSMS in network resource utilization is not obvious compared with FIFO mode. It is because that with the increasing of communication range, the probability node encounter others will go up, so the number of message in buffer will increase. Then, the scheme of sorting node buffer message will consume some network resource. As can been seen there, the overhead of PROPHET Random is lower than others. It is the reason that the order of message forwarding is random. As a result, the Random mode performs unsteadily, especially, TTL is 3 h in the Fig. 3a. As can be seen from the Fig. 3, overhead increases with the increasing of message TTL. It is because when message TTL increases, message will stay more longer in network, which will consume more network resources.

The Fig. 4 depicts the message delay of protocols in different TTLs. It can been seen that the message delay of MFSMS is shorter than PROPHET FIFO mode in the Fig. 4. It is because that MFSMS sorts node buffer message based on message significance. As a result, it makes new message superior to the old message in the order of forwarding. From the Fig. 4a–b, it could clearly see that the advantage of MFSMS is more obvious when communication range increases. The message delay of Fig. 4b is more shorter than Fig. 4a. The reason is that with the increasing of communication range, the probability node encounter others will go up, the number of message in buffer will increase, MFSMS sorts node buffer message according to the message significance.

6   Conclusions

To improve the efficiency of message transmission in the multi-area opportunistic network, this paper proposes the protocol that message forwarding scheme for multi-area opportunistic network based on message significance. It controls the order of message forwarding based on message significance, and transfers message according to the forwarding probability matrix. The simulation results show that MFSMS improves the network performance on the message delivery ratio, network resources utilization and average delay. Since communicating range, message transmission rate and node buffer size are same in area, which appears with a low probability in real life scenario. Considering about those factors, the next work will examine and optimize the performance of MFSMS to make it more applicable.

Acknowledgments. Thanks for the men who give sincere suggestion to the paper. This paper is supported by the National Natural Science Foundation of China (Grant No.61363015, No.61262020), Aeronautical Science Foundation of China (2012ZC56006), and Key Project of Research Program of Jiangxi province (CB-20112038).

References

1. Yongping, X., Limin, S., et al.: Opportunistic networks (In Chinese). J. J. Softw. **20**(1), 124–137 (2009)
2. Becker VD.: Epidemic routing for partially connected ad hoc networks. Technical report, CS-2000-06, Department of of Computer Science, Duke University, Durham, NC (2000)
3. Grossglauser, M., Tse, D.N.C.: Mobility increases the capacity of ad hoc wireless networks. J. IEEE/ACM Trans. Networking **10**(4), 477–486 (2002)
4. Spyropoulos T, Psounis K, Raghavendra CS.: Spray and wait: an efficient routing scheme for intermittently connected mobile networks. In: The 2005 ACM SIG-COMM Workshop on Delay Torlerant Networking, Philaadelphia, pp. 252–259 (2005)
5. Spyropoulos T., et al.: Spray and focus: efficient mobility-assisted routing for heterogeneous and correlated mobility. In: The IEEE PerCom Workshop on Intermittently Connected Mobile Ad Hoc Networks (2007)
6. Lindgren, A., Doria, A., Scheln, O.: Probabilistic routing in intermittently connected networks. 1ACM SIGMOBILE Mob. Comput. Commun. Rev. **7**(3), 19–26 (2003)
7. Dapeing, W., Puning, Z., et al.: Connection status aware cost efficient message transmission mechanism in opportunistic networks (In Chinese). J. J. Commun. 34(3) (2013)
8. Zhen-Jing, Z., et al.: Efficient routing in social DTN based on nodes movement prediction (In Chinese). J. J. Comput. **36**(3), 626–635 (2013)
9. Jianwei, N., Xing, Z., Yan, L., Limin, S.: A message transmission scheme for community-based opportunistic network (In Chinese). J. J. Comput. Res. Dev. **46**(12), 2068–2075 (2009)
10. Jianwei, N., Jin-Kai, G., Yan, L..: An efficient routing algortithm for opportnistic networks based on mobility predition (In Chinese). J.J. Commun. **31**(9) (2010)

11. Haitao, J., Qianmu, L., Jian, X., Hong, Z.: Cross-regional ferry routing design for multiple messagers in opportunistic networks (In Chinese). J. J. Comput. Res. Dev. **49**(4), 700–709 (2012)
12. Qingsong, C., Jianwei. N.: Adaptice data dissemination algorithm for vehicular opportunistic networks (In Chinese). J. Comput. Sci. **38**(6) (2011)
13. Yun, L., Bin-Bin, W., QILie, L., LinJun, T.: Multiple ferry route design based on city-village model in opportunistic networks (In Chinese). J. Appl. Res. Comput. **29**(1) (2012)
14. Yahong, L., Yuan, G., Jinlong, Q., Chuanhua, T.: Communtiy-based message transmission scheme in oppprtunistic social networks (In Chinese). J. J. Comput. Appl. **33**(5), 1212–1216 (2013)

A Dual-Access-Mode Hybrid Routing Strategy
for Energy-Aware Sensor Networks of Grid Topology

Wen-xiang Li[1,2(✉)], Chun-chun Pi[1], and Ya-jie Ma[1,2]

[1] School of Information Science and Technology, Wuhan University of Science and Technology,
Wuhan 430081, China
liwx2006@hotmail.com, pcc11071993ty@yeah.net,
mayajie@wust.edu.cn
[2] Engineering Research Center of Metallurgical Automation
and Detecting Technology of Ministry of Education,
Wuhan University of Science and Technology, Wuhan 430081, China

Abstract. Routing strategy plays important role on energy consumption of wireless sensor networks. This paper analyzed the influencing factors of energy consumption for grid topology, and decomposed the overall energy consumption into two parts, i.e. the energy consumption for node standing-by and that for transmission. Pointed out that delay-minimization routing and load-balance routing can decrease above two types of energy consumptions respectively. However, none of them can minimize the overall energy consumption. With multi-channel and TDMA media-access, this paper proposed a dual-access-mode hybrid routing strategy that adopts different routing methods at different positions of topology. Simulation in OMNet++ showed that this strategy leads to load balance and low transmission delay, and helps to minimize the overall energy consumption.

Keywords: Wireless sensor network · Grid topology · Multi-channel · Routing strategy · Energy consumption

1 Introduction

In wireless sensor networks, Grid topology can provide 4-neighbours connectivity for each node, and achieve efficient surveillance coverage with the least deployment costs [1]. However, its dense deployment of nodes tends to bring about communication conflicts and low energy efficiency. What's more, the convergent mode of many-to-one transmission leads to severe performance bottleneck problem [2]. So routing strategy should be carefully designed to avoid above problems. This paper starts from the modeling and optimization of energy consumption, and explores the impacts of relevant routing protocols on energy consumption. Based on multi-channel and TDMA media-access, we tackle the problem of communication conflicts in both time and space domain for higher transmission efficiency. And we design a hybrid routing strategy that adopts different routing methods at different positions of topology. With the merits

© Springer-Verlag Berlin Heidelberg 2015
L. Sun et al. (Eds.): CWSN 2014, CCIS 501, pp. 393–402, 2015.
DOI: 10.1007/978-3-662-46981-1_38

of load-balance and delay-minimization, this strategy helps to achieved minimized overall energy consumption.

The rest of this paper is organized as follows. Section 2 summarizes the performance of relevant routing methods in Grid topology, Sect. 3 lists the energy consumption model in Grid topology, and Sect. 4 proposes two routing methods for optimizing different types of energy consumption. Analysis shows that neither of these methods can minimize the overall energy consumption. Section 5 proposes dual-access-mode hybrid routing strategy, and simulation results in Sect. 6 shows the effectiveness of the strategy for minimizing overall energy consumption. At last, Sect. 7 gives the conclusion.

2 Related Works

Random walking (RW) is a common routing tactic in Grid topology. Reference [3] obtained the discrete distribution of packet delivery ratio versus transmission hops, and pointed out that RW yields optimal energy efficiency and load balance compared with shortest-path-first routing and flood routing. Taking task cycle ratio, radius of link states propagation, and number of nodes as parameters, [4] gave the close-form expression of average transmission delay for RW. Generally RW can connect to 4 neighbor nodes with unit transmission radius d, while in [5], 8-neighbour and 12-neighbour connectivity can be achieved with $1.414d$ and $2d$ respectively. Simulation results showed that 4-neighbour and 8-neighbour schemes lead to roughly equal energy consumption, however, 8-neighbour scheme yields smaller delay and better path efficiency.

RW leads to relatively low transmission efficiency, so [6] proposed Directional Source-Aware Protocol based on the symmetry of topology. In it, each node is allocated with an identifier indicating the distance to borders. By the calculation of identifiers, the next-hop node for optimizing energy consumption and transmission delay is determined. Simulation results showed that routing by interior paths leads to higher energy consumption than routing by edge paths does.

Reference [7] proposed a routing method for load balance, and this method specifies proper forwarding probability for each link, so the nodes at the same distance to Sink share roughly the same traffic load. Similar work [5] made comparison on load balance of diagonal transmission and straight transmission for one-to-one and many-to-one transmission respectively. Results showed that straight transmission leads to better load balance, and interior nodes bear heavier load than edge nodes do.

Reference [8] designed energy-aware and low-delay broadcast protocol. The one-to-all mode of the protocol selects some nodes as relay, adopts proper tactic for avoiding transmission conflict, and achieves broadcast coverage for all nodes with the smallest hop counts and message overhead. By channel allocation and node grouping, one-to-all broadcast is implemented in each channel, and all-to-all broadcast is implemented for the whole network.

All above studies on routing focus on optimizing transmission efficiency and load balance. However, there is few works on the optimization of routing method for convergent transmission mode in Grid topology.

3 Energy Consumption Model

As shown in Fig. 1, the Grid topology is deployed in the first quadrant of rectangular coordinate, and Sink is located in the origin. There are im columns of nodes in horizontal direction and jm rows of nodes in vertical direction, and each node is represented by coordinate (x,y), $0 \le x < im$, $0 \le y < jm$. Each sensor node starts to gather data and generate packet simultaneously at the beginning of each looping working cycle, and goes to sleep after it has sent all packets that it holds. In each working cycle, the energy consumption of each node consists of two parts. One is the energy consumption for standing-by, and it is the product of fixed standing-by power P_{ON} and variant standing-by time T_{ON}. The other is that for transmission, and it is the product of fixed energy consumption E_{TX} for transmitting one packet and variant number of packets L. And for each node we have the overall energy consumption as

$$E(i,j) = P_{ON} \cdot T_{ON}(i,j) + E_{TX} \cdot L(i,j) \tag{1}$$

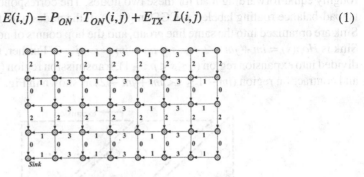

Fig. 1. Timeslot allocation for links in sensor networks of Grid topology

Obviously, the decisive factors for overall energy consumption are T_{ON} and L. The nodes at $(0,1)$ and $(1,0)$ may yield the largest forwarding load and standing-by time, and they are the performance bottleneck of the network. Our optimization target in (2) is to decrease the overall energy consumption on these nodes.

$$\text{Minimize } (\text{Max } (E(0, 1), E(1, 0))) \tag{2}$$

4 Energy Consumption for Typical Routing Methods

4.1 Relevant Media Access Method in Grid Topology

For avoiding the communication conflicts among nodes, we propose a multi-channel and TDMA media-access method based the structural feature of topology. A working cycle is composed of many transmission cycles, and each transmission cycle consists of 4 sequential timeslots numbered by 0, 1, 2, and 3. Figure 1 shows an example for allocating different timeslots (the number near the link) for different links from a node, including 2 timeslots for transmission to down and left neighbors and 2 timeslots for reception from up and right neighbors.

Note that these timeslots are organized in different sequences on different nodes. For example, the four timeslots for node (2,1) are used for sending to down node, receiving from right node, receiving from up node and sending to left node respectively, and the four timeslots for node (3,1) are used for sending to down node, sending to left node, receiving from up node and receiving from right node respectively. By proper allocation of timeslots and multi-channel technique, nodes can achieve interference-free communication and work efficiently at any time.

4.2 Load Balance Routing

Node (0,1) and (1,0) share all packets forwarded to Sink, and the sum of their energy consumption for transmission is fixed. By (2) we conclude that minimal energy consumption for transmission on performance bottleneck node can be achieved by allocating roughly equal forwarding load for these two nodes. The corresponding routing method is load-balance routing labeled as CGD in [9]. In it, the nodes with the same distance to Sink are organized into the same line group, and the hop counts of node (i,j) in group s to Sink is $Hop(s) = im + jm - 2 - s$, $s = im + jm - i - j - 2$. Further, the Grid topology is divided into expansion region $(0 \leq s < jm - 1)$, transmission region $(jm - 1 \leq s < im - 1)$ and contraction region $(im - 1 \leq s < im + jm - 2)$ as shown in Fig. 2.

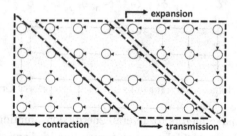

Fig. 2. Region division in grid topology for load balance routing

Let n_t^s be the tth node from edge of line group s, p_t^s be the probability of transmitting to n_t^{s+1}, and $(1 - p_t^s)$ be the probability of transmitting to p_{t+1}^{s+1}. From [9] we get the appropriate probabilities for load balance among the nodes in the same group in (3), with which the nodes in the same group share roughly the same load and energy consumption for transmission. In each transmission cycle, only one transmission timeslot is used for forwarding to left neighbor or down neighbor by (3).

$$p_t^s = \begin{cases} \dfrac{s+2-t}{s+2} & 0 \leq sj < m - 1 \\ 1 & jm - 1 \leq s < im - 1 \\ \dfrac{im + jm - 1 - s - t}{im + jm - s - 2} & im - 1 \leq s < im + jm - 2 \end{cases} \tag{3}$$

4.3   Delay Minimization Routing

By delay-minimization routing labeled as DOR, Sink receives all packets with the smallest T_{ON}. In DOR, both two transmission timeslots are used. In the first transmission timeslot, left neighbor or down neighbor is chosen as destination with equal probability of 0.5. If this transmission fails, the other neighbor is chosen as destination in the second transmission timeslot. If both two chances fail, the transmission is deferred to the next transmission cycle. Given probability of transmission failure ρ, the probability of failure in this transmission cycle is

$$\left(p_{fail}\right)_{DOR} = (1 - \rho)^2 \tag{4}$$

And the probability of successful transmission to left or down neighbor is

$$\left(p_{left}\right)_{DOR} = \left(p_{down}\right)_{DOR} = \left(1 - (1 - \rho)^2\right)/2 \tag{5}$$

4.4   Load on Performance Bottleneck Node

By equal division, the load of performance bottleneck node for CGD is

$$(L(1,0))_{CGD} = (L(0,1))_{CGD} = (im \cdot jm - 1)/2 \tag{6}$$

For DOR, the load of node $(1,0)$ is much larger than that of $(0,1)$ when $im > jm$, so node $(1,0)$ is the performance bottleneck. As shown in Fig. 3, give node (i,j) and (i',j'), we have their hop distance as $h = i + j - i' - j'$, and hop distance in vertical direction as $q = j - j'$. The combination $C_h{}^q$ is the coefficient of item x^q in polynomial $(1 + x)^h$, and 2^h is the sum of coefficients of all items in this polynomial. And the probability of node (i',j') receiving the packet from node (i,j) is $C_h{}^q/2^h$. So we have the load on node $(1,0)$ as

$$(L(1,0))_{DOR} = \sum_{i=1}^{im-1}\left(\sum_{j=0}^{jm-1}\left(\sum_{v=j}^{i+j-1}\frac{C_{i+j-1}^v}{2^{i+j-1}}\right)\right) \tag{7}$$

4.5   Transmission Delay

The transmission of a packet is modeled as a discrete absorbing Markov chain [10]. We denote state $S(i,j)$ as that packet residing in node (i,j), so $S(0,0)$ is the absorbing state, and other states are transient states. As shown in Fig. 4, there exist many different state transition modes according to the difference of locations.

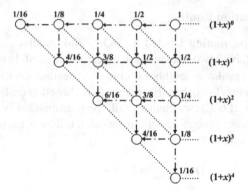

Fig. 3. Accumulative forwarding probability with random equal forwarding

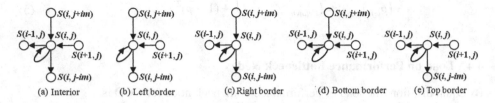

(a) Interior   (b) Left border   (c) Right border   (d) Bottom border   (e) Top border

Fig. 4. State transition of packets transmission in Grid topology

According to Fig. 4, we list the state transition matrix in (8).

$$P = \begin{bmatrix} Q & R \\ 0 & I \end{bmatrix} \tag{8}$$

The sub-matrix I contains the sole absorbing state, and Q is a matrix whose elements are the state transition probabilities. We first get the fundamental matrix of P as $N = (I - Q)^{-1}$. Given $k = i + j \cdot im$, we label h_k as the expectation of transmission hop count from $S(i,j)$ to Sink, and c as a column vector all of whose entries are 1. Then we have h as the column vector whose xth entry is h_x

$$h = N \cdot c = (I - Q)^{-1} \cdot c \tag{9}$$

We label the length of each timeslot as t_0, and get the expectation of transmission delay for packet from node (i,j) with different routing method in (10)

$$delay_k = 4t_0 h_k \tag{10}$$

And the maximal standing-by time in one working cycle is

$$T_{ON} = 4t_0 \text{Max}\left(h_k\right) \tag{11}$$

With 2 transmission timeslots in DOR, we conclude that DOR yields much smaller T_{ON} and energy consumption for standing-by than CGD does. Based on (11), an example of packet transmission delay when $im = 30$ and $jm = 10$ is shown in Fig. 5. In it the transmission delays of packets from the nodes in the same row increase linearly, and 10 rows lead to 10 rising edges. Obviously, the packet from each node takes less time for transmission to Sink by DOR than CGD. However, according to (6) and (7), DOR yields much higher load and energy consumption for transmission on performance bottleneck node than CGD does. And according to (1), it is hard to judge which routing method can achieve the minimal overall energy consumption.

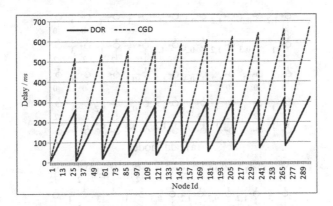

Fig. 5. Theoretical standing-by time for CGD and DOR

5   Hybrid Routing Strategy

A dual-access-mode hybrid routing strategy (DMHR for short) is proposed for selecting proper routing methods for different nodes. In it, the aforementioned routing methods are adopted for different regions of topology.

In contraction region large number of packets concentrate, and it is necessary to forward them to Sink as fast as possible, so DOR routing is adopted. In transmission region the enhanced CGD routing is adopted, in which nodes receive packets only from right neighbor and transmit packets only to left neighbor. So the vertical links in transmission region are not used, and two transmission timeslots and two reception timeslots are all used for doubling transmission efficiency. Considering the traffic congestion in contraction region, it is unnecessary to hasten the packet transmission in expansion region, and CGD routing is adopted for load balance.

Obviously, we can achieve load balance for the nodes of the same group in expansion region and transmission region, but one problem exists in contraction region. For the nodes on the diagonal line from Sink in contraction region, i.e. node (1,1), (2,2)..., fixed allocation of timeslots may lead to unbalance traffic load between left link and down link. Taking Fig. 1 as an example, node (1,1) always sends packets to down link first at timeslot 0, and brings higher load to (1,0) than (0,1). The countermeasure is a dual media-access mode in Fig. 6, in which the odd mode is adopted in the odd transmission cycle, and the even mode is adopted in the even transmission cycle. And the first transmission link used in each transmission cycle interchanges with each other for these two modes. For example, in the odd mode of Fig. 6(a), node (1,1) transmits to left neighbor first at timeslot 1, and transmits to down neighbor at timeslot 2. While, in the even mode of Fig. 6(b), it transmits to down neighbor first at timeslot 0, and transmits to left neighbor at timeslot 3. In this way balanced traffic load on left and down neighbors can be achieved in contraction region. It is required that there is no transmission conflicts among currently allocated timeslots, so the dual-access-mode and proper timeslots-allocation are needed for all three regions.

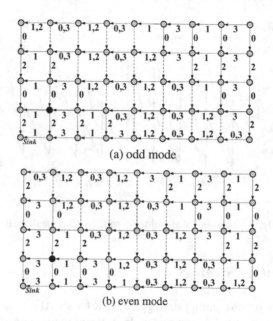

(a) odd mode

(b) even mode

Fig. 6. Timeslot allocation for hybrid routing strategy

6 Numerical Analysis

Simulation experiment is conducted in OMNet++ for performance evaluation. And the parameters are as follows: $im = 30$, $jm = 10$, the duration of working cycle is 5 s, the time needed for transmitting one packet is 1 ms, the number of working cycle is 100, and the typical length of each timeslot increases from 4 ms, 6 ms, ... to 16 ms.

First we get the average transmission delay of each packet. For the case when the length of timeslot is 4 ms, the typical result is shown in Fig. 7. In it, the packets are organized in increasing order of delay. All results demonstrate that CGD leads to the highest transmission delay, and the delays of DHMR and DOR are similar, while, DHMR yields much smaller delay for late arriving packets than DOR does.

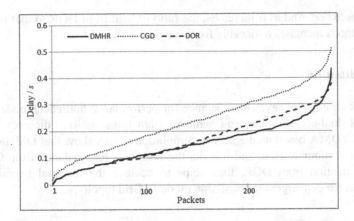

Fig. 7. Average transmission delay to Sink for each packet

The average standing-by time T_{ON} in one working cycle for different timeslots are shown in Fig. 8(a). It is observed that as the length of timeslot increases, T_{ON} increases for all three routing methods, and large length of timeslot may lead to low efficiency of timeslot utilization and high transmission delay. DMHR and DOR yield smaller delay, and unlike the results in Fig. 5, the delay of CGD is only about 1.2–1.3 times as much as that of DMHR or DOR. The reason is that in simulation scenario of using both 2 transmission timeslots, some links cannot work with saturated traffic and may be used inefficiently. So the simulation results of transmission delay are much larger than that of theoretical results for DHMR and DOR.

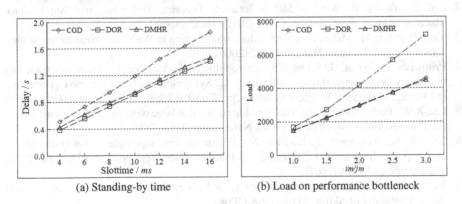

(a) Standing-by time   (b) Load on performance bottleneck

Fig. 8 Performance comparison for routing methods

Assign jm with 10 and assign im with 10, 15, 20, 25 and 30 respectively, we get ratio α of length to width in topology as 1, 1.5, 2, 2.5 and 3 respectively. With different α, we get the number of packets processed on performance bottleneck node in Fig. 8(b). It is observed that as network scale increases, load increases for all three routing methods. DMHR and CGD lead to lower load than DOR does, and can achieve load balance for the whole network. And as α increases, the ratio of load from DOR to that from other routing methods increases noticeably from roughly 1.12 to 1.6.

7   Conclusions

The DMHR strategy achieves load balance for performance bottleneck node by CGD routing and dual-access-mode, and achieves high transmission efficiency by DOR routing and TDMA-based media access. Simulation results show that DMHR leads to conflict-free communication, and inherits the merits of load-balance from CGD and delay-minimization from DOR, thus helps to achieve the minimal overall energy consumption for convergent transmission mode in Grid topology.

Acknowledgement.   This work is supported by the National Science Foundation of China (61104215), the Science and Technology Research Project of Education Department of Hubei Province, China (Q20141110), and Engineering Research Center of Metallurgical Automation and Detecting Technology of Ministry of Education, Wuhan University of Science and Technology (MARC201304, MARC201307), the Training Programs of Innovation and Entrepreneurship for Undergraduates of Hubei Province, China (201410488046), and Students' Renovation Foundation of Wuhan University of Science and Technology, China (14ZRA140).

References

1. Li, W.-X., Ma, Y.-J., et al.: Survey on the deployment and design for regular topology structures in wireless sensor networks. J. Commun. **33**(Z2), 207–216 (2012). (in Chinese)
2. Cui, Y., Zhang, P.: Wireless Mobile Internet- Theories, Techniques and Applications. Machine Industry Press, Beijing, China (2012). (in Chinese)
3. Tian, H., Shen, H., Matsuzawa, T.: Random walk routing in WSNs with regular topologies. J. Comput. Sci. Technol. **21**(4), 496–502 (2006)
4. Prithwisht, B., Saikat, G.: Effect of limited topology knowledge on opportunistic forwarding in ad hoc wireless networks. In: 8th International Symposium on Modeling and Optimization in Mobile, Ad Hoc, and Wireless Networks, pp. 71-80. IEEE Press, Piscataway, USA (2010)
5. Liu, X.W.: Performance analysis and topology control of large wireless networks with fading. Ph. D thesis. University of Notre Dame, Notre Dame, USA (2007)
6. Salhieh, A., Weinmann, J., Kochhal, M.: Power efficient topologies for wireless sensor networks. In: International Conference on Parallel Processing, pp. 156-163. IEEE Press, Washington DC, USA (2001)
7. Mamidisetty, K.K.: Generalizing contour guided dissemination in mesh topologies. Ph.D thesis. University of Akron, Akron, USA (2008)
8. Shen, J.P., Hsu, C.S., Chang, Y.J.: Efficient broadcasting protocols for regular wireless sensor networks. Wirel. Commun. Mob. Comput. **6**(1), 35–48 (2006)
9. Mamidisetty, K.K., Duan, M., Sastry, S., et al.: Multipath dissemination in regular mesh topologies. IEEE Trans. Parall. Distrib. Syst. **20**(8), 1188–1201 (2009)
10. Charles, M., Grinstead, J., Laurie, S.: Introduction to Probability. American Mathematical Society, Providence, USA (1997)

A MIMC Chain-Type Routing Protocol for Wireless Ad Hoc Networks

Jiali Liu[1], Yanjing Sun[2](✉), Yi Jian[1], and Chenglong Feng[1]

[1] School of Information and Electrical Engineering, China University of Mining and Technology, Xuzhou 221116, China
[2] Coal Mine Electrical and Automation Engineering Laboratory of Jiangsu Province, Xuzhou 221116, China
yjsun@cumt.edu.cn

Abstract. To chain routing in the single-channel condition, the performance of wireless Ad Hoc networks will drops sharply along with the increasing routing hops. A novel multi-interface multi-channel OLSR (MIMC-OLSR) protocol is presented based on joint routing and channel assignment in this paper. Moreover, a distributed joint chain-type routing and channel assignment algorithm is given to achieve channel assignment for linear chain wireless Ad Hoc networks. The MIMC-plugin is implemented on OLSRd by adopting MIMC-OLSR protocol, and MIMC-OLSR protocol is evaluated by using a wireless testbed. The testing results show that the MIMC-OLSR protocol has better performance according to throughput, packet loss rate, end-to-end delay and delay jitter.

Keywords: Wireless Ad Hoc networks · OLSR protocol · Multi-interface multi-channel · Channel assignment

1 Introduction

The network topology of underground Ad Hoc networks has the characteristic of chain-type [1]. Meanwhile, safety production and emergency rescue have increasing demand on the capacity of video transmission in underground mines. Gupta et al. [2] demonstrate that throughput would get very low along with the increasing wireless nodes. Hortelano et al. [3] demonstrate that images in video conference cannot be distinguished when the hop count reaches ten. Therefore, it is significant to improve the throughput for wireless Ad Hoc networks.

Currently, many researches use multi-interface multi-channel to improve the network capacity in MAC layer protocols [4,5] and routing layer protocols [6–9]. But the implementation of MAC layer protocol needs the support of cards and other hardwares, which results in the difficulty in application. Sun et al. [10] present a new available transmission time (ATT) routing metric. YUAN et al. [11] present an efficient distributed channel assignment scheme (CA-LQSR) combined with MR-LQSR to improve throughput and end-to-end delay. Joint routing and channel assignment reduces the interference between neighboring

© Springer-Verlag Berlin Heidelberg 2015
L. Sun et al. (Eds.): CWSN 2014, CCIS 501, pp. 403–413, 2015.
DOI: 10.1007/978-3-662-46981-1_39

links without modifying the MAC layer protocol, so as to solve the problem that channel capacity drops sharply along with the increasing routing hops.

This paper presents a multi-interface multi-channel OLSR (MIMC-OLSR) protocol by joint routing and channel assignment on the basis of OLSR protocol [12]. Moreover, a distributed joint chain-type routing and channel assignment algorithm is given to achieve channel assignment for linear chain-type wireless Ad Hoc networks. MIMC-OLSR protocol optimizes the performance of multi-hop transmission for wireless Ad Hoc networks.

2   Distributed Joint Chain-Type Routing and Channel Assignment Algorithm

In MIMC-OLSR, since the network traffic almost converges upon the gateway, a new node must find one or several links to reach the gateway by channel assignment algorithm when it joins into the wireless network. Meanwhile, the channel which has lower interference must be assigned preferentially to establish communication link considering the influence of link quality. In order to guarantee network connectivity, the routing protocol must be able to perceive the change of network topology dynamically and then reallocate the channels.

This paper presents a distributed joint chain-type routing and channel assignment algorithm for MIMC-OLSR protocol to keep good channel discrimination and maintain network connectivity. This algorithm is divided into two parts: channel assignment and routing formation algorithm, channel recovery and routing maintenance algorithm.

To describe the algorithm in linear chain-type network topology, we make several assumptions as follows. (1) In this paper, each node has two network interfaces in linear chain-type network topology, which are uplink interfaces and downlink interfaces. In addition, the gateway only has a downlink interface. (2) This paper takes three orthogonal channels in 2.4 GHz frequency band into account, which are channel 1, channel 6 and channel 11. (3) This paper divides the channel assignment into two problems by referring to literature [13]: nodes are bound to network interfaces, network interfaces are bound to channels.

To describe the algorithm, the following takes a linear chain-type wireless Ad Hoc network as an example, which has five nodes: gateway a, b, c, d and e.

2.1   Channel Assignment and Routing Formation

Channel assignment and routing formation algorithm includes channel initialization CH_IN(), channel switching CH_SW() and handshake HA_SH() phases.

The main pseudocode of algorithm CH_IN(P, C) is shown as below:

```
Algorithm CH_IN(P, C):
  the initial channel is assigned to downlink interface of
each node
  parent node P = gateway
```

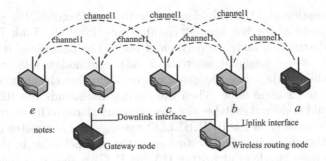

Fig. 1. Initialized channel assignment

```
child node C = NULL
channel assignment of gateway is marked as completed
```

CH_IN(P, C): During initialization phase, each node assigns a fixed initial channel from the three orthogonal channels to downlink interface, such as channel 1. The gateway defaults to be the root node. The channel assignment of gateway is marked as completed (The downlink interface of the gateway is bound to initial channel). Now the gateway is the parent node. That ensures network connectivity before multi-channel assignment. A traditional single-channel wireless Ad Hoc network can be formed by OLSR protocol, as shown in Fig. 1:

The main pseudocode of algorithm CH_SW(P, C) is shown as below:

```
Algorithm CH_SW(P, C):
  If(node n has not completed channel assignment)then
    node n broadcasts REQ_HELLO messages;
  End if
  parent node P receives and handles REQ_HELLO messages
  child node C = a node with highest channel rate
  If(parent node P is gateway)then
    the channel of downlink interface of parent node P is
assigned to downlink interface of parent node P and uplink
interface of child node C;
  Else
    the next circulation channel of uplink interface of
parent node P is assigned to downlink interface of parent
node P and uplink interface of child node C;
  End if
```

CH_SW(P, C): The nodes which have not completed channel assignment broadcast the REQ_HELLO messages periodically through downlink interfaces. Then the parent node receives and handles these messages. The source IP address, MAC address, link identifier and valid time of these messages are saved as one record in the Channel_REQ_Node table. The parent node checks the Channel_REQ_Node table periodically and deletes overdue records. According to the address information and the link identifier in the valid records, the parent node chooses the node which has highest channel rate from the Link Information table as the destination node, namely, child node. The next circulation channel $(1{\to}6{\to}11{\to}1{\to}6{\to}\cdots)$ of uplink interface of the parent node is selected circularly to assign to child node, while the gateway directly assign the channel of downlink interface to its child node. Then the parent node sends the REP_HELLO message to child node and switches the downlink interface to this channel. Meanwhile, child node receives the REP_HELLO message and completes the channel switching of the uplink interface according to the channel value in the message.

The main pseudocode of algorithm HA_SH(P, C) is shown as below:

```
Algorithm HA_SH(P, C):
  child node C sends REQ_ACK message continuously
  If(child node C has received REP_ACK message)
    handshake is successful;
  Else
    handshake is unsuccessful;
  End if
  If(handshake is successful) then
    channel assignment of child node C is marked as completed
    parent node P = child node C
    child node C = NULL
  Else
    the initial channel is assigned to downlink interface of
parent node P and uplink interface of child node C
    child node C = NULL
  End if
```

HA_SH(P, C): The child node sends the REQ_ACK message through uplink interface. After receiving the REQ_ACK message, the parent node sends the REP_ACK message. If the child node receives the REP_ACK message, the handshake phase will be successful. Otherwise, the child node will send the REQ_ACK messages continuously. If the REP_ACK message is still not be received, handshake phase will be unsuccessful.

If the handshake phase of the node is successful, the child node will be marked as a new parent node. The channel switching phase and handshake phase of new parent node are repeated until the last node has completed channel assignment. If the handshake phase is unsuccessful, the original parent node will remain unchanged, but the child node will be reselected. In addition, the downlink interface of the parent node will be switched back to the initial channel, so well as the uplink interface of the child node. Channel switching and handshake phases will be rerun until the channel assignment of the child node has been completed.

The final result of the channel assignment of these nodes is shown in Fig. 2:

2.2   Channel Recovery and Routing Maintenance

The following describes the channel recovery and routing maintenance algorithm on the basis of the assumption that node c fails.

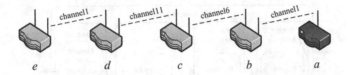

Fig. 2. Final result of the channel assignment

Fig. 3. Result of the channel recovery

The main pseudocode of algorithm RE_CH(P, C) is shown as below:

```
Algorithm RE_CH(P, C):
  the initial channel is assigned to network interfaces
whose links are disconnected
  channel assignment of the node whose uplink interface
is disconnected is marked as uncompleted
  the node whose uplink interface is disconnected and
new node broadcast REQ_HELLO messages
  parent node P = the node whose downlink interface is
disconnected
  child node C = NULL
```

RE_CH(P, C): If node c fails, the downlink interface of node b and the uplink interface of node d will detect the disconnections of link and touch off the reconfiguration. The reconfiguration process is described as follows. All the network interfaces whose links are disconnected are assigned to the initial channel. Then the channel assignment of the node(node d)whose uplink interface is disconnected is marked as uncompleted. This node broadcasts the REQ_HELLO messages through uplink interface according to the channel switching phase. Meanwhile, the node(node b)whose downlink interface is disconnected is marked as the parent node and receives REQ_HELLO message through downlink interface and handles the message. Without a new node joining into network, node b will complete the channel switching and handshake phase with node d according to channel assignment and routing formation algorithm. Finally, channel 6 is assigned between these two nodes. The result is shown in Fig. 3:

If a new node m appears between node b and d, then node b, m and d will recover channels according to channel assignment and routing formation algorithm. The result is the same as Fig. 2.

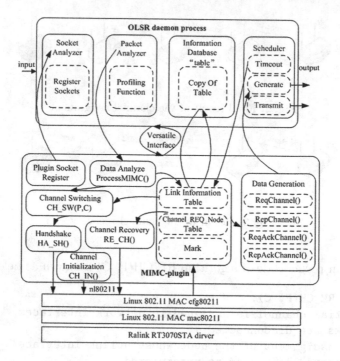

Fig. 4. Structure of MIMC-plugin

3 Implementation of the MIMC-OLSR Protocol

OLSRd (olsr.org OLSR daemon) [14] is written by UniKonstanz (UNIK). MIMC-OLSR protocol is presented on the basis of OLSRd and should be implemented by extensions of OLSRd. This paper implements the MIMC-plugin on OLSRd by referring to the security-plugin [15]. The relation between MIMC-plugin and OLSRd is shown in Fig. 4:

The socket interfaces which are used to send and receive all kinds of the user-defined messages (REP_HELLO, REQ_HELLO, REP_ACK, REQ_ACK) in MIMC-OLSR is registered with the Socket Analyzer module by MIMC-plugin. Meanwhile, ProcessMIMC() function of MIMC-plugin is registered with the Packet Analyzer module of OLSRd in order to complete processing the user-defined messages. In addition, the functions which make the messages send regularly in the distributed joint chain-type routing and channel assignment algo-rithm are registered with the Scheduler module by MIMC-plugin. According to the algorithm, firstly, the CH_IN() function is called to complete the initialized assignment of channels and then a single-channel wireless Ad Hoc network is formed. Then MIMC-plugin exchanges information with the Information Data-base table of OLSRd in order to maintain the Link Information table. The mark in MIMC-plugin is a global variable and is used to mark whether the channel assignment of the node has been completed. The ProcessMIMC() function and the Scheduler module check the Link Information table periodically in order to maintain this mark. Finally, the channel assignment of each node is achieved according to the distributed joint chain-type routing and channel assignment algorithm.

4 Results and Analysis of MIMC-OLSR Protocol

4.1 Testing Environment

In this paper, the network nodes are designed based on embedded OpenWrt system and core module of BCM6358 processor. The RT3070 chip which meets 802.11n standard is adopted to implement multi-interface. This paper runs OLSRd program on OpenWrt system and loads MIMC-plugin to complete the testing of MIMC-OLSR protocol. The wireless cards work in Ad Hoc mode and the bandwidth is 20 MHz. In the testing, Iperf [16] software is adopted to evaluate throughput, packet loss rate and delay jitter of Ad Hoc network. The statistics of return information of *ping* command are adopted to evaluate end-to-end delay. The UDP buffer of iperf is set as 8 KB. Figure 5 shows the topology and the testing environment of the linear chain-type wireless Ad Hoc network. From the gateway to the last node the channels to be assigned are, in order, channel 1, channel 6, channel 11, channel 1 and channel 6.

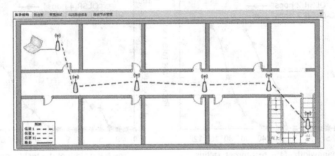

Fig. 5. Testing environment for linear chain structure of the wireless Ad Hoc backbone network

4.2 Performance Testing and Analysis of Network

This paper evaluates the network performance of single-channel OLSR protocol and MIMC-OLSR protocol.

In Fig. 6, the end-to-end throughput for OLSR and MIMC-OLSR protocol is given, which is tested through TCP transmission. In MIMC-OLSR, the throughput under 1-hop and 2-hop are 47.86 Mbps and 42.05 Mbps respectively, which indicates that the throughput under 2-hop declines only 12.14 % than that under 1-hop. In OLSR, the throughput under 2-hop declines 67.16 % than that under 1-hop, which shows the superiority of MIMC-OLSR. Under 5-hop, the throughput

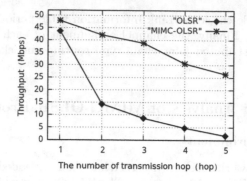

Fig. 6. Throughput under different hops

in MIMC-OLSR is 26.35 Mbps and is over 15 times higher than that in OLSR. The results show that MIMC-OLSR protocol assigns the least interference channel to neighboring links, which reduces the competition of the wireless channels and the interference among nodes. As a result, the end-to-end throughput is improved dramatically.

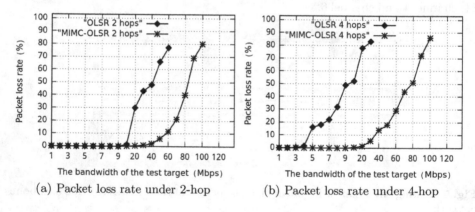

(a) Packet loss rate under 2-hop   (b) Packet loss rate under 4-hop

Fig. 7. Packet loss rate under different bandwidth

In Fig. 7, the packet loss rate of UDP under different bandwidth is given. Figure 7a and b are the testing results under 2-hop and 4-hop respectively. Under 2-hop, the bandwidth in MIMC-OLSR and OLSR are 12 Mbps and 9.4 Mbps respectively when packet loss arises. While under 4-hop, the bandwidths are 9.7 Mbps and 2.9 Mbps respectively. The packet loss rate in MIMC-OLSR is smaller than that in OLSR under the same bandwidth. The results show that the multi-channel in MIMC-OLSR protocol reduces the interference and competition of co-channels, which increases the successful probability of delivering data packets and reduces the packet loss rate.

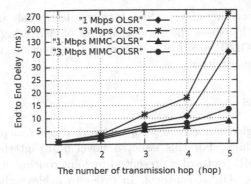

Fig. 8. End-to-end delay under different hops

In Fig. 8, the end-to-end delay under different hops and different network load is given. When the network load is 1 Mbps, the end-to-end delay in OLSR and in MIMC-OLSR are 71.627 ms and 8.98 ms respectively under 5-hop. While the network load is 3 Mbps, the end-to-end delay in OLSR and in MIMC-OLSR are 271.451 ms and 14.28 ms respectively under 5-hop. The results show that MIMC-OLSR protocol can greatly reduce the interference between links for linear chain-type wireless Ad Hoc networks by using the distributed joint chain-type routing and channel assignment algorithm.

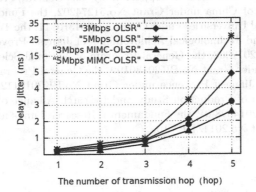

Fig. 9. Delay jitter under different hops

In Fig. 9, the delay jitter under different hops and different bandwidth is given. From the testing result, we can conclusion that delay jitter increases along with the increasing routing hops both in OLSR and MIMC-OLSR, while the delay jitter in MIMC-OLSR increases more slowly. The advantage of MIMC-OLSR protocol is more obvious especially when network load increases. MIMC-OLSR protocol makes neighboring links use different channels, thus greatly reduces the interference of neighboring links. In addition, the multi-interface of nodes achieves receiving and sending data simultaneously without leading to interference, which increases the successful rate of delivering data packets. In conclusion, MIMC-OLSR protocol has an obvious reduction compared with the OLSR protocol in delay jitter.

5   Conclusions

Performance of single-channel multi-hop network drops sharply along with the increasing routing hops. For this issue, a novel multi-interface multi-channel OLSR (MIMC-OLSR) protocol is presented by joint routing and channel assignment on the basis of OLSR protocol. In order to achieve channel assignment for linear chain-type wireless Ad Hoc networks, a distributed joint chain-type routing and channel assignment algorithm is given in this paper. Moreover, MIMC-plugin is implemented on OLSRd to run MIMC-OLSR protocol. OLSR protocol and MIMC-OLSR protocol are evaluated in the experiment by using an embedded wireless testbed on OpenWrt system, which shows that MIMC-OLSR protocol has an obvious improvement according to throughput, packet loss rate, end-to-end delay and delay jitter. The reason for the above is that the distributed joint chain-type routing and channel assignment algorithm is used in MIMC-OLSR protocol to maximally achieve the distinction of channels and reduce the interference between wireless links.

Acknowledgments. This work is supported by the General Program of National Science Foundation of China under Grant No.51274202, the Fundamental Research Funds for the Central Universities under Grant No.2013RC11, the Transformation Program of Scientific and Technological Achievements of Jiangsu Provence (Sub project) under Grant No.BA2012068, the General Program of National Science Foundation of Jiangsu Provence under Grant No.BK20130199, the General Program of National Science Foundation of Jiangsu Provence under Grant No.BK20131124, the Perspective Research Foundation of Production Study and Research Alliance of Jiangsu Province under Grant No.BY2014028-01, the Fundamental Research Funds for the Central Universities under Grant No.2014ZDPY16.

References

1. Haifeng, J., Jiansheng, Q., Yanjing, S., Guoyong, Z.: Energy optimal routing for long chain-type wireless sensor networks in underground mines. Min. Sci. Tech. **21**(1), 17–21 (2011)
2. Gupta, P., Kumar, P.R.: The capacity of wireless networks. IEEE Trans. Inf. Theory. **46**(2), 388–404 (2000)
3. Hortelano, J., Cano, J.C., Calafate, C.T., Manzoni, P.: Evaluating the performance of real time videoconferencing in ad hoc networks through emulation. In: 22nd Workshop on Principles of Advanced and Distributed Simulation, PADS 2008, pp. 119–126. IEEE (2008)
4. Dang, D.N.M., Quang, N.T., Hong, C.S., Hong, J.P.: An enhanced multi-channel MAC protocol for wireless ad hoc networks. In: 2012 14th Asia-Pacific Network Operations and Management Symposium (APNOMS), pp. 1–4. IEEE (2012)

5. So, H.S.W., Walrand, J., Mo, J.: McMAC: A multi-channel MAC proposal for ad hoc wireless networks. In: Proceedings of IEEE WCNC, pp. 334–339 (2007)

6. Liu, T., Liao, W.: Interference-aware QoS routing for multi-rate multi-radio multi-channel IEEE 802.11 wireless mesh networks. IEEE Trans. Wireless Commun. **8**(1), 166–175 (2009)

7. Kajioka, S., Wakamiya, N., Satoh, H., Monden, K., Hayashi, M., Matsui, S., Murata, M.: A QoS-aware routing mechanism for multi-channel multi-interface ad-hoc networks. Ad Hoc Netw. **9**(5), 911–927 (2011)

8. Draves, R., Padhye, J., Zill, B.: Routing in multi-radio, multi-hop wireless mesh networks. In: Proceedings of the 10th Annual International Conference on Mobile Computing and Networking, pp. 114–128. ACM (2004)

9. Sun, Y., He, Y., Zhang, B., Liu, X.: An energy efficiency clustering routing protocol for WSNs in confined area. Min. Sci. Tech. **21**(6), 845–850 (2011)

10. Sun, Y.J., Liu, X., Zhang, B.B.: An available transmission time routing metric for wireless ad-hoc sensor networks. Int. J. Distrib. Sens. Netw. **2011**, 6 (2011)

11. Yuan, F.F., Li, X., Liu, K.M., Liu, Y.A., Du, X., Shi, X.R.: Distributed channel assignment combined with routing over multi-radio multi-channel wireless mesh networks. J. China Univ. Posts Telecommun. **19**(4), 6–13 (2012)

12. Clausen, T., Jacquet, P., Adjih, C., Laouiti, A., Minet, P., Muhlethaler, P., Viennot, L.: Optimized link state routing protocol (OLSR) (2003)

13. Raniwala, A., Gopalan, K., Chiueh, T.C.: Centralized channel assignment and routing algorithms for multi-channel wireless mesh networks. ACM SIGMOBILE Mob. Comput. Commun. Rev. **8**(2), 50–65 (2004)

14. olsr.org OLSR daemon project homepage. http://www.olsr.org

15. Hafslund, A., Tønnesen, A., Rotvik, R. B., Andersson, J., Kure, Ø.: Secure extension to the OLSR protocol. In: Proceedings of the OLSR Interop and Workshop. San Diego (2004)

16. Tirumala, A., Qin, F., Dugan, J., Ferguson, J., Gibbs, K.: Iperf: The TCP/UDP bandwidth measurement tool (2005). http://dast.nlanr.net/Projects

A Hybrid WSN Routing Protocol Based on the Average Degree of Neighborhood

Junhuai Li[1,2(✉)], Xiang Li[1], Kaiming Jiang[1], HuaiJun Wang[1,2],
and Zhixiao Wang[1,2]

[1] Schoool of Computer Science and Engineering,
Xi'an University of Technology, Xi'an 710048, China
lijunhuai@xaut.edu.cn, hjwang006@163.com,
wangzhx@xaut.edu.cn, thaddeusle@126.com,
jiangkm@gmail.com,
[2] Shaanxi Key Laboratory for Network Computing and Security Technology,
Xi'an 710048, China

Abstract. In view of the characteristics of wireless sensor network and existing problems of the routing protocol, we have explored the existing sensor node energy consumption management methods, and proposed a new routing algorithm through quantifying the information of two-hop neighbors, namely, two-hop greedy ellipse routing protocol (GERP). Combining location-based routing protocol and region-based routing protocol, GERP is energy efficient which adopts different routing policies according to the average degree of neighborhood. Simulations have shown that GERP is more efficient than typical methods in reducing the sensor node energy consumption.

Keywords: Wireless sensor network · The average degree of neighborhood · Low energy consumption · Ellipse routing

1 Introduction

As an important underlying network technology of Internet of Things, wireless sensor network (WSN) has the dual heavy responsibility for data sensing and data transmission, which has been more and more concerned nowadays. Currently, most sensor nodes are battery-powered due to the limitations of the technology level, production cost and other factors. In the condition of quite limited energy, one of the most urgent questions is that how to maximally lower the energy consumption and prolong the lifetime of sensor nodes and networks in wireless sensor network [1].

With regard to existing wireless sensor network protocols, including energy efficient MAC protocol, energy efficient routing protocol and node sleep scheduling etc., the primary consideration is to improve the energy efficiency of WSN [2, 3]. Furthermore, the function of a sensor nodes need to perform is relatively simple, with cheap embedded processor and small memory capacity. Under the circumstances, the algorithm design needs to be simpler and more efficient, so as to minimize the requirement of processing, storage and other hardware resources. Designing a low-power routing protocol is one of the primary means to reduce energy consumption in wireless sensor network.

© Springer-Verlag Berlin Heidelberg 2015
L. Sun et al. (Eds.): CWSN 2014, CCIS 501, pp. 414–422, 2015.
DOI: 10.1007/978-3-662-46981-1_40

Most energy of a sensor node is consumed on the radio of transmitting and receiving. With the problem of the network load unbalancing, paper [4] proposed a way to optimize node effective distance of communication by dynamically adjusting the transmission power. But it is applicable only when all sensor nodes are in the one-jump range of the sink node, but most of the sensor networks transmit data by multi-hop. Literature [5] put forward a greedy geographical routing algorithm based on the location information of two-hop neighbors that data can effectively circumvent the dead nodes, and the number of hops and energy consumption will be reduced. However, it is suitable only to the network which has relatively dense distribution of sensor nodes. On the contrary, it wastes a lot of unnecessary energy to maintain the status information neighbors. Literature [6] created an ellipse-hole model to propose the HRAEM protocol which can solve the problem of routing around the hole then reasonably transmit the data to the destination node by greedy forwarding.

In this paper, we analyze the characteristics of typical energy consumption routing protocols, and then propose a new routing algorithm through quantifying the information of the two-hop neighbors (GERP). And it is energy efficient adopting different routing policies according to the average degree of neighborhood. Also GERP is more efficient than typical methods in reducing the energy consumption of the sensor node.

2   Problem Analysis

WSN is large-scale, energy-limited, dynamic, self-organizing, and data-centric, etc. [7], so WSN routing can be divided into neighbor-based routing and region-based routing.

Neighbor-based routing, also called location-based routing, each node knows the location of its next hop nodes or the location of the next two-hop nodes, is suitable to work in a static sensor network [8]. And its disadvantage is that each node needs to communicate frequently to obtain location information of neighbors, resulting in a lot of energy consumption. Although location-based routing algorithm can effectively improve routing efficiency and reduce energy consumption, but also need to consider positioning accuracy, timeliness and accuracy of the neighbors' status, congestion of neighbors, residual energy and other issues.

Region-based routing, each node only needs to know its own, the source node's and the destination node's location information, predetermines an ellipse area and transmits data by flooding [9]. All the nodes in this area should transmit the low power and ensure the communication between source node and destination node. It is only suitable for small-scale network, and the average energy consumption will be extremely high if applied in a large network. Moreover, if holes exist, the region-based routing cannot be restored, and resulting in transmission failure.

For the reduction of the average transmission energy, the energy balance of each node and maximal network lifetime, considering forecasting routing holes, avoiding congested links, greedy policy and average residual energy etc., we integrate the advantages of location-based routing and region-based ellipse routing, and propose a new WSN routing protocol.

In the early time of the network, the sensor nodes are densely distributed, using the neighbor-based routing can be better to save energy; but later some nodes exhaust energy or turn out dead, the distribution of nodes become relatively sparse, region-based routing will be more efficient. We define the density of the node in WSN as average degree of neighborhood.

2.1 Average Degree of Neighborhood

Assuming n nodes are evenly deployed in a square region named Z. Then Z is evenly divided into n small virtual grids, and each grid area has only one sensor node. Each row or column has $\sqrt{n}$ nodes. Only the nodes in adjacent grids can communicate to each other. A node transfers a packet to the adjacent node with the same rule until the sink node get the packet, as shown in Fig. 1.

As can be seen, from any node to sink node in Z, the hop number equals the sum of X and Y coordinate values. So the average hop number to all the nodes in Z is:

$$\bar{H} = \frac{2\sqrt{n}\sum_{i=1}^{\sqrt{n}} i}{n} \tag{1}$$

There are n nodes evenly deployed in region Z, so the parameter n in Eq. (1) is an integer. And Eq. (1) can be simplified as follows:

$$\bar{H} = 1 + \sqrt{n} \tag{2}$$

Equation (2) represents an ideal network topology, but in practice more or less redundant nodes exist. Here we take the idea of cluster-based routing and divide virtual grids according to the transmission radius of sensor node. Supposing n in Eq. (2) as the head of clusters, we got Eq. (3), where a is the side length of region Z, r is transmission radius of sensor node.

$$\bar{H} = 1 + \sqrt{\frac{a}{r}} \tag{3}$$

In order to make the following analysis more straightforward, we give the definition of average degree of neighborhood, ADN for short. It is the number of a node's neighbors, signified with $\bar{N}$. Given the same region Z, n nodes are randomly and independently deployed. To some sensor nodes, like in Fig. 2, they have different $\bar{N}$ value. The broadcast range of node u is completely contained in region Z, so $\bar{N}_u = \frac{\pi r^2}{a^2} n - 1$. Accordingly, to node v, its broadcast region is partly outside region Z, and the ADN is less than $\bar{N}_u$. The worst thing is that a sensor node is just at the vertex of region Z, like node w, it got only quarter of $\bar{N}_u$.

2.2 Energy Consumption Analysis

The energy efficiency of a routing strategy is different as the scale of network changed [10].

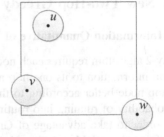

Fig. 1. Network topology   **Fig. 2.** Network deployment positions

Forwarding data with region-based flooding routing, source node and relay nodes transmit packets by broadcasting until the packets reach the destination node. The energy consumption in a routing is given by:

$$E = \bar{N}\bar{H}(E_s + E_R) \tag{4}$$

Parameter E_s is the energy consumption of sensor node sending one byte, and E_R is the energy consumption of node receiving one byte.

Forwarding data with neighbor-based greedy routing, source node and relay nodes select the optimal next-hop node according to the information of neighbors until the packets reach the destination node. The energy consumption in a routing is given by:

$$E = \bar{H}E_s + \bar{N}\bar{H}E_R \tag{5}$$

Neighbor-based greedy routing needs to periodically update its status, and one time updating energy consumption is given by:

$$E = E_s + \bar{N}E_R \tag{6}$$

As WSN is a data-centric network, sensor data collection is regular. Assume sensor data collection interval is T_s, status updating interval is T_M, the average energy consumption of flooding forwarding and greedy forwarding are respectively given by:

$$E_{flood} = \frac{\bar{N}\bar{H}(E_s + E_R)}{T_s} \tag{7}$$

$$E_{greedy} = \frac{\bar{H}E_s + \bar{N}\bar{H}E_R}{T_s} + \frac{E_s + \bar{N}E_R}{T_M} \tag{8}$$

E_s and E_R depend on the electric property of the node. $\bar{H}$ is associated with node transmission radius and deployed area. T_s and T_M are initial parameters of the wireless sensor network. All the energy-related parameters are fixed after the network initialization completed. In the entire lifetime of the network, as old nodes exhaust energy or new nodes join in, the ADN is in dynamic change, which makes the possibility to optimize the routing strategy.

3 A New Two-Hop Greedy Ellipse Routing Protocol

3.1 Information Quantitative of Neighbors

Greedy-2 algorithm requires each node to broadcast its own and its one-hop neighbors' location information to its one-hop neighbors, so that Greedy-2 algorithm can choose next-hop node better according to the two-hop neighbors' information, thus reducing the probability of running into routing holes.

In order to take advantage of Greedy-2 and reduce the cost of hello message for maintaining the neighbors' status information, quantifying the second hop neighbors' information is done to reduce the length of hello message [11]. The basic idea is that dividing the radio propagation area of a node to describe the approximate distribution of its neighbors.

Firstly, the radio propagation area (i is the center, r is the radius of the radio circle) of node i is divided into m sectors, and sector k is $\left[\frac{2\pi k}{m}, \frac{2\pi(k+1)}{m}\right]$, where $0 \leq k \leq m$.

Define $Val(i, j)$ as the node evaluation function of neighbor j, shown by:

$$Val(i, j) = \frac{B_E(j)}{\psi(j)} \tag{9}$$

Among them, $B_E(j)$ is the residual energy of neighbor j; $\psi(j)$ is data congestion of neighbor j, dividing message arrival rate by the service rate. The bigger evaluation value of nodes is, the stronger ability of forwarding data will be. Thus the neighbor sector quantitative information of node i is:

$$\Gamma(i, k) = \max\{Val(i, j)\} \tag{10}$$

where $j \in N^*(i, k)$. $N(i)$ is the neighbor set of node i. $N^*(i, k)$ is a set of neighbors in sector k, and it is a subset of $N(i)$.

3.2 GERP Algorithm

When a wireless sensor network is started, packets sending and receiving will proceed after the node information initialization completed. Assume that the source node S sends a message to the destination node D, the specific strategies of routing forwarding are as follows:

1. Node S checks its own neighbors, if node D is one of its neighbors, then node S sends the passage directly to node D.
2. Otherwise find node v in table $N(i)$ by the following condition:

$$\angle vSD = \min\{\angle iSD\} \tag{11}$$

where $i \in N(i)$. Set a region factor $a(a \geq 1)$, and find node u with the maximum $\angle uSD$ in the range of $a\angle vSD$. So an ellipse area is established, as shown in Fig. 3. Point i in the ellipse area needs to meet the following condition:

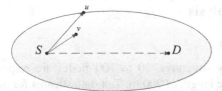

Fig. 3. Ellipse establish

$$d_{Si} + d_{iD} \leq d_{Su} + d_{uD} \tag{12}$$

3. Packet forwarding in the ellipse according to the neighbor sector quantitative information.

   Firstly calculate the evaluation value of neighbors in the ellipse, according to the Eq. (9).

$$W(j) = \frac{B_E(j)}{\psi(j)} \tag{13}$$

   where $j \in N_e(i)$. $N_e(i)$ is the neighbor set of node i in the ellipse.

   Secondly,

$$P_{(j,k)} = \beta W(j) + (1 - \beta)\Gamma(j, k) \tag{14}$$

   where $j \in N_e(i)$, $k = 1, 2, \ldots, m$, m is a positive integer. $P_{(j,k)}$ shows the extent of advancement from neighbors to destination node in the quantified sector k. β is a weight factor.

   At last, find $\max\{P_{(j,k)}\}$, thus node j is the perfect next-hop, and the packet will be sent over.

4. If $N_e(i) = \emptyset$, it means that there is no neighbor to forward packets, usually called routing hole happened. Now redefine the ellipse area by making current node as source node and destination node unchanged, called ellipse redefinition.

5. If the packets still cannot be forwarded after the ellipse redefinition, make a double and go to the second step.

When some nodes leave the network because of energy exhausted or other reasons, the nodes becomes denser, and now forwarding with the region-based routing. Each node maintains a neighbor information table, whenever hello message is received, it will automatically update the table. Update the average degree of neighborhood through the weighted average method at the same time.

Assuming the critical point of the average degree of neighborhood is $\bar{N}_c$. When $\bar{N} < \bar{N}_c$, the node stops regularly sending the hello message, and starts flooding forwarding packets. When $\bar{N} > \bar{N}_c$, the node starts regularly sending the hello message, and use greedy forwarding packets.

4 Simulation Analysis

4.1 ADN Simulation

Nine kinds of topology structures, 20 to 100 nodes are respectively deployed in a square area with the side length of 200 m. Ten data streams for the transmission and 20 node buffer queues, 512-byte sensor data packets, 32-byte neighbor status updating packets, ten seconds transmission interval, four seconds neighbor status updating interval, 6.66 mW transmission power, 4.5 mW receiving power and 0.8 mW idle power, all the parameters are presented. The experimental duration is 200 s, taking an average of 10 results.

The ADN for different nodes number is shown in Fig. 4. We can see that the number of the neighbor nodes increases linearly as the number of nodes deployed increasing. Therefore, the number of neighbor nodes can be used to represent the average degree of neighborhood.

Comparing the average energy consumption between perimeter stateless routing (GPSR for short usually) [12] and MFlood routing, as shown in Fig. 5. GPSR energy consumption rises more slowly as the number of nodes increasing. As can be seen in Fig. 5, 40 nodes is the critical point of average energy consumption. By the calculation, the critical ADN of GPSR and Mflood routing is 3.76. Thus, routing by flooding forwarding when $\bar{N} < 3.76$ and by greedy forwarding when $\bar{N} < 3.76$, the routing energy consumption is more lower.

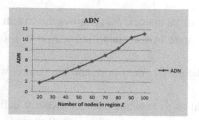

Fig. 4. ADN for different nodes number

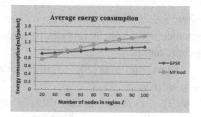

Fig. 5. Average energy consumption for different nodes number

4.2 Performance of GERP

NS-2 simulator is used for GERP simulation and analysis, also the comparison GERP with GPSR and Greedy-2. The evaluation criteria are average energy consumption and packet arrival rate.

100 nodes are deployed in a square area with the side length of 200 m. IEEE802.11 protocol is applied in the MAC layer, and all the sensor nodes have the characters of 50 node buffer queues, 2 MB per second of packet transmission rate, 40 m of node communication radius and 1.5 of region factor. 20 data streams are randomly generated to transmit. Data acquisition cycle is ten seconds, and the transmission cycle of node hello packets is 4 s. The experimental duration is 600 s, taking an average of 10 results.

Figure 6 shows the average energy consumption of a packet transmission in different time periods after the network running. During the first 300 s, the energy consumption of GPSR is less than that of Greedy-2 and GERP. Because Greedy-2's and GERP's hello packets need to exchange two-hop neighbors' information, and the maintenance charge of these information is higher than GPSR. GERP typically chooses suboptimal next-hop node, which also increases the forwarding cost. 300 s later, the energy consumption of GPSR and Greedy-2 increases significantly. Because GPSR and Greedy-2 never consider the residual energy when forwarding, this leads to some specific nodes energy depletion and left network. Thus the number of routing hops increases significantly, and so does the average energy consumption. Moreover, no strategies to avoid routing holes, which makes GPSR waste more energy on routing recovery when routing holes happen. Further increase the energy consumption. On the contrary, thanks to taking energy balance and two-hop neighbors into consideration in a certain area when forwarding, GERP can allocate forwarding nodes reasonably. So the energy consumption of GERP is relatively less during the whole time.

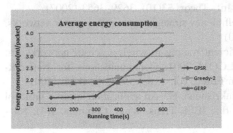 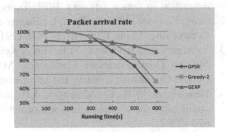

Fig. 6. The contract of average energy consumption

Fig. 7. Packet arrival rate

Figure 7 shows the packet arrival rate at different times. In the first 300 s, the packet arrival rates of the three algorithms are nearly the same, because the energy of every node is in good condition and transmission goes well. As time goes by, GPSR and Greedy-2 make the energy of some key nodes in the network depleted rapidly, resulting in interruption of some data streams and plummeting of the packet arrival rate. But the packet arrival rate of GERP declines less obviously, because of energy balance consideration. 600 s later, the arrival rates of GPSR and Greedy-2 are respectively only 57 % and 64 %. That is nearly half of the packets cannot reach the sink node, which has been unable to reflect the actual deployment environment information. However, the arrival rate of GERP is 85 %, and it still works.

5   Conclusions

The energy consumption in wireless sensor network is a major concern, and researching and designing an efficient routing protocol is practically important. In this paper, combining neighbor-based routing protocol and region-based routing protocol, we have proposed a new low-power hybrid routing protocols for wireless sensor network. All the studies above shows that in the early time of the network, the sensor nodes are densely distributed, using the neighbor-based routing can be better to save energy; but later some nodes exhaust energy or turn out dead, and the distribution of nodes becomes relatively sparse, region-based routing is more efficient. And the GERP simulation result in NS-2 network simulator shows that GERP protocol can effectively reduce more energy consumption of the wireless sensor network than other typical protocols.

Acknowledgments. This work was supported by a grant from the Natural Science Foundation of China (No. 61172018), the Science & Research Plan Project of Xi'an City (No.CXY1340). The authors are grateful for the anonymous reviewers who made constructive comments.

References

1. Bajwa, W., Haupt, J., Sayeed, A., et al.: Joint source-channel communication for distributed estimation in sensor networks. IEEE Trans. Inf. Theor. **53**(10), 3629–3653 (2007)
2. Peng, C., Guo, J., Pei, L., Wen, L.: Energy-efficiency strategies in wireless sensor networks. Control Eng. China **17**(3), 1671–7848 (2010)
3. Schurgers, C., Srivastava, M.B.: Energy efficient routing in wireless sensor networks. In: Military Communications Conference, MILCOM 2001. Communications for Network-Centric Operations: Creating the Information Force, vol. 1, pp. 357–361. IEEE (2001)
4. Heinzelman, W.B., Chandrakasan, A.P., Balakrishnan, H.: An application-specific protocol architecture for wireless micro-sensor networks. IEEE Trans. Wirel. Commun. **1**(4), 560–670 (2002)
5. Wang, J., Zhao, X., Liu, H.: A greedy geographic routing algorithm based on 2-hop neighbors. Acta Electronica Sin. **36**(10), 1903–1909 (2008)
6. Liang, X., Wang, G., Xie, Y.: Ellipse hole-routing algorithm in wireless sensor networks. Comput. Eng. **35**(12), 78–81 (2009)
7. Dong, R., Ma, Z., Guo, Y., Gu, T.: A Markov game theory-based energy balance routing algorithm. Chinese J. Comput. **7**, 1500–1508 (2013)
8. Saad, C., Benslimane, A., Champ, J., et al.: Ellipse routing: a geographic routing protocol for mobile sensor networks with uncertain positions. IEEE Global Telecommunications Conference, IEEE GLOBECOM 2008, pp. 1–5. IEEE (2008)
9. Norouzi, A., Babamir, F.S., Zaim, A.H.: A novel energy efficient routing protocol in wireless sensor networks. Wirel. Sens. Netw. **3**(10), 341–350 (2011)
10. Stojmenovic, I., Lin, X.: Power-aware localized routing in wireless networks. IEEE Trans. Parallel Distrib. Syst. **12**(11), 1122–1133 (2001)
11. Chen, H., Qian, D., Wu, W., Wang, H.: Neighbors quantification based balance routing in wireless sensor networks. J. Xi'an Jiaotong Univ. **46**(4), 1–6 (2012)
12. Karp, B., Kung, H.T.: GPSR: greedy perimeter stateless routing for wireless networks. In: Proceedings of the 6th Annual International Conference on Mobile Computing and Networking, pp. 243–254. ACM (2000)

Adaptive Payload Length Algorithm for Video Transmission Over Wireless Multi-hop Networks

Pengrui Duan[✉], Huadong Ma, and Le Qian

Beijing Key Lab of Intelligent Telecommunications Software and Multimedia,
Beijing University of Posts and Telecommunications, Beijing 100876, China
dpr@bupt.edu.cn

Abstract. Video transmission over wireless multi-hop networks is challenging
due to the varying nature of the wireless channel as well as the inherent
difference between the video data traffic and the general data traffic. A single bit
error in a packet may lead to the packet loss, which results in poor quality of the
entire video frame. In this paper, we first analyze the effect of payload length on
the overhead of bit error, video frame reassembly and network efficiency. Then,
to improve the quality of video transmission, we propose an adaptive payload
length algorithm based on the digital fountain codes while take transmission
efficiency into account. The simulation environment is also designed to evaluate
the performance of multi-hop video transmission, which is based on the ARM
embedded system. Numerical simulations show that adaptive payload length
algorithm can improve the quality of video transmission over wireless multi-hop
networks.

Keywords: Video transmission · Multi-hop · Fountain codes · Payload length

1 Introduction

Transmission of great amount data, i.e. video transmission, is challenging due to the
high Bit Error Rate (BER) and limited bandwidth in wireless multi-hop networks, thus
it is necessary to ensure the transmission quality and throughput in the time-varying
wireless networks.

The digital fountain codes [1], namely one kind of Forward Error Correction (FEC)
codes, are ideally suitable for time-varying wireless transmission, which can be used to
protect the payload at the cost of redundancy. In [2], a data dissemination technique
based on fountain codes for vehicular ad hoc networks was conducted. Fountain codes
were also invoked in wireless networks to protect file transfer by considering 802.11
Media Access Control (MAC) retransmission rate in [3]. Due to the expense of
redundancy, it was observed that fountain codes can improve the performance of data
transmission only when considering the actual application environment in [4]. Carefully selecting the payload length is useful aid in practical fountain codes system in [5].
Aiming at small size Luby Transform (LT) codes, the relationship between the delay
and the redundancy was investigated in [6] through adjusting the parameters of degree
distribute, which can help the real-time applications.

© Springer-Verlag Berlin Heidelberg 2015
L. Sun et al. (Eds.): CWSN 2014, CCIS 501, pp. 423–434, 2015.
DOI: 10.1007/978-3-662-46981-1_41

For contention-based channel access mechanism of IEEE 802.11, the length of payload has great impact on the performance of the network. The relationship between the payload length and the throughput at a certain BER of IEEE 802.11 wireless channels was investigated in [7]. The effect of payload length and retransmission on multimedia over IEEE 802.11 WLANs was studied in [8]. The payload length selection was studied for three multicast solutions by considering the packet overhead in [9]. However, these works mentioned above could not be directly to the video transmission over multi-hop networks.

The rest of this paper is organized as follows. In Sect. 2, we analyze the effect of payload length, and then propose a dynamic adaptation algorithm for payload length. Section 3 describes the evaluation environment and experiment platform. We carry out simulations to evaluate the algorithm. Finally, Sect. 4 concludes this paper.

2 Presented Algorithm

In this section, we analyze the effect of payload length on the overhead of bit error, video frame reassembly, LT codes redundancy and network efficiency. Then, the adaptive payload length algorithm is described in detail.

2.1 The Overhead of Bit Error

Obviously, the packet will be lost when the quality of wireless channel is poor. Let P be the probability of packet loss over the end-to-end wireless transmission. If a packet is lost, retransmitted once and received correctly, the proportion of increased load for retransmission is $P(1 - P)$; If a packet is retransmitted two times and received correctly, the proportion is $2P^2(1 - P)$. In order to successfully transmit a packet, the proportion of total increased load, denoted by R, is given by:

$$R = \sum_{k=1}^{\infty} k \times P^k \times (1 - P) = \frac{P}{1 - P} \qquad (1)$$

In wireless multi-hop networks, let n be the number of multi-hop links and e be BER of the wireless channel. For simplicity of analysis, we ignore the packet collisions, the relationship between P and e is shown below:

$$P = 1 - (1 - e)^{n(L+H)} \qquad (2)$$

In accordance with Eqs. (1) and (2), the proportion of total increased load over a n-hop wireless links, denoted by $R(n)$, is given as follow:

$$R(n) = \frac{1 - (1 - e)^{n(H+L)}}{(1 - e)^{n(H+L)}} \qquad (3)$$

For different value of BER, the relationship between the increased proportion and payload length is illustrated in Fig. 1. Here n is set to 3; H is set to 66 bytes including the overhead of IP layer, UDP layer and the application layer. As can be seen, the same as the payload length, the higher the BER is, the greater the increase is. For the same BER, the larger the payload length is, the greater the increase is. Appropriate payload length can reduce the expense of retransmission load.

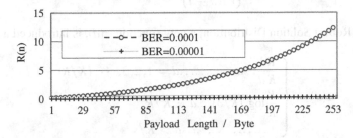

Fig. 1. Total increase in retransmission load over a 3-hop wireless links

2.2 Reconstruction of Video Frame

One I frame of H.264 is usually fragmented into several wireless packets due to Maximum Transmission Unit (MTU). Let a packet set of m wireless packets I = {WP$_1$, WP$_2$, ..., WP$_m$} denote the H.264 I frame, where m is the number of wireless packets from the same I frame, and WP represents wireless packet. At the final receiver, these wireless packets should be reassembled to reconstruct the same I frame.

Evidently, for the same I frame, the less the number of wireless packets is, the higher the reconstruction success rate is. Thus, it is needed to transmit packets with large length. However, considering the impact of BER in wireless medium, the larger packets are not always better than the smaller packets.

In subsequent experiments, the main issue is how to reduce the effect of wireless packet loss on the reconstruction of video frame, and how to reduce the effect of wireless channel access mechanism on the video transmission.

2.3 LT Codes

Retransmission schemes aiming at avoiding packet losses result in larger latency over multi-hop wireless networks. We try to meet the requirement of video transmission latency, and improve the reconstruction success rate by utilizing the FEC technique.

The LT codes [1, 10] are a class of packet-level FEC techniques and suitable for the data recovery in the erasure channel. The design of degree distribution is the key of LT codes, which requires the degree of encoded symbols to be high enough to ensure each source symbol is involved in encoding process. At the same time, it needs most of the degree to be low to ensure decoding process to continue.

Robust Soliton Distribution (RSD) [1] has been widely used in LT encoding and derived from the Ideal Soliton Distribution. For the Ideal Soliton Distribution, the probability that an encoded symbol has degree d, $\rho(d)$, is introduced as follows:

$$\rho(d) = \begin{cases} \dfrac{1}{K}\ldots\ldots\ldots.d = 1 \\ \dfrac{1}{d(d-1)}\ldots d = 2,3,\cdots,K \end{cases} \tag{4}$$

For the Robust Solition Distribution, a new function, $\tau(d)$, is introduced as follows:

$$\tau(d) = \begin{cases} \dfrac{R}{K}\dfrac{1}{d}\ldots\ldots\ldots\ldots.d = 1,2,3,\cdots,(K/R)-1 \\ \dfrac{R}{K}\log_e(R/\delta)\ldots d = K/R \\ 0\ldots\ldots\ldots\ldots.d > K/s \end{cases} \tag{5}$$

where K is the number of source symbols mentioned above; δ is the allowable failure probability of the decoder to recover the data for a given number M of encoded symbols. M is described below.

Add the Ideal Solition Distribution $\rho(d)$ to $\tau(d)$ and normalize to obtain Robust Solition Distribution, $\mu(d)$.

$$\mu(d) = \frac{\rho(d) + \tau(d)}{Z} \tag{6}$$

where

$$Z = \sum_{d=1}^{K} \rho(d) + \tau(d) \tag{7}$$

In order to recover the data successfully with the probability at least $1 - \delta$, the number of encoded symbols that need to be received at the decoder, denoted by M, is $M = K \times Z$. With the same degree distribution, the number of source symbols has great influence on the decoding efficiency. The investigation in [11] points out that the smaller source symbols size is, the larger the number of source symbols is, and the higher the decoding efficiency is.

2.4   Channel Access Mechanism

The efficiency of networks is closely related to channel access mechanism, especially for wireless networks. Figure 2 shows the basic access mechanism for Distributed Coordination Function (DCF) in 802.11 without using Request To Send (RTS) and Clear To Send (CTS) methods [12]. For a station to transmit, it shall sense the medium to determine if another station is transmitting. If the medium is not determined to be busy, and is idle for more than the time gap of DCF InterFrame Space (DIFS), the transmission may proceed. If the medium is determined to be busy, the station shall defer until the end of the current transmission. After deferral, or prior to attempting to transmit again immediately after a successful transmission, the station shall select a random backoff interval and shall decrease the backoff interval counter while the medium is idle. A transmission is successful when an ACK frame is received from the station after the time gap of Short InterFrame Space (SIFS).

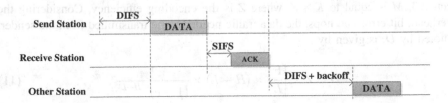

Fig. 2. DCF channel access mechanism

According to the basic access mechanism mentioned above, the transmission includes some overhead. The transmission time of one wireless packet, T, is given by

$$T = DIFS + backoff + T_{DATA} + SIFS + T_{ACK} \tag{8}$$

where T_{DATA} consists of T_{PHY} and T_{data}. T_{PHY} is transmission time of the overhead for Physical Layer Convergence Procedure (PLCP), T_{data} is the overhead including payload, and the header of MAC/IP/UDP. T_{ACK} is transmission time for ACK frame.

Ignoring the influence of BER, the transmission efficiency of 802.11, denoted by η_b, is given by

$$\eta_b = \frac{T_{payload}}{T} = \frac{T_{payload}}{DIFS + backoff + T_{DATA} + SIFS + T_{ACK}} \tag{9}$$

where $T_{payload}$ is the transmission time of payload.

It can be seen that, in the condition of bit error-free, the larger the payload length is, the higher the efficiency is.

2.5   Adaptive Payload Length Algorithm

For the wireless networks, we can see that payload length has great influence on the overhead of bit error, reconstruction of video frame, LT codes redundancy and transmission efficiency. We present an adaptive payload length algorithm which takes the effect of payload length into account. According to the feedback of transmission quality and the number of hops, payload length may be adaptively adjusted.

To generate LT encoded symbols, the data to be transmitted is first divided into K source symbols. K can be calculated by

$$K = \left\lceil \frac{F}{L} \right\rceil \tag{10}$$

where F is the length of total transmission data, and L is equal to the size of LT source symbols.

From these K source symbols, the encoder generates encoded symbols. In order to recover the data successfully with higher probability, the number of encoded symbols that need to be received at the decoder is larger than M. As can be seen from the above Sect. 2.3, M is equal to $K \times Z$, where Z is the encoding efficiency. Considering the overhead, bit error and hops, the data traffic needed to be transmitted from the sender, denoted by D, is given by

$$D = Z \times \left\lceil \frac{F}{L} \right\rceil \times (H + L) \times \frac{1}{(1 - e)^{n(H+L)}} \tag{11}$$

where H is the length of the total header; e is the BER of wireless channels; n is the number of hops. $(1 - e)^{n(L+H)}$ is obtained from Eq. (2).

Due to the constrain of channel access mechanism, the actually available bandwidth to transmit user data, denoted by B_{user}, is given by

$$B_{user} = B \times \frac{t_L}{T} \tag{12}$$

where t_L is the transmission time for the payload with length L; B is the bandwidth of wireless medium. According to the above discussion, the transmission time for data with total length F, denoted by $T(L)$, is given by

$$T(L) = \frac{D}{B_{user}} = Z \times \left\lceil \frac{F}{L} \right\rceil \times (H + L) \times \frac{1}{B \times \frac{t_L}{T}} \times \frac{1}{(1 - e)^{n(H+L)}} \tag{13}$$

where the values of L are sequences of discrete values, which can be set to be 4,8,12, ...,1400. This is because that the size of LT source symbols should be any multiple of 4 bytes and is limited to the MTU of wireless medium. The value of F is the length of data needed to be LT encoded, which includes a series of I frames and P frames.

From the above Eq. (13), we select the exact value of L, s.t. $\min(T(L))$. For the given data with length F, by carefully selecting the payload length, we can minimize the transmission time and maximize the network efficiency.

According to Eq. (2), the receiver can get e, and then back e to the sender. Through calculating the value of $T(L)$ in the sender, the suitable payload length is selected to minimize the transmission time for video frames.

Experiments are conducted to capture YUV video, where the YUV video sequence in the 480*272 format is encoded using H.264. Meanwhile, the value of group of picture (GOP) is set to 5 and the value of quantize parameter (QP) is set to 28, the sum of one Intra-coded frame (I frame) and four predicted frames (P frames) in each scene is about 20000 bytes.

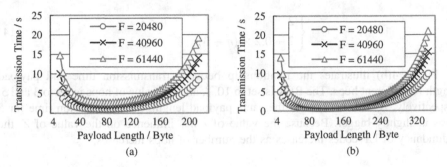

Fig. 3. Transmission time vs payload length over multi-hop wireless links. (a) 5-hop. (b) 3-hop.

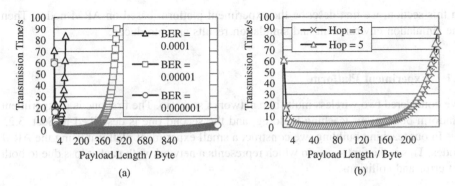

Fig. 4. Transmission time vs payload length over multi-hop wireless links. (a) Comparison among different BERs. (b) Comparison between 3-hop and 5-hop.

For different data size, Fig. 3 shows the relationship between transmission time and payload length. The BER is set to 10^{-5}, as well as the number of hops is set to 5 and 3 in Fig. 3(a) and (b), respectively. We observe from Fig. 3 that there are relatively sharp troughs in transmission time for larger data while a more gradual transition is observed for smaller data. For the 61440 bytes case in Fig. 3(a), there is a small range of payload lengths around 100 bytes that can be selected for optimal performance.

For different value of BER, Fig. 4(a) shows the relationship between transmission time and payload length. The length of data is set to 20480 bytes, the number of hops is set to 3, as well as the BER is set to 10^{-4}, 10^{-5}, and 10^{-6}, respectively. We can see that there are relatively sharp troughs in transmission time for higher BER while a more gradual transition is observed for lower BER. This suggests that the payload length adaptation is more crucial at higher BER.

LT codes efficiency is high when the value of K is large [10]. However, if the number of frame to be LT encoded is set close to 10^3, it will lead to high latency for the video transmission. In order to reduce the redundancy, we change the expression of R [11] from $R = 2 + 8\sqrt[4]{K}$ to $R = 2 + r\sqrt[4]{K}$, where the upper limit for the value of r is 8 and the lower limit for the value of r is 2. The value of r can be adjusted according to the formula given as follows.

$$r = \begin{cases} 2 & n < 3 \\ 2 + 0.2 \times (n - 3) & n \geq 3 \end{cases} \qquad (14)$$

Figure 4(b) illustrates the relationship between transmission time and payload length for different hops. The BER is set to 10^{-5}, and the value of hops is set to 3 and 5, respectively. As can be seen, at the same payload length, the transmission time for 5 hops is slightly bigger. Because the value of r has influence on the value of Z, the redundancy of LT codes increases as the number of hops increases.

3   Evaluation

In this section, we first describe the experiment platform based on ARM nodes. Then the simulation environment and simulation results are introduced.

3.1   Experiment Platform

We considered two wireless multi-hop networks scenario. The first one is a experiment platform built in our teaching building, and the second one is described in Sect. 3.2.

In our teaching building, we construct a small experiment platform using the ARM nodes. This is the first scenario which represents a network with packet loss due to both bit error and collisions.

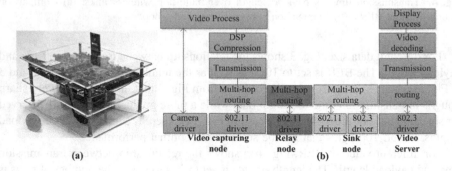

Fig. 5. Experiment platform

Figure 5(a) shows the video capturing node developed by our laboratory. The node is an embedded module based on the S3C6410 ARM11 processor and Linux 2.6.28 operating system. In order to realize the real-time video capture, it photographs with OV3640 digital camera chip supported by Linux. Meanwhile, the H.264 encoder inside the ARM processor achieves real-time video compression. The node supports the IEEE 802.11b standard with the GM320 wireless chip. We also develop Ad hoc On-demand Distance Vector routing (AODV) wireless multi-hop protocol supported by Linux, then the node can act as ad hoc relay node as well as sink node.

Figure 5(b) shows the function blocks of the nodes and video server. OV3640 digital camera captures video stream, and video stream is encoded using H.264, and then appropriate payload length is determined to transmission encapsulation. Multi-hop path is found through AODV, and GM320 chip relays the payload to final sink node link by link. At the video server based on MS Windows, H.264 frame is decoded, and then the live video stream is shown.

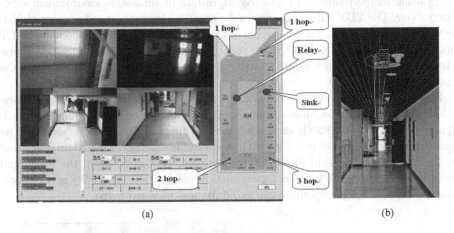

(a)   (b)

Fig. 6. The deployment of the platform

The deployment of the platform is illustrated in Fig. 6(a). The platform is on the 9th floor of the building. We deploy four video capturing nodes at four corners of the floor, one relay node and one sink node. The example of video node hanged on the ceiling is given in Fig. 6(b), and the four video windows are in the left part of Fig. 6(a). Due to the limitation of the site, the number of hops for these video capturing nodes are one, one, two, three, respectively.

3.2 Simulation Environment

In order to evaluate the performance of transmission scheme, we design simulation environment, this is second scenario. It is a network without packet collisions, and packet loss is entirely due to the bit error of channels. Video data traffic is 240 kbps. Data communications are based on the 802.11b. The system consists of the video capturing node, wireless relay nodes, the video server and video quality measurement tool.

We capture a cartoon video sequence of *Ice Age* as original video frames to guarantee the quality of the evaluation consistent criteria. Meanwhile, it is necessary to guarantee the stable wireless channel environment and avoid the interference from devices with WiFi function (i.e. laptop, mobile phone, etc.) in the evaluation environment. We design the simulation wireless channels based on Gilbert model, and thus, the stable wireless channels are achieved.

The video server is developed on the Windows operating system, which is used in experiment platform mentioned above. Just like most video software, the server can decode the H.264 frames, play the video and save YUV frames as log file.

3.3   Simulation Results

We evaluate the performance of adaptive algorithm in simulation environment mentioned above. The YUV video sequence in the 480*272 format is encoded using H.264, the value of GOP is set to 5 and the value of QP is set to 28. The original data to be LT encoded is the sum of one GOP video scene, which includes one Intra-coded frame (I frame) and four predicted frames (P frames). The bit error rate is set to 10^{-4}, and the burst length is set to 100.

Experiment 1 compares the quality of adaptive payload length transmission scheme with the quality of traditional transmission scheme, where the number of hops is set to 3. Figure 7(a) illustrates the PSNR variation at the two different transmissions scheme. The video screen comparison of two different transmissions scheme for the 204th frame and the 233rd frame is show in Fig. 7(b), respectively. As can be seen, the traditional transmission scheme leads to lower reconstruction success rate, the quality is very poor. Adaptive payload length algorithm can avoid the loss of video frame.

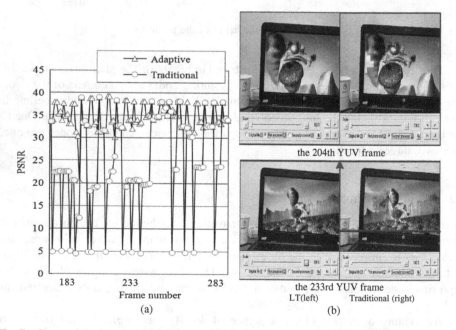

Fig. 7. Comparison between adaptive transmission scheme and traditional transmission scheme

In experiment 2, the adaptive payload length transmission scheme is compared with the fixed length LT codes transmission scheme, where the number of hops is set to 3 and fixed length is set to 1000. Figure 8(a) shows the PSNR variation at the two different transmissions scheme. From Fig. 8(a), we observe that the adaptive payload

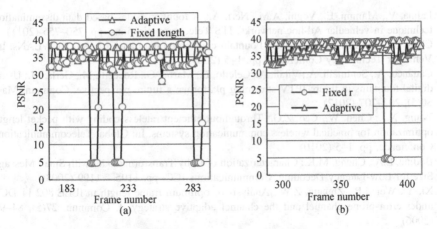

Fig. 8. Comparison of PSNR

length transmission scheme has more advantages than the scheme with fixed length LT codes, dynamic adaptation of payload length can improve the video transmission performance.

We also compared the adaptive payload length transmission scheme with scheme using fixed r value, where r is set to 2 and the number of hops is set to 5. As can be seen from Fig. 8(b), the adaptive transmission scheme can maintain high quality of video, because the value of r is adjusted to 2.4 according to Eq. (14) when the number of hops is 5. The increase for the redundancy of the LT codes can compensate the loss of more hops.

4   Conclusion

In this paper, we investigate the effect of payload length on the overhead of bit error, reconstruction of video frame, LT codes redundancy and network efficiency. Then, we propose an adaptive payload length algorithm to improve the video transmission quality over wireless multi-hop networks. We also design the simulation environment based on the ARM embedded system. Simulations show that carefully selecting the payload length can improve the video quality over wireless multi-hop networks.

Acknowledgments. This work is supported by the Key Technologies R&D Program of China under Grant No. 2013BAK01B02, the National Natural Science Foundation of China under Grant No. 61332005, No.61100207 and No. 61133015, the Specialized Research Fund for the Doctoral Program of Higher Education under Grant No.20120005130002, and Jiangsu Provincial Natural Science Foundation of China under Grant No. BK2011170.

References

1. Luby, M.: LT Codes. In: Proceeding 43rd Annual IEEE Symposium Foundations of Computer Science, Vancouver, pp. 271–280 (2002)

2. Palma, V., Mammi, E., Vegni, A.M., Neri, A.: A fountain codes-based data dissemination technique in vehicular Ad-hoc networks. ITS Telecommunications, pp. 750–755 (2011)
3. Chen, H., Maunder, R., Hanzo, L.: Fountain-code aided file transfer in 802.11 WLANs. In: Vehicular Technology Conference, pp. 1–5 (2009)
4. Cattaneo, A., Sentinelli, A., Vitali, A., Celetto, L., Marfia, G., Roccetti, M., Gerla, M.: Using digital fountains in future IPTV streaming platforms: a future perspective. Commun. Mag. **50**(5), 202–207 (2012)
5. Wang, X.J., Chen, W., Cao, Z.G.: Throughput-efficient rateless coding with packet length optimization for practical wireless communication systems. In: Global Telecommunications Conference, pp. 1–5 (2010)
6. Bodine, E.A., Cheng, M.K.: Characterization of Luby Transform Codes with Small Message Size for Low-Latency Decoding. Communications ICC, pp. 1195 – 1199 (2008)
7. Xi, Y., Wei, J.B., Zhuang, Z.W.: Analysis of optimum frame length in IEEE 802.11 DCF under error-prone channel and the channel adaptive strategy. J. Commun. **27**(5), 84–94 (2006)
8. Choudhury, S., Sheriff, I., Gibson, J.D., Belding-Royer, E.: Effect of payload length variation and retransmissions on multimedia in 802.11a WLANs. International Conference on Wireless communications and mobile computing, pp. 377–382 (2006)
9. Zhu, F., Wu, L.S., Gu, Y.T.: Optimal payload lengths of reliable multicast schemes. J. Commun. **32**(6), 101–106 (2011)
10. MacKay, D.J.C.: Fountain codes. In: Communications, IEE Proceedings, pp. 1062–1068 (2005)
11. Zhu, H.P., Zhang, G.X., Xie, Z.D.: Suboptimal degree distribution algorithm of LT codes of digital fountain. J. Appl. Sci. **27**(1), 6–11 (2009)
12. IEEE Computer Society.: Part 11: Wireless LAN Medium Access Control (MAC) and Physical Layer (PHY) Specifications. (2007)

Wireless Communication Protocols and Sensor Data Quality, Integrity and Trustworthiness

A WSN Data Aggregation Method
with Linear Regression Model

Liping Chen[1,3(✉)], Jie Kan[2], Ruirui Zhang[1,3], and Gang Xu[1,3]

[1] Beijing Research Center of Intelligent Equipment for Agriculture,
Beijing Academy of Agriculture and Forestry Sciences, Beijing, China
{chenlp, zhangr, xug}@nercita.org.cn
[2] College of Information Engineering,
Capital Normal University, Beijing, China
kanjie128@163.com
[3] National Research Center of Intelligent Equipment for Agriculture,
Beijing, China

Abstract. Wireless sensor networks consist of sensor nodes with sensing and communication capabilities, which differ from traditional communication networks in several ways: sensor networks have severe energy constraints, redundant low-rate data, and many-to-one flows. Conduction of data aggregation is required. By the way of extracting reference data set and constructing linear regression mode, a data aggregation algorithm was proposed for WSN which composed of many correlated sensors. Taking a greenhouse air temperature, relative air humidity and soil temperature data sample collected by WSN in a demonstration base as research object, we analyzed performance of the algorithm. Results show that data compression ratio could reach as high as 40.72 % when the RMSE between restored data and raw data are respectively 0.622 °C and 0.853 % for soil temperature and relative air humidity.

Keywords: WSN · Data fusion · Linear regression · Correlation analysis

1 Introduction

Wireless sensor networks have a numerous number of sensor nodes that possess the abilities of communicating, monitoring and calculating Sensor nodes work corporately to gather, analyze and transmit sensor data to ensure the real-time data applications [1, 2]. Sensor network is limited by the limited energy and transmission bandwidth which confront a difficult situation of transferring big amount of data collected by sensors. Energy control has become a bottleneck in WSNs application. How to effectively diminish the data transmission to improve the lifetime of WSNs is one of the most important research issues [3, 4]. Data compression technology is an effective way to solve the problem [5–7].

In this paper, our study builds on the observation that different quantities on the same node have similar change rule over time. Taking [8] as reference and considering the situation that collected data of multi-quantities show strong correlation and

© Springer-Verlag Berlin Heidelberg 2015
L. Sun et al. (Eds.): CWSN 2014, CCIS 501, pp. 437–443, 2015.
DOI: 10.1007/978-3-662-46981-1_42

redundancy, we proposed a data compression algorithm using linear regression model based on node-station separating mode. By excavating correlation among multi-quantities, our algorithm reduces data transmission largely.

2 Algorithm Model Description

Data collected by WSNs node can be depicted in matrix structure as (1). X is the newest sampled data of time m in one node. Each row vector in X stored collected data of a disparate quantity. The matrix has N rows and M columns, where N is the number of sampled quantities.

$$
X = \begin{bmatrix} Y_1 \\ Y_2 \\ \vdots \\ Y_n \end{bmatrix} = \begin{bmatrix} y_{11} & y_{12} & \cdots & y_{1m} \\ y_{21} & y_{22} & \cdots & y_{2m} \\ \vdots & \vdots & \ddots & \vdots \\ y_{n1} & y_{n2} & \cdots & y_{nm} \end{bmatrix} \tag{1}
$$

For quantities that have strong correlation, we always use the standard linear regression to build mathematical estimation equation model like (2). The equation regression coefficient (a, b) can be determined by least square method. Then $Y[j]$ can be defined as base-data (call it BD) and transmitted to base station. For $Y[i]$, we can send regression coefficient (a, b) instead and base station can exploit Eq. (2) to restore its values. But taking the whole series of row vector may lead to lager error for data restore, which performed at two aspects: (i) quantities performed different degree of correlation at different periods of time. (ii) The mutual effect among quantities often has the lag property. So it is hard to meet a high precision application.

$$
\vec{Y}_i = a * \vec{Y}_j + b + \vec{\varepsilon} \ (1 < = i, j < = n) \tag{2}
$$

In this paper, we break sampled data series into intervals (assuming their length is l) and each interval will do standard linear regression with one explicit interval of base-data. Then we define our structural simple set S as definition 1 to describe the feature of each interval.

Definition 1. Structural simple set S has following parts

- Start: the interval's start index in vector. For example, $Yi[start, start + l]$ represents for one interval of $Y[i]$.
- Migration: the migration on base data when doing standard linear regression, for example, BD [migration, migration + l] represents for one base interval of BD.
- a, b: (a, b) represent for the coefficient of regression equation build by one interval and BD set.

When the latest n × m sampled data is collected, sensor node process data compression. Firstly, it's necessary to choose base data (see below), then we break all row vector of

X into m/l intervals. Each interval searches on BD to find out the best interval to process the regression operation and generate its simple set. So, each row of X would have m/l simple sets except the BD vector. Then node sent all simple sets and the whole BD to base station where sampled data matrix X would be restored based on BD and regression coefficient. Assuming BD is the base-data vector, the interval Yi *[start, start + l]* in *Y[i]* can be depicted as:

$$a * \vec{Y}_j[migration, migration + l] + b \tag{3}$$

After data compression, the amount of data transmission is {BD, simple sets}. If measurement data and the member of simple set have the same memory space, we can define data compression ratio of the node as:

$$Ratio = \frac{\frac{M}{l} * 4 + M}{N * M} = \frac{\frac{4}{l} + 1}{N} \tag{4}$$

Ratio is approximate to $1/N$ when l is lager.

3 Algorithm Implementation

The algorithm implementation includes two parts: initialization and maintenance.

Algorithm initialization: using historical collected data as data source, we firstly analyze correlation among quantities to define correlation contribution evaluation model (CCEM, see Eq. 5) on base station that has enough energy. Then based on CCEM, we choose base data set and find the optimal interval number to build interval linear regression model. At last, base station send model parameters to nodes.

Algorithm maintenance: according to parameter received from base station, WSN nodes process data compression calculation and then send compressed data simple set to base station. After collecting data for a period of time, WSN base station will change model parameters timely and update parameters on nodes. Because the parameters selection is processed on base station, WSN nodes only need to do data mapping operation.

Firstly, it is necessary to choose a quantity as base-data. We here use historical sampled data to do CCEM calculation and choose the highest one as BD. In (1), X has n row quantities. In order to calculate CCEM, we define CCEM as:

$$CCEM(i) = \sum_{j=1, j \neq i}^{n} r_{i,j} \tag{5}$$

In which $r_{i,j}$ represent for the correlation coefficient of row i and j.

We will choose Yi as BD if it has the highest CCEM. We do it in two steps:

1. r_{ij} calculation. We use simple sample correlation coefficient calculation method like Eq. (6).

$$r_{ij} = \frac{\sum\limits_{k=1}^{t} (x_{ik} - \bar{x}_i)(x_{jk} - \bar{x}_j)}{\sqrt{\sum\limits_{k=1}^{t} (x_{ik} - \bar{x}_i)^2}\sqrt{\sum\limits_{k=1}^{t} (x_{jk} - \bar{x}_j)^2}} \tag{6}$$

2. We calculate all CCEM of each row in X and sort them. The highest one of CCEM will be chosen as BD.

Then we process linear regression based on BD. Assuming that the newest X has data amounts of N*M and every interval has the length of l, so each row has (M/l)intervals. After we break each row into intervals, algorithm search on BD to do linear regression of length l for each interval. After each search, the corresponding simple set S will be initialized if it has the minimized regression error. We can obtain data transmission set as Data = {∑∑Si, BD} at last.

Because our algorithm takes intervals as units to do linear regression, different number of intervals has different performance. Theoretically, the more the number of intervals leads to the less error when base station restores data. The error would be zero of each interval has only one element. Actually, the error's descent rate is large when interval number is small. But with the increase of the number, the error's descent rate will slow down. Moreover, the compression ratio keeps increase with the raise of the interval number. That brings a negative effect of PWLR. So it is not always profitable if the number of intervals is large. We here use local optimum method to make a tradeoff between error and compression ratio of PWLR. If the error satisfy the threshold we need, it is beneficial to stop increasing the intervals.

4 Experiments

The simulation experiments sample data are chosen from national precision agriculture demonstration base in Beijing Xiao Tangshan at 2013-9-1∼9-10. Sample data include environment temperature, air relative humidity and soil temperature. The sampling period is 1 min. The time span of sampled data matrix X is 5 days. We use data from 9-1∼9-5 to calculate initialization parameters on base station. The data from 9-6∼9-10 is used as algorithm simulation data. Root mean square error (RMSE) is used to evaluate the performance of PWLR in (7).

$$RMSE = \sqrt{\frac{1}{n}\sum (\hat{d}_t - d_t)^2} \tag{7}$$

Firstly, we use historical collected data to calculate CCEM of all quantities to choose BD. Result is shown in Table 1. Obviously, environment temperature is selected as BD.

Table 1. CCEM of simulation quantities

Quantity	CCEM
Temperature	1.73
Air relative humidity	1.26
Soil temperature	1.12

In experiments, we set different interval numbers as input variables and the RMSE error as output. The simulation results of air relative humidity and soil temperature are shown where the interval numbers are set from 1 to 30. From the results we can see that the RMSE error reaches the highest values of 5 °C and 3.2 % when we do not break data set into intervals. When experiments increase interval numbers, the descent rate of RMSE goes fast in the beginning. The RMSEs reaches the local optimal values at 13 (for soil temperature) and 15 (for air relative humidity). After that, the RMSE changes stably with the increase of interval numbers. It obviously brings less promotion of PWLR's performance and result in the increase of compression ratio on the contrary. In this paper, we use local optimal method to choose BD.

When soil temperature and air relative humidity respectively have the interval number of 13 and 15, base station restores data based on structural simple set S received from nodes. Figures 1 and 2 show the restored results of soil temperature and air relative humidity. We can see that PWLR gains a good feature description of compressed data set. For soil temperature and air relative humidity, restored data and original data have the RMSE errors of 0.622 °C and 0.853 % respectively. The whole compression ratio of X reaches 40.72 %. Our technology significantly reduces data transmission of WSN.

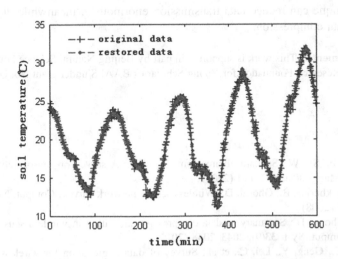

Fig. 1. Restored data versus raw data of soil temperature under the optimal segmentation

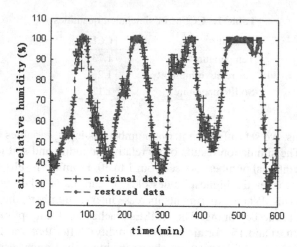

Fig. 2. Restored data versus raw data of relative air humidity under the optimal segmentation

5 Conclusion

Distributed nodes with high density in the sensor network produce a huge amount of data transmission. How to effectively compress the data in response to the resource-constrained WSN application research is a challenging topic. According to the characteristics of the correlation among quantities, we proposed a data compression algorithm based linear regression named PWLR. Simulation results show that, PWLR break sampled data into intervals to do optimal linear regression search taking base data as reference. This can minimize the error when doing data restoration on base station. So our technique can reduce data transmission enormously, meanwhile, it ensure the quality of data compression.

Acknowledgements. This work is supported in part by Beijing Natural Science Foundation ID: 4121001 and Research Foundation for Young Scholar of BAAFS under grant No. QNJJ201217.

References

1. Akyildiz, I.F., Su, W., Sankarasubramaniam, Y., et al.: A survey on sensor networks. IEEE Commun. Mag. **40**(8), 102–114 (2002)
2. Yick, J., Mukherjee, B., Ghosal, D.: Wireless sensor network survey. Comput. Netw. **52**(12), 2292–2330 (2008)
3. Wei, L., Lihong, H.: Summary of data compression algorithm in wireless sensor networks. J. Chin. Comput. Syst. **33**(9), 2043–2048 (2012)
4. Zhengyu, C., Geng, Y., Lei, C., et al.: Survey of data aggregation for wireless sensor netwoeks. Appl. Res. Comput. **28**(5), 1601–1604 (2011)
5. Kang, J., Zuo, X., Tang, L., et al.: Survey on data aggregation of wireless sensor networks. Comput. Sci. **37**(4), 31–35 (2010)

6. Nakamura, E.F., Loureiro, A.A.F., Frery, A.C.: Information fusion for wireless sensor networks: methods, models, and classifications. ACM Comput. **39**(9) (2007)
7. Zhang, R., Du, S., Chen, L. et al.: Data compression method with Piece-wise linear regression in WSN. J. Transduction Technol. (Accepted paper)
8. Deligiannakis, A., Kotidis, Y., Roussopoulos, N.: Compressing historical information in sensor networks. In: Proceedings of ACM SIGMOD Conference (2004)

An Energy-Efficient Data Gathering Scheme for Unreliable Wireless Sensor Networks Using Compressed Sensing

Yi-hua Zhu[1(✉)], Yan-yan Wang[1], Kai-kai Chi[1], and Lin Xu[2]

[1] School of Computer Science and Technology, Zhejiang University of Technology,
Hangzhou 310023, Zhejiang, China
{yhzhu,kkchi}@zjut.edu.cn, wangyan1575@sina.com
[2] College of Business Administration, Zhejiang University of Technology,
Hangzhou 310023, Zhejiang, China

Abstract. The main task of wireless sensor network (WSN) is to collect data from the environment. Sensor nodes usually are powered by batteries with extremely limited energy, which makes energy conservation critical for a WSN to run longer. The energy-efficient Data Gathering Scheme based on Compressed Sensing (DGS-CS) is presented, which enables the sensor nodes to efficiently and evenly expend energy so that the lifetime of the WSN is prolonged. The maximum, minimum, and average energy consumptions of the proposed DGS-CS and those of the Traditional Routing Scheme (TRS) are derived. The numeric analysis shows the proposed DGS-CS outperform the TRS in terms of energy consumption.

Keywords: Wireless sensor network (WSN) · Energy conservation · Data gathering · Compressed sensing

1 Introduction

Wireless Sensor Network (WSN) is widely used in various areas such as environment monitoring, poison gas surveillance, smart house, and more. A WSN is used to collect data captured by its sensor nodes with extremely limited computation power, battery energy, memory space, and communication ranges. In a WSN, the data captured by a sensor node are delivered to the sink in multi-hop manner, i.e., the data are forwarded by the sensor nodes on the route from the sensor node to the sink. Hence, energy exhaustion of a node may lead the data captured by the nodes far away from the sink unable to deliver their data to the sink. As a result, it is significant to conserve energy in sensor nodes of a WSN so that the WSN have a longer running time.

Hitherto, numerous energy-efficient data gathering schemes are presented for WSNs, such as LEACH [1], HEED [2], TEEN [3] etc. It is observed that the sensor nodes around the sink usually consume much more energy in forwarding

© Springer-Verlag Berlin Heidelberg 2015
L. Sun et al. (Eds.): CWSN 2014, CCIS 501, pp. 444–455, 2015.
DOI: 10.1007/978-3-662-46981-1_43

data packets than those far from the sink, which leads them to deplete their battery energy quickly, causing the sink unreachable from the sensor nodes. Hence, researchers seek other means to deal with the problem of the above energy uneven consumption. In last years, Compressed Sensing (CS), which was initiated in 2006 by two ground breaking papers [4,5] written by Donoho and Cand'es et al., respectively, has been used in data gathering in WSNs because CS enables to recovery signal from incomplete information [6–8]. Up to date, some CS based data gathering schemes are presented to conserve energy in WSNs, such as the paper who first proposed compressive data gathering is able to reduce global scale communication cost in large scale wireless sensor networks [9], investigating the application of CS to multihop networking scenarios and minimizing the network energy consumption through joint routing and compressed aggregation in [10], analyzing the network energy consumption theoretically and propose a novel data collection algorithm using compressive sensing [11]. The problem of improving throughput for WSNs by CS is investigated in [12].

In fact, some popular CS-based data gathering schemes [13–15] exist a fatal shortcoming that the sink will fail in recovering the original signal, i.e., the sink cannot recover the data sensed by the sensor nodes, if a packet is lost at an intermediate node on the route to the sink. Currently, most WSNs adopt IEEE 802.15.4 standard designed for low-rate and low-power wireless personal area network. Hence, WSNs are prone to packet loss. In a large-scale WSN, the probability of successful delivering a packet from a sensor node to the sink is extremely low. Obviously, in the case that the sink is not able to recover the original signal, the sensed data may be discarded due to memory space limitation in the sensor nodes, which may cause the critical event missed, or need to be redelivered or even, which consumes extra energy.

Therefore, it is significant to address the packet loss problem existing in the CS-based data gathering schemes so that energy can be efficiently expended. This is the main motivation of the paper. The main contributions are as follows:

(1) The energy-efficient Data Gathering Scheme based on Compressed Sensing (DGS-CS) is presented;
(2) The maximum, minimum, and average energy consumptions of the proposed DGS-CS and those of the Traditional Routing Scheme (TRS) are derived;
(3) Numeric analysis is conducted to analyze the performance of the proposed DGS-CS and compare DGS-CS with TRS.

2   DGS-CS

2.1   Preliminary

Before presenting our DGS-CS, we describe the compressed sensing theory used in the scheme. In a WSN, a signal captured by a sensor can be represented by a vector $x^* \in R^n$, where R^n stands for the vector space with n elements. A set $\{\varphi_1, \varphi_2, \ldots, \varphi_n\}$ is called a basis of R^n if the set spans R^n and its elements are linearly independent ($\varphi_i \in R^n, i = 1, 2, \ldots, n$). With the basis, the signal x^* can be represented by

$$x^* = x_1\varphi_1 + x_2\varphi_2 + \ldots + x_n\varphi_n = \Phi x \tag{1}$$

where $x = (x_1, x_2, \ldots, x_m)^T \in R^n$ and the $n \times n$ matrix $\Phi = \{\varphi_1, \varphi_2, \ldots, \varphi_n\}$ is called the *representation matrix*.

In nature, signal possesses sparse property so that signals are often well approximated by a linear combination of just a few elements from a basis [6]. Therefore, an $m \times n$ matrix $\Psi = \{\psi_1, \psi_2, \ldots, \psi_n\}$, called observation matrix, can be used to observe signal x, in which $m \ll n$ and $\psi_i \in R^m$, $i = 1, 2, n$. Let $y = (y_1, y_2, \ldots, y_m)^T \in R^m$ be vector consisting of the observed values of signal x^* with the observation matrix Ψ. Then, we have

$$y = \Psi x^* \tag{2}$$

which leads to (3) using (1).

$$y = \Psi \Phi x = Ax \tag{3}$$

where $A = \Psi\Phi$ is an $m \times n$ matrix with $m \ll n$. Matrix A, referred to as *sensing matrix* below, represents a *dimensionality reduction*, i.e., it maps R^n into R^m, where m is typically much smaller than n [16].

To make the recovered signals less sensitive to noise, sensing matrix A should meet Restricted Isometry Property (RIP). It is said that matrix A satisfies the RIP of order k if there exists a constant $\delta_k \in (0, 1)$ such that (4) holds for all $x \in \{x : \|x\|_0 \le k\}$ [16].

$$(1 - \delta_k)\|x\|_2^2 \le \|Ax\|_2^2 \le (1 + \delta_k)\|x\|_2^2 \tag{4}$$

Here, $\|x\|_p = (\sum_{i=1}^n |x_i|^p)^{1/p}$ $(p \ge 1)$ and $\|x\|_0$ represents the number of nonzero elements of x. Clearly, $\|x\|_2^2$ is the distance between point x and the origin in the Euclid space. Hence, we define the length of vector x as $\|x\|_2^2$. In fact, (4) can be transformed into

$$\left| \frac{\|Ax\|_2^2}{\|x\|_2^2} - 1 \right| \le \delta_k \tag{5}$$

Hence, $\|Ax\|_2^2 \to \|x\|_2^2$ when $\delta_k \to 0$, which indicates that sensing matrix A maps signal x (with at most k nonzero elements) into Ax and keeps the length of Ax very close to the length of x when δ_k takes a value close to 0. It has been proved that the standardized normal distribution $N(0, 1)$ is suitable for the sensing matrix.

With sensing matrix A, the original sparse signal x^* with k sparsity level can be found by solving the following optimization problem [16]:

$$\min_x \|x^*\|_{l_1} \tag{6}$$

$$s.t. \|Ax^* - y\|_{l_2} \le \varepsilon$$

where ε is the size of error term e.

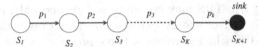

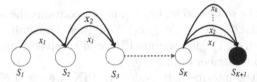

(b) Packet delivery over the route from to S_1 to S_{K+1}

Fig. 1. Gathering data over a route

To measure energy consumption, we adopt the energy dissipation model presented in [2]. That is, the energy consumption for transmitting an l-bit packet over distance d is

$$E_{Tx}(l, d) = l[\varepsilon_0 + f(d)] \tag{7}$$

where

$$f(d) = \begin{cases} \varepsilon_{fs}d^2, & d < d_{co} \\ \varepsilon_{mp}d^4, & d \geq d_{co} \end{cases} \tag{8}$$

Here, $d_{co} = \sqrt{\varepsilon_{fs}/\varepsilon_{mp}}$ [17]; ε_0 denotes the energy consumption resulting from digital coding, modulation, filtering, and spreading of the signal, etc.; and ε_{fs} and ε_{mp} are the energy consumed by the transmitter power amplifier in free space channel and multipath fading channel, respectively. In addition, the energy expended to receive an l-bit packet is [2]

$$E_{Rx}(l) = l\varepsilon_0 \tag{9}$$

For the sake of easy description, we adopt the energy dissipation model with free space channel, which leads to

$$E_{Tx}(l, d) = l(\varepsilon_0 + \varepsilon_{fs}d^2) \tag{10}$$

2.2   DGS-CS for WSN

In any data gathering scheme for WSN, there exists a route between the source and destination nodes, which is illustrated in Fig. 1a, where the circle labeled by S_i is a sensor node, the black circle labeled by S_{K+1} is the sink, and p_i is the probability of successful delivering a packet over link $S_i \rightarrow S_{i+1}(i = 1, 2, \ldots, K)$. Let x_i be the data sensed by node $S_i, i = 1, 2, \ldots, K$. Assume retransmission/acknowledgement (ACK) mechanism with N retrials is applied in the MAC layer to improve reliability (i.e., N is the *macMaxFrameRetries* parameter defined in IEEE 802.15.4 standard [15]).

Under the traditional routing scheme (TRS), node S_i forwards the data sensed by the nodes S_{i-1} in addition to its own data $(i = 2, 3, \ldots, K)$, which is illustrated in Fig. 1b. TRS may consume energy unevenly, causing some key nodes in the WSN died of energy exhaustion. This drawback is overcome by the proposed DGS-CS, which consists of three procedures: the Procedure of the Source Node (PSN), the Procedure of Intermediate Nodes (PIN), and Procedure of the Sink (PoS).

PSN is used in the source node, i.e., S_1, and it contains the steps: S_1 produces vector $v_1 = (a_{1,1}x_1, a_{2,1}x_1, \cdots, a_{m,1}x_1)$ and then transmits v_1 to S_2, where $A_1 = (a_{1,1}, a_{2,1}, \cdots, a_{m,1})^T$ is generated by and received from the sink and its elements are random numbers from $N(0, 1)$.

PIN is used in the intermediate nodes. In PIN, we use a Null-Vector Frame (NVF) to inform the next-hop node of no nonzero data being captured. The NVF only contains a header and a tail and a bit in the header is used as a No-DATA flag set to 1 (see Sect. 4 for the details). The main steps of PIN used in node $S_i (i = 2, 3, K)$ are as follows, where v_null is a variable initialized to 0 and x_i is the data sensed by S_i.

Step 1. If S_i receives a NVF, it acknowledges with an ACK frame, and then it sets $v\_null = 1$ and $v_{Rx} = (0, 0, \cdots, 0)_{1 \times m}$; otherwise, it sets v_{Rx} to the received vector.

Step 2. If $x_i = 0$ and $v\_null = 1$, then S_i generates a NVF and sends it to the next-hop node S_{i+1}. Go to Step 5.

Step 3. If $x_i = 0$, S_i sets $v_{Tx} = v_{Rx}$; otherwise, is makes vector $v_i = (a_{1,i}x_i, a_{2,i}x_i, \cdots, a_{m,i}x_i)$ and sets $v_{Tx} = v_i + v_{Rx}$, where vector $A_i = (a_{1,i}, a_{2,i}, \cdots, a_{m,i})^T$ is generated by and received from the sink and its elements are random numbers from $N(0, 1)$.

Step 4. Transmit the vector v_{Tx} to the next-hop node S_{i+1}.

Step 5. End.

PoS is used in the sink, which calculates the original sparse signal $x^* = (x_1, x_2, \cdots, x_K)$ by solving the optimization problem of CS in (6).

Figure 2 shows the received and transmitted vectors v_{Rx} and v_{Tx} in DGS-CS when all the nodes on the route capture nonzero data. The feature of the DGS-CS can be clearly seen from the figure that each node only transmits one vector to its next node, which enables the node to expend energy evenly. The main difference between an intermediate node and the source node is in that the former needs to receive a vector from its preceding node whereas the latter does not. In fact, with sparse signal, most of the intermediate nodes do not capture nonzero signal. Hence, they only forward the received vector to the next-hop node rather than generate a new vector.

3   Performance Analysis

In this section, we analyze the performance of DGS-CS and compare it with TRS. Generally, in WSN applications, such as capturing temperature, moisture, etc., data packets generated by sensor nodes usually have similar structure. Hence, we assume the number of bits contained in the sensed data x_i is a constant $b(i = 1, 2, \ldots, K)$. For instance, $b = 32$ when floating point representation is

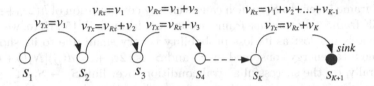

Fig. 2. DGS-CS

adopted, in which a real number is expressed as $\pm z \times 2^e$ and a 32-bit word is divided into 3 fields: 1 bit for the sign "$\pm$", 8 bits for the exponent "e", and 23 bits for the significant "z". With this representation, any transmission vector v_{Tx} generated by a node in the above PIN possesses 32 bits.

To fairly compare DGS-CS with TRS, their energy consumptions are obtained on the condition, referred as *successful arrival condition* below, that all the packets carrying the sensed data reach the sink successfully so that the sink can obtain the original signals. Let N_i be the average (expected) number of transmissions over the link $S_i \rightarrow S_{i+1}$ on the successful arrival condition ($i = 1, 2, \ldots, K$). Noting that the probability that a packet is successfully transmitted over the link $S_i \rightarrow S_{i+1}$ at the j-th trial is $(1 - p_i)^{j-1} p_i, (j = 1, 2, \ldots, N + 1)$, and the probability of successful transmission over the link within $N + 1$ trials is $1 - (1 - p_i)^{N+1}$, where N is the maximum number of retrials defined in the MAC layer, we obtain

$$v_{Rx}N_i = \sum_{j=1}^{N+1} j \frac{(1 - p_i)^{j-1} p_i}{1 - (1 - p_i)^{N+1}}$$

$$= \frac{1 - (N + 2)(1 - p_i)^{N+1} + (N + 1)(1 - p_i)^{N+2}}{p_i[1 - (1 - p_i)^{N+1}]} \qquad (11)$$

With k level sparsity (i.e., at most k elements are nonzero in signal x^*), either in DGS-CS or TRS, there exist two extreme cases: one, referred to as MaxE case below, in which the data sensed by the first k nodes S_1, S_2, $\cdots$ and S_k are all nonzero so that each intermediate nodes have data packets to forward, which expends the maximum energy; and the other, called the MinE case below, in which the data sensed by the last k nodes are all nonzero (i.e., the first $K - k$ nodes captures zero) so that only the last k nodes are involved in forwarding data packets, which consumes the minimum energy.

3.1   Energy Consumption of TRS

In MaxE case, under TRS, on the successful arrival condition, over the lossy link $S_1 \rightarrow S_2$ with the successful delivering probability p_1, the packet containing data x_1 with b bits is transmitted to S_2 with N_1 transmissions, which causes S_1 to expend energy of $N_1(b + h)(\varepsilon_0 + \varepsilon_{fs}d_{1,2}^2)$ for transmitting and S_2 to expend energy of $N_1(b + h)\varepsilon_0$ for receiving according to (9) and (10), where h is the sum of the sizes of frame header and frame tail in bits. Upon the packet is received by

S_2, ACK frame is sent to S_1, which causes energy consumption of $h(2\varepsilon_0 + \varepsilon_{fs}d_{1,2}^2)$ since ACK frame only contains frame header and frame tail [15]. Here, we assume ACK frame is not lost as its loss probability is very small due to its short size. Hence, the total energy consumed by S_1 and S_2 is $(2\varepsilon_0 + \varepsilon_{fs}d_{1,2}^2)[N_1(b+h) + h]$.

Generally, on the successful arrival condition, over link $S_i \to S_{i+1}$, i packets containing $x_1, x_2, \ldots, x_i$, respectively, with each having the same size of $b + h$ bits, are transmitted with N_i trials. Likely, we obtain the total energy consumed by S_i and S_{i+1} as $i(2\varepsilon_0 + \varepsilon_{fs}d_{i,i+1}^2)[N_i(b+h) + h], i = 1, 2, \cdots, K$.

Moreover, in MaxE case, the $K - k$ nodes $S_{k+1}, S_{k+2}, \cdots, S_K$ do not sense nonzero data and only forward the k data packets generated by the nodes $S_1, S_2, \ldots$ and S_k. Hence, on the successful arrival condition, they consume energy of $\sum_{i=k+1}^{K} k(2\varepsilon_0 + \varepsilon_{fs}d_{i,i+1}^2)[N_i(b+h) + h]$.

Thus, the total energy expended by the nodes over the route from S_1 to the sink in the MaxE case under TRS on the successful arrival condition is

$$\overline{E}_{TRS} = \sum_{i=1}^{k} i(2\varepsilon_0 + \varepsilon_{fs}d_{i,i+1}^2)[N_i(b+h) + h]$$

$$+ \sum_{i=k+1}^{K} k(2\varepsilon_0 + \varepsilon_{fs}d_{i,i+1}^2)[N_i(b+h) + h] \qquad (12)$$

$$= \sum_{i=1}^{K} min(i,k)(2\varepsilon_0 + \varepsilon_{fs}d_{i,i+1}^2)[N_i(b+h) + h]$$

Similarly, we obtain the total energy expended by the nodes over the route from S_1 to the sink on the successful arrival condition in the MinE case under TRS as follows:

$$\underline{E}_{TRS} = \sum_{i=K-k+1}^{K} (i - K + k)(2\varepsilon_0 + \varepsilon_{fs}d_{i,i+1}^2)[N_i(b+h) + h] \qquad (13)$$

With (12) and (13) in hands, the average energy consumption of TRS on the successful arrival condition is

$$E_{TRS} = \frac{1}{2}(\underline{E}_{TRS} + \overline{E}_{TRS})$$

$$= \frac{1}{2}\{\sum_{i=1}^{K} min(i,k)(2\varepsilon_0 + \varepsilon_{fs}d_{i,i+1}^2)[N_i(b+h) + h] \qquad (14)$$

$$+ \sum_{i=K-k+1}^{K} (i - K + k)(2\varepsilon_0 + \varepsilon_{fs}d_{i,i+1}^2)[N_i(b+h) + h]\}$$

3.2   Energy Consumption of DGS-CS

Now, we move on to deriving the energy consumption of the proposed DGS-CS. In DGS-CS, each intermediate node may be involved in adding the received vector v_{Rx} to the vector generated by its own data. Surely, this computation operation expends energy. However, it is well-known, compared to communication energy consumption, energy consumption arising in computing can be ignored. Hence, we ignore computing energy consumption.

We stress that the proposed DGS-CS has an advantage over TRS. That is, each node only transmits a vector v_{Tx} (see Fig. 2) with the same size of $bm + h$ to its next-hop node as there are m $b-$bit elements in the transmitted vector. Specially, only the NVF with size less than v_{Tx} is transmitted by a node if the node and its preceding node (if any) do not capture nonzero data. Hence, in DGS-CS, on the successful arrival condition, it consumes energy of $N_i(bm + h)(\varepsilon_0 + \varepsilon_{fs}d_{i,i+1}^2)$ for S_i to transmit vector v_{Tx} and energy of $N_i(bm + h)\varepsilon_0$ for S_{i+1} to receive the vector v_{Tx} over link $S_i \rightarrow S_{i+1}$; and besides, ACK frame consumes energy of $h(2\varepsilon_0 + \varepsilon_{fs}d_{i,i+1}^2)$. Therefore, over link $S_i \rightarrow S_{i+1}$, the total energy consumed by S_i and S_{i+1} is $(2\varepsilon_0 + \varepsilon_{fs}d_{i,i+1}^2)[N_i(bm + h) + h]$, $i = 1, 2, \ldots, K$. Especially, energy consumption is $(2\varepsilon_0 + \varepsilon_{fs}d_{i,i+1}^2)h$ when an NVF is transmitted as it only contain the frame header in which the No-DATA flag is set (see Sect. 4 for the implementation).

In the MaxE case under DGS-CS, the total energy expended by the nodes over the route from S_1 to the sink on the successful arrival condition is

$$\overline{E}_{CS} = \sum_{i=1}^{K} (2\varepsilon_0 + \varepsilon_{fs}d_{i,i+1}^2)[N_i(bm + h) + h] \tag{15}$$

In addition, in the MinE case under DGS-CS, the nodes $S_1, S_2, \ldots, S_{K-k}$ only transmit the NVF to their respective next-hop nodes, which causes energy consumption of $\sum_{i=1}^{K-k}(2\varepsilon_0 + \varepsilon_{fs}d_{i,i+1}^2)h$ and each of the last k nodes transmits a vector v_{Tx} to their respective next-hop nodes, which consumes energy of $\sum_{i=K-k+1}^{K}(2\varepsilon_0 + \varepsilon_{fs}d_{i,i+1}^2)[N_i(bm + h) + h]$.

Hence, the total energy expended by the nodes over the route on the successful arrival condition is

$$\underline{E}_{CS} = \sum_{i=1}^{K-k} (2\varepsilon_0 + \varepsilon_{fs}d_{i,i+1}^2)h + \sum_{i=K-k+1}^{K} (2\varepsilon_0 + \varepsilon_{fs}d_{i,i+1}^2)[N_i(bm + h) + h]$$

$$= \sum_{i=1}^{K} (2\varepsilon_0 + \varepsilon_{fs}d_{i,i+1}^2)h + (bm + h) \sum_{i=K-k+1}^{K} (2\varepsilon_0 + \varepsilon_{fs}d_{i,i+1}^2)N_i \tag{16}$$

Thus, the average energy consumption under DGS-CS on the successful arrival condition is

$$E_{CS} = \frac{1}{2}(\overline{E}_{CS} + \underline{E}_{CS}) = \frac{1}{2}\{\sum_{i=1}^{K}(2\varepsilon_0 + \varepsilon_{fs}d_{i,i+1}^2)[N_i(bm + h) + h]$$

$$+ \sum_{i=1}^{K}(2\varepsilon_0 + \varepsilon_{fs}d_{i,i+1}^2)h + (bm + h) \sum_{i=K-k+1}^{K} (2\varepsilon_0 + \varepsilon_{fs}d_{i,i+1}^2)N_i\} \tag{17}$$

3.3   Comparison of TRS and DGS-CS

To compare DGS-CS with TRS, we define Energy Saving Efficiency (ESE) as (ETRS-ECS)/ETRS.

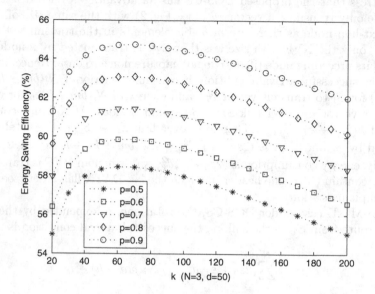

Fig. 3. Energy saving efficiency

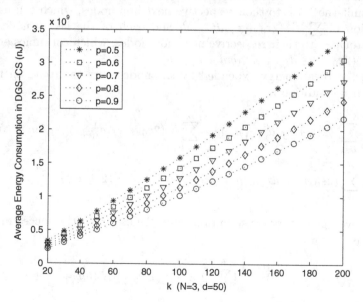

Fig. 4. Average energy consumption in DGS-CS vs the parameter k

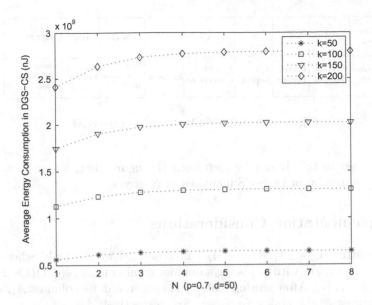

Fig. 5. Average energy consumption in DGS-CS vs the parameter N

As in [17], we choose $\varepsilon_0 = 50\,(\text{nJ/bit})$ and $\varepsilon_{fs} = 10\,(\text{pJ/bit/m2})$. Considering that, in IEEE 802.15.4 standard, frame header and tail occupy 25 Bytes and the number of frame retries in the MAC layer (i.e., the parameter *mac-MaxFrameRetries* defined in [15]) is defaulted to 3, we set $h = 25 \times 8 = 200$ bits and $N = 3$. In addition, we fix $K = 1000$ and $d_{i,i+1} = d = 50$ and $p_1 = p_2 = \ldots = p_K = p, (i = 1, 2, \ldots, K)$. Here, p is a constant. Moreover, we set $m = 4k$, which guarantees the sink to recovery the original signals with high probability close to one [9].

Letting k vary from 20 to 200 and $p = 0.5, 0.6, \ldots, 0.9$, we obtain Figs. 3 and 4. From the two figures, we obtain the following observations. Firstly, DGS-CS significantly outperforms TRS in terms of energy consumption, i.e., it could gain more than 50 percent energy saving compared to TRS. Secondly, for a given p, energy saving exhibits up-and-down tendency as k grows, i.e., ESE grows gradually when k increases from a relatively small values and then decreases when k continues to grow (see Fig. 3). The reason is that the average energy consumption of DGS-CS increases as k grows (see Fig. 4), which indicates that the proposed DGS-CS degrades when the sparsity level in the original signal is high. Lastly, for a given k, as p grows, ESE increases (see Fig. 3) while the average energy consumption decreases (see Fig. 4), which agrees with our intuition that the number of packet retransmissions reduces with link quality being improved so that energy consumption is reduced as well.

In practice, parameters of p and k depend on the environment. Hence, they are hard to be adjusted. The only parameter we can turn is N, which ranges from 0 to 7 [15]. The impact of the parameter N on E_{CS} is shown in Fig. 5,

Bits: 0-2	3	4	5	6	7-9	10-11	12-13	14-15
Frame Type	Security Enabled	Frame Pending	Ack Requset	PAN ID Compression	Reserved	Dest Addressing Mode	Frame Version	Source Addressing Mode

Fig. 6. Mote with 802.15.4 wireless transceiver

where p is set to 0.7. It can be seen from the figure that, for given k and p, energy consumption in DGS-CS increases as N grows.

4 Implementation Considerations

Sensing matrix $A = (A_1, A_2, \ldots, A_K)$ is generated at the sink, where $A_j = (a_{1,j}, a_{2,j}, \ldots, a_{m,j})^T$ with $a_{i,j}$ being a random number from $N(0,1)(i = 1, 2, \ldots, m; j = 1, 2, \ldots, K)$. After sensing matrix A is generated, its columns $A_1, A_2, \ldots, A_K$ are unicast to the nodes $S_1, S_2, \ldots, S_K$, respectively.

In addition, the 2-octet frame control field defined in the IEEE 802.15.4 frame is shown in Fig. 6 [15], where the bits 7–9 are reserved. Hence, we use Bit 7 as the No-DATA flag needed in the proposed DGS-CS (refer to the PIN presented in Sect. 2.2).

5 Conclusion

The proposed DGS-CS allows sensor nodes to energy-efficiently deliver their sensed data to the sink along a route in large scale WSNs since the nodes expend their energy evenly. In fact, tree-based routing protocols, such as the Collection Tree Protocol (CTP), are usually used in WSNs. The proposed DGS-CS can be applied with tree-based protocols by allowing each node to generate a vector using PIN given in Sect. 2.2 and then send the vector to its parent node.

Acknowledgement. This project is supported in part by National Natural Science Foundation of China under Grants No. 61379124 and No. 61001126, in part by Ph.D. Programs Foundation of Ministry of Education of China under grant No. 20123317110002, and in part by Zhejiang Provincial Natural Science Foundation of China under grant number LY13F020031.

References

1. Heinzelman, W.B., Balakrishnan, H.: An application-specific protocol architecture for wireless microsensor networks. IEEE Trans. Wireless Commun. **1**(4), 660–670 (2002)
2. Younis, O.: HEED: a hybrid, energy-efficient, distributed clustering approach for ad hoc sensor networks. IEEE Trans. Mob. Comput. **3**(4), 366–379 (2004)

3. Manjeshwar, A., Agrawal, D.P.: TEEN: A routing protocol for enhanced efficiency in wireless sensor networks. In: Proceedings of 15th International Parallel and Distributed Processing Symposium, pp. 2009–2015 (2000)
4. Donoho, D.L.: Compressed sensing. IEEE Trans. Inf. Theory **52**(4), 1289–1306 (2006)
5. Cand'es, E., Romberg, J., Tao, T.: Robust uncertainty principles: exact signal reconstruction from highly incomplete fourier information. IEEE Trans. Inf. Theory **52**(2), 489–509 (2006)
6. Candes, E.: An introduction to compressive sampling. IEEE Sig. Process. Mag. **25**(2), 21–30 (2008)
7. Candes, E., Romberg, J., Tao, T.: Stable signal recovery from incomplete and inaccurate measurements. Commun. Pure Appl. Math. **59**(8), 1207–1223 (2006)
8. Haupt, J., Bajwa, W.: Compressed sensing for networked data. IEEE Sig. Process. Mag. **25**(2), 92–101 (2008)
9. Luo, C., Wu, F.: Compressive data gathering for large-scale wireless sensor networks. In: Proceedings of the 15th Annual International Conference on Mobile Computing and Networking, pp. 145–156. ACM (2009)
10. Xiang, L., Luo, J.: Compressed data aggregation for energy efficient wireless sensor networks. In: Proceedings of the 8th IEEE SECON, pp. 46–54 (2011)
11. Luo, J., Rosenberg, C.: Does compressed sensing improve the throughput of wireless sensor networks? IEEE Int. Conf. Commun. (ICC) **2010**, 1–6 (2010)
12. Wang, X., Zheng, H., Xiao, S.: Capacity and delay analysis for data gathering with compressive sensing in wireless sensor networks. IEEE Trans. Wireless Commun. **12**(2), 917–927 (2013)
13. Xu, L., Wang, Y.: Major coefficients recovery: a compressed data gathering scheme for wireless sensor network. In: IEEE Global Telecommunications Conference (Globecom 2011), pp. 1–5 (2011)
14. Wu, X., Xiong, Y., Huang, W.: Distributed spatial-temporal compressive data gathering for large-scale WSNs. In: IEEE Computing, Communications and IT Applications Conference (IEEE ComComAp), pp. 105–110 (2013)
15. IEEE Computer Society. IEEE 802.15.4 Standard for Wireless Medium Access Control (MAC) and Physical Layer (PHY) Specifications for Low-Rate Wireless Personal Area Networks (WPANs) (2006)
16. Candes, E.J., Tao, T.: Stable signal recovery from incomplete and inaccurate measurements [J]. Commun. Pure Appl. Math. **59**(8), 1207–1223 (2006)
17. Moussaoui, O., Naimi, M.: A distributed energy aware routing protocol for wireless sensor networks. In: Proceedings of the 2nd ACM International Workshop on Performance Evaluation of Wireless Ad Hoc, Sensor, and Ubiquitous Networks, pp. 34–40 (2005)

Minimum-Latency Broadcast in Multi-channel Duty-Cycled Wireless Sensor Networks

Xianlong Jiao[1]($\boxtimes$), Weidong Xiao[1], Bin Ge[1], and Yuli Chen[2]

[1] College of Information System and Management,
National University of Defense and Technology, Changsha, China
xljiao@nudt.edu.cn, wilsonshaw@vip.sina.com, gebin1978@gmail.com
[2] Chongqing Guanyinqiao Elementary School, Chongqing, China
Chenyulihyn@163.com

Abstract. Broadcast has critical significance for wide application of wireless sensor networks (WSNs). Minimum-latency broadcast (MLB) studies how to devise a broadcast schedule, which can achieve minimum broadcast latency with no signal interference. In multi-channel duty-cycled WSNs, nodes can exploit multiple channels to communicate, and periodically fall asleep after working for some time. Nevertheless, most solutions to the MLB problem either focus on non-sleeping scenarios, or only exploit one single channel. Therefore, we investigate the MLB problem in multi-channel duty-cycled WSNs in this paper, and call this problem as MLBCD problem. We prove that MLBCD problem is NP-hard. We propose a new concept of active interference graph (AIG). Based on AIG, we present one Novel Approximation Broadcast algorithm called NAB to solve the MLBCD problem. We prove that our proposed NAB algorithm achieves provable performance guarantee. The results of our extensive evaluations show that, NAB algorithm can significantly improve the broadcast latency.

Keywords: Broadcast · Wireless sensor networks · Multi-channel · Duty cycle

1 Introduction

Broadcast has critical significance for wide application of wireless sensor networks (WSNs). WSNs usually consist of many sensor nodes, which communicate through radio transmissions on multiple channels [19]. Sensor nodes often have limited energy, and to make effective use of the limited energy, these nodes periodically fall asleep after working for some time. In many scenarios, nodes independently determine their sleep/active cycles without coordination [4,7,11,23].

X. Jiao—We would like to thank the anonymous reviewers for their insightful comments. This work is supported in part by Hunan Provincial Natural Science Foundation of China Grants No. 14JJ3006 and China Postdoctoral Science Foundation Grant No. 2014M552686.

L. Sun et al. (Eds.): CWSN 2014, CCIS 501, pp. 456–466, 2015.
DOI: 10.1007/978-3-662-46981-1_44

Moreover, since the data of WSNs may be outmoded very quickly, broadcast should be completed with low latency. However, in duty-cycled scenarios, a node can receive data only at its active state, which brings a great challenge for designing efficient broadcast schemes.

Minimum-latency broadcast (MLB) studies how to devise a broadcast schedule, which can achieve minimum broadcast latency with no signal interference. This problem has attracted plenty of researches during recent years. Gandhi et al. [5] have proved the NP-hardness of MLB problem in WSNs without sleep/active cycles in single-channel scenarios. Researchers have proposed many solutions to this problem [2,5,6,12,13,16]. Nevertheless, most solutions to the MLB problem either focus on non-sleeping scenarios, or only exploit one single channel. Sensor nodes in duty-cycled scenarios can only receive data when they are active. Moreover, nodes can exploit multiple channels to communicate without signal interference. Existing most algorithms may incur high latency with simple extension. Thus we are motivated to study the MLB problem in multi-channel duty-cycled WSNs (we call it as MLBCD problem), and to propose an efficient solution to this problem.

The transmissions are affected by signal interference. Protocol interference model is adopted as the interference model in this paper, which is a commonly used model in many researches [2,12,16]. Under this model, the interference range and the transmission range of one node are two disks, and the interference range of one node is usually larger than its transmission range. A node's data transmission may prevent other nodes in its interference range from correctly receiving data.

To avoid the signal interference among the data transmissions, we need to choose some nodes as the forwarding nodes and carefully schedule the time when these nodes transmit the message. Multi-channel duty-cycled scenarios have the following special features. First, the transmitter node can only send data to its receiver node when the receiver node is active. Second, it may require several times of data transmission for a node to inform all its receiver nodes. Third, multiple channels can be used to avoid interference. Therefore, it is critical to design efficient algorithms based on these special features.

This paper investigates the MLBCD problem, and to the best of our knowledge, our work is the first solution to this problem. To solve this problem, we present a new concept of Active Interference Graph (AIG). This graph shows the interference relationship among the broadcast links and is associated with the nodes' active time-slots. Based on AIG, we are motivated to devise an efficient approximation algorithm called NAB for the MLBCD problem under protocol interference model, which can provide an interference-free broadcast scheduling and can achieve provable performance guarantee.

In this paper, we have done the following contributions.

1. We give the formulation of MLBCD problem and prove that this problem is NP-hard. Thus it is hard to devise an efficient polynomial-time algorithm which can minimize the broadcast latency without interference.

2. We propose a new concept of Active Interference Graph (AIG), which facilitates the design of our interference-free scheduling algorithm.
3. We present an algorithm called NAB with a approximation ratio of ($\lceil \frac{\chi_{\alpha+2}}{m} \rceil +$ $\lceil \frac{\chi_{\alpha+1}}{m} \rceil)|T|$, where α denotes the ratio of a node's interference radius to its transmission radius, m denotes the number of channels, and $|T|$ denotes the amount of time-slots in one scheduling period. χ_λ is a function of λ, which equals to $\frac{\pi}{\sqrt{3}}\lambda^2 + (\frac{\pi}{2} + 1)\lambda + 1$,
4. We implement our algorithm, and evaluate its performance. The results of our extensive evaluations show that, NAB algorithm can significantly improve the broadcast latency.

2 Related Work

Broadcast is a critical operation in WSNs, and thus has attracted plenty of researches [1–3, 8–10, 12, 14, 16, 18, 21] on this operation. In this paper, we only focus on the work which solves the MLB problem due to the space limit.

Many algorithms [2, 12, 16] have been proposed to address the MLB problem under protocol interference model. An efficient algorithm is proposed in [2], which achieves a ratio of $2\pi\alpha^2$ and turns out to be 26 if α equals to 2. To solve the MLB problem, Mahjourian et al. [16] further take the carrier sensing range into consideration, and prove that if the carrier sensing range is equal to the interference range, their algorithm achieves a ratio of $O(\alpha^2)$, and the constant before α^2 is 4. A better approximation algorithm is proposed in [12] with a ratio of $6\lceil \frac{2}{3}(\alpha + 2) \rceil^2$. However, all these algorithms discussed above are based on the assumption that, all the nodes do not fall asleep.

The broadcast problem in duty-cycled scenarios has been studied in [8, 10, 14, 15, 17, 21, 22]. The MLB problem in duty-cycled scenarios is investigated in [10, 14, 15, 22]. Hong et al. [10] propose ELAC-SC algorithm, which achieves a ratio of $O(\alpha^2)$, and the constant before α^2 is $4|T|$. Nevertheless, the ELAC-SC algorithm incurs high broadcast latency because of leaving a large number of idle scheduling periods unused.

Another piece of work [14] gives a better solution with a ratio of $17|T|$ but is not suitable for protocol interference model. Xu et al. [22] develop a delay efficient broadcast scheduling algorithm for duty-cycled multihop wireless sensor networks with a small ratio, but they assume that a node's interference range equals to its transmission range. An efficient solution for the MLB problem in duty-cycled scenarios under protocol interference model is proposed in [15], which achieves low broadcast latency.

However, all the solutions discussed above only consider the single-channel scenarios, and are not suitable for multi-channel scenarios. Wan et al. [19] propose an efficient broadcast algorithm in multi-channel scenarios, but their work assumes that all nodes are active. Hence, this paper focuses on devising an efficient solution to the MLBCD problem, which can provide an interference-free broadcast scheduling and can achieve a small approximation ratio.

3   Preliminaries

3.1   Network Model and Assumptions

In this paper, we consider a multi-channel duty-cycled wireless sensor network, and model it as a UDG $G = (V, E)$, where V denotes the set of all the n nodes in this network, and E denotes the set of edges among these nodes, which are in the transmission range of other nodes. Protocol interference model is adopted as the interference model. We denote the transmission radius and the interference radius by r and r_f respectively. α denotes the ratio of r_f to r, and we call it as the interference ratio. Each node can use m channels to communicate, and we use Ch_1, Ch_2, ..., Ch_m to denote different channels. The transmissions on different channels can be carried out simultaneously without interference.

We suppose that nodes decide when to sleep without coordination in advance. We divide the whole scheduling time into several scheduling periods with the same number of time slots. We denote one scheduling period by T, which contains several time slots 0, 1, ..., $|T| - 2$, and $|T| - 1$. The active time slot of each node v is a time slot of T. A node can wake up to send data at any time slot as required, but can only receive data when it is active. We define the duty cycle as the ratio of the a node's active time to the whole scheduling time. In this paper, the duty cycle equals to $\frac{1}{|T|}$.

We assume that a node cannot send and receive data at the same time. R_s denotes the maximum depth of the breadth-first-search (BFS) tree, which is rooted at the source node s.

3.2   Problem Formulation

This paper investigates the broadcast problem in multi-channel duty-cycled scenarios, where a source node s sends its message to all the other sensor nodes at time slot 0. The broadcast task completes when all the sensor nodes receive the message. The broadcast scheduling problem is modeled as assigning each node's transmitting time slot. Interference-free broadcast scheduling aims to minimize the latency when each node is informed without signal interference. Therefore we can formulate the MLBCD problem as follows:

Definition 1. *MLBCD Problem: given a multi-channel duty-cycled wireless sensor network $G(V, E)$ and a single source node s, find a broadcast scheduling S such that the broadcast latency is minimized and all the nodes can be informed without interference.*

Next we prove the NP-hardness of MLBCD problem.

Lemma 1. *MLBCD problem is NP-hard.*

Proof. If we set the interference ratio α as 1 and set the number of channels as 1, then the MLBCD problem will reduce to the MLB problem under the single-channel scenario without sleeping cycles, which has been proved to be NP-hard in [10]. Since the special case of the MLBCD problem is NP-hard, this lemma holds.

3.3   Graph-Theoretic Definitions

In this subsection, we give some graph-theoretic definitions. $G[U]$ denotes a subgraph of G, which is induced by V's subset U. An *Independent Set* (IS) U of G satisfies that, the edge set of $G[U]$ is empty. A *Maximal Independent Set* (MIS) U of G satisfies that, U is not a subset of G's any other IS. According to [20], in a half-disk of radius r_1, the number of points with mutual distances at least r_2 is at most $\chi_{\frac{r_1}{r_2}}$.

Coloring of a graph G is to assign natural numbers to each node in this graph. If two nodes are adjacent in this graph, then their assigned numbers are different. First-fit coloring of a graph is to assign each node with the smallest number which is not used by its neighboring nodes. Specially, the first-fit coloring in smallest-degree-last ordering requires at most $\phi(G) + 1$ colors, where $\phi(G)$ is the maximum value of the minimum degrees of all subgraphs in G [20].

4   Approximation Algorithm

In previous section, we have proved that the MLBCD problem is NP-hard. In this section, we propose an approximation algorithm called NAB. Before detailing NAB algorithm, we present a new concept of Active Interference Graph (AIG). Recall that a node can transmit its data to its receiver node only when its receiver node is active. If there are some broadcast links for scheduling, we construct several interference graphs as follows. For each active time-slot t of all the receiver nodes, we construct an interference graph $G_t = (V_t, E_t)$. V_t includes the transmitter nodes if at least one of their receiver nodes is active at time-slot t. The interference relationship only involves the links between these transmitter nodes and their receiver nodes with active time-slot t.

Based on AIG, we propose NAB algorithm. The main steps of NAB algorithm are as follows.

1. Construct the BFS tree T_{BFS}, which is rooted at source node s.
2. Set R_s as $MaxDepth(T_{BFS})$, and divide all the nodes in V into different layers $L_0, L_1, ..., L_{R_s}$.
3. Construct the maximal independent set MIS layer by layer, and choose some connector nodes in T_{BFS} to connect the nodes in MIS based on the minimal cover rule.
4. Construct the broadcast tree T_B based on MIS.
5. Schedule the broadcast based on T_B layer by layer. At each layer, first schedule father nodes of nodes in MIS to broadcast the message to nodes in MIS, and then schedule the broadcast from nodes in MIS to their children nodes.
6. Construct AIG based on these broadcast links, and adopt the first-fit coloring method to color the nodes in the smallest-degree-last ordering of AIG.
7. Schedule the transmitting time-slots of father nodes based on their colors on different channels.

Then we detail this algorithm. The first step is to construct the BFS tree T_{BFS} rooted at source node s, and the second step is to divide all the nodes into different layers according to these nodes' depths in T_{BFS}. We denote the maximum depth of T_{BFS} by R_s.

Since MIS has special geometric features, we then make the best of these features. The third step is to construct the maximal independent set MIS from the top layer to the bottom layer in T_{BFS}. Since the nodes in MIS are not connected, we choose some connector nodes in T_{BFS} to connect these nodes layer by layer based on the minimal cover rule.

The fourth step is to construct the broadcast tree T_B based on MIS. The connector nodes are assigned as the father nodes of nodes in MIS. For the other nodes, which are neither connector nodes nor in MIS, we choose some nodes in MIS at the same layer or at the topper layer as their father nodes.

The fifth step is to schedule the broadcast based on T_B layer by layer. At each layer, we first schedule father nodes of nodes in MIS to broadcast the message to nodes in MIS, and then schedule the broadcast from nodes in MIS to their children nodes. Note that each broadcast link is related to a node in MIS.

We then construct AIG based on these broadcast links. To avoid interference, we require a coloring method to color the nodes in AIG. Nodes with different colors cannot broadcast the data at the same time-slot on the same channel. To use the features of MIS, we adopt the first-fit coloring method to color the nodes in the smallest-degree-last ordering of AIG.

Finally, we schedule the transmissions from the father nodes to their children nodes as follows. The scheduling works from the top layer to the bottom layer. The scheduling time t_s start at time-slot 0. At each layer L_i, the message is first delivered to nodes in MIS, and t_s proceeds to the smallest times of $|T|$ when the previous scheduling finishes. Then nodes in MIS broadcast the message to their children nodes. Similarly, t_s proceeds to the smallest times of $|T|$ when the scheduling finishes.

To avoid the interference among the transmissions, we schedule the transmissions based on the colors of father nodes in AIG. For father nodes with the different colors in G_i ($0 \leq i \leq |T|-1$), we schedule the transmissions on different channels. If the number of colors n_c is smaller than the number of channels m, the transmissions are scheduled on channels Ch_1, Ch_2, ..., Ch_{n_c} at time-slot $t_s + i$. Otherwise, father nodes with the first m colors are scheduled on channels Ch_1, Ch_2, ..., Ch_m at time-slot $t_s + i$. Father nodes with next m colors (if have) are scheduled on channels Ch_1, Ch_2, ..., Ch_m at time-slot $t_s + |T| + i$. We repeat this process until all the father nodes are considered. The transmission time-slot increases $|T|$ time-slots in each loop.

5   Performance Analysis

In previous section, we detail our NAB algorithm. In this section, we analyze the correctness and the approximation ratio of NAB algorithm. To analyze the approximation ratio, we first give the lower bound of the broadcast latency for the MLBCD problem and the worst-case latency of NAB algorithm.

Theorem 1. *NAB algorithm is correct and provides an interference-free broadcast scheduling.*

Proof. NAB algorithm first layers all the nodes and constructs the broadcast tree based on MIS. NAB algorithm then schedules the broadcast layer by layer. At each layer, the message will be first delivered to nodes in MIS, and then these nodes broadcast the message to their children nodes at the same layer or at the lower layer. Therefore all the nodes can receive the broadcast message. The transmitting time-slots are scheduled based on the colors of nodes in AIG. According to the scheduling method, interfering broadcast links are scheduled at different channels or at different scheduling periods. Thus, the scheduled transmissions are interference-free.

Lemma 2. *The lower bound of the broadcast latency for the MLBCD problem is at least R_s time-slots.*

Proof. Since the maximum depth of the BFS tree rooted at source node s is R_s, it is easy to prove that node s requires at least R_s transmission time-slots to finish the broadcast task. Hence, this lemma holds.

Lemma 3. *If the transmitter nodes are all nodes in MIS, then for these broadcast links, the number of colors of nodes in AIG is at most $\chi_{\alpha+1}$.*

Proof. Consider the leftmost transmitter node v in MIS. If other nodes in MIS interfere node v, then these nodes must lie in a half-disk of radius $r + r_f$ centered at node v. The number of these nodes is at most $\chi_{(r+r_f)/r+1} - 1 = \chi_{\alpha+1} - 1$. Thus the minimum degree of the subgraph of AIG is bounded by $\chi_{\alpha+1} - 1$. The number of colors of nodes in AIG is at most the minimum degree plus one. Hence, this lemma holds.

Lemma 4. *If the receiver nodes are all nodes in MIS, then for these broadcast links, the number of colors of nodes in AIG is at most $\chi_{\alpha+2}$.*

Proof. Consider the leftmost transmitter node v. If another transmitter node u interferes node v, then this node must have one child node w in MIS. This child node must lie in the half-disk of radius $r_f + 2r$ centered at node v. The number of all the children nodes like node w is at most $\chi_{(r_f+2r)/r+1} - 1 = \chi_{\alpha+2} - 1$. Thus the minimum degree of the subgraph of AIG is bounded by $\chi_{\alpha+2} - 1$. The number of colors of nodes in AIG is at most the minimum degree plus one. Hence, this lemma holds.

Theorem 2. *The worst-case latency of NAB algorithm is $(\lceil \frac{\chi_{\alpha+2}}{m} \rceil + \lceil \frac{\chi_{\alpha+1}}{m} \rceil)|T|$ $R_s - (\lceil \frac{\chi_{\alpha+2}}{m} \rceil + \lceil \frac{\chi_{\alpha+1}}{m} \rceil - 1)|T|$.*

Proof. At the top layer, there is only one node s. Thus the time for node s to inform all the nodes at layer 1 is at most $|T|$ time-slots. From layer 2 to layer R_s, the process splits into two phases. In the first phase, nodes in MIS receive the broadcast message from their father nodes. According to Lemma 4 and the scheduling method, we have that the first phase takes at most $\lceil\frac{\chi_{\alpha+2}}{m}\rceil|T|$ time-slots. In the second phase, nodes in MIS broadcast the message to their children nodes. According to Lemma 3 and the scheduling method, this phase takes at most $\lceil\frac{\chi_{\alpha+1}}{m}\rceil|T|$ time-slots. We combine the time of these two phases, and the worst-cast latency of NAB algorithm follows that,

$$
\begin{aligned}
Latency(NAB) &\leq |T| + \sum_{i=2}^{R_s}(\lceil\frac{\chi_{\alpha+2}}{m}\rceil|T| + \lceil\frac{\chi_{\alpha+1}}{m}\rceil|T|) \\
&= (\lceil\frac{\chi_{\alpha+2}}{m}\rceil + \lceil\frac{\chi_{\alpha+1}}{m}\rceil)|T|R_s \\
&\quad - (\lceil\frac{\chi_{\alpha+2}}{m}\rceil + \lceil\frac{\chi_{\alpha+1}}{m}\rceil - 1)|T|
\end{aligned}
$$

Theorem 3. *The approximation ratio of NAB algorithm is at most* $(\lceil\frac{\chi_{\alpha+2}}{m}\rceil + \lceil\frac{\chi_{\alpha+1}}{m}\rceil)|T|$.

Proof. First, according to Lemma 2, we have the lower bound R_s for broadcast latency of the MLBCD problem. Theorem 2 gives the worst-case latency of NAB algorithm. Note that $(\lceil\frac{\chi_{\alpha+2}}{m}\rceil + \lceil\frac{\chi_{\alpha+1}}{m}\rceil - 1)|T|$ is larger than 0. Thus we have that the approximation ratio is at most $(\lceil\frac{\chi_{\alpha+2}}{m}\rceil + \lceil\frac{\chi_{\alpha+1}}{m}\rceil)|T|$.

6   Performance Evaluation

In this section, we implement our NAB algorithm, and evaluate its performance through extensive simulations. Our simulations focus on the effect of various network conditions on the performance of our NAB algorithm. The existing two broadcast algorithms ELAC-SC [10] and IFB [15] solve the MLB problem in single-channel duty-cycled scenarios under protocol interference model. Therefore we compare our NAB algorithm with these two algorithms, and show how our NAB algorithm benefits from multi-channel scheduling.

In the simulations, all the nodes are randomly deployed in a 1000×1000-m^2 area. The transmission radius is 300 m. We evaluate the broadcast latency of three algorithms, and study the effect of different network conditions including the duty cycle, the interference ratio and the number of channels on the performance of three algorithms.

In each simulation scenario, we adopt three network sizes of 100, 200 and 300, and adopt three numbers of channels of 1, 3 and 5. First, we evaluate the effect of different duty cycles. We adopt 10, 20, 30, 40 and 50 as the number of time slots in T, and thus the duty cycle changes between 0.1 and 0.02. Then we evaluate the effect of different interference ratios. The interference ratio ranges from 2 to 6. In each experiment, we change one parameter and fix the other three parameters.

We use 20 different graph topologies to conduct these experiments. Moreover, 10 times of experiments are run on each graph topology, and the source node is randomly chosen in each experiment. Each data point reported in the figures results from an average of these simulation results. Since the gap among the simulation results of three algorithms is large, we show the denary logarithm of the results.

6.1 Impact of Different Duty Cycles

First, we study the impact of different duty cycles on the performance of three algorithms. In this simulation scenario, we set the interference ratio α as 3. Figure 1 illustrates the broadcast latency of three algorithms under different duty cycles. This figure also gives the results of our NAB algorithm under different numbers of channels.

From Fig. 1, we can see that, with the decrease of the duty cycle, the broadcast latency of three algorithms increases. The reason is that, one node may wait more time-slots until its receiver node wakes up when the duty cycle decreases. Our NAB algorithm outperforms the other two algorithms notably even when only one channel can be used. This is because we well separate the transmissions of broadcast links based on AIG. When more channels can be used, more transmissions can be carried on at the same time-slot, and thus the broadcast latency is decreased.

From Fig. 1(a), (b) and (c), we can also find that, when the network size increases, the broadcast latency of three algorithms all increases. The reason is that, more nodes require to be covered. In all these three figures, our NAB algorithm performs the best.

6.2 Impact of Different Interference Ratios

In this subsection, we study the impact of different interference ratios on the performance of three algorithms. The number of time slots in T is set as 20. The results are shown in Fig. 2. When the interference ratio increases, a node's interference range becomes larger, and hence fewer transmissions can be simultaneous. Therefore the broadcast latency of all the three algorithms increases when the interference ratio increases.

Note that, the increase of the broadcast latency is not as notable as that in previous subsection. The reason is that, when the network size and the duty cycle

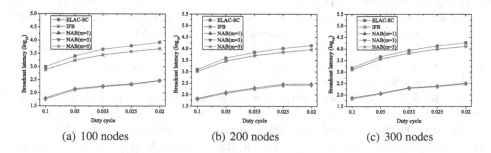

(a) 100 nodes   (b) 200 nodes   (c) 300 nodes

Fig. 1. Broadcast latency under different network sizes and duty cycles

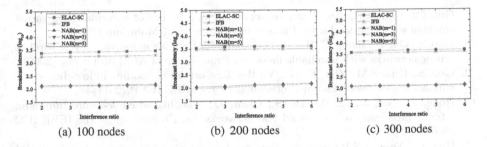

(a) 100 nodes   (b) 200 nodes   (c) 300 nodes

Fig. 2. Broadcast latency under different network sizes and interference ratios

are fixed, the number and waiting time-slots of transmitter nodes do not change notably. The results in Fig. 2 also verify that, when the network size increases, all the algorithms' broadcast latency increases, and our NAB algorithm outperforms the other two algorithms notably.

7   Conclusion

This paper investigates the MLBCD problem when protocol interference model is adopted as the interference model. We prove the NP-hardness of this problem and present one efficient algorithm NAB. We also prove that NAB algorithm is correct and provides an interference-free broadcast scheduling. The broadcast latency of NAB algorithm is bounded by $(\lceil \frac{\chi_a+2}{m} \rceil + \lceil \frac{\chi_a+1}{m} \rceil)|T|R_s - (\lceil \frac{\chi_a+2}{m} \rceil + \lceil \frac{\chi_a+1}{m} \rceil - 1)|T|$. NAB algorithm achieves a ratio of $(\lceil \frac{\chi_a+2}{m} \rceil + \lceil \frac{\chi_a+1}{m} \rceil)|T|$. The results of extensive simulations show that, our NAB algorithm achieves lower broadcast latency than existing algorithms even when only one channel can be used.

References

1. Baghaie, M., Krishnamachari, B.: Delay constrained minimum energy broadcast in cooperative wireless networks. In: Proceedings of the IEEE INFOCOM (2014)
2. Chen, Z., Qiao, C., Xu, J., Lee, T.: A constant approximation algorithm for interference aware broadcast in wireless networks. In: Proceedings of the IEEE INFOCOM (2007)
3. Cheng, L., Gu, Y., He, T., Niu, J.: Dynamic switching-based reliable flooding in low-duty-cycle wireless sensor networks. In: Proceedings of the IEEE INFOCOM (2013)
4. Dousse, O., Mannersalo, P., Thiran, P.: Latency of wireless sensor networks with uncoordinated power saving mechanisms. In: Proceedings of the ACM MobiHoc (2004)
5. Gandhi, R., Parthasarathy, S., Mishra, A.: Minimizing broadcast latency and redundancy in ad hoc networks. In: Proceedings of the ACM MobiHoc (2003)
6. Gandhi, R., Kim, Y.-A., Lee, S., Ryu, J., Wan, P.J.: Approximation algorithms for data broadcast in wireless networks. In: Proceedings of the IEEE INFOCOM (2009)

7. Gui, C., Mohapatra, P.: Power conservation and quality of surveillance in target tracking sensor networks. In: Proceedings of the ACM MobiCom (2004)
8. Guo, S., Gu, Y., Jiang, B., He, T.: Opportunistic flooding in low-duty-cycle wireless sensor networks with unreliable links. In: Proceedings of ACM MobiCom (2009)
9. Guo, S., Kim, S.M., Zhu, T., Gu, Y., He, T.: Correlated flooding in low-duty-cycle wireless sensor networks. In: Proceedings of the IEEE ICNP (2011)
10. Hong, J., Cao, J., Li, W., Lu, S., Chen, D.: Sleeping schedule-aware minimum latency broadcast in wireless ad hoc networks. In: Proceedings of the IEEE ICC (2009)
11. Hua, C., Yum, T.S.P.: Asynchronous random sleeping for sensor networks. ACM Trans. Sens. Netw. 3(3), 15 (2007)
12. Huang, S.C.H., Wan, P.J., Deng, J., Han, Y.S.: Broadcast scheduling in interference environment. IEEE Trans. Mob. Comput. 7(11), 1338–1348 (2008)
13. Huang, S.C.H., Wan, P.J., Jia, X., Du, H., Shang, W.: Minimum-latency broadcast scheduling in wireless ad hoc networks. In: Proceedings of the IEEE INFOCOM (2007)
14. Jiao, X., Lou, W., Ma, J., Cao, J., Wang, X., Zhou, X.: Minimum latency broadcast scheduling in duty-cycled multihop wireless networks. IEEE Trans. Parallel Distrib. Syst. 23(1), 110–117 (2012)
15. Jiao, X., Wang, X., Lou, W., Cao, J., Xia, X., Zhou, X., Xia, G.: On minimizing interference-free broadcast latency in duty-cycled wireless sensor networks. Ad Hoc Sens. Wireless Netw. 18(3–4), 293–309 (2013)
16. Mahjourian, R., Chen, F., Tiwari, R.: An approximation algorithm for conflict-aware broadcast scheduling in wireless ad hoc networks. In: Proceedings of the ACM MobiHoc (2008)
17. Miller, M., Sengul, C., Gupta, I.: Exploring the energy-latency tradeoff for broadcasts in energy-saving sensor networks. In: Proceedings of the IEEE ICDCS (2005)
18. Ni, S.Y., Tseng, Y.C., Chen, Y.S., Sheu, J.P.: The broadcast storm problem in a mobile ad hoc network. In: Proceedings of the ACM MobiCom (1999)
19. Wan, P.-J., Wang, Z., Wan, Z., Huang, S.C.-H., Liu, H.: Minimum-latency schedulings for group communications in multi-channel multihop wireless networks. In: Liu, B., Bestavros, A., Du, D.-Z., Wang, J. (eds.) WASA 2009. LNCS, vol. 5682, pp. 469–478. Springer, Heidelberg (2009)
20. Wan, P.J., Huang, S.C.H., Wang, L.: Minimum-latency aggregation scheduling in multihop wireless networks. In: Proceedings of the ACM MobiHoc (2009)
21. Wang, F., Liu, J.: Duty-cycle-aware broadcast in wireless sensor networks. In: Proceedings of the IEEE INFOCOM (2009)
22. Xu, X., Cao, J., Wan, P.-J.: Fast group communication scheduling in duty-cycled multihop wireless sensor networks. In: Wang, X., Zheng, R., Jing, T., Xing, K. (eds.) WASA 2012. LNCS, vol. 7405, pp. 197–205. Springer, Heidelberg (2012)
23. Zheng, R., Kravets, R.: On-demand power management for ad hoc networks. In: Proceedings of the IEEE INFOCOM (2003)

Outlier Detection Method of Environmental Streams Based on Kernel Density Estimation

Pengfei Wu[1,2], Guanghui Li[1(✉)], Hong Zhu[1], and Wenwei Lu[1]

[1] School of Information Engineering, Zhejiang A & F University,
Hangzhou 311300, China
lgh@zafu.edu.cn
[2] School of Internet of Things, Nanjing University of Posts
and Telecommunication, Nanjing 210003, China

Abstract. Environmental monitoring is a typical application in wireless sensor networks (WSNs), the outlier detection of the sensor data streams is especially important. We put forward an outlier detection algorithm based on multidimensional kernel density estimation. Based on the hierarchical network model, the algorithm estimates the normal distribution model in the cluster head nodes with the latest data sample. Each distributed node computes the new data to identify the abnormal data by the kernel density estimation model. The proposed algorithm can compute the result online. It only spends little time to adjust the appropriate threshold to reduce its complexity. In addition, We also take the spatial and temporal correlation, multiple attribute correlation of sensor data into account, such that the result of outlier detection is very reliable. Theoretical analysis and simulation experimental results demonstrate that the outlier detection accuracy of the proposed algorithm is more than 98 % when the outlier rate p is within a reasonable range. With the increase of p, the outlier detection accuracy will decline gradually.

Keywords: Wireless sensor network · Outlier detection · Kernel density estimate-on · On-line detection

1 Introduction

With the constant development of information technology, wireless sensor networks have become a new method for the information acquisition in the physical world. Has been deployed in large scale environment, the sensor nodes utilize wireless communication ability to build the self-organizing network. Once the network has been established, the nodes will collect the information around their physical world, such as pressure, temperature, humidity, noise. The network should be able to detect the abnormal change in the physical world. Guaranteeing the accuracy and reliability of the data collected by the sensor network is of great significance during the data processing.

In WSNs, when the actual sampling data is inconsistent with the expected data, we call it as outlier data. Some possible factors that result in the outlier data are as follows.

© Springer-Verlag Berlin Heidelberg 2015
L. Sun et al. (Eds.): CWSN 2014, CCIS 501, pp. 467–480, 2015.
DOI: 10.1007/978-3-662-46981-1_45

- The node itself exists software or hardware fault. For example, the battery power is insufficient or the node encounters malicious attack;
- The external environment happen some events such as a forest fire, environmental pollution, etc. The above situation will cause corresponding change of the environmental parameters.

We adopt the statistical method to define the outlier data. The normal data falls within the range of the high probability of some data distribution model, and the abnormal data appears in the low probability interval of the above model [1]. According to whether the parameter exists, the outlier detection can be divided into two cases: parameter and non-parametric.

In centralized wireless sensor network, all nodes will send the collected data to one node, which is the simplest method in processing data. However, the drawback of this is that the whole network communication overhead is large, and the procedure of data acquisition and processing increase the response time against the responding event. Distributed data processing method can well solve the above problems, our paper mainly studies the distributed outlier detection based on nonparametric methods in wireless sensor networks.

We puts forward an outlier detection algorithm using kernel density estimator, its characteristics can be described as follows:

- In-network computation. When the outliers come into the nodes' sliding window, the algorithm can identify them from normal data. It is no necessary for the outliers to be sent to the sink nodes, which can save much time.
- Non-parametric statistical method. This method spends little time in adjusting the appropriate threshold, which can reduce the complexity of the algorithm.
- Spatial-temporal correlation, multiple attribute correlation. The algorithm can get a more reliable effect because it has taken spatial-temporal correlation, multiple attribute correlation of sensor data into account.

This paper is organized as follows: Sect. 2 introduces the existing related work; Sect. 3 presents a hierarchical model of sensor network, and gives mathematical description of the research question; Sect. 4 gives outlier detection algorithm based on kernel density estimate in detail; the experimental results and its analysis have been presented in Sect. 5; Finally, we summarized in Sect. 6.

2 Related Work

The most important design goal in WSNs is to effectively use the energy of sensor nodes, under the premise of completing application requirements, prolong the lifetime of the whole network as soon as possible. Traditional centralized data processing can't satisfy the requirement of low communication overhead, and we have to adopt the distributed method to detect the sensor data streams.

Outlier detection in WSNs is a new studied problem, and its research methods have been thoroughly described in several studies [2, 3]. An outlier is an observation that appears to deviate markedly from other members of the sample in which it occurs.

Outlier detection methods can be divided into statistical based, nearest neighbor based, clustering based, classification based, and spectral decomposition based approaches.

Sheng et al. [3] present a kind of outlier detection algorithm based on histogram, they collect data feature set in the base station to build histogram. If the distance between the data point and the k nearest neighbor point in the range of the threshold value, they concern this data point as normal. The algorithm has higher accuracy, and it reduces the communication overhead compared with the centralized method. However, in some cases, the monitor object can only be one dimension. Besides, the algorithm will increase the running time, even result in an infinite loop, especially when the parameters are not selected appropriately.

Luo et al. [4] study the distributed outlier detection algorithm when the environment noise and sensor nodes failure happen at same time, and they mathematically prove that the increase of nodes' number in the neighborhood will improve the accuracy of outlier detection. In addition, they analysis the abnormal data source from the spatial correlation of node deployment, studies the event boundary detection algorithm. Outlier detection is often associated with the event detection, article [5] have carried on the thorough analysis of the event detection.

Min et al. [5] propose the distributed outlier detection algorithm which concerns the outlier's statistical definition. This method is suitable for large scale sensor network. It is limited by the proportion of fault nodes in the network. If half of the nodes are fault, the algorithm is unable to achieve the desired result. Besides, the algorithm also demanded to get the geographical location of each node by the way of GPS or other positioning system. Chen et al. [6] diagnose the state of other nodes by the reliable nodes. Their outlier detection algorithm has no requirement to the location. Even if the percentage of fault nodes is more than half, the fault nodes can still be detected fully.

Palpanas et al. [7] present the online outlier detection in sensor data streams based on kernel density estimator. This method does not need to get the prior knowledge of the distribution. It can calculate the data distribution based on kernel density estimator. Therefore, the nodes can decide whether it is abnormal data by that the difference between the new arrive data and the original distribution model is beyond threshold. The drawback of this method is difficult to set the appropriate threshold. However, they don't consider the update maintenance problem of the sensor data streams. Therefore, Subramaniam [8] had made corresponding improvement, solved the problem that the single threshold can't satisfy the outlier detection against the multidimensional data object. They updated and maintained the data distribution model with kernel density estimator. Subramaniam introduce another method to detect outlier using Multi Granularity Deviation Factor (MGDF). However, the above method can't detect the spatial abnormal data.

On the basis of the above documents, our paper presents the outlier detection algorithm based on non-parametric method. Our algorithm is appropriate to the multidimensional sensor data streams (means that each data point contains multiple attributes, such as temperature, humidity, air pressure).

3 Hierarchical Sensor Network Model

To acquire accurate information, there are a large number of sensor nodes densely deployed in the monitoring area. In the study of large-scale wireless sensor networks, we introduce the hierarchical sensor network model because of the requirement of extensibility [9, 10].

The hierarchical sensor network model is shown in Fig. 1. It is a virtual network of overlapping, whose communication topology is a tree. The closer to the root of the tree, the better the performance of nodes is, and the more abundant energy the nodes carry. In the hierarchical sensor network model, each node has distributed processing capability. The hierarchical sensor network model divided the close node to the same cluster. Each cluster has a cluster head that is responsible for dealing with data collected by its subset nodes. The higher level, the wider area can be monitor by the cluster head.

As shown in Fig. 1, the node A at the third level is the cluster head of the second level, responsible for handing the data uploaded by node A1, A2, A3, A4.

Without loss of generality, the outlier detection in the hierarchical sensor network can be simplified into distributed outlier detection in the sensor data streams. As shown in Fig. 2, assume that some cluster is mainly composed of a cluster head Nd_c and n sensor nodes Nd_1, Nd_2, ..., Nd_n. The nodes' data streams is respectively DS_1, DS_2, ..., DS_n. Correspondingly, the sliding window for each sensor node is W_1, W_2, ..., W_n. The abnormal data set is indicated as O_1, O_2, ..., O_n. We set $DS = \bigcup_{i=1}^{n} DS_i$ as the union set of all data streams, namely global data streams. We assume that $O = \bigcup_{i=1}^{n} O_i$ is the union of outlier in each sensor data stream, and that $W_c = \bigcup_{i=1}^{n} W_i$ is the sliding window for the cluster head node. Assume that the continuous time series data stream collected by the node Nd_j ($j = 1,2,...,n$) can be presented as $DS_j = \{X_1^{(j)}, X_2^{(j)}, X_3^{(j)}, ..., X_p^{(j)}, ...\}$, $X_p^{(j)}$ is the data collected by the Nd_j at t_p, which is presented as $X_p^{(i)} = \{x_{1p}^{(i)}, x_{2p}^{(i)}, ..., x_{mp}^{(i)}\}^T$.

In the environment monitoring, the sensor data streams generally has the characteristics of temporal correlation. And it is difficult to detect a certain moment with the

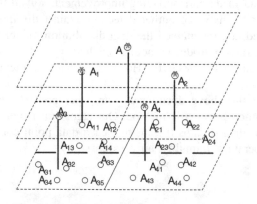

Fig. 1. The hierarchical sensor network model

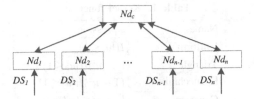

Fig. 2. Distributed outlier detection in sensor data streams

high accuracy and low overhead for the reasons that there is large number of data uploading in the cluster head at same time. Therefore we introduce the sliding window mechanism to observe the change of data stream in the recent period.

4   Outlier Detection Algorithm Based on Multidimensional Epanechnikov Kernel Density Estimator

4.1   Kernel Density Estimator

Our paper presents a kind of outlier detection based on multidimensional kernel density estimator, which is designed for the phenomenon that the communication cost is far greater than their computational overhead between nodes. Our algorithm can reduce the energy consumption in resource-constrained large scale wireless sensor networks. The algorithm mainly includes two processes: the sampling process and the data distribution estimation process. Here is a brief introduce to the kernel density estimator model.

Definition 1. Assuming that $X_1, X_2, \ldots, X_n$ is the independent random variables in R^d (the d dimension Euclid space), $X_i = (x_{11}, x_{12}, \ldots, x_{1d})$ has d dimension attributes. Let k (x) be a d-dimensional function of $X = (X_1, X_2, \ldots, X_n)$, such that $\int_{R^d} k(X)dX = 1$. We call $k(x)$ the kernel function. The distribution density function $f(X)$ of kernel density estimator is defined as follows:

$$\hat{f}_h(X) = \frac{1}{|n|} \sum_{i=1}^{|n|} k(x_1 - x_{i1}, x_2 - x_{i2}, \ldots, x_d - x_{id}) \tag{1}$$

Kernel density estimator depicts the distribution of the data model. It also can be called as kernel density estimator model. Kernel function has a variety of difference forms, commonly used is as shown in Table 1, which does not much affect the estimates.

Our algorithm selects Epanechnikov kernel function which is easier for integrating to calculate the distribution of the data. Besides, when the Epanechnikov kernel function exceeds the limited range, the kernel density estimation is zero. We can approximate the distribution f(x), according to which the values in X were generated, using the following function

Table 1. Kernel function

Name	Expression
Uniform	$\frac{1}{2}I(|u| \leq 1)$
Triangle	$(1 - |u|)I(|u| \leq 1)$
Epanechnikov	$\frac{3}{4}(1 - u^2)I(|u| \leq 1)$
Gaussian	$\frac{1}{\sqrt{2\pi}}\exp(-\frac{1}{2}u^2)$

$$
k(X) = \begin{cases} \left(\frac{3}{4}\right)^d \frac{1}{h_1\ldots h_d}\prod_{1 \leq i \leq d}\left(1 - \left(\frac{x_i}{h_i}\right)^2\right), \left|\frac{x_i}{h_i}\right| \leq 1 \ for \ 1 \leq i \leq d \\ 0, \left|\frac{x_i}{h_i}\right| > 1 \end{cases}
\tag{2}
$$

Where h_i is the bandwidth of the kernel function, it can be presented as $h_i = \sqrt{5} \cdot \sigma_i \cdot n^{-\frac{1}{d+2}}$, where σ_i is the standard deviation of the values in X in dimension i.

The sensor nodes Nd_j sent recent N normal measurements to the cluster head Nd_c, so Nd_c has received S_c normal measurements. We calculate the kernel density estimator model with the S_c normal measurements according definition 2:

$$
\hat{f}_{h,c}(X) = \frac{1}{|S_c|}\sum_{i=1}^{|S_c|} k(x_1 - x_{i1}, x_2 - x_{i2}, \ldots, x_d - x_{id})
\tag{3}
$$

4.2 The Sampling Algorithm Based on K-th Nearest Neighbor (ODBKNN)

We use the outlier detection based on the k nearest neighbor to acquire normal measurement samples in sliding window of each node.

Definition 3. Let DS_i presents the data stream collected by Nd_i. $X_p^{(i)}$ is the block collected at moment t_p by node Nd_i. $X_q^{(i)}$ is the block collected at moment t_q by node Nd_i. Then

1. We can define the distance between $X_p^{(i)}$ and $X_q^{(i)}$ is

$$
d(p,q) = \sqrt{\left(x_{1p}^{(i)} - x_{1q}^{(i)}\right)^2 + \left(x_{2p}^{(i)} - x_{2q}^{(i)}\right)^2 + \ldots + \left(x_{mp}^{(i)} - x_{mq}^{(i)}\right)^2}
\tag{4}
$$

2. The k nearest neighbor distance of the block $X_p^{(i)}$ is defined as $D\left(k, X_i^{(j)}\right)$.

The detail steps for the ODBKNN algorithm can be described as follows. Let the measurements in the sliding window for Nd_j is $X^{(j)} = X_1^{(j)}, X_2^{(j)}, \ldots, X_N^{(j)}$. To begin with, it calculates the $d(p,q)$ $(p,q = 1,2,\ldots,N)$, and sets $A(p,q) = d(p,q)$, which A is a matrix. After that, each line of A can be sorted in ascending order, and we let the sorted matrix be presented as E. And then, the algorithm judges whether $E_{mk} \geq \theta$ is set up, where E_{mk} is the k-th datum in the m-th row, and θ is the predetermined threshold. If the inequality is set up, the algorithm considers the m-th datum in $X^{(j)}$ as the outlier. The nodes delete the outliers and send the normal data to the cluster head nodes.

Considering that the normal measurements collected by the nodes usually fall in a fixed area, we could set the tolerance to identify obviously outliers. Our algorithm utilizes the tolerance δ to filter the outliers from the data streams. So that it decreases the computation complexity. Let the next measurement entering into the sliding window be X_{new}, the data set in the sliding window can be presented as $\left\{ X_1^{(j)}, X_2^{(j)}, \ldots, X_N^{(j)} \right\}$, k, d and θ is the given parameters. The algorithm can be described in follows.

```
program ODBKNN( )

    init( X^(j) );

    calculate  D(k,X_i^(j)) of all points in  X_new^(j);

    if   D(k,X_i^(j)) ≥ d

set X_i^(j) as outlier and insert into O_j;

    end if

    acquire the normal sample S_j=X^(j)-O_j

return;

program init()

    when the new data X_i^(j) arrives

    if   X_si^(j) ≥ δ(s),s∈ (1,2,...,m)

set X_i^(j) as outlier and insert into O_j;

    end if

return;
```

4.3   Outlier Detection Algorithm Based on Multidimensional Epanechnikov Kernel Density Estimator (ODBKDE)

The method of estimating the data distribution model in the cluster heads is the key point for our paper. If the data distribution is known, it is effectively detected by the all nodes. In addition, the data distribution model can fuse multiple kinds of sensors effectively and decrease the communication overhead. Provided the data distribution of cluster head nodes can quickly be computed online, we can identify the outliers by the model. After that the kernel density estimator for some cluster is generated, the cluster head node sends the parameters of the model to the other nodes in the cluster. Then each node recognizes the outliers by the download model parameters effectively.

The Epanechnikov kernel function has the characteristic that the kernel density estimation equals to zero when X exceeds the limited range. So the decision is whether $\hat{f}(X_{new}) = 0$ is true for the new coming data X_{new}. When the events or other cases cause the change of the data distribution, the kernel density estimator model should be updated in the cluster head nodes at regular intervals. We introduce two kinds of update schemes: active update scheme and passive update scheme. In active update scheme, the cluster head nodes request the other nodes upload the latest normal measurement in time interval T. The selection of T reflects the compromise between the network traffic and the algorithm precision. The steps can be described in follows.

```
program   ODBKDE( )

when the new data Xnew arrives Ndj;

if  f̂(Xnew)=0

    set Xnew as outlier and insert into outlier set A;

    program  update( f̂ );

    end if

    if T spillover

      T=0;

      program  update( f̂ );

    else

      T=T+1;

    end if

  return

program  update( );

    each node update the sliding window;

    ODBKNN(data in the sliding window);

    set sample Sj to the cluster head node;

    update the new model f̂new;

  return
```

5 Experimental Evaluation

In this paper, all the simulations are performed on MATLAB. The sensor network contains 90 nodes which are randomly deployed in a square region of size 30 × 30 units. Without loss of generality, we assume that the ninety nodes can be divided into nine small clusters by the location. Each cluster contains a cluster head V_i ($i = 1, 2, ..., 9$) and nine other nodes $V_{i1}, V_{i2}, ..., V_{i9}$. The cluster node is responsible for processing measurements uploaded by other nodes. At the same time it also collects measurements nearby. As shown in Fig. 3, there are two types of nodes, where the hollow circle represents the underlying sensor nodes and the star represents the cluster head nodes in the second layer.

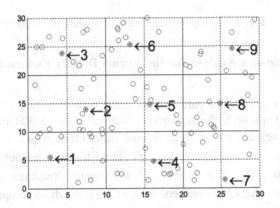

Fig. 3. The deployment of sensor nodes

The article [10] has introduced the clustering methods in detail. The clustering technologies usually utilize the spatial correlation. We do not focus on the clustering methods in our paper. We directly divide the square region into nine clusters averagely. And on this basis we analyze the whole network.

5.1 The Influence on the Choice of K

The choice of k for the outlier detection in the sliding window has some effects on the performance of the algorithm. Let the width of the sliding window be $|W| = 20$, in which the number of the outliers are a. Changing the value of a, we can observe that the appropriate value of k should fall into the shadow part in Fig. 4. Otherwise the algorithm in the sampling process cannot find all outliers. When $k = |W|/2$, the maximum number of the outliers detected can be $a/2$.

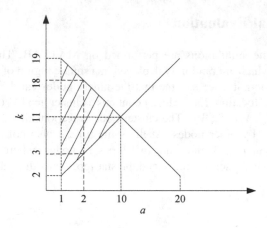

Fig. 4. The appropriate range of k when $|W| = 20$

5.2   The Performance Analysis for the Kernel Density Estimator Algorithm

Assuming that measurements collected by each node has two attributes (such as temperature and humidity), the network collect the data of 300 moments. Normal temperature readings are drawn from normal distribution $N(\mu_{,1}, \sigma_1^2)$, while normal humidity readings are drawn from $N(\mu_{,2}, \sigma_2^2)$. The outliers of temperature readings are drawn from $N(\mu_{,2}, \sigma_2^2)$, The outliers of temperature readings are drawn from $N(\mu_{,1}, \sigma_1^2)$. The occurrences of outliers account for p in whole sampling moments. In the simulation, we set $\mu_1 = 10, \mu_2 = 30$, $\sigma_1 = \sigma_2 = 1$. In order to have better understand for the process, we analyze the cluster marked 1 in the Fig. 5. Same thing as above, the cluster contains a cluster head node V_1 and nine sensor nodes $V_{11}, V_{12}, \ldots, V_{19}$. Each node eliminates the outliers in the sliding window according the ODBKNN algorithm at the beginning. The cluster head nodes receive the normal data and establish the data distribution by kernel density estimator. The characteristic parameters in sliding window W_c for the cluster head are shown in Table 2. The kernel density estimation model for the temperature is shown in Fig. 5.

Table 2. The characteristics of the sample

Attribute	Minimum	Maximum	Mean	Variance
Temperature	6.7680	12.9745	9.9691	1.0120
Humidity	17.7985	22.7304	20.1119	0.9015

In the Fig. 5, we can see that the choice of kernel density function has few effects on the estimation. However, there are some different cases in the sample of maximum and minimum in Fig. 6. The Gaussian kernel function has the smooth estimation curve. It needs to set the threshold or use other ways to identify the outliers, such as the use of

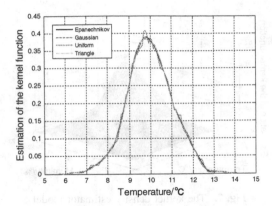

Fig. 5. The kernel density estimator graph of the temperature

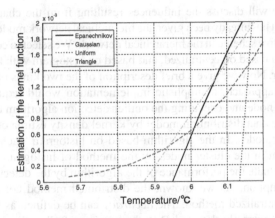

Fig. 6. The difference of Epanechnikov、Gaussian、Uniform and Triangle kernel

multi-granularity deviation factor. The Epanechnikov, Uniform and Triangle kernel function can identify outliers directly by whether $\hat{f}(X) = 0$ is true, but they have different zero boundary point. In this paper, we choose the Epanechnikov kernel density estimator to build the data distribution model.

Compared with that the histogram can only be applied to one attribute, the kernel density estimator is able to deal with multidimensional measurements. The Fig. 7 gives the kernel density estimator model with the temperature and the humidity samples in the sliding window of the marked cluster head node. The kernel density estimator can reflect the multiple attribute objects to one dimension, which reduces the computational complexity of the algorithm.

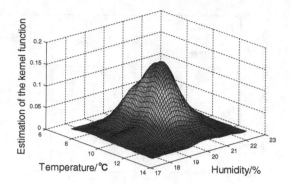

Fig. 7. The kernel density estimator model

5.3   The Influence of P

In this section, we will discuss the influences resulting from the change of the outlier appearance rate p. It has already been given the hierarchical network model in Sect. 3. There is no viable alternative scheme in the hierarchical network. We select to compare the outlier detection algorithm based on centralized, and based on histogram with the algorithm presented in this paper. Now we give a brief description of the two kinds of method.

In centralized approach, a simplistic implementation would require collecting all data at one central node and executing the outlier detection algorithm there. The central node calculates the data distribution model by kernel density estimator, and downloads the model to other nodes. In the algorithm based on histogram, each node carries the detection algorithm in the cluster nodes by the method of histogram.

We mainly evaluate the performance of the algorithm by the detection accuracy and the energy consumption. As we known, the distributed method consumes much less energy than the centralized method. The *accuracy* can be defined as the rate of actual number of outliers correctly detected D to the number of all outliers A.

$$accuracy = \frac{D}{A} \tag{5}$$

Figures 8 and 9 shows the relation between *accuracy* and p. As can be seen from Fig. 8, two kinds of outlier detection algorithms based kernel density estimator have better accuracy than the histogram algorithm at beginning, and the centralized method is better than the hierarchical method. The central node has a larger sample than the other nodes in the sliding window. For this reason, the centralized method can approximate the data distribution as close as possible. However, it increases the communication overhead. In addition, the algorithm will not be able to detect all outliers when the number of outlier exceeds half of the width of the sliding window. So once p exceeds certain critical point, the accuracy of the detection algorithm based on kernel density estimator is lower than the algorithm based on histogram. To prevent the effect resulting from the ODBKNN algorithm, the normal data sample should be pre-prepared, instead of acquiring the normal sample instantly.

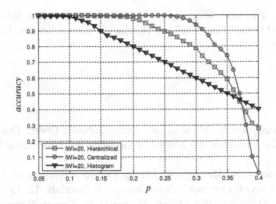

Fig. 8. The relation between *accuracy* and *p* in different methods

Figure 9 shows the relationship between the width $|W|$ of sliding window and *p*. When *p* is constant, the detection accuracy increases along with $|W_c|$. For the hierarchical network model, it is convenience to improve the detection accuracy by increasing the width of sliding window $|W_c|$. We can see from Figs. 8 and 9, the detection accuracy keep almost 100 % when p is below 20 %. It means our algorithm has high detection accuracy in large scale sensor networks.

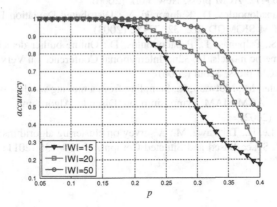

Fig. 9. The relation between *accuracy* and *p* in different $|W|$

6 Conclusion

We put forward a kind of outlier detection algorithm based on non-parametric estimation, which is aimed at the hierarchical wireless sensor network. The algorithm constructs the normal samples and calculates the distribution with ODBKDE. Each node identifies outliers by the download model. The simulation results verify the effectiveness of our algorithm. Compared with centralized algorithms, our algorithm reduces the energy consumption. Compared with the algorithm based on histogram, our algorithm has higher accuracy.

Acknowledgments. This work was supported by the National Natural Science Foundations of China (Grant No. 61174023) and Zhejiang Provincial Natural Science Foundation of China (Grant No. Y1110791).

References

1. Zhang, Y., Hamm, N.A.S., Meratnia, N.: Statistics-based Outlier Detection for Wireless Sensor Networks. J International Journal of Geographical Information Science. **26**, 1373–1392 (2012)
2. Zhang, Y., Meratnia, N., Havinga, P.: Outlier Detection Techniques for Wireless Sensor Networks: A Survey. J. Communications Surveys & Tutorials. **12**, 159–170 (2010)
3. Sheng, B., Li, Q., Mao, W.: Outlier Detection in Sensor Networks. In: 8th ACM International Symposium on Mobile Ad Hoc Networking and Computing, pp. 219–228. ACM press, Canada (2007)
4. Luo, X., Dong, M., Huang, Y.: On Distributed Fault-tolerant Detection in Wireless sensor networks. J. Computers, IEEE Transactions on 55, 58–70 (2006)
5. Ding, M., Chen, D., Xing, K.: Localized Fault-tolerant Event Boundary Detection in Sensor Networks. In: 24th Annual Joint Conference of the IEEE Computer and Communications Societies, pp. 902–913. IEEE press, Piscataway (2005)
6. Chen, J., Kher, S., Somani, A.: Distributed Fault Detection of Wireless Sensor Networks. In: 2006 Workshop on Dependability Issue in Wireless Ad Hoc Networks and Sensor Networks, pp. 65–72. ACM press, New York (2006)
7. Palpanas, T., Papadopoulos, D., Kalogeraki, V.: Distributed Deviation Detection in Sensor Networks. J. ACM SIGMOD Rec. **32**, 77–82 (2003)
8. Subramaniam, S., Palpanas, T., Papadopoulos, D.: Online outlier detection in sensor data using non-parametric models. In: 32nd International Conference on Very Large Data Bases, pp. 187–198. ACM press, Seoul (2006)
9. Babcock, B., Datar, M., Motwani, R.: Sampling from a moving window over streaming data. In: 13th Annual ACM-SIAM Symposium on Discrete Algorithms, pp. 633–634. ACM press, Germany (2002)
10. Boyinbode, O., Le, H., Takizawa, M.: A survey on clustering algorithms for wireless sensor networks. Int. J. Space-Based and Situated Comput. **1**, 130–136 (2011)

A Robust Sparsity Estimation Method in Compressed Sensing

Shaohua Qin[1][(✉)] and Juan Yin[2]

[1] College of Physics and Electronics, Shandong Normal University, Jinan, China
qinshaohua@sdnu.edu.cn
[2] Medical Engineering Department, Shandong Provincial
Qianfoshan Hospital, Jinan, China

Abstract. Compressed sensing has been widely used in wireless sensor networks. In compressed sensing field, many aspects depend on the sparsity of the sparse signal, and we usually assume that the sparsity is known in advance, but the sparsity is unknown and not fixed in practice. So it is necessary to estimate the sparsity before we use it. In this paper, we propose a new method to estimate the sparsity, we use greedy algorithm and relative threshold to estimate the sparsity. Comparing with the traditional method, our method does not need reconstruct the whole signal, needes fewer number of measurements and estimation times, has better performance in low SNR scenarios or when the signal is changing. The simulation indicate the advantages of the new method.

Keywords: Compressed sensing · Sparsity · Estimation

1 Introduction

The compressed sensing is a signal process theory about the sparse or compressive signal [1,2], it has been widely used in wireless sensor networks [3–6]. The sparsity of the sparse signal is an important parameter, many aspects in compressed sensing are associated with the sparsity, such as the signal reconstruction algorithm, the quantity of measurements needed in reconstructions and the design of sensing matrices. But the sparsity is unknown and not fixed in practice, these applications have to use the maximum value of the sparsity, this will affect the performance of these applications. So it is necessary to estimate the sparsity and get an exact value. There are a few of papers discussing the sparsity estimation problem in compressed sensing literature. In paper [7], an optimization reconstruction method is proposed based on the sparsity estimation, this reconstruction needes fewer number of measurements than traditional method owing to the estimation of the sparsity. The method to estimate the sparsity in this paper is based on the Base pursuit (BP) reconstruction [8], of course, the measurements used to estimate the sparsity is fewer than the one

S. Qin—This paper is supported by Shandong Normal University Education Innovation Grants.

L. Sun et al. (Eds.): CWSN 2014, CCIS 501, pp. 481–488, 2015.
DOI: 10.1007/978-3-662-46981-1_46

needed to reconstruct the whole signal. This is a good attempt to estimate the sparsity, but there are still some aspects need to be improved:

1. The sparsity is defined as the number of nonzero coefficients, and the signal reconstruction needes not only the number of nonzero coefficients, but also the amplitude and position of the coefficients. So it is not necessary to reconstruct the whole signal in order to estimate the sparsity, there should be a simple method to estimate the sparsity without reconstructions.
2. The threshold of sparsity estimation in paper [7] is related to the power of the signal and the noise, but the power of the signal is not available or varying with time in some scenarios, this will affect the accuracy of the estimation.

In order to improve the performance of the sparsity estimation, we proposed a robust method, which has some improvements:

1. Our estimation method uses greedy algorithm to find larger coefficients and computes the sparsity, do not need to reconstruct the whole signal. So this method is simpler than traditional methods, and needs fewer number of measurements.
2. Our estimation uses relative threshold to determine the larger coefficients, the threshold is not related to the power of the signal or the noise, so this method is robust when the power of the signal is not available or varying with time.

The remainder of this article is as follows. The sparsity is described in Sect. 2. In Sect. 3, this sparsity estimation method is proposed. The simulations results are given in Sect. 4. Conclusions are offered in the last section.

2   Related Works

2.1   Compressed Sensing

For a signal $\mathbf{x} \in \mathbb{R}^N$, if it can be expressed in an orthogonal basis $\mathbf{\Psi} \in \mathbb{R}^{N \times N}$ as

$$\mathbf{x} = \mathbf{\Psi}\theta, \tag{1}$$

and the number of nonzero coefficients θ is not more than K, then we can call the signal $\mathbf{x} \in \mathbb{R}^N$ is a K-sparse signal.

The compressive measurements $\mathbf{y} \in \mathbb{R}^M$ can be got from the sensing matrix $\mathbf{\Phi} \in \mathbb{R}^{M \times N}(M < N)$

$$\mathbf{y} = \mathbf{\Phi}\mathbf{x} = \mathbf{\Phi}\mathbf{\Psi}\theta, \tag{2}$$

Let $\mathbf{A} = \mathbf{\Phi}\mathbf{\Psi}$, if the matrix $\mathbf{A}$ satisfies the restricted isometry property (RIP) [9]

$$(1 - \delta_K) \|\mathbf{x}\|_2^2 \le \|\mathbf{A}\mathbf{x}\|_2^2 \le (1 + \delta_K) \|\mathbf{x}\|_2^2, \tag{3}$$

where δ_K is the isometry constant in matrix $\mathbf{A}$ about sparsity K [2], then from the compressive measurements $\mathbf{y}$, the signal $\mathbf{x}$ could be accurately recovered.

Some random matrices could follow the restricted isometry property, such as Bernoulli and Gaussian random matrices.

For any reconstruction algorithm, the lower bound of the minimum number of measurements used to recover the sparse signal can be written as

$$M > CK \log(N/K),\tag{4}$$

where C determined by the measurements matrix [2], it is a constant.

Convex optimization and greedy pursuits are two primary reconstruction algorithms in compressed sensing [10]. Convex optimization replace the l_0-norm minimization with the l_1-norm minimization, such as Basis Pursuit (BP) [8], which seeks a set of sparse coefficients θ by solving the convex optimization program.

$$\hat{\theta} = \arg \min \|\theta\|_1 \text{ subject to } \mathbf{y} = \mathbf{\Phi x} = \mathbf{\Phi \Psi} \theta.\tag{5}$$

The greedy reconstruction algorithm makes locally optimal decisions to recover the sparse signal, it builds up the signal approximation iteratively. There are many greedy reconstruction methods, for example Matching Pursuit (MP) [11], and the improved version Orthogonal Matching Pursuit (OMP) [12].

2.2 Sparsity

The sparsity of the signal is defined as the number of the nonzero coefficients, i.e.

$$\mathbf{S} = \|\theta\|_0,\tag{6}$$

Many aspects of compressed sensing are related to the sparsity, such as the signal reconstruction algorithm, the quantity of the measurements needed in reconstructions and the design of sensing matrices [13]. But the sparsity is often unknown or dynamically varying in practice, so it is necessary to estimate the value of sparsity.

There are a few papers considering the sparsity estimation problem. The paper [13] discusses the problem of unknown sparsity, and in order to estimate the sparsity stably, the l_0-norm is replaced with a soft definition, but this estimation method needs measuring the signal two times with Cauchy distribution sensing matrix and Gaussian distribution sensing matrix respectively. In paper [7], in order to reduce the number of measurements needed to reconstruct the sparse signal, a different estimation method based on the threshold is proposed,

$$S = \sum_{i=1}^{N} (|\theta_i| > \gamma),\tag{7}$$

where γ is the threshold, which is defined as $\gamma = (\mu + \delta)/2$, in this definition, δ is the standard deviation about the noise, and μ is the average absolute value about the sparse signal. The coefficients θ is computed using the basis pursuit (BP) algorithm. Affecting by the noise and the algorithm accuracy, many coefficients of the sparse signal are not exact zero. So the sparsity is defined as the number of larger coefficients and not the number of the nonzero coefficients in practice.

As mentioned in Sect. 1, this estimation method in paper [7] has some inadequacies in the threshold definition and the coefficient computation. In this paper, we proposed a robust sparsity estimation method. We use greedy algorithm to find the larger coefficient and do not need to reconstruct the whole signal, the threshold is defined as a relative value and not related to the power of the signal and noise. The detail of our method is discussed in Sect. 3

3 Sparsity Estimation Methods

For a sparse signal, most of the coefficients are close to zero. The coefficients of a sparse signal sorted by the amplitude are represented in Fig. 1. From Fig. 1 we find that the amplitude of coefficients decay rapidly, there is a sharp descent between the larger coefficients and the smaller ones, and the number of the larger coefficients is equal to the sparsity. So we can estimate the sparsity through computing the number of larger coefficients, and not consider other smaller coefficients. The larger coefficients can be determined by comparing with other coefficients.

The greedy reconstruction algorithm, which builds up the signal approximation iteratively by finding the larger coefficient one by one. Motivated by this algorithm, we use greedy algorithm to find the larger coefficient, different from the MP or OMP algorithm, we only care about the larger coefficients and not other smaller coefficient, so we do not need to reconstruct the whole signal and need fewer number of measurements and iterative times. In the process of finding the larger coefficient, the key point is the threshold to define the larger coefficients. In Eq. 7, the threshold is related to the power of the signal and noise.

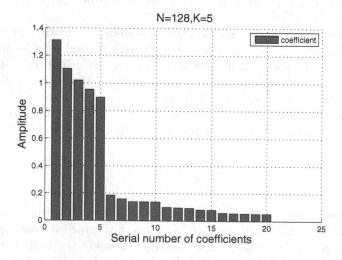

Fig. 1. The coefficients of the sparse signal sorted by amplitude

So this threshold will be affected by the varying of the signal. From Fig. 1 we can find there is a sharp descent between the larger coefficients and the smaller ones, so the larger coefficients can be determined by comparing with the threshold, and the threshold is defined as the average of the previous larger coefficients,

$$\gamma_t = \frac{\sum\limits_{i=2}^{t} \theta_{i-1}}{2(t-1)},$$ (8)

where the θ_i is the larger coefficient selected, the t is the selected times. In the process of estimation, the coefficients of the sparse signal are sorted by amplitude, one new larger coefficient is selected by comparing with the threshold in every iterative time, and the threshold is defined as half of the average of the larger coefficients selected before, as shown in Eq. 8. If this coefficient is greater than the threshold, it is determined as a new larger coefficient; if this coefficient is less than the threshold, then the finding process is finished, and the sparsity is equal to the number of the larger coefficients. The algorithm of our sparsity estimation is given as follows:

1. First, we initialize the residual $r_0 = y$, and the measurement matrix is defined as $A = \Phi\Psi$. The iteration counter is initialized as $t = 1$, and the sparsity of the signal is defined as $S = 0$. $A(t)$ is the set of selected vectors of the measurement matrix in t times, $\theta(t)$ is the approximation coefficients in t times.
2. Select the measurement vector that maximizes the value of the projection of the residual onto A,

$$a_t = \arg \max_{i=1,......,N} \frac{< r_{t-1}, a_i >}{\|a_i\|}.$$ (9)

$$A(t) = [A(t-1), a_t].$$ (10)

3. Update the residual and the estimate of the coefficient for the selected vector

$$\theta_t = \frac{< r_{t-1}, a_t >}{\|a_t\|^2}.$$ (11)

$$\theta(t) = [\theta(t-1), \theta_t].$$ (12)

$$r_t = r_0 - \theta(t)A(t).$$ (13)

4. If $\theta_t > \gamma_t$ then $S = S+1$, where γ_t is the threshold defined in Eq. 8; If $\theta_t < \gamma_t$ then end the algorithm. (γ_0 is defined as zero, we suppose the sparsity is not zero)
5. Increase t, In case $t < T$ (where T is the iteration times, for the sake of reliability, we can make $T = 2K$), then go to Step 2 again; otherwise the algorithm is ended.

4 Simulations

Our estimation method uses greedy algorithm and relative threshold to find larger coefficients and computes the sparsity, does not need to reconstruct the whole signal and does not rely on the power of the signal. So our estimation method needs fewer number of measurements and iteration times, runes well in low SNR scenario, and avoids being affected by the varying of the signal's power. We compare our estimation method with the traditional method in paper [7] in different scenarios. For a sparse signal $\mathbf{x} \in \mathbb{R}^N, N = 128$, which is mixed with a Gaussian noise, and the sparsity of this signal is $K = 5$. In this paper, we use the identity matrix as the representation basis, i.e., $\mathbf{\Psi} = \mathbf{I}^{N \times N}$. The compressive measurements $\mathbf{y} \in \mathbb{R}^M$ are acquired from the random matrix $\mathbf{\Phi} \in \mathbb{R}^{M \times N}, M < N$. Bernoulli and Gaussian random matrices all follow the restricted isometry property, the entries of the random matrix in this simulation are independent and identically distributed according to Gaussian probability distributions, the Bernoulli matrix can also be selected as another measurement matrix. The iterative times in our estimation method is $m = 2K$.

We use the correct rate as the property to evaluate the performance of different estimation methods, the correct rate CR is defined as

$$CR = 1 - \frac{|S - K|}{K} \tag{14}$$

where S is the estimation sparsity and K is the actual sparsity.

Figure 2 indicates the estimation correct rate with the number of measurements. From Fig. 2, we can find that the proposed estimation method has higher correct rate than the traditional method. When the measurements is enough, both methods have perfect performance, as the number of measurements is

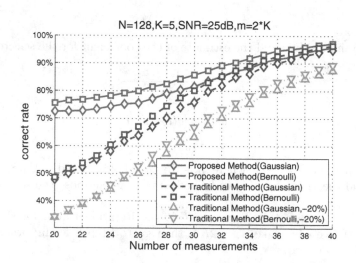

Fig. 2. The estimation correct rate with the number of measurements

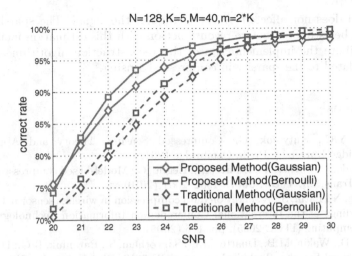

Fig. 3. The estimation correct rate with SNR

reducing, the performance of both methods are decreasing. The correct rate of our method is still higher than 70 % even when the number of measurements becomes 20, but the correct rate of the traditional method is lower than 50 %. This is because our method only computes the quantity of coefficients and not needs to reconstruct the whole signal, so it needs fewer measurements to estimate the sparsity, especially when the measurements is less, our method's performance is better than traditional method.

When the power of the signal is changed, From Eq. 7, we know that the threshold will also change. But in the process of estimation, we don't know the change of the power prior, then the performance of estimation will be affected; and From Eq. 8, we find the threshold is not related to the power of the signal, so the performance of our method will not be affected. Figure 2 indicates the performance of the traditional estimation when the power of signal is reduced by 20 %.

Figure 3 indicates the correct rate with SNR. When the quantity of the measurements is enough, the performance of the estimation will be defected by the SNR of the measurements. From Fig. 3 we find that when the SNR is 30 dB, the performance of both method are perfect, but with the reduction in SNR, the performance is getting worse. The correct rate of the proposed method is better than the traditional method when the SNR is reduced, even when the SNR is 20 dB, the correct rate of our estimation can still reach more than 75 %.

5 Conclusion

From the simulation results, we can find the proposed method has good performance in different measurements and SNR scenarios. Compared with the traditional method, our method needs fewer number of measurements and iterative times, and does not affected by the change of the signal. The sparsity of the signal can be estimated before reconstruction with this estimation method, this will contribute the implementation of the reconstruction algorithm and other aspects related to the sparsity in compressed sensing.

References

1. Eldar, Y.C., Kutyniok, G.: Compressed Sensing: Theory and Applications. Cambridge University Press, Cambridge (2012)
2. Baraniuk, R., Cevher, V., Duarte, M., Hegde, C.: Model-based compressive sensing. IEEE Trans. Inf. Theor. **56**(4), 1982–2001 (2010)
3. Kimura, N., Latifi, S.: A survey on data compression in wireless sensor networks. In: Proceedings of the International Conference on Information Technology: Coding and Computing (ITCC 2005), pp. 1–6 (2005)
4. Baron, D., Wakin, M.B., Duarte, M.F., Sarvotham, S., Baraniuk, R.G.: Distributed Compressed Sensing, Technical report ECE-0612. Rice University, Electrical and Computer Engineering Department (2006)
5. Zheng, H., Xiao, S., Wang, X., Tian, X., Guizani, M.: Capacity and delay analysis for data gathering with compressive sensing in wireless sensor networks. IEEE Trans. Wirel. Commun. **12**(2), 917–927 (2013)
6. Quer, G., Masiero, R., Pillonetto, G., Rossi, M., Zorzi, M.: Sensing, compression, and recovery for WSNs: sparse signal modeling and monitoring framework. IEEE Trans. Wirel. Commun. **11**(10), 3447–3461 (2012)
7. Wang, Y., Tian, Z., Feng, C.: Sparsity order estimation and its application in compressive spectrum sensing for cognitive radios. IEEE Trans. Wirel. Commun. **11**(6), 2116–2124 (2012)
8. Chen, S.S., Donoho, D.L., Saunders, M.A.: Atomic decomposition by basis pursuit. SIAM Rev. **43**(1), 129–159 (2001)
9. Candes, E.J., Tao, T.: Decoding by linear programming. IEEE Trans. Inf. Theor. **51**(12), 4203–4215 (2005)
10. Tropp, J.A., Wright, S.J.: Computational methods for sparse solution of linear inverse problems. Proc. IEEE **98**(6), 948–958 (2010)
11. Mallat, S.G., Zhang, Z.: Matching pursuits with time-frequency dictionaries. IEEE Trans. Sig. Process. **41**(12), 3397–3415 (1993)
12. Tropp, J.A., Gilbert, A.C.: Signal recovery from random measurements via orthogonal matching pursuit. IEEE Trans. Inf. Theor. **53**(12), 4655–4666 (2007)
13. Lopes, M.E.: Estimating unknown sparsity in compressed sensing. In: Proceedings of the 30th International Conference on Machine Learning, JMLR W&CP, Atlanta, Georgia, USA, vol. 28, no. 3, pp. 217–225 (2013)

The Method of Data Aggregation for Wireless Sensor Networks Based on LEACH-CS

Yuanyuan Liu, Wentao Zhao[✉], Lu Zhu, Baishan Ci, and Suhua Chen

School of Information Engineering, East China Jiao Tong University,
Nanchang 330013, China
wentao199012040126.com

Abstract. A novel data aggregation method of WSN based on low-energy adaptive clustering hierarchy compressed sensing (LEACH-CS) is presented to resolve the contradiction between data accuracy and energy consumption in sensor nodes. It considers the sparsity of the sensed data in wireless sensor networks (WSNs). At the proposed method, the LEACH protocol is adopted to select cluster head and cluster formation from the random arrangement of sensor nodes, and the Gaussian random matrix is utilized to linearly compress sensor data by each cluster head. Then the compressed information is transmitted to the base station (BS). It reduces data transmission and energy consumption, thus improving the lifetime of network. According to sensor data being of regional smoothness, the differential transformation regularization is adopted to reconstruct receiving linear compression projection information by the BS. Simulation experiments show that the data aggregation method of WSNs based on cluster compressed sensing can guarantee data accuracy collected, and improves the network lifetime at the same time.

Keywords: Wireless sensor networks · Compressed sensing · Cluster · Data aggregation

1 Introduction

Wireless sensor networks (WSNs) was widely used in many areas recently, such as environmental monitoring, intelligent household and precision agriculture and so on. Sensor nodes of WSNs sense the information of monitoring area. The base station (BS) receives data in the network by wireless communication [1]. Data aggregation is one of the important operations in WSNs. Whether the BS can collect data effectively or not is directly related to the application performance. However, the nodes are usually energy limited. And it is hard for second supplementary of energy after deployment, especially in the long-term and wide range applications. There exists a serious energy constraint problem in WSNs. So the main problem of data aggregation is reducing the energy consumption with ensuring the accuracy of acquired data.

© Springer-Verlag Berlin Heidelberg 2015
L. Sun et al. (Eds.): CWSN 2014, CCIS 501, pp. 489–498, 2015.
DOI: 10.1007/978-3-662-46981-1_47

To ensure the accuracy of sensed data and maintain the communication connectivity of the entire network, it needs a certain distribution density of sensor nodes even multiple nodes overlapped in the same monitoring area. The high density distribution of sensor nodes can guarantee the robustness of the system, but it also leads to data redundancy. Then the data of multiple nodes is of some spatial correlation. The in-network data aggregation techniques [2] process the large amount of acquired raw data through a certain algorithm. It removes the redundant data and only keeps a small amount of meaningful data to send to BS. The in-network data aggregation can reduce the data transfer between the nodes to prolong the network lifetime. References [1,3] use some simple data aggregation methods such as average, maximum and minimum. It compresses data by extracting the statistical characteristics of data of nodes. However, it loses some other information. These methods can only be used in the field without high data accuracy. References [4,5] compress the wavelet coefficient after wavelet transform of the sensed data. Most environmental monitoring signal exist the feature of sparsity in the wavelet domain. The wavelet transform can realize the in-network data compression. The data aggregation based on wavelet transform can improve the efficiency of data. However, the computational complexity of wavelet transform compression algorithm is so high that it is not suitable for the nodes with limited processing capacity. Reference [6] compresses the data of nodes by the method of distributed source coding (DSC). DSC can compress the data independently without communication in nodes. And it can get the similar compression efficiency with the joint coding through mining the spatial correlation of data at the receiving end. However, it is a great challenge to get the joint probability model and the distribution function of nodes in a lot of applications of WSNs, especially without the information of the network topology.

Compressed sensing (CS) [7] uses the non-adaptive linear projection to complete compressive sampling of data based on the sparse characteristic of source data. Then it can reconstruct the raw data by optimization method. CS can reduce the complexity of the data acquisition through complex reconstruction algorithm. The nodes of WSNs are resource-constrained. But the BS is usually not affected by this restriction. So CS can solve the contradiction between the compressed sampling and accuracy of data aggregation. The data has high spatial correlation for the WSNs with high density of sensor nodes. This is the precondition when the CS theory applies to data compression in WSNs. The applications of CS are mainly concentrated in planar routing structure in WSNs. References [8–10] encoding the data of nodes based on CS. Its principle is shown in Fig. 1. The sampling point of node is expanded into m dimensional vector by the Gaussian random vector. Then the m dimensional vector is send to the parent node. The sampling point of parent node is also expanded into m dimensional vector. The sum of the m dimensional vectors can be a new vector to be forwarded. At last the load of entire network is N*m. This method can solve the problem of unbalance network load. The farther the node nears the BS, the larger the amount of data needs to be send. However, it may need more amount of data for the entire network.

Fig. 1. The data aggregation based on CS in planar routing structure

Hierarchical routing structure can solve the limitation issue of planar routing network scale by clustering way. It can support a larger network. LEACH (Low-energy adaptive clustering hierarchy) [11] is the classical clustering routing algorithm. The neighboring nodes can become one cluster. The random selection cluster head compresses the sensed data in cluster and transmit it to BS. There is correlation in the data of neighboring nodes. So the data has the feature of sparsity. This paper introduces the data aggregation method of CS on the basis of LEACH. Each cluster head uses gauss random matrix to observe the nodes' data of cluster. Then observational data will be transmitted to BS. It can decrease transmitted data amount and lower energy use. So the network lifetime will be prolonged effectively. The raw data can be reconstructed efficiently from the observation data by using the prior knowledge of node data in BS. Therefore it can solve the conflict between the accuracy of data aggregation and network lifetime.

2 System Model

Assuming N nodes are placed in the square area (100 m*100 m) randomly. And the WSNs has the following properties.

(1) Sensor nodes don't change after deployed. The structure and initial energy of the each node are same. There is only one base station. And the energy is not restricted. Each node has a certain storage capacity. All the nodes can send data to BS directly.

(2) The energy consume model at receiving and transmitting data are the follows [11].

$$E_{Tx}(L,d) = \begin{cases} 8L * \left(E_{elec} + \xi_{fs} * d^2\right), d \leq d_{threshold} \\ 8L * \left(E_{elec} + \xi_{mp} * d^4\right), d > d_{threshold} \end{cases}$$

$$E_{Rx}(L,d) = 8L * E_{elec} \tag{1}$$

$E_{Tx}(L,d)$ is the consumption energy of transmitting data. $E_{Rx}(L,d)$ is the consumption energy of receiving data. The amount of data is L. E_{elec} is the consumption energy per bit. ξ_{fs} and ξ_{mp} are the radio energy parameters that will be used for simulation. $d_{threshold}$ stands for the distance threshold value.

The WSNs data aggregation method based on LEACH-CS is shown in Fig. 2. First it uses clustering routing protocol to select cluster heads. Then the ordinary nodes join the cluster according to the signal correlation or distance. The cluster heads get the linear compressed projection of the in-cluster data. The linear compressed projection data will be transmitted to BS. At last the raw data can be reconstructed efficiently in BS.

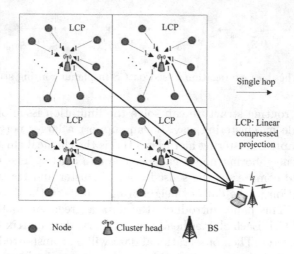

Fig. 2. Data aggregation method based on EACH-CS

3   The Data Aggregation of LEACH-CS

3.1   LEACH Routing Protocol

LEACH is on the based of round. Each round is composed of two parts, namely the establishment of the clusters and the data communication process. In the process of the establishment of the cluster, the cluster heads are confirmed randomly. Then ordinary nodes determine which cluster to being joined through distance. In this paper, we consider the residual energy and average energy factors to optimize the selection mechanism of cluster heads in LEACH. The threshold value of cluster head selection is as follow.

$$G\left(n\right) = \begin{cases} \frac{q}{1-q*\left[r \bmod \left(\frac{1}{q}\right)\right]} * \frac{E_{remaining}}{\bar{E}}, when \ n \in O \\ 0, \ else \end{cases} \tag{2}$$

in which the proportion of setting cluster head node and all nodes is q. O is the node that has not become the cluster head in round $1/q$. The number of round is r. The remaining energy of each node is $E_{remaining}$. And the average residual energy of all the nodes is $\bar{E}$. The node is cluster head when the threshold $G(n)$ is smaller than the random number.

3.2   Basic Idea of CS

CS mainly includes sparse representation, coding measurement and reconstruction. Consider a signal vector $\mathbf{x} = [x_1, x_2, \cdots, x_N]$. Suppose that $\mathbf{x}$ can be represented as $\mathbf{x} = \sum_{i=1}^{N} \theta_i \psi_i$ in domain $\psi = [\psi_1, \psi_2, \cdots, \psi_n]$, where θ_i are the transform coefficients in ψ. We say that $\mathbf{x}$ is k-sparse if there are only k non-zero entries in $\theta_i = [\theta_1, \theta_2 \cdots \theta_N]$. Not directly sampling $\mathbf{x}$, We get the compression $\mathbf{y}$ by a measurement matrix, i.e., $\mathbf{y} = A_{m*n}\mathbf{x}$, in which A_{m*n} is $m \times n$ measurement matrix with $m << n$. The CS theory shows that the k-sparse data $\mathbf{x}$ can be reconstructed from m measurements with high likelihood if $m \geq ck \log n$, in which c is a constant. Recovering the data $\mathbf{x}$ from $\mathbf{y}$ can be finished by solving an l_0-minimization issue:

$$\begin{cases} \min_{w} \|w\|_0 \ w = \mathbf{x} or \theta \\ s.t. A\mathbf{x} = \mathbf{y} or A\psi\theta = \mathbf{y} \end{cases} \tag{3}$$

It shows $\mathbf{x}$ is spare when w is $\mathbf{x}$ in formula (3). If w is θ, $\mathbf{x}$ is spare in the transform domain.

3.3 Linear Compressed Projection and Data Reconstruction

Assuming N nodes are randomly placed in monitoring region. Firstly, the non-head nodes send sensory data to the corresponding cluster head. Then the cluster head transmit it to BS with its own data. The cluster head consumes more energy than non-head node. Therefore, reducing the data transmission is the key to reduce the energy consumption. The clustering CS of cluster head is based on the sparse characteristics of in-cluster data. All the cluster heads generate the Gaussian random observation matrix to compress data. The model of linear compressed projection can be show as follow.

$$\mathbf{y}_m(I) = A_{m*n}(I) * x(I) \tag{4}$$

$\mathbf{y}_m(I)$ is the random projection data by cluster head I. $A_{m*n}(I)$ stands for the Gaussian random observation matrix of cluster head I. n is the number of nodes. m is the number of linear compressed projection data. If there are $Cluster\_h$ clusters in one round, the size of data transferred after linear compressed projection is $n+m-1$. Then the communication load is $Cluster\_h * (n + m - 1) = N + Cluster\_h * (m - 1)$. Because of $m << n$, the communication load of LEACH-CS is far less than N*m.

The difference transformation can get the difference between one element and previous element. If the setting threshold is smaller than the difference value, the data don't change. Or the output is zero. The operation of differential transform is as follow.

$$\mathbf{L} = Q \left\{ \begin{bmatrix} -1 & 1 & 0 & 0 & 0 \\ \cdot & \cdot & \cdot & \cdot & 0 \\ \cdot & \cdot & \cdot & -1 & 1 \\ 0 & \cdot & \cdot & 0 & \lambda \end{bmatrix} \right\} \ \lambda \leq 1 \tag{5}$$

In the last line of $\mathbf{L}$ is artificially added. It can guarantee the continuity of the difference. Q shows the truncation processing to the difference data. Equation (4) is underdetermined. If we directly reconstruct by Eq. (4), there are countless solutions. The in-cluster data has sparse features in differential transformation. The optimal solution can be get through adding this prior knowledge to the model of data. Then BS can generate the reconstruction model for each cluster.

$$(P0) \begin{cases} \min \|L\left[x_I\left(n\right)\right]\|_0 \\ \text{s.t. } \mathbf{y}_m\left(I\right) = A_{m*n}\left(I\right) x_I\left(n\right) + e_i \end{cases} \tag{6}$$

$\mathbf{y}_m\left(I\right) \in \mathbf{R}^m$ shows the compressed data. L is the operation of differential transform. $x_I\left(n\right) \in \mathbf{R}^n$ is the acquired data of cluster I. $A_{m*n}\left(I\right) \in \mathbf{R}^{m\times n}$ is Bernoulli or Gaussian random sampling matrix. The model of $P0$ can reconstruct the raw data accurately. However, it is a NP problem. The solution of l_0 norm can be equivalent to the solution of l_1 norm under the certain conditions. So model $P0$ equals model $P1$.

$$(P1) \begin{cases} \min \|L\left[x_I\left(n\right)\right]\|_1 \\ \text{s.t. } \mathbf{y}_m\left(I\right) = A_{m*n}\left(I\right) x_I\left(n\right) + e_i \end{cases} \tag{7}$$

l_1 norm is convex function. It can be solved by using convex optimal method. But the differential of l_1 norm is difficult to solve in Eq. (7). So we generate a new equation by introducing a auxiliary variable w_I.

$$\begin{cases} \min \|w_I\|_1 \\ \text{s.t. } \mathbf{y}_m\left(I\right) = A_{m*n}\left(I\right) x_I + e_i \ and \ w_I = L\left[x_I\left(n\right)\right] \end{cases} \tag{8}$$

The Eq. (8) is equivalent to unconstraint equation by extended Lagrange method.

$$\min_{w_I, x_I} \ell_A\left(\mathbf{w}_I, x_I\right) = \|w_I\|_1 - v^T\left(L\left[x_I\left(n\right)\right] - w_I\right) + \frac{\beta}{2} \|L\left[x_I\left(n\right)\right] - w_I\|^2$$
$$- \lambda^T\left(A_{m*n}\left(I\right) x\left(I\right) - \mathbf{y}_{\text{ap}}\left(I\right)\right) + \frac{\mu}{2} \|A_{m*n}\left(I\right) x\left(I\right) - \mathbf{y}_m\left(I\right)\|^2. \tag{9}$$

Finally the Eq. (9) is decomposed into two subproblems about w_I and x_I by ADM (Alternating Direction Method) [12]. The raw data can be reconstructed through combining the contraction iterative and steepest descent method to solve Eq. (9). The step of data reconstruction is organized as follows.

Initialization: $v_0, \beta_0, \lambda_0, \mu_0, w_I^0, x_I^0$

Do the iteration while it do not meet the conditions of termination:

(1) Fix x_I^k, solve w_I^{k+1} by contraction iterative method

(2) Fix w_I^{k+1}, solve x_I^{k+1} by steepest descent method

(3) Update

$$\begin{cases} v_{k+1} = v_k - \beta_k * \left(L\left[x_I\left(n\right)\right] - w_I\right) \\ \lambda_{k+1} = \lambda_k - \mu_k * \left(A_{m*n}\left(I\right) x\left(I\right) - \mathbf{y}_m\left(I\right)\right) \\ \beta_{k+1} \geq \beta_k, \mu_{k+1} \geq \mu_k \end{cases}$$

End

---

4   Simulation and Analysis

The definition of the network lifetime is the time that the network provides data or other services. It is one of the most important performance indexes.

Generally, we defined the network lifetime as the time when first node, 10 % or all nodes is death [13]. To validate the performance of LEACH-CS, we evaluate it on the Matlab simulation platform. And it is compared with LEACH and DEEC protocol. In the simulation scenario, 200 nodes are randomly deployed in the area with 100 m*100 m. The position of BS is (50 m, 150 m). In this paper, the improvement of network lifetime and data reconstruction is tested in the simulation of LEACH-CS. The simulation parameter settings are show in Table 1.

Table 1. The parameters of network simulation

Parameter	Default value
Network size(m^2)	100*100
Position of sink node(m)	(50,150)
Number of sensor node	200
Initial energy	0.5 J
E_{elec}	50 nJ/bit
E_{fs}	10 pJ/bit/m^2
E_{mp}	0.0013 pJ/bit/m^2
Data packet size (L)	128 bytes

4.1 Analysis of Network Lifetime

For the simulation of network lifetime, the network will be working until 1500 rounds. The simulation result of network lifetime is shown in Fig. 3. The round when the first node, 10 % nodes and all nodes are death is recorded in the simulation. The corresponding round is 261, 350 and 624 in LEACH respectively. For DEEC algorithm, it is 290, 435 and 738 respectively. And the round of LEACH-CS is 656, 727 and 1217 respectively. If the network lifetime is the round when first node is death, the lifetime of LEACH-CS is about 150 % higher than EACH. If the lifetime is the round when 10 % are death, the lifetime of LEACH-CS is about 100 % higher than LEACH. In short, LEACH-CS can prolong double lifetime at least, relative to LEACH algorithm.

4.2 Simulation of Data Reconstruction

In the simulation of data reconstruction, assuming the node equip with the temperature sensor. The temperature settings of the whole monitoring area are between 25 to 28 degrees. The acquired data of all nodes per round is piecewise constant signal that the simulation data are sparse in the difference transformation. For the sake of simplicity, the two-dimensional data is changed into one-dimensional data in simulation. In every round of data transmission, the ordinary node sends the sensory data to the corresponding cluster head. And the cluster head transmits the linear compressed projection data to BS. Then

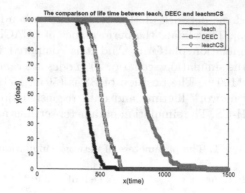

Fig. 3. The result of network lifetime in different algorithms

the raw data can be reconstructed by the method of Sect. 3.3 in BS. To reduce the effects of the noise fluctuation, the result is the average value of 100 times of simulations. Using different compression ratio to compressed data, the corresponding error of the reconstruction data can be get:

$$error = \|x(I) - \hat{x}(I)\|_2 / \|x(I)\|_2 \tag{10}$$

which x(I) is raw data. $\hat{x}(I)$ is the reconstruction data in BS. We firstly verify the effectiveness of LEACH-CS data aggregation method by making 200 nodes generate one cluster. Then we test the accuracy of data aggregation through generating five clusters.

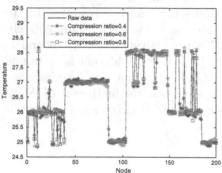
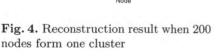
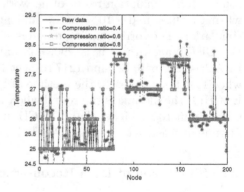

Fig. 4. Reconstruction result when 200 nodes form one cluster

Fig. 5. Reconstruction result when 200 nodes form five clusters

Figure 4 shows that 200 nodes form one cluster. The sparse ratio of raw data is 0.24. Then the BS reconstructs the linear compressed projection data at the compression ratio of 0.4, 0.6 and 0.8 respectively. The compression ratio is defined as the radio of sampling data size to raw data size. And the sparse ratio is the ratio of the number of non-zero data to the number of raw data. For the different compression ratio of 0.4, 0.6 and 0.8, the errors of reconstruction data using total variation (TV) method are 0.0007, 0.0001 and 0.00009 respectively. When the compression ratio is 0.8 that is about four times larger than sparse ratio, the reconstruction data and raw data are the same essentially. This is consistent with the theory of CS. The results indicate that the clustering CS method works well for data aggregation.

Figure 5 shows that 200 nodes form five clusters. The BS reconstructs the linear compressed projection data at the compression ratio of 0.4, 0.6 and 0.8 respectively. The corresponding errors of reconstruction data using TV method based on difference transform are 0.0007, 0.0001 and 0.00009. And the errors in the algorithms of orthogonal matching pursuit (OMP) and optimal orthogonal matching pursuit (OOMP) are show in Fig. 6. We can see from Fig. 6 that the TV reconstruction algorithm is better than OMP and OOMP. TV uses convex optimal method to reconstruct data. OMP and OOMP are greedy algorithm that they are easy to trap in local optimum and cannot guarantee the accuracy of reconstruction data. However, it can be found that the effect in Fig. 4 is better than Fig. 5. And the error in Fig. 4 is smaller. When there is a small amount of data in cluster, the sparse ratio is usually large in space. So the data is hard to be reconstructed efficiently. If we want to improve the accuracy, we should consider the temporal-spatial sparse characteristic. From the above simulations, the LEACH-CS method can resolve the conflict between network lifetime and accuracy of reconstruction data to some extent.

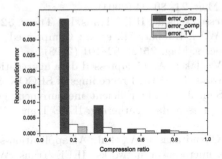

Fig. 6. Reconstruction errors in different algorithms and compression ratios

5   Conclusion

In this paper, a data aggregation method based on LEACH-CS is proposed for wireless sensor networks. The method uses LEACH to form clusters and compressed sensing to compress data. Each cluster head gets the linear compressed projection of in-cluster data by under determined Gaussian random matrix. Then it can reduce the sensed data transmitted to BS. The network lifetime will be prolonged efficiently. And we present reconstruction algorithm based on TV regularization to improve the accuracy of reconstruction. We only study the data aggregation method under LEACH protocol. But it also can be applied to other clustering protocols. The actual data acquired by nodes has the temporal-spatial sparse characteristic. The next work is using distributed compressed sensing to reconstruct the actual data.

Acknowledgments. This work is supported by National Natural Science Foundation of China (No. 31101081, No. 61162015).

References

1. Madden, S., Franklin, M.J., Hellerstein, J.M., et al.: TAG: a tiny aggregation service for ad-hoc sensor networks. ACM SIGOPS Operating Syst. Rev. **36**(SI), 131–146 (2002)
2. Fasolo, E., Rossi, M., Widmer, J., et al.: In-network aggregation techniques for wireless sensor networks: a survey. Wirel. Commun. **14**(2), 70–87 (2007)
3. Cheng, S., Li, J., Ren, Q., et al.: Bernoulli sampling based (ε, δ)-approximate aggregation in large-scale sensor networks. In: Proceedings of the 29th IEEE INFOCOM (2010)
4. Ciancio, A., Pattem, S., Ortega, A., et al.: Energy efficient data representation and routing for wireless sensor networks based on a distributed wavelet compression algorithm. In: Proceedings of IPSN, pp. 309–316 (2006)
5. Zhou, S.W., Lin, Y.P., Zhang, J.M., et al.: A wavelet data compression algorithm using ring topology for wireless sensor networks. J. Softw. **18**(3), 669–680 (2007)
6. Xiong, Z., Liveris, A.D., Cheng, S.: Distributed source coding for sensor networks. IEEE Sig. Process. Mag. **21**, 80–94 (2004)
7. Donoho, D.: Compressed sensing. IEEE Trans. Inf. Theor. **52**(4), 1289–1306 (2006)
8. Haupt, J., Bajwa, W.U., Rabbat, M., et al.: Compressed sensing for networked data. IEEE Sig. Process. Mag. **25**(2), 92–101 (2008)
9. Xiang, L., Luo, J., Vasilakos, A.: Compressed data aggregation for energy efficient wireless sensor networks. In: IEEE Proceedings of SECON, Salt Lake (2011)
10. Luo, C., Wu, F., Sun, J., et al.: Efficient measurement generation and pervasive sparsity for compressive data gathering. IEEE Trans. Wirel. Commun. **9**(12), 3728–3738 (2010)
11. Heinzelman, W.R., Chandrakasan, A., et al.: An application-specific protocol architecture for wireless microsensor networks. IEEE Trans. Wirel. Commun. **1**(4), 660–670 (2002)
12. Yang, J.F., Zhang, Y., Yin, W.: A fast alternating direction method for TVL1-L2 signal reconstruction from partial fourier data. IEEE J. Sel. Top. Sig. Process. Spec. Issue Compressive Sens. **4**(2), 288–297 (2010)
13. Liu, A.F., Zhang, P.H., Chen, Z.G.: Theoretical analysis of the lifetime and energy hole in cluster based wireless sensor networks. J. Parallel Distrib. Comput. **71**(10), 1327–1355 (2011)

Robust Monitor Assignment for Large Scale Sensor Network Tomography

Xiaojin Liu, Yi Gao, Wenbin Wu, and Wei Dong$^{(\boxtimes)}$

College of Computer Science and Technology,
Zhejiang University, Hangzhou, China
{liuxj0208,gaoyi,wuwb,dongw}@zju.edu.cn
http://www.emnets.org

Abstract. In wired networks, monitor-based network tomography has been proved to be an effective technology for network internal state measurements. Existing wired network tomography approaches assume that the network topology is relatively static. However, the network topology of sensor networks are usually changing over time due to wireless dynamics. In this paper, we study the problem to assign a number of sensor nodes as monitors in large scale sensor networks, so that the end-to-end measurements among monitors can be used to identify hop-by-hop link metrics. We propose RoMA, a Robust Monitor Assignment algorithm to assign monitors in large scale sensor networks with dynamically changing topology. RoMA includes two components, confidence-based robust topology generation and cost-minimized monitor assignment. We implement RoMA and evaluate its performance based on a deployed large scale sensor network. Results show that RoMA achieves high identifiability with dynamically changing topology and is able to assign monitors with minimum cost.

Keywords: Robust · Monitor assignment · Sensor networks

1 Introduction

Network tomography techniques [1] use *end-to-end* measurements to calculate *hop-by-hop* link metrics, such as delay and packet reception ratio. Recent advances in network tomography techniques [2–4] show that cycle-free measurement paths among *monitors* can be used to form a linear system on the internal unknown link metrics. Then these unknown link metrics can be calculated by solving the linear system. In order to successfully solve the linear system, sufficient linearly independent measurement paths should be able to be conducted among the monitors, requiring the monitors assignment to comply with certain conditions.

Existing works assume relatively static network topologies and uniform cost of assigning monitors, since they all focus on wired communication networks. Then these works focus on calculating the minimum monitor assignment to enable sufficient linearly independent measurement paths. In wireless sensor networks (WSNs), however, the network topologies keep changing over time [5] due

© Springer-Verlag Berlin Heidelberg 2015
L. Sun et al. (Eds.): CWSN 2014, CCIS 501, pp. 499–508, 2015.
DOI: 10.1007/978-3-662-46981-1_48

to the wireless dynamics. Further, assigning a monitoring node to different nodes in a deployed network usually requires different cost, depending on the environmental conditions, the distance to the sink node, and etc. Therefore, existing techniques cannot be applied into WSNs directly.

In this paper, we focus on calculating a minimum cost monitor assignment in a WSN, given the dynamic changing network topology. In particular, we propose RoMA, a Robust Monitor Assignment algorithm to assign monitors with minimum cost in large scale sensor networks with dynamically changing topology. RoMA includes two components, confidence-based robust topology generation and cost-minimized monitor assignment. The confidence-based robust topology generation merges multiple historical topologies based on a confidence value. It generates a robust topology, which captures the dynamic changing topology over time. Based on this robust topology, the cost-minimized monitor assignment component of RoMA assigns monitors with minimum overall cost.

We implement RoMA and evaluate its performance through extensive simulations based on a deployed large scale sensor network. Compared with a baseline approach, RoMA assigns much less monitors with high link metric identifiability and achieves a much smaller overall cost.

The rest of the paper is organized as follows. Section 2 describes the related work of RoMA. Section 3 formulates the problem. Section 4 describes the design of RoMA. Section 5 presents evaluation results. Finally, Sect. 6 concludes the paper.

2   Related Work

Based on the model of link metrics, existing work on measuring the network internal state can be broadly classified as *hop-by-hop* and *end-to-end* approaches. *Hop-by-hop* approaches, use diagnostic tools such as *traceroute*, *pathchar* [6], and *Network Characterization Service (NCS)* [7] to measure *hop-by-hop* link metrics directly. By sending multiple probes with different time-to-live fields, *traceroute* can measure the delay of each hop on the probed path. *Pathchar* uses a similar approach to measure *hop-by-hop* delays, capacities and loss rates. *NCS* also reports available capacities of each hop.

End-to-end approaches, use *end-to-end* metrics to calculate internal link metrics. They assume the network is controllable, otherwise, the minimum monitor assignment problem has been proved to be NP-hard [8–10]. The basic idea is to build a linear system from the path measurements and use linear algebraic techniques to calculate the unknown link metrics [11,12]. When cyclic measurement paths are allowed, Gopalan et al. [13] give the necessary and sufficient conditions on the network topology. Since routing along cycles is typically prohibited in real networks, Ma et al. [2] give the necessary and sufficient conditions on the network topology when only cycle-free measurement paths are used.

However, in WSNs, the network topologies keep changing over time and exiting techniques cannot be applied into WSNs directly. In this paper, we focus on calculating a minimum cost monitor assignment in a WSN, given the dynamic changing network topology. We propose RoMA, a Robust Monitor Assignment algorithm to assign monitors with minimum cost in large scale sensor networks with dynamically changing topology.

3   Problem Formulation

We model the network topology as an undirected graph $G = (V, L)$, where V is the set of nodes and L is the set of links. Each link $l_i \in L$ is associated with an unknown metric w_{l_i}. We assume that link metrics are symmetric in both directions. We also assume that the link metric w_{l_i} does not change during the measurement period. Take delay as an example, Gao et al. [14] show that the delays of the same link within a relatively short period of time are similar. Monitors are certain nodes in V which can initiate/collect cycle-free measurements. They can control the routing of measurement packets.

Let $w = (w_{l_1}, ..., w_{l_n})^T$ denote the column vector of all link metrics and $c = (c_{p_1}, ..., c_{p_r})^T$ the column vector of all available path measurements, n and r are the number of links and measurement paths respectively and c_{p_i} is the sum of metrics along measurement path p_i. Then we can get a linear system as follow:

$$Rw = c,$$

where $R = (R_{ij})$ is a $r \times n$ matrix, with each $R_{ij} \in \{0,1\}$ means whether link j is on path i. A link is identifiable if we can solve its metric from the above linear system. If and only if $rank(R) = n$, the network G is completely identifiable. If $rank(R) < n$, it may still be possible to identify some of the link metrics.

We want to assign a number of nodes in the network as monitors to initial/ collect measurement packets. Since assigning a node as a monitor usually needs non-negligible operational cost (e.g., hardware/software, human efforts), we focus on assigning monitors with minimum cost to identify most of the link metrics.

4   Design

The design of RoMA includes two components: confidence-based robust topology generation and cost-minimized monitor assignment. The confidence-based robust topology generation algorithm uses instant topologies to generate a robust topology. The cost-minimized monitor assignment algorithm provides a subset of nodes in the robust graph as monitors with the minimized cost. The set of monitors can identify all of the link metrics in the robust graph and the majority of link metrics in future topologies.

4.1   Confidence-Based Robust Topology Generation

Due to wireless dynamics and interference, a node usually transmits its packets to different receivers at different time. Therefore, RoMA first generates a robust topology of a WSN for monitor assignment. The input of RoMA is a number of packets received by sink. In each packet k, there are three data fields related to RoMA, which are the origin $o(k)$, the parent $p(k)$ and global packet generation time $t(k)$. Origin $o(k)$ and parent $p(k)$ are the first two hops of k's routing path. The global packet generation time can be obtained by packet timestamping technique without global time synchronization [15]. By using each packet's origin and parent, we can construct the topology of the WSN. Let G_i denote an instant topology constructed by a set of packets sent by nodes to their parents in a period t. With a set of packets having different sending time, a number of instant topologies can be constructed. Then we use a set of instant topologies $\{G_1,...,G_i,...\}$ to generate a robust topology. As described in Algorithm 1, the inputs are a set of packets $P = \{P_1,..., P_k\}$ received by sink, period t and confidence C_{min}. These packets have different sending time so that we can get a set of instant topologies $\mathcal{G} = \{G_{t_1},..., G_{t_n}\}$ (line 1). Let L be a set, which contains all instant topologies' links in $\mathcal{G}$ (line 2). For each link l in set L, we compute link l's confidence C_l and compare it with the minimum confidence C_{min}. $|\mathcal{G}|$ denote the number of instant topologies in $\mathcal{G}$, n_l the number of instant topologies in $\mathcal{G}$ which contain link l. If C_l is larger than C_{min}, we select l as a link in the robust topology G_r (line 4–7).

Algorithm 1. Confidence-based Robust Topology Generation

Input: a set of packets $P_1,..., P_k$, confidence C_{min}, period t

Output: A robust topology G_r

1: Construct a set of instant topologies $\mathcal{G} = \{G_{t_1},..., G_{t_n}\}$ according to t
2: $L = L(G_{t_1}) \cup L(G_{t_2}) \cup ... \cup L(G_{t_n})$
3: set $G_r = \emptyset$
4: **for** each link l in L **do**
5:     $C_l = n_l/|\mathcal{G}|$
6:     **if** $C_l \geq C_{min}$ and l is not in G_r **then**
7:         select l as an link in G_r
    return G_r

4.2 Cost-Minimized Monitor Assignment

Then RoMA assigns monitors with minimum cost in the robust topology G_r. Before describing the algorithm, we first introduce several graph theory concepts.

- A graph is *connected* if there is a path from any point to any other point in the graph.
- A *k-connected component* of G is a maximal sub-graph of G that is either (i) k-vertex-connected, or (ii) a complete graph with up to k vertices. The case of $k = 2$ is also called a biconnected component, and $k = 3$ a triconnected component.
- A *cut-vertex* is a vertex whose removal will disconnect the graph.

- A *2-vertex* cut is a set of two vertices $\{v1, v2\}$ such that removing $v1$ or $v2$ alone does not disconnect G, but removing both disconnects G. Each vertex of $\{v1, v2\}$ is a 2-cut-v.
- Nodes that are *cut-vertices* or part of 2-vertex cuts are called separation vertices.

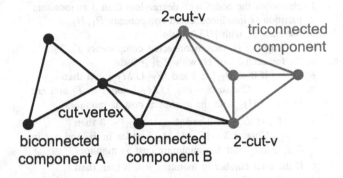

Fig. 1. An example that illustrates several graph theory concepts

Figure 1 shows an example which illustrates the above concepts. In this example, the whole graph is a connected graph. It contains two biconnected components, which are separated by a cut vertex. There is also a triconnected component shown in the figure, which is connected to the graph by a 2-vertex cut.

If all vertices are assigned as monitors, it is obvious that all links are identifiable. However, assigning a node as a monitor usually needs non-negligible operational cost (e.g., hardware/software, human efforts), RoMA tries to assign monitors with minimum cost to identify most of the link metrics. A recent work MMP [2] assigns the minimum number of monitors to identify all links in a connected graph. It is actually a special case when all vertices have the same cost to be assigned as monitors. Different with MMP, RoMA calculates a subset of nodes in the robust graph as monitors with the minimum cost.

Ma et al. [2] show that there are 4 rules must be satisfied to identify a topology with the minimum number of monitors.

i. A node whose degree is one must be a monitor.
ii. A node on a tandem of links (degree is two) must be a monitor.
iii. For a sub-graph with two cut-vertices or a 2-vertex cut, at least one node other than those cuts must be a monitor.
iv. Similarly, for a sub-graph with one cut-vertex, at least two nodes other than the cut-vertex must be monitors.

As shown in Algorithm 2, the cost-minimized monitor assignment method follows rules i and ii to select all vertices with degree less than three as monitors (line 1). Then it partitions the graph into a number of biconnected components. For each biconnected component, it further partitions the biconnected component into a number of triconnected components. Note that there are efficient algorithms to accomplish the above biconnected components and triconnected components partitioning [16,17].

Algorithm 2. Cost-minimized Monitor Assignment

Input: Connected graph G and the set of nodes' cost
Output: A subset of nodes in G as monitors
1: choose all the nodes with degree less than 3 as monitors
2: partition G into biconnected components $B_1, B_2...$
3: **for** each B_i with $|B_i| \geq 3$ **do**
4:     partition B_i into triconnected components $T_1, T_2...$
5:     **for** each T_j of B_i with $|Tj| \geq 3$ **do**
6:         **if** $0 < |S_{T_j}| < 3$ and $|S_{T_j} \cup M_{T_j}| < 3$ **then**
7:             Choose $3 - |S_{T_j} \cup M_{T_j}|$ nodes in T_j and not in $S_{T_j} \cup M_{T_j}$ with the minimum cost as monitors
8:         **if** $0 < |C_{B_i}| < 3$ and $|C_{B_i} \cup M_{B_i}| < 3$ **then**
9:             Choose $3 - |C_{B_i} \cup M_{B_i}|$ nodes in B_i and not in $C_{B_i} \cup M_{B_i}$ with the minimum cost as monitors
10: **if** the total number of monitors $k < 3$ then **then**
11:     Choose $3 - k$ non-monitors nodes with the minimum cost as monitors

---

For each triconnected and then biconnected component that contains three or more nodes, the cost-minimized monitor assignment makes sure that: (i) each triconnected component has at least three nodes that are either separation vertices or monitors with the minimum cost in the component (line 5–7), and (ii) each biconnected component has at least three or more nodes that are either cut-vertices or monitors with the minimum cost in the component (line 8–9). Finally, Algorithm 2 selects additional monitors with the minimum cost as needed to ensure that the total number of monitors is at least three (line 10–11). As described in Algorithm 2, for a component D, let S_D denote the number of separation vertices, C_D the number of cut-vertices, and M_D the number of (already selected) monitors in D.

5 Evaluation

In this section, we evaluate the performance of RoMA through a set of simulations based on a deployed large scale sensor network, the CitySee project.

5.1 Evaluation Setup

CitySee is deployed in an urban area to collect multidimensional sensing data such as carbon emission, temperature and humidity. All nodes in CitySee are organized as four sub-nets. Each sub-net has one sink and these four sink nodes transmit data packets to a base station through 802.11 wireless links. And each node in the network transmits 4 data packets back to the sink node every 10 min. We use the trace from one sub-net to evaluate the performance of RoMA. The main performance metrics are the number of monitors and identified ratio of links.

We construct a set of instant topologies using period t and merge N topologies into a robust topology with different confidence C_{min}. Getting a set of monitors of the robust topology and then using these monitors to identify other instant topologies.

In the simulations, we study the impacts of different parameters to the performance of RoMA. There are several parameters such as confidence C_{min}, period t and number of merged topologies N. When changing one parameter, we keep the other parameters as constant.

5.2 Simulation

First we evaluate the performance of cost-minimized monitor assignment and compare it with MMP [2]. Assuming that each node has a steady cost, we select several topologies at random and use two algorithms: MMP [2] and cost-minimized monitor assignment to assign monitors. After computing the total cost of two monitor sets, we show the results in Fig. 2. The y-axis is the cost of monitors. From Fig. 2, we can see that the monitors' cost of RoMA is always not more than MMP's.

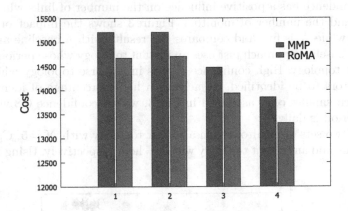

Fig. 2. The cost of MMP and RoMA

While $N = 1$, we set the period t hour, semi-daily and daily respectively. From Table 1 we can see that with different temporal resolutions (hour, semi-daily and daily), there is a very drastic change in the number of monitors. That is because with a high temporal resolution, the topology is sparse and needs more monitors to be identified.

Table 2 shows the impact of different numbers of merged topologies N. The relationship between N and identifiability isn't linear. That is to say, a larger N does not mean a better performance. On the other hand, to identify more links needs more monitors, which results in a higher cost. Considering the cost, it is unreasonable to assign a lot of monitors. To achieve a balance between the number of monitors and the percentage of identified links, we set N five while t = daily.

Table 1. Impact of temporal resolutions

Period	t=daily	t=semi-daily	t=hour
Identifiability	0.896	0.951	0.966
Monitors	46	117	168

Table 2. Impact of the number of merged topologies

N	3		5		7		10	
Confidence	0.6	0.8	0.6	0.8	0.6	0.8	0.6	0.8
Identifiability	0.905	0.940	0.896	0.919	0.909	0.933	0.895	0.926
Monitors	43	92	29	58	38	71	28	57

The confidence has a positive influence on the number of links which can be identified and the number of monitors. Figure 3 shows the impact of different confidence while N is five and compares the results with a baseline approach's result. The baseline approach just uses an instant topology whose period t is hour as a robust topology. High confidence results in a sparse topology which needs more monitors to be identified. To achieve a high percentage of identifiability with a much smaller cost, as shown in Fig. 3, we set confidence 0.8 while N is five and period is daily.

We get two sets of monitors from a robust topology with $N = 5$, $C_{min} = 0.6$ and $t = $ daily and an instant topology with $t = $ hour respectively. Using these two

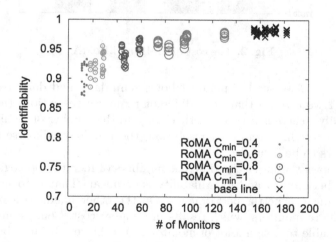

Fig. 3. Impact of different confidences

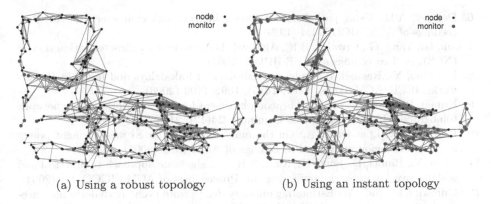

(a) Using a robust topology   (b) Using an instant topology

Fig. 4. Compare with base line (Color figure online)

sets of monitors to identify a future topology, the results are shown in Fig. 4. Figure 4(a) shows the result of using the robust topology, Fig. 4(b) using the instant topology. These red links cannot be identified by those monitors marked as blue. Obviously, RoMA can identify most links of a topology with a minimum monitors.

6   Conclusion

In this paper, we propose RoMA, a robust monitor assignment algorithm to assign monitors in large scale sensor networks with dynamically changing topology. RoMA merges instant topologies into a robust one and uses the cost-minimized monitor assignment algorithm to get a set of nodes as monitors with the minimum cost. We then analyze the performance of RoMA and the analysis results show that RoMA achieves high percentage of identifiability with a minimum cost.

References

1. Lawrence, E., Michailidis, G., Nair, V.N., Xi, B.: Network tomography: a review and recent developments. In: Frontiers in Statistics (2006)
2. Ma, L., He, T., Leung, K.K., Swami, A., Towsley, D.: Identifiability of link metrics based on end-to-end path measurements. In: Proceedings of ACM IMC (2013)
3. Ma, L., He, T., Leung, K.K., Towsley, D., Swami, A.: Efficient identification of additive link metrics via network tomography. In: Proceedings of IEEE ICDCS (2013)
4. Ma, L., He, T., Leung, K.K., Swami, A., Towsley, D.: Link identifiability in communication networks with two monitors. In: Proceedings of IEEE Globecom (2013)
5. Gao, Y., Dong, W., Chen, C., Bu, J., Guan, G., Zhang, X., Liu, X.: Pathfinder: robust path reconstruction in large scale sensor networks with lossy links. In: Proceedings of ICNP (2013)

6. Downey, A.B.: Using pathchar to estimate internet link characteristics. In: Proceedings of ACM SIGCOMM (1999)
7. Jin, G., Yang, G., Crowley, B.R., Agarwal, D.A.: Network characterization service (NCS). In: Proceedings of IEEE HPDC (2001)
8. Bejerano, Y., Rastogi, R.: Robust monitoring of link delays and faults in IP networks. IEEE/ACM Trans. Netw. 14(5), 1092–1103 (2006)
9. Kumar, R., Kaur, J.: Practical beacon placement for link monitoring using network tomography. IEEE J. Sel. Areas Commun. 24(12), 2196–2209 (2006)
10. Horton, J.D., Lpez-Ortiz, A.: On the number of distributed measurement points for network tomography. In: Proceedings of ACM IMC (2003)
11. Chen, Y., Bindel, D., Song, H., Katz, R.H.: An algebraic approach to practical and scalable overlay network monitoring. In: Proceedings of ACM SIGCOMM (2004)
12. Gurewitz, O., Sidi, M.: Estimating one-way delays from cyclic-path delay measurements. In: Proceedings of IEEE INFOCOM (2001)
13. Gopalan, A., Ramasubramanian, S.: On identifying additive link metrics using linearly independent cycles and paths. IEEE/ACM Trans. Netw. 20(3), 906–916 (2012)
14. Gao, Y., Dong, W., Chen, C., Bu, J., Chen, T., Xia, M., Liu, X., Xu, X.: Domo: passive per-packet delay tomography in wireless ad-hoc networks. In: Proceedings of IEEE ICDCS (2014)
15. Dong, W., Zhang, X., Wang, J., Gao, Y., Chen, C., Bu, J.: Accurate and robust time reconstruction for deployed sensor networks. In: Proceedings of ACM SIGMETRICS (poster) (2014)
16. Tarjan, R.E.: Depth-first search and linear graph algorithms. SIAM J. Comput. 1(2), 146–160 (1972)
17. Hopcroft, J.E., Tarjan, R.E.: Dividing a graph into triconnected components. SIAM J. Comput. 2(3), 135–158 (1973)

Sampling Based Approximate τ-Quantile Computation Algorithm in Sensor Networks

Ran Bi$^{(\boxtimes)}$, Jianzhong Li, and Hong Gao

School of Computer Science and Technology,
Harbin Institute of Technology, Harbin 150001, China
biranhit@gmail.com, {lijzh,honggao}@hit.edu.cn

Abstract. A fundamental issue for detecting rare event or small probability event is to generate the description for the tail probability distribution of the sensed data. Tail quantile can effectively describe the tail probability distribution. However, most of the existing works focus on the computation of approximate quantile summary, and they are inefficient in calculating tail quantile. This paper develops an algorithm based on sampling technique for computing approximate tail quantile, such that the approximate result can satisfy the requirement of given precision. A more accurate estimator is given first. For given upper bound of relative error, this algorithm satisfies that the probability of the relative error between the exact tail quantile and the returned approximate result being larger than the specified upper bound is smaller than the given failure probability. Experiments are carried out to show the correctness and effectiveness of the proposed algorithms.

Keywords: Approximate quantile · Sampling based algorithm · Sensor networks

1 Introduction

Wireless sensor networks (WSNs) bridge the physical world and the computing systems, which open up the potential to span and monitor large geographical areas inexpensively. With the advances in sensing technology and wireless communication, WSNs are witnessed to deploy thousands of nodes for various applications, such as habit monitoring [1], environment monitoring [3] and alarm system for forest-fire prevention [2], And the scale of WSNs is envisioned to achieve even larger in the future. However, sensor node whose power source is on-board battery has significant energy constraint, which poses great challenges on large-scale deployment of sensor networks.

In practice, more attention is paid to the detection of rare event or small probability event in monitoring applications. Then a fundamental problem in this type of monitoring is to generate descriptions for the tail probability distribution of the sensed data. For any $0 < \phi < 1$, a quantile summary enables users to extract the ϕ-quantile of the whole sensed data. Quantiles can be regarded

© Springer-Verlag Berlin Heidelberg 2015
L. Sun et al. (Eds.): CWSN 2014, CCIS 501, pp. 509–519, 2015.
DOI: 10.1007/978-3-662-46981-1_49

as the cumulative distribution function of the underlying data [4]. Suppose that set S consists of n elements from an ordered set. The ϕ-*quantile* of set S is the element with rank $\lfloor \phi n \rfloor$ for given $0 < \phi < 1$, where rank of an element x, $r(x)$, is the number of elements in S larger or smaller than x. Quantiles can characterize the data distribution and they are the mostly widely used nonparametric representation for data distributions [5].

An exact quantile summary that enable users to exact the accurate quantiles requires all the sensed data to be collected at the sink, which is inefficient in terms of bandwidth and energy usage. Due to the noise and inherent low sensitivity to the physical world, sensed data often has measurement error and noise [6,7]. Therefore, approximate quantile result with accuracy guarantee can meet the requirement of most practical applications. The widely used notion of approximation for this problem is as following. For given $0 < \varepsilon < 1$, an ε-*approximate* ϕ-*quantile* is any element, whose rank ranges from $(\phi - \varepsilon)n$ to $(\phi + \varepsilon)n$. There are plentiful research works that focus on the computation of approximate quantile summary over distributed data [4,8,9], such that the returned quantiles satisfy the given precision requirement with constant probability. However, all the existing works do not consider the efficient computation for the tail quantile, and the collected sensed data are high redundancy for tail quantile computation which are not efficient in term of communication cost.

In this paper, an algorithm based on sampling technique for computing approximate tail quantile is designed, such that the approximate result can meet the requirement of given precision. For given failure probability δ and relative error ε, the result of the approximate τ-quantile computation algorithm satisfies that the probability of the result with rank between $(\tau - \tau\varepsilon)n$ and $(\tau + \tau\varepsilon)n$ is larger than $1 - \delta$. Different from previous works, the estimator for τ-quantile is more accurate. According to the given precision requirement ε, δ and quantile τ, the proposed algorithm determines the optimal sample size firstly, and then sensed data are uniformly sampled from the sensor networks. After collecting the sample data, the approximate τ-quantile is calculated based on the sample. The main contributions of the paper are summarized as following.

- The (ε, δ)-estimator for τ-quantile is proposed in this paper. The mathematical formula to compute the optimal sample size according to the given quantile τ and precision requirement ε, δ is derived.
- According to the given precision requirement ε, δ and quantile τ, a sampling based algorithm for approximate τ-quantile computation is proposed.
- Experiments are carried out to show the correctness and effectiveness of our algorithms.

The rest of this paper is structured as following. The related works on quantile summary computation are surveyed in Sect. 2. In Sect. 3, an optimal sample size is proved first, and a sampling based algorithms for approximate τ-quantile computation is provided. Experimental results are illustrated in Sect. 4, and Sect. 5 concludes this paper.

2   Related Works

In the Sawzall language that is the basis for all of Google's log data analysis, quantile computation is one of the seven basic operators defined (the others including sum, max, top-k, and count-distinct) [10]. Quantile computation is an essential issue in data management and analysis. And the problem is sometimes investigated under the name of order statistics in database community. The early work by using random sampling to identify frequent items in a set is that of Gibbons [11]. Two techniques of constructing and incrementally maintaining random samples were introduced. However, no explicit tradeoffs were provided between the sample size and failure probability. A sparse sampling based algorithm was proposed to identify the elements whose frequency exceeds a particular threshold in [12]. Reference [13] aimed at the problem of approximately identifying the most frequent item. These works focus on identifying the item of greater frequency, which is different from that of τ-quantile computation. The proposed algorithms are for centralized access, then they can not be straightly applied in sensor networks.

The problem of calculating quantile summary also attracts attention in the streaming model, in which the data elements arrive one after another in a streaming fashion. The streaming algorithm only has limited memory to work with, then approximate quantile computation algorithms using sublinear space were designed. Vapnik and Chervonenkis [14] provided a randomized algorithm and state that a random sample of size $O\left(\varepsilon^{-2}\log\varepsilon^{-1}\right)$ preserves all quantiles within ε error with a probability guarantee. This fact was also proved in [15], and the proposed algorithm supposes that the size, n, of data set is known as a priori knowledge, which is not available in streaming model. The latest literature [16] provided a more complicated algorithm with a space complexity of $O\left(\varepsilon^{-1}\log^{1.5}\varepsilon^{-1}\right)$. Reference [5] presented an extensive experimental comparison of the competing methods for quantiles over data streams. But the streaming model is quite different from the distributed environment. The proposed algorithms are not suitable for sensor networks.

Shrivastava [8] and Agarwal [17] respectively investigated the problem of computing approximate quantile summaries in sensor networks. The size of $q\text{-}digest$ summary is $O\left(\varepsilon^{-1}\log u\right)$, in which u is the size of the whole data set. Then the total communication cost is $O\left(k\varepsilon^{-1}\log u\right)$, in which k is the size of sensor network. The GK $summary$ has size $O\left(\varepsilon^{-1}\log^2 n\right)$, where n is the total number of data values of the sensed data. And the total communication cost is $O\left(k\varepsilon^{-1}\log^2 n\right)$. The communication cost of the two algorithms are not comparable. GK $summary$ is more general since it is in favor of unbounded universe. Recently, Huang [4] proposed a new algorithm for computing quantile summaries in sensor networks, with an expected total communication of $O\left(\varepsilon^{-1}\sqrt{kh}\right)$, where h is the height of routing tree. However, these works focus on the computation of quantile summaries and they are inefficient for tail quantile computation in term of communication cost.

3   Sampling Based Algorithm for Approximate τ-Quantile Computation

τ-quantile is useful in the description for the tail probability distribution of the sensed data. Collecting all sensed data from WSNs results in excessive communication. In this section, (ε, δ)-estimator for τ-quantile is proposed firstly. According to the given precision requirement ε, δ and quantile τ, an optimal sample size is proved. Then a sampling based algorithm for approximate τ-quantile computation is provided.

3.1   Problem Definition

In this paper, we suppose that the sensor networks consists of n sensor nodes, and each node has a unique ID in range of $[1, n]$. For ease of algorithm description, we assume that the sensor network is partitioned into k disjoint clusters logically, indicated by $C_1, C_2, ..., C_k$. Let $s_i(t)$ denote the sensed data of node i at time t, the set $S(t) = \{s_1(t), s_2(t), ..., s_n(t)\}$ is composed of all the sensed data of time t. Let the set $S(t_0, t_{h-1}) = \{S(t_0), S(t_1), ..., S(t_{h-1})\}$ denote the sensed data, which are collected by the network at time interval $[t_0, t_{h-1}]$. It is assumed that all values in $S(t_0, t_{h-1})$ are distinct, and this assumption can be removed through consistent tie-breaker technique [4].

Definition 1. *Rank $r(x, S)$: For given set S with N data values, the rank $r(x, S)$ is the number of elements in S larger or equal to x, that is $r(x, S) = |\{y \geq x | y \in S\}|$.*

Definition 2. *τ-quantile of set S: Suppose that S consists of N data values and all values in S are distinct. For a given $\tau \in \{1/N, 2/N, ..., 1\}$, the τ-quantile of set S is the value α, that satisfies the following conditions:*

1. α belongs to set S;
2. The rank of α, $r(\alpha, S)$, is τN.

When the context is clear, the τ-quantile of set S is denoted as $\tau(S)$.

Definition 3. *(ε, δ)-Estimator: For any given $\varepsilon > 0, \delta > 0$ and set S, if $\Pr\left[\frac{|r(\alpha, S)/|S| - \tau|}{\tau} \geq \varepsilon\right] \leq \delta$ is hold, then α is called as (ε, δ)-estimator for τ-quantile of set S, denoted as $\widehat{\tau(S)}$.*

Definition 4. *(ε, δ)-Approximate τ-quantile: For given $\tau \in (0, 1)$ and set S, if $\widehat{\tau(S)}$ is the (ε, δ)-estimator for τ-quantile of set S, then $\widehat{\tau(S)}$ is called as (ε, δ)-approximate τ-quantile result.*

Let $S_i(t_0, t_{h-1})$ denote the data set $\{s_i(t_0), ..., s_i(t_{h-1})\}$, which consists of sensed data collected by node i at time interval $[t_0, t_{h-1}]$. The problem of (ε, δ)-approximate τ-quantile computation is described as following.

Input:

1. Precision requirement $\varepsilon > 0, \delta > 0$ and quantile $\tau \in (0, 1)$.
2. The sensed data set $S(t_0, t_{h-1})$, which are collected by the network at time interval $[t_0, t_{h-1}]$.

Output:
(ε, δ)-approximate τ-quantile result.

Since the uniform sampling methods are widely used in approximate quantile estimation [5,18], an algorithm based on uniform sampling technique for computing approximate tail quantile is designed. The main steps of this algorithm is described as following.

1. According to given ε, δ and quantile τ, the sink determines the sample size.
2. We implement uniform sampling in the wireless sensor network. The samples are collected by cluster-head.
3. According to the sample data sent by cluster-head, the sink computes (ε, δ)-approximate τ-quantile result.

It is easily known that when $h = 1$, the algorithm returns the approximate τ-quantile result of snapshot at time t_0. Based on the above analysis, the key point of the algorithm is to compute the optimal sample size and estimate the approximation of τ-quantile based on the sample data, such that the estimator satisfies the (ε, δ)-precision requirement. In the following section, an optimal sample size is proved first. Based on the sample data, the (ε, δ)-estimator of τ-quantile is derived.

3.2 Determination of Sample Size and Estimator

Theorem 1. *(Sanov Theorem)* [19] *Let Π be a set of distributions on A. For the empirical distribution of a sample from a strictly positive distribution P on A, we have*

$$-\frac{1}{n} \log \Pr\left(\hat{P}_n \in \Pi\right) \leq D(\Pi|P) \tag{1}$$

in which, n is the sample size and $D(\Pi|P)$ is the KL Divergence of Π and P.

Theorem 2. *Suppose that the size of set $S(t_0, t_{h-1})$ is N. Let $U^{(m)} = \{s_{i1}(t_{j1}), s_{i2}(t_{j2}), ..., s_{im}(t_{jm})\}$ be a uniform sample of $S(t_0, t_{h-1})$. For any given $\varepsilon > 0, \delta > 0$, if the sample size, m, is larger than $\frac{\ln(\tau N - \tau \varepsilon N) - \ln(\delta/2)}{\ell(\tau, (1-\varepsilon)\tau)}$, then the following inequality is hold,*

$$\Pr\left[\frac{\tau - r\left(\alpha, S(t_0, t_{h-1})\right)/N}{\tau} \geq \varepsilon\right] \leq \frac{\delta}{2} \tag{2}$$

in which α is the τ-quantile of sample set $U^{(m)}$, $\ell(\tau, (1 - \varepsilon)\tau) = \tau \ln\left(\frac{1}{1-\varepsilon}\right) + (1 - \tau) \ln\left(\frac{1-\tau}{1-(1-\varepsilon)\tau}\right)$.

Proof. According to the definition of τ-*quantile of set* S, it can be inferred that $\alpha \in U^{(m)}$ and the rank of α in set $U^{(m)}$, $r\left(\alpha, U^{(m)}\right)$, is τm. Then it is easily known that the rank of α in set $S(t_0, t_{h-1})$, $r\left(\alpha, S(t_0, t_{h-1})\right)$, is no less than τm. Therefore, the following equality is derived.

$$\Pr\left[N\tau - r\left(\alpha, S(t_0, t_{h-1})\right) \geq \varepsilon N\tau\right] = \sum_{\theta \leq N\tau - \varepsilon N\tau} \Pr\left[r\left(\alpha, S(t_0, t_{h-1})\right) = \theta\right]$$

$$\leq \sum_{\theta = \tau m}^{N\tau - \varepsilon N\tau} \Pr\left[r\left(\alpha, S(t_0, t_{h-1})\right) = \theta\right] \quad (3)$$

For given θ, the rank of α in set $S(t_0, t_{h-1})$ is θ. Then for any $s \in S(t_0, t_{h-1})$, the probability of $s \geq \alpha$ is θ/N. According to random sample $U^{(m)}$, $\forall s \in U^{(m)}$ follows the empirical distribution, $\Pr[s \geq \alpha] = \tau$. Based on Sanov theorem [19], the following formula can be derived,

$$\Pr[r\left(\alpha, S(t_0, t_{h-1})\right) = \theta] \leq e^{-m\ell(\tau, \theta/N)} \quad (4)$$

in which, $\ell(\tau, \theta/N) = \tau \ln\left(\frac{\tau}{\theta/N}\right) + (1-\tau)\ln\left(\frac{1-\tau}{1-\theta/N}\right)$.

Taking the derivative of $\ell(\tau, \theta/N)$ with respect to θ/N, we have $\frac{\partial \ell(\tau, \theta/N)}{\partial \theta/N} = \frac{\theta/N - \tau}{\theta/N(1-\theta/N)}$. Since θ/N is bounded in $(0,1)$, then $\ell(\tau, \theta/N)$ is a monotonic decreasing function, when $0 \leq \theta/N \leq \tau$. Therefore, for any $\theta/N \in \left[\frac{\tau m}{N}, \tau - \tau\varepsilon\right]$, we have that $\ell\left(\tau, (1-\varepsilon)\tau\right) \leq \ell(\tau, \theta/N)$. Then, for any integer $\theta \in [\tau m, N\tau - \varepsilon N\tau]$, the following inequality is obtained.

$$\Pr[r\left(\alpha, S(t_0, t_{h-1})\right) = \theta] \leq e^{-m\ell(\tau, (1-\varepsilon)\tau)} \quad (5)$$

Therefore, the following inequality can be achieved.

$$\sum_{\theta = \tau m}^{N\tau - \varepsilon N\tau} \Pr\left[r\left(\alpha, S(t_0, t_{h-1})\right) = \theta\right] < (N\tau - \varepsilon N\tau)e^{-m\ell(\tau, (1-\varepsilon)\tau)} \quad (6)$$

Based on the above analysis, when the sample size, m, is larger than $\frac{\ln(\tau N - \tau\varepsilon N) - \ln(\delta/2)}{\ell(\tau, (1-\varepsilon)\tau)}$, we know that $\Pr\left[N\tau - r\left(\alpha, S(t_0, t_{h-1})\right) \geq \varepsilon N\tau\right] \leq \frac{\delta}{2}$. Then $\Pr\left[\frac{\tau - r(\alpha, S(t_0, t_{h-1}))/N}{\tau} \geq \varepsilon\right] \leq \frac{\delta}{2}$ is hold.   □

Theorem 3. *Suppose that the size of set* $S(t_0, t_{h-1})$ *is* N. *Let* $U^{(m)} = \{s_{i1}(t_{j1}),$ $s_{i2}(t_{j2}), ..., s_{im}(t_{jm})\}$ *be a uniform sample of* $S(t_0, t_{h-1})$. *For any given* $\varepsilon > 0, \delta > 0$, *if the sample size,* m, *is larger than* $\frac{\ln(N - \tau N - \tau\varepsilon N) - \ln(\delta/2)}{\ell(\tau, (1+\varepsilon)\tau)}$, *then the following formula is hold,*

$$\Pr\left[\frac{r\left(\alpha, S(t_0, t_{h-1})\right)/N - \tau}{\tau} \geq \varepsilon\right] \leq \frac{\delta}{2} \quad (7)$$

in which α *is the* τ-*quantile of sample set* $U^{(m)}$, $\ell(\tau, (1+\varepsilon)\tau) = \tau \ln\left(\frac{1}{1+\varepsilon}\right) + (1-\tau)\ln\left(\frac{1-\tau}{1-(1+\varepsilon)\tau}\right)$.

Proof. The proofs of the theorem is alike with that of Theorem 2, then some details will be omit. Since α is τ-quantile of set $U^{(m)}$, it can be inferred that the rank of α in set $U^{(m)}$, $r\left(\alpha, U^{(m)}\right)$, is τm. Then it is easily known that there exist $m - \tau m$ elements belonging to $S(t_0, t_{h-1})$ at least, whose value is smaller than α. Then the rank of α in set $S(t_0, t_{h-1})$, $r\left(\alpha, S(t_0, t_{h-1})\right)$, is no more than $N - m + \tau m$. Therefore, the following inequality can be known.

$$\Pr\left[r\left(\alpha, S(t_0, t_{h-1})\right) - N\tau \geq \varepsilon N\tau\right] = \sum\nolimits_{\theta \geq N\tau + \varepsilon N\tau} \Pr\left[r\left(\alpha, S(t_0, t_{h-1})\right) = \theta\right]$$

$$\leq \sum\nolimits_{\theta = N\tau + \varepsilon N\tau}^{N + m(\tau - 1)} \Pr\left[r\left(\alpha, S(t_0, t_{h-1})\right) = \theta\right] \quad (8)$$

For given θ, the rank of α in set $S(t_0, t_{h-1})$ is θ. Then for any $s \in S(t_0, t_{h-1})$, the probability of $s \geq \alpha$ is θ/N. According to random sample $U^{(m)}$, $\forall s \in U^{(m)}$ follows the empirical distribution, $\Pr[s \geq \alpha] = \tau$. Based on Sanov theorem [19], we know that $\Pr[r\left(\alpha, S(t_0, t_{h-1})\right) = \theta] \leq e^{-m\ell(\tau, \theta/N)}$, in which $\ell(\tau, \theta/N) = \tau \ln\left(\frac{\tau}{\theta/N}\right) + (1 - \tau)\ln\left(\frac{1-\tau}{1-\theta/N}\right)$.

Taking the derivative of $\ell(\tau, \theta/N)$ with respect to θ/N, we have $\frac{\partial \ell(\tau, \theta/N)}{\partial \theta/N} = \frac{\theta/N - \tau}{\theta/N(1-\theta/N)}$. Then $\ell(\tau, \theta/N)$ is a monotonic increasing function, when $\tau \leq \theta/N < 1$. Therefore, for any $\theta/N \in \left[\tau + \tau\varepsilon, 1 + \frac{m(\tau-1)}{N}\right]$, we have that $\ell(\tau, (1+\varepsilon)\tau) \leq \ell(\tau, \theta/N)$. Then, for any integer $\theta \in [N\tau + \varepsilon N\tau, N + m(\tau - 1)]$, the following inequalities can be derived.

$$\sum\nolimits_{\theta = N\tau + \varepsilon N\tau}^{N + m(\tau - 1)} \Pr\left[r\left(\alpha, S(t_0, t_{h-1})\right) = \theta\right]$$

$$\leq \left(N + m\tau - m - N\tau - \varepsilon N\tau + 1\right) e^{-m\ell(\tau, (1+\varepsilon)\tau)}$$

$$\leq N(1 - \tau - \varepsilon\tau) e^{-m\ell(\tau, (1+\varepsilon)\tau)} \quad (9)$$

Based on the above analysis, when the sample size, m, is larger than $\frac{\ln(N - \tau N - \tau\varepsilon N) - \ln(\delta/2)}{\ell(\tau, (1+\varepsilon)\tau)}$, we have $\Pr\left[\frac{r(\alpha, S(t_0, t_{h-1}))/N - \tau}{\tau} \geq \varepsilon\right] \leq \frac{\delta}{2}$. □

Corollary 1. *For any given $\varepsilon > 0$ and $\delta > 0$, if the size of random sample $U^{(m)}$, m, satisfies that*

$$m \geq \max\left(\frac{\ln(\tau N - \varepsilon\tau N) - \ln(\delta/2)}{\ell(\tau, (1-\varepsilon)\tau)}, \frac{\ln(N - N\tau - \varepsilon N\tau) - \ln(\delta/2)}{\ell(\tau, (1+\varepsilon)\tau)}\right) \quad (10)$$

then the τ-quantile of sample set $U^{(m)}$ is the (ε, δ)-approximate τ-quantile result of $S(t_0, t_{h-1})$.

Proof. It is obvious that $\Pr\left[\frac{|r(\alpha, S(t_0, t_{h-1}))/N - \tau|}{\tau} \geq \varepsilon\right] = \Pr\left[\frac{\tau - r(\alpha, S(t_1, t_h))/N}{\tau} \geq \varepsilon\right]$ $+ \Pr\left[\frac{r(\alpha, S(t_1, t_h))/N - \tau}{\tau} \geq \varepsilon\right]$. Let α be the τ-quantile of sample set $U^{(m)}$. According to Theorems 2 and 3, it is easily known that the τ-quantile of sample set $U^{(m)}$, α, is the (ε, δ)-approximate τ-quantile result of $S(t_0, t_{h-1})$, when the sample size, m, satisfies formula (10). □

3.3   Sampling Based Algorithm For Approximate τ-Quantile Computation

According to formula (10), the sink computes the optimal sample size, which is indicated by m. The algorithm based on sampling from the set $S(t_0, t_{h-1})$ collected by the sensor network with n nodes is described as follows.

1. m random numbers in $[1, nh]$ are generated independently by the sink. Suppose that random numbers are separated into n disjoint sets, indicated as $R_1, R_2, ..., R_n$, in which R_i consists of the random numbers, whose value belongs to $[(i-1)h+1, ih]$. And the sink broadcasts $R_1, R_2, ..., R_n$ into the WSN.
2. When node i receives the set R_i, for each element r belonging to R_i, node i sends $s_i(t_{\mathrm{mod}(r)})$ to the sink, in which $\mathrm{mod}(r)$ is r moduled by h.
3. When the sink receives all the sample data, it computes the τmth largest value of the sample data.

It leads to high communication cost in sending sample size to cluster-head and member nodes. Less random but energy efficient strategies can be introduced in the sampling process. For example, the sink can periodically broadcast the sequence generating function to the WSN, such as module function. Then each node automatically generates the number sequence and sends the corresponding data to the cluster-head.

4   Performance Evaluation

To evaluate the performance of the proposed approximate τ-quantile computation algorithm, a series of experiments are implemented based on the sensed data set collected from the application of environment monitoring. The data is sampled by TeloB motes. The temperature data is used in the experiments. Each simulation is repeated 100 times and the simulation result corresponds to the average value over 100 times.

The first group of experiments is to investigate the relationship between the accuracy of approximate τ-quantile computation algorithm and the sampling

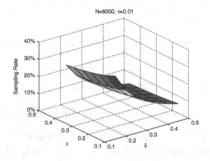

Fig. 1. The relationship between precision requirement and sample size

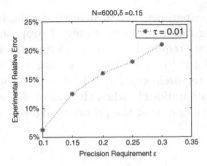

Fig. 2. The relationship between relative error and precision requirement ε

rate, where sampling rate is the sample size divided by the size of set $S[t_0, t_{h-1}]$.
Figure 1 depicts the relationship between the precision requirement and the optimal sample size, which is calculated according to formula (10). As shown in Fig. 1, the sample size is little compered with the set $S[t_0, t_{h-1}]$. For example, for given quantile $\tau = 0.01$, when $\varepsilon = 0.2, \delta = 0.15$, we sample 25.4% sensed data uniformly from the whole data set, then the probability that the relative error of the approximate τ-quantile result is smaller than 0.2 is larger than 0.85. Since τ is very small, then the rank of the approximate τ-quantile result belongs to $[(1-\varepsilon)\tau N, (1+\varepsilon)\tau N]$ with high probability. Therefore, the rank of the approximate result is very close to that of exact τ-quantile.

The second group of experiments is to investigate whether the accuracy of the approximate τ-quantile result computed by the proposed algorithm can achieve the given precision requirements, in which the precision requirements are represented by ε and δ. The experimental results depicted in Fig. 2 demonstrate that the approximate tail quantile can meet the requirements of given precision. For example, when $\tau = 0.01$ and the size of data set is 6000, the relative error of the returned result by our algorithm is below than 16%, where the precision requirements ε and δ are 0.2 and 0.15 respectively. Then the proposed algorithm can achieve given precision.

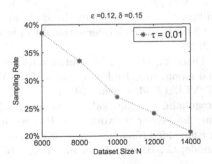

Fig. 3. The relationship between sampling rate and dataset size

The third group of experiments is to investigate the impact of sensed data set size on the sampling rate and the accuracy of proposed algorithm. Figure 3 presents the sampling rate required by ε and δ, where the size of the whole data set is enlarged from 0.6×10^4 to 1.4×10^4. As shown in Fig. 3, for given quantile $\tau = 0.01$ and precision requirements $\varepsilon = 0.12, \delta = 0.15$, our algorithm needs to sample 33.5 % sensed data uniformly when the size of sensed data set is 0.8×10^4. The experimental results show that the proposed algorithm is efficient for larger scale sensor networks.

5   Conclusion

In practice, more attention is paid to the detection of rare event or small probability event in monitoring applications. Then a fundamental problem in this type of monitoring is to generate descriptions for the tail probability distribution of the sensed data. An algorithm based on sampling technique for computing approximate tail quantile is designed in this paper, such that the approximate result can satisfy the requirement of given precision. For given failure probability δ and relative error ε, the result of this algorithm satisfies that the probability of the result with rank between $(\tau - \tau\varepsilon)n$ and $(\tau + \tau\varepsilon)n$ is larger than $1 - \delta$. Simulation experimental results indicate that our algorithm has better performance in terms of effectiveness and accuracy.

References

1. Habitat monitoring on great duck island. http://www.greatduckisland.net/
2. The firebug project. http://firebug.sourceforge.net
3. James reserve microclimate and video remote sensing. http://www.cens.ucla.edu
4. Huang, Z., Wang, L., Yi, K., et al.: Sampling based algorithms for quantile computation in sensor networks. In: Proceedings of the 2011 ACM SIGMOD International Conference on Management of Data. ACM (2011)
5. Wang, L., Luo, G., Yi, K., et al.: Quantiles over data streams: an experimental study. In: Proceedings of the 2011 ACM SIGMOD International Conference on Management of Data. ACM (2013)
6. Tang, M., Li, F., Phillips, M., et al.: Efficient threshold monitoring for distributed probabilistic data. In: 2012 IEEE 28th International Conference on Data Engineering (ICDE). IEEE (2012)
7. Cao, Z., Sutton, C., Diao, Y., et al.: Distributed inference and query processing for RFID tracking and monitoring. In: Proceedings of the VLDB Endowment, vol. 4, no. 5, pp. 326–337. VLDB Endowment (2011)
8. Shrivastava, N., Buragohain, C., Agrawal, D., et al.: Medians and beyond: new aggregation techniques for sensor networks. In: Proceedings of the 2nd International Conference on Embedded Networked Sensor Systems (SenSys). ACM (2004)
9. Agarwal, P.K., Cormode, G., Huang, Z., et al.: Mergeable summaries. In: ACM PODS (2012)
10. Pike, R., Dorward, S., Griesemer, R., et al.: Interpreting the data: parallel analysis with sawzall. Dyn. Grids Worldwide Comput. **13**(4), 277–298 (2005)

11. Gibbons, P.B., Matias, Y..: New sampling-based summary statistics for improving approximate query answers. In: Proceedings of ACM SIGMOD 1998, pp. 331–342. ACM (1998)
12. Chaudhuri, S., Motwani, R., Narasayya, V.: Random sampling for histogram construction: how much is enough? In: Proceedings of ACM 1998 SIGMOD, pp. 436–447. ACM (1998)
13. Mannor, S., Tsitsiklis, J.N.: The sample complexity of exploration in the multi-armed bandit problem. J. Mach. Learn. Res. 5, 623–648 (2004)
14. Vapnik, V.N., Chervonenkis, A.Y.: On the uniform convergence of relative frequencies of events to their probabilities. Theor. Probab. Appl. 16, 264–280 (1971)
15. Manku, G.S., Rajagopalan, S., Lindsay, B.G.: Approximate medians and other quantiles in one pass and with limited memory. In: Proceedings of ACM SIGMOD 1998. ACM (1998)
16. Agarwal, P.K., Cormode, G., Huang, Z., et al.: Mergeable summaries. In: Proceedings of ACM PODS 2012. ACM (2012)
17. Greenwald, M., Khanna, S.: Power conserving computation of order-statistics over sensor networks. In: Proceedings of ACM PODS 2004. ACM (2004)
18. Huang, Z., Yi, K., Zhang, Q.: Randomized algorithms for tracking distributed count, frequencies, and ranks. In: Proceedings of the 31st Symposium on Principles of Database Systems. ACM (2012)
19. Cover, T.M., Thomas, J.A.: Elements of Information Theory. Wiley, New York (2012)
20. Li, Y., Chen, C.S., Song, Y.Q., et al.: Enhancing real-time delivery in wireless sensor networks with two-hop information. Trans. Ind. Inf. 5(2), 113–122 (2009)
21. Kadri, A., et al.: Wireless sensor network for real-time air pollution monitoring. In: 1st International Conference on Communications, Signal Processing, and their Applications, pp. 1–5. IEEE (2013)

Data Aggregation in 6LoWPAN

Juan Luo[1]([⊠]), Jinyu Hu[1], Yuxi Zhang[2], and Yu Liu[1]

[1] College of Computer Science and Electronic Engineering, Hunan University,
Changsha 410082, Hunan, China
juanluo@hnu.edu.cn
[2] Department of Electronics and Information Engineering,
Huazhong University of Science and Technology,
Wuhan 430074, Hubei, China

Abstract. Traditional CSMA/CA in MAC layer causes transmission control and time cost on listening and competing for channels. And the header of IPv6 packet in 6LoWPAN is usually larger than the data in it, which leads to low efficient channels. To overcome these shortages, in this paper, we proposed a novel data aggregation model. By adding a data aggregation model to 6LoWPAN stack, we aggregated data from the network layer according to the MAC layer queuing delay. When the queuing delay is larger, more packets could be dynamically aggregated into one packet to increase the proportion of application data. When the queuing delay is smaller, the amount of packets involved in aggregation will decrease to improve channels utilization. The proposed model can improve transmission performance and enhance the efficiency of channel utilization and data transformation. Simulation results show that our approach could provide better real-time guarantees, and reduce data amount and energy consumption efficiently.

Keywords: 6LoWPAN · Adaptation layer · Data aggregation · Real-time

1 Introduction

The Internet of Things (IoT) [1] is a novel application that has gained extensive attention in modern wireless telecommunications scenario. However, the limited resources of embedded device, such as energy, computing ability and storage capacity, greatly restrict IoT application. Meanwhile, the communication mechanism between heterogeneous embedded devices and the Internet is still a challenge for IoT.

As a solution for above problems, 6LoWPAN [2,3] (IPv6 over Low Power Wireless Personal Area Network) firstly introduced IPv6 to the wireless personal area network. This technology combines the IEEE 802.15.4 MAC layer with the IPv6 network layer, which effectively solved the communication problem between heterogeneous embedded devices and the Internet. As a special kind of wireless sensor network, 6LoWPAN networks have the following characteristics:

© Springer-Verlag Berlin Heidelberg 2015
L. Sun et al. (Eds.): CWSN 2014, CCIS 501, pp. 520–529, 2015.
DOI: 10.1007/978-3-662-46981-1_50

(1) Massive nodes, wireless communication, limited bandwidth; (2) Encapsulating upper-layer protocol data unit by using IPv6 header; (3) Limited-power nodes affect the network performance; (4) Different applications requires different QoS; (5) The amount and redundancy of collected data are very high.

Therefore, we should reduce the amount of data transferred in the network, improve the efficiency of data transmission and save node energy when researching the 6LoWPAN network.

Data aggregation [4–8] which can reduce the redundancy and amount of data saves the bandwidth when sending and receiving data, and also can improve the efficiency of data collection of the network as well. Zhang et al. [8] proposed a novel data aggregation algorithm, which could re-construct the aggregation tree adaptively according to the types of sensed data. Chen et al. [4] studied the impact of Minimum Data Aggregation Time (MDAT) problem, and provided a $(\Delta - 1)$ R-approximation algorithm to solve this problem. However, the latency is still very high. Scott et al. [5] designed another aggregation scheduling algorithm aiming at reducing the latency bound, which has the latency bound of $23R + \Delta - 18$ less than Chen et al.

However, little works on the in-node aggregation and existing aggregation algorithms almost all runs on the intermediate node. Based on the analysis of 6LoWPAN stack, we add the data aggregation function to the adaptation layer of 6LoWPAN protocol stack, and proposed a dynamic data aggregation mechanism which can aggregate the data adaptively according to the network status. Through this mechanism, we can reduce obviously the number of transmitted data, and promote effectively the real time performance of network.

The remainder of the paper is organized as follows. In Sect. 2, we describe briefly the relevant background knowledge of 6LoWPAN. And our data aggregation mechanism are detailed in Sect. 3. Section 4 analyzes the simulation results of the proposed mechanism. Finally, the conclusions are presented in Sect. 5.

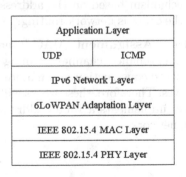

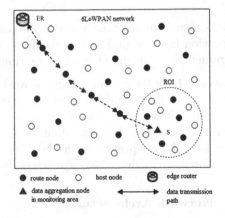

Fig. 1. 6LoWPAN stack structure.   **Fig. 2.** Data monitoring diagram in 6LoWPAN.

2   System Model

2.1   6LoWPAN Protocol Stack

Figure 1 shows the structure of 6LoWPAN protocol stack. 6LoWPAN requires that its MAC layer and physical layer must comply with IEEE 802.15.4 standard, and its network layer must use IPv6 Protocol. In order to run IPv6 on IEEE 802.15.4 standard, 6LoWPAN adds an adaptation layer [9] between IPv6 network layer and IEEE 802.15.4 MAC layer. The basic functions of 6LoWPAN, such as header compression, multicast support, fragmentation and reconstruction, address distribution and network topology construction are implemented in the adaptation layer [10]. The adaptation layer provides medium access for the upper IPv6 layer, and controls over the lower layer function such as network construction, topology control, and MAC routing etc.

Header Compression. The adaptation layer of 6LoWPAN compresses the header and subsequent header of IPv6 packets by using context-based method and stateless compression methods, which could improve the transmission efficiency and reduce the energy consumption of nodes. In order to satisfy the maximum transmission unit (MTU) of IPv6 under the IEEE 802.15.4 MAC layer, 6LoW-PAN has been expanded and improved in [11] based on early definition in [12].

Multicast Support. Multicast technology plays a very important role in IPv6 protocol. Many functions in Neighbor Discovery Protocol rely on it. IEEE 802.15.4 MAC layer only provides limited broadcast. Therefore, the multicast function of adaptation layer can be realized by using controllable broadcast flooding.

Fragmentation and Restructuring. IPv6 stipulates that the MTU size is no less than 1280B [13]. Those links that don't support this MTU must realize the fragmentation and restructuring function, so that the adaptation layer of 6LoW-PAN realizes this function to cope with the frame whose length is bigger than MTU.

MAC-layer Routing. Due to the absence of multi-hop routing in MAC layer, adaptation layer defines two kinds of routing mechanism based on the address assignment mechanism. One is tree routing, and the other is network routing.

Network Topology Construction and Address Assignment. MAC layer provides abundant primitives, including network maintenance, channel scanning, and so on. While MAC layer is not responsible for the construction and maintenance of network topology by calling these primitives. Therefore, these works will be achieved by adaptation layer. Adaptation layer implements a 16bits address allocation mechanism to identify each node in the network.

2.2   Network Architecture

6LoWPAN network shows in Fig. 2, Edge Routers(ER) request data and select multi-hop paths to node S in Region of Interest (ROI), then node S start to collect data from the area. When sink node S receives a service request, it uses a spanning tree algorithm for data aggregation to generate a tree topology which uses S as root node.

6LoWPAN could be represented as an undirected *graph G(N, L)* that composes of a set of nodes N and a set of links L where $\{(i,j) \in L \mid i,j \in N, j \in S_i\}$, for each node $i \in N$, S_i represents the set of neighbor node, i could communicate with any node in S_i. H is the set of hosts, R stands for the set of routers, and ER is the set of edge routers, where $N = ER \cup R \cup H$. We assume that the nodes do not move, in other word, the network is a static network.

2.3   Energy Model

In 6LoWPAN, whether node i sends service data to edge routers is determined by the service request on the edge routers. If the edge routers request service, node i would send service data to edge routers, otherwise node i would not send any. We assume that nodes in network are supplied by batteries and different nodes have same initial energy. Transmit power could be changed dynamically between *(0, P)*, where P is the maximum Transmit power of node i. According to First Order Radio Model, the node energy consumption includes the transmission and receiving energy cost modes. The energy dissipated per bit in the transmission mode is defined as E_s, and E_r represents the energy dissipated per bit in the receiving mode. E_s is given by

$$E_s = E_{elec} + E_{emp}d^n(i,j). \tag{1}$$

Where E_{elec} is the transmission power of nodes, and E_{emp} is the power gain. Upper and exponent n $(2 \leq n \leq 4)$ for transmission radius d indicates attenuation factor. Edge routers are not energy limited nodes, total data for transmission over $L(i,j)$ per unit time is $D_{i,j}$, thus the total energy dissipated over this link $E_{i,j}$ is:

$$E_{i,j} = \sum D_{i,j}(E_s + E_r). \tag{2}$$

3   Data-Aggregation-Based 6LoWPAN Stack

3.1   Data Aggregation Model

In order to reduce the amount of control messages, as well as the costs of channel listening and competition, we add an aggregation model to the adaptation layer of 6LoWPAN stack. The architecture of aggregation model is shown in Fig. 3. It consists of two sub modules: aggregation processing module and aggregation control module. The aggregation processing module includes an input queue, a data aggregation unit and an output queue. By setting aggregation parameters which include aggregation-condition (P), aggregation-degree (D), time-granularity (T) and aggregation-content (C), the aggregation control module could adjust the aggregation dynamically.

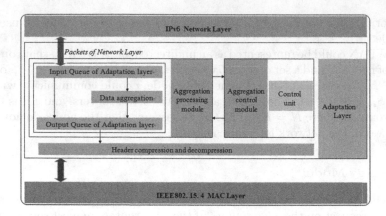

Fig. 3. Aggregation architecture.

3.2   Aggregation Strategy

In this paper, we use the four-tuple $< P, D, T, C >$ to represent the aggregation strategy.

P is the aggregation condition which consists of Traffic Class and Destination Address. Traffic Class is used to identify real-time data or any data requiring to be handled specially. Destination Address is utilized to identify the packets with the same IPv6 address.

D is the aggregation degree. The definition is shown as $D = N_r/N_s$, where N_r represents the total number of received packet, and N_s represents the number of packet involving aggregation.

T is a fixed time granularity. We set the parameter according to $T = \alpha M/S$, where M is the actual monitoring time of application, S is the accuracy requirement of application, and the factor α is related to specific application, valued from 0 to 1.

C is the content of aggregation which is from the network layer to the adaptation layer.

We use the output queuing delay (Queuing Delay) to represent MAC layer delay, and adopt loop control method to adjust **D** dynamically which will reduce the collision probability and waiting time in wireless channels. We can get real-time Queuing Delay by monitoring the output queue of the adaptation layer and then use it to adjust **D**.

The detail operation is: we set up a timer with initial value of 0 at the output queue, and it starts when the first packet comes into the output queue. If the output queue is empty, it will be set to 0. At the beginning, the traffic load is low, and the aggregation degree is set to 1. With the collected data growths, the traffic load will increase as well. Assuming that the $Queuing\ Delay = T$ when the output queue suffers from congestion, if $Queuing\ Delay \geq T$, **D** will add by $T * D/Queuing\ Delay$ to increase the packet number involving aggregation, which will lead to reduce the packet number and the speed the packet pushed into output queue. In the same way, if *Queuing Delay* $< T$, **D** will minus by $T * D/Queuing\ Delay$ to reduce the packet number involving aggregation, which will lead to reduce the aggregation delay and the free time of MAC layer.

According to the Traffic Class field of the packet, we divide data into high-priority Real Time Data (RTD) and low-priority Non Real Time Data (NRTD). The output queue of adaptation layer contains two independent sub-queues, one is the Real Time Queue (RTQ) for RTD and the other one is the Default Queue (DQ) for NRTD. Each RTD will be sent to the MAC layer by RTQ in real-time speed, it ensures that RTD will not encounter unexpected queue delays and congestion. On the other hand, NRTD in DQ will do the best on data output, it probably experiences a significant delay and high levels of congestion.

The packets need to aggregate according to their destination address. First, we should classify the input data into different groups. When the number of the packets with the same destination address reaches the aggregation-degree D, these packets will be sent to the aggregation processing module. The DAA algorithm maps the packet into a Hash-Table using the destination address as the Key. Within the pre-setting time-granularity T, if the length of the list reaches the aggregation-degree D, we will output whole list into aggregation processing module, and sent the aggregated result to the DQ for MAC layer transmission.

DAA works as follows:

Step 1. The adaptation layer receives the packets from the output queue in the network layer, and pushes them into the input queue. Then we check the Traffic Class in the packet, if it is RTD, go to Step 8, otherwise, go to Step 2;

Step 2. The aggregation control module maps NRTD packet into Hash-Table based on the destination address and check if the destination address has the same value. If exists, go to Step 3, otherwise, go to Step 4;

Step 3. The aggregation control module adds the packet to the packet list with the same address. If the length of the list is 0, restart the timer related to the list, otherwise, calculate the length of the packet list. Then go to Step 5;

Step 4. The aggregation control module constructs a new packet list in the Hash-Table for the new destination address, adds the packet into the list, and starts a new timer for this list. Then go to Step 5;

Step 5. If the timer of the packets list is end, go to Step 9, otherwise, go to Step 6;

Step 6. If the length of the packets list equals with aggregation-degree D, the aggregation control module outputs the list to the aggregation processing module, and then go to Step 7;

Step 7. The aggregation processing module aggregates multiple packets and outputs the results into DQ, then go to Step 9;

Step 8. The aggregation control module outputs the RTD to the RTQ directly. Then go to Step 9;

Step 9. The adaptation layer calls the sending module of the MAC layer to send the data.

4   Simulation Results and Analysis

4.1   Simulation Parameters Setting

To investigate the performance of the proposed Aggregation Algorithm, the simulation environment is set to MyEclipse 8.5, using JAVA programming language. 100 sensor nodes are distributed in a square of 100 m × 100 m, which consists of 30 host nodes and 70 routing nodes. We assume that the initial energy of each node is 1J, and energy consumption per unit is 50 nJ. The maximum transmission distance of each node is 30 m. Consistently, the packet length is fixed at 4000 bits. In this paper, we compare the DDA algorithm with NOA (Non-data aggregation Algorithm) and FIXA (data aggregation algorithm with Fixed aggregation degree) algorithms on two aspects. One is the end-to-end delay of packet, and the other is the energy consumption.

4.2   End-to-End Delay

The end-to-end delay is the main factor of the network real-time performance. Therefore, under the same network load conditions, the shorter the end-to-end delay is, the higher the network real-time performance will be.

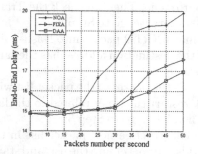 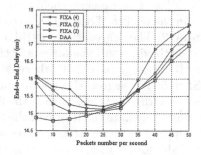

Fig. 4. Packets sent per second compared with the end-to-end delay.

Fig. 5. The end-to-end delay comparison of DAA and FIXA with different aggregation degrees.

The end-to-end delay changed with the packet number sent per second of the DAA, NOA and FIXA algorithms is shown in Fig. 4. When the network load is low, the number of packets sent per second is less than 15, and the end-to-end delay of NOA and DAA algorithm is less than FIXA. This is because the DAA algorithm can reduce the aggregation degree, but FIXA must consume a certain time to meet a fixed aggregation degree. When the number of packets sent per second happens between 20 and 30, the DAA and FIXA algorithms have the same end-to-end delay, and the aggregation degree of them is almost similar. However, when increasing the number of packets sent per second is to more than 30, the DAA algorithm will continue to increase the aggregation degree to meet the increased network load.

But the aggregation degree of FIXA algorithm is fixed, it can not adapt to the network load. Therefore, the DAA algorithm is superior to the NOA and FIXA algorithms on the aspect of end-to-end delay.

Figure 5 shows the end-to-end delay comparison of DAA and FIXA algorithms with different aggregation degrees. When the aggregation degree of FIXA Algorithm is 2, 3 or 4, with the increase of network load, the end-to-end delay of FIXA algorithm is obviously greater than DAA at the beginning , then comes to approximate, and at last is greater again. In particular, when the number of packets sent per second is less than 30, the end-to-end delay when the aggregation degree is 2 is smaller than that when the aggregation degree is 4. When the rate is between 20 and 30, they have similar end-to-end delay. When the rate is higher than 30, the end-to-end delay with an aggregation degree of 4 is smaller. Thus, the DAA algorithm can adjust the aggregation degree dynamically. Therefore, we can conclude that DAA is superior to FIXA and more suitable to the networks whose load changes dynamically, and could get more effective network bandwidth utilization and transmission delay.

4.3 Energy Consumption

The relationship between network load and the energy consumption which is generated to transfer a packet successfully under three algorithms is shown in Fig. 6. We can see that NOA and FIXA have no obvious changes in energy consumption when the sending rate of packet increases. But the energy consumption of the DAA algorithm reduces by 30 % than the NOA algorithm. This is because that the DAA algorithm adopts data aggregation operation, which can reduce the number of header and the length of the data efficiently, and hence, the transmission power is lower. When the network load is low, the DAA algorithm has the similar energy consumption to the NOA, as it doesn't execute any aggregation. With the increase of network load, the DAA algorithm increases its aggregation degree dynamically, which makes its energy consumption per packet lower than NOA and FIXA.

Figure 7 shows the energy consumption required to transfer a packet of the FIXA with different aggregation degree and the DAA. As the network load changes, the change in the energy consumption of FIXA algorithm is gradual. However, with aggregation degree increases, the energy consumption declines obviously. When the aggregation degree is 3, the energy consumption decreases about 20 % more than the degree of 2. When the aggregation degree is 4, the energy consumption decreases about 28 % more than the degree of 2. This is because that, the higher the aggregation degree is, the more the data packets which share the same header will be, the energy consumption per packet decreases.

Based on the analysis of the delay and energy consumption performance of these algorithms, we conclude that the network performance would not keep improving with the aggregation degree increases. DAA algorithm would increase more energy consumption to reduce the transmission delay during low network load. But with the network load increases, the algorithm could adjust the aggregation mechanisms dynamically to provide better latency and energy consumption.

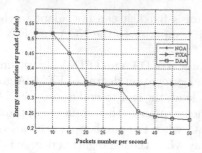
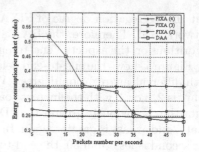

Fig. 6. Comparison of different algorithms for energy consumption in the network.

Fig. 7. DAA with different degrees of polymerization of FIXA energy consumption compared.

5   Conclusions

In this paper, we have designed an aggregation model in the adaptation layer of 6LoWPAN Protocol stack to reduce the transmission control overhead and the MAC layer delay. We proposed the Dynamic Aggregation Algorithm (DAA) based on aggregation conditions. DAA could obtain the network load in real time by monitoring the MAC layer delay and adjust the aggregation degree dynamically by monitoring the network load. DAA divides IPv6 packets into different priorities based on the aggregation strategy that reduces the impact of delay on real-time data. For real-time data, DAA will aggregate it directly to the MAC layer without executing any aggregation. For non-real-time data, DAA will aggregate it according to the aggregation degree. Clearly, the algorithm can not only effectively reduce the data amount and the energy consumption of 6LoWPAN networks, but also provide better real-time guarantees for data in networks to meet the applications of 6LoWPAN networks.

Acknowledgments. This work was partially supported by National Key Technology R&D Program(2012BAD35B06); Program for New Century Excellent Talents in University (NCET-12-0164); National Natural Science Foundation of China (61370094); Natural Science Foundation of Hunan (13JJ1014).

References

1. Chui, M., Löffler, M., Roberts, R.: The internet of things. McKinsey Q. **2**, 1–9 (2010)
2. Shelby, Z., Bormann, C.: 6LoWPAN: The Wireless Embedded Internet, vol. 43. Wiley, New York (2011)
3. Chaudhry, S.A., Akbar, A.H., Ki-Hyung, K.: On the interplay of service proximity and ubiquity. IEICE Trans. Commun. **90**(12), 3470–3479 (2007)
4. Chen, X., Hu, X., Zhu, J.: Minimum data aggregation time problem in wireless sensor networks. In: Jia, X., Wu, J., He, Y. (eds.) MSN 2005. LNCS, vol. 3794, pp. 133–142. Springer, Heidelberg (2005)

5. Scott, C.H.H., Peng-Jun, W., Chinh, T., et al.: Nearly constant approximation for data aggregation scheduling in wireless sensor networks. In: Proceedings of INFO-COM, pp. 366–372 (2007)
6. Akkaya, K., Demirbas, M., Aygun, R.S.: The impact of data aggregation on the performance of wireless sensor networks. Wirel. Commun. Mob. Comput. **8**(2), 171–193 (2008)
7. Pandey, V., Kaur, A., Chand, N.: A review on data aggregation techniques in wireless sensor network. J. Electron. Electr. Eng. **1**(2), 01–08 (2010)
8. Zhang, J.h., Peng, H., Yin, T.t.: Tree-adapting: an adaptive data aggregation method for wireless sensor networks. In: 2010 6th International Conference on Wireless Communications Networking and Mobile Computing (WiCOM), pp. 1–5. IEEE (2010)
9. Luo, j., Pan, C., Wang, P.W.: Data aggregation method based on 6lowpan protocol stack (2013) CN Patent App. CN 201,310,233,531
10. Ma, X., Luo, W.: The analysis of 6lowpan technology. In: 2008 IEEE Pacific-Asia Workshop on Computational Intelligence and Industrial Application, vol. 1, pp. 963–966 (2008)
11. Hui, J., Thubert, P., et al.: Compression format for ipv6 datagrams in 6lowpan networks. draft-ietf-6lowpan-hc-13 (work in progress) (2010)
12. Montenegro, G., Kushalnagar, N., Hui, J., Culler, D.: Transmission of ipv6 packets over ieee 802.15. 4 networks. Internet Proposed Standard RFC 4944 (2007)
13. Deering, S., Hinden, R.: Internet protocol, version 6 (ipv6) specification. RFC1883 (1998)

Internet of Things

Machine Tool Vibration Fault Monitoring System Based on Internet of Things

Yilin Zheng[1,2(✉)], Hu Lin[2], Qingxu Deng[3], Weijie Yang[3], and Xianli Su[3]

[1] University of Chinese Academy of Sciences, Beijing 100049, China
zhengyl@sict.ac.cn
[2] Shenyang Institute of Computing Technology, Chinese Academy of Sciences,
Shenyang 110168, China
[3] College of Information Science and Engineering, Northeastern University,
Shenyang 110819, China

Abstract. To solve the problem such as the difficulty in node wiring and noisy vibration information in the traditional machine tool vibration monitoring system, a machine tool vibration fault monitoring system based on Internet of Things (IoT) is studied and established. According to the characteristics of the star topology network, a wireless ad hoc network protocol is designed based on the handshaking communication protocol and the absolute survival time. In order to filter the noise of the vibration information in real time and monitor the gradual faults of the machine tools online, a simplified Kalman filtering algorithm is achieved on the sink node. An application example applied to the ball screw of CNC-lathe indicates that the monitoring system could monitor the machine tool vibration fault effectively.

Keywords: Internet of things · Vibration fault monitoring · Wireless ad-hoc network · Kalman filtering

1 Introduction

The high precision is the core technical requirement of CNC machine tools. The physical state of machine parts, such as temperature, vibration and noise, will be affected by the cutting motion of the tools and the workpieces in the machining process. If the status parameter exceeds the safety threshold, the machining precision will be significantly reduced, and even the processing failures and security incidents will occur [1]. Monitoring vibration information is currently the most widely used as a monitoring method [2], for its technical means and theory has been relatively mature. The wired sensor network collecting and manual monitoring is used traditionally. This method has the problems such as the difficulty in sensor node wiring and the heavy reliance on the monitoring experience of the technical staff [3].

The Internet of Things is a new kind of technology which connects the sensors to the Internet. This new technology has four characteristics such as sensing, knowing, connecting and controlling so that it can achieve the collection and processing of the sensor information [4]. The Internet of Things can be deployed more quickly, conveniently and

© Springer-Verlag Berlin Heidelberg 2015
L. Sun et al. (Eds.): CWSN 2014, CCIS 501, pp. 533–547, 2015.
DOI: 10.1007/978-3-662-46981-1_51

efficiently by the self-organizing wireless network protocol. Because the traditional wired sensor network system is not suitable for the real-time vibration monitoring of large equipment, the machine tool vibration fault monitoring system based on Internet of Things is studied in this paper. The real-time monitoring and fault diagnosis of the important machine components such as guide rails, ball screws and spindle can be achieved by Internet of Things technology, sensor technology and digital filter algorithms.

2   System Architecture Design

The machine tool vibration fault monitoring system based on Internet of Things can be divided into two parts: the wireless sensor network part and the Internet part. In the wireless sensor network part, the wireless acquisition nodes attached to the spindle and ball screws send the vibration information to the sink node. The sink node processes the received wireless data by the digital filtering algorithm, and then sends the vibration information which is packaged into the TCP segment to the local CNC system via the Ethernet module. The vibration information node can be also sent to the remote fault diagnosis system via the GPRS module so that the machine manufacturer can monitor the equipment remotely. The overall structure of the system is shown in Fig. 1.

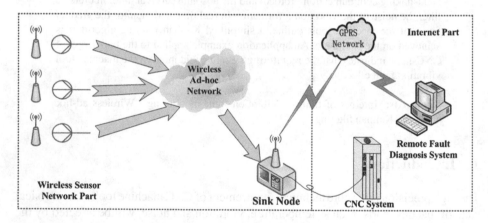

Fig. 1. The general structure of the system

3   System Hardware Design

3.1   Radio Frequency Chip Selection

As the hardware core part of the Internet of Things system, a suitable kind of RF (radio frequency) chip plays an important role in the entire system. In accordance with the carrier frequency, the RF chip on the market is currently divided into two categories: 433 MHz and 2.4 GHz. The two types of chips mentioned above have advantages and disadvantages: the former's wireless signal has stronger penetration with less attenuation during transmission; the latter has the faster transmission speed but using the global public frequency band which often has overlaps and interferences with other RF chip channels. According to the contrast experiment in the machine shop, the large machine usually blocks the transmission of 2.4 GHz wireless signal. Because there is a small amount of data transmitted by the vibration information acquisition nodes (generally less than 10 bytes), the transmission rate of RF chip has little effect on system performance. Taking these two above-mentioned aspects into consideration, the ultra-low power RF transceiver chip CC1101 which works in the 433 MHz carrier frequency is used as the RF chip of the wireless sensor network part.

3.2 Hardware Design of Acquisition Node

The hardware structure of the acquisition node is divided into four parts: MCU, the RF chip, the vibration information acquisition chip and the battery voltage detection chip. As the acquisition node hardware design target is low power consumption, low cost, high integration and small volume, the ultra-low power 16-bit processor MSP430F2011 is selected as MCU. The vibration information of the machine can be described by several physical quantities such as displacement, acceleration and velocity. The first two physical quantities are poor and difficult to obtain, but the acceleration information has the remarkable advantages such as strong real-time, mature technology and product variety [5]. Therefore, the three-axis accelerometer ADXL345 is used in the vibration information acquisition chip for the absolute acceleration collection of the machine components on the XYZ three axis direction. ADXL345 has the features such as the small size, low power consumption, high resolution and suitable for mobile devices [6]. In order to repair or replace the battery in the acquisition nodes in time when its voltage is low, the XC61CC2802 chip is used for real-time monitoring of the battery voltage. The output pin of this chip will be pulled down when the external power supply voltage is lower than 2.5 V. The acquisition node hardware structure is shown in Fig. 2.

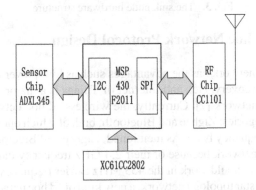

Fig. 2. The acquisition node hardware structure

3.3 Hardware Design of Sink Node

The sink node hardware structure is divided into MCU, RF chip and Ethernet controller. As the core part of the star network, the sink node needs to complete the digital filtering process of the vibration information and the conversion of the communication protocol between the sensor network part and the Internet part. For this reason, the MCU of the sink node should have high processing speed and large-capacity storage space. The ARM Cortex-M3 based microprocessor STM32F103VET6, which has the highest 72 MHz clock speed and 512 K of Flash, is used in this design. The RF chip and 10Mbps Ethernet controller ENC28J60 are connected to the microprocessor by the bus interface of SPI1 and SPI2. The GPRS module based on the SIM900 chip communicates with the ARM microprocessor via a serial interface, while the 16-bit parallel LCD interface can realize the real-time display of the collected vibration information on the LCD screen. The sink node hardware structure is shown in Fig. 3.

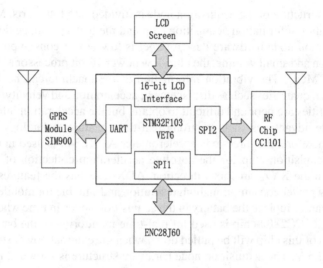

Fig. 3. The sink node hardware structure

4   Wireless Ad-hoc Network Protocol Design

The wireless ad hoc network has the advantages such as low-power consumption, self-management, self-discovery, etc., and Internet of Things is a major application area of the wireless ad hoc network [7]. Currently, the wireless ad hoc network technology is divided into two categories: Zigbee and Bluetooth, both of which operate in the 2.4 GHz global free public frequency band. As mentioned, Zigbee and Bluetooth do not apply to the machine ad hoc network because of their 2.4 GHz frequency band, so the network designed in this paper should work in the 433 MHz carrier frequency. According to the characteristics of the star topology network, a new kind of ad hoc network protocol based on the machine Internet of things is designed.

4.1   Objective and Basic Principle of Protocol

The machine ad hoc network is similar with other ad hoc networks [8], for its devices can be also divided into full function devices (FFD) and reduced function devices (RFD).

As the sink node at the core of star network, the full function device is generally responsible for establishment and management of the ad hoc network through the adoption of full duplex communication mode. The reduced function device, whose power is supplied by the 3.3 V lithium battery, is mainly responsible for sending the sensor information to the sink node periodically. The RFD usually stays in the sleep mode to save battery power, for it receives the wireless packets rarely. Therefore, the design objective of machine ad hoc network protocol is to achieve the self-management function of the network at the situation of minimizing the power consumption of acquisition nodes [9]. It means that the designed protocol could connect the active nodes to the ad hoc network and delete the connected nodes which have been no response within a period of time. In order to achieve the above design goal, a new kind of machine self-organizing network protocol on the handshaking communication protocol and the absolute survival time is studied in this paper. The basic principle of this network protocol is that the sink node connects the acquisition nodes to the ad hoc network via the three-way handshake, and maintains an array of structures based on the absolute survival time to remove the unresponsive nodes in the network. The absolute survival time is expressed as the survival time threshold of the connected nodes by using the network system time, which equals the last confirmed active time of the acquisition nodes in the network plus the relative survival time. The absolute survival time of the acquisition nodes is different from each other because it is closely related to the time when the machine connects these nodes to the network system. The relative survival time mentioned above is defined as the waiting maximum delay of waiting for the activities of connected nodes. This means that if the sink node had not received any wireless data from a connected node for the relative survival time, this connected node should be considered as an unresponsive node and removed from the network. The relative survival time of all acquisition nodes is a time constant based on the specific application environment of the network.

4.2   Protocol Realization on the Acquisition Node

In order to extend the battery life of acquisition nodes, the major part of the network protocol is implemented on the sink node which has high processing speed, large memory space and using the DC power. But the acquisition nodes only complete the small parts of the protocol, such as broadcasting the connecting requests and sending the sensor data. Therefore, the data packets collected by the sink node can be divided into two categories: the connecting broadcast packets and the sensor information packets. The connecting packet is used for the acquisition nodes joining the ad hoc network. The source address of these packets is the default initial address (0xFF) and their destination address is the broadcast address (0x00). The sensor information packets collected by the connected nodes contain the six-byte three-axis acceleration data which needs to be sent to the sink node. The source address of the sensor information packets is the acquisition node's ID assigned by the self-organizing network protocol, and their destination address is the sink node's ID.

The acquisition node enters the initialization state after power-up. In this state, the acquisition node will send the broadcast packets periodically to look for the self-organizing network which can be connected. In the time gap between two times of sending packets, the RF chip CC1101 turns into the receiving mode to monitor the connected acknowledgment packets from the sink node. The connected acknowledgment packets contain the acquisition node's ID assigned by the protocol and the sink node's ID. When the acquisition node receives the connected acknowledgment packets, it turns into the connected state and uses the node ID assigned by the protocol as the source address of the sensor information packets, and its destination address will be updated to the sink node's ID in the connected acknowledgment packets. Then the three-axis acceleration acquisition nodes collect the acceleration data and send the sensor information packets periodically. The acquisition nodes begin the normal collection and transmission work without receiving any wireless data packets in the connected status, so these nodes should close the external interrupt and enter the sleep mode in the time gap between two times of sending packets to reduce the power consumption. In order to ensure that the sink node can receive the response from the active connected nodes within the maximum waiting time, the maximum time gap of the acquisition node sending packets in this protocol must be less than the node's relative survival time. The protocol realization on the acquisition node is shown in Fig. 4.

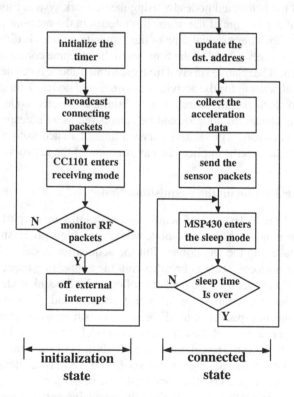

Fig. 4. The realization of the protocol on the acquisition node

4.3 Protocol Realization on the Sink Node

Since the sink node uses the selected processor which has the higher performance with no consideration of the power consumption, the machine Things of Internet realizes the major part of self-organizing network protocol on the sink node. The sink node should have the functions such as the three-way handshaking communication with the acquisition nodes and the management of the absolute survival time. The structure named Node is designed to manage the connected acquisition nodes. The Node structure contains two member variables: a Boolean variable Active and an integer variable Max_Time. The former is used to represent the active state of the acquisition nodes; the latter stores the absolute survival time of this node for checking whether its lifetime has been over or not. The sink node initializes a contiguous array space of the Node structure to store the information of acquisition nodes after power-up. The Active member variable of each array element is initialized to 0. After initializing the structure array, the CC1101 chip on the sink node turns into the receiving mode to wait for the wireless data packets from acquisition nodes. In the receiving mode, the CC1101 chip's address filtering function is open so that the sink node can only receive the sensor information packet which uses the node's ID number as its destination address or the connecting broadcast packet which uses the default broadcast address (0x00) as its destination address. When the sink node receives a wireless data packet from an acquisition node, the destination address of this packet will be analyzed first. If the destination address is the default broadcast address (0x00), it indicates that the received wireless data packet is the connecting broadcast packet (the first handshake). Otherwise, the received packet is a sensor information packet and its source address is the ID number of the acquisition node assigned by the self-organizing network protocol.

After receiving a connecting broadcast packet, the sink node immediately checks whether the current number of the active nodes is equal to the maximum number of nodes named Max_Node which is predetermined by the ad hoc network. The equation of the two numbers indicates that all of the acquisition nodes needed by the machine monitoring system has been connected. Otherwise, the sequential query of Active member variables in the Node structure array should be executed for finding the inactive element which has the smallest array index. The array index of this element will be used as the ID number of this acquisition node and sent with the sink node's ID number by the connected acknowledgment packets (the second handshake). At this time, the connected acquisition nodes close the external interrupt so that they cannot receive any wireless data packets. Therefore, the acquisition nodes can receive the connected acknowledgment packets only in the initialization state. The acquisition nodes, which have received the connected acknowledgment packets, will update their ID numbers to the number assigned by the network protocol and send the sensor information packets to the sink node periodically.

When the sink node receives a packet containing the acquisition node ID number, the element whose array index is the acquisition node's ID number will be found and the Active member variable of this element will be checked. The zero value of variable indicates that this node has not connected to the network yet, so this node should be seen as the new connected node and the Active member variable of the corresponding array element will be set to one (the third handshake). In order to achieve the self-management function of the ad hoc network, the Max_Time member variable of this element will be updated to the sum of the current system time (Ticks) and the relative survival time (Life_Time). Then, the reading and processing of the six-byte triaxial acceleration data from the sensor information packets can be completed on the sink node.

When the connected acquisition nodes in the network could not work due to the electrical faults or the exhaustion of the dead battery, the sink node needs to delete these "dead" nodes from the network. A new kind of approach, which is used to judge whether the acquisition node is active in the network, is realized by updating and checking the absolute survival time periodically. The essence of this approach is the software watchdog realized on the basis of the system tick timer interrupt. Similar with the "feeding the dog" operation of the software watchdog, when the sink node receives a sensor information packet, the absolute survival time of the corresponding element Node structure array will be updated based on the current system time and the node's relative survival time. The absolute survival time Max_Time of these elements will grow together with the system time Ticks. So the lifetime of the acquisition node is extended, and the time gap between the node's absolute survival time and its last active time in the network can be the constant-the relative survival time Life-time. The Systick timer of STM32 processor, which can be seen as the system tick timer, is able to provide the periodic hardware timer interrupt to the software system. In the system tick timer interrupt handler, the system time Ticks should be added one automatically, and the Tick_Check function is called to find the connected acquisition node whose absolute survival time is equal to the current system time. Because the survival time threshold of the acquisition node mentioned above acquisition node has reached the current system time, as the manager of the self-organizing network, the sink node should remove this "dead" acquisition node from the network immediately. On the specific implementation of the protocol, the Tick_Check function will find the active element whose Max_Time is equal to Ticks in the Node array elements, and then reset the Active variable to 0. The protocol realization on the sink node is shown in Fig. 5.

5 Online Processing Algorithm of Vibration Information

In the case of the acquisition nodes powered by battery, the sensor chip manufacturer of ADXL345 recommend sets the Low_Power bit of the chip's internal BW_RATE register to one so that ADXL345 can work in the low-power mode. The power consumption of ADXL345 can be reduced by a third at the expense of signal-noise ratio in this mode, so the lifetime of the battery will be extended. In the 25 Hz data transfer rate, the working current of ADXL345 can be reduced from 60 uA to 40 uA because of the low-power mode. In order to obtain the true value of the sensor information and reduce the noise impact on the measurement result in the low-power mode as far as possible, a kind of online processing algorithms based on the Kalman filtering is realized on the sink node in the machine monitoring system.

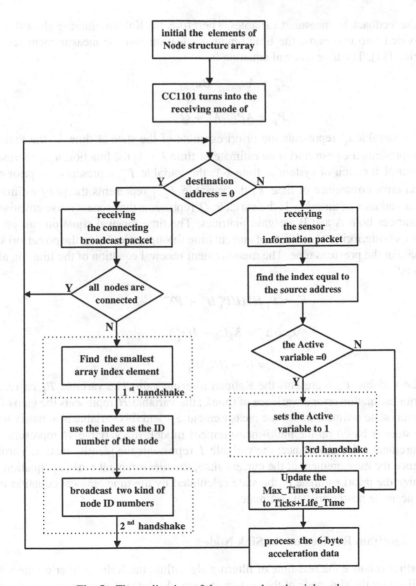

Fig. 5. The realization of the protocol on the sink node

5.1   Introduction to the Kalman Filtering

The Kalman filtering, which can estimate the current status of system based on the previous time state, is a digital filtering algorithm with the minimum variance estimation for the state sequence of dynamical system [10]. Because the iterative method is used for reducing the amount of computations and improving the processing speed, the Kalman filtering algorithm is very suitable for the occasions of high real-time requirements. The algorithm estimates the running status of the system at a moment, and then gets the feedback by measured variables. Therefore, the Kalman filtering algorithm can be divided into two parts: the time renewal equation and the measurement renewal equation [11]. The time renewal equation is:

$$x_k^- = Ax_{k-1} + Bu_{k-1} \tag{1}$$

$$P_k^- = AP_{k-1}A^T + Q \tag{2}$$

The variable x_k^- represents the priori estimate of the state at time k; the variable x_{k-1} represents the posteriori state estimate of time $k-1$; the function u_{k-1} represents the control function of system at time k-1; the variable P_k^- represents the prior estimation error covariance of time k; the variable P_{k-1} represents the prior estimation error covariance of time $k-1$; the variable Q represents the process noise covariance; the matrices both A and B are gain matrices. The time renewal equation can get the system's posteriori state estimate of current time through calculating the posteriori state estimate of the previous time. The measurement renewal equation of the filtering algorithm is:

$$K_k = P_k^- H^T (HP_k^- H^T + R)^{-1} \tag{3}$$

$$x_k = x_k^- + K_k(z_k - Hx_k^-) \tag{4}$$

$$P_k = (I - HK_k)P_k^- \tag{5}$$

The variable K_k represents the Kalman filtering gain; The variable P_k represents the prior estimation error covariance of time k; the variable H represents the gain of the posteriori state estimate x_k for the measurement z_k, and this variable is a matrix when the system is based on the multi-measurement model; the variable R represents the measurement noise covariance; the variable I represents the identity matrix. Through reference the measurement of the current state, the measurement renewal equation can optimize the priori estimate of the state calculated by the time renewal equation for a more accurate posteriori state estimate.

5.2   Algorithm Realized on the Sink Node

To further enhance the real-time of filtering algorithm, the Kalman filtering algorithm is realized on the sink node of the bottom system. As the system coprocessor, the sink node is mainly responsible for filtering noise and vibration information online and sending it to the local CNC systems or remote fault diagnosis system. Due to the limited storage capacity and processing power of embedded devices, the whole matrix operations of the Kalman filtering algorithm realized on the sink node will need to consume a lot of time and code space so that the efficiency of the sink node will be reduced. Therefore, a simplified Kalman filter algorithm is designed in this paper and implemented on the ARM embedded processor.

Because the vibration intensity changes irregularly without the time, the gain matrix is simplified as the constant 1 in the filtering algorithm; the measurement z_k is fully reflected in the state estimate x_k of time k, so the weight of z_k to the variable x_k is 1 and the gain variable H is also equal to the constant 1; because the mechanical vibration is an inherent property of the device movement and irrelevant to the external factors [12], the function u_{k-1} and its gain variable B are zero. The filtering algorithm for the matrix I is the first-order matrix, for the monitoring system is the single model and measurement system which treats the vibration acceleration as a single object of research. The measurement noise covariance R and the process noise covariance Q are set to the constants. The measurement noise covariance R represents the fluctuation extent of the object. Because the variance of the random variables can be expressed as its fluctuation extent under certain conditions, the simplified filtering algorithm can get the value of R through calculating the variance of vibration acceleration collected by the acquisition nodes in the stationary state. The calculation method of the measurement noise covariance R is:

$$R = \frac{\sum_{i=1}^{n}(x_i - \bar{x})^2}{n} \tag{6}$$

The variable n is the total number of the vibration acceleration samples collected by the acquisition nodes in the stationary state. The variable x_i presents the first sample. $\bar{x}$ is the average of the samples. The process noise covariance Q in the Kalman filtering is determined by the experience based on a lot of monitoring data. If the variable Q is larger, the Kalman filtering gain K_k will be larger together and the state estimate x_k will prefer to the measurement z_k. Otherwise if Q is smaller, x_k will prefer to the priori estimate x_k^-. Because the weight of z_k and x_k^- to x_k is influenced by the value of Q, the appropriate model according to the actual needs of the system will be established for the best value of Q. In order to accelerate the convergence process of the posteriori state estimate x_k, the initial value x_0 of the posteriori state estimate x_{k-1} is set to the first vibration acceleration collected by the monitoring system. The simplified Kalman filter algorithm is:

$$K_k = (P_{k-1} + Q)(P_{k-1} + Q + R)^{-1} \tag{7}$$

$$x_k = x_{k-1} + K_k(z_k - x_k^-) \tag{8}$$

$$P_k = (1 - K_k)(P_{k-1} + Q) \tag{9}$$

The simplified filtering algorithm turns the matrix operations into the constant values in these equations mentioned above. Therefore, the number of variables involved in the operations is reduced to improve the acceleration efficiency of the information processing on the sink node.

6   Experimental Analysis

Taking example for the more common lathe, a machine tool vibration fault monitoring system based on Internet of Things is studied in this paper. In order to facilitate the data analysis and fault diagnosis, the acquisition nodes are devised the side of the lathe spindle box, the surface of X-axis and Z-axis of ball screw and some other key parts of the lathe. The X-axis vibration acceleration of ball screw is studied and the motion characteristics and failure causes of the ball screw are analyzed on this paper. As an important part of the machine feed system, the ball screw is mainly responsible for turning the rotary motion into the linear motion of nut brackets. Through the real-time online monitoring of the operational status of the ball screw, the reliability and the location precision of the machine feed system can be improved significantly [13].

The mechanical failure, according to their forming speed, can be divided to the gradual failures and sudden failures. The gradual failure is the failure such as aging and mechanical wear which changes slowly with the time growth [14]. When the gradual failure has occurred on the ball screw, the trend of the vibration information presents a slow drift. Because there is a mount of noise in the acceleration sensor information under the ADXL345's low-power mode, the vibration information drift caused by the gradual failure is often difficult to monitor. Because the Kalman filtering is an iterative estimation algorithm based on the dynamic time-domain model, it can be applied to the gradual fault monitoring of the ball screw to filter the noise of the acceleration data so that the current work status can be evaluated on line [15]. In the specific implementation, the acquisition node is fixed on the X-axis nut bracket so that the X-axis direction of the acceleration sensor can be parallel to the axial direction of the ball screw. The variance of the axial vibration acceleration collected within two minutes in the stationary state can be calculated as 9.225 mg, and this value will be used for the measurement noise covariance of the Kalman filtering algorithm. After several experiments and observations, the program will encourage the process noise covariance is set to 0.1 mg to achieve better filtering effect. The process noise covariance will be set to 0.1 mg for the better filtering effect.

The monitoring data from the lathe processing site shows that the gradient fault of the ball screw is mainly from the mechanical wear and poor lubrication between the ball and the ball-return track. The axial vibration of the ball screw with the gradual fault has the characteristics of slow growth and fluctuating when the noise in the information has been removed by the filtering algorithm. But because of the less friction under normal conditions, the ball screw feed motion can be approximately considered as the uniform or uniform plus (or minus) speed movement. Therefore, the vibration acceleration almost has no change after filtering noise. The X axial vibration acceleration of the lathe ball screw is sampled and filtered twenty times under the normal condition and the poor lubrication condition. Under the two conditions mentioned above, the original sampling data and filtered acceleration data with the sampling period for 1 second is shown in Fig. 6.

The obvious conclusion can be drawn from Fig. 6 that the waveform of the filtered axial vibration acceleration is approximated as a straight line under the normal condition. And the acceleration average of twenty samples is 33.26 mg and its standard deviation is about 2.67 mg. But the waveform of the axial vibration acceleration under the poor lubrication state is a fluctuating curve. And the acceleration average of twenty samples is 30.03 mg and its standard deviation is about 9.89 mg. By the comparison between the vibration acceleration data and waveforms under the two different conditions, the conclusion can be drawn that the latter's axial acceleration is smaller (small average)

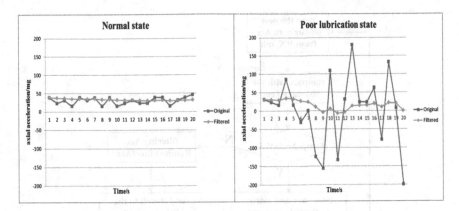

Fig. 6. The axial vibration acceleration waveforms in the both states

and undulating larger(large variance) as a whole because of the larger reverse friction in the process of the ball screw's movement. The local CNC system and the remote fault diagnosis system can conclude whether there has been the gradual failure on the ball screw through analyzing the characteristics of the vibration information mentioned above. So that the lathe operators can replace the worn ball or inject the lubricating oil into the nut in time.

In the process of machining parts on the lathe, the ball screw might encounter several sudden failures such as the ruptured steel ball, depression of the return pipe and the shoulder fracture of ball screw. These failures have large destructive power, short duration and difficult prediction. Because of the dramatic change of the axial vibration acceleration caused by the sudden failure(600 mg or more), the sudden failure information can be distinguished from the ordinary noise information. The difference between the two acceleration data can be calculated for the sudden failure monitoring. When a new acceleration data (Acc) is received, the sink node will compare Acc with the last received data (Temp). If the absolute value of the difference between the two values over the alarm threshold of the sudden failure of (usually set to 600 mg), the aggregation node should send the alarm information to upper computers. Otherwise, the acceleration data will be filtered and stored in the sink node for the next comparison. The algorithm flowchart of vibration information processing is shown in Fig. 7.

When the lathe operators get the alarm information of sudden failures through the upper computer, the lathe work should be stopped immediately for the further examination of ball screw to reduce the losses. The axial vibration acceleration waveforms of the burst fault caused by the ruptured steel ball are shown in Fig. 8.

It can be shown from Fig. 8 that the axial vibration acceleration of ball screw has dropped from 78 mg of the 30th sampling data to -670.8 mg of the 31st sampling data. The difference between the two sampling data is 748.8 mg, which is larger than the alarm threshold of the sudden failure (600 mg), can be inferred that the ball screw should have happened some sudden failure in the two sampling interval.

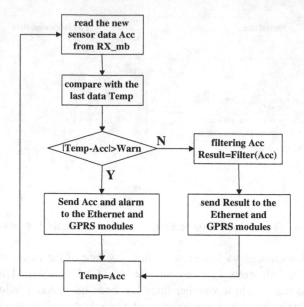

Fig. 7. The algorithm flowchart of vibration information processing

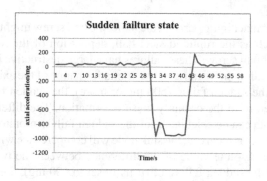

Fig. 8. The axial vibration acceleration waveforms of the burst fault

7 Conclusions

In order to solve various problems generated by the use of wired network, the machine vibration fault monitoring system based on Internet of Things is studied in this paper. The self-management capabilities of the machine Internet of Things is realized base on the handshaking communication protocol and the absolute survival time. A simplified Kalman filtering algorithm is designed and applied on the sink node to remove noise of the vibration information so that the efficiency and instantaneity of the monitoring system can be improved. The lathe ball screw is considered as the monitoring objects and the system reliability in condition monitoring and fault diagnosis has been validated in this paper. Due to the emergence of multi-sensor fusion technology, how to use the variety of physical quantities (such as vibration, temperature, noise, etc.) for the more accurate diagnosis of machine failures needs further research in the follow-up work [16].

Acknowledgments. The project is supported by the National Key Basic Research Program funded (Mathematical mechanization method and its application in digital manufacturing: No. 2011CB302400-G).

References

1. Gao, H.L., Liu, Q.J., Huang, B.Q., et al.: Key techniques of fault prediction and health management system in NC machine tool. Comput. Integr. Manuf. Syst. **16**(10), 2217–2226 (2010)
2. Li, J.B., Lu, Y.X., Li, H.J., et al.: CNC Machine Fault Diagnosis and Maintenance Quick Reference, pp. 503–520. Chemical Industry Press, Beijing (2009)
3. Liu, J., Qin, D.L., Yu, D.J.: Intelligent condition monitoring system based on wireless sensor networks. Comput. Integr. Manuf. Syst. **14**(10), 2047–2051 (2008)
4. Song, C.P., Wu, B.J., Wang, P.F.: Study on safety management of condition-based maintenance based on Internet of Things technology. China Saf. Sci. J. **21**(1), 77–81 (2011)
5. Zhang, B.Q., Lei, B.Z., Zhao, L.H., et al.: Research on vibration method of fan blade fault forecasting. J. Electron. Meas. Instrum. **28**(3), 285–291 (2014)
6. Zhu, J., Yang, Z.Y.: Design of wireless vibration monitoring sensor node based on CC2530. Instrum. Tech. Sens. **8**, 56–58 (2012)
7. O'Brein, W.J., Julien, C., Kabadayi, S., et al.: An architecture for decision support in ad hoc sensor networks. Electron. J. Inf. Technol. Constr. **14**, 309–327 (2009)
8. Wheeler, A.: Commercial applications of wireless sensor networks using ZigBee. IEEE Commun. Mag. **45**(4), 70–77 (2009)
9. Song, Y.H., Li, F.B., Li, Z.M.: Survey on energy-efficiency technology for wireless sensor networks. Chinese J. Sci. Instrum. **27**(6), 1665–1674 (2006)
10. Zhao, C.S.: Kalman filter under the correlated noise of dynamic and observation. Bull. Surv. Mapp. **1**, 14–15 (2013)
11. Deng, H.B., Zhang, L., Wu, Y., et al.: Research on track estimation based on Kalman filtering algorithm. Transducer and Microsystem Technologies **31**(5), 4–7 (2012)
12. Li, S.M., Guo, H.D., Li, D.R.: Review of vibration signal processing methods. Chinese J. Sci. Instrum. **34**(8), 1615–1907 (2013)
13. Wu, X.X., Gao, H.L., Yan, J.M., et al.: Fault diagnosis technology for NC machine screw based on hyper-sphere support vector machines. Comput. Int. Manuf. Syst. **16**(12), 2661–2667 (2010)
14. Wang, H.B., Tang, K.M., Xu, R.L., et al.: Diagnosis of soft fault of electronic transformer in digital substation. Power Syst. Prot. Control **40**(24), 53–58 (2012)
15. Yan, X.Z., Luo, Q.H.: dynamic sensor data stream estimation method based on Kalman filtering. Chinese J. Sci. Instrum. **34**(8), 1847–1854 (2013)
16. Zhan, H., Tan, J.W., Du, Y.: Diagnosis research of high-speed motorized spindle with vibration fault symptom based on multi-sensors information fusion. Manuf. Autom. **35**(12), 30–32 (2013)

A Novel Urban Traffic Prediction Mechanism for Smart City Using Learning Approach

Xiaoguang Niu[1](✉), Ying Zhu[1], Qingqing Cao[1],
Lei Zhao[1], and Wei Xie[2](✉)

[1] Computer School, Wuhan University, Wuhan, China
{xgniu,yingzhu91,cqq,leizhao}@whu.edu.cn
[2] Computer School, Central China Normal University, Wuhan, China
xw@ccnu.edu.cn

Abstract. Traffic flow condition prediction is a basic problem in the transportation field. It is challenging to play out full potential of temporally-related information and overcome the problem of data sparsity existed in the traffic flow prediction. In this paper, we propose a novel urban traffic prediction mechanism namely C-Sense consisting of two parts: CRF-based temporal feature learning and sequence segments matching. CRF-based temporal feature learning exploits a linear-chain condition random field (CRF) to explore the temporal transformation rule in the traffic flow state sequence with supplementary environmental resources. Sequence segments matching is utilized to match the obtained state sequence segments with historical condition to get the ultimate prediction results. Experiments are evaluated based on datasets obtained in Wuhan and the results show that our mechanism can achieve good performance, which prove that it is a potential approach in transportation field.

Keywords: Traffic flow condition prediction · Temporal feature learning · Environmental resources · Smart city · Intelligent transportation system

1 Introduction

Predicting the urban traffic flow condition can offer the best routes for travelers [1] and provide the foundational basis for balancing the traffic flow, optimizing traffic management schemes [2] and improving traffic control. Therefore, it is necessary to solve this problem which can coordinate traffic congestion, protect environment and save energy.

There is an underlying rule in the temporal evolution of traffic flow condition, which can be explored by making use of the method such as state transition probability. Through the fine-grained analysis of the prediction results of the existing works, we find that they have suffered from the problem of data sparsity. Although the condition of a road segment follows a certain pattern on the time dimension, the previous works cannot play a good role in some situations especially when there are not sufficient taxi GPS traces. Feature learning for traffic prediction used to extract and select some representative features from traffic flow sequence which can reflect the traffic flow condition, while it has not been utilized to extract extra data except traffic information.

© Springer-Verlag Berlin Heidelberg 2015
L. Sun et al. (Eds.): CWSN 2014, CCIS 501, pp. 548–557, 2015.
DOI: 10.1007/978-3-662-46981-1_52

Based on the above findings, we can combine taxi GPS traces with other dimensions of information for traffic prediction, i.e. utilize supplementary features such as environmental resources which contain temporal changes that can also reflect the traffic flow condition of current road.

In this paper, we propose a temporal traffic flow feature learning mechanism, namely C-Sense. Firstly, it uses an undirected graphical model, known as linear chain conditional random fields (CRFs), to estimate the current state through the previous state in the temporal sequence and supported observations. With supplementary environmental information, the CRF model capture correlations among state transitions over time and the relationship that observations support states. Secondly, a DTW-based segment matching algorithm is applied to match the state sequence segment obtained by CRF with historical traffic flow condition sequence segments to get the result at the predicted time.

The main contributions of this paper are concluded as the following aspects:

1. Through the fine-grained analysis of the prediction results on the time dimension, we combine temporally-related environmental resources which are utilized in CRF and segment matching to further improve the prediction accuracy. The approach makes the utmost of temporally-related information for traffic forecasting and effectively overcomes the problem of data sparsity.
2. Our mechanism evaluates the experiments comprehensively with large scale taxi GPS traces and environmental information obtained in Wuhan. Experimental results manifest that C-Sense mechanism can obtain robust performance in prediction precision.

2 Related Works

Many approaches existed have utilized time-dependent pattern of traffic flow evolution for traffic flow prediction. Auto regressive integrated moving average (ARIMA) model [3, 4] use time-series features, i.e. previous traffic flow of a specific segment, to predict the future traffic flow, which do not use extra data except traffic information. Yuan and Zheng [5] propose constructing an m_{th}-order Markov chain, which combines current traffic condition and state transition probability to predict the traffic condition after a period of time. The state transition probability is counted with historical data of the predicted road segment. However, this approach, exploring the evolution of traffic pattern in time sequence using historical and real-time traffic flow, is only a statistic method and has some uncertainty. The variance-entropy-based clustering approaches [6, 7] estimate the predicted time of objected road segments according to the travel time distribution in various time slots obtained by clustering historical data. These approaches utilize the main idea of clustering with generality.

The feature learning based approach about traffic flow condition prediction is considered in [8], which learns features without any prior knowledge through training a Deep Belief Network. However, the resources for abstracting features in this deep architecture only consist of the transportation information. It does not consider other traffic-related information to play out its potential for traffic prediction.

3 C-Sense: Temporal Feature Learning Based Traffic Prediction

Our mechanism includes two main steps: CRF-based temporal feature learning and sequence segments matching. With learning supplementary pre-extracted environmental features, CRF approach is trained to estimate the current state of traffic flow. And then, the temporal state sequences obtained from CRF can be matched with historical state sequence segments for future state prediction.

3.1 Preliminary

Taxi Trajectory: A trajectory denotes a temporal sequence of GPS points in a trip, where each consecutive point contains a geospatial coordinate set and a timestamp. Spatial trajectories collected by GPS-equipped taxis are mapped onto a road network using a map matching algorithm [10] and then they are stored into a traces database.

Road Segment/Link: A road segment/link is a directed edge including a direction symbol, two terminal points and a length between two crossroads.

Traffic Flow Condition: Traffic flow is utilized to indicate traffic condition of road segments. Because of different road situations and flow limits on distinct road segments, classifying traffic states according to absolute flow value is apparently erroneous. We classify the traffic conditions into five states based on the degree of traffic congestion, denoted as $\Omega = \{$congesting (Cg), slow (Sl), normal (Nm), moderate (Md), unimpeded $(Un)\}$.

Specifically, considering the road segment R from 0 o'clock to 24 o'clock, we collect the traffic flow o_i after per time interval Δt (e.g. 15 min). Hence, a sequence of traffic flow observations O (e.g. o_1, o_2, o_3, $\cdots$, o_{96}) can be acquired. Then we adopt K-means algorithm to categorize these traffic flow observations into five states as mentioned before. By applying the average values of the 5 subsets, we can get the corresponding traffic flow conditions.

Environmental Feature Extraction: We select some environmental features that related to the traffic—road noise, temperature, wind speed, PM2.5 and rainfall, denoted by a 5-dimensional vector $E_m = [e_1, e_2, e_3, e_4, e_5]$, where e_i ($i = 1, 2, ..., 4, 5$) is the value of each feature.

3.2 CRF-Based Temporal Feature Learning

The characteristic mode and temporal evolution rule of the traffic flow state of a segment or road are investigated by using linear-chain CRF method [9], considering the temporal-related features such as E_m of the segment. CRF, a kind of conditional probability model for annotation and segmentation of data in order, is a discriminative probability undirected graphical learning model based on hidden Markov models and maximum entropy Markov models. Whereas HMM is necessarily local in nature because they are constrained to binary transition and emission feature functions, which force each state to depend only on the current label and each label to depend only on the previous label, then CRF can use more global features. Normalizing each node, MEMM can only find the local optimal value with the problem of label bias, i.e. any condition which does not appear in training corpus is all ignored. However, CRF can obtain the global optimal value with the global normalization of all features. Building the special case of a linear-chain CRF, features are restricted to dependence on only the current and previous labels instead of arbitrary labels throughout.

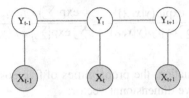

Fig. 1. Temporally-related feature learning CRF model

As shown in Fig. 1, an undirected graph G consists of two kinds of nodes. The white nodes $Y = \{Y_1, Y_2, \cdots, Y_n\}$ represent traffic flow state variables at continuous time stamps, connected with supplementary features represented by blue nodes $X = \{X_1, X_2, \cdots, X_n\}$, $X_t = \{E_m, t\}$. Under observation sequence x, each random variable Y_i obey the Markov property, i.e. $p(Y_v|X, Y_u, u \neq v) = p(Y_v|X, u \sim v)$ (u and v are adjacent nodes in G). Given observation sequence x at time t, the probability of each possible state for Y_t is defined as follows:

$$P(y|x, \lambda) = \frac{\exp(\sum_j \lambda_j t_j(y_{t-1}, y_t, x, t) + \sum_k \mu_k s_k(y_t, x, t))}{\sum_l \exp(\sum_j \lambda_j t_j(y_{t-1}, y_t, x, t) + \sum_k \mu_k s_k(y_t, x, t))} \quad (1)$$

where $t_j(y_{t-1}, y_t, x, t)$ is the transfer feature function depending on the current time t and previous time $t - 1$, $s_k(y_t, x, t)$ represents the state feature function depending on the time t, y_t denotes the traffic flow state at time t. When meeting the known deterministic feature conditions, the value of t_j or s_k is 1, otherwise 0. λ_j and μ_k can be estimated from training data.

Assuming that there is a bunch of samples which are independent of each other in training data set $Data = \{x^{(q)}, y^{(q)}\}$, $q = 1, \cdots, n$, maximum likelihood estimation learning $p(y|x, \lambda)$ is used to learn the parameters λ by gradient descent algorithm [11].

$$L(\lambda) = \sum_q [\log \frac{1}{\sum_y \exp[\sum_j \lambda_j f_j(y_{t-1}, y_t, x, t)]} + \sum_j \lambda_j f_j(y_{t-1}, y_t, x, t)] \quad (2)$$

Writing $s_k(y_t, x, i) = s_k(y_{t-1}, x, t)$, two feature functions are unified into $f_j(y_{t-1}, y_t, x, t)$, which includes an observation sequence x, the time t, the current state y_t and the previous state y_{t-1}. Assuming that there are K_1 transfer feature functions and K_2 state feature functions under the given deterministic feature conditions, $K = K_1 + K_2, f_j(y_{t-1}, y_t, x, t)$ is represented as follows:

$$f_j(y_{t-1}, y_t, x, t) = \begin{cases} t_j(y_{t-1}, y_t, x, t), & j = 1, 2, \cdots, K_1 \\ s_k(y_t, x, t), & j = K_1 + k; k = 1, 2, \cdots, K_2 \end{cases} \tag{3}$$

Assigning each feature function f_j a weight λ_j and given an observation sequence x, Eq. 1 can be transformed as follows:

$$P(y|x, \lambda) = \frac{\exp[p(y|x, \lambda)]}{\sum_y \exp[p(y|x, \lambda)]} = \frac{\exp[\sum_j \lambda_j f_j(y_{t-1}, y_t, x, t)]}{\sum_y \exp[\sum_j \lambda_j f_j(y_{t-1}, y_t, x, t)]} \tag{4}$$

Through the above equation, the probabilities of five possible states for Y_t can be informally denoted as a five-dimensional vector:

$$P(t) = [p(y_t = Cg), p(y_t = Sl), p(y_t = Nm), p(y_t = Mo), p(y_t = Un)] \tag{5}$$

3.3   Sequence Segments Matching

After applying CRF classifier to output a state vector of traffic flow at each time stamp, a state sequence segment can be obtained. Through finding similar state segments in history, we can obtain the state of traffic flow at the predicted time stamp according to the sequence matching with historical sequence segments. Because there may be no identical state sequence segments, measuring the similarity between sequence segments is necessary for sequence matching. Commonly used Euclidean distance is not suitable for the distance measurement of time-series sequences, which leads to the utilization of a non-linear time alignment approach, namely dynamic time warping (DTW).

In the process of state sequence segment matching, assuming that the current time is t_{ct}, a traffic state sequence segment obtained from CRF classifier in advance is represented as $S = (s_{t_{ct}-n\cdot\Delta t+1}, \cdots, s_{t_{ct}-\Delta t}, s_{t_{ct}})$ and a predicted traffic state after time t_l can be denoted as $s_{t_{ct}+t_l}$. DTW-based segment matching algorithm, shown in Algorithm 1, is employed to procure adequate matching segments through measuring DTW distances between the given state sequence segment and historical segments $S^* = (s^*_{t_{ct}-n\cdot\Delta t+1}, \cdots, s^*_{t_{ct}-\Delta t}, s^*_{t_{ct}})$. In this algorithm, the predicted sequence segment is warped non-linearly in time dimension to determine the similarity with historical segments. A constant threshold ε is defined to filter adequate traffic flow state segments in history according to the DTW distances which are less than the chosen threshold, i.e. $DTW^{(i)}[t_{ct}][t_{ct}] \leq \varepsilon$. Assuming there are m adequate historical segments chosen through DTW-based segment matching algorithm, so we can get m state probability vectors of 5-dimensional at the predicted time $t_{ct} + t_l$, where i_{th} probability vector is represented as $P^{(i)}(t = t_{ct} + t_l) = [p^{(i)}(s^*_t = Cg), p^{(i)}(s^*_t = Sl), p^{(i)}(s^*_t = Nm), p^{(i)}(s^*_t = Mo), p^{(i)}(s^*_t = Un)]$. In the above formula, $S^{*(i)}$ is the i_{th} adequate historical sequence segment, $P^{(i)}(s^*_t = s)(s \in \Omega)$ represents the probabilities of five possible states at the predicted time $t_{ct} + t_l$ according to the i_{th} historical segment $S^{*(i)}$. Since $w^{(i)}$ is the weight of i_{th} historical segment and can be calculated as:

$$w^{(i)} = \frac{DTW^{(i)}[t_{ct}][t_{ct}]}{\sum\limits_{i=1}^{m} DTW^{(i)}[t_{ct}][t_{ct}]} \tag{6}$$

we can compute the weighted vector at the predicted time t ($t = t_{ct} + t_l$) as the final state result:

$$P(t = t_{ct} + t_l) = \sum_{i=1}^{m} w^{(i)} \cdot p^{(i)}(t = t_{ct} + t_l) \tag{7}$$

Algorithm 1. DTW-based segment matching algorithm

Input: Historical segments:

$\qquad S^{*(i)} = (s_{t_{ct}-n\cdot\Delta t+1}^{*(i)}, \cdots, s_{t_{ct}-\Delta t}^{*(i)}, s_{t_{ct}}^{*(i)})$ $(i=1,2,\cdots,m)$

$\qquad$ Predicted segment: $S = (s_{t_{ct}-n\cdot\Delta t+1}, \cdots, s_{t_{ct}-\Delta t}, s_{t_{ct}})$

Output: Adequate historical segments
Procedure:
1: **for** $S^{*(i)}$ $(1 \le i \le m)$
2: $\quad$ **for** $t_{ct}-n\Delta t+1 < j,k \le t_{ct}$ do
3: $\qquad$ Distance$^{(i)}[j][k] == 0$;
4: $\qquad$ DTW$^{(i)}[j][t_{ct}-n\Delta t+1] ==$ inf;
5: $\qquad$ DTW$^{(i)}[t_{ct}-n\Delta t+1][k] ==$ inf;
6: $\quad$ **end;**
7: $\qquad$ DTW$^{(i)}[t_{ct}-n\Delta t][t_{ct}-n\Delta t] == 0$;
8: $\quad$ **for** $t_{ct}-n\Delta t+1 < j,k \le t_{ct}$ do
9: $\qquad$ Distance$^{(i)}[j][k] = (s_{k-1}-s_{j-1}^{*(i)})*(s_{k-1}-s_{j-1}^{*(i)})$
10: $\quad$ **end;**
11: $\quad$ **for** $t_{ct}-n\Delta t+1 < j,k \le t_{ct}$ do
12: $\qquad$ DTW$^{(i)}[j][k]$ = Distance$^{(i)}[j][k]$ + Min(DTW$^{(i)}[j-1][k-1]$,
$\qquad\qquad\qquad\qquad\qquad\qquad\qquad$ DTW$^{(i)}[j][k-1]$,
$\qquad\qquad\qquad\qquad\qquad\qquad\qquad$ DTW$^{(i)}[j-1][k]$);
13: $\quad$ **end;**
14: $\quad$ **if** DTW$^{(i)}[t_{ct}][t_{ct}] \le \varepsilon$
15: $\qquad$ output $S^{*(i)}$;
16: $\quad$ **end;**

---

4 Performance Evaluation

4.1 Datasets

We utilize the datasets of Wuhan for our traffic flow prediction and select a representative region to evaluate the performance of our mechanism. Three available datasets are used as following:

(1) Road Network: We adopt the road network of Wuhan to perform the experiments. Figure 2 shows a snapshot of the road network of the Wuchang district in Wuhan at the rush hour (5 pm).
(2) Taxi Trajectories: We perform the evaluations based on the trajectory data sets of 30,000 taxis covering three months from January to March in 2013. In the dataset, the total space is about 450 million kilometers, and the whole number of GPS points reaches 890 million. The sampling interval is 4.5 min between two consecutive points.
(3) Environmental data: We collect environmental resources consisting of road noise, PM2.5, wind speed, rainfall and temperature from a public website.
(4) Ground truth: The ground truth we used in our paper is the actual traffic flow which can be achieved from camera sensors on the road.

Fig. 2. The road network of Wuchang district in Wuhan

4.2 Performance

We define five numbers for five states to indicate the forecasted state and its corresponding probability, e.g. $\Omega = \{$congesting $(Cg) = 1$, slow $(Sl) = 2$, normal $(Nm) = 3$, moderate $(Md) = 4$, unimpeded $(Un) = 5\}$. The state number n_r^t represents the valued road segment state of the road segment r at the time stamp t. If a road segment traffic flow state is predicted as the state n_r^t and the probability is p, the predicted state value of the road segment is defined as $n_r^t - 1 + p$, e.g., when the predicted state of a road segment is Nm and the corresponding probability is 0.9 generated by C-Sense approach, then the predicted state value is 2.9.

Figure 3 shows the traffic flow condition prediction of temporal feature learning approach with the prediction time $\varphi = 15$ min. It is obvious that the prediction values are more close to the actual values especially in the early morning hours (from 1:00 am to 5:00 am). In addition, Fig. 4 represents that the comparison about the traffic flow condition prediction of three different approaches in a day with the prediction time $\varphi = 60$ min. Existing approaches cannot perform well when it is early in the morning. It can be inferred that in the morning hours, without enough taxi trajectories which can provide us sufficient data to learn the conditions of traffic flow, temporal feature learning approach can effectively extract the temporally-related features of traffic flow to make a supplement and obtain higher prediction accuracy, rather than only utilizing traffic information like in the other two approaches. However, the traffic prediction accuracy of C-Sense in the rush hours is lower because of complicated environmental information containing some noisy data. It can be seen that temporal feature learning approach have better prediction effect on compensating for sparse data since it takes full advantage of supplementary information especially such as road noise that provides effective information to improve the prediction accuracy when in the midnight time.

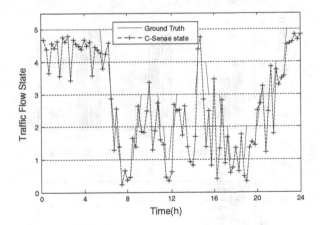

Fig. 3. Traffic state prediction of C-Sense mechanism

The precision and the recall of three approaches is shown in Fig. 5. As is shown in Fig. 5(A) and (B), under the same prediction time, C-Sense can obtain higher precision and recall than two other approaches. C-Sense comprehensively uses traffic flow information and temporally-related supplementary features in the traffic network. We can also conclude that combining temporally-related supplementary features used by CRF to overcome the problem of sparse data, the prediction result of C-Sense can be further improved.

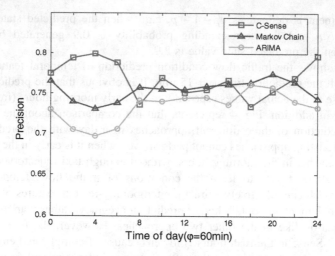

Fig. 4. Precision of different methods in a day

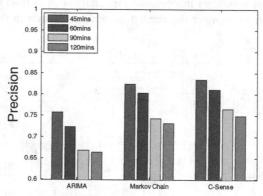

A) Precision of three different methods

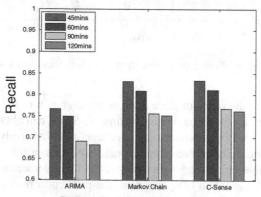

B) Recall of three different methods

Fig. 5. Study on three different methods

5 Conclusions

This paper presents a temporal traffic flow feature learning mechanism, namely C-Sense, for traffic condition prediction with large scale taxi GPS traces and environmental information. C-Sense effectively overcomes the problem of data sparsity and takes full advantage of temporally-related information for traffic forecasting. In C-Sense, environmental features which can reflect traffic flow change is utilized by CRF as a supplement. Our approach is evaluated using trajectory data of 30,000 taxis in Wuhan, which manifests that our method can improve the prediction accuracy efficiently.

Acknowledgements. This work was partially supported by National Key Basic Research Program of China "973 Project" (Grant No. 2011CB707106), Development Program of China "863 Project" (Grant No. 2013AA122301), National Natural Science Foundation of China "NSFC" (Grant No. 61103220, 61303212) and the Program for Changjiang Scholars and Innovative Research Team in University (Grant No. IRT1278).

References

1. Yuan, N.J., Zheng, Y., et al.: T-finder: a recommender system for finding passengers and vacant taxis. IEEE Trans. Knowl. Data Eng. **25**(10), 2390–2403 (2013)
2. Liu, S., Liu, Y., Ni, L.M., et al.: Towards mobility-based clustering. In: Proceedings of 16th ACM SIGKDD, pp. 919–928 (2010)
3. Van Der Voort, M., Dougherty, M., Watson, S.: Combining Kohonen maps with ARIMA time series models to forecast traffic flow. Transp. Res. Part C Emerg. Technol. **4**(5), 307–318 (1996)
4. Moorthy, C.K., Ratcliffe, B.G.: Short term traffic forecasting using time series methods. Transp. Plan. Technol. **12**(1), 45–56 (1988)
5. Yuan, J., Zheng, Y., Xie, X., et al.: Driving with knowledge from the physical world. In: Proceedings of the 17th ACM SIGKDD International Conference on Knowledge Discovery and Data Mining, pp. 316–324. ACM (2011)
6. Yuan, J., Zheng, Y., Zhang, C., et al.: T-drive: driving directions based on taxi trajectories. In: Proceedings of the 18th SIGSPATIAL International Conference on Advances in Geographic Information Systems, pp. 99–108. ACM (2010)
7. Yuan, J., Zheng, Y., Xie, X., et al.: T-drive enhancing driving directions with taxi drivers' intelligence. IEEE Trans. Knowl. Data Eng. **25**, 220–232 (2013)
8. Huang, W., Hong, H., Li, M., Hu, W., Song, G., Xie, K.: Deep architecture for traffic flow prediction. In: Motoda, H., Wu, Z., Cao, L., Zaiane, O., Yao, M., Wang, W. (eds.) ADMA 2013, Part II. LNCS, vol. 8347, pp. 165–176. Springer, Heidelberg (2013)
9. Lafferty, J., McCallum, A., et al.: Conditional random fields: probabilistic models for segmenting and labeling sequence data. In: Proceedings of 18th International Conference on Machine Learning, pp. 282–289, June 2001
10. Thiagarajan, A., Ravindranath, L., LaCurts, K., et al.: VTrack: accurate, energy-aware road traffic delay estimation using mobile phones. In: Proceedings of the 7th ACM Conference on Embedded Networked Sensor Systems, pp. 85–98. ACM (2009)
11. Liu, L., Feig, E.: A block-based gradient descent search algorithm for block motion estimation in video coding. IEEE Trans. Circ. Syst. Video Technol. **6**(4), 419–422 (1996)

Security of Cyber Physical System

Yaowen Zheng[1,2], Hong Li[1,2], Zhiqiang Shi[1], and Limin Sun[1(✉)]

[1] Institute of Information Engineering, Chinese Academy of Sciences, Beijing, China
{shizhiqiang,sunlimin}@iie.ac.cn
[2] University of Chinese Academy of Sciences, Beijing, China
{zhengyaowen,lihong}@iie.ac.cn

Abstract. Cyber Physical System (CPS), which is based on the environment perception, combines computing, communications, and control processes effectively. Through the interaction and the feedback loop between physical space and cyber space, it implements the function of real-time sensing and dynamic control. The view of this paper will firstly describe the structure of CPS and its security issues in industry applications. Then it explains the security threats and defines the security goal, comprehensively analyses the key technologies to solve the system's security issues from the perspective of system's protection, detection and resilience, and finally expects the development of cyber physical system's security.

Keywords: Cyber physical system · Information flow security · Authentication · Patch management · Privacy preserving · Risk assessment · Detection · Resilience

1 Introduction

With the development of computer and network technologies, people's life becomes more and more convenient. Nowadays, people's requirement for computer equipment and systems is not just the extension of system function. They pay more attention to rational allocation of system resources and system's operational performance [1]. In this context, an intelligent system named CPS starts to develop.

CPS is a developing networking and intelligent system consisting of 3C (calculation, communication, control) modules, and its goal is to realize the deep integration and cooperation of 3C and to achieve the function of real-time sensing and dynamic control [2]. It mainly consists of a physical layer and a cyber layer (Fig. 1). The physical layer is composed of sensors, actuators, and devices that integrate the functionality of both sensors and actuators. These devices tightly interconnect with the physical world and effectively sense and control the physical process. They also have capability of autonomous coordination and computation. Sometimes, the actuator in the physical layer can represent human and other life entities. The cyber layer interconnects physical devices by means of wired or wireless connection, which promotes the communication and feedback control of devices.

© Springer-Verlag Berlin Heidelberg 2015
L. Sun et al. (Eds.): CWSN 2014, CCIS 501, pp. 558–567, 2015.
DOI: 10.1007/978-3-662-46981-1_53

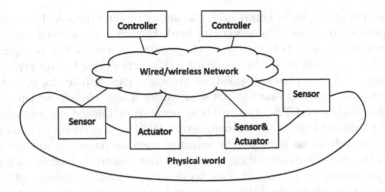

Fig. 1. Structure of CPS [1]

As we know, CPS is widely used in many fields. In smart grid, CPS interconnects distributed generators which are unstable and adjusts electricity load dynamically and accurately, so as to assure the real-time matching between the electricity generation and consumption. In intelligent transportation system, CPS interconnects the sensors and actuators that are spread among automobiles, roads and people. It realizes autonomy and corporation between automobiles which will reduce the number of traffic accidents and ease traffic congestion. In medical treatment, CPS helps doctors monitor and record patient's physiological status remotely. And CPS can make the portable medical equipment complete some simple treatment such as injecting drug automatically and accurately according to the patient's condition.

However, CPS faces serious security challenges and they will bring great threaten to people's life and property. In American DEF CON 21, two researchers demonstrate how to intrude the automobile's inner electronic control unit (ECU) and launch the high privileged operations such as break failure and crash protection, which will threaten passenger's life [3]. Also, a hacker named Jack claimed that he implements intruding the heart pacemaker nine meters away and control it to send out 30 V voltage which can kill a patient [4]. It is observed that the research on CPS security is extremely urgent.

So in the Sect. 2, we will firstly analyze security threats of CPS which do not exist in traditional IT network, and then define the goal of CPS security. And in the Sect. 3, we summarize the key technologies that achieve CPS security goal. Finally, there will be a concluding part in the Sect. 4.

2   The Goal of CPS Security

As CPS has some particular characteristics that traditional IT network does not have, it faces many unique security threats. Different with traditional IT network, the device in the physical layer of CPS need to provide computation resources for the whole system, which will carelessly leak private information to public. For example, in smart grid, the smart meter's data will be employed by the system to balance the electricity load. However, if the data leaks to the public, the consumer's behavior (e.g., sleep patterns, number of occupants) at home will be deduced. Also, the operation in the cyber layer is strongly coupling with variation in the physical world, so attackers can deduce the operation in the cyber layer by observing the physical world. These threats seriously affect the confidentiality of CPS. And in CPS, because of limited computation and memory resources, Public Key Infrastructure (PKI) is too costly to be deployed on CPS. So only some light weight schemes such as password authentication are used to ensure authentication. But it is quite insecure that attackers can easily masquerade as privileged roles to enter into system. Besides, CPS is a real time system, that means the system works almost all the time and has very transient downtime. Different with IT network, CPS only has little time to patch vulnerabilities. So we do not have enough time to test whether the patch will affect the regular operation or not. And we also have no enough time to fix all the vulnerabilities. Therefore, existing attack will continue threatening the system for a long time until the next patch.

Above are some threats that do not exist in traditional IT network. So the objective of the paper is to analyze and solve the threats that do not exist in traditional IT network. Therefore, we will summarize some technologies that can protect system from known threats that are mentioned above. Then, to some unknown attacks which are also threatened to CPS, We cannot figure out them, so we must have robust detection technologies to identify them. Moreover, when the damage caused by attacks has entered into system, we must need some technologies to guarantee the system resilient to it and reduce the loss as much as possible. So the goal of CPS security in the paper is to protect the system from known threats that only exist in CPS, to detect unknown attacks and to keep the system resilient to attacks.

3 Key Technologies of CPS Security

In order to achieve the security goal of protecting the system from known threats that only exist in CPS, detecting unknown attacks and keeping the system resilient to attacks, we will analyze and summarize the technologies in these three aspects respectively.

3.1 System Protection

In system protection, we will study the technologies that relate to the particular threats in CPS. So we will study privacy preservation, information flow security, authentication mechanism, patch management and risk assessment these five representative aspects.

Privacy Preservation. These years, there are two main technical routes for privacy preservation: secure multi-party computation and data anonymization.

Secure multi-party computation is a privacy preservation technique based on data encryption. It refers that each of multiple parties calculates according to a certain agreement, and only knows its inputs and results after computation, so the technique ensures that computation does not leak the private information. Two algorithm prototypes are included: secure accumulative agreement and privacy homomorphism [5]. In WiFi Fingerprint-Based Localization, [6] employed the technology of privacy homomorphism to keep client's location and the server's data private. Data anonymization is a privacy preservation technique based on constraints. It refers not to release or selectively release low precision information to achieve privacy preservation. Of course, this technology makes a trade off between losing integrity and exposing privacy. A method of data anonymization named k-anoymization can ensure data privacy and at the same time reduce the information loss as much as possible. Reference [7] proposed a localization privacy preservation mechanism based on k-anoymization technology.

In the future, these two technologies will have their limitation. Traditional secure multi-party computation is not efficient. As CPS has high demand for timeliness, the deployment of traditional way will affect the efficiency of regular operation. A homomorphic encryption algorithm based on ideal lattice was proposed [8]. The algorithm is implemented on hardware circuit, so it will be efficient for CPS. In wireless sensor network and Internet of Things, sensor data is just collected for analysis, data error is tolerable. But in CPS, sensor data will be used as an input of decision-making machine to control the physical world, it needs high accuracy. So how to extend k-anoymization technology and make it suitable for CPS privacy preservation is a meaningful research work in the future. Besides, to some particular CPS, there will be some other strategies to preserve the privacy. In smart gird, the system can take advantage of battery and make it charged and discharged at strategic time to hide the appliance loads from smart meters [9].

Information Flow Security. In CPS, the operation in the cyber layer is strongly coupling with variation in the physical world, so we can deduce the operation in the cyber layer by observing the variation in the physical layer. Because of the characteristic of information flow in CPS, traditional access control mechanism may fail in preventing information leaking from the high-level region to the low-level region, and in this way information confidentiality in high-level region is tampered [10]. And this problem is defined as information flow security. Reference [11] presented a theory of event compensation which enforces the information flow security for CPS and verifies this concept by testing it on DC circuit. Reference [12] employed trace-based and automated process-algebra-specification-based analysis approaches to analyze the information flow security. Reference [13] proposed a self-obfuscating system based on the concept of nondeducibility. By understanding and reconstructing the interactive semantics between the cyber and physical layer, the high-level region's information is kept secret to the low-level observer.

Compared to traditional IT network, information flow security is a particular security issue in CPS. No matter how robust other security mechanisms are, if this mechanism is not well guaranteed, the system is still insecure. The research on the construction of semantic model and analysis approach is mature, and the future work may be focused on employing the approach to different systems.

Authentication Mechanism. In CPS, actuators in the physical layer may be people or other life entities. As they own specific properties (e.g., pulse, iris, fingerprint), we can use them to produce keys for authentication. And they are difficult to be cracked and forged by others, so the authentication mechanism constructing on these properties has high-level security. Reference [14] took the ECG signal that is measured by heart pacemaker to produce the key for authentication, to verify whether the accessor is a legitimate doctor or not. In addition, the material derived by pseudo random source can also be used for authentication. Reference [15] proposed an approach to verify whether the data origin belongs to the same power gird by comparing the feature called Electrical Network Frequency.

On one hand, the key material derived by biological features or pseudo random sources need to have large entropy, so as to avoid the brute force attack. On the other hand, we must prevent others stealing the key material by social engineering or other illegal ways. Reference [16] proposed an approach to estimate patient's inter-pulse interval using a web cameral at the distance of nearly 50 cm from human subjects. The approach brings serious threat to authentication in medical CPS. We need to solve these two issues in the future.

Patch Management. When the known vulnerability is found on the system, we will patch to fix the system and protect it from security attacks. Compared with traditional IT network, CPS is a real time system, that means the system works almost all the time and has very transient downtime. Then it results in very limited time for patching. Therefore, we need to conduct patch management in a different way in CPS. In industrial control fields, the system requires at least 99.999 % uptime. This requirement relates to 5 min and 35 s downtime every year [17]. So it is very important to conduct patch management effectively.

In [17], it described the whole procedures that form a good patch management program. To patch testing, Edison Electric Institute advised that patching firstly need to be applied on some unimportant devices for testing and then on critical devices [18]. To vulnerable analysis, [17] developed four primary elements (Impact, Exposure, Deployment, Simplicity) to identify the risk level of vulnerabilities. Besides, the risk associated with the patch also includes the potential impact to business operations.

The research work of patch management about CPS is rare, and it will be a meaningful work to quantify the impact the patching affecting the system's availability.

Risk Assessment. Nowadays, we have limited budgets and resources to protect CPS's security. We must put them to the most critical or weakest component. Therefore, we need conduct risk assessment to find the most critical or weakest component. So we need risk assessment. And the first step is to develop attack model, assuming the attack method and its legality. Then we get all the possible attacks' consequences by experiment. Finally, we can find out which part in system need to be protected urgently.

In smart grid, [19] simulated the function of real-time data reading and dynamic change of current and voltage, and evaluated the delayed price information's impact on the advanced meter infrastructure, modified load information's impact on load distribution and dispatch, and composite data's impact on energy management. Based on vulnerability of closed loop in pricing system, [20] assessed the impact of integrity attack including scaling and delayed attack on real-time pricing system. Reference [21] assessed the impact of integrity and DoS attack on Tennessee-Eastmanprocess control system, and found out the most significant sensor and that system should prioritize defenses against integrity attacks rather than against DoS attacks. From another perspective, although CPS is opened and interconnected, information asymmetry results in the fact that the local optimal decision is not consistent with the global optimal decision. In order to solve the problem, [22] proposed a game-theoretic approach to benchmark this problem.

3.2 System Detection

As we cannot figure out all the security attacks threatened to CPS, we need a robust system to detect unknown security attacks. System detection techniques in CPS can be classified into two categories: network-based detection and device-based detection.

Network-Based Detection. Network-based detection is to develop the model based on network flow and log data, which can distinguish attack patterns from normal patterns. In traditional IT network, there are three approaches to detect attacks: signature-based, anomaly-based, and specification-based approaches [23]. The first approach is blacklist-based and needs to set up a feature database of malicious attacks while the latter two approaches are whitelist-based and need to train normal behaviors. In whitelist-based approaches, specification-based model has higher accuracy than anomaly-based model.

As the number of operation and state in CPS is few, the manager often adopts specification-based model. In [24] and [25], it explains the reason why advanced meter infrastructure and medical CPS use this detection model. Furthermore, we need to keep two issues in mind. First, what features to select that can effectively distinguish attacks from normal behaviors. In the advanced meter infrastructuremodeling the collected log data using 4 rand markov chains in smart collectors, and using linear temporal logic to set up features, the detection module can effectively detect mimicry and evasion attacks [26]. Then, we need to distinguish attacks from malfunction. In smart grid, the price's changing will lead to a situation that when price is low, consumers will frequently use high power appliances, finally it will promote a new load peak or even blackout.

It belongs to system malfunction, but the method can be utilized by adversary to launch an attack. So we need to distinguish them. Reference [27] proved that fault-detection algorithms do not work against attackers, so it may provide some ideas about how to distinguish attacks from malfunctions.

As we know, network will produce a large amount of logs and warning messages every day. One piece of warning message cannot provide detail information about system condition. We need an effective scenario to analyze them and extract the useful information which can help the manager fully recognize the features and the path of attack. At present, the detection module often employs the data reduction model to analyze the logs and warning messages. The model will lose much useful information which affects the overall analysis. One feasible way is to use data containing model which does not require the data normalization. It can complete the function of real-time searching and is easy for statistics, relevance and analysis [28].

Device-Based Detection. Due to heterogeneity of physical devices, each device in physical layer has differences on protocol processing and character interpretation. The network-based detection cannot take all various devices into account, and some detection evasion technologies can bypass the network-based detection module. For example, Due to different ways of interpretation of character set between the intrusion detection module and some physical devices, it is possible to transmit strings that are harmful for physical devices but cannot be recognized by the network detection module. So we need to detect attacks by analyzing status of physical devices. That is device-based detection. As CPS has high demand on timeliness, if parts of code operates much longer than it does in usual time, the warning of attacks need to be launched. Reference [29] proposed an approach to estimate whether or not the system suffers from code injection attack according to the running time of code. In addition, detecting compromised node in CPS is very important. When sensors or actuators are compromised, an attacker can obtain the session keys which will make other security mechanisms break down. Reference [30] described several approaches to detect compromised nodes in wireless network.

However, device-based detection has its limitation. For example, in advanced meter infrastructure, due to limited computation capability and memory resources of smart electric meters, it is not suitable to embed the detection module into meters. Simultaneously, operator and hardware vendors cannot allow the widely embedding of detection modules in smart meters because of the costs increment in redevelopment.

3.3 System Resilience

In CPS, system's resilience is important. It requires that CPS can continue completing the task normally when attacked, and that means it is quite tolerated to security attacks. There are some schemes to improve the resilience of CPS. Redundancy of physical devices can prevent a single-point failure [31].

Diversity can prevent that one attacked vendor will compromise all the physical devices and the separation of privilege and the principle of least-privilege can reduce the privilege an attacker will have when he or she corrupts the device [31]. To redundancy, [32] analyzed the ring topology of network which can raise the capability of system's redundancy and self-recovery. Besides, the capability of situation awareness and fine-grained isolation are also important.

Situation Awareness. In CPS, the capacity of situation awareness can promote the system's resilience. Sensors are widely distributed in remote places, so they may suffer attacks or malfunctions and the intrusion detection module inner them will work in abnormal condition. In this way the wrong detection results will affect the judgment at cyber layer which then give false feedback to devices. Therefore, CPS need have the capability of situation awareness, and distinguish which parts of the sensors are trusted. Reference [33] constructed the graph structure of equipment alarm and found sensors that are truly trustworthy so that we can get meaningful alarm from them. Reference [34] not only considered the heterogeneity of devices, also gave different semantics to different types of data so that the model can develop different algorithm for different device's reputation.

Fine-Grained Isolation. Fine-grained isolation in CPS can also promote the intrusion tolerance capability [35]. In smart grid, the system is divided into several subsystems according to the business logic which can resist many attacks expanding such as flooding attack. In industry control fields, the system is divided to 5 regions that are cooperate network, demilitarized zone, process network, control network and field devices. Different regions are isolated by firewall gateways, which can prevent damage propagating between different regions. The gateway must make a trade off between efficiency and security. If the firewall is simply package filtering or state detection, it cannot discover the threat at application layer. But if the firewall pays more attention to the security, the configuration will be complex and will affect the performance of network. So it remains an issue.

4 Summary

To conclude, we firstly introduce the physical structure of CPS and claim the importance of CPS security. Then we explain the CPS's security particular threats and the goal. Next, the core of the paper, is to address the CPS security issues from the perspective of system protection, detection and resilience. Our security solutions are related to the technologies of information communication, and do not contain control theories. The future work need to take them into account. In addition, many security mechanisms are not referred in the paper, because we think they are nearly the same in CPS and traditional IT network. CPS is at beginning of development, so some technologies and ideas still remain open to questions. We are aimed at bringing interests and attention to more and more scientists, and laying the foundation of follow-up work.

References

1. Wang, Z.J., Xie, L.L.: Cyber-physical systems: a survey. Acta Automatica Sin. **37**(10), 1157–1166 (2011). (in Chinese)
2. Li, Z.: Security threats and measures for the cyber-physical systems. Tsinghua Univ. (Sci. Tech.) **52**(10), 1396–1408 (2012). (in Chinese)
3. DEF CON 21 Hacking Conference. http://www.defcon.org/html/defcon-21/dc-21-index.html
4. black hat USA (2013). http://www.blackhat.com/us-13/
5. Oleshchuk, V.: Internet of things and privacy preserving technologies. In: 2009 1st International Conference on Wireless Communication, Vehicular Technology, Information Theory and Aerospace & Electronic Systems Technology, vols. 1 and 2, pp. 297–301 (2009)
6. Li, H., Sun, L.M., Zhu, H.J., Lu, X., Cheng, X.Z.: Achieving privacy preservation in WiFi fingerprint-based localization. In: 2014 Proceedings of IEEE INFOCOM, pp. 2337–2345 (2014)
7. Yang, D., Fang, X., Xue, G.: Truthful incentive mechanisms for k-anonymity location privacy. In: 2013 Proceedings of IEEE INFOCOM, pp. 2994–3002 (2013)
8. Gentry, C.: Fully homomorphic encryption using ideal lattices. In: Proceedings of the 41st Annual ACM Symposium on Theory of Computing (STOC 2009), pp. 169–178 (2009)
9. Yang, W., Li, N., Qi, Y., Qardaji, W., McLaughlin, S., McDaniel, P.: Minimizing private data disclosures in the smart grid. In: Proceedings of the 2012 ACM Conference on Computer and Communications Security, pp. 415–427 (2012)
10. Gamage, T., Akella, R., Roth, T., McMillin, B.: Information flow security in cyber-physical systems. In: Proceedings of the Seventh Annual Workshop on Cyber Security and Information Intelligence Research, p. 52 (2011)
11. Gamage, T.T., McMillin, B.M., Roth, T.P.: Enforcing information flow security properties in cyber-physical systems: a generalized framework based on compensation. In: 2010 IEEE 34th Annual Computer Software and Applications Conference Workshops (COMPSACW), pp. 158–163 (2010)
12. Akella, R., Tang, H., McMillin, B.M.: Analysis of information flow security in cyberCphysical systems. Int. J. Crit. Infrastruct. Prot. **3**, 157–173 (2010)
13. Gamage, T.T., Roth, T.P., McMillin, B.M.: Confidentiality preserving security properties for cyber-physical systems. In: 2011 IEEE 35th Annual Computer Software and Applications Conference (COMPSAC), pp. 28–37 (2011)
14. Rostami, M., Juels, A., Koushanfar, F.: Heart-to-heart (H2H): authentication for implanted medical devices. In: Proceedings of the 2013 ACM SIGSAC Conference on Computer & Communications Security, pp. 1099–1112 (2013)
15. Chuang, W.-H., Garg, R., Wu, M.: How secure are power network signature based time stamps? In: Proceedings of the 2012 ACM Conference on Computer and Communications Security, pp. 428–438 (2012)
16. Poh, M.Z., McDuff, D.J., Picard, R.W.: Non-contact, automated cardiac pulse measurements using video imaging and blind source separation. Opt. Express **18**, 10762–10774 (2010)
17. Tom, S., Christiansen, D., Berrett, D.: Recommended practice for patch management of control systems. In: DHS Control System Security Program (CSSP) Recommended Practice (2008)
18. Edison Electri Institute. http://www.eei.org

19. Wei, M., Wang, W.: Greenbench: a benchmark for observing power grid vulnerability under data-centric threats
20. Tan, R., Badrinath Krishna, V., Yau, D.K., Kalbarczyk, Z.: Impact of integrity attacks on real-time pricing in smart grids. In: Proceedings of the 2013 ACM SIGSAC Conference on Computer & Communications Security, pp. 439–450 (2013)
21. Cardenas, A.A., Amin, S., Lin, Z.-S., Huang, Y.-L., Huang, C.-Y., Sastry, S.: Attacks against process control systems: risk assessment, detection, and response. In: Proceedings of the 6th ACM Symposium on Information, Computer and Communications Security, pp. 355–366 (2011)
22. Amin, S., Schwartz, G.A., Hussain, A.: In quest of benchmarking security risks to cyber-physical systems. IEEE Netw. **27**, 19–24 (2013)
23. Berthier, R., Sanders, W.H., Khurana, H.: Intrusion detection for advanced metering infrastructures: requirements and architectural directions. In: 2010 First IEEE International Conference on Smart Grid Communications (SmartGridComm), pp. 350–355 (2010)
24. Berthier, R., Sanders, W.H.: Specification-based intrusion detection for advanced metering infrastructures. In: 2011 IEEE 17th Pacific Rim International Symposium on Dependable Computing (PRDC), pp. 184–193 (2011)
25. Mitchell, R., Chen, R.: Behavior rule based intrusion detection for supporting secure medical cyber physical systems. In: 2012 21st International Conference on Computer Communications and Networks (ICCCN), pp. 1–7 (2012)
26. Ali, M.Q., Al-Shaer, E.: Configuration-based IDS for advanced metering infrastructure. In: Proceedings of the 2013 ACM SIGSAC Conference on Computer & Communications Security, pp. 451–462 (2013)
27. Liu, Y., Ning, P., Reiter, M.K.: False data injection attacks against state estimation in electric power grids. ACM Trans. Inf. Syst. Secur. (TISSEC) **14**, 13 (2011)
28. Concept and characteristics of Next Generation Security. NSFOCUS (2013)
29. Zimmer, C., Bhat, B., Mueller, F., Mohan, S.: Time-based intrusion detection in cyber-physical systems. In: Proceedings of the 1st ACM/IEEE International Conference on Cyber-Physical Systems, pp. 109–118 (2010)
30. Mathews, M., Song, M., Shetty, S., McKenzie, R.: Detecting compromised nodes in wireless sensor networks. In: Eighth ACIS International Conference on Software Engineering, Artificial Intelligence, Networking, and Parallel/Distributed Computing, SNPD 2007, pp. 273–278 (2007)
31. Cardenas, A., Amin, S., Sinopoli, B., Giani, A., Perrig, A., Sastry, S.: Challenges for securing cyber physical systems. In: Workshop on Future Directions in Cyber-Physical Systems Security (2009)
32. Yang, G.: A topological analysis of industrial ethernet redundancy and self-recovery, automation Panorama (2009). (in Chinese)
33. Tang, L.-A., Yu, X., Kim, S., Han, J., Hung, C.-C., Peng, W.-C.: Tru-alarm: trustworthiness analysis of sensor networks in cyber-physical systems. In: 2010 IEEE 10th International Conference on Data Mining (ICDM), pp. 1079–1084 (2010)
34. Li, W., Jagtap, P., Zavala, L., Joshi, A., Finin, T.: Care-cps: context-aware trust evaluation for wireless networks in cyber-physical system using policies. In: 2011 IEEE International Symposium on Policies for Distributed Systems and Networks (POLICY), pp. 171–172 (2011)
35. Codella, C., Hampapur, A., Li, C.-S., Pendarakis, D., Rao, J.R.: Continuous assurance for cyber physical system security. In: Workshop on Future Directions in Cyber-Physical Systems Security (2009)

Design and Implementation of Smart Home Linkage System Based on OSGI and REST Architecture

Shanyan Gao[1], Hongsong Zhu[2(✉)], Xinyun Zhou[2],
Yan Liu[1], and Limin Sun[2]

[1] School of Software and Microelectronics, Peking University,
Beijing 102600, China
gaoshanyan001@126.com, ly@ss.pku.edu.cn
[2] Institute of Information Engineering, Chinese Academy of Sciences,
Beijing 100095, China
{zhuhongsong,zhouxinyun,sunlimin}@iie.ac.cn

Abstract. Smart Home, a typical application scene of Internet of Thing, recently has attracted wide attention from industry to academic circles. There are many heterogeneous devices in smart home environment, which makes it difficult to integrate, make united management and work with each other for different subsystems. Based on the above issues, this paper designs and implements a smart home linkage system based on the OSGI and REST architecture. It consists of four subsystems, which are as follows: environment perception subsystem, home appliances control subsystem, video monitoring subsystem and intelligent analysis and linkage control subsystem. Combined the advantages of OSGI and REST, the software architecture of it has solved three issues mentioned above. On the basis of prototype system, this paper makes several concerning experiments in the overall system delay and linkage delay to verify the performance of it.

Keywords: Internet of Thing · Smart home · REST · OSGI · Software architecture · Linkage rules

1 Introduction

The concept of smart home first appeared in the United States. With the platform of residence, smart house is a kind of the efficient, safe, convenient and environmental living environment collecting system, structure, service and management, something of construction equipment, network communications, information appliances and equipment automation. It is the instrumented embodiment under the influence of the Internet, which is also the inevitable result of infiltrating development from computer technology, network technology, and control technology from the traditional home. Through the Internet of Things technology, it connects various home devices (such as audio equipment,

© Springer-Verlag Berlin Heidelberg 2015
L. Sun et al. (Eds.): CWSN 2014, CCIS 501, pp. 568–582, 2015.
DOI: 10.1007/978-3-662-46981-1_54

lighting systems, curtain control, AC control, etc.) together to provide a variety of functions like appliance control, lighting control, curtain control, etc. At present, smart home is defined as a system organically combining the various subsystems related to home life through the family information management platform, with the use of computers, networks, and the sum of cabling technology. Compared with ordinary home, smart home not only has a traditional residence features, but also helps us to keep information exchange smoothly between families and outside, to optimize people's lifestyles, to arrange a time effectively, and to enhance the security of home life, even to save funds for various energy cost [1].

In the smart home application scenarios, the heterogeneity of subsystems for various access devices have resulted in large difficulties to the systems integration. So how to shield the heterogeneity of the various subsystems and use a unified platform for management and collaborative work between various subsystems calls for immediate solution. Firstly, this paper analyzes briefly for the current background of smart home, raising the issue that it is necessary to integrate each application subsystem and to manage and publish services uniformly, as well as the collaborative work in the home-made scenarios. Then it analyzes the study progress of other domestic and foreign experts and scholars on this issue. After that, this thesis proposes smart home linkage system architecture based on OSGI and REST, and describes the design and implementation of the system in details. Finally, the system is validated to show its value.

2   Related Works

At home and abroad, many researches about system integration, service united management and release, and cooperative work problem in the household scenario have been made in one or more aspects. The gateway model proposed by Zhu Qian provides a solution of how heterogeneous devices connect to the IOT and highlights the importance of the gateway in the communication between sensor network and the IOT [2]. Ma Shiming puts forward a converged system architecture of smart home based on SOA which can integrate the different services together in application scenario. However, users can not manage various services effectively and the collaborative problem between different services was not mentioned [3]. For the application scenario of device heterogeneity and service diversity, Choonhwa Lee comes up with OSGI architecture to establish an open service platform [4] which is controllable, extensible and can access multiple devices. Zhanghaitao raises three-layer smart home control system architecture [5]. Wuchaolin presentes a service-oriented smart home software architecture which addresses the complex communication problem resulted from the dynamic changes of the mobile terminals and servers [6]. These three articles all emphasize that OSGI architecture has positive effect on the integration of subsystems and users can manage kinds of applications in the home scenario. However, they rarely mention the cooperative service among systems. In the term of Internet of Things, Zhang Xinshuang proposes the design of IOT Platform based on

REST architecture [7]. Regrettably, he just formulates the constraints of REST architecture and the feature of its URI, but not verify them in the real smart home system.

From the point of technology, Web Service finishes abstraction from a higher level and realizes the communication across software on different platform. But its key communication protocol SOAP, as the standard is put forward continually, becomes more and more bloated, more and more complicated to operate. When encountering some complicated requirements, Web Service technology seems very heavy which leads to cumbersome user interaction and device management in application scene, and the centralized management ability of the service becomes weaker. Compared with the Web Service, OSGI implements a local, centralized and service-oriented architecture. By maintaining a built-in service registry, components can make use of the service registry to find and use service, thus a dynamic architecture orienting service is formed within the framework. So, the OSGI performs well in system integration and unified management of various services in application scene. REST is a resource-oriented architecture and it can uniquely identify one kind of resource application scenario. At the same time according to a unified interface constraint, it sets the unified interface of communication, through which users can conduct all kinds of operations for resources. REST architecture provides a lightweight Web services solution case, through providing a unified interface, it gives great support on all the integrated services release.

Based on the above analysis, we designes and implemented a smart home linkage system of the architectural style based on OSGI and REST. The system realizes the centralized management of three different application scenario using OSGI architecture, releases external unified interfaces and manages the resources in the application scene based on REST architecture. Besides, through the message queue mechanism, it also makes a try on service collaboration.

3 System Architecture Design

3.1 System Architecture

The system is divided into four parts: wireless sensor node, smart home gateway, business platform and mobile user terminal. They are respectively located in device layer, device access layer, business platform layer and application layer. The whole architecture is as Fig. 1.

Sensor nodes mainly realize the control of home appliance and the data interaction among home gateway, upload the sensor data and accept user commands. The home gateway is the bridge of communication between sensor nodes and business platform, and plays a role in the collection and report of sensor data, collection and distribution of control command, and the conversion of communication protocol. Business platform plays a role of the service provider in this system, whose core tasks are the data management, service management and business logic processing. In the implementation process, it provides a unified URI interface externally (to the smart terminals and home gateway) based on

Fig. 1. Smart home system overall architecture

REST architecture style. The main functions of user terminal include providing users with interactive interfaces, sending control commands to the business platform, and obtaining data from the business platform. Namely getting the relative data from the business platform, providing the interactive interface to the user, and then sending the user's control operation to the business platform to process.

In this architecture, terminals of different communication protocol carry out the report of perceived data through accessing home gateway. The business platform provides a unified access interface to shield the heterogeneity of terminals and realizes the undifferentiated process with intelligent terminal and home gateway.

3.2 REST

REST is short for Representational State Transfer, which establishes the unified interface among communication according to the unified interface constraints, provides kinds of operations on the resources through these interfaces and only one group of operations are allowed for one kind of resource. HTTP limits the kinds of operations on resources to four interfaces: GET, PUT, POST and DELETE. This is the way that service provider maintains a group of resource and provides the corresponding unified operation interface to operate. In the application scenario of smart home, the business platform is designed and accomplished in the form of REST architecture style. URI, namely Uniform Resource Identifier, is a method to identify resource address in the REST architecture. The defined format of traditional URI doesnt have strong regularity and high flexibility, resulting in the great difficulty in maintaining, which is even worse with the number of resource access interfaces increasing. In the process of URI design in the business platform, according to the different characteristics of data, we redefine a new URI format to achieve the easy maintenance and easy management after reconstructing the data.

The actual business flow data can be divided into three levels: Feed, DataStream and DataPoint. The Feed refers to the space or device owning sensors, which can be physical environment like room, mobile phone, forest, etc. DataStream stands for the sensors in the environment, such as temperature, humidity, illumination, infrared, acceleration, switches, etc. These can be regarded as different type of DataStream. DataPoint represents the data in data flow at a specific time point. For example, a piece of real-time temperature data reported from temperature node. Based on this, the URI design of Feed, DataStreams and DataPoints in business platform. Taking the DataPoint Request URI for example: http://.../version/feeds/feedId/datastreams/datastreamId/datapoints/time stamp. In the above example, the data contained in " " are variables, varying with the version of the application system. This kind of design nearly covers the operation of adding, deleting, updating and searching on the data in the smart home environment. For example, to get all the device information in the scene, the URI is "http://.../vl/feeds/all", and to delete the data (each kind of node can obtain one or more kinds of perceiving data at same time) from the temperature flow whose Id is 70 (assume the Id of temperature flow is 10), the URI is "http://... /v1/feeds/70/datastreams/10". Therefore, this model effectively implements a unified interface, and has certain popularization value.

Business platform adopts REST architectural style. By redesigning the URI model, it not only manages resources effectively, but also shields the heterogeneity of the underlying devices. It can make terminals which have different operating system, implementation methods and communication protocol accessing in a unified way, thus greatly improving the extensibility and maintainability of the system.

3.3   OSGI

OSGI is short for Open Service Gateway Initiative, which is a typical representative of plugin architecture, and it is a series of service specification based on Java formulated by the OSGI alliance. Besides, it accomplishes OSGI Service Platform according to these specifications. The OSGI platform has the features of dynamic software components management, components remote control, security implementation link and simplify deployment. It provides developers the mechanism of dynamic operation module, and the dynamically module adding, deleting, updating mechanism at running time.

In the business platform of the system, REST provides all the management of resources in the application scenarios, including searching, updating, deleting, adding and so on. These devices are distributed in different application subsystems. The OSGI conducts a unified management on each subsystem, including service registration, release and deletion to make user can grasp the real-time running state of each subsystem in the application scene.

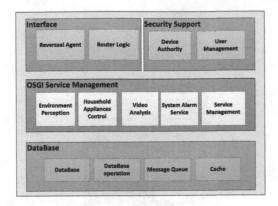

Fig. 2. Function block diagram of business platform

4   System Implementation

4.1   Business Platform Implementation

Business platform mainly includes four parts: Interface Layer, Security Support Layer, OSGI Service Layer and Data Layer. The structure diagram is as shown in Fig. 2.

The interface layer mainly includes the reverse proxy module and the routing logic module. Generally speaking, the Reverse Proxy refers to the way that the proxy server receives connections requests from the Internet, then forwards the request to the server in the internal network, and returns the result obtained from the server to the client requesting connection in the Internet. At the time, the proxy server functions as a server for external. At this point, the reverse proxy is an access interface to the client provided by the business platform. Because of the statelessness of business platform, it is responsible for receiving the request from client (the mobile clients or gateways) in the process of implementation, and then passes the requests to go through authority certification for the judgments of next step. For the routing logic, as the introduction of the information URI model in Sect. 3.1, the same type of URI may take on different types of data requests, especially the request using POST method, which is necessary to determine the parameters passed. According to the type of request, it will call different processing logic to response the user request. As a result of the complexity and changing of request type, in order to maintain the good extensibility, we encapsulate the routing process into routing processing module to achieve the implementation depends on abstraction rather than concreteness, which also conforms to the principles of design pattern.

Security support layer mainly includes two modules: authority certification and user management, which mainly provide the security support to the user and device accessed in the whole system. Authority certification mainly realizes the judgments on the access permissions of users and devices. User management mainly realizes the user registration and the deletion, updating or searching of

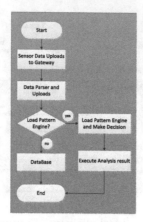

Fig. 3. System linkage rule functional flow diagram

user information. User information module includes not only the basic information, but also the permission information owned by the user in the system.

The OSGI service management layer has the core function in the business platform which associates user interface and data layer. It not only deals with the user request, including controlling the household appliances, reporting the perceived data, managing the sensors itself device information or user information, analyzing and reporting alarm information, but also realizes the functions of service management, such as registration, deletion and query of service. All these functions make various application services integrated, uniformly managed and published. In order to make the service to work together, this layer implements the intelligent analysis and alarm service. This service is mainly realized by rule engine, which are mainly used for the real-time analysis and alarm of the data reported from sensor node. When a sensor node receives any exceptional formation, users can get alarm information in real time. Linkage business process rules are shown in Fig. 3. The rules set by the system are as follows: When someone gets close to the infrared node, the user will receive real-time information notification from the mobile terminal and the corresponding light will be opened at the same time; When indoor humidity is lower than the threshold value set by user, the humidifier automatically opens; when the indoor illumination is less than the threshold value of user setting, indoor lights will automatically open, otherwise, shut down lights automatically. All the thresholds can be configured in the mobile client.

Data layer belongs to the underlying business platform, it provides users with data adding, querying, updating and deletion support, which mainly contains database, related operation module, message queue (RabbitMQ) and cache (Memcache). Message queue is based on the Publish/Subscribe architecture, which can make the traditional data transmission changes from C/S mode to the C/S/C mode. The transition of data transmission mode makes data transmission more effective and directly, which to meet the requirements of strong

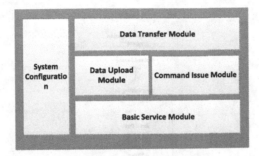

Fig. 4. Function block diagram of gateway

real-time data transmission. Cache is designed for the requirement that users frequently request a large number of database data, such as get the current sensory value from temperature node every 3 s. Cache can speed up the client response time.

Electronic Map is realized by Web ArcGIS and gets source data through AJAX. Those data define the campus information. According to the specific data of different attributes of each campus, this map can display the student's number respectively. It can also be added to a given campus dynamically which should be added the latitude and longitude of the name attributes. Each of the campus icons has two buttons, "video monitoring" and "statistics", which respectively jump to the personnel technical page.

4.2 Home Gateway Implementation

Home Gateway is an important subsystem of system communication layer. It solves the communication and interaction between the sensor network and Ethernet communication, which are heterogeneous network. Home Gateway could allow the upper application layer to get the sensory data from senor network, and transfer the control command from application layer to sensor node through sensor network.

Figure 4 describes the function module of Home gateway. Gateway and sensor network data commutation with each other via reading and writing the serial port. The module of reading and writing serial port listens the serial port of Zigbee communication module, read sensory network data from serial port, transfer the data to data manage module and write the control command from command manage module to the serial port of Zigbee communication module for sending the data to sensor network. Protocol conversion module is responsible for data parsing and encapsulation, which means parse and encapsulate the data from data source into the data format that the receiver needs. On the business requirements, it can transform the sensor data of Zigbee protocol which from sensor network into the data of Ethernet TCP/IP protocol and also transform the data of Ethernet from business platform into data of Zigbee protocol. Data management module manage and storage the data which is obtained from

Fig. 5. Data reporting flow of gateway

sensor network. Ethernet communication module is responsible for the communication among the business platforms. Order management module is responsible for receiving and processing the commands of business platform. It sends the configuration management command from business platform to configure management module and also sends the node control commands from business platform to protocol conversion for issuing the data in package. Configuration management module records the gateway hardware and software configuration information and modifies the configuration information (IP, port, etc.) according to the configuration management commands from business platform.

Figure 5 describes the process of gateway submits data. Firstly, it starts the communication agent for preparing for the data that is submitted to business platform. Secondly, if there exists data from sensor nodes in serial port, including equipment status and node acquisition data, system will parse the data, encapsulate the data into data format which business platform required, and writing the data into the report queue. Finally, system will upload data of report queue to the business platform to process through the communication agent. Figure 6 describes the process of gateway commands issues commands. Firstly, it starts the communications agent for preparing the commands that issued by business platform. Secondly, if the serial ports revives the command, system will parse the command data, encapsulate the data according to the sensor network communicate protocol and write in the issued command queue. Finally, the program of reading and writing from serial port will write the date from issued command queue into serial port. The above two business processes are executing in circle, so there is no exit step.

4.3 Sensor Nodes Implementation

Sensor nodes are at the bottom of subsystems. It is not only responsible for data acquisition, which undertakes the work of data entry, but also completes the commands that upper layers issue. Sensor nodes collect data and submit

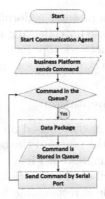

Fig. 6. Data sending flow of gateway

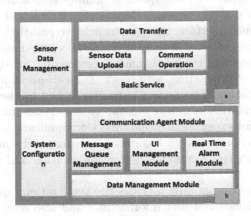

Fig. 7. Sensory node function block diagram/function block diagram of mobile client

to Home Gateway through wireless, and need get user control command from gateway at the same time to complete the command control operation.

(a) Diagram of Fig. 7 describes the function module of sensor nodes. Basic service module is responsible for collecting sensory data periodically. The object of collecting data is different according to different types of nodes, such as temperature, humidity, illumination, gate magnetism, switch node status, etc. Data upload module is responsible for uploading the data that the nodes obtain, including basic sensory data and network status data. If the node is common node, the data will upload to the cluster head nodes. If the node is cluster head node, the data will directly write into the serial port that connected with the gateway. Data transmission module is a wireless sensor network transmission protocol management module, which completes the interaction communication among sensor network. Command agent module is responsible for parsing the sensor node control command issued by gateway and execute these commands, such as parsing the switch command to control intelligent switch to control home appliances, time synchronization or enter a dormant state, etc. Sensor network management module is responsible for collecting the network information relate with sensor network, including network topology, signal strength, etc. And then send all the information in heartbeat packets to cluster head node.

4.4 Android Client Implementation

Intelligent mobile client is implemented based on the android system, it mainly realizes the interaction between the user and the business platform. The function block diagram is shown as (b) diagram of Fig. 7.

(b) Diagram of Fig. 7 describes the functional module of android mobile client. Data management module is responsible for data analysis in the process of system initialization and the cache or update operations of parameters in the process of the operation. Message queue is mainly responsible for transferring server-side distributed alarm message. Because the REST is stateless, there is no initiative data sending interface. In order to achieve real-time delivery of alarm information, we have adopted queue mechanism which has a good real-time capability. UI management module is mainly responsible for the switch of interface in the process of interaction with users. Data display module shows users the following information: The devices currently owned by the user, the current and historical information of sensory data, video stream information and the alarm information for exceptional situations. Communication agency is responsible for communications between business platforms, and communication data types include user control command, device information and real-time pushing alarm data, etc.

System configuration not only includes the registration, update, modify and delete function of device and user information, and also reserves for customers the function of linkage parameters configuration, which can make linkage rules changing with user choice. According to seasonal changes, for example, the appropriate data of temperature and humidity which the users feel comfortable is changing. At the time user can configure these parameters through the mobile terminal in real time. According to user's configuration, business platform will automatically adjust the linkage rule. Users can also custom linkage rules. According to the system default options, users can dynamically configure to generate the new rules, and submit them to the business platform. Then, the system will run in accordance with the newly added rules. The number of rules configuration is not unique, which can be multiple and rules engine will load all the rules for execution. If conflicts between rules are caused by human negligence, the rules engine will automatically dispose to avoid system crash.

5   System Verification

5.1   Testing Environment

This testing environment is set up according to the system deployment diagram, it contains the following devices:

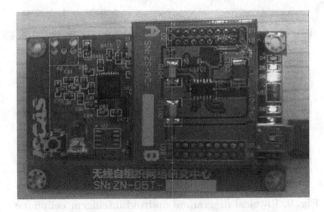

Fig. 8. Physical diagram of temperature and humidity sensor node

Sensory Node: There are 11 sensory nodes. Among them, there are two temperature sensor nodes, two humidity sensor nodes, one light sensor node, one acceleration node, and five intelligent switch node. The physical diagram are shown in Fig. 8.

Home Gateway: One Mina6410 ARM development board from the Youshanzhibi company in Guangzhou.

Business Platform: A business platform system which deployed on PC. It runs on JDK 1.6 runtime environment and Windows XP operating system.

User Terminal: A user terminal which deployed on android intelligent cellphone. Its physical diagram is shown in Fig. 9.

5.2 System Delay Analysis

As a real-time linkage system, this system has a high requirement on time delay. Overlong time delay will have a great impact on the linkage effect. Therefore, in order to test the delay of this system, we proceed in two aspect: system overall time delay and linkage time delay.

System Overall Delay Testing. For this test, the testing method is as follows: We send control commands (on or off) to a normal running switch node for 100 times continuously through the Android client, then calculate the average of the delay of gateway, the delay of platform and the total delay. Repeat eight times, record the result and do some analysis. The system overall delay testing is divided into two parts, the first part is the delay from Android terminal to the business platform, this contains the time delay of network transmission

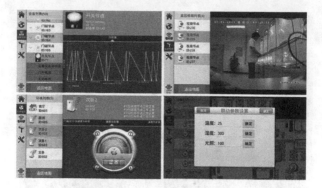

Fig. 9. Physical diagram of android intelligent cellphone

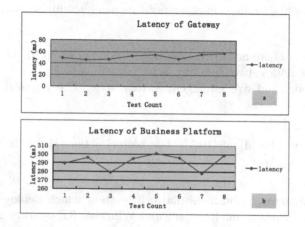

Fig. 10. Curve chart of gateway delay/curve chart of platform delay

and program delay; The second part is the delay from business platform to operations performed by the control nodes, the delay of network transmission and node response time delay are also included in this part. Due to the restricted laboratory environment, the second part of the network time delay may exist some error from the real network time delay. The final testing results are shown in (a) of Fig. 10, (b) of Fig. 10 and (c) of Fig. 11.

Linkage Delay Testing. For this test, we set the linkage rule is when someone is shaking acceleration node, the signal will submit to business platform and the platform responds immediately to open the lamp to prompt the user. The test method is as follows: Prepare a well running acceleration node and five switch node. Shake the infrared node every 2 s for 50 times continuously to calculate the average total delay from people begin shake to lamp open every time. Repeat eight times, record the result and do some analysis. Linkage delay contains two parts: first is the delay of shaking signal transmission to the business platform,

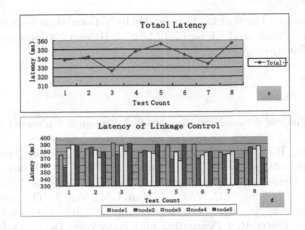

Fig. 11. Curve chart of total delay/bar chart of linkage delay

which includes the delay of receiving signals and the network transmission delay. Second is the delay from business platform to the switch node, which includes the delay of signal processing on business platform, command transmission delay and command execution delay. The final testing results are shown in (d) of Fig. 11.

(c) of Fig. 11 shows that the total delay is controlled in 350 ms, and the gateway delay accounts for 10 %–20 %, while the delay of platform accounts for 80 %–90 %. This also shows that in the system, the delay of data sending from home gateway to the sensor network and data receiving delay is not very high. The main time delay comes from the communication time delay between business platform and gateway, or between business platform and user terminal. Because this kind of time delay is much influenced by the Internet signal, it is not stable. From (d) of Fig. 11 shows the total linkage delay is around 380 ms, 30 ms higher than the total system delay. The main reason is that the linkage requires to across the gateway for two times (to report sensory signals and control command of node through the gateway) which leads to increasing delay. From the test, we can conclude that the total delay and linkage delay have small impact on the users experience, which can meet user requirements in general.

6 Conclusion

This paper describes the design and implementation of smart home linkage system based on OSGI and REST architecture in detail. The architecture design of this system makes use of the powerful management functions for service from OSGI architecture as well as the great advantages of resource management from REST architecture. A combination of both provides a feasible solution on system integration of different applications, unified management publishing of service, and cooperative work among services in home scenario. However, further research on user management, resources permission management and system security management are still needed.

Acknowledgement. The work has been funded by National High Technology Research and Development Program of China (2012AA050804) and National Natural Science Foundation of China(61202066).

References

1. Sun, L.M.: Wireless Sensor Networks, pp. 6–8. Tsinghua University Press, Beijing (2006)
2. Zhu, Q., Wang, R.C., Chen, Q., Liu, Y., Qin, J.: IOT gateway: bridging wireless sensor networks into internet of things. In: 2010 IEEE/IFIP 8th International Conference on Embedded and Ubiquitous Computing (EUC), pp. 347–352 (2010)
3. Ma, S.N., Chen, X., Song, G.C., Wang, J., Sun, L.M., Yan, J.: The converged service oriented architecture in smart home service. In: 2012 International Conference on Cyber-Enabled Distributed Computing and Knowledge Discovery (CyberC), pp. 237–240 (2012)
4. Lee, C., Nordstedt, D., Helal, S.: Enabling smart spaces with OSGi. IEEE Pervasive Comput. **2**(3), 89–94 (2003)
5. Zhang, H.T., Wang, F.Y., Ai, Y.F.: An OSGi and agent based control system architecture for smart home. In: 2005 IEEE Proceedings of the Networking, Sensing and Control, pp. 13–18 (2005)
6. Wu, C.L., Liao, C.F., Fu, C.: Service-oriented smart-home architecture based on OSGi and mobile-agent technology. In: IEEE Transactions on Systems, Man, and Cybernetics, Part C: Applications and Reviews, vol. 37, no. 2, pp. 193–205 (2007)
7. Zhang, X.S., Wen, Z.G., Wu, Y.X., Zou, J.W.: The implementation and application of the internet of things platform based on the REST architecture. In: 2011 International Conference on Business Management and Electronic Information (BMEI), vol. 2, pp. 43–45 (2011)

Wireless Mobile Network Architecture, In-Vehicle Network

Reliability and Real-Time Analysis of Safety-Related Messages in VANET

Wei Sun, Hesheng Zhang[✉], and Cheng Pan

School of Electrical Engineering, Beijing Jiaotong University, Beijing, China
{10117350,hszhang,09117354}@bjtu.edu.cn

Abstract. In vehicular ad hoc network (VANET), IEEE 802.11p protocol has been adopted for transmitting the information through vehicle-to-vehicle and vehicle-to-infrastructure communication. Due to the dynamic topology and the real-time constraints, broadcast is an effective approach to deliver the safety-related messages. The reliability and real-time analysis of the safety-related messages can make better decisions on the adaptation and improvement of the standard. In this paper, a Markov chain model has been proposed to investigate the broadcast performance of IEEE 802.11p with two access categories (ACs). Based on the proposed model, closed form expressions, such as packet delivery ratio (PDR) and total delivery delay are derived, taking different ACs, hidden terminal problem and frozen mechanism into account. The obtained numerical results can be used to determine a good tradeoff between the implementation and the network parameters and also help to analyze the capabilities and limitations of the standard.

Keywords: VANET · IEEE 802.11p · Safety-related messages · Reliability and real-time analysis

1 Introduction

Vehicular ad hoc network (VANET) aims to improve road safety and effectives by applying the advanced information and communication technologies [1]. Safety applications provided by VANET are crucial to improve road safety. Broadcast is an effective approach to deliver the safety-related messages to notify the neighbor vehicles. The IEEE 802.11p protocol [2] based on enhanced distributed channel access (EDCA) mechanism has been adopted for delivering the safety-related messages in vehicular environments.

The reliability and real-time analysis of the safety-related message can help the protocol developers to analyze the capabilities and limitations of the IEEE 802.11p protocol. The performance analysis, which is an important and challenging problem, has been partially investigated in some recent publications.

In [3–5], the authors present a Markov chain to analyze the broadcast performance incorporating the backoff procedure and hidden terminal problem. The shortcoming of those papers is that the frozen mechanism is not considered. Yin et al. [6] propose a simi-Markov-Process considering the frozen mechanism to evaluate the performance of

© Springer-Verlag Berlin Heidelberg 2015
L. Sun et al. (Eds.): CWSN 2014, CCIS 501, pp. 585–592, 2015.
DOI: 10.1007/978-3-662-46981-1_55

broadcast service. A mean-decoupling approximation has been proposed in [7] to calculate the collision probability. However, the performance analysis of these papers focus on the IEEE 802.11 distributed coordination function (DCF) mechanism that is different from the IEEE 802.11p EDCA mechanism. In [8, 9], multiple types of the messages using EDCA mechanism are considered.

Comparing with the existing publications, the contribution of this paper can be summarized as follows: unsaturated traffic analytical model based on Markov chain has been proposed to investigate the broadcast performance of IEEE 802.11p. The performance metrics, such as packet delivery ratio (PDR) and the total delivery delay are derived for the reliability and real-time analysis, taking different ACs, hidden terminals and frozen mechanism into account.

The remainder of this paper is organized as follows: In Sect. 2, the analytical model is developed. We verify the proposed analytical model and discuss the obtained results in Sect. 3. Finally, the conclusion is given in Sect. 4.

2 Analytical Modeling and Performance Analysis

2.1 Model Assumptions

The safety applications aim to improve road safety by broadcasting two types of safety-related messages: event driven messages and period messages. Event driven messages are triggered by the vehicle which experiences or detects the dangerous behavior. Period messages are disseminated regularly to notify the current status information. Therefore, the former has the higher priority than latter, and all the messages should be received timely and reliable. In order to analyze the performance easily, we give the following assumptions:

1. A highway environment has been considered. And it can be abstracted into a one dimensional model, as shown in Fig. 1.

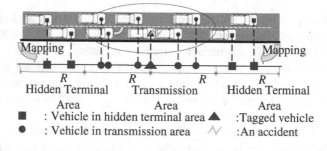

Fig. 1. Highway topology model

2. The vehicles are dispersed on the highway following a Poisson process with a parameter of β vehicles per unit meters.
3. The highest priority AC[3] is used for the event driven messages, while the lower priority AC[2] is for the routine messages. Both types of messages are generated according to a Poisson process with ratio λ_3 and λ_2, respectively.

4. All vehicles have the same range of R meters, such as sensing, transmission and receiving range. Let N_{tr} and N_{ph} denote the average number of vehicles in the transmission range and the hidden terminal area of the tagged vehicle, respectively. Then, $N_{tr} = N_{ph} = 2\beta R$.

Hence, according to the assumptions, each AC can be modeled as an M/G/1 queue.

2.2 Analytical Model

A Markov chain has been used to construct the broadcast model of AC[i] ($i = 3, 2$), one for event driven messages and the other for routine messages. Firstly, we should differentiate four following situations that a newly generated message may confront under unsaturated traffic condition [7]:

- A generated message of AC[i] finds its buffer empty and senses the channel idle for the AIFS[AC[i]], at this time the higher priority ACs do not initiate the transmission sequences.
- A generated message of AC[i] finds its buffer empty and senses the channel idle for the AIFS[AC[i]]. However, at this time the higher priority ACs initiate the transmission sequences. For AC[3], this situation cannot be encountered, due to the highest priority.
- A generated message of AC[i] finds its buffer empty but detects the busy channel during AIFS[AC[i]] period.
- A generated message of AC[i] finds its buffer nonempty.

The process can be represented using a Markov chain model, as shown in Fig. 2.

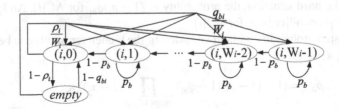

Fig. 2. Markov chain model for AC[i] ($i = 3, 2$)

The message will be sent when the backoff counter reaches zero. Hence, the transmission probability τ_i for AC[i] in any given slot time can be given as follows:

$$\tau_i = \frac{2(1 - p_b)}{2(2 - \rho_i)(1 - p_b) + (W_i - 1)[\rho_i + (1 - \rho_i)q_{bi}]} \tag{1}$$

The channel busy probability p_b during a slot time can be expressed as:

$$P_b = 1 - \sum_{j=0}^{\infty} \left\{ \left(1 - \sum_{i=2}^{3} \rho_i \tau_i\right)^j \frac{(N_{tr} - 1)^j}{j!} e^{-(N_{tr}-1)} \right\}$$

$$= 1 - e^{-(N_{tr}-1) \sum_{i=2}^{3} \rho_i \tau_i}$$

(2)

The probability q_{bi} that AC[i] detects the channel as busy during the AIFS[AC[i]] period, and it can be expressed as:

$$q_{bi} = 1 - (1 - P_b)^{\left\lceil \frac{AIFS[AC[i]]}{\sigma} \right\rceil}$$

(3)

Where $\lceil x \rceil$ represents the minimum integer no less than x, σ is a slot time.

The expression of queue utilization ρ_i is given as $\rho_i = \lambda_i E[S_i]$. Where $E[S_i]$ is the average service time of AC[i] and will be derived lately.

2.3   The Collision Probability Without Considering Hidden Terminal Problem

In this section, we derive the collision probability without considering hidden terminal problem, which means all vehicles are located at the transmission range of the tagged vehicle.

In the following, we give the probability of the four situations mentioned above. The probability for the first situation is $(1 - \rho_i)(1 - q_{bi}) \prod_{j \in hp(AC[i])} (1 - \tau_j)$, where $hp(AC[i])$ is a set of AC with the priority higher than AC[i]. For the second situation, the probability is $(1 - \rho_i)(1 - q_{bi})[1 - \prod_{j \in hp(i)} (1 - \tau_j)]$, except for the highest priority AC[3] which is zero. For the third situation, the probability is $(1 - \rho_i)q_{bi}$ for AC[i]. And for the last situation, the probability is ρ_i for AC[i].

The collision probability without considering the hidden terminals can be expressed as:

$$P_{dci} = (1 - (1 - \rho_i)(1 - q_{bi}) \prod_{j \in hp(AC[i])} (1 - \tau_j))P_b$$

(4)

The PDR is defined as the ration of the number of successfully received messages to the number of transmitted by the tagged vehicle [4, 6]. Consequently, we have:

$$PDR_i = 1 - P_{dci} \quad i = 3, 2$$

(5)

2.4   The Collision Probability Considering Hidden Terminal Problem

The collision between the tagged vehicle and the hidden terminals only occurs during the vulnerable period of AC[i] that is expressed as [3]:

$$T_{\text{vu ln } i} = \frac{2(E(L_i) + L_{\text{H}})}{R_{\text{d}}} \tag{6}$$

Where $E(L_i)$ is the average packet length of AC[i]; L_{H} is the length of message header including the physical layer header and the MAC layer header; R_{d} is data rate.

Therefore, the probability p_{phi} that no message from the hidden terminal collides with the message of AC[i] is expressed as:

$$p_{\text{phi}} = \left\{ \sum_{j=0}^{\infty} (1 - \sum_{i=2}^{3} \rho_i \tau_i)^j \frac{(N_{\text{ph}})^j}{j!} e^{-N_{\text{ph}}} \right\}^{\frac{T_{\text{vu ln } i}}{\sigma + P_b T_i}}$$
$$= e^{-N_{\text{ph}} \sum_{i=2}^{3} \rho_i \tau_i \frac{T_{\text{vu ln } i}}{\sigma + P_b T_i}} \tag{7}$$

Then, the collision probability due to the hidden terminals is given as:

$$p_{ci} = 1 - (1 - p_{dci})p_{\text{phi}} \tag{8}$$

The PDR considering the hidden terminal problem can be expressed as:

$$PDR_{\text{phi}} = 1 - p_{ci} \tag{9}$$

2.5 The Total Delivery Delay

The total delivery delay of AC[i], denoted by D_i, consists of the queuing delay Q_i, the access delay A_i and the transmission delay T_i. The sum of access delay and transmission delay is termed as service time and denoted as S_i. Hence:

$$D_i = Q_i + S_i = Q_i + A_i + T_i \tag{10}$$

$$T_i = \frac{(E(L_i) + L_{\text{H}})}{R_{\text{d}}} + AIFS[AC[i]] + \delta \tag{11}$$

Where δ is the propagation delay and it can be ignored.

The access delay is different for different ACs, and it can be expressed as:

$$A_3 = \begin{cases} 0 & \text{w.p. } (1 - \rho_3)(1 - q_{b3}) \\ B_3 + T_{cb} & \text{w.p. } (1 - \rho_3)q_{b3} \\ B_3 & \text{w.p. } \rho_3 \end{cases} \tag{12}$$

$$A_2 = \begin{cases} 0 & \text{w.p. } (1 - \rho_2)(1 - q_{b2})(1 - \tau_3) \\ B_2 + T_3 & \text{w.p. } (1 - \rho_2)(1 - q_{b2})\tau_3 \\ B_2 + T_{cb} & \text{w.p. } (1 - \rho_2)q_{b2} \\ B_2 & \text{w.p. } \rho_2 \end{cases} \tag{13}$$

Where, A_3 and A_2 are the access delay of AC[3] and AC[2], respectively; T_{cb} is the remaining channel busy duration, it assume equal to T; B_i is the backoff process duration, including the suspend time due to channel busy.

The duration of B_i can be derived in the following [7]:

$$B_i = \sum_{j=1}^{U_i} (\sigma + Y_i) \tag{14}$$

Where, U_i is the backoff counter of AC[i] and is uniformly chosen in range [0, W_i - 1]; Y_i is the interruption time caused by other messages transmission.

In the following, the expression of the service time and queuing delay are derived. $E[X]$ and $E[X^2]$ are the average and second moment of X, respectively. According to the independence of access delay and the transmission delay, we have:

$$E[S_i] = E[A_i] + E[T_i] \tag{15}$$

$$E[S_i^2] = E[A_i^2] + E[T_i^2] + 2E[A_i]E[T_i] \tag{16}$$

The average queuing delay $E[Q_i]$ of AC[i] can be obtained by the Pollaczek-Khintchine formula [10]:

$$E[Q_i] = \frac{\lambda_i E[S_i^2]}{2(1 - \lambda_i E[S_i])} \quad i = 3, 2 \tag{17}$$

3   Model Validation and Discussion

In this section, the numerical results regarding the analysis have been presented, and validated by NS-2 [11].

Figures 3, 4 and 5 presents the numerical results varied with the vehicle density, AC[i] (i = 3, 2) queue, the packet arrival rate, data rate and packet length. It can be observed that the analytical results agree well with the simulation results. Another observation from Fig. 3 is that the PDR is above 97 % for all AC when $\lambda = 2$; however, when $\lambda = 10$, the PDR decreases sharply as the vehicle density increases. Under the

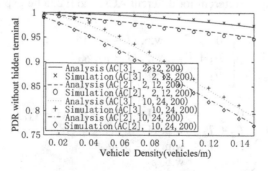

Fig. 3. PDR without considering hidden terminal

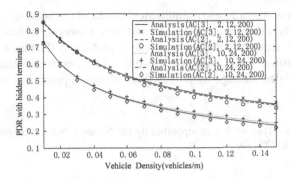

Fig. 4. PDR with considering hidden terminal

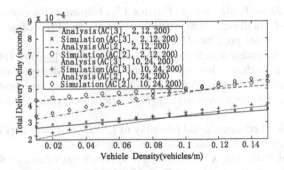

Fig. 5. Total delivery delay

same packet arrival rate condition, we also observe that AC[3] has a larger packet delivery ratio than AC[2].

From Fig. 4 we can observe that, the PDR drops when the vehicle density increases, and its value is below 90 %, which dissatisfy the safety application requirements of ASTM. However, little difference exists between ACs, because there is no priority differentiation for the messages among vehicles. Comparing Fig. 3 with Fig. 4, the results show that the hidden terminal problem is the major factor affecting the PDR.

As shown in Fig. 5 the total delivery delay almost increases linearly with the increase of vehicle density. Comparing with the $\lambda = 2$ case, the slope for $\lambda = 10$ is larger. The value of total delivery delay for higher priority AC is smaller than the lower one due to the internal schedule mechanism. And the results of the total delivery delay satisfy the real-time constraints.

4   Conclusion

In this paper, the unsaturated traffic analytical model based on Markov chain has been proposed to investigate broadcast performance of IEEE 802.11p and the results are validated by simulation. The performance metrics including PDR and the total delivery delay are derived for the reliability and real-time analysis. The proposed model is validated by simulation. According to the numerical results, it can be observed that the IEEE 802.11p can easily satisfy the real time constraints; however, it difficult to meet the reliability requirements. And the hidden terminal problem is the major factor affecting the PDR performance. In our future work, we should focus on the reliability improvement of safety-related message by proposed an effective approach to solve the hidden terminal problem.

Acknowledgments. This work was supported by the National Natural Science Foundation of China under Grant 61174179.

References

1. Figueiredo, L., Jesus, I., Machado, J., Ferreira, J.R., Martins de Carvalho, J.L.: Towards the development of intelligent transportation systems. In: Proceeding IEEE Intelligent Transportation System, pp. 1206–1211(2001)
2. IEEE 802.11p. Amendment to Standard for Information Technology Telecommunications and Information Exchange Between Systems Local and Metropolitan Area Networks-Specific requirements - Part11: Wireless LAN Medium Access Control (MAC) and Physical Layer(PHY) Specifications-Amendment 7: Wireless Access in Vehicular Environment (2010)
3. Ma, X., Chen, X.: Performance and reliability of DSRC vehicular safety communication: a formal analysis. EIRASIP J. Wirel. Commun. Netw. 1–13 (2009)
4. Chen, X., Refai, H.H., Ma, X.: A quantitative approach to evaluate DSRC highway inter-vehicle safety communication. In: IEEE GLOBECOM, Washington DC, USA, pp. 151–155 (2007)
5. Ma, X., Chen, X.: Performance analysis of IEEE 802.11 broadcast scheme in ad hoc wireless LANs. IEEE Trans. Veh. Technol. **57**(6), 3757–3768 (2008)
6. Yin, X., Ma, X., Trivedi, K.S.: An interacting stochastic models approach for the performance evaluation of DSRC vehicular safety communication. IEEE Trans. Comput. **62**(5), 873–885 (2013)
7. Hassan, M.I., Vu, H.L., Sakurai, T.: Performance analysis of the IEEE 802.11 MAC protocol for DSRC safety applications. IEEE Trans. Veh. Technol. **60**(8), 3882–3896 (2011)
8. Hafeez, K.A., Zhao, L., Liao, Z., Ma, B.N.: Performance analysis of broadcast messages in VANETs safety application. In: IEEE GLOBECIM, pp. 1–5 (2010)
9. Gallardo, J.R., Makrakis, D., Mouftah, H.T.: Mathematical analysis of EDCA's performance on the control channel of an IEEE 802.11p WAVE vehicular network. EURASIP J. Sel. Areas Commun. 485–529 (2010)
10. Trivedi, K.S.: Probability and Statistics with Reliability, Queuing and Computer Science Application, 2nd edn. Wiley, New York (2002)
11. http://www.isi.edu/nsnam/ns/

A Position Prediction Based Beacon Frequency Control Scheme for Vehicular Ad-Hoc Network

Jizhao Liu[✉] and Quan Wang

School of Computer Science and Technology, Xidian University,
No.2, South Taibai Road, Xi'an, Shanxi, China
liujizhao2009@163.com, qwang@xidian.edu.cn

Abstract. In VANET, frequent beacon broadcasting can lead to high bandwidth consumption and channel congestion. In this paper, a position prediction based beacon approach is proposed to reduce beacon frequency and decrease bandwidth consumption. Vehicles track their neighbors using the predicted position instead of beacon broadcasting periodically. Only when the prediction error is higher than predefined tolerance will a event-driven beacon broadcasting be triggered. We extract two typical vehicular motion statuses: the constant speed status and the maneuvering status. A motion detecting module is used to dynamically recognize current motion status, and an adaptive Kalman filter is employed to generate position prediction which can switch dynamically between the two statuses. The simulation results show the proposed scheme can significantly reduce beacon frequency. The beacon interval over 800 ms account for more than 80 % of the total in three traffic scenarios.

Keywords: Vehicular ad-hoc networks · Beacon message · Position prediction · Kalman filter

1 Introduction

Vehicular Ad-hoc NETworks (VANET) are receiving more and more attentions from academia and industry, since various kinds of applications can be provided for improvement of road safety and other potential benefits. VANET generally consist of on-board unit (OBU), road side unit (RSU) and a central trusted authority (TA). Vehicles can connect to each other (Vehicle-to-Vehicle: V2V), as well as with a nearby RSU (Vehicle-to-Infrastructure: V2I) [1].

In VANET, vehicles frequently broadcast beacon messages to inform neighbors with their status (position, speed, direction, etc.) for supporting various applications. This operation uses the WAVE/IEEE 802.11p technologies on the 5.9 GHZ band [2], and beacon messages are broadcasted periodically on a common channel (control channel). In some highly dense areas, frequent beacon broadcasting can cause high bandwidth consumption and channel congestion. It is important for the 802.11p standard that is based on the CSMA/CA protocol which could cause instability. We assume a single 10 MHz wide control channel

© Springer-Verlag Berlin Heidelberg 2015
L. Sun et al. (Eds.): CWSN 2014, CCIS 501, pp. 593–602, 2015.
DOI: 10.1007/978-3-662-46981-1_56

is used, the data rate of IEEE 802.11p standard is from 3 to 27 Mbps. According to previous works, the beacon frequency can be 1 to 10 times per second [3]. The size of a beacon message can reach more than 800 Bytes due to security-related overhead (signature, certification). In a highly dense area, there may be more than 200 vehicles within the wireless transmission range of a vehicle. If vehicles broadcast beacon at a frequency of 10 Hz, the channel load may be higher than 3Mb bandwidth provided by IEEE 802.11p standard.

2   Related Work

To avoid channel congestion caused by beacon messages, researchers have focused on the adapted beacon mechanism in various prospects, and some solutions have been proposed to reduce the channel overhead [4]. We classify existing solutions into two categories: transmission power control based schemes and frequency control based schemes.

M.T. Moreno et al. [5] assume that two kinds of messages (beacon and alert message) are broadcasted in the control channel for road safety related applications: beacon messages and alter messages. To avoiding channel congest caused by frequent beacon broadcasting, a distributed power control scheme is proposed to reduce the channel load caused by periodic beacon broadcasting. Y.P. Fallah et al. [6,7] argue that the tight mutual dependence of vehicular mobility, vehicles tracking applications and communication between vehicles should be paid more consideration. A scheme is proposed for this design process to simplify this coupled system. The proposed scheme consists of subcomponent model, devising interaction and a new algorithms for tightly coupled them.

Since frequent beaconing may lead to channel congestion, K.Z. Ghafoor et al. [8] proposed a adaptive beacon frequency control scheme which is based on fuzzy logic approach. The proposed scheme considers traffic characteristics, vehicular mobility (such as velocity, heading) and status of vehicles. They is used as the inputs of the fuzzy decision making system to dynamically adjust beacon frequency. S. Rezaei et al. [9] proposed a beacon frequency control scheme which is based on position prediction approach. Vehicles run a Kalman filter to predict future position for itself and all of its neighbors. A beaconing is triggered only if the prediction error is higher than predefined maximum tolerant error. Since reducing beacon rate can decrease accuracy of shared position information, R. Schmidt [10] et al. proposed a scheme for adapt beacon rate according to the VANET traffic behavior, and tried to make a trade off between accuracy of position information and channel occupancy.

3   System Model

As shown in Fig. 1, the system consists of three modules: motion detecting module, Kalman filter and error estimation module. Firstly, we assume the time is divided into discrete time slots, and two typical motion statuses are extracted from vehicular mobility to improve the accuracy of prediction: the constant speed

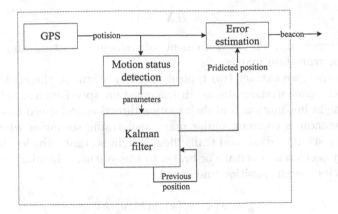

Fig. 1. System architecture

status and the maneuvering status. The work flow of the system is as follows: the motion detecting module obtains the real-time position information from GPS. It monitors motion parameters (speed, acceleration, direction) and recognizes dynamically which status vehicles are currently. According to current motion status, the Kalman filter runs at corresponding mode and generates position prediction for future N time slots. Finally, the error estimation module calculates prediction error by comparing the predicted position and the GPS position. Only when the prediction error is higher than the predefined maximum tolerable error will a beacon message be broadcasted. Moreover, vehicles run a same position prediction algorithm for each their neighbors. At each time slot, if no new incoming beacon, the predicted position is used as the position estimation for this neighbor. Upon receiving a new beacon, the Kalman filter is updated using received position information to improve the accuracy of the position prediction.

In real traffic scenarios, many kinds of factors have impact on vehicular mobility. These factors should be taken into consideration for ensuring the accuracy of the position prediction. We classify these factors into two categories: deterministic factors (vehicular history status such as its past position, speed) and unpredictable factors (driver's ongoing action, such as acceleration, brake, etc.). We use vector X_k to represent vehicular status at time slot k, the historical status at time $k-1$ is denoted by X_{k-1}, and the unpredictable factors is modeled as a random stimulation W_{k-1}. A Markov sequence model based vehicle motility model can be established.

$$X_k = \Phi_{k|k-1}X_{k-1} + GW_{k-1} \tag{1}$$

where, $\Phi_{k|k-1}$ and G are the status-transition matrix and the input matrix of the random stimulation respectively. At each time slot, a vehicle obtains the observation value of its current status from GPS. We assume that it consists of the vehicular status X_k and the observation noise V_k. A observation equation can be established as follows.

$$Z_k = HX_k + V_k \tag{2}$$

where, Z_k represents the measurement of vehicular status, and H is the measurement-transition matrix.

In this paper, we extract two typical mobility statuses: the constant speed status and the maneuvering status. In the constant speed status, vehicles keep uniform straight line motion, and their motion direction and speed rarely change. This phenomenon is common under many real traffic scenarios when vehicles traveling at a straight road, and traffic flow is light so that vehicles do not have to frequently accelerate, overtake or brake. In this status, vehicular status vector X_k^c includes its current position and speed.

$$X_k^c = [x(k), v_x(k), y(k), v_y(k)]^T \tag{3}$$

where, $x(k)$ and $y(k)$ are x-axis and y-axis position of vehicle at timeslot k, $v_x(k)$ and $v_y(k)$ are corresponding x-axis and y-axis velocity. The status-transition matrix and the input matrix of random stimulation are defined as follows.

$$\Phi^c = \begin{bmatrix} 1 & T & 0 & 0 \\ 0 & 1 & 0 & 0 \\ 0 & 0 & 1 & T \\ 0 & 0 & 0 & 1 \end{bmatrix}, \quad G^c = \begin{bmatrix} \frac{T^2}{2} & 0 \\ 1 & 0 \\ 0 & \frac{T^2}{2} \\ 0 & 1 \end{bmatrix}, \tag{4}$$

The motion detecting module monitors vehicular transverse or lengthways speeds. If vehicular speed change reaches a predefined threshold, the system switches to the maneuvering status. For instant, when a traveling vehicle comes to an intersection with a red light, it will brake and stop to wait for a green light. Its speed and instantaneous acceleration fluctuates significantly. For ensuring the accuracy of the position prediction, The acceleration should be taken into consideration. Therefore, we define the extend status vector X_k^a of the maneuvering status as:

$$X_k^a = [x(k), v_x(k), y(k), v_y(k), a_x(k), a_y(k)]^T \tag{5}$$

where, $a_x(k)$ and $a_y(k)$ are vehicular acceleration at x-axis and y-axis at time k. Vehicular state-transition matrix and input matrix of random stimulation at the maneuvering status are defined as follows:

$$\Phi^a = \begin{bmatrix} \Phi & G^c \\ 0_{2 \times 4} & I_2 \end{bmatrix}, \quad G^a = \begin{bmatrix} G^c \\ 0_{2 \times 2} \end{bmatrix}, \tag{6}$$

4 Position Prediction Based Beacon Scheme

4.1 Motion Pattern Recognition

As shown is Fig. 2, a decision logic window is used to recognize vehicular motion status. Assuming a vehicle is currently in constant speed status. The vehicle calculates its instantaneous acceleration a at every time of beacon message is

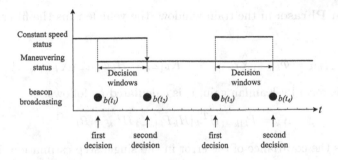

Fig. 2. Decision window

sent. If a is higher than a pre-defined threshold η, a decision window with a length of W_d time slots is triggered to determine if vehicular motion status has been changed. During this decision window, the vehicle predicts future vehicular position using both the constant speed status and the maneuvering status. Before the decision window finishes, the vehicle takes the second decision if the next beacon is broadcasted: it compares the prediction error of two statuses, and the status with lesser error will be used to perform the following prediction. If no beacon is broadcasted till the decision window ends, the vehicle does not change its current status. The decision from the maneuvering status to the constant speed status is as follows: the condition for starting a decision window is that vehicular acceleration drop to below the threshold η, the condition to switching to the constant speed status is that the acceleration a in the second beacon message also is lower than η.

The threshold η is calculated as follows.

$$P\{a \geq \eta\} < \delta \tag{7}$$

where δ is the significance parameters. The Eq. (7) means that the probability that vehicular instantaneous acceleration reach η is less than δ.

4.2 Position Prediction

In this paper, we use a kalman filter [11] to estimate vehicular current status and generate forward position prediction. The algorithm consists of three phrase: initialization phrase, estimation phase and prediction phrase.

Initialization phrase: since Kalman filter is a kind of self-recursive optimize estimation process, a warm-up period is necessary for the convergence of the estimation error. For reducing the error level in this phrase, we use a training window with a length of W_t time slots. It means that the Kalman filter starts from $k - W_t$ instead of current time k. At the starting of the filter, vehicles set the initial value $\hat{X}_0$ and the covariance matrix of filter estimation $P(0) = cov(\hat{X}_0)$.

Estimation Phrase: in the train window, the vehicle runs the filter according to Eq. (8).

$$\hat{X}_{k|k} = \Phi_{k|k-1}\hat{X}_{k-1|k-1} + K_k[Z_k - H_k\Phi_{k|k-1}\hat{X}_{k-1|k-1}] \tag{8}$$

where, K_k is term by Kamlan gain, it is calculated as follows.

$$K_k = P_{k|k-1}H^T{}_k[H_kP_{k|k-1}H^T{}_k + R_k]^{-1} \tag{9}$$

$P_{k|k-1}$ is the covariance of the error in the single step estimation. it is calculated as follows

$$P_{k|k-1} = \Phi_{k|k-1}P_{k-1|k-1}\Phi^T{}_{k|k-1} + Q_{k-1} \tag{10}$$

$$P_{k|k} = [1 - K_kH_k]P_{k|k-1} \tag{11}$$

Prediction Phrase: when Kalman filter runs to current time k, the vehicle performs a fix N time slots forward position prediction. The system status of the time $t + n$ is calculated according Eq. (12).

$$\hat{X}_{k+n|k} = \Phi_{k+n|k}\hat{X}_{k|k} \tag{12}$$

where $n = 1, 2, \dots N$, and

$$\Phi_{k+n|k} = \Phi_{k+n|k+n-1}\Phi_{k+n-1|k+n-2}\cdots\Phi_{k+1|k} \tag{13}$$

5   Simulation

In this section, we analyze the temporal stability of vehicular mobility using publicly available large-scale real vehicular traces. Furthermore, we establish three traffic scenarios, and use beacon interval as measure to evaluate the performance of the proposed scheme.

5.1   Real Traces Based Vehicular Mobility Analysis

To validate the temporal stability of vehicular mobility, we analyze the publicly available real vehicular traces collected by Microsoft China Research Institute [12]. The dataset contains the GPS trajectories of 10,357 taxis during 7 days at Beijing, China. The sampling time interval of two consecutive points is from 1 s to 10 min, and the interval below 10 s account for 23.6 % of the total. Because we only focus on the short-period position prediction, these points with the interval above 10 s are abandoned.

We denote vehicular velocity vector by $\vec{v}(i,t)$. a Normalized Velocity Change (NVC) [13] is calculated:

$$NVC(i,t) \triangleq \frac{\|\vec{v}(i,t) - \vec{v}(i,t-1)\|_2}{mean_{i,t}\|\vec{v}(i,t)\|_2} \tag{14}$$

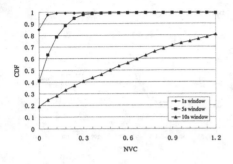

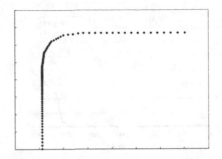

Fig. 3. Normalized velocity change   **Fig. 4.** A sample of vehicular traces

Figure 3 shows the Cumulative Distribution Function (CDF) of NVC under various size of time windows. The results show that the probability for NVC does not change is 84.9 %, 40.8 % and 19.1 % respectively under 1 s, 5 s and 10 s time window. Under 1 s time window, NVCs below 0.1 account for more than 99 % of the total. It illustrates a fact that vehicles rarely change their speed and direction in a short time window. It can be view as the vehicle is in the constant speed status. In this situation, the high accuracy can be achieved easily in position prediction algorithm.

5.2 Beacon Interval Analysis

We evaluate the performance of the proposed scheme by analyzing what degree beacon frequency can be reduced. We use three traffic scenarios: intersection scenario, straight road scenario and real traces scenario. Where fore two scenarios are generated by the traffic simulation software SUMO [14] and latter one is based on real vehicular traces introduced in Sect. 5.1. We set maximum beacon interval as 2 s, the position tolerance is 0.5 m, the length of the decision window W_d and the training window W_t is 5 s.

Intersection Scenario: we establish an intersection scenario with traffic light control which includes four two-way, 4-lane roads. When a vehicle comes to a red light, it must brake, stop and wait for a green light. Figure 4 shows a sample of vehicular trace.

Figure 5 shows the realtime speed of a vehicle at x-axis and y-axis respectively. Vehicular motion can be divided into four phases: the constant speed status (0–63 s), the deceleration status (64–160 s), the stop status (161–208 s), and acceleration and turning direction status after 208 s.

Figure 6 shows the beacon interval in the intersection scenario. The results show that the predefined maximum beacon interval can be reached under the constant speed status and the deceleration status. Under the deceleration status, the minimum of beacon interval is 600 ms. The beacon interval of the acceleration and turning direction status is 400 ms. In the two scenarios, vehicular x-axis and y-axis acceleration change simultaneously. It increase the error level of predicting position, thus the vehicle must broadcast beacon messages more frequently.

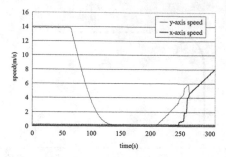

Fig. 5. Vehicular real-time speed

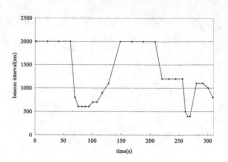

Fig. 6. Intersection scenario

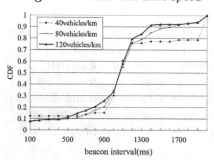

Fig. 7. Straight road scenario

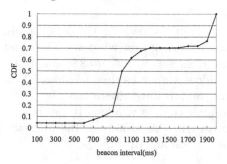

Fig. 8. Real trace scenario

Straight Road Scenario: we generate a two-way, 4-lane, 2 km length straight road traffic scenario. The average vehicle density is variable from 40 to 120 vehicles/km. Figure 7 shows the CDF of beacon interval under different vehicle density. The results show that the beacon interval above 700 ms account for more than 80 % of the total, and the beacon interval above 1200 ms account for more than 20 % of the total. Moreover, the beacon interval does not increase significantly when vehicle density increase from 80 to 120 vehicles/km. The beacon interval above 800 ms account for 80.1 % and 82.7 % of the total respectively. It proves that the proposed algorithm provides robustness against changing of vehicle density. There are no severe performance degrade with increasing vehicle density.

Real Traces Scenario: we evaluate the performance of the proposed scheme under real vehicular traces. We choose traces of 50 vehicles from Beijing taxi data set. The sampling duration of each vehicle is 100 s. For obtaining fine-granularity, we apply linear interpolation to each trace, and interval of points after interpolation processing is 0.1 s. The CDF of the beacon interval is shown in Fig. 8. The results show beacon intervals above 800 ms account for 89.3 % of the total. The beacon intervals within 800–1300 ms account for 60.3 % of the total. It proves that the proposed scheme can significantly reduce beacon frequency under real vehicle trace scenario.

6   Conclusion

In VANET, vehicles need to exchange information to support various applications. Frequent beacon broadcasting leads to heavy channel load and even causes channel congestion. Since vehicular mobility exhibit temporal stability, a short-period position prediction can be used to update the position of the neighbors, thus the beacon frequency can be reduced effectively. This paper proposes a position prediction based beacon approach. Each vehicle runs the position prediction algorithm to obtain real time position estimation for its neighbors. Only the estimation error is higher than tolerance will a beacon broadcasting be triggered. For decreasing the error level of position prediction, we divide the vehicular movement into the constant speed status and the maneuvering status. Vehicles dynamically detect current motion status and switch prediction mode. The adapted Kalman filter is used to improve the accuracy of the position prediction. A real vehicular traces based analysis show that the probability that the vehicles do not change speed and direction is 84.9 % and 40.8 % respectively under 1 s and 5 s time window. The simulation results show the proposed scheme can significantly reduce beacon frequency. The beacon interval over 800 ms account for more than 80 % of the total in three traffic scenarios.

References

1. Hartenstein, H., Laberteaux, K.P.: VANET: Vehicular Applications and Inter-Networking Technologies. Wiley, UK (2009)
2. IEEE standards association. http://standards.ieee.org
3. Fallah, Y.P., Huang, C.L., Sengupta, R., Krishnan, H.: Analysis of information dissemination in vehicular ad-hoc networks with application to cooperative vehicle safety systems. IEEE Trans. Veh. Technol. **60**, 233–247 (2011)
4. Ghafoor, K.Z., Lloret, J., Bakar, K.A., Sadiq, A.S., Mussa, S.A.B.: Beaconing approaches in vehicular ad hoc networks: a survey. Wireless Pers. Commun. **73**, 885–912 (2013)
5. Torrent-Moreno, M., Mittag, J., Santi, P., Hartenstein, H.: Vehicle-to-vehicle communication: fair transmit power control for safety-critical information. IEEE Trans. Veh. Technol. **58**, 3684–3703 (2009)
6. Fallah, Y.P., Huang, C.L., Sengupta, R., Krishnan, H.: Design of cooperative vehicle safety systems based on tight coupling of communication, computing and physical vehicle dynamics. In: 1st ACM/IEEE International Conference on Cyber-Physical Systems. ACM Press, New York (2010)
7. Fallah, Y.P., Huang, C.L., Sengupta, R.: Analysis of information dissemination in vehicular ad-hoc networks with application to cooperative vehicle safety systems. IEEE Trans. Veh. Technol. **60**, 233–247 (2011)
8. Ghafoor, K.Z., Bakar, K.A., Eenennaam, M., Khokhar, R.G., Gonzalez, A.J.: A fuzzy logic approach to beaconing for vehicular ad hoc networks. Telecommun. Syst. **52**, 139–149 (2013)
9. Rezaei, S., Sengupta, R., Krishnan, H.: Reducing the communication required by DSRC-based vehicle safety systems. In: Intelligent Transportation Systems Conference, pp. 361–366. IEEE press, New York (2007)

10. Schmidt, R.K., Leinmuller, T., Schoch, E., Kargl, F.: Exploration of adaptive beaconing for efficient intervehicle safety communication. Network **24**, 14–19 (2010)
11. Rutan, S.C.: Adaptive kalman filtering. Anal. Chem. **63**, 1103–1109 (1991)
12. Yuan, J., Zheng, Y., Xie, X., Sun, G.: Driving with knowledge from the physical world. In: 17th ACM SIGKDD International Conference on Knowledge Discovery and Data Mining. ACM Press, New York (2011)
13. Rallapalli, S., Qiu, L., Zhang, Y., Chen, Y.: Exploiting temporal stability and low-rank structure for localization in mobile networks. In: 16th Annual International Conference on Mobile Computing and Networking, pp. 161–172. ACM press, New York (2010)
14. Institute of Transportation Systems, German Aerospace Center. http://sumo-sim.org

Indoor Positioning
and Location-Based Services

The Location Fingerprinting and Dead Reckoning Based Hybrid Indoor Positioning Algorithm

Ruiyun Yu[1(✉)], Pengfei Wang[1], and Zhijie Zhao[2]

[1] Software College, Northeastern University, Shenyang 110819, China
yury@mailneu.edu.cn, wangpengfei_top@163.com
[2] Information and Technology Center, China Mobile Group Liaoning Co., LTD,
Shenyang 110179, China
zhaozhijie@ln.chinamobile.cn

Abstract. With the developing of mobile applications based on indoor location based services (LBS), the higher accuracy of indoor positioning is required. The Location Fingerprinting and Dead Reckoning based hybrid indoor positioning (HIP) algorithm is proposed to calculate the current indoor location more precisely. During the whole process of indoor positioning, WiFi modules and inertial sensors, which are mounted in smart devices, are used to obtain essential sensing data to position. HIP algorithm calculates the initial location through the weighted fingerprinting K nearest neighbor (WFKNN) algorithm using RSSI signals of WiFi firstly, and then starts to update the current location through both the WFKNN algorithm and the dead reckoning technique. The experiments are implemented several smart phones with Android system, the results show the HIP algorithm performs much better than KNN and dead reckoning algorithm on positioning accuracy.

Keywords: Indoor positioning · Location based service · Dead reckoning · Fingerprinting

1 Introduction

Location Based Service [1] (LBS) is a kind of service which utilizes wireless networks or other localization methods, such as using GPS, to gain the location information of mobile terminal users, and provides a kind of value-added services by using geographical coordinates or geodetic coordinates with the support of GIS platform.

Outdoor positioning technique is much more mature than before, and the earlier Location Based Service is passive, self-referential, goal-singular and oriented by simple content. With the rapid development of positioning with low-power dissipation, middleware technology for LBS [2, 3] and 3G mobile networks, companies become much

This work is supported by the National Natural Science Foundation of China under Grant No. 61272529; the Fundamental Research Funds for the Central Universities under Grant No. N120417002, 2014.

© Springer-Verlag Berlin Heidelberg 2015
L. Sun et al. (Eds.): CWSN 2014, CCIS 501, pp. 605–614, 2015.
DOI: 10.1007/978-3-662-46981-1_57

easier to provide Location Based Service than before [4]. Besides the GPS positioning for outdoor positioning, the Cell ID technique based triangulation positioning is also used widely for outdoor positioning [5].

However, there hasn't been a mature solution to solve acquire the precise position for the indoor positioning. Up to now, the indoor positioning methods are mainly based on infrared [6], ultrasonic wave [7], RFID [8], magnetic field [9], etc. Although these methods can provide a partial solution for indoor positioning, these methods or solutions need additional equipment, or the system complexity is very high, or the positioning accuracy is very low. So how to get the position accurately without additional equipment is a major problem to solve.

With the popularization of smart mobile devices, indoor positioning with smart mobile devices becomes possible. The usually feasible solution is to utilize WiFi signal strength [10] or inertial sensors to attain the position data with smart mobile devices.

The current indoor positioning with WiFi signal includes measuring the actual distances or angles between nodes or using RSSI (Received Signal Strength Indicator). Indoor wireless positioning technology is divided into range-based methods and range-free methods by configuring weather the technology measures the distances between the positioning nodes and anchor nodes or not [11]. The former get the location by measuring the travel time of signals or angles between anchor nodes and unknown nodes, which mainly includes: Time of Arrival Based (TOA) [6, 12, 13], Time Difference of Arrival (TDOA) [6], Angle of Arrival (AOA) [14]. The later doesn't need to measure the length or angle, and it only uses the connectivity of the networks to calculate the current location.

Also, there are some impure positioning techniques, such as TOA/AOA, TDOA/AOA, TDOA/TOA, RSSI/TOA, RSSI/TDOA and so on. Because of the complexity of environment of the indoor positioning, TOA, AOA and TDOA cannot satisfy the requirement of indoor positioning.

Reversely, indoor positioning methods with RSSI can decrease the multipath effects, and it only needs to measure the strength of signals without adding extra equipment, so it is better than other methods in positioning.

We use both inertial sensors and WiFi modules which are equipped in smart mobile devices to find the position indoor. And we improve the fingerprinting algorithm [16] and dead reckoning algorithm.

The basic theory of fingerprinting is based on K-nearest neighbor algorithm (KNN). KNN is very classical, its main theory is: If a sample is similar with other K known samples in feature space, and these K known samples belongs to one type, and the unknown sample is also belongs to this type.

The main progress of indoor positioning with KNN is as follows: Firstly, build a train sets measuring the known WiFi signal strengths. And the location can be obtained by measuring the distance between the RSSI matrix of the sample $[s_1, s_2, ..., s_n]$ and all RSSI matrix of reference points (RP) $[s_1, s_2, ..., s_N]$ in database. The K nearest neighbors can be obtained by calculated distances.

Dead Reckoning (also ded (for deduced) reckoning or DR) calculates the accurate location of vessels originally, and it is the process of calculating one's current position by using a previously position which has been known before, or revising and advancing that position based upon known or estimated speeds over elapsed time and ship route. There are mainly two solutions to get the location when people walk by adopting the dead reckoning algorithm. One method is to gain the current acceleration to calculate the velocity of walking, and obtain the displacement. The other method is to calculate the steps by inertial sensors. The first method doesn't sound well, because the acceleration is changing rapidly when people walk. The second scheme is much better to calculate the displacement when people walk. However, the step length and the number of steps should take into consideration.

A hybrid indoor positioning algorithm (HIP) is proposed to solve the problem of indoor positioning without adding extra equipment and obtain a good result. The practical experiment shows that the HIP is much better than only using one positioning algorithm.

The remainder of this paper is organized as follows. The HIP algorithm is designed in Sect. 2; practical experiments have been done in Sects. 3 and 4 concludes the paper.

2   Hybrid Indoor Positioning Algorithm Design

2.1   Main Process of HIP Algorithm

The fingerprinting and dead reckoning based hybrid indoor positioning algorithm (HIP) includes two parts. One part is to obtain the location by fingerprinting and the other part is to get the position by dead reckoning, and they revise the results by each other.

The signal strength of WiFi is used to measure the initial location, and the location is obtained by both WiFi and inertial sensors.

The HIP algorithm first obtains the initial value by using weighted fingerprinting K nearest neighbor (WFKNN) algorithm which will be elaborated below, and uses both WFKNN and improved dead reckoning algorithm to calculate the indoor position. The improved dead reckoning algorithm enhances the accuracy of only using WFKNN, and WFKNN algorithm eliminates the accumulative errors that the dead reckoning technique has.

The HIP algorithm is shown in Algorithm 1.

Algorithm 1. HIP algorithm

1: Use WFKNN to obtain the initial position;

2: **while**(people walk one step)

3:   calculate the position by WFKNN

4:   **if**(obtain the maximum signal strength of one AP)

5:     The position of this AP is set to the sample, eliminate the accumulative error of dead reckoning , and adjust step

6:   **else**

7:     **if**(not the initial position)

8:       dead reckoning

9:       get the average location with WFKNN

10:    **end if**

11: **end if**

12: **end while**

The weighted fingerprinting K nearest neighbor (WFKNN) algorithm which is first introduced, and after that the improved dead reckoning is elaborated in detail.

2.2 WFKNN and Improved Dead Reckoning Algorithm

The KNN algorithm has a satisfactory result when the train set is big enough, otherwise it will lead a huge error. A weighted fingerprinting K nearest neighbor algorithm is designed to solve this kind of problem.

The main steps of WFKNN are as follows. After getting K nearest neighbors, calculate each RSSI of AP, and set a selected range [RSSI-Σ, RSSI + Σ], Σ is an experimental value, and if there has n nodes meet the condition, the weight of each node is 1/n, and others are set 0. After traversing all Access Points (APs), the weight of each neighbors is calculated by the weights that obtains divides the whole number of APs.

The computational formulas of dead reckoning algorithm are shown as formula (1) and (2).

$$E(l) = \sum_{n=1}^{l} d(n) \bullet \sin \theta n \tag{1}$$

$$N(l) = \sum_{n=1}^{l} d(n) \bullet \cos \theta n \tag{2}$$

Fig. 1. Coordinate axis of smart mobile device

Where E(l) stands for the horizontal displacement, N(l) stands for the vertical displacement, d(n) is the step length. The directions of x, y, z axis of a smart mobile device are defined as Fig. 1. And the values of accelerations of three axes are shown as Fig. 2.

We can find out that the acceleration of z axis change periodically with the time passing. The acceleration of z axis is near 9.8 m/s^2 because of the gravity.

However, it is hard to count steps only by the acceleration of z axis. There are two difficulties. One is we cannot always put the mobile devices horizontally; the other is the range of acceleration may be little, and it is not easy to detect the change.

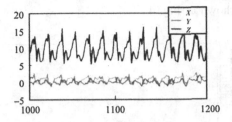

Fig. 2. Change of acceleration when people walk

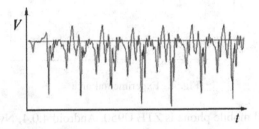

Fig. 3. Vector sum of acceleration on three axes

In order to solve the above problems, an improved dead reckoning algorithm is proposed. Use the vector sum of three axes to count steps.

The sum of acceleration on three axes is shown as Fig. 3. What can be obtained from analyzing the vector sum of acceleration on three axes is that the acceleration sum also changes periodically. Counting steps by sum of acceleration can solve the problems counting steps above easily.

Therefore, the improved counting step is designed by the above analysis. There has a flag F, and when the sum acceleration reach to a value, F will be set true; after sum acceleration decrease to another value, F will be set false and count one step.

3   Performance Test

3.1   Experiments Settings

HIP algorithm is programed in smart mobile with Android system [17], and the common android phones have integrated the Wi-Fi module and inertial sensors module.

The core controller of the system includes three parts: initial module, inertial system module and Wi-Fi scan module.

The main classes in Android system are Wifi, LoationDao, LocPoint and MAP-View. Wifi is an entity class for Wi-Fi, LocationDao operates the database, LocPoint stores the location information, and MAPView is a map class for drawing on mobile screen.

The system is deployed in science building in Northeastern University, there are five access points: TP-LINK TL-WR845 N 300 M, TP-LINK TL-MR12U 150 M, TP-LINK TL-WR740 N 150 M, FAST FWR310 300 M, FAST FW150RM 150 M.

The open area is shown as Fig. 4.

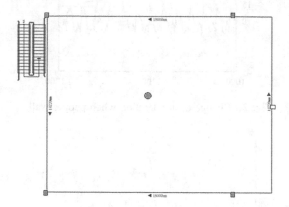

Fig. 4. Experimental area

The experimental mobile phone is ZTE U950, Android 4.0.4, Nvidia Tegra 3 quad cores. The interface of experimental applications is shown as Fig. 5.

Fig. 5. Interface of experimental application

3.2   WFKNN Performance Analysis

The contrasts between using WFKNN and KNN are shown in Table 1, and Fig. 6 is the diagram for illustrate the differences between WFKNN and KNN. Bounded by x = 6.4, the left part is the part that we store the fingerprinting data which interval is 1.6 m in both x and y axis, and the right part is 3.2 m.

The filled circle stands for the actual position, and empty circle stands for the positioning results using KNN, and the star stands for the positionin results using WFKNN.

Table 1. Experimental results of localization

No.	Actual axis		KNN			WFKNN		
	x	y	x	y	No.	x	y	No.
1	0	0	2.1	1.0	J-01	0.4	0.7	Y-01
			1.0	0.5	J-02	0.4	0.8	Y-02
			1.0	1.0	J-03	1.0	0.4	Y-03
2	1	1	4.2	3.7	J-04	2.9	1.9	Y-04
			4.8	6.4	J-05	3.1	1.6	Y-05
			5.3	4.8	J-06	0.9	0.5	Y-06
3	3	4	5.3	2.1	J-07	3.5	3.0	Y-07
			5.3	5.3	J-08	3.9	3.9	Y-08
			8.5	3.7	J-09	2.0	4.2	Y-09
4	5	5	3.2	4.8	J-10	3.8	4.1	Y-10
			4.3	4.8	J-11	5.6	4.9	Y-11
			5.3	5.3	J-12	5.9	5.0	Y-12
5	7	7	7.4	6.9	J-13	6.8	6.6	Y-13
			6.4	6.9	J-14	6.0	6.6	Y-14
			6.4	6.4	J-15	6.6	6.8	Y-15
6	7	14	12.8	12.7	J-16	10.0	10.0	Y-16
			5.3	9.0	J-17	11.2	13.6	Y-17
			6.4	11.2	J-18	6.3	11.1	Y-18
7	14	14	11.7	11.5	J-19	10.0	12.5	Y-19
			11.7	12.5	J-20	11.6	13.0	Y-20
			10.6	11.7	J-21	11.7	12.5	Y-21

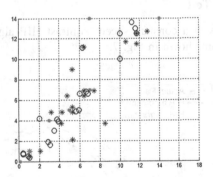

Fig. 6. Illustration of localization precise

The experiments show that the more data in fingerprinting database the more accuracy both KNN and WFKNN are. At the same time, the accuracy of indoor positioning with KNN algorithm is worse than with WFKNN algorithm, especially when the unknown location is far away from APs.

3.3 Counting Steps Algorithm Performance Analysis

Counting steps algorithm is mainly by contrasting the errors using z axis step counting and three axes step counting. The experimental results are shown in Table 2.

Table 2. Errors of step counting (Left: z axis step counting, Right: three axes step counting)

No.	Counting steps	Actual steps	Error	No.	Counting steps	Actual steps	Error
J-01	38	44	6	Y-01	20	20	0
J-02	38	44	6	Y-02	21	20	1
J-03	49	48	1	Y-03	23	23	0
J-04	40	43	3	Y-04	19	20	1
J-05	36	42	6	Y-05	20	22	2
J-06	43	44	1	Y-06	24	24	0
J-07	27	44	17	Y-07	20	20	0
J-08	46	50	4	Y-08	20	21	1
J-09	36	43	7	Y-09	23	22	1
J-10	40	44	4	Y-10	20	21	1

The initial length of step refers the Chinese standard length of steps [18], and it adjusts dynamically by Wi-Fi singals which has been mentioned above.

By contrasting the Table 2, what we conclude is that counting steps using three axes is much better than counting steps using z axis. And counting steps using three asxes overcomes the weaks that using z axis has to put the mobile horizontialy.

3.4 HIP Integration Test

Data collection: walk with a constant speed, contrast HIP algorithm with the KNN algorithm. The results are shown in Fig. 7.

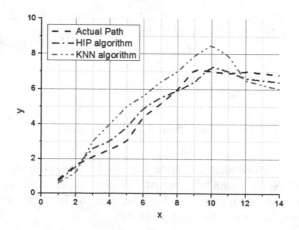

Fig. 7. Performance of HIP algorithm

The results show the HIP algorithm is much better than KNN algorithm, and the test path with HIP algorithm is closer to the actual path.

4 Conclusion

HIP algorithm refers the classical KNN algorithm, and a kind of weighted method is proposed to solve the problem. The dead reckoning is applied to the indoor positioning, and improved the counting steps algorithm. HIP algorithm is proposed, and it is combined with both WFKNN and improved dead reckoning.

WFKNN can eliminate the accumulated errors that dead reckoning algorithm generates, and dead reckoning improves the accuracy of WFKNN. The experiment shows that HIP is much better than other indoor positioning algorithm without adding any other equipment.

References

1. Barkhuus, L., Dey, A.K.: Location-based services for mobile telephony: a study of users' privacy concerns. In: Proceedings of 9th IFIP TC13 International Conference on Human-Computer Interaction, pp. 709–712 (2003)
2. Kupper, A., Treu, G., Linnhoff-Popien, C.: TraX: a-device-centric-middleware framework for location-based services. IEEE Comm. Mag. **44**, 14–120 (2006)
3. Bellvist, P., Corradi, A., Giannelli, C.: Coupling transparency and visibility: a translucent middleware approach for positioning system integration and management (PoSIM). In: Proceedings of International Symposium Wireless Communication Systems (Iswcs06), IEEE Press, pp. 179–184 (2006)
4. Bellavista, P., Kupper, A., Helel, S.: Location-based services: back to the future. Pervasive Comput. **7**(2), 85–89 (2008)
5. Zandbergen, A.: Accuracy of iphone locations A comparison of assisted gps, wifi and cellular positioning. Trans. GIS **13**, 5–25 (2009)
6. Sun, L., Li, J.: Wireless Sensor Networks. Tsinghua University Press, Beijing (2005)
7. James, M.Z., Steen, A.P., Julian, J.B., Karen, D.M.: Providing universal location servies using a wireless E911 location network. IEEE Commun. Mag. **36**(4), 66–71 (1998)
8. He, T., Huang, C., Blum, B.M., Srankovic, J.A., Abdelzaher, T.: Range-free localization schemes for large scale sensor networks. In: Proceedings of the 9th ACM Annual International Conference on Mobile Computing and Networking (MobiCom' 2003), San Diego, CA, USA, ACM, pp. 81–95 (2003)
9. http://web.indooratlas.com/web/WhitePaper.pdf
10. Honkavirta, V.: Location Fingerprinting Methods in Wireless Local Area Networks. Tampere University of Technology, Tampere (2008)
11. Kushiki, A., Plataniotis, K.N., Venetsanopoulos, A.N.: Kernel-based positioning in wireless local Area networkds. IEEE Trans. Mob. Comput. **6**(6), 689–705 (2007)
12. Girod, L., Estrin, D.: Robust range estimation using acoustic and multimodal sensing. In: Proceedings of IEEE International Conference Intelligent Robots and Systems (IROS'01), vol. 3, pp. 1312–1320. Muai, Hawaii, USA, (2001)

13. Caffery, J.J., Caftery Jr., J.J.: Wireless Location in CDMA Cellular Radio Systems. Kluwer Academic Publisher, Boston (1999)
14. Stansfield, G.: Statistical theory of DF fixing. J. IEE **94**(15), 762–770 (1947)
15. Wang, J.: Research on Wireless Sensor Network Positioning. University of Science and Technology of China, Baohe (2009)
16. Kushiki, A., Plataniotis, K.N., Venetsanopoulos, A.N.: Kernel-based positioning in wireless local area networks. IEEE Trans. Mob. Comput. **6**(6), 689–705 (2007)
17. http://developer.android.com/index.html
18. Xiangping, L.I., Bin, S.H.U., Xiaohong, G.U., et al.: The analysis of Normal steps parameter for Chinese adult. Chin. J. Rehabil. Med. **27**(3) (2012)

Maintenance of Wi-Fi Fingerprint Database by Crowdsourcing for Indoor Localization

Yanjun Li$^{(\boxtimes)}$, Kaifeng Xu, Jianji Shao, and Kaikai Chi

School of Computer Science and Technology, Zhejiang University of Technology,
Hangzhou 310023, China
yjli@zjut.edu.cn

Abstract. Wi-Fi fingerprint localization has been well accepted to solve the indoor localization problem, while the most important part in this method is the construction and maintenance of the fingerprint database. A timely update of the fingerprint database is required due to the fluctuation of the received Wi-Fi signal strength. However, having professionals updating the fingerprint database is costly in terms of time and effort. In this paper, a crowdsourcing approach is proposed where the users themselves can evaluate and correct the localization result, thus training and using the localization system at the same time. Particularly a clustering based error detection method is adopted to detect the erroneous input location data, which can effectively avoid the contamination of the fingerprint database. Finally an indoor localization system is developed and practical experiments in real indoor environment show that the proposed approach achieves satisfying localization accuracy over a long time.

Keywords: Crowdsourcing · Location fingerprint · Clustering · Indoor localization

1 Introduction

With the increase of large urban buildings and the popularization of smart phones, the need for indoor location service is growing rapidly. In most of today's applications such as public security, pervasive medicare, smart space, crowd surveillance etc., location is one of the most essential contexts. While GPS is widely used to provide outdoor location information, it does not work well indoors. Some early indoor localization technologies used infrared, laser, ultrasonic, etc., yielding fairly good system performance in field tests. The disadvantages of such an approach are its size, complexity, and cost, which render it infeasible for mobile devices. Wi-Fi network infrastructure is found in many public facilities and can be used for indoor localization. In addition, the ubiquity of Wi-Fi-capable devices makes this approach especially cost-effective.

For most Wi-Fi localization system, a fingerprinting approach is commonly used based on the Received Signal Strength (RSS) transmitted by nearby Wi-Fi Access Points (APs) [1,2,5]. Typically, such an approach consists of two

© Springer-Verlag Berlin Heidelberg 2015
L. Sun et al. (Eds.): CWSN 2014, CCIS 501, pp. 615–624, 2015.
DOI: 10.1007/978-3-662-46981-1_58

phases: off-line training phase and real-time localization phase. In the training phase, each survey position is characterized by location-related Wi-Fi RSS properties called Wi-Fi RSS fingerprints. Engineers record the fingerprints and accordingly build a fingerprint database. In the localization phase, when a user sends a location query with its current RSS fingerprint, localization algorithms retrieve the fingerprint database and return the corresponding location of the most matched fingerprint. For Wi-Fi fingerprinting, fine-grained system training is normally required to achieve high accuracy and resolution. However, various effects, including interference from interposing objects as well as reflections of neighboring objects, make the RSS fluctuates over time. This results in significant costs in terms of ongoing maintenance in order to continuously adapt to Wi-Fi environmental changes and Wi-Fi infrastructure alterations. A great deal of effort has been made by researchers to reduce such costs. A potentially effective way is to let users provide feedback to facilitate the maintenance of the RSS fingerprint database. This paper proposes a crowdsourcing-based approach, making the users not only enjoy the localization service but also participate in the maintenance of the RSS fingerprint. Furthermore, an indoor localization system is developed on Android platform. Practical experiments in a real indoor environment have validated the effectiveness of this approach in keeping the localization accuracy comparatively firm.

2   Related Work

Wi-Fi fingerprint-based indoor localization approach is first proposed by Microsoft researchers with a corresponding system called RADAR [1]. As Wi-Fi APs and smart phones are more and more popular, this localization approach has caught extensive contentions. By this approach, the position of a mobile user is estimated by comparing online RSS readings with off-line observations. One solution is the k-nearest neighbor algorithm (kNN), which estimates the users location by computing the centroid of the k closest neighbors that have the smallest Euclidean distance to the online RSS reading [1]. This method is easy to implement but the estimation is not very accurate. Another solution is to solve the problem by a statistical method, in which the probability of each potential position is analyzed using the Bayesian theory and kernel functions [2,5]. However, an explicit formulation of RSS distribution is challenging. In the localization phase, random propagation effects of signal propagation introduced by complex indoor environments may result in large RSS fluctuations or AP loss. These shortcomings imply a high fingerprint maintenance cost. Park et al. [6] propose a method by prompting users to label the places around them that need coverage, and conveys to them the level of localization precision they can expect in their current vicinity. This method can proceed with an empty fingerprint database, but it may interrupt users very frequently at the beginning and degrade the user experience. Bolliger et al. [3] propose an asynchronous interval labeling technique that extends the applicability of a user-provided label from an instant to an interval over which the device is stationary. The stationary state is detected using an accelerometer, which allows the

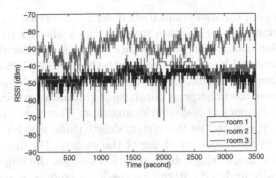

Fig. 1. RSS measurements over time.

system to collect stationary interval measurements without explicit user intervention. The shortcoming of this method is that they fail to detect user's erroneous labels. Different from their work, the fingerprint database of our system is built by professionals initially and users could provide feedback to the localization service based on their knowledge of the surroundings. They may choose to accept or modify the results after being given the estimated position. A clustering-based method that automatically discards erroneous user input through outlier detection is also proposed.

3   The Crowdsourcing-Based Approach

3.1   Motivation

The localization method using RSS fingerprint assumes that the pattern of mean signal strengths received in one location differs from the pattern observed in another location. However, the mean RSS of a fixed location is nonstationary. To study the significance of the variations in RSS, we performed a small experiment. We positioned three smart phones in three rooms of our office building. Each phone maked an active Wi-Fi scan every 5 s and recorded the APs' SSID and RSS. Figure 1 shows the RSS variation of the APs inside three different rooms over a period of time. The variance of the RSS measurements are 8.1, 4.0 and 3.9 respectively. These fluctuations are unavoidable, which may get worse with the lapse of time. The solution to short-term variation is to average the RSS measurements taken during a short time. However, long-term variation cannot be solved without the update of the fingerprint database.

3.2   Overview of the Approach

Crowdsourcing is a method that can solve a tedious problem distributively [4]. Our proposed crowdsourcing-based approach consists of three phases: off-line training phase, real-time localization phase and fingerprint updating phase. The first two phases are similar to traditional approach. In the third phase, if the user is satisfied with the localization result, the current RSS fingerprint will be included in the database. Otherwise if the user is unsatisfied with the service, he/she can choose to make a correction. The localization server decides whether to accept or reject the user's correction using a detection method. If the server decides to accept the correction, the corrected location binding with the current RSS will be stored in the database as a new fingerprint. Otherwise the correction will be ignored. During this phase, the size of the fingerprint database is gradually growing and will eventually reduce the efficiency of real-time localization. Therefore, we set a period of valid for each fingerprint and let the system delete those which are overdue. This setting is related to the frequency of use of the system. By this approach, when there are quite a few users using this localization system, the fingerprint database can be automatically updated without professional engineers and thus adapt to Wi-Fi environment changes.

3.3   Localization Algorithm

We adopt the localization algorithm specified in [7]. Since the focus of our work is the maintenance approach of the fingerprint database, we do not consider complicated localization algorithm. However, our proposed fingerprint maintenance approach is compatible with any other localization algorithm. We denote the sets of APs scanned at locations l_1 and l_2 as A_1 and A_2, respectively. Also, let $A = A_1 \cup A_2$. Let $f_i(a)$ denote the RSS of AP a, $a \in A$, scanned at location l_i; if a is not scanned at l_i, then $f_i(a) = 0$. We now define the similarity $S_{l_1,l_2} \in [0,1]$, between locations l_1 and l_2 as:

$$S_{l_1,l_2} = \frac{1}{|A|} \sum_{a \in A} \frac{\min\left(|f_1(a)|, |f_2(a)|\right)}{\max\left(|f_1(a)|, |f_2(a)|\right)} \tag{1}$$

The rationale for Eq. (1) is that a larger S_{l_1,l_2} indicates a more adjacent geographic relation between locations l_1 and l_2, and vice versa. We illustrate the computation of the similarity by the following instance. Suppose there are 5 APs in an indoor environment, numbered from 1 to 5. The MAC address and RSS of the APs scanned at location 1 and location 2 are listed in Tables 1 and 2. According to Eq. (1), the similarity is computed as $S_{1,2} = (0/80 + 55/75 + 60/75 + 0/85)/4 \approx 0.383$.

Let L denote the set of fingerprints in the database. The user's estimated location $\tilde{P}_j$ is supposed to be the corresponding location that maximizes the

Table 1. APs scanned at location 1

AP	MAC address	RSS (dBm)
1	14:e6:e4:d2:35:6a	−80
2	34:08:04:b9:0f:10	−75
3	84:4b:f5:8c:f6:37	−75

Table 2. APs scanned at location 2

AP	MAC address	RSS (dBm)
2	34:08:04:b9:0f:10	−55
3	84:4b:f5:8c:f6:37	−60
4	56:f0:6d:7c:57:80	−85

similarity between the observed RSS measurements and the RSS fingerprints in L, i.e.,

$$\tilde{P}_j = \arg\max_{i \in L} S_{i,j}. \tag{2}$$

3.4 Fingerprint Maintenance Approach

After the user obtains the estimated localization result from the localization sever, he/she is encouraged to make an evaluation. If the user is satisfied with the service, the RSS measurements with the localization result will be stored into the database. Otherwise the user can make a correction. If the correction is accepted, the corrected location binding with the RSS measurement will be stored into the database. Obviously, the system needs a discrimination mechanism to avoid careless or malicious corrections. It is worth noting that the initial configuration of the fingerprint database by professional engineers is of high quality and the system can achieve over 90 % localization accuracy in the initial stage. Due to the time-varying properties of the Wi-Fi signals, the localization accuracy gradually decreases. But the deviation is not supposed to be significant all of a sudden. Inspired by this fact, we believe that the if the user chooses to make a correction, the corrected location should still be in the "vicinity" of the localization result given by the system. In other words, if the corrected location is deviated far from the localization result, the correction cannot be trusted. Finally, the problem is transformed to determine the "vicinity" of a location. We use a clustering algorithm to group the location set in the database together with the corrected location by the user into different clusters. Those location points grouped in the same cluster are supposed to be "adjacent" to each other. Therefore, if the corrected location is in a different cluster with the localization result, the correction will not be accepted by the system. In the following, we elaborate on the clustering algorithm and how to choose related parameters.

Clustering Algorithm. Since the rooms in an indoor environment have irregular shapes and the activity space of the users is uncertain, the number of clusters cannot be determined a priori. Therefore, centroid-based or hierarchical clustering algorithms are not appropriate. The advantage of density-based clustering algorithm, e.g., DBSCAN [8], is that it does not require one to specify the number of clusters in the data a priori and it can find arbitrarily shaped clusters, which makes it fully satisfy our requirement. We therefore adopt DBSCAN as the clustering algorithm. DBSCAN starts with an arbitrary starting point p that has not been visited. The circular region with center p and radius ε is called p's ε-neighborhood. Point p's ε-neighborhood is retrieved, and if it contains at least a minimum number of $MinPts$ points, a cluster is started. Point p is thus a core point. Otherwise, point p is labeled as noise. If a point is found to be core point, its ε-neighborhood is also part of that cluster. Hence, all points that are found within the ε-neighborhood are added, as is their own ε-neighborhood when they are also core points. This process continues until the density-connected cluster is completely found. Then, a new unvisited point is retrieved and processed, leading to the discovery of a further cluster or noise. DBSCAN requires two parameters: the neighborhood radius ε and the minimum number of points required to form a dense region $MinPts$. How to determine the two parameters is crucial to the algorithm.

Determining the Parameters. First, we determine the parameter ε. In Fig. 2, suppose the black rectangle L is the localization result while the user corrects it to L'. If ε is given a too small value, as shown in Fig. 2a, the points inside the circle form a cluster and the size of the cluster is much smaller than that of the room. Obviously point L' is not in cluster A and the user's correction will be rejected by the system. In such a case, a user's right correction are very likely to be rejected, which is not beneficial to the update process. On the contrary, if ε is given a too high value, as shown in Fig. 2b, the size of the cluster is much larger than that of the room and may even cover several rooms. It is easier for the system to accept a user's correction. An extreme case is that if ε goes to infinity, all the points will be in the same cluster, the system will accept all the corrections no matter it is right or wrong. In such a case, the system has no capability of discrimination. Weighing these cases, we propose to set ε to half of the smallest room's diagonal length. The reason is as follows: as aforementioned, the initial configuration of the fingerprint database by professional engineers is of high quality and the system can achieve over 90 % localization accuracy in the initial stage, which indicates a small probability of having a localization error larger than the size of a room. Therefore, setting ε to half of the smallest room's diagonal length is a neutral choice for minimizing the system's discrimination error.

Second, we determine the value of $MinPts$. This problem can be transformed to the Neyman-Pearson decision problem. Let L_s denote the computed localization result, L_c denote the corrected location by the user. Then the erroneous correction detection problem can be transformed to test the following two hypotheses:

$$H_1: L_s \text{ and } L_c \text{ are from different rooms}$$
$$H_2: L_s \text{ and } L_c \text{ are from the same room}$$

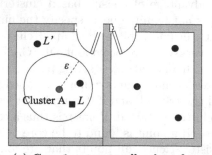 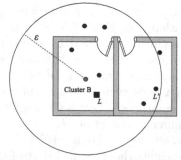

(a) Case 1: a too small value of ε (b) Case 2: a too high value of ε

Fig. 2. Cases of different ε values.

We assume that an appropriate value of $MinPts$ can achieve the following effect: if L_s and L_c are from different rooms, the system actually groups them into different clusters and vice versa. Let x denote the values of $MinPts$ when L_s and L_c are grouped into different clusters. Therefore, $P_D = P(x \leq MinPts|H_1)$ represents the detection rate of a different cluster under the condition that the two points are from different rooms while $P_{FA} = P(x < MinPts|H_2)$ represents the false alarm rate of a different cluster under the condition that the two points are from the same room. Under the Neyman-Pearson model, we expect to find a best $MinPts$ that can maximize the detection rate under a given false alarm rate. As we cannot directly obtain the distribution of x, we will find the best $MinPts$ through extensive experiments in the following Sect. 4.2.

4   Experimental Results

To evaluate the performance of the our proposed approach, we have developed an indoor localization system on Android platform and conducted extensive experiments. The experimental field is located on the 4th floor of an office building in Zhejiang University of Technology, as shown in Fig. 3. The floor has dimension of 95.4 m by 26.4 m. Upon testing, we find there are in total 14 APs in this field, as marked in Fig. 3. They are autonomously placed by the staff in the offices, not for the purpose of the experiments. We use Samsung Galaxy S7562 as the end device whose OS is Android 4.0.4. In the off-line training phase, a total of 40 fingerprints are collected. They are fairly scattered in the hallway and different rooms. We use "localization accuracy" as a metric to evaluate the localization performance, which is defined as the ratio of the localization result conforming with the real room. For the hallway, we also divide them into different regions, as shown in Fig. 3. In the following, we first give an overview of the system. Then we obtain the parameters for DBSCAN clustering algorithm through experiments. Finally we compare the localization performance of our approach with the other two approaches: non-updating approach and non-error-detection approach.

4.1   System Overview

The indoor localization system consists of two major components: the end device and the server. The end device collects the Wi-Fi information and provides the

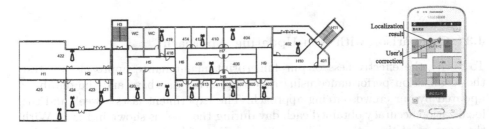

Fig. 3. Experimental field.   **Fig. 4.** User interface.

interactive interface for the users. The server provides three kinds of services: fingerprint sharing, satisfying user's localization requirement and discriminating user's correction. To reduce the short-term instability of RSS, the end device takes the average of three scans, where all the RSS are larger than -80dBm. To encourage the users to contribute to the fingerprint maintenance, we design a user-friendly interactive interface, as shown in Fig. 4. A user can load the plan of the building and view his/her position visually. If he/she is not satisfied with the localization result, he/she can correct it by simply dragging the location bubble, as shown in Fig. 4.

4.2   Determination of DBSCAN Parameters

To find the best $MinPts$, we conduct extensive experiments. Figures 5 and 6 show the performance of P_{FA} and P_D with the increase of $MinPts$ from 1 to 4. For each $MinPts$, we take 50 testings. When $MinP = 1$, both P_{FA} and P_D is 100 %, which means all the user's corrections will be accepted by the system. With the increase of $MinPts$, P_{FA} decreases. When $MinP = 4$, P_{FA} approaches 0, which means when $MinP$ is sufficiently large, the system will not accept any correction. Weighing the tendency of both P_{FA} and P_D, we find that for any given P_{FA}, there is a best $MinPts$ which maximizes P_D. For example, if P_{FA} is set to 14 %, the best $MinPts$ should be 3 so that a maximized P_D of 80 % can be reached. In the following experiments, $MinPts$ is set to 3 accordingly.

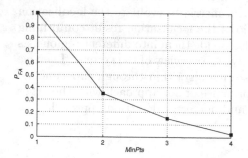
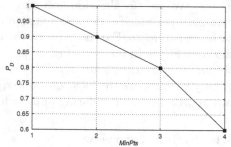

Fig. 5. False alarm rates under different values of $MinPts$.

Fig. 6. False alarm rates under different values of $MinPts$.

4.3   Comparison with Non-Updating Approach

To verify the effectiveness of our fingerprint maintenance approach, we test the localization performance using a non-updating database and the database updated by our crowdsourcing approach. The experiment lasts a week and the localization accuracy obtained each day during the week is shown in Fig. 7. With the passage of time, the localization accuracies of both approaches are declining. However, with the non-updating fingerprint database, the declining range

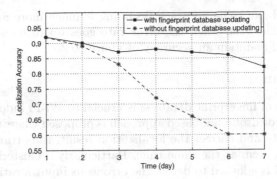

Fig. 7. Our approach compared with non-updating approach.

is significantly larger. On the whole, our crowdsourcing-based approach keeps an accuracy of over 80 % in a week. It is worth mentioning that, the volunteers engaged in the experiments are small in number, and thus the potential of updating of the database are not fully explored. However, we believe that in practical use when there are sufficient users, the localization accuracy of the system can achieve a higher level.

4.4   Comparison with Non-Error-Detection Approach

Discrimination between user's right and wrong correction is the key to our system. To verify the effectiveness of our proposed approach, we let the volunteers maliciously alter the localization result and compare our approach to non-error-detection approach. As shown in Fig. 8, with the increase of the error rate, the localization accuracy of both approaches declines. However, by non-error-detection approach, the localization accuracy declines much more rapidly. When the input error rate goes to 40 %, the localization accuracy has fallen to below 50 %. Thank to the clustering algorithm, our approach is effective in detecting

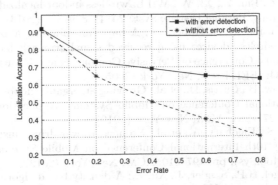

Fig. 8. Our approach compared with non-updating approach.

user's erroneous input. The accuracy declining is much more gradual. We can see from Fig. 8 that even when the error rate goes up to 80 %, our proposed approach can still maintain an accuracy of above 60 %.

5   Conclusion

The maintenance of fingerprint database is crucial to Wi-Fi indoor localization. In this paper, a crowdsourcing-based approach is proposed where the users themselves can evaluate and correct the localization result, thus training and using the localization system at the same time. Particularly a clustering based error detection method is adopted to detect the erroneous input location data, which can effectively avoid the contamination of the fingerprint database. Finally an indoor localization system is developed and practical experiments in real indoor environment show that the proposed approach achieves satisfying localization accuracy over a long time. Our proposed approach can solve the labor cost issue in fingerprint maintenance. If sufficient number of users use the system and engage in the maintenance, the prospect of application and extension of Wi-Fi localization will be vast and bright.

Acknowledgments. This work is supported in part by China NSF No.61003264 and Zhejiang Provincial NSF No.LY13F020028.

References

1. Bahl, P., Padmanabhan, V.N.: Radar: an in-building RF-based user location and tracking system. In: 9th Annual Joint Conference of the IEEE Computer and Communications Societies (INFOCOM), pp. 775–784. IEEE Press, New York (2000)
2. Bruno, L., Robertson, P.: WiSLAM: improving FootSLAM with WiFi. In: International Conference on Indoor Positioning and Indoor Navigation (IPIN), pp. 1–10. IEEE Press, New York (2011)
3. Bolliger, P., Partridge, K., Chu, M., Langheinrich, M.: Improving location fingerprinting through motion detection and asynchronous interval labeling. In: Choudhury, T., Quigley, A., Strang, T., Suginuma, K. (eds.) LoCA 2009. LNCS, vol. 5561, pp. 37–51. Springer, Heidelberg (2009)
4. Wu, C., Yang, Z., Liu, Y., Xi, W.: WILL: wireless indoor localization without site survey. IEEE Trans. Parallel Distrib. Syst. **24**(4), 839–848 (2013)
5. Seshadri, V., Zaruba, G.V., Huber, M.: A bayesian sampling approach to in-door localization of wireless devices using received signal strength indication. In: 3rd IEEE International Conference on Pervasive Computing and Communications (PerCom), pp. 75–84. IEEE Press, New York (2005)
6. Park, J., Charrow, B., Curtis, D., et al.: Growing an organic indoor location system. In: 8th International Conference on Mobile Systems, Applications, and Services (MobiSys), pp. 271–284. ACM, New York (2010)
7. Wang, H., Sen, S., Elgohary, A., et al.: No need to war-drive: unsupervised indoor localization. In: 10th International Conference on Mobile Systems, Applications, and Services (MobiSys), pp. 197–210. ACM, New York (2012)
8. Ester, M., Kriegel, H.P., Sander, J., Xu, X.: A density-based algorithm for discovering clusters in large spatial databases with noise. In: 2nd International Conference on Knowledge Discovery and Data Mining (KDD), pp. 226–231. AAAI Press (1996)

Applications of Wireless
Sensor Networks

Wireless Sensor Networks Based Heritage Deformation Detection Algorithm

Zhijun Xie[1(⊠)], Hongwu Ye[2], and Rong Yu[1]

[1] College of Information Science and Engineering Ningbo University,
Ningbo 315021, China
xiezhijun@nbu.edu.cn, xiezhijun888@163.com
[2] Zhejiang Fashion Institute of Technology, Zhejiang,
People's Republic of China

Abstract. Wireless sensor networks, comprising many small sized, low cost, low power intelligent sensor nodes, are more useful to detect the deformation of every small part of the heritage objects. Deformation is the direct cause of the heritage object collapse. It is significant to monitor and signal an early warning of the deformation of heritage objects. In this paper, we provide an Effective Heritage Deformation Detection using wireless sensor networks (EffeHDD) method. In EffeHDD, we propose a heritage object boundary detecting mechanism. Both theoretical analysis and experimental results demonstrate that our EffeHDD method outperforms the existing methods in terms of network traffic and precision of the deformation detection.

Keywords: Sensor networks · Heritage monitoring · Heritage deformation · Deformation detection

1 Introduction

A culture heritage site is often an invaluable historical legacy. Different from the stone ruins in European, many of the heritage sites in Asia (e.g., China) are often damaged due to some part of natural-deformation-caused collapse since they are built using clay and have complicated structures that are composed of a large number of surfaces inside and outside or range along a very long zigzag way; typical examples include the ancient Great Wall, Xi'an imperial city wall ruins of the Sui and Tang Dynasties, Terracotta Army, Yang Mausoleum of the Han Dynasty and Dunhuang Mogao Grottoes. Deformation, which causes the split, collapse and destruction of parts or whole heritage sites, is mainly responsible for heritage site damage. Therefore, it is significant to monitor and signal an early warning of the deformation of heritage objects.

The existing monitoring methods are not sustainable for surveillance of the heritage clay sites since they only roughly monitor a simple heritage object as a whole, but cannot monitor heritage objects with complicated structures (i.e., with a large number of surfaces inside and outside). Although wireless sensor network was applied in the protection of heritage for its characteristics of easy deployment and extended, For example, in recent years, researchers have deployed sensor network in clay sites but only for environmental status monitoring, such as collecting data of temperature and humidity [1–4].

© Springer-Verlag Berlin Heidelberg 2015
L. Sun et al. (Eds.): CWSN 2014, CCIS 501, pp. 627–637, 2015.
DOI: 10.1007/978-3-662-46981-1_59

In this paper, we propose an effective heritage detection (EffeHDD) method to tackle these challenges. The EffeHDD method mainly comprises the following two phases. In the initialization phase, EffeHDD determines the initial boundary of the heritage object; In the monitoring phase, the EffeHDD measure those tiny slow deformations of precious and small heritages by detecting the changing of anchor node's RSSI value periodically. As for those large and established in the wild relatively poor environment heritages, the EffeHDD detects and tracks the boundary of the heritage object periodically. We detect the deformation and collapse of the heritage object through checking whether a part of or the whole heritage boundary moves out of the sensing range of the current boundary sensors; note that the membership of heritage boundary node set must be updated to responsible for a new boundary location.

The rest of this paper is organized as follows. Section 2 briefs an overview of related works. Section 3 details the EffeHDD method. Section 4 conducts an experimental study to validate the effectiveness of the proposed method. Section 5 concludes the paper.

2   Related Works

In this section, we conduct a survey of the sensor networks that are applied for monitoring the culture heritage objects and object tracking technology of sensor networks. The sensor networks become popular to monitor culture heritage objects. Casciati et al. in Italy Pavia University proposed a wireless sensor network technology to protected cultural heritage in Italy in 2004 [1]. The researchers in the Trento University deployed a WSN monitoring system in TorreAquila tower to monitor its structure and environment. The researchers in Madeira University of Portugal developed a WSN in Fortaleza Sho Tiago Museum for monitoring and protecting the art environment. Jongwoo Sung from The South Korean deployed a sensor network around the temple for the forest fire detection [5]. The researchers from Institute of Computing Technology, Chinese Academy of Sciences deployed a sensor network to monitor the imperial palace cultural relics exhibition hall [1–4]. However, these applications are simply collected the site environmental data but there is no study on detecting the deformation of heritage sites. Fu Y et al. proposed the judgment of heritage deformation method based on cloud model, but the heritage deformation method based on cloud model did not define deformation accuracy and predict the deformation trends.

Our EffeHDD method overcomes the limitations of existing communication-consuming sensor networks and focuses on detecting the deformation of the heritage objects and continuously tracking the deformation changing with time.

3   Effective Heritage Deformation Detection (EffeHDD) Algorithm

The main idea of EffeHDD is as follows. In Step 1, the EffeHDD is divided into initial stage and monitoring stage, in the initialization phase, the EffeHDD determines the initial boundary of heritage site, deploys the anchor nodes on the heritage; while in the monitoring phase, the EffeHDD detects and tracks the deformation of the heritage periodically. Then, after the sensor networks having been deployed in the heritage site, the EffeHDD forms domain head and gateway for those precious and small heritages, such as Buddha, stored in a museum or the temple, where the environment is better than outdoors, the deformation is very small. We measure these tiny slow deformations by detecting the changing of node's RSSI value periodically. But some large heritages, such as Chinese ancient Great Wall and Mount Li Buddha, are established in the wild relatively poor environment, and thus are vulnerable to earthquakes, landslides and other disasters that may induce sudden and greater collapse. If the deformation is not timely detected and treated, the partially collapsed of heritage will lead to large-scale collapse and even the whole heritage collapse. We measure these large-scale and sudden deformations by detecting the change of the heritage's boundary. In Step 2, when a heritage site deformed and, a portion of or the whole heritage boundary moves out of the sensing range of the current boundary sensors, the membership of heritage boundary node set must be updated to responsible for the new boundary location. The domain heads identified the nodes within its domain which detect the new boundary sensors of the heritage by executing the boundary detection method in Sect. 3.2 and the heritage boundary node set must be updated to responsible for the new boundary location.

3.1 Boundary Detection

The key point for detection and tracking of deformation is to construct a set of connected core nodes [9] in the sensor networks during the initial phase. The node within each domain is nominated as the head and plays the role of a local controller. The normal nodes get the sensor data of the environment and send or relay the sensing data to the Domain Head (DH). The DH collects the data from the normal nodes and generates sensing data of its own in the domain, fuses and transfers this information to the sink [9].

When the DH receives the location information from all of the normal nodes in the domain, the DH detects the sensors located around at the boundary of the heritage object and notifies them that they are the boundary sensors of the heritage object. The boundary sensors are selected from the normal nodes in a domain through finding the minimum convex polygon that contains the heritage object. For a subset S of n-dimensional space R, t convex MCP(K) is defined as the smallest convex set in R. For example, the convex polygon represented by red line as shown in Fig. 1 is the minimum convex polygon of convex set $Q = \{p_0, p_1....p_{12}\}$. We present the algorithm for finding boundary sensors in Sect. 3.3.1; the method for finding the minimum convex polygon in geometry refers to [6].

Finding the Boundary Sensors (FBS) Algorithm. Let all the nodes in a domain represent the subset S of n-dimensional space R, and the DH distinguishes the boundary sensors among them by using the finding the boundary sensors (FBS) algorithm in Table 1.

Definition 1. Rotation Direction of the Path: Let $o = (x_o, y_o)$, $p = (x_p, y_p)$, $q = (x_q, y_q)$ are any three nodes in the domain, vector $D(o,p,q)$ denote the rotation direction of the path.

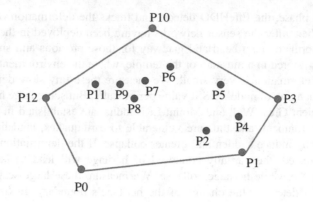

Fig. 1. The minimum convex polygon.

$$D(o,p,q) = \begin{vmatrix} x_o & y_o & 1 \\ x_p & y_p & 1 \\ x_q & y_q & 1 \end{vmatrix} = x_o y_p + y_o x_q + x_p y_p - x_q y_p - y_q x_o - x_p y_o \quad (1)$$

If $D > 0$, then the path $< o, p, q, o >$ forms an anti-clockwise loop; if $D < 0$, then the path (o, p, q, o) form a clockwise loop; if $D = 0$, o, p, q are collinear.

We first identify the smallest y coordinate of nodes in S, assumed p_0, and establish a coordinate axis whose origin is p_0, (if two nodes p_i and p_j have the same smallest y coordinate and $p_i.x < p_j.x$, we select p_j as its origin). The other nodes are mapped to the p_0 origin coordinate axis system. After mapping all the nodes into the p_0 origin coordinate axis system, we compute all the node's slope and sort all the nodes in ascending order according node's slope, and get the sorted nodes set $T = \{p_1, p_2, ...P_n\}$, where p_1 and P_n have the smallest and largest slope respectively.

Second, we establish the stack $ST(S)$, which is initialized to $ST(S) = \{P_n, p_0\}$. Without loss of generality, We assume that at a time the $ST(S) = \{ P_n, p_0...p_i p_j p_k\}$, where p_k is on the top of ST, and the nodes in ST have constituted a semi-closed convex polygon (Fig. 2a), p_l is the next node in the T. If the rotation direction D $(p_j, p_k, p_l) > 0$, then we push p_l into stack ST(S), since the path $< p_j, p_k, p_l >$ forms an anti-clockwise loop and $< p_j, p_k, p_l >$ forms a convex polygon, and the p_k, p_l are a convex polygon edge. If D $(p_j, p_k, p_l) > 0$, then we pop p_k out of stack $ST(S)$ (Fig. 2b and c), since the path $< p_j, p_k, p_l >$ forms an clockwise loop and p_k, p_l are not a convex polygon edge. Finally, the nodes in ST are the boundary sensors which determine the boundaries of a heritage object.

3.2   Boundary Detection

1. Heritage Deformation Detecting by Check the RSSI of Anchor Nodes

The wireless signal energy will decay with increasing distance in the process of communication. The signal energy received by the node is the RSSI. According to the log path loss model in [8], the received signal energy decay in a logarithmic trend with distance increases. If both the transmission energy and the received signal energy can

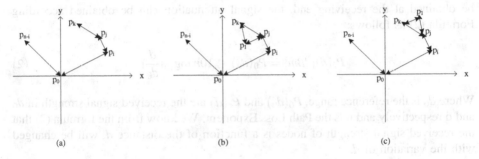

Fig. 2. finding the boundary sensors

Table 1. Finding the boundary sensors (FBS) algorithm

Algorithm: Finding the boundary sensors

1: Input a set of sensors $S=\{p_0, p_2, ...P_{n-1}\}$

2: Select the rightmost and lowest sensor p_0 as the original, and establish a coordinate axis whose origin is p_0.

3: Map the other sensor s into the p_0 origin coordinate axis system.

4: Compute the slope of the sensor s

5: Let $T[n]$ be the sorted array S in ascending order.

6: Push $T[n-1]$ and p_0 onto a stack ST, and sp denote the stack point of ST.

7: WHILE i<n

8:      IF D($ST[sp]$,$ST[sp-1]$,$T[i]$)$\geq$0 THEN

9:      Push $T[i]$ into ST

10:      i++

11:   ELSE

12:      Pop the $ST[sp]$ off the ST

13 :   sp=sp-1

14:      ENDIF

15:ENDWHILE

16:Output:ST

---

be obtained at the receiving end, the signal attenuation can be obtained according Formula (2) as follows:

$$P_r(d)[dBm] = P_0(d_0) - 10n \log_{10}\left(\frac{d}{d_0}\right) \tag{2}$$

Where d_0 is the reference range, $P_0(d_0)$ and $P_r(d)$ are the received signal strength in d_0 and d respectively and n is the Path Loss Exponent. We know from the formula (2) that the received signal strength of nodes is a function of the distance d, will be changed with the variation of d.

Transform the formula (2) to formula (3):

$$d = \left(10^{\frac{P_0(d_0)[dBm]-p_r(d)[dBm]}{10n}}\right) \times d_0 \tag{3}$$

According to formula (3), given $P_r(d)$, d_0 and $P_0(d_0)$, we can get the new reference range d, where the path loss exponent n is a fixed value and can be measured in experiment if the environment unchanged.

For example, In Fig. 3, The new position of anchor node P_0 is P, the distance between P and B_1, B_2, B_3 is d, d_1, d_2 respectively, and the coordinate of B_1, B_2, B_3 is $(x_1,y_1),(x_2,y_2)(x_3,y_3)$ respectively. We can get the new position of P's coordinate (x,y) according to formula (4). By fusing the RSSI data of anchor nodes which deployed on the heritage, we can accurately calculate the heritage deformation size and angle. According to our actual experiment, the average positioning error is 0.115 m.

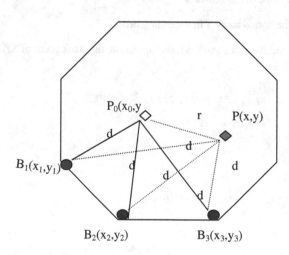

Fig. 3. Changes position of anchor nodes after deformation

$$\begin{cases} (x - x_1)^2 + (y - y_1)^2 = d^2 \\ (x - x_2)^2 + (y - y_2)^2 = d_1^2 \\ (x - x_3)^2 + (y - y_3)^2 = d_2^2 \end{cases} \tag{4}$$

We get the P's coordinate (x,y) by transform the formula (4).

$$\begin{bmatrix} x \\ y \end{bmatrix} = \begin{bmatrix} 2(x_1 - x_3) & 2(y_1 - y_3) \\ 2(x_2 - x_3) & 2(y_2 - y_3) \end{bmatrix}^{-1} \begin{bmatrix} x_1^2 - x_3^2 + y_1^2 - y_3^2 + d_3^2 - d^2 \\ x_2^2 - x_3^2 + y_2^2 - y_3^2 + d_3^2 - d_1^2 \end{bmatrix}$$

In the actual environment, the signal attenuation model is influenced by the influence factors such as temperature, humidity, wind and other environmental factors such as voltage and antenna. The signal attenuation model is not an ideal type as the formula (2), but in line with the normal distribution related to the distance [8] as shown in formula (5).

$$P_r(d)[dBm] = P_0(d_0) - 10n \log_{10}(\frac{d}{d_0}) + X_\sigma \tag{5}$$

Where X_σ is the random variable in line with normal distribution; σ is the noise factor under specific circumstances. When the environment is stable, the path loss exponent n and noise factor σ can be considered as a fixed value and can be obtained in experiment. Therefore, The $P_r(d)$ is a function of d and the X_σ, and in line with the normal distribution. In order to improve the accuracy of calculation, we replace $P_0(d)$ and $P_r(d)$ with $E(P_0(d))$ and $E(P_r(d))$, replace X_σ with $\overline{X_\sigma}$, where $E(P_0(d))$ is the expected value of the received signal strength of $P_0(d)$, $E(P_r(d))$ is the expected value of the received signal strength $P_r(d)$, $\overline{X_\sigma}$ is the mean value of X_σ, we can get the formula (6) from formula (3).

$$d = \left(10^{\frac{E(P_0(d_0)[dBm]) - E(P_r(d)[dBm]) + \overline{X_\sigma}}{10n}} \right) \times d_0 \tag{6}$$

2. Heritage Deformation Detecting by Boundary Detection of Heritage Site

When the DH finds the boundary of the domain, the DH determines the sensors located at the boundary of the domain and notify them be the boundary sensors of the domain. The DH determines the boundary sensors among the normal nodes in the domain by the FBS algorithm in Table 1. Hereafter, the boundary sensors of the domain are referred to as Domain-boundary-sensors (DBs), while the other remaining nodes are referred to as normal-sensors (Ns).

The control messages are used to send the detecting information to the DH when the object is detected. There are "Detecting" and "Domain" in the control message.

"Detecting" is used by the DBs only and is sent to the DH when the DBs detects the target heritage. For example, when the DBs detect the collapse of the large heritage and parts of the heritage move into the domain, The DBs will set the "Detecting" to '1' and send to DH.

"Domain" is used by the Ns only. It is set to 'n' when the detected heritage is identified within domain n.

When the collapse or the deformation of the heritage object is detected, a DBs talks with all the one hop neighboring DBs in other domains to get their detection information. Once the DBs has received this information, it sets the "Domain" to 'n' in the control message and sends it to the DH such that the DH can determine all of the domains within which the heritage has spread (Tables 2, 3).

Table 2. Heritage boundary detection algorithm.

Algorithm: Heritage boundary detection (HBD) algorithm

---

1 : **IF** the heritage within a single domain **THEN**

2:   get the heritage boundary by executing FBS

3: **ELES**

4: DHs estimates the portion of the object boundary lying within its own domain by executing the BPE(the Boundary Portion Estimation algorithm).

  6: All DHs fuses the boundary information in a compact data format and then relays it to the sink.

  7: The Sink determines the entire boundary of the heritage by compiling the integrated boundary information received from all the DHs in the network.

  9:**ENDIF**

Table 3. The boundary portion estimation algorithm

Algorithm: The Boundary Portion Estimation algorithm (BPE)	
Step 1	DHs distinguish the domain boundary sensors among all of the sensors which have detected the heritage by FBS
Step 2	DHs identify and eliminate the redundant sensors in domain boundary set
Step 3	DHs eliminate any non-boundary sensor(s) from the heritage boundary set

4   Performance Evaluation

In this section, we demonstrate the effectiveness and efficiency of EffeHDD by real nodes experiment. Typically, the preservation of cultural relics or heritage has higher requirements on the environment. This experiment is in the laboratory that store precision instruments, which are very similar to the place to save the precious cultural relics or heritages, there are specialized equipment to keep indoor temperature, wind and dust stable and keep dry, at the same time, there are special equipments to screen out strong electric and magnetic fields.

  In the experiment, we use the Micaz node of Crossbow to collect on the RSSI value and create a sample database. 10 anchor nodes are deployed randomly in the 10 m × 10 m region which around by 30 boundary nodes. The average of the 3 boundary nodes corresponds to 1 anchor node to calculate the RSSI value. In order to simulate the random heritage deformation, we move the position of anchor node randomly and the distance of each movement is limited to 0.2 meters. We collect 1000 data at each distance, 60 % of them are treated as the sample data for training, and the remaining 40 % are treated as test data, the abnormal data are processed before the training samples.

The average weighted distance is calculated following formula (6) acted as estimation distance between boundary nodes and anchor nodes. We define distance error as follow: distance error = actual distance- estimation distance. The actual distance is the line measuring distance between boundary nodes and anchor nodes. Figure 4 shows the distance error results of EffeHDD fluctuates between 0.015 and 0.025, which is a reasonable error range for site deformation decision [7].

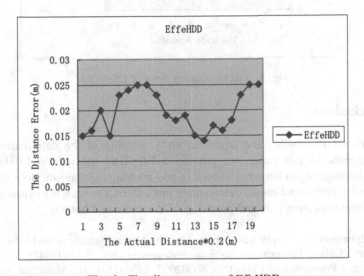

Fig. 4. The distance error of EffeHDD

We carry out a positioning error experiment to test the positioning accuracy of EffeHDD. If anchor node P's coordinates in the P_i position is (x_i, y_i) and was moved by K times, the final estimated position coordinate is (x_i', y_i'). The definition of positioning error γ for the anchor node is:

$$\gamma = \frac{\sum_{i=1}^{k} \sqrt{(x_i - x_i')^2 + (y_i - y_i')^2}}{k} \tag{7}$$

Figure 5 shows the positioning error results of EffeHDD fluctuates between 0.018 and 0.042, which is a reasonable error range for site deformation decision [7].

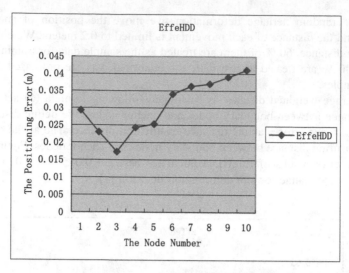

Fig. 5. The positioning error of EffeHDD

5 Conclusions

It is significant to monitor and signal an early warning of the deformation of the heritage objects. In this paper, we provide a EffeHDD method. In EffeHDD, we develop a heritage object boundary detecting and tracking mechanism. Both theoretical analysis and experimental results demonstrate that EffeHDD excels the existing work in terms of communication cost and precision of the estimated boundary.

Acknowledgements. This work was supported by The Major Scientific & Technology Specific Programs of Zhejiang Province for key industrial project (No. 2011C11042); The National Natural Science Foundation of China (No. 60902097, 51303157); The Municipal Natural Science Foundation of Ningbo (No. 2012A610013, 2013A610044); The Ningbo Municipal Technology Innovation Team (2011B81002)

References

1. Ceriotti, M., Mottola, L., Piceo, G.P., et al.: Monitoring heritage buildings with wireless sensor networks: The torre Aquila deployment. In: Proceedings of the 2009 International Conference on Information Processing in Sensor Networks IEEE 2009, pp. 277–288 Washington, DC (2009)
2. de Brito, L.M.P., Peraha, L.M.R, Santos, F.E.S., et al.: Wireless sensor networks applied to museums environmental monitoring. In: Proceedings of the 4th International Conference on Wireless and Mobile Communication, IEEE 2008, pp. 364–369, Washington, DC (2008)
3. Li, D., Liu, W, Zhao, Z. et al.: Demonstration of a WSN application in relic protection and an optimized system deployment tool. In: Proceeding of the 7th the International Conference on Information Processing in Sensor Networks, IEEE 2008, pp. 541–542 Washington, DC (2008)

4. Ming, X., Yabo, D., Dongming, L., et al.: A wireless sensor system for long-term micro-climate monitoring in wild land cultural heritage sites. In: Proceedings of the 2008 IEEE International Symposium on Parallel and Distributed Processing with Applications, IEEE 2008, pp. 207–214, Washington, DC (2008)
5. Mechitov, K., Kwon, Y., Sundresh, S., Agha G.: Poster abstract: Cooperative tracking with binary-detection sensor networks. In: Proceedings of the First International Conference on Embedded Networked Sensor Systems, pp. 332–333, Los Angeles, CA, USA (2003)
6. Eddy, W.: A new convex hull algorithm for planar sets. ACM Trans. Math. Softw. 3(4), 398–403 (1977)
7. Li, Z., Wang, X., et al.: A reinforcement test of the earthern sites of Qin's terra-cotta Army pit. Dunhuang Res. 4, 151–158 (1998)
8. Guoqiang, M., Baris, F., Brian, D.: Wireless sensor network localization techniques. Comput. Netw. 51(10), 2529–2553 (2007)
9. Xie, Z.J., Wang, L., Lin, Y.P., Chen, H.: An algorithm of data aggregation based on data compression for sensor networks. J. Softw. 17(4), 860–867 (2006)

Recognizing Human Activities in Real-Time Using Mobile Phone Sensors

Boxuan Jia[1] and Jinbao Li[2]([envelope])

[1] School of Computer Science and Technology, Heilongjiang University,
Harbin 150080, Heilongjiang, China
jiaboxuan1177@163.com
[2] Key Laboratory of Database and Parallel Computing of Heilongjiang Province,
Harbin 150080, Heilongjiang, China
jbli@hlju.edu.cn

Abstract. To overcome the defects that previous research cannot recognize human activities accurately in real-time, we proposed a novel method, which collects data from the accelerator and gyroscope on a mobile phone, and then extracts features of both time domain and frequency domain. These features are used to learn random forest models offline, which make our mobile app can recognize human activities accurately online in real-time. Verified by theoretical analysis and a large number of contrast experiments, the recognition is rapid and accurate on mobile phones with accuracy at 97 %.

Keywords: Activity recognition · Random forests · Mobile sensors · Real time

1 Introduction

Human activity recognition is a very extensive and meaningful research. It can be used to detect human health, predict human social behavior, do context-aware computing, etc. It also promotes the development of research of human behavior and human motion measurement, human biology, and other related disciplines. There are many ways to recognize human activity, and people can make use of different kinds of information to perform Human activity detection, recognition and analysis. In these cases it generally needs a video or audio information, infrared sensor, acceleration sensor and so on. Even people's social activities are helpful to identify the activities of the human body. The popularization of smart phones equipped with an accelerometer, gyroscope sensor, brings a new platform and opportunity for human activity recognition.

This work is supported in part by the National Natural Science Foundation of China(NSFC) under Grant No.61370222 and No.61070193, Heilongjiang Province Founds for Distinguished Young Scientists under Grant No.JC201104, Natural Science Foundation of Heilongjiang Province of China No.F201225, Technology Innovation of Heilongjiang Educational Committee under grant No.2013TD012.

© Springer-Verlag Berlin Heidelberg 2015
L. Sun et al. (Eds.): CWSN 2014, CCIS 501, pp. 638–650, 2015.
DOI: 10.1007/978-3-662-46981-1_60

Essentially, human activity recognition is actually a process of classification, and there are a variety of classifiers. In recent years, the dominant method is broadly divided into discriminative classifiers and generative classifiers. Generative classifiers try to generate a model to describe how the different physical activity data generated. Depending on erent physical activity data generated. Discriminative models, as opposed to generative models, do not allow one to generate samples from the joint distribution, but depending on boundary or mathematical functions in the feature space to distinguish between different activities. Bayesian network (Naive Bayes classifier) is an example of generative classifier; while K nearest neighbor classification algorithm, decision tree algorithms, neural networks and support vector machines are discriminative ones. These classifiers have different characteristics. Support vector machines are very sensitive to noise in high-dimensional space. The performance of the Naive Bayes model in the high dimension is not good enough. Compared to these above traditional models, random forest (RF) as a discriminative classifier is an effective method. It uses Bootstrap re-sampling method to extract a collection of multiple samples from the original sample, then builds decision tree model for each bootstrap sample collection, and finally combines trees to make predictions by majority voting mechanism. Lots of theoretical research and practice proved that Random Forest has a higher prediction accuracy of outliers and noise with good tolerance, and not prone to over-fitting [2].

Extracting feature data on activity recognition is a very important job. Typical characteristic data includes time domain and frequency domain features. The time-domain features include statistical maximum, mean, variance, etc. Fourier transform or wavelet transform extracts frequency domain features such as FFT coefficients, frequency domain entropy and so on. The above information can be generated from the activities of acceleration signals.

In order to obtain a better accuracy and do quicker identification, we propose a novel method named DTR (DWT + Time-domain features + RF) to recognize human activities. The main idea is to combine time-domain and frequency domain features together to recognize human activity by Random Forest. We select the maximum, minimum and mean as the time-domain characteristics, and frequency-domain feature selection method bases on wavelet transformation, in order to avoid noise interference.

The paper is organized as follows: The next section is about related work; the third section describes some preliminaries of the method used in this article; Sect. 4 describes the data collection process, analyzing process and the algorithms DTR; Sect. 5 describes the experiments and results; Sect. 6 concludes the whole paper.

2   Related Works

Advances in ubiquitous and pervasive computing have resulted in the development of a number of sensing technologies for capturing information related to human physical activities. Previous researchers have already done a lot of different exploration in human activity recognition. To identify human mobility,

L. Song et al. used Wifi access points as data source for localizing and predicting user mobility [14]. Song et al. studied the predictability of human mobility from very coarse location data of GSM tower IDs [13]. However, this method limited deployment of sensors. Yu-Jin Hong et al. using RFID technology for activity recognition, they tied Tag on some household items, in addition, the human body was equipped with some basic sensor equipments and also wore Reader device, when the body is doing some daily activities, Reader would use Tags to identify human activities [7]. LiDan et al. proposed a recognition algorithm which is less sensitive to sensor position, the sensor may be worn on one of the waist, pocket, the pocket of the jacket, by only one acceleration sensor can be realized on the activity recognition, having strong practical [3]. We refer to LiDan's work for the difference of recognition accuracy on every sensor's position and choose to place the phone in waist. T.M, T. Do and D. Gatica-Perez, took advantage of combination Bluetooth network [5] and topic model to recognize human activity. This method is very practical, but due to environmental impact, it will be overfitting easily. Zhengyi Chao firstly converted the time domain features into the frequency domain by Fourier transformation, and applied it to an improved KNN algorithm. The activity recognition accuracy has been greatly improved [8]. Use the same frequency domain information, Yavuz et al. proposed a activity recognition mothod using wavelet transform. Compared with the Fourier transform, wavelet transform in the frequency domain retains the same frequency characteristics, but also keeps the time-domain characteristics, so the recognition of making short-term activities with a higher degree of accuracy [11]. This paper selected wavelet transform in the frequency domain information processing.

With smart phones, Nike wristbands, Google glasses wearable sensor devices are widely used, the application of mobile phone activity recognition gets more and more attention. Bingchuan Yuan et al. Who collected the data on the phone, then process the data on a computer to identify activities, but his method requires a large amount of computation, high dependence on the server, the phone can not be used to identify activities independently [16]. Stefan et al. try to identify some more complex mobile activities, but with limited performance [4]. Jussi Leppänen et al. try to use GMM identify activities on the phone, but the recognition rate on seven basic activities' such as upstairs, downstairs was only 72.6 % [10]. Young-Seol Lee attempted to introduce unlabeled data for training, but the model was too complex to implement on phones [9].

Aiming to resolve problems in the existing research, we propose a novel activity recognition method named DTR, with considering the data size and model which mobile phones can handle, so that the DTR method can accomplish recognition of simple activities on the fly in real time.

3   Preliminaries

This section describes some basic knowledge of the proposed activity recognition methods, including the discrete wavelet transform and random forests.

3.1 Discrete Wavelet Transform

The wavelet transform is the time (space) localization analysis of frequency, it shifts operation on it by stretching signal (function) and multiscale gradually refined, can automatically adapt to the requirements of time-frequency signal analysis.

We adapt the Haar wavelet [15] because the computation consumption is affordable for such a limited platform like smartphones.

3.2 Random Forests

Random forests is an ensemble learning method for classification (and regression) that operate by constructing a multitude of decision trees at training time and outputting the class that is the majority of the classes output by individual trees [2].

3.3 Error Analysis

Kappa Statistic. This indicator is used to judge the degree of difference between classifier results with random classification. It is calculated by the following formula:

$$k = \frac{p(A) - p(E)}{1 - p(E)} \tag{1}$$

where $P(A)$ is the ratio of classifier's agreement, $P(E)$ is a random assortment agree ratio. When $K = 1$ it indicates that the classifier decisions completely different with random classification. $K = 0$ indicates that classifier is the same with random classification. $K = -1$ indicates it is even worse than random classification. In general, it is positively correlated with the accuracy, so the closer to 1, the better.

Mean Absolute Error. MAE is a quantity used to measure how close forecasts or predictions are related to the eventual outcomes. The mean absolute error is given by:

$$\text{MAE} = \frac{1}{n} \sum_{i=1}^{n} |f_i - y_i| = \frac{1}{n} \sum_{i=1}^{n} |e_i| \tag{2}$$

In (2)–(5), f_i is the predictive value, y_i is the true value, and $\bar{y} = \frac{1}{n} \sum_{i=1}^{n} y_i$ is the average of y_i.

Relative Absolute Error. It reflects the predictive value and the actual value of the relative deviation. It is calculated by the following formula:

$$\text{RAE} = \frac{1}{n} \sum_{i=1}^{n} \left| \frac{f_i - y_i}{y_i} \right| \tag{3}$$

Root Mean Squared Error. It is given by the following formula:

$$\text{RMSE} = \sqrt{\frac{\sum_{i=1}^{n} (f_i - y_i)^2}{n}} \tag{4}$$

Root Relative Squared Error. It is Similar to the root mean square error, given by formula:

$$\text{RRSE} = \sqrt{\frac{\sum_{i=1}^{n} (f_i - y_i)^2}{\sum_{i=1}^{n} (y_i - \bar{y})^2}} \tag{5}$$

4   Data Collection and Processing

4.1   Data Collection

Depending on the type of motion, we select activities such as upstairs and downstairs, walking, running, jumping and stationary. The phone used to collect data is the Mi2, running Android 4.4.2.

Mobile sensors used are: *TYPE_LINEAR_ACCELERATION*, *TYPE_GRAVITY* and *TYPE_GYROSCOPE* [6].

The sampling rate is 100Hz. We record linear acceleration, gravity and gyroscope value as described above, each sensor has three dimensions, so a single sample has 9 components. Figure 1a shows the MI2 phone's accelerometer, gyroscope axes, which Pitch, Roll, Azimuth is the three-axis rotation component.

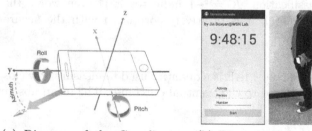

(a) Diagram of the Coordinate System

(b) Diagram of Data Collection

Fig. 1. Coordinate system and data collection

In this paper, we collected activity data from 20 individuals, age range from 19 to 50, including 11 males and 9 females, each collected six events, which are upstairs, downstairs, walking, running, jumping and still, each one was lasting one minute, each activity was collected twice.

The app was used to collect data on the mobile phone and where the phone places are shown in Fig. 1b.

4.2   Data Processing

The size of sliding window is set to 512. We treat a single window as a training sample, and every two adjacent windows overlaps $\frac{1}{2}$ of the window size, that is, 256. Our experiment collected a total of 3892 samples. We get the 512 frequency-domain features from the wavelet transform. By calculating the maximum, minimum and average value of the original window data as time-domain characteristics. Therefore, a single sample contains $(512 + 3) * 9$ features. We use 10-fold cross-validation to learning arguments in our model. After training offline on the computer, the app only needs to load the model, and promise the phone can recognize activities on the fly.

There are two typical methods, time domain analysis and frequency domain analysis to extract features. If only use features in time domain, it has lower performance almost like random guessing. Moreover, when the signal transformed into the frequency domain, it can effectively separate the noise from the signal.

For frequency-domain analysis, FFT and DCT are two classical methods, the DWT is an efficient frequency domain analysis method proposed in the last 30 years.

Figure 2 shows the frequency domain information of the y axis of jumping and downstairs (the data size is a window), in which Fig. 2a is a s a time-domain waveform of jumping, Fig. 2c is the frequency domain information about the jumping, Fig. 2b is the time domain waveform of downstairs, Fig. 2d shows information on the frequency domain of that activity. As can be seen from Fig. 2, the differences in time domain between jumping and downstairs are not significant (including the maximum, minimum and mean of acceleration), but from the waveform and spectral observations, the frequency signals of these two activities distribute very differently.

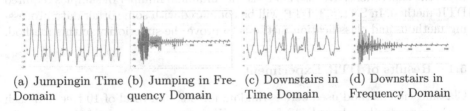

(a) Jumpingin Time Domain   (b) Jumping in Frequency Domain   (c) Downstairs in Time Domain   (d) Downstairs in Frequency Domain

Fig. 2. Time and frequency domain signal of jumping and downstairs

In fact, human activities, such as going downstairs, jumping, are often composed by a number of cyclical movements including breathing, waving hands, kicking or other periodicity movements. The period of these movement varies with different activities. Moreover, even same cyclical movements in different activities are not same, such as breathing and leg swing. These different cyclical actions will affect the value of the acceleration and gyroscope. After the frequency domain analysis, these values will be separated into signals of different frequencies. The spectral differences between different activities is the theoretical foundation of recognizing activities by frequency features. Therefore, we attempt to combine frequency-domain and time-domain information for activity recognition.

Since we abstract activity recognition to a multi-classification problem, it is inevitable to select an appropriate classifier. Considering the phone's computing ability, we examined the Naïve Bayes, Support Vector Machines and Random Forests, and several other candidates. We finally chose Random Forests, which performs the best under limited resources like a phone.

4.3   Data Processing Algorithms

Learning Method. In this section we will elaborate the learning process. Firstly, we need to handle the data obtained from phones. We divide the whole data sequence into data windows and extract time and frequency domain features of every window. And then, random forests are set up using these data. The details of the algorithm are shown in Algorithm 1.

Recognition Method. The activity recognition algorithm aims to classify an unknown datum using the random forests obtained by the former step. Data processing is same with the learning method. The details are shown in Algorithm 2.

5   Results and Discussion

In Sect. 5.1, we will use the collected data in Sect. 4.1 and use the DTR method to do the experiment. We also analysis the minimum number of samples required DTR method. In Sect. 5.3, DTR will be compared with some other data processing methods and classification methods to prove the superiority of this method.

5.1   Results of DTR Experiment

Classification method used here is random forests, in a total of 10 tree and each of them randomly selected 512 features. We set the number to 512 to promise recognition accuracy as well as reducing the cost of computation. 10-fold cross-validation is used in our experiments, and the results are shown in Fig. 3.

We can observe that, where Kappa index is 0.96. Kappa is close to 1, indicating that it is a good enough classification. The average absolute error is 0.05, and root mean square error is 0.1171, indicating a low misclassification rate. We also calculate the out-of-bag error, which is 0.0843, showing that this method is more effective.

Confusion matrix of our experiment is shown in Table 1. From Table 1, we find that jumping, sitting have a high recognition accuracy, the classification of running is also relatively accurate, while walking is easily mistaken assigned into

---

Algorithm 1. DTR Learning Algorithm

1: **procedure** DTRLEARN$(S = \{(x_1^i, x_2^i, \ldots, x_9^i, y^i)\}_{i=1}^N)$ ▷ S is the training set with N as its size; $x_1^i, x_2^i, \ldots, x_9^i$ are the linear acceleration values, gravity acceleration values, gyroscope values in the three axes respectively; y^i is the activity label for the ith window.

2:   $W_j \leftarrow \left\{(x_1^i, x_2^i, \ldots, x_9^i)_{i=1+(j-1)*256}^{512+(j-1)*256}\right\}$ ▷ Separating data sequence into windows, the window size is 512, and neighbor windows overlap 1/2.

3:   $Y_j \leftarrow \text{Major}\left(\{y_i\}_{i=1+(j-1)*256}^{512+(j-1)*256}\right)$ ▷ The activity label of a window is the major activity of that window.

4:   **for** $j \leftarrow 1, n$ **do**   ▷ Extract feature vector Features$_j$ for every window, where $1 < j < J$, J is the total number of windows.

5:    **for** $k \leftarrow 1, 9$ **do**

6:     $\text{FF}_k \leftarrow \text{Wavelet}\left(\{x_k^i\}_{i=1}^{512}\right)$ ▷ Using Haar wavelet transform to extract frequency domain features.

7:     $\text{TF}_k \leftarrow \left\{\max\left(\{x_k^i\}_{i=1}^{512}\right), \min\left(\{x_k^i\}_{i=1}^{512}\right), \text{avg}\left(\{x_k^i\}_{i=1}^{512}\right)\right\}$ ▷ The time Domain Features.

8:    **end for**

9:    Features$_j \leftarrow \left(\{\text{FF}_k, \text{TF}_k\}_{k=1}^9\right)$ ▷ Vectorization

10:   **end for**

11:   $S' \leftarrow \{\text{Features}_j, Y_j\}_{j=1}^J$ ▷ S' is the new training set.

12:   **for** $m \leftarrow 1, 10$ **do**

13:    $S_m' \leftarrow \text{Sample}(S')$ ▷ Using bootstrap to resample S' to form the new 10 training sets $\{S_m'\}_{m=1}^{10}$

14:    $T_m \leftarrow \text{C4.5}(S')$ ▷ For every resampled set, apply the C4.5 algorithm to set up a decision tree.

15:   **end for**

16:   $M \leftarrow \{T_m\}_{m=1}^{10}$ ▷ The 10 trees form the final random forests.

17: **end procedure**

Algorithm 2. DTR Recognition Algorithm

Require: $W = \left\{(x_1^i, x_2^i, \ldots, x_9^i)_{i=1}^{512}\right\}$ is the data window to recognize, ModelFile is the result of Algorithm 1.

  procedure DTRRECOGNIZE$(W, \text{ModelFile})$

   for $k \leftarrow 1, 9$ **do**

    $\text{FF}_k \leftarrow \text{Wavelet}\left(\{x_k^i\}_{i=1}^{512}\right)$

    $\text{TF}_k \leftarrow \left\{\max\left(\{x_k^i\}_{i=1}^{512}\right), \min\left(\{x_k^i\}_{i=1}^{512}\right), \text{avg}\left(\{x_k^i\}_{i=1}^{512}\right)\right\}$

   end for

   Features $\leftarrow \left(\{\text{FF}_k, \text{TF}_k\}_{k=1}^9\right)$

   $M \leftarrow \{T_m\}_{m=1}^{10}$

   $M \leftarrow \text{load}(\text{ModelFile})$ ▷ Load the Model file.

   for $m \leftarrow 1, 10$ **do**

    $y_m \leftarrow \text{Classify}(T_m, \text{Features})$

   end for

   $Y \leftarrow \text{Major}\left(\{y_m\}_{m=1}^{10}\right)$ ▷ The final activity label is obtained by majority voting

  end procedure

Correctly Classified Instances	3758	96.557 %
Incorrectly Classified Instances	134	3.443 %
Kappa Statistic		0.9587
Mean Absolute Error		0.0455
Root Mean Squared Error		0.1171
Relative Absolute Error		16.3764 %
Root Relative Squared Error		31.4337 %
Out-of-bag Error		0.0843

Fig. 3. DTR performance

downstairs and upstairs, and downstairs and upstairs can easily be mistaken assigned walking label. In fact, due to the limitation of experimental locations in the test downstairs and upstairs, when reaching at the corner of the staircase, subjects need to walk a few steps before proceeding to the next stairs movement, resulting in accelerator and gyroscope values becoming similar. In addition, the age, gender, physical condition of the selected subjects, can also cause some impact on the classification results.

Table 1. Confusion matrix

	Jumping	Downstairs	Upstairs	Walking	Running	Sitting
Jumping	586	2	0	0	3	0
Downstairs	3	673	6	11	7	1
Upstairs	0	2	626	23	0	0
Walking	0	26	29	624	1	0
Running	5	5	7	1	598	0
Sitting	0	2	0	0	0	651

To complete a basic human activity needs about five seconds, so we need every 5 s to identify an event. Reference [12] also identified activities around five seconds and get a good recognition accuracy.

5.2   Minimum Requirements for of Training Samples

The random forests model is built offline, so the number of samples in training set dominates the accuracy of the model. We studied the minimum number of samples required for the DTR method in detail.

In Fig. 4, the horizontal axis is the number of samples and the vertical axis represents the corresponding number of data sets in the 10-fold cross validation accuracy of recognition. The data is randomly generated. We can see from Fig. 4, with the increase in the number of samples, the recognition accuracy is increasing, but the growth trend slows down after reaching the 2048 sample and the recognition accuracy has stabilized. Thus to guarantee accuracy while reducing modeling time, 2048 samples should be use at least.

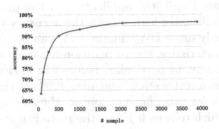

Fig. 4. Experiment on samples number and identification accuracy

5.3   Contrast Experiments

In this section we will test different features and different models. At the end, the DTR will be compared with other known methods.

Contrast Experiment on Feature Selection. In addition to the discrete wavelet transform, another frequently used method for extracting characteristic frequency domain signal is DCT. The data processing method in this paper were compared with the DCT, the DCT will also be added with time-domain features. The relationship between accuracy and numberof features is shown in Fig. 5a, the modeling time and the number of different treatment methods characteristic relation are shown in Fig. 5b.

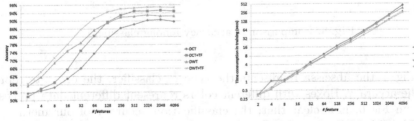

(a) Comparison of Identification Accuracy among Features

(b) Comparison of Modeling Time among Features

Fig. 5. Comparison of different feature set

From Fig. 5 to Fig. 6, TF represents only using time domain features, including the maximum, minimum and average values of a sliding window. In Fig. 5, the horizontal axis represents the number of features, while the vertical axis represents the recognition accuracy. In Fig. 6, the horizontal axis represents the number of characteristics, and the vertical axis represents the time required to train the model. These data using random forest classification.

As can be seen from Fig. 5, the application of the proposed method DTR (DWT + TF) was significantly higher than the accuracy of the DCT, DCT + TF, also higher than only using DWT method. As can be seen, with the increase of the number of characteristics, the recognition accuracy of four kinds of data processing rising gradually, in particular, before 512 it rises significantly, after 512, the accuracy enters a stable stage, and after 4096 the characteristic accuracy rate will drop. Reasons for this phenomenon are the emergence of the phenomenon of over-fitting, which tells us it is not the more features the better. On the modeling time, when the number of features increases, it grows exponentially.

From Fig. 5 we can know that, using time-domain characteristics in the frequency domain characteristics, the accuracy was significantly higher than only using the frequency-domain information, and the modeling time grows not too much. After the above analysis, we chose 512 as the number of features to ensure accuracy rate, while its modeling time is also in acceptable range.

Comparison of Classifiers. In this section, we compare DTR with some other classifiers, including SVM and Naïve Bayes. These two methods usually as the comparative experiment baseline. The results are shown in Fig. 6:

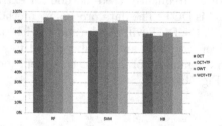

Fig. 6. Comparison of accuracy among classifiers

In Fig. 6, the abscissa represents the type of classifier, the ordinate represents the accuracy. Boxes with different colors represent different data processing. From Fig. 6, it is clear that, the classification accuracy of our method is higher than the other two baseline. Due to limitations of Bayesian method, it cannot capture the TF information correctly, which makes the useful TF information for Naive Bayes be equivalent to populate the noise, leading to decreased classification accuracy, which explains why when TF added to DCT/DWT, the accuracy of DCT and DWT drops. In this paper, the number of features used is big, which led to the dimension of the SVM classifier feature space is very large, very complex feature space, although parameters have been tuned, the accuracy is still not high enough. In summary, our method is better than the baselines.

Comprehensive Experiments. In this section we will compare DTR with some known methods. The results shown in Table 2.

Table 2. Comparison of recognition methods

	GMMs	Hybrid Classifiers	MC-HF SVM	DTR
Walking	76.7 %	98.4%	95.6 %	91.7 %
Running	95.7 %	97.0 %	–	97.5%
Sitting/Still	94.3 %	100%	96.4 %	99.5 %
Upstairs	–	–	72.1 %	95.1%
Downstairs	–	–	79.7 %	96.0%

The GMMs derived from the literature [9]. It extracts cepstrum features and mixture Gaussian model to identify activities, but recognition accuracy is very limited. Hybrid Classifiers are from the literature [4]. The method first uses a threshold to determine motionless, and it gains high accuracy in recognizing motionless, but the biggest disadvantage of this approach is that the model is too complex and must rely on complex calculations to be performed on the server to recognize activity, so when offline the phone cannot do recognition independently. Despite it has higher recognition accuracy, it also pays large and cannot run on limited platforms like phones; MC-HF SVM method comes from the literature [1]. It uses the SVM model with transformation, with recognition accuracy for walking and still, but accuracy is lower to distinguish upstairs between downstairs; Recognition accuracy of DTR for all activities are more than 90 %, does not have any instability of performance like other methods.

6 Conclusion and Future Work

According to the characteristics of human activities, we present a novel method for activity recognition on mobile phones, named DTR. The experiment results show the accuracy of our method is significantly higher than some other methods of data processing, classification. It can also accomplish accurate recognition of simple activities on mobile phones in real time with better practicality. We only studied simple activities at present, but we will attempt to identify some more complex activities in future. With the continuous improvement of the performance of mobile phone hardware, some more complex models can be introduced to further improve the recognition accuracy.

Acknowledgments. This work is supported in part by the National Natural Science Foundation of China(NSFC) under Grant No.61370222 and No.61070193, Heilongjiang Province Founds for Distinguished Young Scientists under Grant No.JC201104, Natural Science Foundation of Heilongjiang Province of China No.F201225, Technology Innovation of Heilongjiang Educational Committee under grant No.2013TD012.

References

1. Anguita, D., Ghio, A., Oneto, L., Parra, X., Reyes-Ortiz, J.L.: Human activity recognition on smartphones using a multiclass hardware-friendly support vector machine. In: Bravo, J., Hervás, R., Rodríguez, M. (eds.) IWAAL 2012. LNCS, vol. 7657, pp. 216–223. Springer, Heidelberg (2012)
2. Breiman, L.: Random forests. Mach. Learn. **45**(1), 5–32 (2001)
3. Dan, L., Yan-yan, C., Zhi-ming, Y., Hui-liang, Y.: Recognition system of human daily physical activity based on a 3d acceleration sensor. Instrum. Technol. **9**, 002 (2013)
4. Dernbach, S., Das, B., Krishnan, N.C., Thomas, B.L., Cook, D.J.: Simple and complex activity recognition through smart phones. In: 2012 8th International Conference on Intelligent Environments (IE), pp. 214–221. IEEE (2012)
5. Do, T.M.T., Gatica-Perez, D.: Contextual grouping: discovering real-life interaction types from longitudinal bluetooth data. In: 2011 12th IEEE International Conference on Mobile Data Management (MDM), vol. 1, pp. 256–265. IEEE (2011)
6. Google: Sensors overview – android developers. http://developer.android.com/guide/topics/sensors/sensors_overview.html (2014). Accessed 28 July 2014
7. Hong, Y.J., Kim, I.J., Ahn, S.C., Kim, H.G.: Mobile health monitoring system based on activity recognition using accelerometer. Simul. Model. Pract. Theor. **18**(4), 446–455 (2010)
8. Kose, M., Incel, O.D., Ersoy, C.: Online human activity recognition on smart phones. In: Workshop on Mobile Sensing: From Smartphones and Wearables to Big Data, pp. 11–15 (2012)
9. Lee, Y.S., Cho, S.B.: Activity recognition with android phone using mixture-of-experts co-trained with labeled and unlabeled data. Neurocomputing **126**, 106–115 (2014)
10. Leppanen, J., Eronen, A.: Accelerometer-based activity recognition on a mobile phone using cepstral features and quantized gmms. In: 2013 IEEE International Conference on Acoustics, Speech and Signal Processing (ICASSP), pp. 3487–3491. IEEE (2013)
11. Maekawa, T., Watanabe, S.: Unsupervised activity recognition with user's physical characteristics data. In: 2011 15th Annual International Symposium on Wearable Computers (ISWC), pp. 89–96. IEEE (2011)
12. Ravi, N., Dandekar, N., Mysore, P., Littman, M.L.: Activity recognition from accelerometer data. In: AAAI, vol. 5, pp. 1541–1546 (2005)
13. Song, C., Qu, Z., Blumm, N., Barabási, A.L.: Limits of predictability in human mobility. Science **327**(5968), 1018–1021 (2010)
14. Song, L., Kotz, D., Jain, R., He, X.: Evaluating next-cell predictors with extensive wi-fi mobility data. IEEE Trans. Mob. Comput. **5**(12), 1633–1649 (2006)
15. Wikipedia: Haar wavelet – wikipedia, the free encyclopedia. http://en.wikipedia.org/w/index.php?title=Haar_wavelet&oldid=616502668 (2014). Accessed 28 July 2014
16. Yuan, B., Herbert, J., Emamian, Y.: Smartphone-based activity recognition using hybrid classifier. In: Proceedings of the 4th International Conference on Pervasive and Embedded Computing and Communication Systems (PECCS 2014) (2014)

The Model of Malware Propagation in Wireless Sensor Networks with Regional Detection Mechanism

Jintao Hu and Yurong Song[✉]

Institute of Automation, Nanjing University of Posts and Telecommunications,
Nanjing 210046, China
hujintao88@163.com, songyr@njupt.edu.cn

Abstract. The characteristics of wireless sensor networks can be programmed over the air interface lead to a serious threat to its security. This paper proposed susceptible - infectious - recovered model of propagation based on two - dimensional cellular automata, which analyzes the characteristics of dynamic propagation in the wireless sensor networks with regional detection mechanism. Numerical simulation analysis shows that regional detection mechanism not only makes the wireless sensor networks regionalization, but also can inhibit the malware propagation in the wireless sensor networks by allowing the sensor to implement detecting strategy, thereby reducing the risk of large-scale outbreak of virus in wireless sensor networks.

Keywords: Wireless sensor networks · Malware · Cellular automata · Regional detection · Propagation model

1 Introduction

Wireless sensor networks (WSN) are new network system developed by multidisciplinary highly crossing [1], which are constituted by a large number of sensor nodes deployed in the perceived object, and perceive, collect and process the information of network coverage area. WSN widely used in areas such as military field, health care, environment monitoring and target tracking [2, 3].

In addition to the wide range of applications of wireless sensor networks, the research scope is relatively broad, and researchers have studied from different angles.

For example, as a result of limited energy, they have studied how to maximize the energy conservation and effective use of wireless sensor nodes [4]. Considering the real-time performance of data collection and transmission, the choice of routing policy is very important [5]. In addition, the topology control has also been taken more and more

Supported by the National Natural Science Foundation of China (Grant Nos. 61373136, 61374180), the Ministry of Education Research in the Humanities and Social Sciences Planning Fund of China (Grant No. 12YJAZH120), the Six Projects Sponsoring Talent Summits of Jiangsu Province, China (Grant No. RLD201212).

© Springer-Verlag Berlin Heidelberg 2015
L. Sun et al. (Eds.): CWSN 2014, CCIS 501, pp. 651–662, 2015.
DOI: 10.1007/978-3-662-46981-1_61

attention [6]. Considering all kinds of network security attacks, the malware propagation problem of wireless sensor network is in focus. Wireless sensor network generally applied in rugged environment, no man land and hostile area, and high-density deployment of wireless sensor contributes to the malware propagation, coupled with its limited resources the wireless sensor networks lack of reliable virus defense mechanism, so the safety and reliability of the wireless sensor networks cause the great attention of scholars, which is the problem to be solved. From the security angle of the wireless sensor networks, this paper established the malware propagation model based on wireless sensor networks, and carries on the analysis, explore the mechanism of inhibition of malware propagation.

In recent years, virus spreading in wireless sensor network is growing popularity in this field, and there are a large number of research results. For example, [7, 8] use the theory of epidemic and related theory of virus spreading in wireless environment [9] to study the dynamic propagation of virus in the wireless sensor networks. In the literature [10] the author has established worm propagation model with topological perception, which described both the spatial and temporal dynamics of the worm propagation. The literature [11] established worm propagation model based on theory of epidemics, and built the discrete equation to describe the worm propagation. In [12], the model of SEIRS-V (Susceptible - Exposed - Infectious - Recovered - Susceptible with a vaccination compartment) was established to describe the dynamic characteristics of worm propagation in wireless sensor networks, and analyzed the stability of the worm propagation. In [13], virus propagation model of improved SI (Susceptible - Infective) was established, this model described the sensor node would do system maintenance before going to sleep, which improved the antiviral ability of the networks without increasing hardware cost and signaling overhead. In [14], the SIS model (Susceptible - Infective - Susceptible) was established in another article, each sensor node in the model installed antivirus program, which would start to restore infected nodes on a regular basis. The model described the space-time dynamic characteristics of virus spreading and was suitable for all kinds of network, such as wireless networks, social networks and computer networks. In [15], monitoring nodes was added in the WSN to establish model of virus spreading, which described that packets with virus could trigger the monitoring node to broadcast antiviral packets in the network, thus suppressing the virus spreading. In [16], the small world of wireless sensor network structure based on the tree was established, the virus propagation in this network was studied, and virus outbreak threshold in the network was analyzed. In [17], considering the Media Access Control mechanism (MAC) model of SI was established, the theoretical analysis showed that MAC could reduce the number of infected nodes in wireless sensor network, this view have been verified through the simulation analysis in this paper.

To sum up, although there are a lot researches curbing malware propagation in wireless sensor networks now, but most of them establish spread model based on the planar structure of WSN. Although [18] established malware propagation model based on GAF of clustering network, the simulation analysis showed the GAF clustering network architecture could inhibit the malware propagation, but the model only verified the network topology could inhibit malware propagation, but without any defense mechanism. From the perspective of inhibiting virus spreading, this paper regionalized the network and added detection node in the regionalized area except using the broadcast routing protocol, and studied the process of malware propagation. We established malware propagation model of SIR (Susceptible-Infected-Recovered) Using 2–D cellular (CA) [19, 20]. We also analyze the impact of regional detection node on malware propagation.

2   Structure and Model of Wireless Sensor Networks with Detection Mechanism

2.1   Model of Wireless Sensor Networks

In a wireless sensor network, N wireless sensor nodes equipped with Omni-directional antenna distributed in a planar grid randomly and evenly. From the perspective of complex network theory, the wireless sensor network is a network of spatial-temporal correlation, the interaction between nodes in a network is a function of their space distance [21]. The strength of signal that is node n receives from node m will decay with the increase of the distance between them. Shown by the following:

$$P_{mn} = \frac{P_m}{Cd_{mn}^{\alpha}}$$ (1)

Where P_m denotes the transmitted power of node m, d_{mn} denotes the Euclidean distance between node m and n, C denotes the attenuation factor of inter-node communication channel (a constant affected by transmission frequency and other factors), P_{mn} denotes the received power of node n to receive signals from nodes m, Usually for free space propagation, α is 2, according to the different transmission environment, for the range of 2–5 [4]. When (2) was founded, the node m and n is to establish a communication link, i.e. node n can receive data from the node m correctly and node m also can receive data from the node n.

$$\frac{P_{mn}}{l} = \frac{P_m}{Cd_{mn}^{\alpha}l} \geq \beta_0$$ (2)

where l denotes the noise level of node n, and β denotes the attenuation threshold. The maximum transmission distance of node m can be obtained by (2), as follows:

$$d_{mn} = (\frac{P_m}{C\beta_0 l})^{\frac{1}{\alpha}}$$ (3)

2.2   Regional Detection Mechanism and Media Access Control Method (MAC)

Assume that wireless sensor nodes can know their own physical location information according to the GPS. The deployment area of wireless sensor network is divided into several virtual square cell, all the nodes are divided into the corresponding cell. Regularly detection nodes are elected in each cell to detect packets for the safety. Then data are transmitted in accordance with the broadcast routing protocol: when the source node transmits the data packet, the data packet was sent to the detection node within the scope of their neighbors (except the detection node of cell source node is in), then detection node receives packet and detect them, it will broadcast the packet to nodes of cell it is in if the packet detected are normal packet, and if the packet is detected for abnormal (infected) it discards the packet.

It will inevitably occurs that collision data signals when wireless channel is regarded as the transmission medium of the wireless sensor network, so the problem of sensor node contention channel must be solved for ensuring the data is sent accurately. Wireless medium access control (MAC) specific method for: when a sensor node monitors the channel free, it once again sends data after a random retreat time. A node could not send data to its neighbor nodes, unless it monitors the channel free. The malware propagation also must follow the media access control method in wireless sensor network, and we adopt collision avoidance method for media access control in this paper.

2.3   Topology of Wireless Sensor Networks

The structure of wireless sensor network is shown in Fig. 1. If r_0 denotes the communication radius, a denotes the virtual cell length, in order to ensure the sensor nodes can build communication link with detection nodes in the adjacent cell, communication radius and virtual cell side need to satisfy the following conditions:

$$a^2 + (2a)^2 \leq r_0^2 \Rightarrow a \leq \frac{r_0}{\sqrt{5}} \tag{4}$$

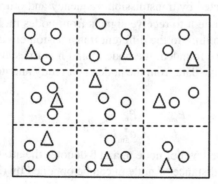

Fig. 1. The topology of networks

Dot in the Fig. 1 represent general sensor nodes, triangle said the detection node of corresponding cell.

Generation of wireless sensor network topology passes through three stages: division of virtual cell, election of detection node, identity. Generation of wireless sensor network topology process is as follows:

Step 1.   first initialized the network, all nodes in the preset is a regular nodes, each node is assigned a unique identifier ID. Each node according to the GPS gets their location information.

Step 2. the network will be divided several square cell according to the location information of nodes and the relationship of communication radius and side length
of virtual cell.

Step 3. the nodes in each cell elect detection nodes through negotiation method.

Step 4. detection node broadcasting HELLO (g, ID) message to notice other nodes in
a network after detection node of each cell is determined.

3 Propagation Model Based on Cellular Automata is Established

Two - dimensional cellular automaton is discrete dynamic systems composed of finite
number of the same cell object which is random distributed; each cell has a state, state
will changes in each time step according to the corresponding rules. In this paper, the
state of cell determined by the state of cell itself at time t and the state of its neighbors
at time t − 1. Cellular automata CA can be defined by a quad (C, Q, V, and f). Where C
denotes cellular space, Q denotes cell set of state, V denotes node neighborhood, and f
denotes the rules of state transition function.

3.1 Definition of Cellular Space

Suppose that a sensor network consists of N sensor nodes, which are random distributed
evenly in unit consists of a two - dimensional space, each unit only hold a sensor node
at most, ρ denotes the density of sensor nodes, $\rho = N/L^2$, and each sensor node occupy
a cell in the cellular space. Cell can be represented with coordinate vector, we use C_{ij}
denotes a sensor node with coordinates (i, j), cellular space consists of L*L cell which
can be expressed as follow:

$$C = \{(i,j)|1 \le i \le L, 1 \le j \le L\} \tag{5}$$

3.2 Cellular Neighborhood

There are three types about cellular neighborhood in cellular automata. For example,
Von Neumann neighborhood, Moore neighborhood, Extension Moore neighborhood.
The corresponding neighborhood is Von Neumann neighborhood when the largest
communication radius of the node for one unit, Moore neighborhood when the largest
communication radius of the node for 1.5 unit. So cellular neighborhood in cellular
automata i.e. communication neighbor of nodes in wireless sensor network can be
defined as:

$$V_{ij} = \{(x,y): \sqrt{(x-i)^2 + (y-j)^2} \le r_0, (x,y) \in C\} \tag{6}$$

3.3 Set of State and Transition Function

We use the model of SIR for propagation model here, so at any time t spread states of each cell C_{ij} should be in one of the three states: susceptible, infected, recovered. Spread states of node are defined as follows:

$$SS_{ij}(t) = \begin{cases} 0 & susceptible \\ 1 & infected \\ 2 & recovered \end{cases} \tag{7}$$

At any time t detection states of each cell should be in one of two states: detection state, normal common state. Detection states of nodes are defined as follows:

$$JS_{ij}(t) = \begin{cases} 0 & normal\ common\ state \\ 1 & detection\ state \end{cases} \tag{8}$$

There are two kinds of sensor node's channel states: busy and idle. Channel states are defined as follows:

$$MAC_{ij}(t) = \begin{cases} 0 & idle \\ 1 & busy \end{cases} \tag{9}$$

Transition function f1 of detection state and transition function f2 of spread state for any cell in cellular space are as follows:

$$JS_{ij}(t) = f1(JS_{ij}(t-1), JS_{Vij}(t-1)) \tag{10}$$

$$SS_{ij}(t) = f2(SS_{ij}(t-1), SS_{Vij}(t-1)) \tag{11}$$

where JS_{Vij} denotes detection state of all the neighbors of node, SS_{Vij} denotes spread state of all the neighbors of node.

Node state is determined by the state of itself at time t and the state of its neighbors at time $t-1$ in accordance with the rules of f1 and f2. For the of transformation detection state, a node used to detect packets is selected randomly for detection node in each cell at time t, and we use parameter p to measure the detection strength, i.e. the probability of a packet is detected to be a packet with virus is p. For propagation model of SIR, the susceptible node will be infected with probability β when the detection node of its virtual cell cannot detect the received packet with virus with probability $(1-p)$. Because sensor nodes can be installed with patch, so the node will be immunized with probability γ, the state of the node is called recovered state after immunized by installed with patch.

S (t), I (t), R (t) denote the total number of susceptible nodes in network, the total number of infected nodes and the total number of recovered nodes respectively at time t, so the follow formulas set up:

$$N = S(t) + I(t) + R(t) \tag{12}$$

where:

$$S(t) = \sum_{i,j} (SS_{ij}(t) = 0)$$

$$I(t) = \sum_{i,j} (SS_{ij}(t) = 1)$$

$$R(t) = \sum_{i,j} (SS_{ij}(t) = 2)$$

4   Simulation and Analysis

In this section we analysis the influence of regional detection mechanism on virus spreading in the WSN. N sensor nodes are distributed randomly and evenly in the area of L*L, the density is 0.5, the biggest communication radius is r_0, and we take the average of 20 times simulation results averaged to get the final simulation results. Steps of simulation are as follows:

(1) Selecting the side length of a virtual cell according to (4), a is half the communication radius. And then electing detection nodes by negotiation of the nodes of virtual cells.
(2) Three nodes are selected randomly from WSN as the initial infected nodes.
(3) Infected sensor nodes find the detection nodes in the scope of their biggest communication radius (except their own cell), and then broadcasting the packet with malware to the detection nodes, detection node receives packet and detects for malware, the packet detected as packet with malware will be discarded, else the packet is sent to all nodes within the cell, all the nodes within the cell are infected according to the state transition function.
(4) Infected sensor nodes in network continue to spread malware by the above way.
(5) Selecting the detection node of each cell after a period of Ta, repeating the above steps (1)–(4).

4.1   Influence of Regional Detection Mechanism on Propagation

The following analysis of the malware propagation in WSN without any defense mechanism, with clustering of GAF and with regional detection mechanism has the same probability of infection, recovery, radius of communications and initial infection node, i.e. the probability infection is 0.5, the probability of recovery is 0.01, communication radius is 4, the initial number of infected nodes is 1. The period of election of cluster Ta is 10 in the WSN with clustering of GAF, the probability of detection p is 0.8 and the period of election of detection node Ta is 10. Figure 2(a) and (b) on behalf of evolution trend of the proportion of infected nodes and susceptible nodes respectively in the above networks. Figure 2(a) shows that the speed of malware propagation is the fastest and the number of infected nodes is most in the WSN without any defense mechanism and the speed of malware propagation is the slowest in the WSN with regional detection mechanism, which shows that the regional detection mechanism can effectively curb the malware propagation. Figure 2(b) shows that the declines speed of susceptible nodes is the fastest in the WSN without any defense mechanism, but the slowest in the WSN with regional detection mechanism, which also shows that the curb effect of regional detection mechanism is better than others. The reason is that the regionalized WSN change the topology of the network, which affects the speed of malware propagation, and then the detection mechanism is used for data transmission, the using of detection node decreases the probability of infection. Therefore regional detection mechanism can effectively curb the malware propagation.

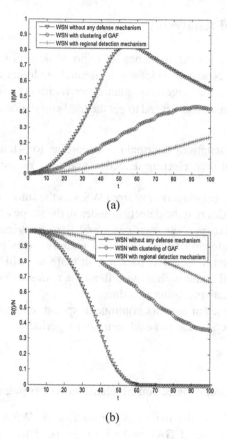

(a)

(b)

Fig. 2. (a). The changes of i(t) in three kinds of network. (b). The changes of s(t) in three kinds of network

4.2 Influence of Detection Strength on Propagation

Here we analyze the influence of different kinds of detection strength on the propagation when $\beta = 0.5$, $\gamma = 0.01$, $r_0 = 4$, $Ta = 10$. The results of simulation are the same to expected results. As shown in Fig. 3, the stronger detection strength, the less the number of infected nodes, and the slower speed of malware propagation. This is because the bigger the detection probability of detection node, the bigger the probability of a packet is detected to be a packet with malware; the packet will be discarded when it is detected to be a packet with malware, which results in the probability of infection is reduced in the cell, then the speed of propagation will be slow down, and the number of infected nodes will be reduced. The number of infected nodes will be close to zero when the detection probability reaches to a certain extent, i.e. the packets with malware can't be sent out, so which also reduces the energy consumption of the network.

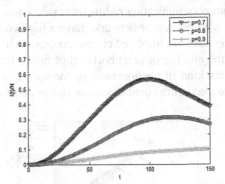

Fig. 3. The influence of detection probability on propagation

4.3 Influence of Election Period of Detection Nodes on Propagation

The simulation parameters as follows: $\beta = 0.5$, $\gamma = 0.01$, $r_0 = 4$, $p = 0.7$, then we analyze the influence of election period of detection nodes on propagation. As shown in Fig. 4, the bigger the election period, the slower speed of malware propagation, and the less the number of infected nodes. This is because the smaller the election period, the bigger the probability of detection nodes is infected nodes. They broadcast packets without detected, which lead to that the speed of propagation will be slow down and the number of infected nodes will be more.

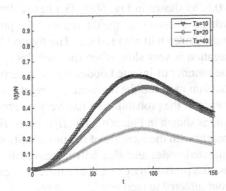

Fig. 4. The influence of election period of detection nodes on propagation

4.4 Influence of the Maximum Communication Radius on Propagation

The simulation parameters as follows: $\beta = 0.5$, $\gamma = 0.01$, Ta = 10, p = 0.8, then we analyze the influence of the maximum communication radius on propagation. As shown in Fig. 5, the speed of malware propagation and the number of infected nodes will increase with the increase of maximum communication radius, which is conceivable. But when the maximum communication radius on propagation increased from 4 to 5, 6, the speed of malware propagation and the number of infected nodes change faintly, this is because the maximum communication radius increased equal to the average degree of node increased, and wireless sensor networks have a high clustering coefficient and the interaction between nodes has localized characteristics, so the high clustering coefficient of nodes make the number of neighborhood of nodes tends to saturation state, which would lead to this kind of phenomenon of the speed of malware propagation change faintly when the maximum communication radius on propagation increased.

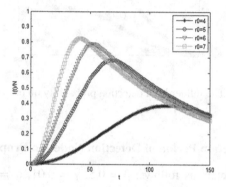

Fig. 5. The influence of the maximum communication radius on propagation

4.5 Influence of the Probability of Infection and Recovery on Propagation

We analyze the influence of the probability of infection on propagation when $r_0 = 4$, $\gamma = 0.01$, Ta = 10, p = 0.8, as shown in Fig. 6(a). The figure depicts that the speed of malware propagation will slow down with the decrease of the probability of infection, and the number of infected nodes will also reduce. The figure also represents that the speed of malware propagation is very slow when the probability of infection decrease from 0.4 to 0.35, and the number of infected nodes tends to zero, which indicates that regional detection mechanism can curb the malware propagation.

We analyze the influence of the probability of recovery on propagation when $r_0 = 4$, $\beta = 0.5$, Ta = 10, p = 0.8, as shown in Fig. 6(b). The figure describes that the influence on propagation is unapparent with the increase of the probability of recovery, but it will reduce the number of infected nodes and also will increases the speed of recovery to recovered, this is because the probability of recovery increased can increase the probability of nodes' states from infected to recovered, which results in the speed of recovery increased, it is easy to understand.

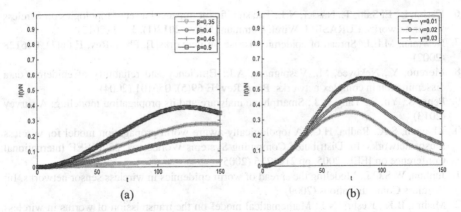

Fig. 6. (a). The influence of the probability of infection on propagation, (b). The influence of the probability of recovery on propagation

5 Conclusion

We put forward a kind of regional detection mechanism, established the malware propagation model of SIR in WSN based on two - dimensional cellular automata, analyzes the characteristics of dynamic propagation in wireless sensor networks with regional detection mechanism, and compared it with the malware propagation in WSN without any defense strategy and with clustering of GAF. Simulation results show that the regional detection mechanism can effectively inhibit the malware propagation in the wireless sensor networks, reduce the risk of virus outbreak, and ensure the normal operation of the network system. Simulation results also point out that increasing the ability of detection node, extending the election period of detection nodes and reducing the probability of infection can effectively restrain the malware propagation.

Acknowledgments. The authors thank the National Natural Science Foundation of China (Grant Nos. 61373136, 61374180), the Ministry of Education Research in the Humanities and Social Sciences Planning Fund of China (Grant No. 12YJAZH120), the Six Projects Sponsoring Talent Summits of Jiangsu Province of China (Grant No. RLD201212) for supporting this work.

References

1. Akyildiz, I.F., Su, W., Sankarasubramaniam, Y.J.: Wireless sensor networks: a survey. Comput. Netw. **38**(4), 393–422 (2002)
2. Chong, C.Y., Kumar, S.P.J.: Sensor networks: evolution, opportunities, and challenges. Proc. IEEE **91**(8), 1247–1256 (2003)
3. Akyildiz, I.F., Su, W., Sankarasubramaniam, Y.J.: A survey on sensor networks. Commun. Mag. IEEE **40**(8), 102–114 (2002)
4. Pantazis, N.A., Vergados, D.J., Vergados, D.D.J.: Energy efficiency in wireless sensor networks using sleep mode TDMA scheduling. Ad Hoc Netw. **7**(2), 322–343 (2009)
5. Xu, Y., Ren, F., He, T.J.: Real-time routing in wireless sensor networks: A potential field approach. ACM Trans. Sensor Netw. (TOSN) **9**(3), 35 (2013)

6. Karim, L., El Salti, T., Nasser, N.J.: The significant impact of a set of topologies on wireless sensor networks. EURASIP J. Wirel. Commun. Netw. **2012**(1), 1–13 (2012)
7. Newman, M.E.J.: Spread of epidemic disease on networks[J]. Phys. Rev. E **66**(1), 016128 (2002)
8. Moreno, Y., Nekovee, M., Vespignani, A.J.: Efficiency and reliability of epidemic data dissemination in complex networks. Phys. Rev. E **69**(5), 055101 (2004)
9. Peng, S., Yu, S., Yang, A.J.: Smartphone malware and its propagation modeling: A survey (2013)
10. Khayam, S.A., Radha, H.C.: A topologically-aware worm propagation model for wireless sensor networks. In: Distributed Computing Systems Workshops. 25th IEEE International Conference on IEEE, 2005, pp 210–216 (2005)
11. Junhua, W.S.C.J.: Modeling the spread of worm epidemics in wireless sensor networks. In: Wireless Communications (2009)
12. Mishra, B.K., Keshri, N.J.: Mathematical model on the transmission of worms in wireless sensor network. Appl. Math. Model. **37**(6), 4103–4111 (2013)
13. Tang, S.J.: A modified SI epidemic model for combating virus spread in wireless sensor networks. Int. J. Wireless Inf. Netw. **18**(4), 319–326 (2011)
14. Tang, S., Myers, D., Yuan, J.J.: Modified SIS epidemic model for analysis of virus spread in wireless sensor networks. Int. J. Wireless Mob. Comput. **6**(2), 99–108 (2013)
15. Kechen, Z., Hong, Z., Kun, Z.C.: Simulation-based analysis of worm propagation in wireless sensor networks/multimedia information networking and security (MINES). In: 2012 Fourth International Conference on. IEEE, pp. 847–851 (2012)
16. Vasilakos, A.V.J.: Dynamics in small worlds of tree topologies of wireless sensor networks. J. Syst. Eng. Electr. **3**, 001 (2012)
17. Ya-Qi, W., Xiao-Yuan, Y.J.: Virus spreading in wireless sensor networks with a medium access control mechanism. Chin. Phys. B **22**(4), 040206 (2013)
18. Xiao-Ping, S., Yu-Rong, S.J.: A malware propagation model in wireless sensor networks with cluster structure of GAF. J. Telecommun. Sci. **27**(8), 33–38 (2011)
19. Georgoudas, I.G., Sirakoulis, G.C., Andreadis, I.J.: Modeling earthquake activity features using cellular automata. Math. Comput. Model. **46**(1), 124–137 (2007)
20. Cunha, R.O., Silva, A.P., Loureiro, A.A.F.C.: Simulating large wireless sensor networks using cellular automata. In: Proceedings of the 38th annual Symposium on Simulation. IEEE Computer Society, pp. 323–330 (2005)
21. Mickens, J.W., Noble, B.D.C.: Modeling epidemic spreading in mobile environments. In: Proceedings of the 4th ACM workshop on Wireless security. ACM, pp. 77–86 (2005)

An Adaptive Step Detection Algorithm Based on the State Machine

Fang Zhao[1], Xinran Li[1(✉)], Jiabao Yin[1], and Haiyong Luo[2]

[1] Beijing University of Posts and Telecommunications, Beijing, China
zfsse@bupt.edu.cn, {lxrhzmlh,yinjiabao1991}@gmail.com
[2] Institute of Computing Technology Chinese Academy of Sciences, Beijing, China
yhluo@ict.ac.cn

Abstract. This paper addresses an adaptive step detection algorithm using inertial sensors commonly found on commodity mobile phone. After analyzing the acceleration data collected by the accelerometer in mobile phone, the step detection is completed by using the state machine combined with other subsidiary conditions. This step detection algorithm can also dynamically change the thresholds based on the acceleration data features to achieve the goal of detecting the steps adaptively. The experimental results show that this step detection algorithm not only has high accuracy, but also solid robustness. It can eliminate the error count caused by the shaking and flipping.

Keywords: Step detection · Accelerometer · State machine · Mobile phone

1 Introduction

Along with social economy development and people living standard enhancement, people pay more and more attention to health quality. Pedometer is available to detect the walk steps and helps people directly know the physical exercising in real time [1]. With the gradual development of the indoor positioning, it is able to apply the pedometer to the field of the indoor positioning [2–4]. Combining the measured walk steps with the step estimation method, it is easily to get the walking distance [5]. The indoor positioning requires more accurate function which the existing pedometer can't offer [6]. Therefore, a high-precision pedometer is needed to ensure the precision of the indoor positioning.

In recent years, with the functions of the mobile phone increasing, the use of it is more extensive in the daily life [7,8]. It is common to use the built-in sensors of the mobile phone to develop the pedometer. The main advantage of inertial sensor-based pedometer is that it is environment-independent and more convenient than the traditional pedometer since the life of people and mobile phone is closely bound up. But the existing pedometer also couldn't eliminate the error count caused by the shaking and flipping, and they can detect the walk steps accurately only in the condition of carrying the phone

© Springer-Verlag Berlin Heidelberg 2015
L. Sun et al. (Eds.): CWSN 2014, CCIS 501, pp. 663–672, 2015.
DOI: 10.1007/978-3-662-46981-1_62

in the specified location [9,10]. In addition, the accelerometers of the different brands of mobile phone have different sensitivity and parameters, so the same pedometer algorithm applied to different mobile phones may computes various numbers of steps.

The purpose of this article is attempt to overcome shortcomings of existing techniques by providing an accurate step detection algorithm using the data collected by the accelerometers of the carry-on mobile phones. Compared with the current technology, the algorithm proposed in this paper has the following advantages:

1. This algorithm can combat the effects of the shake and quiver of the sensor, so realize accurate step detection.
2. It is not directed at a certain person or a certain status and is able to adaptively adjust the parameters and count the steps accurately, in despite of the athletic forms of different people or the different athletic forms of the same person.
3. This algorithm is particularly suitable for the mobile phones or other common mobile smart devices and is compatible with various different types of mobile phone and other mobile smart devices.
4. At the data acquisition stage, this algorithm doesn't limit the position or the way the user carry the device. For example, when using the mobile phone as the accelerometers data acquisition device, this algorithm can adaptively adjust the parameters and count the steps accurately no matter where the user put the mobile phone, such as trouser pocket, shirt pocket, handbag or backpack, or how you hold the mobile phone, such as holding the phone in hand and swinging back and forth or using the phone while walking.

2   System Design

Figure 1 shows the flow chart of this step detection method includes the following steps:

Step 1: Use the 3-axis linear accelerometer data collected by the carry-on accelerometer in real-time to calculate magnitude of the linear acceleration vector. The existing smart mobile devices usually have built-in 3-axis linear accelerometer, which can measure the linear acceleration in three perpendicular directions. The magnitude of the linear acceleration vector formed by these three linear accelerations can be calculated. For ease of description, all linear acceleration mentioned in this paper refers to the magnitude of the linear acceleration vector.

Step 2: The main task of this step is to pre-process the raw data collected in Step 1. The curve of the raw linear accelerometer data changing in time which is the sample sequence in fact has large high-frequency noise. In order to eliminate the effect of noise, a low-pass filter is used to cut unwanted high-frequency noise in this step.

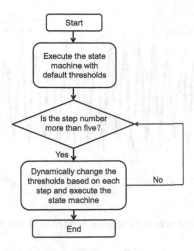

Fig. 1. Flow chart of the System

Low-pass filter provides a smoother form of a signal, removing the short-term fluctuations, and leaving the longer-term trend. The equation of low-pass filtering is shown as the following:

$$Y_n = a * X_n + (1 - a) * Y_{n-1} \tag{1}$$

where X_n is the current sample, Y_{n-1} is the previous output, Y_n is the output and a is the filter coefficient.

In the normal walking state of human, the maximum walking frequency is 3 Hz. The cut-off frequency f_c of the low-pass filter is 3 Hz [8]. The cut-off frequency (in hertz), is determined by the time constant τ. The equation is shown as following:

$$\tau = 2\pi f_c \tag{2}$$

Then the time constant can be obtained. The Eq. 3 is used to obtain the filter coefficient a, where the dt is the sampling period, for example, 20 ms.

$$a \approx \frac{\tau}{\tau + dt} \tag{3}$$

These numerical values are substituted in above equations to calculate the filter coefficient which is used to filter the high-frequency noise of the linear accelerometer data that is collected while walking. The filter coefficient is 0.84. The Fig. 2 shows comparison of results before and after the filtered. The values shown in Fig. 2 are the values after the gravitational acceleration subtracted. It is observed that this filter has a prefect effect on removing the high-frequency noise.

Step 3: In this step, a state machine mode is used to simulate people's walking pattern and the steps are counted according to the cycle numbers of this state machine [11]. The multiple states of linear acceleration curve correspond to the

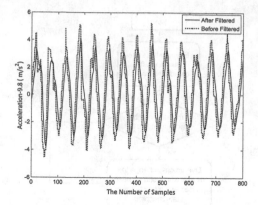

Fig. 2. The comparison of results before and after the filtering

Fig. 3. The whole process of walking one step

multiple walking states and drive the state machine to change different states. At the same time, each cycle of the state machine generates one step of the person. In this way, the steps number can be calculated based on the state transition of the state machine.

Figure 3 shows the whole process of walking one step. Through the analysis of the walking process, it is found that the variation of linear acceleration has certain regularity and periodicity. When the linear acceleration is equals to gravitational acceleration, it is recognized that the person is not influenced by the driving forces upwards, so only the gravitational acceleration is collected and particular point can be regarded as the splitting point between two steps. For ease of description, this paper calls this splitting point the balance point. Based on the balance point to do the analysis, when a person walks one step, the linear acceleration rises from the balance point to the maximum value, drops to the minimum value, and then comes back to the balance point. This process is similar to changing trend of the sine curve. In this way, if the feature points of the acceleration curve are found and the walking process is divided into multiple stages based on these feature points, the different states of the state machine can be used to simulate these stages and the each cycle of the state machine corresponds to one step. Based on the collected linear acceleration to execute the state machine, the transfer of the state simulates the transfer of the stages while people are walking. When the state machine completes a cycle, it means that the person walks one step.

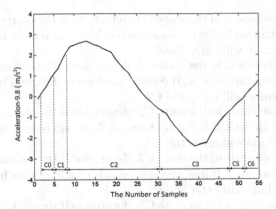

Fig. 4. The curve of the linear acceleration

The Fig. 4 shows the curve of the linear acceleration collected by the three-axis acceleration sensor in the phone varies with time while a person is walking one step. According to the Fig. 4, the state machine includes the state C0, C1, C2, C3, C5 and C6. The different state corresponds to the different stage of one step and they form the whole process of one step. There C1 is the equilibrium state of the linear acceleration, C1 is the increasing state, C2 is the peak state, C3 is the declining state, C5 is the valley state and C6 is the completion state. In order to drive the state machine, four thresholds Str1, Str2, Str3, Str4 are set, which are correspond to the upper limit of the equilibrium stage, the lower limit of the peak stage, the upper limit of valley stage and the lower limit of the equilibrium stage.

The process of the state machine includes the initialization of the counter whose value is considered as the step number. Then the collected linear acceleration stream is imported into the state machine and run the state machine based on the rules (a)–(f) as shown in Fig. 5.

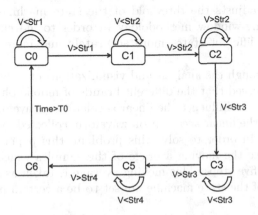

Fig. 5. State transition diagram

(a) If the state machine is in the state C0, determine if the current linear acceleration is less than Str1. If it is, the state machine will remain in C0; otherwise, the state machine will enter the C1.

(b) If the state machine is in the state C1, determine if the current linear acceleration is less than Str2. If it is, the state machine will remain in C1; otherwise, the state machine will enter the C2.

(c) If the state machine is in the state C2, determine if the current linear acceleration is less than Str3. If it is, the state machine will remain in C2; otherwise, the state machine will enter the C3.

(d) If the state machine is in the state C3, determine if the current linear acceleration is less than Str3. If it is, the state machine will remain in C3; otherwise, the state machine will enter the C5.

(e) If the state machine is in the state C5, determine if the current linear acceleration is less than Str4. If it is, the state machine will remain in C5; otherwise, the state machine will enter the C6.

(f) If the state machine is in the state C6, add 1 to the counter and jump to the state C0. It can be inferred that the state C5 is a virtual state. When the state machine enters the state C6, it can be considered that the collected acceleration sequence has gone through the previous state C1, C2, C3 and C5 completely. This acceleration sequence is effective, so we can add 1 step to the counter directly and the state machine jump to the next cycle.

Whats more, in state C6, we can determine whether count one step or not according to the subsidiary conditions. In the above (f), if the state machine is in the state C6, determine if the period of the most recent process from C0 to C6 is satisfied with subsidiary conditions. If it is, add 1 to the counter and jump to the state C0; otherwise, the value of the counter remains the same and the state machine jumps to the state C0. The subsidiary conditions include that the period of the most recent process from C0 to C6 should be in the time interval that a person walks one normal step. In this way, the influence of the shaking or other interference factors can be reduced and the accuracy will be improved.

This paper also provides an adaptive step counting method. Based on the above method, it adjusts the threshold of the state machine dynamically by adopting the sliding-window methodology in order to movement of the state machine between different states more accurately and more like the walking process.

Specifically, through the analysis and visualizations of collected linear acceleration, it can observed that the different brands of mobile phone and different placement method can influence the linear acceleration waveform. For example, Figs. 6 and 7 show the linear acceleration waveform collected by HTC and SAMSUNG separately. In order to solve this problem, this paper adopts a sliding window to calculate the moving average of the samples which are larger than zero in the recent five steps. This moving average is taken as a baseline. Some of the thresholds of the state machine are set to be a certain percentage of this moving average.

These percentages are set based on the empirical analysis and multiple tests. After experimental analysis, it can be divided into two kinds of situations no

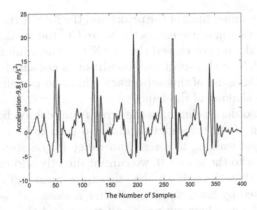

Fig. 6. The linear acceleration waveform collected by HTC

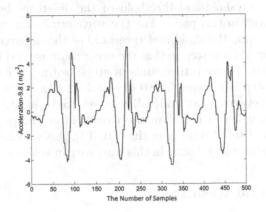

Fig. 7. The linear acceleration waveform collected by SAMSUNG

matter how the phone is placed: when the average of the peaks exceeds $2.5 \, \text{m/s}^2$, Str1 and Str2 are set to 50 % and 75 % of the average respectively; when the average of the peaks is between $1.0 \, \text{m/s}^2$ and $2.5 \, \text{m/s}^2$, Str1 and Str2 are set to 33 % and 100 % of the average respectively. Meanwhile, the valleys of the linear acceleration waveform show little change, so Str3 and Str4 are set to the fixed value $-0.5 \, \text{m/s}^2$ and $-0.4 \, \text{m/s}^2$.

In addition, through data analysis, it shows that the restriction of thresholds can only eliminate the slight shaking of hands. When a person is holding the phone in hand, the great shaking of the hand could easily affect the judgment of the normal steps. To solve this problem, another subsidiary condition is added to our judgment based on the previous subsidiary condition. The specific method is to set the maximum MAX and minimum MIN [8] which are set to be twice the value of the peaks and the valleys of the average of the recent five steps, respectively. Its worth noting that the valleys equal to the linear acceleration minus the gravitational acceleration. The peaks are positive and the valleys are negative. MAX it he upper limit of the peaks and the MIN is the lower limit of the valleys. When the state machine enters the state C0, the maximum values of the linear acceleration should not exceed the MAX and the minimum values should not go below the MIN. If this subsidiary condition is not satisfied, we should not count one step. Making use of this subsidiary condition can effectively avoid the interference by the shaking of the hand.

Furthermore, in order to eliminate the error count caused by the shaking and flipping, the setting of the threshold should also need to be combined with the time characteristic of walking to set a time range for on step. When the state machine comes back to the state C0, we cannot directly add one step, since not all the waveforms that through all the states are meaningful, some complete waveforms are caused by hand shaking or other reasons.

Because the difference between peak and valley and the corresponding time length produced by hand shaking is different from that produced by the normal walking, the time threshold and threshold of the difference between peak and valley are introduced in this paper. For the waveforms that satisfy the all the states but not the time threshold and threshold of the difference between peak and valley, we dont add one step so that the error count caused by the accidental acts can be avoided. Through thousands of steps testing, it can be found that the time for one step is between $T0=0.41\,s$ and $T1=1\,s$ [12] and the threshold of the difference between peak and valley is set to $1.1\,m/s^2$. If the difference between peak and valley is less than the threshold or the period of the most recent process from C0 to C6 is not in the $[T0, T1]$, this waveform is determined to be caused by the accidental acts. In this way, we can achieve the desired effect.

3   Experimental Results

In order to confirm the effectiveness of this step detection method, different people took different models of smartphones to collect the acceleration data in different condition. The models of smartphones include GT - S7562i (Android 4.0.4) and HTC S720t (Android 4.0.4). The conditions include:

1. Hold the phone in the front of the chest and check the message.
2. Put the phone in the pocket or bags.
3. Holding the phone in hand and swing back and forth.

Test 1 refers to the (f) without any subsidiary conditions. Test 2 refers to (f) with the condition that the period of the most recent process from C0 to C6 should be in valid time interval $[T0, T1]$. Test 3 refers to (f) with the conditions that the period of the most recent process from C0 to C6 should be in valid time interval $[T0, T1]$ and in this period the peak value should not exceed the upper limit of the peaks MAX and the valley value should not go below the lower limit of the valleys MIN. Test 4 refers to (f) with the all the subsidiary conditions. The subsidiary conditions include that the period of the most recent process from C0 to C6 should be in valid time interval $[T0, T1]$, in this period the peak value should not exceed the upper limit of the peaks MAX and the valley value should

Table 1. The test results of the four tests

Model of Smartphone	Condition	Accuracy of Test 1	Accuracy of Test 2	Accuracy of Test 3	Accuracy of Test 4
Samsung	coat pocket	94.80%	96.40%	98.20%	99.00%
Samsung	coat pocket	95.60%	97.80%	98.60%	99.60%
Samsung	coat pocket	95.20%	97.00%	98.80%	99.40%
Samsung	coat pocket	96%	98.60%	98.60%	100.00%
Samsung	coat pocket	96%	97.80%	98.80%	100.00%
HTC	coat pocket	95.20%	97.20%	98.00%	99.00%
HTC	coat pocket	94.40%	96.20%	97.60%	98.60%
HTC	coat pocket	90.40%	92.40%	95.20%	99.80%
HTC	coat pocket	94.40%	96.00%	97.60%	98.40%
HTC	coat pocket	96%	98.60%	99.00%	100.00%
Samsung	trouser pocket	94.80%	96.40%	98.60%	99.00%
Samsung	trouser pocket	93.00%	99.40%	99.40%	100.00%
Samsung	trouser pocket	94.40%	96.20%	97.40%	99.60%
Samsung	trouser pocket	93%	99.80%	98.00%	99.40%
Samsung	trouser pocket	95.60%	98.00%	99.40%	99.60%
HTC	trouser pocket	95.60%	97.20%	98.60%	99.60%
HTC	trouser pocket	95%	99.40%	99.10%	100.00%
HTC	trouser pocket	94.60%	97.00%	99.40%	99.60%
HTC	trouser pocket	96.00%	98.20%	99.20%	100.00%
HTC	trouser pocket	95.80%	97.00%	98.40%	99.80%

not go below the lower limit of the valleys MIN and the difference between peak and valley should not less than the threshold $1.1\,\text{m/s}^2$. The following table shows the test results of the four tests.

From the above table it can be seen that testing results are more accurate along with conditions to be improved. The Table 1 shows this step detection method has high accuracy and adapt to various placement conditions and different models.

4 Conclusion

This paper puts forward a step detection method using the state machine model. In this paper, the individual processes of one step are defined as different status while the thresholds are regarded as trigger conditions, which determine a finite state machine. The acceleration data collected by the accelerometer in mobile phone is taken as the input. Moreover, the paper also introduces the design thought and structure of the state machine. The setting of the subsidiary conditions also is based on the feather of the step. The experiment result proves that this step detection method is efficient and robust. But this method also has its shortcomings: when the people are walking too fast or too slow, the accuracy of this method is not very high. So, the future research will be aimed at analyzing the feature of the acceleration data from other perspectives to solve these kinds of extreme cases.

Acknowledgments. This work was supported in part by the National Natural Science Foundation of China (61374214), the Major Projects of Ministry of Industry and Information Technology (2014ZX03006003-002), the National High Technology Research and Development Program of China (2013AA12A201) and Taiyuan-Zhongguancun Cooperation special Project (130104).

672   F. Zhao et al.

References

1. Lu, Y.Y., Lin, W.B., Huang, J.J., Cheng, K.S.: The fulfillment of a three step-size models pedometer based on accelerometer and embedded system. Artif. Life Rob. **17**(1), 7–10 (2012)
2. Woodman, O., Harle, R.: Pedestrian localisation for indoor environments. In: Proceedings of the 10th International Conference on Ubiquitous Computing, pp. 114–123 (2008)
3. Krach, B., Robertson, P.: Integration of foot-mounted inertial sensors into a bayesian location estimation framework. In: 5th Workshop on Positioning, Navigation and Communication, pp. 55–61 (2008)
4. Alberto, S., Davide, C., Valentina, M.: Indoor pedestrian navigation system using a modern smartphone. In: 12th International Conference on Human-Computer Interaction with Mobile Devices and Services, pp. 397–398 (2010)
5. Constandache, I., Choudhury, R., Rhee, I.: Towards mobile phone localization without war-driving. In: Proceedings of IEEE INFOCOM 2010, pp. 1–9 (2010)
6. Hu, W.Y., Lu, J.L., Wu, M.Y.: Indoor positioning system based on RSSI and inertial measurement. Comput. Eng. **39**(11) (2013)
7. Wu, S.S., Wu, H.Y.: The design of an intelligent pedometer using android. In: 2011 2nd International Conference on Innovations in Bio-Inspired Computing and Applications, pp. 313–315 (2011)
8. Zhong, S., Wang, L., Bernardos, A.M., Song, M.: An accurate and adaptive pedometer integrated in mobile health application. In: IET International Conference on Wireless Sensor Network 2010, IET-WSN 2010, pp. 78–83 (2010)
9. Klingbeil, L., Wark, T.: A wireless sensor network for real-time indoor localisation and motion monitoring. In: 2008 International Conference on Information Processing in Sensor Networks, pp. 39–50 (2008)
10. Li, F., Zhao, C.S., Ding, G.Z., Gong, J., Liu, C.X., Zhao, F.: A reliable and accurate indoor localization method using phone. In: Inertial Sensors UbiComp 2012 - Proceedings of the 2012 ACM Conference on Ubiquitous Computing, pp. 421–430 (2012)
11. Moustafa, A., Moustafa, Y.: Ubiquitous pedestrian tracking using mobile phones. In: 2012 IEEE Wireless Communications and Networking Conference, pp. 3204–3209 (2012)
12. Cai, J.M., Chen, X.W.: The research of time-history response analysis of footbridge vibration based on stimulation of group walking. Steel Constr. **7**, 16–20 (2009)

An Individual Service Recommendation Model Based on Social Network and Location Awareness

Tingting Zhao, Ning Ye[✉], Ruchuan Wang, and Qiaomin Lin

College of Computer, Nanjing University of Posts and Telecommunications,
Nanjing 21003, China
yening@njupt.edu.cn

Abstract. With the rapid development of Web technology and mobile devices, it is necessary to provide efficient models for service recommendation. In connection with the problems of existing systems and LBS (Location Based Service), we propose a model composed of three modules. In social network module, we detect community from the social network, classify users by computing the shortest length and filter users according to the destination. The location awareness module collects the history trace of users with the positioning algorithm based on mobile anchor node. In the module of LBS, we unify the description of user traces using locations obtained from extracting and clustering the key points. After that, we compute the relevance between two locations to realize the location recommendation service. At last, we provide some simulations to verify the validity and enforceability of the model we proposed.

Keywords: Individual · Service recommendation · Social network · Location awareness · LBS · Location relevance

1 Introduction

With the development of Web technology in recent years, the number of Web-based services increases exceptional rapidly leading to the urgent need of putting forward kinds of efficient service recommendation mechanisms and models. But the existing methods of service recommendation pay more attention to service performance and QoS (Quality of Service) like the response time. For instance, Blake and Nowlan proposed an algorithm to compute a score for each Web service based on their performance when interacting with users [1]. And in [2], Zhu et al. proposed a QoS prediction framework based on landmarks and presented two developed algorithms for service recommendation based on clustering. In addition, the authors of [3] designed a collaborative filtering approach to infer the QoS value of a Web service based on its past performance. However, those methods may offer the same service results to users with similar requirements, lacking of individuals. In [4], the authors designed a model to characterize the

© Springer-Verlag Berlin Heidelberg 2015
L. Sun et al. (Eds.): CWSN 2014, CCIS 501, pp. 673–684, 2015.
DOI: 10.1007/978-3-662-46981-1_63

interactions of Web service and emphasized the performing resources of had impacts on individual Web service. By analyzing the contextual information of user-service interactions, such as location and network delay, a region-sensitive recommendation method was provided in [5] to infer the individual QoS value of a service for each user. But these individual predictions mainly based on information about QoS properties still ignoring users' individual needs largely. Searches about LBS mainly view GPS as the data collection sources, the authors of [6] proposed the method analyzing GPS sequences of vehicles and points of interest nearby to predict possible paths and related traffic information on the way to the destinations. Some vehicle tracking systems mentioned in [7] monitored and collected GPS data to estimate some points of interest. However, GPS is limitedly used in the outdoor environment without any shelter. Whats more, the devices with GPS function are usually bulky with high energy consumption that will result in higher costs and sometimes need fixed infrastructures [8].

In this paper, we provide an individual location-based service recommendation model by combining community detection in social network and data in location awareness. In the following Chap. 2, we describe the background of the social network, community detection, location awareness and location based service (LBS). In Chap. 3, we present the framework of the model we proposed as well as a separate flow chart of data processing in LBS module. Chapter 4 presents the main algorithm and AlgorithmDijkstra used in our model. Chap. 5 presents simulation results using a corpus of experimental data in the application background of tourism. At the last, Chap. 6 concludes the paper and shows the outlines of future research.

2   Background

2.1   Social Network and Community Detection

A group of people or groups associated by a relationship is called a social network. The social network is often represented as a complex graph consisting of nodes and edges, where nodes represent people and edges represent various social relationships [9]. With the constant join of new nodes or establishment of new links, the social network continues to evolve [10]. With the large-scale local interaction of individuals in a network, the social network emerges several characteristics that are the small world property, the scale-free property and the self-similarity. Figure 1 shows a graph which represents a complex social network with a very significant difference between the intensities of the regional linkages. A few regions are particularly concentrated while others are not. The network communities called a cluster or a module are defined as the dense connectivity branches of network, they have the characteristics that the dense connections in the community and relatively sparse connections between communities [11]. For example, we can abstract the WWW (World Wide Web) as a weighted directed graph, and the cluster consists of multiple websites with common properties called the online community [12]. There are many methods used to community detection, including optimization-based method and heuristic method [13].

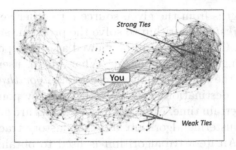

Fig. 1. Social network

2.2 Location Awareness and Location Based Service

Location Awareness is a key issue embedded into widespread computing environments to develop the autonomous entities [14], which means it can obtain the position of a particular individual or object by using the navigation apparatus to provide the corresponding location-based services [15]. The wide use of location awareness device like mobile phones makes the obtaining of individual movement trajectory with long sequences and mass high-precision become a possibility [16]. Although the position function can be achieved through GPS, its scope of applications is limited to the outdoor environment without any shelter. Then in the case that GPS is limited or in more complex environments, the position sensors with characteristics like small size, low power consumption and suitable prices began to be applied [8]. Here we use a position algorithm based on mobile anchor node that can update their coordinates at any time in the process of moving. We assume that these sensor nodes with position ability and mobility are placed with the human to obtain location information. The *LocationBasedServices(LBS)* get the location information as geographical coordinates of mobile users through radio communications network (like GSM or CDMA network) of the Mobile and Telecommunications network or external position means like GPS to provide a value-added service, which is also known as position service or mobile position service system [17]. LBS is based on the combination of mobile communication networks and computer networks that are interacted by gateways. The main characters are the high coverage both indoor and outdoor, and changeable position accuracy in light of different service needs for various users [18].

3 Model Framework

The model proposed in this paper takes advantage of existing mature community detection method to detect the community that the center user belongs to. The community will be expressed as an undirected graph $G = (V, E)$ without weight, where V is the set of all users, and links between users compose of edge set E. In the next, the user classification problem will be converted into a single-source shortest path problem, which is used to turn up the shortest paths and the shortest lengths from the given source v to other vertices. And we will make changes to $Dijkstra$ algorithm to solve the problem, and then we give the $AlgorithmDijkstra$. Central user will be viewed as source point v to obtain the shortest path and length starting from it. Whats more, users will be classified into different sets by the way of using the results of $AlgorithmDijkstra$. For the user filtered out with destination, we will extract the key points where the users stayed more than a certain time. Next all the key points are going to be clustered into locations with clustering algorithm and each history track will be described as location history. An iterative algorithm is used to obtain users experiences that will be applied to calculate the relevance between every two locations to provide an individual recommendation. The proposed model framework is shown as Fig. 2, including the social network module, the location awareness module and LBS module, and the input of model only includes the center user and his destination. The final recommendation will be provided after data processing. The flow chart of LBS module is as depicted in Fig. 3. The history trace will be described as sequence of locations. The location history will be used to infer the user experience with an iterative algorithm. Finally, we can calculate the relevance in matrix Rel for recommendation.

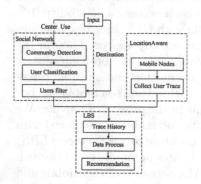

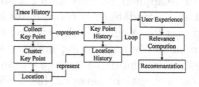

Fig. 2. Model framework   **Fig. 3.** Flow chart of LBS module

4   Algorithm Design

4.1   Module Algorithm Design

The algorithm will be divided into community detection, user classification, location relevance calculation based on the general idea of this paper. We firstly give detailed analysis and algorithms of every part and the overall algorithm framework will be provided at last of this chapter.

Community Detection: We take advantage of the idea about community detection using ordinary clustering algorithms like K-means to divide the whole social network to extract the small community related to the center user u_c, such as $C = CommunityDetection(N, u_c)$[19]. Then we can get community

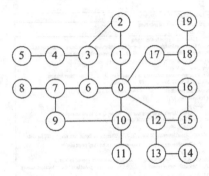

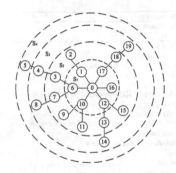

Fig. 4. u0-Centered community   **Fig. 5.** User classification

$C = \{U, u_c\}$ where U represents the users related to u_c, and it is also a sub-network, therefore we still express the community as graph. The community shown in Fig. 4 contains 20 users represented by numbers from 0 to 19 who respectively have direct or indirect contact with u_0. Edges in the graph only represent an association between the two connected users but not distinguish the intimacy of connections, so that the intimacy between u_1 and u_0 is the same as that between u_{10} and u_0.

AlgorithmDijkstra: Now we will introduce *AlgorithmDijkstra* used in this paper, as depicted in Fig. 6. Since the adjacency list representation is relatively complex, we use an adjacency matrix A of $n * n$ to express the graph so that *AlgorithmDijkstra* is more concise and easier to understand. While solving the shortest path storing in array L, we use an array $Path$ to save the vertices through which we can reverse trace back to each shortest path step by step. Note that the path lengths this paper refers to mean the number of edges. *AlgorithmDijkstra* related definitions are as follows. $G = (V, E)$ is an undirected graph without weight. s is a one-dimensional array whose element value is 1or -1 used to respectively indicate the vertex in or out of set S.

User classification: In order to improve the individual significance of the recommendation, we will classify all users in the community according to the length of the shortest path. The nodes of a length of 1 in L are the closest to center user, the nodes of a length of 2 are the second closest. We can divide all vertices into several set sequentially, $S_1 = \{u|L(u) = 1\}$, $S_2 = \{u|L(u) = 2\}$ and so on. Representation of U finally becomes $U = \{S_1, S_2...\}$. In order to improve the proportion of users closest to the center user, we need to set a threshold Q. If the users satisfy a condition in S_1 reach this value, we only need to make historical data of these users for further analysis but not to continue searching other collections. It saves the time of finding unnecessary historical data of users, in a sense shortens the whole recommended time. After seeking the shortest path and classifying users, Fig. 4 is converted into the form shown in Fig. 5 from which we can clearly see that users are divided into collections of $S_1 = \{1, 6, 10, 12, 16, 17\}$,

AlgorithmDijkstra(G, v)
Input: Adjacent Matrix A
Output: L, Path
1. { int i, j, k, u, n;
2.   n= number of nodes in graph G;
3.   for(i=0, i<n, i++)   // Initialize the array L
4.   { s[i]=-1;
5.   if(A[v][i]=1)
6.   L[i]=A[v][i]; // L[u] is shortest path length from node v to u.
7.   else L[i]=∞;
8.   if(i=v && L[i]=1)
9.   Path[i]=v; // Path[u] stores the previous vertex from v to u
10.   else Path[i]=-1; }
11. s[v]=1;//Add resource node v into set S
12. L[v]=0;
13. for(j=1, j<n, j++;)   //Longest path length of nodes is n-1
14. { foreach L[u]=j do   // Solving the shortest path to the remaining nodes
15.   {.s[u]=1;//Add vertex u into set S storing the end of shortest path obtained.
16.   for(k=0; k<n;K++)   //Modify values in array L and array Path
17.   { if(!s[k]&& L[u]+A[u][k]<L[k])
18.   { L[k]=L[u]+A[u][k];
19.   Path[k]=u; }
20.   }
21.   }
22. }
23. }

Algorithm LocationRelation(u_c , Destination, $Trace_j$, D_t , T_t)
Input: A center user u_c and a destination
Output: Matrix Rel
1. { Ka=KPh=LH=∅ ;   // Initialization
2.   int q=0; // Used to calculate the number of users satisfying the condition, initialized to 0
3.   C=CommunityDetection(N, u_c);   //Detect the community whose center user is u_c
4.   A=AlgorithmDijkstra(C;v) ;   // A={L, Path}
5.   Foreach node v in V do
6.   Insert v corresponding value in L is i into the set Si;   // User Classification
7.   Foreach node v' in S1 do   //Retrieval set S_i
8.   if v'meet the condition   // Condition can be a city or location
9.   { Insert v' into U';
10.   q++; }
11. if q<Q   // Q is a threshold of user number. We set Q = 5 as an example.
12.   earch S2, S3 etc. successively until q>=Q; // Judge after each search of a collection
13. Foreach u_c in U' do
14.   { KP=KeyPointDetection($Trace_j$, D_t , T_t); //Detect Key Point, referring to[20] for detail
15. KPh_c =TracePresent(KP);   // Converted trace into key point history
16.   Ka=Ka∪KP; }
17. L=Clustering(Ka);   // Clustering the key point to extract a set of locations
18. { Lh_i =LacationHistoryPresent(Lh_i ,L); // Converted key point history into location history
19.   LH=LH∪ Lh_i ; }
20. E=UseExperience(U', L, LH);   // Iterative user experience
21. Foreach Lh_c in LH do
22. { For(i=0; i<| Lh_c |; i++) //| Lh_c	indicates the number of Lh_c
23.   For(j=i+1; j<| Lh_c |; j++)
24.   { $\alpha = b^{-(i-i-1)}$;   // Attenuation factor, b=2
25.   Rel(l_i , l_j)= αs_{a_c} ; } }
26. }
27. For(p=0;p<|L|;p++)   // Calculate the relevance of every two locations
28.   For(q=0; q≠ p && q<|L|;q++)
29.   { Rel(l_p , l_q)= $\sum_{s_a e U'}$ Rel(l_p , l_q); }// Sum the relevance of the same two locations
30. }

Fig. 6. *AlgorithmDijkstra*   **Fig. 7.** Algorithm *LocationRelation*

$S_2 = \{2, 3, 7, 9, 11, 13, 15, 18\}$, $S_3 = \{4, 8, 14, 19\}$ and $S_4 = \{5\}$. Due to the small number of users in our example, we set the threshold $Q = 5$ and the selection criteria is that the user must once visit Nanjing.

4.2 Relevance Calculation

Basic definitions: (a) $User$: $U = (u_0, u_1, ..., u_m)$ is a set used to describe users, where $u_k \in U, 0 \le k \le m$ is a user whose corresponding trace, location history and experience respectively is $Trace_k, Lh_k, e_k$. (b) $Trace$: $Trace_j = \langle p_0, p_1, ..., p_k \rangle$ is trace of user u_j that is a set of point coordinates with timestamps, where $p_i = (x_i, y_i, t_i)$ is the two-dimensional coordinates of point i, t_i is a timestamp and $t_i < t_{i+1}, 0 \le i < k$.

$$s.x = \frac{1}{|P|} \sum_{i=m}^{n} p_i.x, \quad s.y = \frac{1}{|P|} \sum_{i=m}^{n} p_i.y \qquad (1)$$

(c) $KeyPoint$: A key point s is a geographical region where the user stayed among the distance threshold D_t over the time threshold T_t so that the detection of key point depends on the twos thresholds. We suppose that $D(p_m, p_i)$ represents the true geographical distance between point p_m and p_i point, $Int(p_m, p_n) = |p_n \cdot t_n - p_m \cdot t_m|$ indicates the time interval between these two points. In the following, the stay point will be described formally as a set $P = \langle p_m, p_{m+1}, ..., p_n \rangle$ with collected consequent points, where $D(p_m, p_i) \le D_t, m < i \le n, D(p_m, p_{n+1}) > D_t$ and $Int(p_m, p_n) \ge T_t$. And $s = (x, y, t_a, t_l)$, where $s.t_a = p_m \cdot t_m$ shows the time user arrived s, $s.t_l = p_n \cdot t_n$ is the time user left $s.x$ and $s.y$ respectively represents the mean average value of x coordinate and y coordinate of the points in set P whose calculation formula is as shown in Eq. (1). Compared to the origin point p_i in trace, the key point has more special semantics which may mean that the point is a possible shopping mall or hotel visited by the user. For instance, $P = \langle p_1, p_2, ..., p_6 \rangle$ represents the user trace shown in Fig. 8. We assume that if $d < D_t$, $Int(p_2, p_3) \geq T_t$, then the key point s will be selected in the region with radius and must be one of the points in $\{p_2, p_3, p_4, p_5\}$.

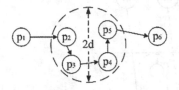

U_1	Lh_1		U_2	Lh_2		U_3	Lh_3	
X	Y	Z	Y	Z	X	Y	X	Z
O→O→O			O→O→O			O→O→O		
0	1	2	0	1	2	0	1	2

Fig. 8. Key point detection   **Fig. 9.** Example for relevance calculation

(d) *KeyPoint* History: On the basis of key point detection, the user trace will be expressed as a set of key points visited in the range of arrival and leaving time which is named as key point history KPh represented as the following Eq. (2), where $s_i, 0 \leq i < n$ is a key point and $\Delta t_i = s_{i+1}.t_a - s_i.t_i$ is the time interval between two key points. Because that key points still can not describe the KPh in a comparable space, we need to classify the key points for obtaining *Location* to describe KPh uniformly. All key points are set up into data set Ka that will be divided into several categories of clusters by using a cluster algorithm, so that the similar key points will be in the same cluster called *Location*.

$$KPh = \langle s_0 \xrightarrow{\Delta t_1} s_1 \xrightarrow{\Delta t_2} ... \xrightarrow{\Delta t_{n-1}} s_n \rangle \tag{2}$$

(e) *Location*: $L = \{l_0, l_1, ..., l_n\}$ is a set of locations where $l_i = \{s | s \in Ka\}, 0 \leq i \leq n$ is a location and $l_i \cap l_j = \emptyset, i \neq j$. After the cluster, we transform $KeyPointhistory$ into the location history Lh indicated with location l_i that the key points belong to. For $s_0 \in l_i, s_1 \in l_j, s_n \in l_k$, Eq. (2) is transformed as Eq. (3). So far, different location histories of users become comparable. In the following, we will use the location histories to infer use experience and calculate the relevance between every two locations.

$$Lh = \langle l_i \xrightarrow{\Delta t_1} l_j \xrightarrow{\Delta t_2} ... \xrightarrow{\Delta t_{n-1}} l_k \rangle \tag{3}$$

Experience inference: From examples in our Life, we can find that every user can appear in many places, and each location will be visited by a lot of different users. If representing the user as a point and viewing the visit as a directed connection, we can find that there are connections from a user point to different locations. Meanwhile, a location will be connected by numbers of users.

Figure 10 shows us the interdependence relationship between user experience and location interest, where the solid line circle indicates a key point, the dotted circle represents a location. For instance, location l_0 consists of two key points that respectively extracted from trace of u_0 and that of u_1, that means both u_0 and u_1 have visited location l_0. All in all, there is an inseparable relation between the user experience and location interest.

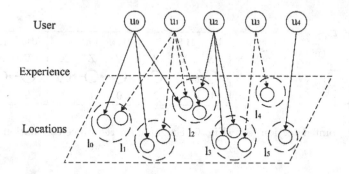

Fig. 10. User experience inference model

We use a column vector $E = (e_0, e_1, ...e_n)^T$ to show the user experiences, where e_i is the experience of u_i and $n = |U|$. Vector $I = (I_0, I_1, ...I_m)^T$ is used to represent the location interest, where I_j is the corresponding interest of location l_j and $m = |L|$. When knowing the location history Lh_k of user u_k, we can get the correlation matrix M between users and locations, where m_{ij} indicates the times that user $u_i, 0 \leq i < n$ visited location $l_j, 0 \leq j < m$. In fact, it is the number of key points detected from u_i in l_j. The correlation matrix of Fig. 10 shows as the following.

$$M = \begin{array}{c} \\ u_0 \\ u_1 \\ u_2 \\ u_3 \\ u_4 \end{array} \begin{array}{c} l_0\, l_1\, l_2\, l_3\, l_4\, l_5 \\ \begin{bmatrix} 1\,1\,1\,0\,0\,0 \\ 1\,1\,2\,0\,0\,0 \\ 0\,0\,1\,2\,0\,0 \\ 0\,0\,0\,1\,1\,0 \\ 0\,0\,0\,0\,0\,1 \end{bmatrix} \end{array}$$

The interdependence relationship between E and I is as depicted in Eq. (4). The interdependence relationship is further converted into the matrix form shown in Eq. (5). We presume that the initial state is $I_0 = E_0 = (1, 1, ..., 1)$, user experience and location interest is E_n and I_n after n iterative algorithm, the iterative process is shown as Eq. (6). We can use a matrix power iteration algorithm to calculate the final results of E.

$$e_i = \sum_{0 \leq j < m} m_{ij}.I_j, I_j = \sum_{0 \leq i < n} m_{ji}.e_i \qquad (4)$$

$$E = M \bullet I, I = M^{\mathrm{T}} \bullet E \tag{5}$$

$$I_n = M^{\mathrm{T}} \bullet M \bullet I_{n-1}, E_n = M \bullet M^{\mathrm{T}} \bullet E_{n-1} \tag{6}$$

Location relevance: The relevance between X and Y is represented as Eq. (7), where is e_i the experience of $u_i \in U'$. The attenuation factor $\alpha = b^{-(|j-i|-1)}$ and $0 < \alpha \leq 1$, where b is a constant, i and j are respectively indexes of X and Y. We can find more discontinuously two locations are visited, smaller α will be and smaller the help provided for the relevance calculation will be. We use a weighted approach to distinguish the contribution for relevance calculation to improve the rationality of results. We can calculate the relevance of every two locations in one user location history in advance, and then sum relevance of the same two locations to obtain the relevance matrix Rel. In this paper we take $b = 2$ for analysis, as shown in Fig. 9, three users (u_1, u_2, u_3) visited location (X, Y, Z) in different orders so as to produce three different location histories (Lh_1, Lh_2, Lh_3). Note that figures below the nodes are the index values of the locations in the sequence.

$$Rel(X, Y) = \sum_{u_i \in U'} \alpha.e_i \tag{7}$$

From the figure, we find that X and Y are two locations accessed continuously by user u_1 as well as Y and Z, i.e. the difference between their indexes is 1 so that $\alpha = 1$. According to the location history Lh_1 of u_1, we can calculate the results that $Rel(X, Y) = c_1$ and $Rel(Y, Z) = e_1$. However, there is a location between X and Z, so the difference between their indexes is 2, $\alpha = \frac{1}{2}$ and $Rel(X, Z) = \frac{1}{2}e_1$.

Here we demonstrate the conclusion that the relevance of two locations accessed continuously is stronger than that of locations the user visited non-continuously. In the same way, we can obtain results in the light of Lh_2 of u_2 and Lh_3 of u_3. Through summing the results of the same two locations, we can calculate the location relevance as Eqs. (8) and (9).

$$Rel(X, Y) = e_1, Rel(X, Z) = \frac{1}{2}e_1 + e_3, Rel(Y, X) = \frac{1}{2}e_2 + e_3 \tag{8}$$

$$Rel(Y, Z) = e_1 + e_2 + \frac{1}{2}e_3, Rel(Z, X) = e_2, Rel(Z, Y) = 0 \tag{9}$$

4.3   Main Algorithm Design

Algorithm $LocationRelation$ related definitions are as follows. S_i is a collection storing the nodes whose length of shortest path is i. U' is a collection of users satisfying the conditions. The definitions of KPl, L, Lh and Ka has been given above. $LH = \{Lh_k\}$ is a collection of all location histories. Rel is a matrix used to describe the location relevance. The proposed idea of Algorithm $LocationRelation$ shown in Fig. 7 is starting from the center user and destination. First of all, the user is viewed as the center cluster to detect community of the user (line 3), using $AlgorithmDijkstra$ to solve the shortest path and the shortest length from the community center to the nodes (line 4), that is the result $A = \{L, Path\}$ of the algorithm consists of two parts. Next, according to the shortest path length of seeking to classify users (line 5–6), and then click search to the collection of user traces of each category based on the destination to extract the user meets the requirements (line7–12), where selecting the number of users will be involved in the threshold Q, this article will set it to 5. For the analysis of user's historical trace, we need to extract key points through (line 13–16), clustering the key points (line 17) to make all users into comparable space to unify the expression of user traces to get location history (line 18–19). In the following, it is to calculate the relevance between locations to obtain a relevance matrix between every two locations in Rel (line21–30), which could not avoid the need to iteratively infer the relationship between the user experience and the location (line 20). Finally, we will achieve recommendation according to the output of Algorithm *LocationRelation*, by first traversal the entire correlation matrix *Rel* to retrieve the largest value, and the starting point is recommended as the first location to the second location and then view it as the starting point to retrieve for all correlations to find the third position, and so on until you can get 5–10 recommended locations, arranged in order to be a sequence that is the result of the feedback to the user.

5   Simulation

We generated multiple sets of data as the user historical trace via Matlab according to the needs, and then combined them with the generated social network relationship graph to analyze results. These simulations were done on a Toshiba L537 computer with dual processor CPU of Intel Core i3 330M Processors, running at 2.13 GHz. All simulative approaches were implemented by us in Matlab.

Settings: (a) *Dataset*: We randomly design five social network communities, which are Community 1 contains 20 users, Community 2 contains 30 users, Community 3 contains 50 users, Community 4 contains 100 users and Community 5 contains 200 users. To Nanjing for tourism as the background, we can generate the corresponding user traces with the timestamp in a reasonable geographic scope, and the location points composing of the same user trace reflect the user's journey sequentially according to the size of the timestamp. (b) *KeyPoint* Detection: In the key point extraction algorithm, we will set the distance threshold D_t to 300 m and set the time threshold T_t to 20 min. (c) *Clustering*: In this paper we use the global K-means clustering algorithm to divide the extracted key point into clusters, forming a variety of location areas. The method selects the densely distributed sample point as the cluster center. Then, we select the sample point far away from the existing ones as the next initial center to avoid interference generated the cluster centers, and shorten the clustering time without affecting the effect.

Simulation Results: Simulation 1 sequentially uses 10 %, 20 %, 30 %, 50 % and 100 % of the users in each community as the users satisfying the condition to generate recommendations. Figure 11 shows the simulation results, from the figure we can clearly see that if choosing 50 %-60 % of the users, we can basically get the same results with all users recommended jointly, that gives the proof to confirm the rationality of our model classifying users in community and selecting an appropriate number of users. This paper fully reflects the necessity of filtering users in the social network module and the significance of selecting appropriate users according to intimacy. Simulation 2 uses Community 1 of 20 users and their historical traces as the application background, and the city of Nanjing as a tourist destination to extract and cluster the key points, and calculate the location relevance through the proposed algorithm. Finally, the recommendation results are shown in Fig. 12.

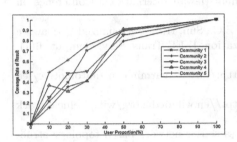

Fig. 11. Coverage rate of result with different user proportion

Fig. 12. Recommendation result

6 Conclusion

This paper generally integrates the social network data and location-aware data in IoT and achieves the location-based recommendation services. From the data analysis we can find that apart from the geographical association between locations, another relevance of locations can be described by human behavior in a different way. With using the calculated location relevance, we generate a sequence of the most relevant locations as results recommended for users. The simulations verify the validity and enforceability of the proposed method. The future work will focus on giving more evidence to prove that services achieved by the connected relationship of users in social network are more effective and individual.

Acknowledgments. The research is support by National Natural Science Foundation of P. R. China (No. 61170065 and 61003039), Peak of Six Major Talent in Jiangsu Province(No. 2010DZXX026), Jiangsu Planned Projects for Postdoctoral Research Funds (No. 1302055C), Science &Technology Innovation Fund for higher education institutions of Jiangsu Province (No. CXZZ11-0405), China Postdoctoral Science FoundationNo. 2014M560440), the Natural Science Foundation of Jiangsu Province (BK20130882)Project sponsored by Jiangsu Provincial Research Scheme of Natural Science for Higher Education Institutions (12KJB520009).

References

1. Brian, M.B., Nowlan, M.F.: A Web service recommender system using enhanced syntactical matching. In: Proceedings of the IEEE International Conference on Web Services, pp. 575–582, July 2007
2. Zhu, J.M., Kang, Y., Zheng, Z.B., Lyu, M.R.: A clustering-based QoS prediction approach for Web service recommendation. In: Proceedings of the 15th IEEE International Symposium on Object/Component/Service-Oriented Real-Time Distributed Computing Workshops, pp. 93–98, April 2012
3. Zheng, Z.B., Ma, H., Lyu, M.R., King, I.: QoS-aware web service recommendation by collaborative filtering. IEEE Trans. Serv. Comput. 4(2), 140–152 (2011)
4. Maamar, Z., Mostefaoui, S.K., Mahmoud, Q.H.: Context for personalized Web services. In: Proceedings of the 38th Annual Hawaii International Conference on System Sciences (2005)
5. Chen, X., Zheng, Z.B., Liu, X.D., Huang, Z.C., Sun, H.L.: Personalized QoS-aware Web service recommendation and visualization. IEEE Trans. Serv. Comput. 6(1), 35–47 (2003)
6. Garmin, Premium Navigation Features. http://www8.garmin.com/automotive/features/
7. Vehicle Tracking System, Wikipedia. http://en.wikipedia.org/wiki/Vehicle_tracking_system
8. Gu, J.J., Chen, S.C., Zhuang, Y.: Wireless sensor network-based topology structures for the internet of things localization. Chin. J. Comput. 33(9), 1548–1556 (2012)
9. Wen, Y.: Architecture of internet of things based on social networks. Mod. Electron. Tech. 36(3), 34–36 (2013)
10. Guo, R., Zhong, N., Bin, L.W.: Social network evolution analysis based on graph entropy. Pattern Recognit. Artif. Intell. 22(3), 360–365 (2009)
11. Pizzuti, C.: A multiobjective genetic algorithm to find communities in complex networks. IEEE Trans. Evol. Comput. 16(3), 418–430 (2012)
12. Lin, Y.F., Wang, T.Y., Tang, R., Zhou, Y.W., Huang, H.K.: An effective model and algorithn for commuity detection in social networks. J. Comput. Res. Develpoment 49(2), 337–345 (2012)
13. Fortunato, S.: Community detection in graphs. Phys. Rep. 486(3), 75–174 (2010)
14. Tesoriero, R., Tebar, R., Gallud, J.A., et al.: Improving location awareness in indoor spaces using RFID technology. Expert Syst. Appl. 37(1), 894–898 (2010)
15. Liu, Y., Xiao, Y., Gao, S., Kang, C.G., Wang, Y.L.: Summary of human mobility studies based on location-aware devices. Geogr. Geo-Info. Sci. 27(4), 8–13 (2011)
16. WANGD: Conjoint Approaches to Developing Activity Based Models. Eindhoven University of Technology, Netherlands (1998)
17. Schiller, J., Voisard, A.: Location-Based Services, pp. 1–10. Elsevier, San Francisco (2004)
18. Kolodziej, K.W., Hjelm, J.: Local positioning systems: LBS applications and services. CRC Press, Boca Raton (2010)
19. Krumm, J., Horvitz, E.: Predestination: inferring destinations from partial trajectories. In: Dourish, P., Friday, A. (eds.) UbiComp 2006. LNCS, vol. 4206, pp. 243–260. Springer, Heidelberg (2006)

A Distributed Wireless Sensor Network for Online Water Quality Monitoring

Shu Shen[1,2]($\boxtimes$), Jiao Hu[1,2], Zhiqiang Zou[1,2], Jian Sun[1,2], Siyu Lu[1,2], and Xiaowei Wang[1,2]

[1] College of Computer, Nanjing University of Posts and Telecommunications, Xin Mofan Road No. 66, Nanjing 210003, China
[2] Jiangsu High Technology Research Key Laboratory for Wireless Sensor Networks, Xin Mofan Road No. 66, Nanjing 210003, China
{shens,b11020603,zqzou,q11010114,b11030501}@njupt.edu.cn,
lusiyu90@163.com

Abstract. An application of distributed wireless sensor network for online water quality monitoring is proposed. In this paper, the architecture, hardware and software designs of the system are presented. A friendly WUI and HUI are developed to allow the users monitor the water parameters being measured in real time via Internet by PC or remote smart mobile devices. Several preliminary results of test to evaluate the reliability and effectiveness of the system are also discussed. The work in this paper is devoted to provide a feasible solution to the problem of water pollution monitoring with advantages such as low cost, real time, easy installation and maintenance and so on.

Keywords: WSN · Water quality monitoring · Zigbee · WUI · HUI · MCU · Arduino

1 Introduction

In the last decade, the problems of water pollution are increasingly gaining attentions from both academia, industries and government. As a result, the situation of water source became worse and worse with the rapid development of economy in China. The surface and underground water environments, such as rivers, lakes, oceans, springs, and deep underground waters have been and being polluted because of the large amount of unprocessed life and industrial waste water.

To the best of our knowledge, each of present ways for monitoring water environments has its own merits and drawbacks, which are summarized in [1]. Meanwhile, wireless sensor network (called WSN in short) plays an increasingly

S. Shen—Please note that this project is supported by the National Natural Science Foundation of China No. 61401221, Jiangsu province science and technology plan project No. BE2014718, and a Nanjing University of Posts and Telecommunication research project No. NY213037.

© Springer-Verlag Berlin Heidelberg 2015
L. Sun et al. (Eds.): CWSN 2014, CCIS 501, pp. 685–697, 2015.
DOI: 10.1007/978-3-662-46981-1_64

important role in the environmental monitoring. Compared with the present water quality monitoring methods, an online water quality monitoring system based on WSN provides a feasible solution, supported by many previous related works on the applications of WSN in the domain of water environment monitoring [2–6]. It can be concluded from these previous works that this solution meets several positive points like low cost, small size, high accuracy and sensitivity, low power consumption, real time, easy installation and maintenance.

In the project we are discussing now, we have emphasized the advantages of WSN. WSN is an ad-hoc network system, which composed of a lot of sensor nodes. Each node contains a special processing unit, transceiver, battery, and different kinds of sensors [1,2]. A popular and widely used technology currently based on WSN, known as Zigbee, is used in this project because of its advantages such as flexibility, low cost implementation, reliability [3].

The aim of our work in this paper is to develop a distributed WSN for online water quality monitoring, which is suitable to be applied in the rugged water environment without negative influence to the surroundings. This paper is organized as follows. The design of the whole system is described in Sect. 2. The hardware design of the system is introduced in Sect. 3. Then the software design is discussed in Sect. 4. A web user interface (WUI) for the purpose of monitoring at the data base station is developed as well. Furthermore, in order to let end users use the system easily, an Andriod based handset user interface (HUI) worked on the smart mobile device is designed. Several tests and measurements, as well as the performance analysis are discussed in Sect. 5. At the end, some conclusions are summarized in Sect. 6.

2   Water Monitoring System Design

The proposed distributed WSN for online water quality monitoring in our project is demonstrated in Fig. 1. The whole system includes four parts: Sensor node, sink node, database station, and remote monitoring end device. Two-way communication allows users monitor and control each part in the system structure. On the one hand, a large number of sensor nodes collect several key water parameters such as temperature, depth, pressure, pH, electrical conductivity rate, dissolved oxygen with the help of different kinds of water sensor detectors. The sink node communicates with the sensor nodes via Zigbee network and collects the data carried by each sensor node, then transfers all data to the database station connected. The database station processes and analyzes the water quality parameters, acting as a data processing center. As soon as accidents or emergencies like pollution or contamination occur, the database will give an alarm if any water parameter monitored is abnormal. End users could easily access the system network via Internet and monitor any parameter they are interested in. An Andriod based HUI is designed as well to support smart end device better. On the other hand, end users could control the modules like sensor node, sink node and data base station by sending some specially appointed commands like controlling, polling and management. It also supports user to modify some settings according to their own habits.

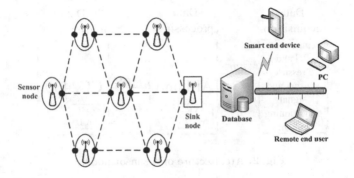

Fig. 1. Structure of the distributed WSN for online water quality monitoring.

3 Hardware Design

The sensor nodes, which have already been introduced in Fig. 1, are the basic units to realize the water environment monitoring function in the distributed environment. Generally speaking, there are following two main functions of the sensor nodes.

- Collecting several key water parameters like temperature, pH value, and water pressure or depth in the monitored area.
- Establishing a WSN network based on Zigbee protocol and realizing the two-way communication between sensor nodes and sink node, following the previous introduction in Sect. 2.

The architecture of a sensor node is illustrated in Fig. 2. The sensor node system could be divided into three major modules: data acquisition module, data processing module and data transmission module. The data acquisition module is responsible for the first function discussed above, which involves temperature, pH and pressure sensors. Since the collected original raw signals via sensors are generally too weak to be processed by MCU directly. Relevant signal conditioning circuits are required and designed here. A popular open source AVR MCU development platform, called Arduino is selected as data processing module, which connected with data acquisition module on the one hand, and connected to the data transmission module on the other hand. We use CC2430 SOC chip from Texas Instrument to design data transmission module, which deals with second function in the previous context.

3.1 Data Acquisition Module

Pressure and Temperature Sensor Unit. The measurement of water depth is always considered as a difficult point in the domain of water environment monitoring applications based on WSN technology, on the other hand, actually it is a key and necessary point especially in the research of underwater 3D monitoring. Normally, the measurement procedure of underwater depth is divided into following two steps:

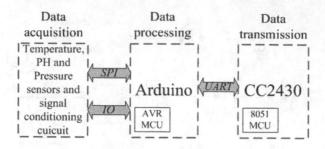

Fig. 2. Architecture of a sensor node.

- Measuring underwater pressure with the help of pressure sensor;
- Calculating the underwater depth according to the relationship of depth and pressure.

To our knowledge, at present there are mainly following two difficulties by applying traditional water pressure transducer together with WSN technology to measure water pressure:

- Power Supply Problem. Traditional water pressure transducer requires high DC voltage supply, normally 24 VDC, which is too high to supply by using battery as power source in WSN applications.
- Communication Protocol Problem. Generally, water pressure transducer is used by connecting with the specially designed compatible device from same manufacture. As a result, the communication protocol is neither unified nor easy to be adopted in other applications. For example, some water pressure transducers apply RS-485 as communication protocol, which is suitable for long range wire communication rather than wireless communication.

In order to overcome above difficulties, our group adopts the novel pressure sensor module called MS5541C from Intersema Corporation. MS5541C contains a precision piezoresistive pressure sensor and an improved version of 16 bit micropower sensor interface IC. The module uses an antimagnetic polished stainless steel ring for sealing with O-ring [9]. Besides pressure, the sensor module also provides temperature data, which supports much higher accuracy than standard solution using analog temperature sensor DS18B20 [8]. MS5541C can be easily interfaced with MCU in data processing module via 3 wire serial interface with SPI protocol [13,14]. Figure 3 shows the hardware link between master device, a MCU in processing module and slave device MS5541C. To decrease the complexity of circuit, MS5541C desired 32.768 kHz master clock signal is generated from a general IO pin of MCU by software coding instead of external oscillator.

pH Value Sensor Unit. The pH value is an important water parameter, being used widely to evaluate the water quality in monitored area. In this work we adopt industrial pH sensor, which converts pH value into electronic signal to

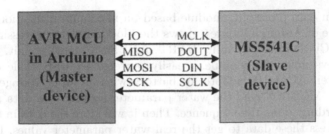

Fig. 3. Hardware link between MCU and MS5541C.

collect and process. The initial raw electronic signal is a weak DC potential signal, from $-414 - 414\,\text{mV}$. Actually, the pH value is linear inversely proportional to the electric potential.

Figure 4 shows pH signal conditioning circuit. CA3140 plays a role as voltage follower. Two operational amplifiers LMC6041 comprise two level amplifier circuit, where the first level is noninverting amplifier circuit as well as the second level is inverting. ICL7660 is used to generate negative potential ($-5\,\text{V}$) for operational amplifier. The relationship of the output of conditioning circuit, denoted V_{OUT} and the input of the circuit from pH sensor, denoted V_{IN} is following Equation:

$$V_{OUT} = V_{REF} - V_{IN}\left(1 + \frac{R3}{R2}\right) \cdot \frac{R7}{R4} \tag{1}$$

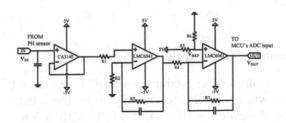

Fig. 4. pH signal conditioning circuit.

3.2 Data Processing Module

Data processing module is developed based on an open source electronics prototyping development platform, named Arduino, with flexible, easy-to-use software and hardware. The heart of Arduino is an AVR MCU Atmega 328, which has 14 digital IO pins, 6 analog inputs and is quite suitable for sensing applications [12]. Besides, Arduino also has a 16 MHz crystal oscillator, a USB connection, a power jack, an ICSP header, and a reset button [12].

We design data processing module based on maximum utilization the hardware resource of Arduino. Figure 5 shows the blocks of data processing module, including MCU unit, power unit, UART unit, flash memory unit, and LCD, LED and keys unit. The module is easily powered by USB cable connecting with computer, AC-to-DC adapter or battery with an input voltage of 5–12 V alternatively. MCU will read the water parameter signals from data acquisition module according to the time sequence. Then it will store the data in flash memory and process these data to get the real water parameter values. LCD, LED and keys unit provides an easy-to-use human-to-machine communication interface for users. At the end, MCU will send the data after processing to the data transmission module via UART.

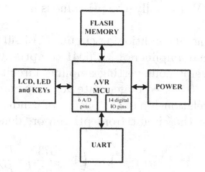

Fig. 5. Blocks of data processing module.

3.3   Data Transmission Module

The heart of data transmission module is a SOC transceiver IC CC2430 from Texas Instrument, which complys to the Zigbee protocol IEEE 802.15.4 standards. CC2430 is integrated with a 8051 MCU with a low power and high performance of 64 KBytes programmable features [13]. The structure of dual processor in this work is also an innovation, which improves the efficiency of the system. The integrated 8051 MCU in CC2430 is responsible of work on the network layer, while the AVR MCU in Arduino is mainly dealing with the sensing layer.

There are two concerns about the design of data transmission module: lower power consumption, and higher RF transmission performance. So we decide to design two types of data transmission modules according to the above concerns, without or with RF front end power amplifier. CC2591 from Texas Instrument too is adopted here as a cost effective and high performance RF front end for low power and low voltage 2.4 GHz wireless applications. Figure 6 shows an application hardware link circuit of CC2430 and CC2591. The output power of CC2591 is controlled by controlling the input power [13,14].

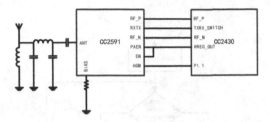

Fig. 6. CC2430 and CC2591 hardware link.

3.4 Sink Node

The sink node consists of a same data transmission module as a coordinator which initializes the Zigbee network and receives the data sent from the sensor nodes. Since the sink node needs to receive data from the sensor nodes, normally it is powered by uninterrupted power supply instead of battery to make sure the stability and reliability of the network. Then the data collected from the sensor nodes is sent to the database station via RS-232 interface.

4 Software Design

According to the introduction in the context, the work of software design is mainly divided into four parts, the data processing module program, the data transmission module program, the WUI program at the database station, and the HUI program at the smart mobile devices.

4.1 Data Processing Module Program

The responsibilities of the data processing module are initializing the system, collecting the signals from sensors, storing and processing the signals to get the real water parameter value, receiving and executing the commands, communicating with the data transmission module. Figure 7 demonstrates the flow chart of data processing module program. The programming environment Arduino IDE uses Arduino programming language, which is similar to C/C++.

As the pressure and temperature sensor MS5541C is a digital module, which is interfaced with MCU in Arduino via SPI, the programming for pressure and temperature reading needs to follow some rules in references [9,10]. The program flow chart for pressure and temperature reading are shown in Fig. 8. Since the procedures of reading pressure and temperature are similar, only an example of reading pressure value is given.

For reading and processing pH value, the program is easier. It is only need to sample the signals from ADC input and calculate the real pH value. The pH value is closely associated with temperature referring to [15], so the temperature compensation effect is added in this project.

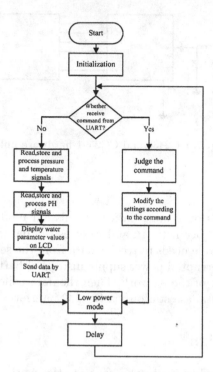

Fig. 7. Flow chart of data processing module program.

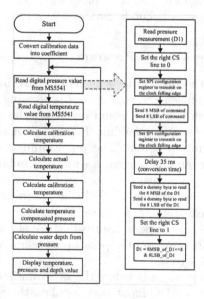

Fig. 8. Flow chart for pressure/temperature reading (left) and an example of reading pressure value (right).

4.2   Data Transmission Module Program

The programming environment for CC2430 in data transmission module is IAR embedded workbench, while the programming language is C. The function of data transmission module is building a communication bridge between sensor node and sink node. Specifically, data transmission module receives the data from data processing module via UART and send to the sink node by wireless. On the other hand, it gets command from sink node by wireless, and send to the data processing module via UART. The flow chart of data transmission module program is shown in Fig. 9. The program is developed based on the Z-stack 2006 sample applications, supported by Texas Instrument, referring to [16].

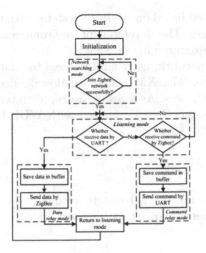

Fig. 9. Flow chart of data transmission module program.

4.3   WUI Program

The WUI platform, which is able to interact with the sink node at the database station, was successfully developed using ASP.NET programming environment while C# is used as programming language.

Administrator could easily realize the system management with full functions, which involve network topology, data search, user management, network setting. For ordinary users, they could remote login the WUI via Internet and look up basic information of network topology and data carried by sensor nodes. The core function of this platform is data search function, which supports querying according to the different ways of time, distributed area or the node numbers. It provides much convenience for users to monitor and analyze the updated water parameters with the help of these functions. Figure 10 shows the flow chart of the WUI program operation and a shot display of data search function interface respectively.

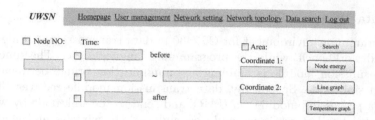

Fig. 10. Display of data search function interface.

4.4 HUI Program

HUI program is developed based on Android system, with the aim of giving more convenience for end users. The development environment is Android SDK IDE with Java adopted as programming language.

Through 3G/WIFI network, users could access the database station by HUI on smart mobile device. The XML files are downloaded from database and resolved on the mobile devices. As a result, a graphic interface is created, which provides real-time data querying. Compared with WUI, HUI focuses on portability rather than functionality.

5   System Test

Some preliminary tests are carried out to evaluate the system performance, including RF test and performance test. The test platform including sensor node is shown in Fig. 11.

5.1   RF Test

Having mentioned before, we designed two types of data transmission modules, CC2430 without or with CC2591. Figure 12 shows the strength of Received Signal

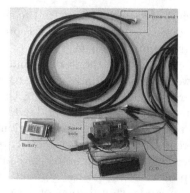

Fig. 11. Photo of the test platform.

Strength Indication (RSSI) for such two types of data transmission modules at distance of 1.2 m, using the tool RF studio from Texas Instruments. Without CC2591, the strength of RSSI is −38 dBm, and this result is −26 dBm with CC2591. In addition, with actual measurement over land, we get a result that the reliable signal could be obtained at 100 % success percentage of packet delivery to the distance of 300 m without CC2591, while with CC2591 this result is increased up to about 600 m. The result in water environment is predicted to be worse because of the complexity of water environment.

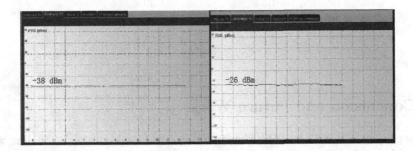

Fig. 12. RF power test without (left) or with (right) CC2591 at distance 1.2 m, using the tool RF studio.

5.2   Performance Test

In this experiment, we deployed 16 sensor nodes in an artificial lake to monitor the water parameters online. The monitor system automatically collects the water temperature, depth, pH and location, as shown in Fig. 13.

Time	NO	Temperature	Depth	PH	X-coordinate	Y-coordinate
2012/7/6 10:03:18	1	27.8	6	6.8	126	34
2012/7/6 10:03:18	2	28.4	6.5	6.8	150	15
2012/7/6 10:03:19	3	26.5	7.2	7	100	250
2012/7/6 10:03:22	4	28.4	8.2	6.9	235	235
2012/7/6 10:03:30	5	27.8	6.7	7.2	324	233
2012/7/6 10:03:44	6	28.4	9.6	7	13	213

Page 1/total 3 pages 1st page previous page next page end page

Fig. 13. A shot of display of monitoring.

As the temperature and pressure sensor is a digital sensor IC, the resolution is very high, as accurate as 0.015 °C for temperature and 1.2 mbar for pressure.

For analog pH sensor, we calibrate and test the pH probe with standard solutions of pH 4, pH 6.86 and pH 9.18 in order to get a reliable test result, as shown in Table 1. From the results in Table 1, we get a conclusion that the accuracy of pH test is good enough to be used in real applications.

Table 1. pH test results under ambient temperature.

Standard pH	V_{OUT} in theory (V)	V_{OUT} in test (V)
4.00	1.34	1.36
6.18	2.16	2.12
9.18	2.80	2.75

6   Conclusion and Future Work

In this project, a distributed WSN system was developed, aiming at dealing with the problems of online water quality monitoring. The architecture, hardware and software designs of the system are designed and introduced. A friendly WUI and HUI are developed to allow the users monitor the water parameters being measured in real time via Internet by PC or remote mobile devices.

For the future work, we will take the power consumption into consideration, which affects the life cycle of sensor nodes heavily as a key factor. Furthermore, some related theory and technology, will be researched to improve the efficiency and reduce the power consumption of the system.

Acknowledgments. The work in this paper is supported by the National Natural Science Foundation of China No. 61401221, Jiangsu province science and technology plan project No.BE2014718, and a Nanjing University of Posts and Telecommunication research project No. NY213037.

References

1. Jiang, P., Xia, H., He, Z., et al.: Design of a water environment monitoring system based on wireless sensor networks. Sensors **9**, 6411–6434 (2009)
2. Rasin, Z., Abdullah, M.R.: Water quality monitoring system using Zigbee based wireless sensor network. Int. J. Eng. Technol. (IJET) **9**(10), 24–28 (2009)
3. O'Flynn, B., Cleary, J., Murphy, H., et al.: SmartCoast: a wireless sensor network for water quality monitoring. In: 32nd IEEE Conference on Local Computer Networks (LCN), Dublin, Ireland, pp. 815–816, October 2007
4. EmNetLLC: Technology Note. http://www.heliosware.com/technology.html
5. CSIRO ICT Centre: Wireless Sensor Network Devices. http://www.ict.csiro.au
6. Seders, L.A., Shea, C.A., Lemmon, M.D., et al.: LakeNet: an integrated sensor network for environmental sensing in lakes. Environ. Eng. Sci. **24**, 183–191 (2007)

7. Alkandari, A., Alnasheet, M., Alabduljader, Y., et al.: Wireless sensor network (WSN) for water monitoring system: case study of Kuwait Beaches. Int. J. Digit. Inf. Wirel. Commun. (IJDIWC) **1**(4), 709–717 (2009)
8. Cheng, C., Mao, X., Lizhen, W.: An online monitoring system of water quality based on Zigbee. Chin. J. Electron Devices **32**(5), 942–945 (2009)
9. Intersema, Inc.: MS5541C datasheet. http://www.meas-spec.com/downloads/ MS5541C.pdf
10. Intersema, Inc.: Using SPI protocol with pressure sensor modules. Application Note. http://www.meas-spec.com/downloads/Using_SPI_Protocol_with_Pressure_ Sensor_Modules.pdf
11. Tatsiopoulos, C., Ktena, A.: A smart Zigbee based wireless sensor meter system. In: 16th International Conference on Systems, Signals and Image Processing (IWS-SIP), Chalkida, Greece, June 2009
12. Atmel Corporation: ATmega328P datasheet. http://www.atmel.com/Images/ Atmel-8271-8-bit-AVR-Microcontroller
13. Texas Instruments, Inc.: CC2430 PRELIMINARY datasheet (2006)
14. Texas Instruments, Inc.: CC2591 datasheet: 2.4GHz RF Front End (2008)
15. Zou, Y., Xing, H.: High precise PH value measurement meter. J. Meas. Control Technol. **29**(9), 1–4 (2010)
16. Texas Instruments, Inc.: Z-Stack Sample Applications (2006)

Author Index

Printed in the United States
By Bookmasters